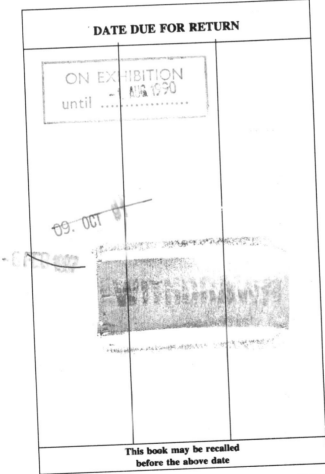

DATE DUE FOR RETURN

ON EXHIBITION
until ...... 1 AUG 1990

09. OCT

This book may be recalled
before the above date

90014

Soviet Ballistic Missile Defense
and the Western Alliance

Soviet Ballistic Missile Defense and the Western Alliance

David S. Yost

Harvard University Press
Cambridge, Massachusetts
London, England
1988

Library of Congress Cataloging-in-Publication Data

Yost, David S. (David Scott), 1948–
Soviet ballistic missile defense and the western
alliance.

Includes index.
1. Ballistic missile defenses—Soviet Union.
2. Europe—Military policy.   3. Soviet Union—Military
policy.   4. United States—Military policy.   I. Title.
UG745.S65Y67   1988   358'.1754'0947   88-2674
ISBN 0-674-82610-8 (alk. paper)

346636

Preface

Although several studies have examined the U.S. Strategic Defense Initiative and others have analyzed U.S.–West European relations and Western security, less attention has been devoted to Soviet military programs and perspectives. This book addresses issues of long-range offense and defense in light of Soviet ballistic missile defense (BMD) capabilities and activities. It also considers apparent Soviet political-military intentions and their possible implications for the Western alliance.

The book is based primarily on published sources; it also draws on off-the-record interviews with scores of scholars and officials in North America and Western Europe since 1980. Interviews with a relatively small and no doubt unrepresentative "sample" of observers constitute an impressionistic source of evidence, to be sure, but they also offer a basis for interpreting the declaratory policies and public assessments of governments regarding politically controversial issues. Moreover, they supply a basis for some confidence in making generalizations. Despite obvious risks of oversimplification, owing to the diversity of views in each country, I have chosen to conform to standard practice by referring to the "West Europeans" as a shorthand for what appear to be dominant trends in contemporary opinion, particularly among attentive observers in Britain, France, and the Federal Republic of Germany.

The interpretive approach in this book—describing Soviet behavior and examining various explanations before turning to possible policy implications—is an organizing framework for the consideration of a number of relatively controversial topics. Topics such as BMD and Soviet political-military intentions have remained contentious because of the gravity of the issues and the continuing disagreements in the West about how to interpret Soviet behavior and define Western security requirements. Responsible Western officials have no alternative but to define strategic policies for their governments, even though (owing to Soviet secrecy and other factors) the evidence about Soviet capabilities and likely intentions is never complete and unambiguous, and the consequences of specific choices cannot be fully foreseen.

Strategic studies are, in other words, subject to the limitations of other fields of political and social analysis. It is, as a practical matter, impossible to escape dependence on qualitative and provisional judgments. While a substantial number of significant technical and operational analytical issues lend themselves to a quantitative approach, many of the more important political and strategic questions cannot be reduced to quantitative terms. In strategic planning, moreover, many of the key factors (such as the specific operational plans that might be employed by adversaries in a potential future conflict) cannot be known, and multiple uncertainties are involved.

It is nonetheless important to attempt to gain a better understanding of Soviet capabilities and possible Soviet choices, in order to improve the West's prospects for successfully deterring and, if necessary, countering aggression. The ideal would be to comprehend Soviet political-military objectives in particular theaters of strategic military action and likely Soviet assessments and decision-making criteria with a due regard for their specific and unique features, rather than to engage in mirror-imaging or, as one of my students put it, "mirror-imagining" about the Soviet Union. At the same time, it would be no less desirable to seek a more profound understanding of U.S. and allied strengths, vulnerabilities, and possible choices in relation to the strategic challenges posed by the Soviet Union.

While ideal levels of discernment will no doubt remain elusive, as a practical matter, some judgments will have to be reached about apparent trends, and responsibilities will have to be shouldered. I hope that this book will contribute to more sober and deliberate assessments of the potential significance of strategic defenses for Western security, especially in the more plausible contingencies in which limited and selective long-range offensive strikes might be threatened or employed.

Despite the talk about fundamental changes in Soviet military thinking under Mikhail Gorbachev, little evidence has so far emerged to suggest that the talk has resulted in action. While such changes cannot be ruled out in the future, the current and foreseeable trends indicate continuing Soviet military force expansion and modernization. Although the April 1988 edition of the U.S. Department of Defense's *Soviet Military Power* survey includes previously unpublished photographs of the large phased-array radar near Pushkino called Pill Box, probably the most remarkable new information about Soviet strategic defenses in this annual report concerns the steady construction over four decades of underground facilities "hundreds of meters deep" and capable of accommodating thousands of Soviet leadership personnel. Such costly investments underscore the need to see Soviet BMD efforts as part of a larger array of Soviet damage-limiting programs.

The book has a long history. Although I have been working on BMD issues affecting Western security since 1980, I gave less attention to Soviet BMD programs until early 1985, when Lieutenant General G. C. Berkhof of the Royal Netherlands Army invited me to prepare a paper on Soviet BMD and NATO for a conference sponsored by the Netherlands Institute of International Relations, Clingendael, at the Hague in April 1985.

When this invitation arrived, I was in Washington, D.C., as a NATO Fellow and National Endowment for the Humanities/International Affairs Fellow of the Council on Foreign Relations. These fellowships made it possible for me to contribute to the Hague conference and to carry forward research on this topic. I would therefore like to express my appreciation to the NATO Fellowship Program, especially its director, Fernand Welter, and to the Council on Foreign Relations. Three members of the council's staff—Alton Frye, David Kellogg, and Paul Kreisberg— provided a great deal of advice and encouragement during the process of research and writing. I am particularly grateful to them for organizing a manuscript review group in March 1986. For their time and counsel, I would like to thank cordially Ambassador Jonathan Dean, who presided at the review group's meeting, and the participants: Alton Frye, David Kellogg, Paul Kreisberg, Michael Krepon, Gale Mattox, Keith Payne, Alan Platt, Alan Tonelson, and Bruce Weinroc. Additional research support, direct and indirect, was provided by the Fritz Thyssen Foundation, the Earhart Foundation, and the Woodrow Wilson International Center for Scholars, Smithsonian Institution.

The fellowships from NATO and the Council on Foreign Relations enabled me to spend a year and a half in the Department of Defense, primarily in the Office of Net Assessment. For his exceptionally valuable advice on this fellowship research project and other endeavors, I would like to thank Andrew W. Marshall, the director of this office. Colleagues in this office who provided advice were David F. Epstein; Lieutenant Colonel John G. Hines, U.S. Army; Commander George F. Kraus, Jr., USN; Lieutenant Colonel Jeffrey McKitrick, U.S. Army; Captain Charles Pease, USN; Dmitry Ponomareff; Commander James J. Tritten, USN; and Lieutenant Colonel Barry Watts, USAF. George Kraus and Dmitry Ponomareff provided particularly helpful advice on technical issues, while John Hines supplied extensive guidance on Soviet affairs.

Indeed, it was largely thanks to John Hines that I became better acquainted with Phillip Petersen and Notra Trulock III. The interpretation of Soviet political-military policy in this book has been influenced by their advice and their work. I have also benefited from discussions with other experts in Soviet affairs, notably Hannes Adomeit, Alexander Alexiev, Robert Bathurst, Sherman Garnett, Harry Gelman, Dennis Gormley, William C. Green, Stanley Kober, Benjamin Lambeth, Malcolm Mackintosh, Lieutenant General William E. Odom, William F. and Harriet Fast Scott, John Van Oudenaren, Peter Vigor, and Gerhard Wettig.

A number of West European officials discussed the issues with me and offered suggestions. Although no attribution can be made for such assistance, I would like to express my gratitude to them. I would also like to thank, for their advice on the issues, Falk Bomsdorf, Jean-François Delpech, Thomas Enders, Hubert Feigl, Michael Forster, Lawrence Freedman, General Georges Fricaud-Chagnaud, Pierre Hassner, François Heisbourg, Hubertus Hoffmann, Veronika Isenberg, Josef Joffe, Karl Kaiser, Joachim Krause, Admiral Pierre Lacoste, Pierre Lellouche, Laurence Martin, Dominique Moisi, Thierry de Montbrial, Harald Müller, Uwe Nerlich, Wolfgang Pfeiler, Hartmut Pohlman, John Roper, Michael Rühle, Reinhardt Rummel, Peter Schmidt, Wolfgang Schreiber, General Franz-Joseph Schulze, Georges-Henri Soutou, Peter Stratmann, Michel Tatu, Hermann Volle, Hans-Heinrich Weise, Stephan von Welck, Stuart Whyte, and Berhard Zepter.

In the United States, I benefited from advice in discussions with Benson Adams, Thomas Brown, Brian Dailey, Patrick Garrity, Colin Gray, William Griffith, Kerry Hines, Fred S. Hoffman, Francis X. Kane, Phillip Karber, Kerry Kartchner, Catherine Kelleher, Edward Kolodziej, Paul Kozemchak, Kevin Lewis, Steven Maaranen, John Matheny, Gordon McCormick, Richard Nuttall, Patrick Parker, Joseph Pilat, Thomas Rona, Henry Rowen, Diego Ruiz Palmer, Mark Schneider, Richard Shearer, Henry Sokolski, James Thomson, William R. Van Cleave, Merrill Walters, Ambassador Seymour Weiss, Samuel F. Wells, Jr., James Wendt, and Albert Wohlstetter. Joseph Pilat in particular read more than one draft of this work and provided many thoughtful and judicious suggestions.

Because I have been working on the subject since 1980, certain ideas have naturally recurred. I would like to thank the following publishers for granting me permission to draw upon work originally presented under their imprints: the MIT Press, for "Ballistic Missile Defense and the Atlantic Alliance," *International Security*, 7 (Fall 1982), 143–174, and "European Anxieties about Ballistic Missile Defense," *Washington Quarterly*, 7 (Fall 1984), 112–129; Lexington Books, D.C. Heath and Co., for "Alliance Strategy and Ballistic Missile Defense," in Sanford Lakoff and Randy

Willoughby, ed., *Strategic Defense and the Western Alliance* (Lexington, Mass., copyright 1987, D. C. Heath and Co.), pp. 63–104, and "Strategic Defenses in Soviet Doctrine and Force Posture," in Fred S. Hoffman, Albert Wohlstetter, and David S. Yost, ed., *Swords and Shields: NATO, the USSR, and New Choices for Long-Range Offense and Defense* (Lexington, Mass., copyright 1987, D. C. Heath and Co.), pp. 123–157; the Woodrow Wilson International Center for Scholars, Smithsonian Institution, for "U.S. and Soviet Views on Prospects for a Cooperative Transition in Strategic Defense," in Samuel F. Wells, Jr., and Robert Litwak, ed., *Strategic Defenses and Soviet-American Relations* (Cambridge: Ballinger, 1987), pp. 163–174; the Center for Strategic and International Studies, Georgetown University, for "Soviet Ballistic Missile Defense and the Atlantic Alliance," in Dan Quayle, Robert E. Hunter, and C. Elliott Farmer, ed., *Strategic Defense and the Western Alliance* (Washington, D.C., 1986), pp. 70–85; the School of International and Public Affairs, Columbia University, for "Western Europe and the U.S. Strategic Defense Initiative," *Journal of International Affairs*, 41 (Summer 1988), 269–323; the School of Advanced International Studies, Johns Hopkins University, for "The Reykjavik Summit and European Security," *SAIS Review*, 7 (Summer-Fall 1987), 1–22; and the Foreign Policy Research Institute for "Soviet Ballistic Missile Defense and NATO," *Orbis*, 29 (Summer 1985), 281–292.

Thanks are also owed to the following publishers for permission for extensive citations from their works: the Fondation pour les Etudes de Défense Nationale, for Groupe X-Défense, *Les défenses anti-missiles, la France et l'Europe* (Paris, 1986); the Brookings Institution. for Sayre Stevens, "The Soviet BMD Program," in Ashton B. Carter and David N. Schwartz, ed., *Ballistic Missile Defense* (Washington, D.C., 1984), pp. 182–220; and the U.S. Strategic Institute, for Manfred Wörner, "A Missile Defense for NATO Europe," *Strategic Review*, 14 (Winter 1986), 13–20.

I would like to express my appreciation to my editor, Jacqueline Dormitzer, for her careful reading of the text and skillful editing. Aida Donald, Virginia LaPlante, and Elizabeth Suttell of Harvard University Press have likewise been most helpful and patient during the lengthy process of book production.

Finally, I am deeply grateful to my wife, Catherine, for her generous and steadfast support and encouragement.

The views expressed in this book are, of course, mine alone and should not be construed to represent those of the Department of the Navy or any U.S. government agency.

D.S.Y.

July 1988

Contents

Soviet Ballistic Missile Defense
and the Western Alliance

Introduction

In March 1985 the British foreign secretary, Sir Geoffrey Howe, made a controversial speech about the long-term security issues raised by strategic-defense programs, particularly research on ballistic missile defense (BMD). His critical remarks about President Reagan's Strategic Defense Initiative (SDI) were widely reported. In a little-noted passage in his speech, however, Sir Geoffrey also referred to "the very considerable research under way in the Soviet Union on a range of potential defensive measures." He added that "not enough attention has been paid to this Soviet research. It is extensive and far-reaching and has been going on for many years. Any discussion of future Western strategies must take full account of it. To ignore or to dismiss what is happening in the Soviet Union would be not only myopic; it would be dangerous."[1]

The specific dangers that enhanced Soviet strategic defenses could imply for Western security are not entirely self-evident. This study examines the strategic implications and policy choices that may face the West, after reviewing Soviet BMD programs and assessing their prospects for further expansion, and after examining various interpretations of Soviet strategic behavior. Caution and circumspection are essential in this inquiry. Much of the evidence is indirect and incomplete, and the issues are much more complex than some advocates for certain policy positions have conceded. The neglect of Soviet BMD capabilities and activities in intra-alliance discussions until relatively recently has promoted a misleading impression, at least in some quarters, that current Soviet BMD activities are mainly reactive to the SDI.

Indeed, some proponents and critics of the SDI seem to share a certain ethnocentrism regarding Soviet BMD prospects. While it may oversimplify their position to put it so baldly, some advocates of the SDI appear to assume that the United States could readily be the first to deploy such defenses on a large scale and that the Soviet Union would not be able to overcome them or match them—unless the United States provided technological assistance to the USSR. Conversely, some who question the value of an improved U.S. BMD research program seem to assume that cutting back U.S. BMD research efforts would provide an assurance of Soviet inaction in the field of ballistic missile defense.

Both of these self-centered assumptions—rarely stated so simply or in such a stark fashion—may in fact be mistaken. Both imply Soviet competitive inferiority and a Soviet propensity to imitate U.S. military behavior. The United States and its partners in the Western alliance may well not have the liberty of choice implied by such reassuring assumptions. The Soviet Union has operational BMD capabilities today, unlike the United States; and the Soviets are better prepared than the Americans to deploy a widespread network of such defenses that would have at least some military and strategic value in the next decade. This value would clearly be substantially greater in defending critically important Soviet military and leadership assets against the limited and selective ballistic missile strikes envisaged in NATO strategy than in countering the larger-scale but less plausible intercontinental attacks that are often emphasized in Western discussions of BMD issues. Although the Soviet Union will no doubt monitor U.S. BMD decisions attentively, Soviet decisions on whether to deploy BMD capabilities on a larger scale (and to select certain types of BMD systems for specific purposes) could well be made on grounds of political-military expediency distinct from emulating U.S. behavior.

On the other hand, it would be unwise to jump to the conclusion that a clear-cut Soviet "breakout" from current arms control limits on BMD is probable. An ambiguous situation may be more likely—that is, a continuing buildup of the Soviet BMD deployment potential within ABM Treaty limitations, in conjunction with equivocal activities that may eventually amount to a "creepout" with respect to certain treaty constraints. Such a situation could also threaten Western security interests in the long term. In this case, prudent response measures would have to be envisaged, and appropriate hedges would have to be made in the interests of stable deterrence, so that any necessary countermeasures could be taken in a timely fashion.

It should also be recognized that BMD is only one form of strategic defense. Although BMD deployments could be of critical significance, depending on their scope and effectiveness, Western discourse about strategic defense has tended to emphasize BMD to the neglect of other forms of strategic defense. Popular analyses of BMD requirements in the

West have typically set very high standards of effectiveness. These standards have often amounted to demands for virtual impermeability. BMD systems incapable of providing such protection to the most vulnerable targets (cities, for example) have been deemed discredited and useless. By the same token, other defenses falling short of such near-perfect criteria—air defenses, civil defenses, hardened command shelters, and so forth—have been slighted in the West.

The Western emphasis on BMD in analyzing strategic-defense issues is understandable, because ballistic missiles have become exceptionally important means of attack. Ballistic missiles began in the late 1950s to supplant bomber aircraft as the most prompt and reliable means of delivering nuclear weapons. Today both the United States and the Soviet Union maintain arsenals of land-based intercontinental ballistic missiles (ICBMs) and submarine-launched ballistic missiles (SLBMs) that surpass their bomber fleets (and their cruise missile platforms) in relative importance (for example, in numbers of deliverable warheads). The USSR and the United States also depend in part on ballistic missiles to threaten targets at shorter ranges (within Europe, for instance). With foreseeable improvements in accuracy, ballistic missiles will also become increasingly important vehicles for delivering conventional and chemical munitions at various ranges. Britain, France, and China have, moreover, placed great emphasis on ballistic missiles in their nuclear force postures, partly because such missile systems have had a high probability of penetrating defenses.[2]

Three other factors also justify special consideration of ballistic missile defense as a leading element of strategic defense. First, unlike other means of strategic defense, U.S. and Soviet BMD deployments are limited by international agreement—the Soviet-U.S. Antiballistic Missile (ABM) Treaty of 1972. Second, President Reagan has made BMD the preeminent focus of research in his Strategic Defense Initiative. This is consistent with U.S. attitudes since the mid-1960s—that is, without relatively effective BMD, air defenses and other forms of strategic defense seem almost pointless; if the principal threat (ballistic missile attack) cannot be contained, the logic holds, other means of defense will be rapidly overwhelmed. Third, from this U.S. perspective, BMD looks like the missing link in the Soviet strategic-defense posture.

The Soviet Union has, in contrast to the United States and its allies, invested heavily in air defenses, civil defenses, hardened command shelters, and so forth. But such defenses appear likely to be ineffective in the most demanding of contingencies (which are almost certainly not the most probable ones)—that is, large-scale intercontinental nuclear debate, however, consensus in expert circles about the foundations of stable deterrence and Western security was undermined by various developments. The credibility of U.S. nuclear guarantees seemed increasingly questionable in view of growing U.S.-Soviet force imbalances. Some perceived dangers in the Soviet buildup of intermediate-range nuclear forces (INF) based in Europe, in the context of what they saw as a stalemate in the Soviet-U.S. competition in intercontinental strike capabilities. Others saw the predictable vulnerability of U.S. ICBMs, owing to improvements in the accuracy of the asymmetrically large Soviet ICBM force, as especially significant. Both developments cast some doubt on assumptions of a coincidence of Soviet and U.S. views on political and strategic stability through mutual vulnerability. Interpretations in the West of the evolution of the Soviet force posture, including Soviet investments in strategic defense as well as in offensive strike forces, were placing BMD on the agenda of the alliance well before President Reagan's speech of March 1983.[4]

West European reactions to the U.S. Strategic Defense Initiative launched in March 1983 have been mainly critical. The criticisms have focused on its far-reaching strategic and arms control implications. Moreover, in Britain, France, and West Germany—the leading military powers of Western Europe (each contributes roughly a quarter of NATO European defense spending)—the SDI has provoked substantial domestic political controversy. The SDI has also contributed to intra-European debates about security policy and Western Europe's future political identity, including prospects for European-American interdependence and high technology industrial competition.[5]

Although serious West European reservations about the SDI persist, there has been a general recognition (at least in government and expert circles) that the true challenges to the military security of Western Europe reside not in the U.S. SDI but in the actual and potential capabilities of the Soviet Union. Soviet military capabilities have been reassessed with increasing earnestness—to some extent because of the SDI, and to some extent despite the inconsistencies and deficiencies that West Europeans discern in recent U.S. analyses of Soviet BMD prospects. Because the SDI has been such a prominent focus of U.S. and allied attention in recent years, concerns about the SDI have overshadowed to some degree analyses of changes in the Soviet force posture, offensive and defensive.

Chapter 1 surveys the historical evolution of Soviet BMD capabilities and apparent "hardware" trends. Soviet BMD programs represent a contrast to U.S. BMD efforts, because the levels of funding and official interest accorded BMD in the United States have fluctuated greatly, with high points (as in the late 1960s and early 1970s) followed by declines. Soviet BMD programs appear, in comparison, as activities sustained steadily over decades with gradual incremental increases in effort. Several types of potential BMD systems have been investigated and developed during the construction of an infrastructure for possible expansion beyond capabilities permitted by the 1972 Antiballistic Missile (ABM) Treaty.

Given the history of Soviet progress in BMD and the potential for further Soviet advances, Chapter 2 considers possible explanations of these developments. The evidence suggests that, while "arms race" and "bureaucratic politics" interpretations throw some light on the subject, they are incapable of fully accounting for the facts. Instead, it appears that a composite interpretation, one integrating BMD "mission requirements" —that is, purposeful political and military rationales—with other factors, could explain the Soviet pattern of behavior more convincingly and could account for Soviet approval of the ABM Treaty. This conclusion supports a working hypothesis about Soviet motives and incentives with respect to competition in BMD: under currently prevailing conditions, the Soviets consider it imperative to keep U.S. BMD efforts under control by perpetuating the ABM Treaty regime, even though this imposes constraints on Soviet BMD activities as well.

At the same time, it is not clear to what extent this policy might be modified under changed circumstances; nor is it clear to what lengths the Soviets are prepared to go—in terms of arms control negotiations and compliance with existing treaties, for example—in order to keep U.S. BMD activities under control by means of the ABM Treaty regime. The Soviet Union has developed an option to deploy ground-based terminal defenses of essentially traditional types more rapidly and more extensively than the United States could deploy such defenses. As Stephen Meyer points out, "the Soviet Union could deploy her nonexotic [BMD] system sooner, and at a much faster pace. The intent, and the result, might well be to raise uncertainty about America's second-strike capability for a significant period before the Soviet deterrent is threatened. This would certainly be a different 'transition phase' than most supporters of SDI have in mind."[6]

Inferences about the potential implications for the security of the Western alliance are drawn in Chapter 3. The most obvious would concern NATO's strategy of flexible response, since it depends heavily on threats of nuclear retaliation, with ballistic missiles as key means of delivery, along with bombers and cruise missiles. Other implications could nonetheless also be important, given Soviet foreign policy objec-

If Soviet behavior necessitated the deployment of BMD capabilities in NATO countries, BMD could help to avert the adverse consequences of what might otherwise be an even larger Soviet advantage in strategic defenses. BMD in Western Europe and North America could deny the Soviets a free ride against critical targets and greatly enlarge Soviet uncertainties about the feasibility of successful countermilitary attacks.

The probable requirements for military security—improved active defenses, more controllable and discriminate long-range strike forces, passive defenses such as hardening and mobility, and enhanced conventional capabilities—amount to an unprecedented challenge for the alliance. The challenge is complicated by the need to maintain Western cohesion while continuing the search for constructive policies, including arms control.

Reassessments of Soviet Strategic Defense

Allied governments have known since the late 1940s that, to a significant extent, all the strategic and diplomatic issues affecting the security of Western Europe hinge on the USSR's military posture and on Soviet strategic and political intentions. The Soviet Union's military options and prospects determine, in short, what level and type of "insurance" the West requires —what "prudent hedges" should be foreseen and developed, in the interests of stable deterrence. The SDI has, however, resulted in a more widespread recognition that Soviet strategic defense capabilities must be included in analyses of the West's security requirements.

Recent West European analyses of Soviet BMD include an August 1985 article by the head of the planning staff in the West German Defense Ministry;[8] a November 1985 paper prepared by the British Defence Ministry;[9] and a January 1986 report to the French Defense Ministry by an officially chartered commission on space weapons, called the Delpech report, after the commission's chairman, Jean-François Delpech.[10] In addition, especially in 1985 and 1986, defense ministers and other officials of Britain, France, and West Germany made public statements about Soviet BMD and Soviet offensive- and defensive-force developments. Finally, important unofficial analyses have recently become available. In June 1986, for example, the Fondation pour les Etudes de Défense Nationale in Paris published a book on BMD and European security authored by a group of experts affiliated with the Ecole Polytechnique, including Jean-François Delpech.[11]

The influence of the SDI on West European reassessments of Soviet strategic defense has been complex. On the one hand, West Europeans have been troubled by apparent inconsistencies in U.S. discussions of Soviet BMD as a justification for the SDI. Moreover, the SDI context seems to have exacerbated, to some degree at least, the long-standing problems in European-American relations that derive from the preeminent role of the United States in technical intelligence collection and evaluation. Partly because the United States has such an important role in this domain, doubts about U.S. competence and objectivity arise from time to time, and West Europeans then become more acutely concerned about their dependence on U.S. sources and analyses.

On the other hand, despite continuing misgivings about the SDI and about U.S. appraisals of actual and potential Soviet progress in strategic defense, West European governments have increasingly recognized the gravity of the issues posed by Soviet strategic defense. Improved Soviet capabilities for limited and discriminate missile attack—possibly with conventional warheads alone—and enhanced Soviet capabilities for active defense against Western missiles and aircraft may well emerge in the next decade, whatever the fate of the SDI. In other words, a number of responsible Europeans have concluded that the peculiarities of the U.S. approach to the SDI do not excuse Western Europe from recognizing the Soviet capacity for autonomous action.

APPARENT INCONSISTENCIES IN U.S. DISCUSSIONS
OF SOVIET BMD

West Europeans have frequently called attention to the apparent contradiction between (1) the initial SDI advocacy by the president and other high-level U.S. officials (a *U.S. initiative* oriented toward ridding the world of nuclear weapons, with little or no reference made to reacting to specific developments in Soviet BMD or to improvements in the Soviet ballistic missile force) and (2) the subsequent emphasis the United States has placed on the SDI as a prudent hedge in response to the expanding BMD activities of the USSR (that is, *a reaction to Soviet exertions* that have necessitated an improved BMD research program in the United States, so that the West may be better prepared to erect defenses against Soviet ballistic missiles and to respond to any eventual expansion of existing Soviet BMD deployments).

Despite the long history of Soviet BMD programs and the continuing modernization of current Soviet BMD deployments, the initial advocacy and the circumstances of the surprise announcement of the SDI established the U.S. program as a U.S. initiative in public perceptions. As a result, West Europeans have noted, the prudent-hedge justification for the SDI has often appeared to be a convenient afterthought or pretext in support of what originated as a U.S. initiative. The U.S. Department of State–Department of Defense document *Soviet Strategic Defense Programs* was published in October 1985, over two years after the president's March 1983 SDI speech.[12] The "response" elements behind the SDI have often been discounted because of the "initiative" perception, although both types of motives have been present.

A related question concerns whether the United States views highly effective Soviet BMD as desirable. The initial U.S. SDI advocacy emphasized "rendering these nuclear weapons impotent and obsolete,"[13] with a concept of "mutual assured security" replacing "mutual assured destruction."[14] These notions implied that the Soviet Union ought to have very heavy—and, indeed, extremely effective—defenses similar to those envisaged for the United States. The president said, "I would like to say to the Soviet Union, we know you've been researching for this same thing longer than we have. We wish you well. There couldn't be anything better than if both of us came up with it."[15] The president even said that, if necessary, the United States would give the relevant technology to the Soviets, again implying that the USSR ought to be intensively pursuing BMD research and development.[16]

European observers maintain that this line of argumentation has tended to legitimize Soviet BMD activities. It undermines the credibility of U.S. warnings about the dangers that Soviet strategic defense could pose. How, they ask, can the U.S. initiative endorse serious Soviet BMD activities and the development of highly effective Soviet defenses and urge Europeans to view Soviet BMD activities with alarm at the same time? In the same vein, some West Europeans have wondered how the U.S. arguments for "deterrence characterized by greater reliance on defensive capabilities that threaten no one"[17] can be squared with U.S. warnings that Soviet strategic defenses could threaten Western deterrence capabilities. Some official U.S. policy statements indicate that "strategic defenses . . . threaten no one" and that Soviet "active and passive defenses . . . provide evidence of the Soviet nuclear warfighting mentality."[18]

Although some West Europeans suspect that these U.S. arguments may be disingenuous or simply incoherent, others see a certain logic in them. That is, while a unilateral Soviet advantage in strategic defense would be harmful to Western security interests, the U.S. administration thinks a U.S.-Soviet strategic relationship of defense dominance would be desirable in the long term. This distinction explains both Secretary of Defense Caspar Weinberger's view, "I can't imagine a more destabilizing factor for the world than if the Soviets should acquire a thoroughly reliable defense against these missiles before we do,"[19] and his statement, "I would hope and assume that the Soviets, with all the work they have done and are doing in this field, would develop about the same time we did the same kind of effective defense, which would then have the effect of totally and completely removing these missiles from the earth and also the fears that they cause."[20]

In other words, U.S. spokesmen have suggested that a simultaneous introduction of highly effective strategic defenses could be generally beneficial, whereas Soviet superiority in strategic defense would be harmful to Western security interests. In President Reagan's words, "I want to make it clear that we welcome the day when the Soviet Union can shoot down any incoming missile, so long as the United States can shoot down any incoming missile, too."[21] This is a concept that many West Europeans have felt unable to welcome.

At various points in the post-1945 period, both U.S. and Soviet commentators have shown interest in a concept of defense dominance assuring strategic stability after the reduction of offensive nuclear forces to extremely low levels. Examples include J. Robert Oppenheimer's suggestions in 1953,[22] the Soviet-proposed "Gromyko plan" of 1962,[23] and the U.S. "strategic concept" for SDI and arms control in 1985. Paul Nitze described this strategic concept in February 1985 as follows:

> During the next 10 years, the U.S. objective is a radical reduction in the power of existing and planned offensive nuclear arms, as well as the stabilization of the relationship between offensive and defensive nuclear arms, whether on earth or in space. We are even now looking forward to a period of transition to a more stable world, with greatly reduced levels of nuclear arms and an enhanced ability to deter war based upon an increasing contribution of non-nuclear defenses against offensive nuclear arms. This period of transition could lead to the eventual elimination of all nuclear arms, both offensive and defensive. A world free of nuclear arms is an ultimate objective to which we, the Soviet Union, and all other nations can agree.[24]

Such concepts have not been applauded in Western Europe, because it is difficult to identify benefits for Western Europe in large-scale Soviet strategic defenses, even if Soviet defenses were matched by equivalent deployments in North America and Western Europe. The gist of some U.S. SDI advocacy has been that a defense-dominant U.S.-Soviet relationship, including highly effective Soviet defenses, would be universally beneficial and necessarily desirable.

According to Weinberger, "a truly stable superpower relationship would be one in which both sides were protected from attack."[25] Many West European strategists would attach reservations to this concept, in view of Soviet advantages in conventional, chemical, and short-range nuclear forces. In their view, Soviet vulnerability to long-range nuclear attack will remain necessary for deterrence and stability.[26] Moreover, there is some concern that, even if a relationship of mutual U.S.-Soviet invulnerability to nuclear attack did not lead to conflicts limited to the territory of third parties, it could imply a U.S.-Soviet condominium and/or an increase in West European dependence on relations between the "two world powers" for their security.

In short, it may well be possible to reconcile the U.S. admonitions about the risks in Soviet superiority in strategic defense and the U.S. advocacy of highly effective strategic defenses on both sides; but West Europeans generally see little reason to welcome the latter. Moreover, the latter vision—the renunciation of any aspiration for U.S. superiority—seems inconsistent with other U.S. statements suggesting that the United States should have superiority in ballistic missile defenses. According to Weinberger, "if we can get a system which is effective and which we know can render their weapons impotent, we would be back in a situation we were in, for example, when we were the only nation with the nuclear weapon and we did not threaten others with it."[27] Other statements implying an intention to build on U.S. technological advantages have also been cited in this context.[28]

These statements, some Europeans maintain, have tended to legitimize Soviet BMD activities in public perceptions because they are congruent with the general impression conveyed by much of the U.S. SDI advocacy—that the United States has taken the "first step" in a new round of the arms race, and that it represents a profound technological challenge for the Soviet Union. It is understandable if the Soviet Union tries to rise to fundamental challenges. The SDI thus appears to be the stimulus responsible for Soviet BMD activities, because the Soviets would not wish to allow the United States to gain superiority. In the words of Sir Geoffrey Howe: "If the technology does work, what will be its psychological impact on the other side? President Reagan has repeatedly made it clear that he does not seek superiority. But we would have to ensure that the perceptions of others were not different."[29]

Precisely because West Europeans cannot see any benefits for them in improved Soviet strategic defenses, they are uncomfortable with U.S. rhetoric implying the desirability of a U.S.-Soviet competition in advanced technologies for strategic defense. The idea of technological and military competition is consistent with the warning that a unilateral Soviet advantage in strategic defense would be threatening to the West. But competitive strategies are not consistent with visions of U.S.-Soviet cooperation and technology sharing to build a mutually beneficial relationship of defense dominance. If the U.S. government intended to solicit public and allied support for a competitive effort, why did it place itself in a role that could be perceived as one of U.S. responsibility for stimulating the arms race? Why did it begin by emphasizing the U.S. initiative and the defense-dominance vision rather than the Soviet challenge to Western security?[30] A widespread tendency in Western Europe has been to discount the defense-dominance vision and to emphasize the U.S. challenge and the likely Soviet response. In 1986 Paul Quilès, then the French minister of defense, declared that "whatever the evolution of the American position, the SDI risks bringing about a reinforcement of Soviet defensive programs."[31]

U.S. CREDIBILITY PROBLEMS

The U.S. government's use of the responding-to-Soviet-BMD-activities argument as a justification for the SDI has been less than fully convincing in Western Europe for reasons distinct from apparent inconsistencies in the conceptual rationales offered in support of the SDI. West European doubts about the objectivity and reliability of U.S. analyses of Soviet BMD activities have also been important.

The U.S. government enjoys relatively high credibility. Even West Europeans who question particular points in the official U.S. depiction of Soviet BMD activities indicate that they tend to rely on U.S. sources. The course of events has usually vindicated U.S. descriptions of Soviet military capabilities. Five problem areas are nonetheless worth noting. Some illustrate general problems of intelligence sharing and public information policy in a coalition of sovereign democracies, whereas others relate more directly to the specific issues posed by Soviet strategic defense.

First, some West Europeans suggest, the U.S. reputation for truthfulness could be more readily maintained if the United States provided more evidence to back up official U.S. views. If more evidence cannot be made available, they suggest, the United States should supply more caveats qualifying statements that appear to be bald assertions, or more background explaining why the evidence is classified or how certain judgments were reached—for instance, regarding Soviet spending on strategic defense.

An example is the issue of photographic evidence and artists' drawings in the annual U.S. Department of Defense publication *Soviet Military*

Power and in other official documents. Except for occasional photographs of a Galosh interceptor missile in its launch tube during parades in Moscow, virtually all U.S. graphic representations of Soviet BMD capabilities—other interceptor missiles, radars, and so forth—consist of artists' drawings. Europeans dissatisfied with the amount or quality of evidence on Soviet BMD made public by the United States call these drawings "cartoons" and indicate that such illustrations often evoke negative reactions. Experts and officials understand, however, that the U.S. government's reluctance to make available more details about Soviet systems is based on concerns about the risk of revealing too much about its intelligence sources.[32] The 1987 edition of *Soviet Military Power* included a photograph of the large phased-array radar at Pechora (similar to the controversial radar at Krasnoyarsk), which the United States had purchased commercially from the French SPOT Image Corporation.[33] A SPOT photograph of the Krasnoyarsk radar has been privately published, and it "broadly corresponds" to the indications given in *Soviet Military Power*.[34]

A second problem is that the "equidistancing" trend in West European attitudes toward the United States and the Soviet Union has extended to U.S. information policy. Opinion poll data suggest that the equidistancing tendency is partly rooted in a perception that "both [the United States and the USSR] employ disinformation techniques."[35] Some journalists have claimed that U.S. government agencies are conducting disinformation programs regarding various military projects, including the SDI, in order to deceive the Soviet Union.[36] Since the United States could not deceive the USSR in this fashion without simultaneously misleading Western publics, these claims may have a corrosive effect on the credibility of official U.S. statements about strategic matters.

A third difficulty resides in the fact that U.S. assessments of Soviet military systems and of the broad strategic challenges posed by Soviet capabilities are subject to change, owing in part to ambiguities in the available evidence and the acquisition of new information over time. In 1981, 1983, and 1984, for example, *Soviet Military Power* indicated that the Soviet SS-12/Scaleboard missile was expected to be replaced by the SS-22, a new missile with similar range (about 900 km) but greater accuracy.[37] In 1985, 1986, and 1987, the SS-22 designation was omitted, and the Soviets were simply attributed new Scaleboards more accurate than the older missiles they replaced.[38] This implied a reappraisal of earlier judgments — that is, the more advanced Scaleboards now seem to amount to simply upgraded versions of the earlier SS-12/Scaleboards rather than a distinctly new category of missile. Other sources continued, however, to refer to the SS-22;[39] and the SS-22 designation is still frequently used to refer to the new and more accurate versions of the Scaleboard.

Attentive West European observers have also noted the U.S. failure to address strategic problems that were once described as exceptionally grave. During the late 1970s and early 1980s, U.S. ICBM vulnerability was widely viewed as one of the most serious strategic infirmities of the United States.[40] In 1983, however, the President's Commission on Strategic Forces (the Scowcroft Commission) underlined the practical operational difficulties that the USSR would have to overcome to mount a coordinated attack on U.S. ICBMs and other strategic nuclear forces.[41] The Scowcroft Commission's findings have been widely interpreted as having "explained away" the problem of ICBM vulnerability, particularly since the Reagan administration has ceased to attach much urgency to its resolution. Indeed, several U.S. officials have specifically ruled out using BMD to defend vulnerable U.S. ICBMs, because this might be seen as inconsistent with the SDI vision of a more comprehensive defense.[42]

Some European experts suspect that changing U.S. appraisals of specific Soviet systems and broad military challenges may be partly influenced by internal political factors. In the late 1970s, for example, the U.S. Joint Chiefs of Staff recommended that the Soviet Backfire bomber be counted in the SALT II ceilings on strategic forces because "it has characteristics and capabilities similar or superior to those aircraft which both sides agree are heavy bombers."[43] President Carter, however, accepted Soviet President Brezhnev's statement that the USSR did not "intend to give this airplane the capability of operating at intercontinental distances," and the Backfire was excluded from the SALT II aggregate ceilings.[44] At the beginning of the Reagan administration, the Department of Defense held that the Backfire "has a strategic capability and cannot be ignored as a potential intercontinental bomber threat."[45] The reference to potential "intercontinental missions against the United States" was repeated in 1983;[46] and in 1984 it was specified that the Backfire has "sufficient range/radius capabilities for it to be employed effectively against the contiguous United States on high-altitude subsonic missions."[47] The word *effectively* was, however, dropped from this formulation in 1985.[48] In 1986 it was simply noted that in-flight refueling "would improve its capabilities against the contiguous United States."[49] In 1987 an additional caveat appeared: in-flight refueling for such missions would be feasible "if sufficient tankers are available."[50]

The apparent downgrading of the Backfire's intercontinental performance potential by the United States in recent years is in one sense irrelevant to West European officials, for no one has ever questioned the Backfire's ability to attack targets in Europe. But the changing U.S. judgments have given rise to speculation about whether the causes could include factors in addition to new information. Were assessments attributing an impressive intercontinental capability to the Backfire influenced by misgivings about the SALT II limitations as a whole? Did lobbying for the B-1 bomber help to dispose U.S. agencies to attribute enhanced potential to the new Soviet bomber? Did the flight tests in the early 1980s of the new Soviet Blackjack bomber, an aircraft larger and potentially faster than the U.S. B-1, help to degrade the perceived intercontinental importance of the Backfire? Did the initial deployments of AS-15 air-launched cruise missiles (with a range of 3000 km) on Soviet Bear H bombers in 1984 make the Backfire seem of secondary importance as an intercontinental air strike threat? Did the institution of regular combat patrols by Bear-H bombers with AS-15 cruise missiles off the coast of North America tend to reinforce this impression? Did more information about maritime and regional assignments of Backfire units become available? Did the increase in Soviet intercontinental ballistic missile capabilities after the conclusion of SALT II make the Backfire appear less useful in U.S. assessments of possible Soviet requirements in attack planning? Whatever the causes, the suspicion that interagency disagreements and internal politics in the United States could affect U.S. judgments about Soviet military capabilities has given some West Europeans what they regard as grounds for caution in accepting U.S. appraisals.[51]

This is a fourth credibility problem for the United States: beyond the fact that honest assessments of Soviet capabilities are subject to change as new evidence and analytical tools become available, at least some West Europeans have become concerned that U.S. agencies might manipulate data to help sell certain programs to the Congress, the public, and allies. Despite the well-documented history of chronic U.S. underestimates of Soviet deployments of ICBMs, SLBMs, and bombers from the early 1960s to the early 1970s,[52] the United States has more often been suspected of overestimating Soviet capabilities. As France's Ecole Polytechnique group recently put it: "It is indisputable that the American intelligence services have been mistaken in the past. It might be added that, the policy of the American administration being what it is, the American services might be tempted to exaggerate."[53] The former West German chancellor, Helmut Schmidt, has even argued that various U.S. administrations have "manipulated" their "satellite photography" data and "arranged the presentations in a way that suited the prevailing strategic doctrine."[54]

The suspicion that the U.S. government might make public only the information it deems opportune, neglecting certain ambiguities and exaggerating some details, has been present for many years. Current doubts about U.S. objectivity regarding Soviet BMD have been encouraged by the administration's SDI advocacy. The implicit allegations of a post-SDI politicization of U.S. assessments of Soviet BMD are not persuasive, however. The historical record shows that the U.S. government has been monitoring improvements in the Soviet BMD potential since the mid-1970s. While some statements regarding the implications of Soviet BMD programs may be viewed as exaggerated (as noted in Chapter 5), most of the recent U.S. government descriptions of Soviet BMD activities have been consistent with a long-standing pattern of reports. More information has, however, been made public in recent years, partly (it appears) because more noteworthy activity has been observed, and partly because of the administration's interest in promoting a higher level of public awareness in the West about Soviet military programs.

A fifth, and closely related, problem area concerns U.S. reports of Soviet BMD activities that may violate the ABM Treaty. These reports bring together the other problems—insufficient public evidence, changing U.S. assessments, the possibility of mistaken judgments or inadvertent exaggeration, and so forth—and add the dimension of possible Soviet noncompliance with an international treaty. ABM Treaty compliance issues are awkward for West European governments for several reasons.

To begin with, there is a fear that a clear alliance consensus on Soviet violations could encourage the United States to abrogate the ABM Treaty in retaliation; this would mean the end of a long-established arms control regime believed to be central to East-West strategic stability. Many judge that this could be more "destabilizing" than the issues of Soviet noncompliance that have been reported to date. Some West European officials reportedly fear that the U.S. government is trying to use Soviet violations "to justify retreat from the A.B.M. Treaty" rather than seeking a negotiated resolution of the noncompliance questions.[55] West Europeans are also uncertain whether the United States will sustain its judgments regarding actual or potential Soviet noncompliance over time; they speculate that the Soviet Union might offer compensatory compromises to resolve the questions in the Soviet-U.S. Standing Consultative Commission. In other words, some West Europeans judge that current U.S. concerns may prove to be temporary and subject to political bargaining.

West Europeans are, moreover, reluctant to be drawn into a dispute about Soviet compliance with a Soviet-U.S. treaty, to which they are not partners, when their technical means for independently verifying treaty compliance are inferior to those of the United States. As a result, West European governments have been circumspect in their statements about reported Soviet ABM Treaty violations. They have generally limited their comments to the Krasnoyarsk radar; this is the only long-standing violation charge for which the United States has declared the evidence to be unambiguous.

To some extent, all these credibility problems flow from the same source: West European dependence on U.S. intelligence collection and analysis, at least insofar as high-technology systems such as satellites are concerned. French officials have for years deplored what they call a superpower "monopoly" on military observation satellites.[56] West European dependence on the United States for certain types of intelligence has been a manageable difficulty in European-American relations, but it could become a serious one if European suspicions about possible U.S. exaggeration grew. U.S. assessments have, however, usually been confirmed by the course of events and by independent analyses made by West Europeans using their own sources of data.

In order to diminish West European dependence on the United States in this regard, the French government has since 1978 called for the creation of an international satellite observation agency. When this proposal was first made, the French favored a United Nations–sponsored agency.[57] Although the French still envisage sharing national data with a U.N. agency as a long-term possibility, more recent French statements have emphasized the need for France to go forward with its own military observation satellite program. The first *Hélios* satellite is to be launched in the early 1990s and is to have sharper resolution capabilities than France's existing civilian SPOT satellite. It will provide electronic as well as photographic and infrared intelligence, for the French are especially interested in understanding the characteristics of Soviet radars.[58] French statements have stressed France's interest in working closely with West Germany and other West European countries, in order to give Western Europe more autonomous intelligence collection and analysis capabilities.[59] Italy has decided to contribute 13 percent of the financing of *Hélios*, while Spain has recently agreed to make a contribution of 7 percent.[60]

The French proposals have been well received by various parties in West Germany, including prominent figures in the Social Democratic party (SPD) and a high-level private study commission.[61] The West German government has, however, indefinitely delayed taking a decision on participation in the *Hélios* satellite program. Some French observers have speculated that the West Germans fear giving offense to the United States, although the West Germans have referred to the cost of such a satellite program and the prevalence of cloud cover over Central and Eastern Europe.[62]

Britain has reportedly made plans to deploy a signals intelligence satellite called *Zircon*. Although some accounts describe the project as intended to diminish British dependence on the United States for technical intelligence,[63] others stress complementary desires: to improve Britain's standing in Western Europe and in its "special relationship" with the United States in intelligence matters.[64] Some French experts have argued that future intelligence satellites will be so costly that no "medium power" will be able to afford them, and that West European cooperation will therefore be necessary.[65]

Strengthened independent West European sources of intelligence might be beneficial for alliance cohesion, in that they could confirm the accuracy of U.S. assessments. But they might also furnish a new source of discord, if conclusions differed. Some Europeans argue that French or jointly devised West European satellite capabilities would be inferior to those of the United States, that West European governments would scarcely be able to match the comprehensive scale of U.S. efforts in various areas of intelligence (including analysis), and that closer cooperation with the United States might be the wiser course.

REASSESSMENTS OF SOVIET STRATEGY AND CAPABILITIES
West European support for the SDI has remained highly qualified, partly because the SDI vision has increasingly been associated with other aspects of U.S. policy that have been interpreted as implying a trend toward the disengagement of U.S. nuclear commitments regarding European security.[66] On the other hand, even if support for the SDI vision has been minimal, West European governments and experts have shown an awareness of the serious issues posed by Soviet strategic defense and foreseeable improvements in Soviet offensive capabilities. In the March 1985 communiqué of NATO's Nuclear Planning Group (NPG), the participating allies "noted with concern the extensive and long-standing efforts in the strategic defence field by the Soviet Union, which already deploys the world's only ABM and anti-satellite systems. The United States strategic defence research programme is prudent in the light of these Soviet activities and is also clearly influenced by the treaty violations reported by the President of the United States."[67] In October 1986, NATO's Nuclear Planning Group reviewed developments in the Soviet offensive-force posture and expressed concern about "the major

Soviet effort into continuing improvements in strategic and tactical anti-missile systems."[68]

The initial tendency was to focus on the SDI, because the U.S. administration made the SDI vision the center of attention. The spotlight on the U.S. initiative diverted attention from developments in the Soviet military posture. With the SDI's implications dominating the debate, most discussions of Soviet capabilities and prospects were filtered through an SDI prism. The assumption that the SDI might well result in improved Soviet strategic defenses was encouraged by the conspicuous U.S. initiative and by the U.S. rhetoric implying that highly effective Soviet strategic defenses could be benign and even beneficial in some circumstances. These aspects of the SDI (and others) naturally led many Europeans to blame the SDI for the undesirable consequences that could follow from improvements in the Soviet military posture.

With time, however, it has been more widely recognized that the SDI is probably only one factor (though an important one) in Soviet decision making about the development of improved defensive and offensive capabilities. In other words, the peculiarities of the U.S. approach to the SDI do not alter the central importance of the Soviet military posture, offensive and defensive, for the security of the Western alliance. The development of the Soviet posture is likely to be influenced by decisions in North America and Western Europe, but autonomous factors probably also play a role. The historical background of the Soviet BMD program shows that it did not result from U.S. initiatives. As George Younger, the British secretary of state for defense, recently noted, "the key point is that this is not a new Soviet programme; it is not a response to the SDI—far from it, it long pre-dates it—it is not something peripheral to the Soviet effort in defence research; it is a key component of it."[69]

West European governments have also recognized more clearly the need to place Soviet BMD activities in the context of other Soviet capabilities, offensive and defensive. The Soviet interest in eroding West European security by degrading the credibility of U.S. "guarantees" has long been acknowledged. But a new awareness of what improved strategic defense capabilities could contribute to the realization of this Soviet objective and others seems to be emerging. That is, Soviet strategic purposes may help to explain Soviet decision making regarding active defenses, not merely arms race responses in imitation of the United States. The Union pour la Démocratie Française grouping of political parties in France recently argued that "ultimately, the French and British strategic nuclear forces are threatened not by the American SDI . . . but by a Soviet ABM system that will be developed whatever the Americans do."[70]

In other words, the Soviet potential for expanded BMD deployments could well improve, even if the United States were to abandon the SDI and cut back its BMD research. Curtailing the SDI would probably not alter the thrust of Soviet BMD activities, given their history and the strategic incentives to carry them forward. This judgment has been invited by recent Soviet behavior. At least some West Europeans regard the Soviet responses to U.S. statements regarding potential Soviet ABM Treaty violations as evasive and unsatisfactory. As France's Ecole Polytechnique group of experts recently noted, "in the absence of a credible Soviet response [to the U.S. statements regarding potential Soviet violations], prudence leads us to take Soviet ABM programs seriously; these programs, moreover, long preceded the famous [U.S. Strategic Defense] Initiative. Nothing would be more incorrect than seeing in these Soviet developments a simple response to the American programs."[71]

1

Soviet BMD Capabilities and Activities

As Sayre Stevens, a former deputy director of the Central Intelligence Agency, has noted, there remain "many uncertainties about the Soviet BMD program, its achievements, technical objectives, and overall intent."[1] Many of these uncertainties derive, of course, from Soviet secrecy and efforts to deny Western intelligence services any knowledge of Soviet BMD.[2] Other uncertainties derive from the difficulty of establishing whether the Soviets intend to use specific systems for BMD purposes or for other purposes (for example, for attacking aircraft or satellites, or simply for surveillance). "We will probably never have absolute proof short of their performance in actual battle."[3] Even if the intended function were clear, the reliability and effectiveness of the system in combat would still be unclear—even, to a lesser degree, to the Soviets themselves.

Even though the Soviets would know more than outside observers about the specific strengths and defects of their BMD systems, they would still face the many uncertainties that could degrade the effectiveness of BMD systems in actual military operations. These uncertainties would include the reliability and endurance of their electronic systems (radars, data processing, communications, and so forth) in a nuclear environment. Nuclear explosions could, after all, result from both the attack and the defense. Although both the Soviet Union and the United States have shown greater interest in recent years in developing highly accurate conventional-warhead ballistic missiles and nonnuclear-kill (NNK) means of BMD, the risk of disabling nuclear effects—either enemy- or self-inflicted—will remain a grave source of uncertainty. Nuclear uncertainties will remain inexorable to some degree, despite attempts to harden facilities and to lessen the impact of nuclear explosions in other ways.

Effectiveness depends, moreover, on the requirements of the specific contingency. It has been known for many years that some targets are far more defensible than others, that the scope and purpose of an attack (and its tactics) could vary significantly, that a defense might be part of a more comprehensive campaign involving preemptive attacks against the enemy's offensive forces, and so forth. The BMD technologies employed are likely to be of varying states of "maturity," and full-scale testing of the entire system under realistic conditions is likely to be impossible. Performance in the field—in war, that is—could fall short of performance on a test range. It might be more feasible to envisage a range of possibilities than a single probable outcome. The U.S. Department of Defense has attempted to conduct studies of Soviet strategic defenses "across a broad range of values, since it is very difficult to get a good assessment of just how capable their systems are now or how capable they might be."[4]

Unintended biases may nonetheless emerge, owing to one's vantage point. Ashton Carter has remarked that "the same BMD system will look very different to the defender, aware of all the system's hidden flaws, and to the attacker, prone to give the system the benefit of the doubt."[5] The reverse could also be true in some circumstances: a system could have flaws unsuspected by the defender, or an attacker might rashly disparage enemy defenses and exaggerate the likelihood of his own success in penetrating them. Western analysts of Soviet BMD seem to have been accused of overstatement more often than of understatement, but one should beware of both pitfalls. The uncertainties about operational performance in a real contingency, either a limited conflict or one of greater scale, should be kept in mind throughout this review of U.S. and West European assessments of Soviet BMD capabilities.

Before the ABM Treaty

The Soviets first began basic research on BMD "shortly after the end of World War II," and work on specific BMD development programs must have been initiated "by the mid-1950s."[6] U-2 reconnaissance pictures of the BMD research center at Sary Shagan in 1958 showed "primitive" BMD radars under construction.[7] U-2 imagery in 1960 established that "a major program was underway and that a considerable amount of progress toward the development of BMD components had already occurred."[8]

Soviet interest in BMD seems to have originated at roughly the same time as Soviet work on long-range ballistic missiles,[9] in accordance with the principle of investigating countermeasures concurrently with the development of new equipment. The interest in BMD may be seen as a logical complement to the expansion and modernization of Soviet air defenses after 1945—an impressive proliferation of interceptor aircraft, antiaircraft artillery, and surface-to-air missiles that was even costlier than the U.S. air defense effort in the 1950s and early 1960s.[10] In 1967 the U.S. secretary of defense, Robert McNamara, estimated that the Soviets had spent two and a half times as much as the United States on air defense.[11] In 1969 Soviet spending on defensive strategic systems was estimated by Secretary of Defense Melvin Laird to be three and a half to four times that of the United States.[12] It appears that a great part of this Soviet spending was in air defense.

Early Soviet BMD efforts were distinctive in that they took operational considerations most seriously. For example, during their atmospheric nuclear test series in 1961–62, the Soviets launched missiles from Kapustin Yar to the impact area associated with Sary Shagan. As Hans Rühle, head of the planning staff in the West German Ministry of Defense, has noted, "on five consecutive days nuclear weapons were detonated at high altitude above the radar system of Sary Shagan in order to investigate the effects of the electromagnetic pulse on electronic components."[13] Such tests could, in other words, supply information on the effects of nuclear explosions on radars, communications, guidance systems, and so forth. The kill radius of the nuclear warheads that would be used for BMD might also be estimated.[14] The Soviet method, trying to replicate conditions comparable to those of a nuclear war in order to test their systems, differed from the U.S. approach, which was one of making inferences about "a wide range of specific operational conditions . . . from more basic data."[15] As a result, U.S. officials were concerned that the Soviets might have surpassed the United States in knowledge about nuclear environments relevant to building BMD systems.[16]

Another distinctive feature of the Soviet approach to BMD has been the preference for prompt operational applications. This has meant deploying capabilities as soon as possible, even if rudimentary and imperfect, so that a basis for developing more effective systems—through incremental improvements—might be established. This approach contrasts with the typical U.S. weapons acquisition process, which demands that high standards of effectiveness be achieved prior to production and deployment decisions. As Stevens notes, the Soviet method has "the advantage that even still flawed systems provide the Soviet Union with a force-in-being that is able partially to fulfill some important missions."[17]

The Soviet preference for early operational deployments and the early initiation of Soviet research on antiballistic missile (ABM) capabilities help to explain why "Soviet ABM deployments preceded those of the

United States."[18] Three systems were deployed in the period before the conclusion of the ABM Treaty in 1972: the Griffon and the SA-5, which appear to have been largely unsuccessful attempts to upgrade air defense surface-to-air missiles to some BMD capability. and the Galosh-based Moscow system, which was clearly dedicated to BMD from the outset.[19] Each deserves a brief discussion before post-1972 developments are considered.

GRIFFON

As many as thirty launch positions for the Griffon surface-to-air missile (SAM) were prepared around Leningrad by 1962. The components of the Griffon system were similar to those tested at Sary Shagan, and the deployment location implied coverage against aircraft and (perhaps) missiles coming from the United States. As with most other names for Soviet systems in use in the West, the designator "Griffon" was provided by NATO. The Soviets did not indicate whether the system was designed for BMD; it may have been intended originally for air defense purposes alone.[20] Although some observers credit the Griffon with having had "a marginal capability against the first-generation Polaris A-1 missile and the medium-range Thor,"[21] others doubt that it would have been effective against strategic missiles. Mark Miller observes that its "more probable mission was against high-altitude threats such as the B-70 [bomber] and tactical ballistic missiles."[22] Even if it had some "very limited" capability for intercepting ballistic missiles, "it was incapable of dealing with emerging new ICBM developments" and may have been unsatisfactory as a high-altitude air defense system as well[23]—perhaps "because of the lack of adequate data processing and poor missile performance."[24] At any rate, the Griffon program was terminated and the deployed systems dismantled by 1964.

SA-5

The Soviets began deploying the SA-5 surface-to-air missile in 1963.[25] The first arc of SA-5 deployments was called the Tallinn Line in the West, owing to its proximity to the Estonian capital. Like the Griffon, it was developed at Sary Shagan, the principal Soviet test and development center for surface-to-air defenses, including BMD as well as air defenses. There were "serious doubts" that the initial versions of the SA-5 had significant BMD capacity, but the Soviets proceeded to extensive deployments, which were probably intended for long-range and high-altitude air defense.[26] Some experts conjecture that the Tallinn Line may have been intended to defend against the Polaris A-1 missile, because this submarine-launched ballistic missile had a range of only 1300 miles and would therefore probably have been launched from the Barents Sea—thus bringing its "flight path to the European USSR directly through the area covered by the Tallinn Line."[27] The Polaris A-1, however, was soon replaced by longer-range (and hence more flexible) SLBMs. Soviet air defenses may have been concentrated in the Tallinn area simply because it was a logical approach route for attacking Western aircraft. The absence of nuclear-warhead storage sites at the Tallinn complexes suggested that no effective BMD kill mechanism for these SA-5s was available.[28]

GALOSH

In addition to Galosh nuclear-armed interceptor missiles (first publicly displayed in 1964), the Moscow BMD system before 1972 included Hen House radars around the periphery of the USSR for early warning and target acquisition, Dog House and Cat House phased-array radars south of Moscow for battle management, and Try Add dish radars for tracking targets and guiding the Galosh interceptor missiles. The range of the Galosh (reported as "hundreds of miles"[29] or "more than 200" miles[30]) and the location of the sites in a ring forty to fifty miles from the heart of Moscow allowed the Moscow system to cover an area far beyond Moscow and to use shoot-look-shoot defense tactics. Such tactics would "make fairly high-confidence intercepts possible."[31]

The system's vulnerability to nuclear effects, however, was a serious shortcoming—for two reasons. First, the number of radars deployed was so limited that any leakage of attacking missiles and warheads could effectively eliminate the radars, either through direct attack or through nuclear effects on the electronic components of the radars (electromagnetic pulse) or on the radar's field of vision (blackout). Second, because of accuracy uncertainties, a nuclear weapon, probably one of "very large yield," had to serve as the kill mechanism on the Galosh interceptor missile.[32] Self-inflicted nuclear effects such as blackout could therefore help to degrade the system's performance, depending on the altitude and location of the nuclear explosions and other factors. The missile's size (it was carried in a canister about twenty meters long), its similarity to the U.S. Spartan system, and Soviet reports—including a Soviet television film—made it apparent that it was intended to destroy attacking missiles outside the atmosphere.[33]

The original Galosh system had three further deficiencies. First, its only credible capacity was against small attacks, but U.S. ICBMs and SLBMs were soon to be equipped with multiple independently targeted reentry vehicles (MIRVs): "while the Galosh system may have been marginally effective against the American missile force of the 1960s, it would be virtually useless against the MIRVed force of the 1970s."[34] As a result, as Rühle notes, "it would not be too difficult to saturate the radar equipment, in other words, engage with more targets than the system could process simultaneously." Second, the system's radars were vulnerable to deception by exoatmospheric decoys and chaff (clouds of thin wires that scatter radar signals). Third, the radars were incapable of scanning all possible "attack corridors" and thus left gaps in the system's protective coverage.[35] Perhaps because of these limitations, the eight complexes (including 128 Galosh missile launchers) that appear to have been planned originally were cut back in 1968 to a total of four complexes with 64 Galosh missile launchers.[36]

Since the ABM Treaty

In the 1972 ABM Treaty, each of the two parties (the Soviet Union and the United States) undertook not to deploy BMD systems "for a defense of the territory of its country and not to provide a base for such a defense" (article I). Whereas the 1972 treaty allowed each side to deploy BMD systems at two sites, including no more than 100 launchers and interceptor missiles at each site (article III), a 1974 protocol to the treaty cut the permitted level of deployment to one such site per side. The ABM Treaty also limited deployments of large phased-array radars for ballistic missile early warning and prohibited potential means of circumvention of the treaty's purpose: for example, the development of mobile land-based BMD systems or components (article V) or the development and testing of non-BMD systems (such as air defense missiles and radars) for use "in an ABM mode" (article VI). Yet the ABM Treaty authorized a certain level of continuing research and development work. Article IV stipulates that article III's limits "shall not apply to ABM systems or their components used for development or testing" and provides for a ceiling of fifteen launchers at agreed test ranges. Moreover, article VII indicates that, "subject to the provisions of this Treaty, modernization and replacement of ABM systems or their components may be carried out."

Soviet behavior under the ABM Treaty regime has differed from that of the United States in several ways. The United States built a Safeguard site at Grand Forks, North Dakota, but dismantled it in 1975–76 and reduced funding for BMD activities. (The Safeguard perimeter acquisition radar was retained for early warning.) In contrast, the Soviet Union retained its Moscow BMD system, which has provided some limited protection to the Soviet command authorities. The continuing operational status of the

Moscow system and its modernization since the late 1970s have probably facilitated the conduct of Soviet BMD research, development, and testing programs. The Moscow system has served as "a test bed for ABM systems and training,"[37] even though BMD research and test activities have remained centered at Sary Shagan.

The Soviets indicated at the outset that their BMD research efforts would continue to be intensive. The minister of defense, Marshal Andrei Grechko, remarked when the treaty was ratified by the Supreme Soviet in 1972 that it "does not place limitations of any kind on the conduct of research and experimental works directed at the solution of the problem of the defense of the country against rocket nuclear strikes."[38] Soviet BMD research and development activities have accordingly proceeded. The Treaty is relatively permissive about the development and modernization of permitted BMD capabilities, and the Soviet Union has generally made fuller use of the scope allowed by the treaty than the United States.

The impact of the ABM Treaty on Soviet BMD activities in the early 1970s was not dramatic. According to Sayre Stevens, "the level of activities at Sary Shagan continued much the same as before the treaty was signed . . . Work on the peripheral network of early warning and acquisition radars continued. Slowly but surely the Soviet Union continued to fill existing gaps in the coverage it provided. In general, this activity had a flavor of steady, unfrenzied progress toward defined development goals."[39] In addition to the radar network expansion, the active program for developing interceptor missiles should be noted: "Between 1972 and 1976, there were 55 ABM test launches, including tests of high-acceleration missiles using both conventional [that is, inertial] and infrared guidance systems."[40] The pace of this Soviet BMD activity differed from that of the United States. In 1976 Malcolm R. Currie, then director of defense research and engineering, remarked: "When the ABM Treaty was signed . . . our test activity of ABM interceptors goes practically to zero, just catastrophically within a couple of years, you know, as we deployed that one Safeguard system. Their activity continues monotonically steadily to go up. So they have an intensive activity in ABM research and development from which they could react at some time in the future."[41]

The Soviet financial investment in BMD research and advanced technology development since 1972 has also shown continued growth, in contrast to that of the United States. In 1978 it was officially estimated that the Soviets were probably spending twice as much as the United States on BMD research and development, without including Soviet BMD operational activities and the construction of new large phased-array radars.[42] According to one source, in fiscal year (FY) 1980 dollars, the United States went from a high point of approximately $1 billion a year in the late 1960s to around $200 million in FY 1980.[43] Although no precise figures on Soviet research are available, E. C. Aldridge and Robert Maust, Jr., suggested in 1979 that the relative "allocation of resources to BMD system technology and development programs changed from an approximate U.S. advantage of 2 to 1 in the late 1960s to a possible Soviet advantage of 5 to 1 in 1980."[44]

The deputy director for scientific and technical intelligence of the Defense Intelligence Agency (DIA), Jack Vorona, offered similar judgments in 1979. Although no exact estimate of Soviet expenditures on BMD could be made, observable Soviet BMD activities suggested that the amount spent was "very, very extensive" and "considerably greater" than that of the United States. Vorona explained that, besides maintaining the Moscow BMD system,

> the Soviets maintain a model Moscow ABM site at their test range which they use, regularly, for troop training. In addition, Soviet ballistic missile early warning radars are deployed much more extensively than U.S. systems . . . The big difference in R & D efforts lies in the fact that U.S. programs are characterized as technology and component programs whereas *the known Soviet programs appear aimed at achieving deployable weapon systems.* The latter requires considerably more cost for construction and testing.[45]

It is possible that the "methodical pace" of the increases in Soviet BMD investment may be explained by the regularity of the Soviet weapons acquisition and research and development planning cycle, which is apparently geared to the five-year plans of the Soviet state budget.[46]

Not even approximate estimates seem to be publicly available regarding Soviet BMD investment since 1979. The available information generally refers to "strategic defense systems" and includes air defenses as well as BMD. The USSR continues to enlarge what has been for many years the largest air defense system in the world, with 9400 SAM launchers (the United States has none defending North America); 1200 fighter-interceptor aircraft (the United States has 300) and 10,000 radars (the United States has 100).[47] The National Air Defense Troops, or Voyska-PVO, number some 371,000 and constitute a separate service of the armed forces of the USSR.[48] The ongoing expansion of the Soviet air defense network is apparent in the fact that the Soviets annually procured fifteen times as many SAMs as did the United States during the period 1980–1984.[49] A U.S.-Soviet air defense comparison omits, of course, the air defense capabilities (and offensive strike forces) of third parties, notably those maintained by China and by U.S. allies in Europe and Asia.

The USSR's high level of air defense effort probably plays a great role in supplementing the cost of BMD activities and helps to explain the estimate that "over the past decade [1975–1985] the dollar cost of Soviet strategic defense procurement has been more than the cost of U.S. strategic offense procurement."[50] Secretary of Defense Weinberger stated that, since signing the ABM Treaty in 1972, "the Soviet Union has spent more on strategic defensive forces than on strategic offensive forces."[51] According to *Soviet Military Power 1987*, during the preceding decade "the Soviets allocated resources equivalent to approximately $400 billion to both strategic offensive and defensive programs in almost equal amounts—about $20 billion per year for each program."[52]

West European observers have noted that such estimates are broad and imprecise. They have regretted the absence of a definition of strategic defense in many U.S. statements regarding Soviet investments. Official statements often fail to acknowledge that, as one CIA spokesman has noted, "estimates of Soviet spending on their military programs are based on an arcane and in absolute terms not particularly reliable science."[53] The problems obviously include incomplete information and the assumptions used (regarding labor costs, for example) in converting possible Soviet ruble costs into dollar values. Recent U.S. statements about Soviet spending on strategic defense have been, some West Europeans suggest, rather vague and less than entirely consistent.

Under Secretary of Defense for Policy Fred C. Iklé, for example, indicated that the Soviet Union "has spent slightly more on active defenses since the signing of the ABM Treaty than on its nuclear offensive forces," adding that "the bulk of it went into air defense."[54] Paul Nitze has referred to "the last two decades" (1965–1985) as a period in which "the Soviet Union has spent roughly as much on strategic defense as it has on its massive offensive nuclear forces." But Nitze's wording implies that his estimate includes not only BMD and air defense but also "a vast political leadership survival program, and nationwide civil defense forces and programs."[55] The Central Intelligence Agency's estimate is comparable to Nitze's in seeing the Soviet defensive effort as roughly equivalent in cost to that for offensive forces. The definition of strategic defense used by the CIA seems, however, to include antisubmarine warfare (ASW) in addition to BMD, air defense, and leadership protection shelters.[56] Except for Iklé's comment about "the bulk" of Soviet spending on active defenses going to air defense, no estimates of the relative magnitude of the Soviet BMD spending effort appear to be publicly available.

In February 1986, however, Secretary of Defense Weinberger indicated that "strategic defense" encompasses both passive and active measures "to blunt the effects of U.S. retaliation . . . The passive measures include both the hardening of ICBM silos and launch facilities to an unprecedented degree (far above the strength of our Minuteman silos), the proliferation of hardened leadership and command, control, and communications (C^3) bunkers, and an extensive civil defense effort . . . Active strategic defense . . . forces include air defense, missile defense, and since the 1960s, antisatellite defense."[57] In January 1987 the Department of Defense definition excluded "wartime mobilization and civil defense programs," and the chart indicated that the Soviet Union had spent $65 billion more than the United States on strategic defense since 1965 (in FY 1988 dollars).[58]

The 1986 definition of strategic defense is, it appears, the basis for the chart released by the Department of Defense indicating that (in FY 1987 dollars) the Soviet Union has spent $80 billion more than the United States on strategic defense since 1970. Weinberger added that the USSR is currently spending "ten times our level of effort on strategic defense."[59] This estimate could be reconciled with the CIA judgment that the Soviets have spent "almost fifteen times" as much as the United States on strategic defense in the decade since 1976, since U.S. spending increased beginning in the early 1980s.[60] But, except for Weinberger's statement that the Soviet BMD research program "represents a far greater investment [than the U.S. SDI] in terms of plant space, capital, and manpower,"[61] no official estimates of Soviet investment in BMD seem to be in the public domain. West European sources—official and unofficial—have generally avoided the investment issue, except to regret the nonexistence of reliable Soviet sources and the scarcity of official U.S. commentary.

Soviet BMD-relevant activities may, at any rate, be grouped under four headings: improved Moscow BMD systems, including transportable components for what is sometimes designated the ABM-X-3 system; potentially BMD-capable SAMs, including the SA-X-12; new large phased-array radars that could support the new interceptor missiles and associated radars; and advanced "exotic" technologies.

MOSCOW BMD SYSTEMS
In 1978 William Perry, the under secretary of defense for research and engineering, testified that the Soviets were developing a "layered defense" consisting of "two different missiles, one for high altitude and the other one which gets the ones which survive, and goes after them at

low altitude." This would represent an advance in that the Moscow system had been dependent on Galosh missiles alone. Perry noted that the two-layer concept was similar to what the United States had deployed in the (then-dismantled) Safeguard system, and said that his "best estimate" was that the Soviets could deploy it in "about five years." He added that "we would have perhaps two or three years' warning, depending on the extent to which they maintained covertness in what they were doing."[62] The missile for lower-altitude interceptions was reported in 1978 to be a silo-based high acceleration missile, then being tested for the first time.[63]

Jack Vorona of the DIA testified in 1979 before the Senate Committee on Armed Services that the Moscow BMD system would need "discrimination radars capable of handling large numbers of targets and high performance interceptor missiles" in order to be able "to counter sophisticated threats." He added, "There is every indication the Soviets are pursuing R & D supportive of these requirements."[64] Secretary of Defense Harold Brown referred in 1979 to the Soviet development of a new interceptor missile,[65] and added the following year that the USSR was "developing a rapidly deployable ABM system."[66] In 1978–1980 the USSR began dismantling half of its sixty-four Galosh ABM-1B launchers, and it became apparent that an upgrading and expansion of the Moscow BMD system was under way.[67] According to the Department of Defense, "when completed, the modernized Moscow ABM system will be a two-layer defense composed of silo-based, long-range, modified GALOSH interceptors; silo-based GAZELLE high-acceleration endoatmospheric interceptors designed to engage targets within the atmosphere; associated engagement, guidance and battle management radar systems; and a new large radar at Pushkino designed to control ABM engagements. The silo-based launchers may be reloadable."[68]

The terminology in use regarding the interceptor missiles in the Moscow system does not, unfortunately, seem to be fully consistent. Some sources imply that the original system consisted of Galosh ABM-1B missiles and that SH-04 (or ABM-2) missiles were then tested and deployed. Descriptions of the modern ABM-X-3 system are sometimes limited to the new high-acceleration endoatmospheric interceptor and sometimes expanded to include the improved Galosh. Stevens refers to "one or the other (or both) of the [latter] missiles" as elements of the ABM-X-3.[69] Some observers refrain from using the ABM-X-3 designation, but all seem to agree that the concept behind the vaguely defined ABM-X-3 is a more advanced and more rapidly deployable system, based on transportable radars and other components.[70] The ABM-X-3 may have originated in the Soviet development, beginning in 1974, of a transportable BMD radar that is reportedly capable of deployment within "several months."[71]

Estimates as to when the upgraded Moscow system could be fully operational, with the 100 launchers permitted by the ABM Treaty, have slipped from 1987 to 1988 or "the late 1980s."[72] The improved Galosh interceptor missile is, like its predecessor namesake, nuclear armed and designed to engage warheads in space before they reenter the atmosphere. The improved Galosh apparently has some features in common with another Soviet system, the SH-04 interceptor missile. The first reported tests of the SH-04 were in 1976,[73] and several sources indicate that the SH-04 "can loiter in space by stopping and restarting its engines, thus giving its land-based radars time to discriminate between live warheads and chaff or decoys."[74] France's Ecole Polytechnique group of experts and some U.S. sources have referred to the improved Galosh interceptor as the SH-11, noting that it could (in conjunction with transportable radars) furnish a basis for a rapid expansion of the Moscow BMD system.[75] According to a French parliamentary report, the full treaty-compliant Moscow system is expected to consist of sixty-four SH-11 exoatmospheric interceptors (with ranges of 150 to 500 km) and thirty-six SH-08 (Gazelle) endoatmospheric interceptors (with ranges of 80 to 300 km).[76]

As suggested above, the silo-based high-acceleration interceptor for engaging targets within the atmosphere is also known as the Gazelle or SH-08; it first appeared in the late 1970s. The SH-08 has given the USSR its first capability to employ "atmospheric sorting" to discriminate genuine warheads from penetration aids such as lightweight decoys and chaff. This would appear to be especially feasible to the extent that the enemy ballistic missiles still depended on chaff as their principal penetration aid. It was reported in 1979, for example, that chaff packages constituted the only penetration aids on U.S. Minuteman ICBMs.[77] The SH-08 could enable the Soviets to wait until the chaff slowed down and "pancaked" on hitting the atmosphere; the real reentry vehicles (RVs) would pierce through the chaff and be readily discernible. The SH-08/Gazelle might also be effective against penetration aids more sophisticated than chaff. All decoys that are significantly lighter than real warheads slow down in the atmosphere. According to an official statement prepared by the British Ministry of Defence, this interceptor's "endoatmospheric" capability "will enable discrimination against all but the most elaborate penetration aids."[78]

The Department of Defense statement that "the silo-based launchers may be reloadable" could logically apply to both the improved Galosh and the Gazelle, but published reports have referred to a "rapid-reload capability" for only the SH-08. Unnamed U.S. officials have reportedly described multiple launches from the same silo, without any reloading or surface launch equipment observed. For some, this has implied "an underground automatic reload system," which "could double or even triple the number of allowed interceptors under the [ABM] treaty."[79] Such tests have reportedly been observed "on more than one occasion."[80] Because the launch equipment is underground, neither the reload method nor the number of reloads can be monitored by national technical means.[81] These reports have suggested to some analysts a possible Soviet violation of article V (2) of the ABM Treaty, which states: "Each party undertakes not to develop, test, or deploy ABM launchers for launching more than one ABM interceptor missile at a time from each launcher, not to modify deployed launchers to provide them with such a capability, nor to develop, test, or deploy automatic or semi-automatic or other similar systems for rapid reload of ABM launchers."

The December 1985 unclassified report of the president to the Congress on Soviet noncompliance with arms control agreements noted that the "rapid reload" possibility is significant because the ABM Treaty "does not limit the number of interceptor missiles that can be built and stockpiled." It concluded that Soviet actions in this respect "constitute an ambiguous situation" and "a serious concern."[82]

Other observers argue that a reloadable launcher should not be considered a rapid reload system unless reloading has been observed to require a "period of less than 15 minutes," on the grounds that "U.S. intelligence believed in 1972 that the Galosh ABM launchers could be reloaded in a period of about 15 minutes." Those holding this viewpoint imply that a "strategically significant" period of time for rapid reload should be based on the consideration that "U.S. SLBM warheads could arrive at Soviet targets in less than 15–20 minutes; U.S. ICBMs could arrive approximately 15 minutes later."[83] This reasoning seems to exclude the possibility that nuclear conflicts could involve scenarios other than well-coordinated salvos involving large numbers of U.S. SLBMs and ICBMs. Declaratory U.S. nuclear strategy has for over a decade included options for selective strikes, with substantial numbers of forces withheld for intrawar deterrence. Soviet BMD launchers might then presumably be reloaded. Moreover, Soviet doctrine has long posited the possibility of protracted nuclear conflict, with nuclear exchanges spaced over weeks and months.

No information seems to have been made public on whether there were indications during the construction phase of an automatic reload system for the interceptor silos. Some observers have speculated that reloading may simply consist of mounting another canisterized missile in a launcher, either above ground or in a silo. If such reloading could be done within the revisit time of a reconnaissance satellite (perhaps ninety minutes or more), this might explain the reports on the absence of observable reloading or launch equipment between launches. Some sources assert that tests of such reloading at Sary Shagan have been accomplished in "much less than a day" for both the improved Galosh and the Gazelle.[84] Decreased reload time could significantly improve the utility of a BMD system.

European sources have generally not commented on the rapid-reload issue. France's Ecole Polytechnique group has described it as an open question.[85] Rather than referring to the possibility that the Soviets might manufacture reload missiles, a well-informed French expert has suggested that the Soviets might produce additional interceptor missiles to defend targets other than the Moscow region, "once the Galosh replacement has been completed."[86] The Soviets are reportedly stockpiling additional BMD interceptor missiles.[87]

The most visible of the new elements in the Moscow complex since 1980 has been the Pushkino radar, a pyramidal structure 152 meters long at the base and 76 meters high. Each of its four faces displays a phased array. The Pushkino radar, also known as Pill Box, is four times larger than the U.S. Pave Paws radar.[88] According to France's Ecole Polytechnique group, the Pushkino radar will increase Soviet BMD battle management capabilities. It will be effective in all directions (360 degrees, in contrast to the radars of the original Moscow system) and is expected to be capable of tracking 1000 to 2000 targets simultaneously, at a range on the order of 2000 km.[89]

Two of the other radars associated with the Moscow system, the Pawn Shop missile guidance radar and the Flat Twin tracking radar, have (particularly the latter) been seen as potential violations of the ABM Treaty. The Flat Twin has been described as "both transportable and modular" in that it could "be disassembled, moved in component stages and reassembled in a period of months," assuming that its relocation site had been suitably prepared in advance; the Pawn Shop is "housed in a van-sized container."[90] These characteristics have for several years raised questions with respect to Common Understanding C for interpretation of the ABM Treaty, for this understanding specifies that all allowed launchers and radars must be "of permanent fixed types."

As long ago as 1978, U.S. Secretary of State Cyrus Vance reported that,

The U.S.S.R. does not have a mobile ABM system or components for such a system. Since 1971, the Soviets have installed at ABM test ranges several radars associated with an ABM system currently in development. *One of the types of radars associated with this system can be erected in a matter of months, rather than requiring years to build* as has been the case for ABM radars both sides have deployed in the past. Another type could be emplaced on prepared concrete foundations. This new system and its components can be installed more rapidly than previous ABM systems, but they are clearly not mobile in the sense of being able to be moved about readily or hidden. *A single complete operational site would take about half a year to construct.* A nationwide ABM system based on this new system under development would take a matter of years to build.[91]

At the request of the Congress, the president in October 1984 forwarded unclassified as well as classified versions of the report on Soviet compliance with arms control agreements by the bipartisan General Advisory Committee on Arms Control and Disarmament. The unclassified report referred to Soviet development and deployment of nonpermanently fixed BMD radars since 1975 as a violation of Common Understanding C regarding article V (1) of the ABM Treaty.[92] In contrast, the president's own February 1985 report to the Congress regarding Soviet noncompliance with arms control agreements concluded that "Soviet actions with respect to ABM component mobility are ambiguous, but the USSR's development of components of a new ABM system, which apparently are designed to be deployable at sites requiring relatively little or no preparation, represent a potential violation of its legal obligation under the ABM Treaty."[93]

Some argue that U.S. component mobility interpretations in 1972 were such that the system would have to be capable of being "disassembled, transported, and reassembled" within a period of "a week or less" for the activity to "be considered inconsistent with the Treaty."[94] Flat Twin radars would not be treaty violations, according to this interpretation, though they might nonetheless have considerable strategic importance in some circumstances. The United States is currently unprepared to deploy BMD radars at a comparable pace.

Other observers, however, are not certain that testing of movable BMD system elements should necessarily be seen as even a potential ABM Treaty violation: "The components of the Soviets' fully tested ABM-X-3 system—the Flat Twin radar and the SH-04 and the SH-08 missiles—are merely 'transportable,' not 'mobile.' The Treaty does not limit mass production or storage of these components. If they are ever deployed *en masse* after a sudden denunciation of the Treaty, the United States would have no legal complaint."[95]

Some experts judge that the USSR has the capacity for such production. The missiles for the new Moscow complex "are reportedly in a production line which normally turns out much larger quantities of equipment than would be required to modernize the Moscow site alone. This suggests that the Soviets have placed themselves in a position to move quickly to a larger system, at a time of their choosing."[96] Stevens agrees that the ABM-X-3 seems "suitable for fairly rapid deployment because of the transportable nature of its components," and that its other characteristics make it "appropriate for widespread deployment." In his view, "substantial expansion of the Moscow defenses beyond treaty limits could occur rapidly. If such an expansion could allow a preferential defense of certain critical components such as hardened command bunkers, a militarily significant capability could be achieved."[97]

France's Ecole Polytechnique group has also underlined the potential significance of the "modular and transportable" Flat Twin and Pawn Shop radars, noting that previously manufactured radars and missiles could be deployed in a few months: "It therefore cannot be excluded that the Soviets could have by 1990 a great number of operational ABM systems, mobile or at least transportable, that would then be in flagrant contradiction with the ABM Treaty. These systems would perhaps not have the capability to cover all Soviet territory. However, they would permit reasonably effective protection for an important number of specific sites."[98]

POTENTIALLY BMD-CAPABLE SAMS

Surface-to-air missiles (SAMs) are normally regarded as intended for defense against aircraft and cruise missiles (which are, after all, simply pilotless aircraft). Three SAMs have, however, been discussed in recent years as potentially BMD-capable systems: the SA-5, SA-10, and SA-X-12. While the SA-X-12 has the most significant BMD potential, the SA-5 and SA-10 continue to receive some analytical attention.

SA-5. The Soviets currently deploy about 2050 SA-5 launchers.[99] The SA-5 has been repeatedly modified and improved since it first appeared in the early 1960s. In the late 1960s and early 1970s, various U.S. officials testified that the SA-5 was such an effective high-altitude air defense interceptor that it might be upgraded to some capability against ballistic missiles if it were supplied with suitable radar guidance.[100]

The SA-5's radars were reportedly tested "some 50" times in conjunction with strategic ballistic missile flights in 1973 and 1974.[101] The Soviet warheads used in the tests "simulated the characteristics of American reentry vehicles."[102] The testing was halted when the United States objected in the SALT Standing Consultative Commission that this might violate the ABM Treaty's prohibitions against testing SAMs in an ABM mode.[103]

Some observers emphasize that the USSR has "continued to produce and deploy the SA-5 Gammon long after [the] U.S. Strategic Air Command . . . shifted its tactics from high-altitude penetration of Soviet air space, to low-altitude penetration. Since the SA-5 Gammon is entirely ineffective in low-altitude defence, this has led to renewed suspicions of the ABM role of this system."[104] In 1986 the Joint Chiefs of Staff listed the SA-5 with the SA-10 and SA-X-12 as SAMs that "may have potential to intercept some types of U.S. ballistic missiles."[105] The SA-5's range may be as great as 300 km. It may be fitted with either a nuclear or a conventional warhead, and "improved terminal maneuvering"—perhaps with an "antiradiation seeker"—has been mentioned.[106] Yet, the Department of Defense *Soviet Military Power* surveys have since 1981 described the SA-5 as simply a long-range interceptor "designed to counter the threat of high-performance aircraft."[107] Although "many . . . still believe that some BMD capability is embodied in the SA-5 or could be achieved rather easily if the Soviet Union chose to do so,"[108] with "the capability to intercept RVs of older generation SLBMs" considered most likely,[109] the predominant opinion is that the SA-5's BMD capability is "probably marginal at best."[110]

SA-10. Deployment of the nonmobile SA-10, described as "probably not fixed, i.e., transportable or semi-permanent,"[111] began in 1980. In April 1984, about 40 sites with almost 350 SA-10 launchers were reported to be operational.[112] In April 1985, it was reported that almost 60 sites were operational, with work under way on "at least another 30."[113] By March 1987, according to the Department of Defense, over 80 sites were reported operational with work progressing on "at least another 20 . . . Nearly half of these sites are located near Moscow. This emphasis on Moscow as well as the deployment patterns noted for the other SA-10 sites suggest a first priority on terminal defense of command-and-control, military, and key industrial complexes."[114] In the meantime, apparently in order to improve prospects for survivability, the Soviets have developed and started to deploy a mobile version of the SA-10. The Department of Defense judges that "this version, designated SA-10b, could be used to support Soviet theater forces and to permit periodic changes in the location of SA-10 sites within the USSR to counter the various kinds of US retaliatory forces more effectively."[115]

Published assessments have, overall, displayed increasing confidence in the SA-10's strategic BMD potential, although some uncertainties seem to persist in this regard. In 1980, without any specification of which Soviet systems were under discussion, the Soviet program to develop BMD against the Pershing II was described by a U.S. senator as "aggressive."[116] But the United States in 1980–1982 attributed the Pershing II "a high assurance of penetrating future Soviet defenses,"[117] partly because the combination of ground-launched cruise missiles and Pershing IIs envisaged in NATO's December 1979 decision for modernization of intermediate-range nuclear forces would stress Soviet defenses, and both would have potential for penetrability measures upgrade.[118] The 1981 and 1983 Department of Defense reports on Soviet military power alluded to potential antitactical ballistic missile capabilities under development, but did not attribute any BMD potential to the SA-10.[119]

In April 1983, however, the Scowcroft Commission's report revealed that "at least one new Soviet defensive system is designed to have capability against short-range ballistic missiles; it could perhaps be upgraded for use against the reentry vehicles of some submarine-launched missiles and even ICBMs."[120] A year later, in April 1984, the Department of Defense specified that "the Soviets are deploying one surface-to-air missile system, the SA-10, and are flight-testing another, the mobile SA-X-12. The SA-X-12 is both a tactical SAM and antitactical ballistic missile. *Both the SA-10 and SA-X-12 may have the potential to intercept some types of U.S. strategic ballistic missiles as well.* These systems could, if properly supported, add significant point-target coverage to a widespread ABM deployment."[121]

In 1985 the Department of Defense omitted attributing any antitactical ballistic missile (ATBM) capability to the SA-10 while stating that the SA-X-12 "may have the capability to engage the LANCE and both the PERSHING I and PERSHING II ballistic missiles."[122] The 1987 edition of *Soviet Military Power* nonetheless reported that the SA-10 has "a capability against low-altitude targets with small radar cross-sections such as cruise missiles, a capability against tactical ballistic missiles, and possibly a potential to intercept some types of strategic ballistic missiles."[123]

The question of the SA-10's BMD potential is, as France's Ecole Polytechnique group has observed, "controversial but important." If the SA-10 had genuine BMD potential, "the Soviet Union would have the possibility of equipping itself with a certain anti-missile capacity without it being visible."[124]

SA-12. The 1987 edition of *Soviet Military Power* revealed that there are two versions of the mobile SA-12. The Soviets have begun deploying the

SA-12A/Gladiator and are testing "an even more capable, longer range, higher altitude complement, the SA-X-12B/GIANT." Both versions are considered "capable of intercepting aircraft at all altitudes as well as cruise missiles and tactical ballistic missiles," while the SA-X-12B "may have the potential to intercept some types of strategic ballistic missiles."[125]

The only other noteworthy official comments elaborate on the statement in 1984 by Robert Cooper, then director of the Defense Advanced Research Projects Agency, that the SA-X-12's mobility could enable the Soviets to "build thousands of these ballistic-missile interceptors" and conceal them in storage until ready to deploy rapidly a "significant capability."[126] In 1986 Defense Department publications said that the SA-X-12 could give the USSR "supplemental ABM capability,"[127] and that widespread deployments of the SA-10 and SA-X-12 in the late 1980s "could, if properly supported, add significant point-target defense coverage to a nationwide Soviet ABM deployment."[128]

The obscure phrase "if properly supported" could well refer to the need for suitable radar internetting and command, control, and communications. According to France's Ecole Polytechnique group, the SA-X-12's performance characteristics (notably its initial acceleration speed) are "such that they are obviously designed for doing much more than air defense . . . In the long term, the ABM capacity of a system based on the SA-12 will depend on the way in which the SA-12s will be coordinated with the large radars that perform the functions of early warning and battle management. If such a coordination proved effective, the deployed system would have a considerably improved ABM capacity."[129] The Department of Defense has indicated that the air surveillance data systems of Soviet surface-to-air missile systems are being internetted and integrated, and that the network includes links with the over-the-horizon BMD radars.[130]

Unofficial sources have reported that the SA-X-12 "was successfully tested in Siberia in 1983 for its defense capabilities against an intermediate-range ballistic missile that showed the same characteristics as the U.S. Pershing-2 which is currently being emplaced in Europe."[131] Other sources report that these tests took place "on several occasions during 1983 and 1984,"[132] and that the SA-X-12 was "tested against the Scaleboard, a short-range [900 km] Soviet ballistic missile."[133] Successful SA-X-12 tests against the Scud and the SS-4, Soviet ballistic missiles with ranges of 300 km and 2000 km, respectively, have also been reported.[134] Some sources contend that such tests have furnished grounds for a capability against older sea-launched ballistic missiles, including U.S. Poseidon SLBMs.[135] While some reports have suggested a low rate of success in such tests (as low as one intercept in twenty attempts),[136] others have noted that no comprehensive test data have been made public. More recent test series may have been more successful than initial indications. Some analysts interpret testing in an "ABM mode" to require actual intercepts of RVs, whereas others suspect that successful tracking tests and the launching of interceptors against notional targets could partially substitute for full-scale intercept exercises.

Although some doubt whether proven capability against intermediate-range missiles would equate to capability against SLBMs, especially those with greater range and reentry velocity,[137] Stevens judges that:

> *The Soviet Union could have, with its new SAMs, a BMD capability able to enhance damage limitation that is not controlled by the ABM Treaty, whereas the United States, with no strategic SAMs, has none* . . . ATBM [antitactical ballistic missile] . . . systems, designed to handle short-range ballistic missiles, must include in their design many of the features apt to be missing and requiring upgrade in SAM systems. Very short reaction times and automated launch commitment processes, for example, must be included in ATBM systems. Soviet development of such systems constitutes a qualitative change in the nature of SAM upgrade concerns, for although these weapons systems are not specifically constrained by the ABM Treaty, *they will almost surely possess some significant capability against long-range strategic ballistic missiles . . . This is particularly true in the case of submarine-launched ballistic missiles (SLBMs).*[138]

The relative vulnerabilities of U.S. ICBMs and SLBMs are significant because U.S. ICBMs, like SLBMs in port, are subject to Soviet counter-force attack. This means that survivable U.S. deterrent capabilities depend heavily on SLBMs at sea. U.S. SLBM RVs, however, are more vulnerable to Soviet BMD than are U.S. ICBM RVs for three reasons. First, it has been reported that no penetration aids—not even chaff—accompany U.S. Poseidon SLBM RVs.[139] (The current operational U.S. SLBM inventory is composed of 256 Poseidons and 384 Trident I's.)[140] Second, SLBMs generally have shorter ranges and slower reentry speeds than ICBMs. Third, SLBM RVs of older design generally have relatively high radar cross sections. This is because the lack of space in SLBM launch tubes and the low throwweights of SLBMs posed especially challenging problems of reentry vehicle design.[141] Although the guidance mechanisms and other features of specific systems differ, intermediate-range missiles such as the Pershing II "have essentially the same re-entry characteristics as SLBMs; thus, an ATBM tends to have inherent capability to defend against SLBMs."[142]

As has already been suggested, the most impressive of the potentially BMD-capable Soviet SAMs and the one most capable of functioning as an ATBM is the SA-X-12B/Giant. It may have been designed from the outset to be capable of engaging both high-performance aircraft and some types of ballistic missiles. It is reportedly equipped with high-acceleration interceptor missiles and radar and data-processing capabilities for automatic launch commitment. According to France's Ecole Polytechnique group,

> with the "Giant," the SA-X-12 would be capable of effectively protecting—against the reentry vehicles of Minuteman II, Poseidon or Pershing I—a ground surface with the dimensions of a circle with a radius of 12 km. It would remain, however, much less effective against the warheads of Minuteman III, MX or [Trident II] D5 [SLBMs], whose re-entry speeds are very superior to the former. This is true for isolated SA-X-12s, that is, ones functioning without information from an early warning radar network. This interconnection is difficult to realize, but it is known that the Soviets have a certain competence in this domain: they are already capable of tracking over a thousand systems simultaneously in the European theater.[143]

Apparently no public U.S. sources, official or unofficial, have offered any information—however speculative—on the SA-X-12's kill mechanism, although it is presumed to have a nonnuclear warhead for air defense missions. The Ecole Polytechnique group noted the absence of publicly available data and suggested that the SA-X-12s might require nuclear warheads with yields on the order of ten kilotons to have BMD capability, but that they might nonetheless have BMD capability with conventional warheads.[144] General Jeannou Lacaze, then chief of staff of the French armed forces, referred in 1985 to possible Soviet deployments of "surface-to-air missiles with nuclear warheads, and even conventional warheads" with BMD potential; but he did not indicate whether he had the SA-X-12 and/or other specific interceptor missiles in mind.[145]

Whether the SA-X-12 would require a nuclear warhead to be effective against ballistic missiles would depend on its accuracy. A large kill radius can compensate for miss distance. The tests that have been reported have presumably been nonnuclear, because the 1963 Partial Test Ban Treaty has forbidden nuclear explosions in the atmosphere. If the tests have been as successful as some reports have suggested, the SA-X-12 may have (1) high accuracy, permitting use of a conventional warhead, or (2) sufficient accuracy to permit the inference that use of a nuclear warhead of suitable yield and design would have resulted in an effective kill. Information on the SA-X-12's accuracy is as scarce as data on its kill mechanism.

The Ecole Polytechnique group has pointed out, however, that an important indicator of Soviet intentions will be where the SA-X-12 is deployed.[146] According to the U.S. Department of Defense, in 1986 the SA-X-12 was still being flight tested and was not yet being operationally deployed.[147] This official information cast doubt on reports in late 1985 that the SA-X-12 had already been deployed to defend SS-25 ICBM sites.[148] The Department of Defense in 1987 indicated that the SA-12A/Gladiator was replacing the SA-4 air defense systems deployed with nondivisional ground force air defense units.[149] Unofficial reports indicate that these deployments are in the Carpathian military district, and that the Soviets are also deploying SA-12A/Gladiators to defend SS-18 ICBM sites.[150]

Such deployments would underline the extent to which past distinctions between strategic and tactical SAMs and between strategic and tactical BMD have been obscured by modern technology. CIA officials have testified that the SA-X-12's "technical capabilities bring to the forefront the problem that improving technology is blurring the distinction between air defense and ABM systems."[151]

These uncertainties help to explain Sayre Stevens' judgment (cited above) that ATBM capability upgradable to defense against strategic ballistic missiles is "not controlled by the ABM Treaty." The U.S. government's position appears to be that the SA-X-12 would be legally allowable under the ABM Treaty if the SA-X-12 were capable only of intercepting "shorter-range ballistic missiles," because the treaty only limits capabilities against "strategic ballistic missiles." Treaty compliance issues arise to the extent that the SA-X-12 may be useful in defense against U.S. ICBMs and SLBMs. In 1983 the deputy under secretary of defense for strategic and theater nuclear forces, T. K. Jones, testified that "it appears the Soviets are developing that [the SA-X-12] to counter the shorter-range ballistic missiles and the ABM Treaty was drafted so that that is a legal development and they could deploy it fully. However, at the margin, a system that has good capability against something like the Pershing II would also have reasonable capability to defend reasonable areas against our ICBMs and submarine-launched ballistic missiles."[152]

The controversy is complicated by the failure of the United States to obtain in the ABM Treaty "an adequately specific definition" of the prohibited testing of air defense radars, launchers, and missiles "in an ABM mode."[153] The only definition attached to the ABM Treaty came in the form of Unilateral Statement E by the U.S. delegation—a statement that was not endorsed by the Soviet delegation and that excluded radars "used for purposes such as range safety or instrumentation." In an attempt to close what some still perceive as a loophole open to Soviet exploitation (because the Soviets might simply assert that U.S. assessments of the purposes of Soviet radar activities are mistaken, and that the activities are in fact allowable), the United States on November 1, 1978, obtained Soviet approval of a secret agreed statement that

> specifies criteria for applying the term "tested in an ABM mode" as used in the ABM Treaty to missiles, launchers, and radars. Finally, the Agreed Statement specifies that the ABM Treaty permits air defense radars located at ABM test ranges to carry out air defense functions, but to avoid ambiguous situations or misunderstandings the sides will refrain from concurrent testing of air defense components and ABM system components co-located at the same test range, and air defense radars utilized as instrumentation equipment will not be used to make measurements on strategic ballistic missiles.[154]

It has been reported that the United States made further (and unsuccessful) attempts in 1982 and 1983 to reach an additional mutual understanding about concurrent operations of SAM and BMD components that would minimize residual ambiguities.[155] In February 1985, the president reported to the Congress that

> evidence of Soviet actions with respect to concurrent [SAM and BMD] operations is insufficient to assess fully compliance with Soviet obligations under the ABM Treaty, although the Soviet Union has conducted tests that have involved air defense radars in ABM-related activities. The number of incidents of concurrent operation of SAM and ABM components indicate *the USSR probably has violated the prohibition on testing SAM components in an ABM mode. In several cases this may be highly probable.* This and other such Soviet activities suggest that the USSR may be preparing an ABM defense of its national territory.[156]

In his December 1985 report to the Congress, the president reached a similar conclusion, adding a reference to the "large number, and consistency over time, of incidents of concurrent operation of ABM and SAM components, plus Soviet failure to accommodate fully U.S. concerns." The December 1985 report also revealed that the classified version of the February 1985 report had "examined whether the Soviet Union has tested a SAM system or component in an ABM mode or given it the capability to counter strategic ballistic missiles or their elements in flight trajectory." The evidence on SAM upgrade was found "insufficient to assess compliance."[157]

Some observers found it surprising that the president's December 1985 report to the Congress did not allude to a U.S.-Soviet agreement in the Standing Consultative Commission in June 1985 regarding concurrent operation of SAM and ABM components. The official press release indicated simply that the USSR and the United States had "signed a Common Understanding intended to further enhance the viability of the ABM treaty."[158] But the Soviets have reportedly agreed that the air defense radars at Sary Shagan "may not be operated during missile tests unless potentially hostile aircraft are clearly in the vicinity, and their operation must then be fully explained."[159] Other observers see deficiencies in the ABM Treaty's definitions with respect to SAM upgrade and testing "in an ABM mode," given advances in air defense technology; they contend that "the ABM Treaty is not being violated so much as it is being left behind by evolving reality."[160]

NEW LARGE PHASED-ARRAY RADARS

New large phased-array radars in the USSR are militarily significant in that they could supplement the Soviet satellite launch-detection system, over-the-horizon radars, and older early-warning radars with hand-over data for the new Moscow-associated systems and for potentially BMD-capable SAMs such as the SA-12.[161] The Flat Twin and Pawn Shop and other new transportable engagement radars would benefit from early warning superior to that which might be provided by the Hen House network of the 1960s, even though the capabilities of the eleven large Hen House radars on the USSR's periphery have been improved since the conclusion of the ABM Treaty.[162] The radar restrictions of the ABM Treaty are particularly important because the treaty does not limit the production of interceptor missiles, which could be built covertly and then deployed relatively quickly. The large phased-array acquisition and tracking radars for optimally effective BMD require years to construct and can be more readily observed than the production and testing of interceptor missiles and transportable engagement and guidance radars.

The Soviet construction of new large phased-array radars (LPARs) to supplement those in existence in 1972, at the conclusion of the ABM Treaty, was apparently first reported in 1978.[163] In 1978 William Perry, under secretary of defense for research and engineering, testified that the Soviets "have engaged in a very significant deployment of very large phased array radars around the periphery of the Soviet Union . . . There is a question as to what the function of the radars is, whether they are early warning and attack assessment radars in the sense of our BMEWs [Ballistic Missile Early Warning System] or PAR [Perimeter Acquisition Radar] radar, or whether indeed they are intended to be used as ———[deleted]."[164] Secretary of Defense Harold Brown in 1979 and 1980 also referred to Soviet efforts to improve their "large phased-array detection and tracking radars."[165] In 1981 the Joint Chiefs of Staff confirmed that new LPARs were "under construction at various locations in the USSR. These radars could perform some battle management functions as well as provide redundant ballistic missile early warning coverage."[166] It has since been revealed that a total of nine such LPARs are under construction.[167]

Of these nine new LPARs, most public attention has been devoted to the one located near Krasnoyarsk, which the United States evidently first detected in mid-1983. This radar has been at the center of BMD discussions since January 1984, when the U.S. government announced that it considered the radar "almost certainly" a violation of the ABM Treaty.[168] The Soviet Union has maintained that the Krasnoyarsk radar is an ABM Treaty–permitted radar for space tracking. The U.S. response has been that the radar's design is "not optimized for a space tracking role" but is "essentially identical to that of other radars that are known—and acknowledged by the Soviets—to be for ballistic missile detection and tracking, including ballistic missile early warning." The Krasnoyarsk radar differs from the other new LPARs in that it is not located on the periphery of the Soviet Union and oriented outward, as required by the ABM Treaty. Instead, it is situated some 750 km from the nearest border and oriented inward, toward the northeast.[169]

U.S. officials have disputed the Soviet contention that the Krasnoyarsk radar is intended to track satellites in space: "If the Soviets [had] set out to build a space track radar at Krasnoyarsk, they would have designed a radar that could look up to a much higher angle and would have oriented the radar almost in the opposite direction."[170] More specifically, it has been reported that the Krasnoyarsk radar's tilt of about twenty degrees from the vertical optimizes it for surveillance of the horizon, whereas a dedicated space-tracking radar would be oriented upward at about forty-five degrees. An unpublished National Security Council (NSC) paper has reportedly concluded that the radar's space track capability would be "limited and redundant," but that its location and capabilities could provide BMD battle management coverage for the defense of critical targets in the central region of the USSR. If the radar had been intended to provide only ballistic missile early warning, the NSC paper reportedly argues, it would have been placed on the Soviet periphery—a location that would have been in conformity with the ABM Treaty and would have gained the USSR six minutes of warning time.[171]

Some observers doubt whether the Krasnoyarsk radar is intended to serve as either an early-warning or battle management radar for BMD, while others see an early-warning role with respect to U.S. SLBMs in the northern Pacific as more likely than a BMD battle management function.[172] These disagreements may stem in part from deficiencies in the ABM Treaty's definitions and the difficulties of verifying the intended functions of what could be a multipurpose radar. According to Robert Buchheim, "this problem was built into the treaty from the day it was written. Call it a loophole if you want—the treaty is simply incomplete. On the one hand, it allows radars built for spacetrack or intelligence, and on the other, it limits those for early warning and ballistic missile defense. The problem is that phased-array radars can do all of these things, and the two sides never reached any agreement on how to tell the difference."[173]

In view of the inherent capabilities that this new LPAR may be expected to have when it becomes operational, the U.S. government in February 1985 announced that it considered Krasnoyarsk a violation of the ABM Treaty:

> In an effort to preclude creation of a base for territorial ABM defense, the ABM Treaty limits the deployment of ballistic missile early warning radars, including large phased-array radars used for that purpose, to locations along the periphery of the national territory of each party and requires that they be oriented outward . . . The U.S. Government judges, on the basis of evidence which continued to be available through 1984, that the new large phased-array radar under construction at Krasnoyarsk constitutes a violation of legal obligations under the Anti-Ballistic Missile Treaty of 1972 in that in its associated siting, orientation, and capability, it is prohibited by this Treaty. Continuing construction, and the absence of credible alternative explanations, have reinforced our assessment of its purpose. Despite U.S. requests, no corrective action has been taken.[174]

This U.S. government position has remained unchanged. The December 1985 and March 1987 reports of the president to the Congress on Soviet noncompliance with arms control agreements reaffirmed the earlier conclusion that Krasnoyarsk represented a treaty violation.[175] The Krasnoyarsk radar has also been judged a violation of the ABM Treaty by the U.S. Senate (in a 93-to-2 vote) and the U.S. House of Representatives (in a 418-to-0 vote).[176]

Krasnoyarsk is the only reported ABM Treaty violation that West

European governments have commented on. In March 1986 Sir Geoffrey Howe, the British foreign minister, called Krasnoyarsk a "cause for deep concern," adding that "double standards over Treaty compliance cannot be accepted."[177] Lord Trefgarne, the minister of state for defence procurement, declared in June 1986 that the siting and orientation of the Krasnoyarsk radar pose "serious questions" about ABM Treaty compliance: "We have raised this matter with the Soviet Union on a number of occasions, and clearly it will be necessary to resolve these questions if the ABM Treaty is to be protected from erosion and the necessary confidence is to be created for concluding new agreements."[178]

Other West European governments have been more circumspect than the British. Paradoxically enough, their reticence seems to stem in part from deference to a reported judgment in January 1985 by Britain's Cabinet Joint Intelligence Committee that it is "unlikely" that the Krasnoyarsk radar would be effective in a BMD battle management role and that the Soviet declarations about its space-tracking role are "plausible."[179] Some West European officials seem to doubt that the reported violation is militarily significant, whereas others consider the relevant treaty provisions rather ambiguous. Other possible factors— inferior national intelligence means, for example—were reviewed in the Introduction.

Whatever their reasons, most NATO European governments have limited their support for U.S. findings about the Krasnoyarsk radar and other issues to vague generalities. The October 1985 communiqué of NATO's Nuclear Planning Group referred to the "evidence of Soviet treaty violations" presented by the U.S. secretary of defense and stated, "We take the most serious view of this and call on the new Soviet leadership to take the steps necessary to assure full compliance with its commitments."[180] West German Chancellor Helmut Kohl has apparently not gone further than stating that the Krasnoyarsk radar is "possibly" in violation of the ABM Treaty.[181]

France's Ecole Polytechnique group has noted that the Krasnoyarsk radar's siting and orientation are inconsistent with the ABM Treaty. It could therefore be more easily defended against enemy attack and could in principle serve as a means of BMD battle management. But, the group concluded, they would prefer to reserve judgment on its true capacities until it becomes operational and begins emitting signals that might throw light on its purposes and potential.[182]

The Krasnoyarsk radar's status as an apparent violation of the ABM Treaty may well be significant for the future of Soviet-U.S. arms control arrangements; but the strategically relevant question is the BMD potential of the entire Soviet network for surveillance and target tracking, not the independent capability of one radar.[183]

Published assessments disagree on the military value of the new Soviet LPAR network. Some describe the radars as unlikely to be effective in BMD roles, especially in the most challenging task of battle management. It has been stated that the separation of the transmitter and receiver arrays at the new LPAR sites is "indicative of the limitations of Soviet radar and signal processing technologies compared to their U.S. counterparts."[184] Others have suggested that the Soviets have assumed the great expense of building separate arrays in order to obtain clearer reception and higher reliability. The Krasnoyarsk radar alone could, it has been estimated, provide battle management coverage sufficient to protect 200 ICBM silos and "over 20 percent of the Soviet ICBM warheads."[185] In March 1987 the Department of Defense noted: "These radars provide significantly improved target-tracking and -handling capabilities and add a redundancy in coverage over the existing HEN HOUSE network. In conjunction with the HEN HOUSE radars, the LPAR near Krasnoyarsk in Siberia, when fully operational, will close the final gap in the Soviet ballistic missile early warning radar coverage. The entire network could become fully operational in the mid-1990s."[186]

France's Ecole Polytechnique group has concluded that the new LPAR network, once operational, could contribute to a BMD system "capable of protecting a zone much larger than the Moscow region alone."[187] Similarly, high officials of the Central Intelligence Agency testified in June 1985 that the new LPAR network will give the USSR "a much improved capability for ballistic missile early warning, attack assessment, and accurate target tracking. These radars will be technically capable of providing battle management support to a widespread ABM system, but there are uncertainties about whether the Soviets would rely on these radars to support a widespread ABM deployment."[188]

No information on the nature of the uncertainties that might put the reliability of the new LPARs in doubt was offered in this testimony. But Robert Gates, the CIA's deputy director, is reported to have indicated that LPARs could be vulnerable to attack: "Because such radars are fixed and they are key nodes for an A.B.M. system's capability, there will always be an issue of whether an A.B.M. system is worth having, which depends to a great extent on a few potentially quite vulnerable facilities."[189] More specifically, the Soviets would have to consider the vulnerability of such radars to nuclear weapons effects, including destruction and blackout.

The Soviets might, however, be able to address these vulnerabilities, at least to some extent. Soviet radars already "operate at higher frequencies and in locations that could reduce blackout effects."[190] Blackout is simply a short-lived ionization cloud created by a nuclear explosion. Although blackout poses genuine performance uncertainties, it may inhibit only part of a radar's field of vision, and may do so only temporarily—only for "tens of seconds," in fact.[191] This duration might be crippling in some contingencies and less relevant in others.

The possible incapacitation of a radar by blackout can be most readily countered by deploying additional radars to cover the same area and "see around" the blackout clouds. This may help to explain the apparent redundancy of part of the Soviet radar network. As the Department of Defense has noted, the "degree of redundancy" under construction in the Soviet LPAR network is "not necessary for early warning. It is highly desirable, however, for ballistic missile defense."[192] Redundancy may be augmented with "frequency agility," an ability to switch to different frequencies and continue to perform effectively—in a single radar or in several radars with redundant coverage over various frequencies. Reductions in the size of electronic systems and in their power requirements have made the proliferation of rapidly deployable and potentially deceptively based radars feasible for the Soviet Union as well as for the United States.[193] Indeed, the Soviets already have transportable phased array radars in the Pawn Shop and Flat Twin, and the Grill Pan radar that is reportedly part of the SA-X-12 system is mobile.[194]

Electromagnetic pulse (EMP) effects from a nuclear explosion may also be countered to some extent. An EMP wave will be picked up by any electrical system that can function as an antenna. The most direct solutions are therefore to ensure that electronic systems are sufficiently grounded, to use electrical components capable of withstanding a large and abrupt shock of electrical current, and to put sensitive components in "Faraday boxes" with automatic switch-off mechanisms to channel away the current—as with shielding against lightning. Advanced target acquisition launch-control radars may in principle be made almost invulnerable to EMP if all the components respect electromagnetic compatibility requirements in order to avoid interference with the radar, and if the support systems—power supplies, computers, and so forth—are hardened against such effects as systems. How well such countermeasures might work in nuclear war conditions is a matter of great controversy in the technical community,[195] but the Soviet Union is known to have taken EMP effects seriously into consideration in the design and construction of its military systems.

Moreover, the Soviets apparently plan to defend the new LPARs and the Pushkino battle management radar.[196] Some experts have speculated that the LPARs could be "heavily defended" if the Soviets deployed an extensive BMD system "consisting of mobile land-based radars and interceptors internetted" with the LPAR network.[197] With the SA-12 and the advanced Moscow system components, such defenses might theoretically be erected within a number of months. Active defense of the LPARs could well be more feasible after an initial Soviet counterforce strike against U.S. ICBMs and command, control, and communications capabilities; it might then be difficult for the United States to mount a "tailored attack" against the LPARs.[198] It would depend on the ability of surviving U.S. command assets to direct attacks against the LPARs. Even if U.S. command assets were still capable of directing attacks against the radars, the Soviets could defend them preferentially to improve the prospects for survival of the most vital ones.[199]

The possible advantages of imbedding antennas in concrete slabs have been recognized for years, and the Soviets are apparently hardening their LPARs against nuclear blast overpressures to be at least partially prepared for such risks.[200] Although the LPARs would be unable to resist focused attacks, they might nonetheless last long enough to provide hand-over data for defense against the initial U.S. retaliatory strikes—data that could be reckoned worthwhile in the Soviet calculus. Finally, the Flat Twin and Pawn Shop radars—smaller phased arrays—might partially substitute for the loss of elements of the LPAR network. It is hard to estimate what level of performance degradation specific attacks might cause when so little is known about the design of the Soviet radars, but the potential benefits of rapidly deployable and deceptively based radars have been more widely recognized in recent years.

The offense-defense "dialectic" is far more complex than suggested above, of course. For example, U.S. authorities have discussed the possibility of developing missile warheads that could "home on and destroy ABM radars with small, low-yield nuclear or nonnuclear weapons."[201] An obvious Soviet countermeasure to radar-seeking U.S. warheads (aside from directly intercepting them) would be to develop passive sensors (infrared or optical sensors) that would diminish dependence on signal-emitting radars. Infrared sensors would, however, be vulnerable to "redout"—thermal radiation and bright light that could blind the sensor.[202] It would, in turn, probably be possible to construct an infrared sensor that could shut off when a certain energy level is reached; but, while this would enhance the sensor's prospects for survival, other sensors would have to serve as means of BMD target tracking and battle management in the interim. It is possible, for example, that laser imaging sensors would be insensitive to blackout and redout effects—though they would have other vulnerabilities.

Although such advanced sensors are a relatively distant prospect, as are the information-processing capabilities that would be necessary for their effective employment, it is premature to rule out the possibility of the Soviets' developing an array of radars and other sensors that could have some military utility, at least for the defense of a limited set of critical targets. The new LPARs represent an enormous investment, and the Soviets have presumably taken their potential vulnerabilities into account. The new ballistic missile early warning radars under construction in the United States, known as Pave Paws, have been described as "much less capable" than the new Soviet LPAR network.[203]

ADVANCED EXOTIC TECHNOLOGIES
Soviet BMD research based on exotic technologies—from hypervelocity kinetic-energy railguns to directed energy systems (lasers, particle beams, and radiofrequency signals)—began in the 1960s.[204] Western discussions of Soviet research in such advanced technologies are usually hedged with more than the normal number of caveats regarding uncertainties in our knowledge. Sayre Stevens writes that the likely utility of such weapons is still unclear—as are the focus and progress of Soviet activities.[205] The Office of Technology Assessment of the U.S. Congress has noted that, although the total Soviet effort in directed-energy research is estimated to be greater than that of the United States,

> the *quality* of that work is difficult to determine, and its *significance* is therefore highly controversial. In large part, we are limited to observing what goes *into* their efforts (e.g., the amount of floor space at various Soviet research laboratories, the observable activity at test sites) and what does *not* come out (e.g., absence or cessation of publication on topics known to be under investigation, indicating that the activity has been classified).[206]

Such research activities are unusually difficult to investigate by national technical means of intelligence: "Unlike missiles, the characteristics which make lasers fit or unfit for strategic warfare are not discernible through mere observation. Observation will yield information on gross size, power plant, and, possibly, wave length. But the laser's power, the quality of its beam, its pointing accuracy, its jitter, the time it needs to retarget and the number of times it can fire can be learned only from direct access to test data."[207] The situation is further complicated by the fact that the Soviets evidently intend to develop directed-energy weapons capable of use against aircraft, cruise missiles, and satellites, as well as against ballistic missiles.

According to a recently declassified U.S. intelligence report, the Soviets "have been working as long [as] and more extensively than the United States on directed energy—laser, radio frequency, and particle-beam—technologies applicable to strategic weapons."[208] In his February 1977 final report as director of defense research and engineering in the outgoing Ford administration, Malcolm Currie expressed concern about observed increases in the Soviet effort in high-energy lasers and particle beam weapons: "We know few details of the Soviet programs, but the scope and degree of commitment of their interests in these weapons of the future is quite large as judged by their investments in physical plant for research and development."[209]

In the late 1970s, U.S. officials were skeptical as to whether this research would lead to any practical results. Secretary of Defense Harold Brown reported that, although the Soviets were conducting research on lasers and charged-particle beams, "there are severe technical obstacles to converting this technology into a defensive weapon system that would offer a capability against ballistic missiles. There is no evidence, furthermore, that the Soviets have yet devised, even conceptually, a way to eliminate these obstacles."[210]

At the same time, the Department of Defense noted that the Soviets were making large investments in military applications of directed energy, especially lasers. In 1980 William J. Perry, under secretary of defense for research and engineering, observed that Soviet laser programs differed from the typical Soviet pattern of gradual incremental improvements in technology in that the laser programs were marked by innovation and "high level policy intervention."[211] Perry had pointed out the year before that annual Soviet spending on high-energy lasers was estimated at $1 billion—five times that of the United States.[212]

The laser programs have been considered especially significant in recent years. Some U.S. authorities regard lasers as an area of Soviet advantage, although others disagree.[213] Lasers enjoy, at any rate, earlier weaponization prospects than other directed-energy technologies. Although some unofficial sources reported in 1984 that the Soviets had already tested ground-based lasers at Sary Shagan against ballistic missile reentry vehicles,[214] the Department of Defense in 1987 did not expect the Soviets to have prototypes for ground-based BMD lasers until "the late 1980s," with the testing of components for a large-scale deployment to begin in "the early 1990s" and deployment of an operational ground-based BMD laser to follow in "the late 1990s or after the year 2000."[215] The estimate of the Central Intelligence Agency in 1985 differed in that it called attention to "major uncertainties . . . concerning the feasibility and practicality of using ground-based lasers for BMD," and suggested that an operational ground-based laser BMD could probably not be deployed "until after the year 2000."[216]

The Joint Chiefs of Staff in 1986 offered an intermediate judgment, suggesting that the Soviets could have a ground-based directed energy BMD capability "in the 1990s."[217] The Department of Defense in 1986 omitted referring to the possibility that had been mentioned the previous year (a ground-based laser BMD system in the "early to mid-1990s") and instead said, "An operational ground-based laser for defense against ballistic missiles probably could not be deployed until the late 1990s or after the year 2000."[218] Reports of the discovery of two new large laser facilities on mountaintops by Dushanbe, near the Soviet-Afghanistan border, suggested uncertainty about whether they could function as antisatellite systems, although some U.S. analysts reportedly believe they "could be upgraded to antiballistic missile lasers with more advanced pointing and tracking systems."[219]

The existing Soviet ground-based laser weapons prototypes seem capable of interfering only with U.S. satellites orbiting at low altitudes, not ballistic missiles[220]—although interfering with U.S. satellites could possibly deny the United States information that would be vital in acquiring targets in the USSR. In October 1985, this potential satellite interference capability was described as an ability to damage "some components of satellites in orbit."[221] General Abrahamson specified that some Soviet chemical lasers may be capable of "reaching up through the atmosphere and damaging—not destroying—some of the sensitive elements of low-flying satellites, like optical elements or solar cells."[222]

Without commenting on such details, the British Ministry of Defence in November 1985 simply stated, "An airborne laser has also been tested which could have ASAT [antisatellite] or air defence applications, and the testing of a ground based laser which could be a prototype ASAT weapon has taken place."[223] In October 1987 General John L. Piotrowski, chief of the U.S. Space Command, said that Soviet ground-based lasers at Sary Shagan could today destroy low-orbiting U.S. reconnaissance satellites (at an altitude of 400 miles) and damage satellites at higher altitudes. Even U.S. satellites in geosynchronous orbits (22,300 miles) are potentially vulnerable, in that sensors and solar panels could be damaged by certain Soviet laser emissions. U.S. geosynchronous military communications satellites may, General Piotrowski stated, become vulnerable to Soviet ground-based lasers within five years.[224]

Space-based antisatellite lasers may be deployed by the USSR in the mid-1990s, but no space-based laser BMD is considered likely until after the year 2000.[225] The assumption seems to be that, although it might be easier to acquire hot missile boosters as targets than cold satellites, a space-based BMD system could well have to contend with far more targets in a short time than would an ASAT system. Indeed, depending on the particular circumstances, ASAT attacks might be feasible at a time chosen by the Soviets, against targets in established and predictable orbits. Moreover, depending on their design, Western satellites might be more vulnerable than warheads hardened against reentry into the atmosphere.

The January 1986 Delpech report to the French Defense Ministry held that the Soviets are unlikely to be able to deploy a space-based chemical laser for BMD until 2010, on the assumption of "extremely rapid technical progress," and with no guarantee of success. Although France could afford the countermeasures (such as increased numbers of missiles and warheads, and possibly a French ASAT) necessary to continue to hold Soviet cities at risk, the report concluded, such a space-based BMD could make it more difficult for the United States to conduct strikes against Soviet military targets. The Delpech report also suggested that the Soviets might try to deploy space-based BMD systems of dubious technical effectiveness in the next few years in order to undermine public confidence in nuclear deterrence.[226] Hans Rühle of the West German Ministry of Defense has also noted the possibility that a Soviet laser weapon could be tested in space "in the early 1990s," even though a comprehensive space-based BMD system would still be far away.[227]

These forecasts are based in part on the size and accomplishments of the Soviet high-energy laser program, which is "much larger" than that of the United States.[228]

> They have built over a half-dozen major R & D facilities and test ranges, and they have over 10,000 scientists and engineers associated with laser development. They are developing chemical lasers and have continued to work on other high-energy lasers having potential weapons applications—the gas dynamic laser and the electric discharge laser. They are also pursuing related laser weapon technologies, such as efficient electrical power sources, and are pursuing capabilities to produce high-quality optical components. They have developed a rocket-driven magnetohydrodynamic (MHD) generator which produces 15 megawatts of short-term electric power—a device that has no counterpart in the West.[229]

Official sources have also indicated that Soviet laser weapons research includes other types of lasers (such as excimer and free-electron lasers) "that the United States had not seriously considered for weapons applications until very recently."[230] Soviet laser research encompasses advanced optical systems, including large segmented mirrors.[231]

Despite all the uncertainties attending Western assessments of Soviet laser research, the Soviet contribution to laser physics and technology has been described as "both significant and pervasive. There are practically no areas of laser technology where the USSR has not either been at the forefront of developments, or even leading the way."[232] The Soviets disclosed their interest in BMD applications of lasers in 1962, and investments in military lasers apparently increased after the Soviet academicians N. G. Basov and A. M. Prokhorov shared the 1964 Nobel Prize for physics with Charles Townes of the United States, for their work in maser and laser physics. The Soviets in 1967 publicly reported obtaining neutron generation in laser-induced nuclear fusion experiments (an achievement not duplicated in the United States until 1974), and they operated the world's first excimer laser in 1970. Yet the Soviets may also face severe deficiencies in their research infrastructure and supply industries that necessitate financial and personnel investments that are unnecessary in the West and that make simple quantitative comparisons of U.S. and Soviet investments in military laser research efforts misleading.[233]

Aside from high-energy lasers, two other types of directed-energy weapons may have BMD applications: particle beams and radiofrequency signals. Particle beams consist of high-energy subatomic particles that are generated in accelerators, or "atom smashers." If particle beams could be applied to BMD, they could melt the target's nuclear materials and detonate its high explosives or damage its electronic components.[234]

U.S. concern about possible Soviet development of particle beam weapons first became public in the 1977–1979 period.[235] In 1979 a panel of scientists appointed by the Department of Defense placed the USSR five to seven years ahead of the United States in this area.[236] Intense Soviet research on military applications of particle beams has been under way since at least the early 1970s.[237] Indeed, "much of the U.S. understanding as to how particle beams could be made into practical defensive weapons is based on Soviet work conducted in the late 1960s and early 1970s."[238] The Soviet Union is widely, but by no means universally, regarded as in advance of the United States in research on particle beam weaponry.[239] With regard to both lasers and particle beams, Albert Carnesale judges that, "although the Soviet effort in this area has been more intense than that of the United States, neither seems to be ahead."[240]

Practical military applications for particle beams will evidently be more difficult to develop than for lasers. Official U.S. statements on the timing of weaponization prospects show some variations. According to Paul Nitze's June 1985 statement, "for the ASAT mission they may be able to test a prototype space-based particle-beam weapon intended to disrupt satellite electronic equipment in the mid- to late 1990s. One designed to destroy satellites could be tested by the year 2000. Early in the next century, the Soviets could have a prototype space-based BMD system ready for testing."[241]

The October 1985 joint Department of State–Department of Defense document on Soviet strategic defenses offered similar but less precise timing judgments (that is, simply "the 1990s" for disrupting satellite electronics, "later" for an ability to destroy satellites, and "probably . . . several additional years" for BMD capability).[242] The June 1985 Central Intelligence Agency testimony said, "We believe the Soviets will eventually attempt to build a space-based PBW [particle beam weapon], but the technical requirements are so severe that we estimate there is a low probability they will test a prototype before the year 2000."[243] This implies a judgment that not even an ASAT prototype is likely to be tested in the 1990s. The British Ministry of Defence in November 1985 referred, however, to a possible prototype space-based particle beam weapons system "by the late 1990s."[244] Stephen Meyer has suggested that, although the Soviet Union might precede the United States in deploying such systems, the performance prospects of the initial Soviet systems could well be less than fully satisfactory.[245]

The Soviet interest in radiofrequency (RF) or electromagnetic pulse weapons for BMD was mentioned by U.S. officials as early as 1979, when they were also referred to as "millimeter waves or electromagnetics."[246] The Department of Defense in 1981 referred to the Soviet open literature on radiofrequency weapons and the Soviet development of "very high peak-power microwave generators."[247] Such weapons could damage critical electronic components of enemy military systems and "inflict disorientation or physical injury on personnel."[248]

Apparently no estimates have been made public on when the Soviets could have RF weapons capable of damaging or destroying the components of enemy missiles or warheads. The Department of Defense has indicated that the Soviets could test a ground-based RF weapon capable of damaging satellites in "the 1990s,"[249] a judgment that the British Ministry of Defence has amended to "the mid-1990s."[250] Paul Nitze has added that a space-based RF antisatellite system will "probably not be tested until after the year 2000,"[251] while the June 1985 CIA estimate includes no indications as to timing: "we judge they are probably capable of developing a prototype RF weapon system."[252] RF weapons would work, it appears, by overloading electronic receivers. Because incoming warheads would have no such receivers (except perhaps for radar fusing systems, which might be supplemented by barometric and impact fuses), RF weapons might not be as useful for terminal BMD as other approaches. RF weapons could, however, disrupt guidance and RV release systems. Soviet capabilities to devise RF weapons are judged to be "on a par [with] if not superior to those of the United States."[253]

Finally, the Soviets have research programs of long standing in advanced kinetic energy weapons. The kill mechanism consists of the high-speed collision of a small mass against the target. As early as 1966, the Soviets had developed an experimental "gun" that could shoot streams of particles of heavy metals (such as tungsten or molybdenum) "at speeds of 25 kilometers per second in air and over 60 kilometers per second in a vacuum."[254] According to the U.S. Defense and State Departments, long-range space-based BMD systems employing such kinetic-energy weapons "probably could not be developed until the mid-1990s or even later," but the USSR could "deploy in the near-term a short-range, space-based system useful for satellite or space station defense or for close-in attack by a maneuvering satellite."[255] The British Ministry of Defence has confirmed the Soviet development of "electromagnetic railguns to accelerate projectiles to extra high velocities," but contends that there is "no evidence of work on space based systems."[256]

The Delpech report to the French Ministry of Defense concluded in January 1986 that, despite all the publicity given to possible space-based directed energy weapons in the U.S. SDI, "the USSR has been working for a long time on corresponding technologies, and it has been possible to follow some of its advances, which have been substantial at times, in its open-literature scientific publications, at least until 1979 . . . it is reasonable to acknowledge that they are making an effort analogous to that of the United States, with comparable realization prospects."[257]

If advanced technologies for BMD were to be space based, in order to seek the leverage obtainable from boost-phase interceptions, the Soviets would require extensive space transportation assets. The Soviet military space program, the world's largest by various measures, would probably be capable of providing the necessary logistical and communications support. According to a 1980 U.S. Senate report, "the launch tonnage capacity of Soviet rockets measured cumulatively is about 90 percent more than the United States and is currently running about ninefold the U.S. annual level."[258] This comparison has remained valid. The Soviets launch five to six times as many satellites per year as does the United States, owing in part to the fact that the lifetimes of Soviet satellites (especially reconnaissance satellites) are shorter than those of U.S. satellites.[259]

Soviet space-transportation means under development include ten types of expendable launch vehicles and two reusable manned space vehicles.[260] According to the British Ministry of Defence, the new Soviet heavy-lift booster system "should be able to lift as much as 150 tonnes into low earth orbit, adequate to launch the components needed for a large manned space complex or elements of space based weapons systems."[261] The new heavy-lift booster, named *Energia*, was successfully tested in May 1987.[262]

Soviet manned space programs are relevant to BMD because, as the British Ministry of Defence notes, the Soviets are "acquiring experience" in "maintaining complex platforms in space."[263] In 1985 the Soviets conducted the first space-station crew rotation in history. This was followed in February 1986 with the launch of a larger space station with six docking ports. Soviet space stations and reusable manned space vehicles could support BMD systems and ancillary reconnaissance and ASAT capabilities.[264] Soviet cosmonauts have reportedly used a laser in a space station to track a Soviet ICBM test flight.[265] Soviet sources have suggested that the power for permanent space stations might be derived from innovative concepts.[266] Soviet plans for the construction of large solar energy satellites have raised the possibility of large power sources in space that could be applied to various purposes, including BMD and antisatellite systems.[267]

Overall Soviet BMD Prospects

Two rough but basic measures of Soviet BMD prospects would be (1) where Soviet BMD technology stands in relation to U.S. technology and (2) which government is more likely to be able to deploy useful BMD capabilities in the near to medium term.

In terms of technology, most U.S. and West European authorities would probably reject or highly qualify the appraisal made in 1984 by Richard DeLauer, then under secretary of defense for research and engineering. DeLauer estimated that the Soviet Union was "about a decade" ahead of the United States in "defensive systems," including mobile ATBMs, radars, lasers, and particle beam technology.[268] DeLauer may have been referring to the duration of certain engineering investments rather than to basic technological capabilities.

At any rate, the 1985 judgment of the Office of Technology Assessment (OTA) of the U.S. Congress is far more generally accepted: "The United States clearly remains ahead of the Soviet Union in key areas required for advanced BMD systems, including sensors, signal processing, optics, microelectronics, computers and software. The United States is roughly equivalent to the Soviets in other relevant areas such as directed energy and power sources."[269] This OTA judgment is consistent with that of the under secretary of defense for research and engineering in 1986. That is, in the twenty most important areas of basic technology, the United States is equal or superior to the Soviet Union.[270]

U.S. retention of overall superiority (or at least parity) in the key areas of basic technology does not mean that Soviet BMD investments have been ineffectual. As long ago as 1978, U.S. Secretary of Defense Harold Brown noted that "the lead enjoyed by the United States in BMD at the time we entered into the ABM Treaty has greatly diminished."[271] Brown's view is compatible with the conclusion reached by Sayre Stevens in 1984—that is, the Soviet BMD program "really has only now achieved the level of technology that was available to the United States ten years ago. The main difference now is that Soviet technology is much closer to application."[272]

The application angle probably helps to explain why the Department of Defense rates deployed Soviet technology as superior to that of the United States in both SAMs and BMD.[273] The October 1985 joint State-Defense document on Soviet strategic defense suggested that U.S. superiority in sensor and computer technologies relevant to BMD helps to account for Soviet interest in acquiring such technologies through all means, including clandestine and illegal channels.[274] Documents obtained by French intelligence sources reportedly include data on KGB-directed technology acquisition programs in support of the Soviet Union's Military Industrial Commission. These documents from 1979–80 imply that the Soviets have been interested in obtaining information regarding BMD-relevant technologies, including lasers and electronics.[275]

In one of the few official comparisons of Soviet and U.S. BMD technology made public in Western Europe, a British Ministry of Defence official testified as follows to the House of Commons Defense Committee in 1985: "The relative capabilities vary according to which research area you are looking at. There are some areas where clearly the Americans have an advantage now. This is true of computers and computer software. There are some areas where perhaps the Russians have a lead———— [deleted] . . . It is very difficult to make an assessment of what the longer term position might be."[276]

The British Ministry of Defence has also noted that "the most serious deficiency in Soviet capability is in the electronic systems required to manage the operations involved in detecting, tracking and recording all the missile movements covered by a ballistic missile defense system."[277]

French sources seem to have generally disregarded the question of the relative standing of Soviet and U.S. BMD technology. This question is, after all, less salient than the issue of whether France will continue to be able to penetrate Soviet defenses. The Ecole Polytechnique group has, however, offered a judgment about the relative prowess of the Soviet Union and the United States in "traditional" BMD technologies—that is, ground-based interceptor missiles and radars: "Soviet technology is generally considered as being behind American technology: the figure of ten years is often advanced. But we should not let this mislead us: ten years ago Western technology was already of quite honorable quality."[278]

Western experts generally agree that U.S. and Soviet behavior under the ABM Treaty regime has differed. Aside from issues of reported noncompliance, the Soviet Union has invested more resources in BMD and other forms of strategic defense and has taken fuller advantage of the treaty's permissiveness. Unlike the United States, the USSR has maintained an operational BMD system that provides some minimal protection not only to military forces but also to command centers of the top leadership and other vital assets. The Moscow BMD site has probably enabled the USSR to cultivate a more active research, development, and testing program for advanced BMD concepts. The Soviet lead in operational experience may give the USSR "a distinct advantage in any possible expansion of strategic defenses."[279] In addition to the Moscow site, the Soviet Union has maintained two BMD test ranges—at Sary Shagan and on the Kamchatka Peninsula[280]—with phased-array radars and missile launchers that could be militarily useful; they could in the future form part of an expanded BMD system covering highly valued assets and could, if suitably prepared for such a role, help to provide the USSR with protection against small attacks.

Soviet BMD research has included a strong emphasis on improving ground-based terminal defenses of traditional types—that is, interceptor missiles and radars—with an apparent view toward developing capabilities that could be deployed fairly quickly. In 1980 Secretary of Defense Harold Brown indicated that "their main concentration appears to be on improving the performance of their large phased-array detection and tracking radars, and on developing a rapidly deployable ABM system which includes a new interceptor."[281]

The Soviets have also taken full advantage of the treaty's imposing no ceilings on numbers of new large phased-array radars (only their location, orientation, and purpose are limited). In contrast to the United States, the USSR has developed an extensive air defense network that includes radars and surface-to-air missiles with at least some capability against ballistic missiles. Although the United States has retained superiority in BMD-relevant technologies, the Soviet Union has taken precedence in applying such technologies to BMD and getting BMD capabilities fielded. The bipartisan Scowcroft Commission pointed out in 1983 that "their vigorous research and development programs on ballistic missile defense provide a potential . . . for a rapid expansion of Soviet ABM defenses, should they choose to withdraw from or violate the ABM Treaty."[282]

The modernization of the Moscow complex, the potentially BMD-capable SAMs, and the new LPARs make it plausible that the Soviets could obtain significant partial BMD coverage in the next decade, well before the United States could achieve comparable capabilities, given current U.S. programs. Because of the transportable and concealable nature of some of the key components, the actual deployments could be made in months, if the new LPARs were in place—and their construction could probably be completed by the mid-1990s. The radar network could permit the Soviets to track far more objects than the 100 treaty-permitted launchers could intercept.[283] According to the Department of Defense,

> the Soviets are developing a rapidly deployable ABM system to protect important target areas in the USSR. They have been testing all the types of ABM missiles and radars needed for widespread ABM defenses beyond the 100 launcher limit of the 1972 ABM Treaty. Within the next 10 years, the Soviets could deploy such a system at sites that could be built in months instead of years. A typical site would consist of engagement radars, guidance radars, above-ground launchers, and the high-acceleration interceptor. The new, large phased-array radars under construction in the USSR, along with the HEN HOUSE, DOG HOUSE, CAT HOUSE, and possibly the Pushkino radar, appear to be designed to provide support for such a widespread ABM defense system. *The aggregate of the USSR's ABM and ABM-related activities suggests that the USSR may be preparing an ABM defense of its national territory.*[284]

The ABM Treaty has, in short, not prevented the Soviet Union from making progress toward substantial BMD capabilities. The Soviet progress may be largely explained by the high level of Soviet effort under the ABM Treaty regime. In addition, in the U.S. government's judgment, the Soviets have engaged in actual and potential violations of certain treaty provisions. CIA officials have testified that "the Soviets have the major components for an ABM system that could be used for widespread ABM deployments well in excess of the ABM Treaty limits . . . The potential exists for the production lines associated with the upgrade of the Moscow ABM system to be used to support a widespread deployment. We judge they could undertake rapidly paced ABM deployments to strengthen the defenses at Moscow and cover key targets in the western USSR, and to extend protection to key targets east of the Urals, by the early 1990s."[285]

In other words, the strategically relevant BMD asymmetry between the United States and the Soviet Union in the near term (that is, the next decade) does not reside primarily in either side's advantage in specific technologies but rather in the Soviet option for widespread and militarily useful BMD deployments. These deployments would not consist of space-based exotic systems but of ground-based radars and interceptor missiles of essentially traditional types. The Office of Technology Assessment has noted that, "although the level of Soviet 'traditional' BMD technology probably does not exceed our own, the Soviets, with a working BMD production base, are almost certainly better equipped in the near-term to deploy a large-scale, 'traditional' BMD system than we are."[286]

French officials in 1985 and 1986 repeatedly expressed similar views. The most likely Soviet BMD deployments in the near term are "terminal defenses" consisting of ground-based interceptors and radars.[287] France's Ecole Polytechnique group has also concluded that, although the Soviets probably cannot develop a "leak-proof space shield," they could "very probably" develop and deploy, with the SA-X-12 and the new large phased array radars, "a system capable of effectively serving in a strategy of 'damage limitation.' "

> These systems would perhaps not be capable of covering all Soviet territory. However, they would permit a reasonably effective protection of an important number of specific sites . . . the Soviets have attained a stage of development that would permit them, more rapidly than the Americans, to pass to the stage of large-scale deployment. To be sure, these ABM systems would be—for a certain time still—of the "traditional" type: ground-based components and nuclear-armed missiles.[288]

West German officials have disclosed comparable judgments. Manfred Wörner, the minister of defense, has written that it is "possible that the combination of ground-to-air SA-10 missiles and modernized radars already is providing the Soviets with a defense capability of greater effectiveness than that represented in the present ABM system around Moscow."[289] Hans Rühle, the head of the Planning Department in the Ministry of Defense, has suggested that the USSR has been "building up a network of communications systems, mobile air- and missile-defence radar installations together with operational radar equipment, as a basis for a nation-wide missile defence system capable of rapid deployment."[290]

Such judgments have not, however, won universal endorsement in either Western Europe or North America. Doubts about whether the Soviets could gain any usable military or political advantage through BMD deployments of traditional types remain fairly widespread. To some extent, these doubts are rooted in the factors discussed in the Introduction. For a number of Europeans, the SDI context has cast suspicion on official U.S. assessments of Soviet BMD. Dissatisfaction persists regarding the publicly available evidence about, for example, Soviet radar and interceptor production capacity, the scope of BMD system component stockpiling, the training of personnel and the logistical support for a possible large-scale deployment, and internetting between the new LPAR network and the radars of the Moscow system and the SA-10 and SA-12 systems.[291]

Three sources of technical skepticism are, moreover, often mentioned. First, it is frequently assumed that the United States could readily match any Soviet BMD capabilities if it concentrated on doing so and exploited its technological and economic advantages. Sayre Stevens and other experts have argued that the Soviet Union's continually enhanced BMD infrastructure has endowed it with an option "to deploy limited ABM defenses widely and rapidly at a time of its choosing. The United States has no comparable option and is at least five years away from having one."[292] In interviews, however, some West Europeans have argued that such estimates are debatable, because a "five-year lead" could turn out to be much briefer if the United States was aroused to a serious competitive effort. Indeed, it is generally presumed that American technological superiority (in electronics, above all) could enable the United States to surpass the USSR relatively quickly, especially with respect to sophisticated sensors and data processing.

Second, West Europeans can point to possible offensive countermeasures to justify doubts about the plausibility of the Soviets' gaining any usable BMD advantage with traditional ground-based interceptors. The U.S. government has historically expressed confidence in its ability to defeat Soviet BMD with improved penetration aids. In 1978 William Perry, under secretary of defense for research and engineering, said that "we have no need for penetration aids unless there is an ABM system out there to penetrate. Our approach on ABRES [Advanced Ballistic Reentry System] is to keep that technology on stand-by . . . Our technical capability in penetration aids is first-class and far superior to anything the Soviet Union has or is likely to have in the foreseeable future."[293] In 1986 the under secretary of defense for research and engineering maintained that the U.S. government was "confident" that the penetration aids under development "will meet the near-term threat posed by Soviet ABM capabilities."[294]

U.S. assessments of the feasibility of offensive countermeasures can, in other words, be used to buttress skepticism about the utility of expanded Soviet BMD deployments. The impression that Soviet BMD capabilities would not be so reliable and effective that U.S. penetration aids and other countermeasures could not overcome them is reinforced by confidence in U.S. technological superiority. It has been hypothesized, for example, that U.S. advantages in electronic systems could enable the United States to disable, jam, deceive, and otherwise thwart Soviet sensors and battle management systems. It is argued that, in a competition between the SA-X-12B/Giant and the Moscow interceptors (the improved Galosh and the Gazelle), on the one hand, and future U.S. offensive forces (for example, MX and Trident II), on the other, U.S. offensive forces should be able to penetrate to a sufficient number of targets to maintain the credibility of U.S. deterrent threats.

Third, some West Europeans doubt that the Soviets could have sufficient confidence in the reliability of their BMD capabilities, owing to the impossibility of testing the entire system in realistic simulations of operational conditions, the multiplicity of nuclear effects involved, the battle management challenge, the possibility of U.S. countermeasures, and so forth. It is widely believed that any BMD system that depends on a nuclear-kill mechanism is futile and self-defeating because of the effects of nuclear explosives on one's own territory—above all, the self-blinding of radars. As noted earlier, however, the Soviets are no doubt aware of the steps that can be taken against effects such as blackout and electromagnetic pulse, and appear to be pursuing at least some of these countermeasures.

Countermeasures would be essential because the kill mechanisms on the USSR's ground-based interceptor missiles are believed to be predominantly—if not exclusively—nuclear.[295] Few Western officials have referred publicly to the possibility that the Soviets may be developing nonnuclear-kill mechanisms, but French authorities have indicated that this may be possible in the near future.[296] While knowledge of the nuclear yields on Soviet interceptors is uncertain. it is possible that the yield could be much smaller than that of the offensive warhead intercepted—for example, a yield of perhaps fifteen kilotons or less could be used to neutralize a U.S. warhead with a yield of several hundred kilotons. France's Ecole Polytechnique group has referred to the possibility of Soviet yields on BMD interceptor missiles as low as ten kilotons or "some tens of kilotons,"[297] and British publications indicate that the Gazelle's warhead may be in the "single figure kiloton range."[298]

Moreover, such relatively low-yield warheads on the Soviet interceptor missiles could well be designed to cause x-rays and an enhanced radiation or neutron flux, which could leave little residual radioactivity and be effective in incapacitating the target warhead.[299] An airburst explosion would also cause much less fallout than a ground-burst or near ground-burst explosion, which would create more fission fragments.[300] All in all, an effective defense with such nuclear kill mechanisms would be preferable to receiving a nuclear attack without defenses, even if the enemy's offensive warheads were salvage fused.[301]

The appeal to U.S. technological superiority as a reason for discounting the potential significance of Soviet BMD may also be ill founded. It assumes that the United States would be politically capable of acting in a timely fashion, and that highly sophisticated and complex systems are necessarily more militarily effective than cruder pieces of equipment. The technological quality of the traditional ground-based BMD systems deployed and under development in the Soviet Union may be inferior to the more exacting standards that the United States would establish for such systems, but this technical inferiority need not rule out the acquisition of strategically useful capabilities. The Soviet lag in microelectronics, for example, need not be a crippling disadvantage: "Much of the necessary hardware needed can get along quite well using older circuitry and components. This use of older technologies can even demonstrate some benefits such as greater 'hardness' with respect to the effects of Electromagnetic Pulses generated by nuclear detonations (EMP)."[302]

Similarly, the argument that offensive countermeasures would probably be able to defeat any Soviet defenses may be no more than a half-true broad-brush generalization. The more plausible contingencies in which Soviet BMD capabilities would matter probably would not concern all-out intercontinental nuclear war, but cases of coercion and limited conflict. The United States would, for example, be more likely to attempt limited and selective retaliation in the event of Soviet aggression in Europe than a large-scale attack intended to overwhelm Soviet BMD systems. Sweeping judgments about the feasibility of inundating Soviet BMD capabilities usually do not consider the specific target sets at issue in selective attacks, the required probability of sufficient target coverage, or other operational factors—to say nothing of the political and strategic implications of large-scale nuclear attacks.

Soviet BMD capabilities more substantial than those currently deployed could supplement an extensive array of active and passive defenses in the USSR. The effectiveness and reliability of such capabilities would be, to some degree, uncertain even for the Soviets. But they could notably degrade U.S. prospects for striking certain targets in the Soviet Union. Because the USSR's "target set" differs so dramatically from that of the United States—in its dispersion and hardness, among other factors—imperfect BMD capabilities of traditional types might endow the Soviet Union with strategic advantages that identical BMD capabilities would not provide the United States.

Having a near-term BMD deployment option that might be strategically useful in certain contingencies does not place the Soviet Union under any obligation to exercise it, however. Exercising the option—and engaging in a clear-cut breakout from the ABM Treaty—could be strategically disadvantageous for the USSR in the longer term if it resulted in vigorous and timely countermeasures by the United States and its allies. If these Western countermeasures included significantly improved offensive capabilities and passive and active defenses (air defenses as well as BMD), the Soviet Union could find itself in a less favorable situation than the current one.

As the Office of Technology Assessment has noted, even though Soviet BMD activities have sometimes been interpreted as the groundwork for a potential decision for a relatively rapid breakout, another possibility is a gradual and ambiguous Soviet "creepout" from the ABM Treaty: "That is, they might feign adherence to the ABM Treaty but gain a significant unilateral ballistic missile defense capability through treaty violations and through technical advances in systems (e.g., theater ballistic missile defenses) nominally permitted by the treaty."[303]

There are thus three possible avenues for the improvement of Soviet BMD capabilities: (1) infrastructure expansion and system modernization within the constraints of the ABM Treaty; (2) the creepout approach noted by the Office of Technology Assessment; and (3) an overt breakout from treaty constraints, either illegal or legal (upon treaty abrogation). While each of these possibilities could obviously involve significant variations and choices, the customary shorthand is to refer to basic alternatives such as creepout and breakout. In order to gain a better understanding of the factors that might affect the Soviet Union's possible decision making about its near-term BMD options, we must examine various interpretations of Soviet BMD policy, including the Soviet decision to approve the ABM Treaty.

2

Interpretations of
Soviet Behavior

The Soviet buildup of BMD capabilities and other BMD-relevant activities in the USSR have led, as noted in Chapter 1, to a situation in which the Soviet Union may be several years ahead of the United States in its potential for relatively rapid and widespread deployments of ground-based BMD systems of traditional types. Moreover, the mobility of the SA-X-12B/Giant and the transportable character of some of the radars and other components associated with the Moscow system represent notable qualitative improvements in comparison with BMD systems of the late 1960s and early 1970s.

The continuing process of building up this potential has been termed a creepout from the ABM Treaty's constraints by some observers, owing to the variety of noncompliance issues raised by Soviet behavior. Some would even characterize the aggregate of Soviet BMD activities as a virtual breakout from the treaty's constraints. While this interpretation might be correct, depending on the nature of undisclosed Soviet intentions and on the relationship of Soviet activities to Soviet capabilities (that is, are the Soviets in fact moving as quickly as they might?), the term *breakout* should probably be reserved for more clear-cut and extensive deviations from the treaty than the Soviets appear to have undertaken so far. The issue at hand could then be formulated as the problem of superior Soviet BMD breakout potential, at least with respect to ground-based defenses of essentially traditional types, coupled with activities that steadily enhance the Soviet BMD infrastructure and breakout potential.

Before examining possible strategic implications of the Soviet BMD breakout potential (the subject of Chapter 3), various interpretations of the behavior in question should be considered. It would be precipitate simply to presume that the Soviets have built up a certain BMD breakout potential with specific deployment plans in mind. If the breakout-preparation hypothesis appeared doubtful, however, it would still be necessary to account for the continuing improvement of deployed Soviet BMD capabilities, the treaty-compliant infrastructure expansion, and other activities that may over time amount to a creepout from certain ABM Treaty provisions, including the declaration of intent in article I — "not to provide a base" for large-scale BMD deployments. The question implies reaching confident conclusions about the origins and purposes of Soviet choices in military investments. While no definitive and unqualified judgments can be made (causation is ultimately indeterminate, and information always incomplete —especially with respect to Soviet decision making), it is possible to consider what light three of the most standard interpretations of Soviet military policy may throw on the matter.

These three explanations differ in the degree of conscious deliberation and purposeful autonomy attributed to Soviet decisionmakers. The first category, that of "arms race" interpretations, typically includes contentions of Soviet reactiveness and dependence on the lead shown by foreign governments (notably the United States) for guidance regarding Soviet force requirements. Some versions of the second category, "bureaucratic politics," might imply that seemingly coherent Soviet BMD activities result in fact from ill-coordinated bureaucracies in competition over policies and resources; Soviet BMD efforts might not, from this perspective, raise exceptional concern. The third category, a composite hypothesis emphasizing "mission requirements," suggests a higher degree of deliberate and central control over Soviet military investments. The Soviets may well, in other words, be pursuing their own political-military aims while responding to U.S. behavior. The first and third categories are similar in that both interpret the Soviet Union's behavior as coherent and purposeful; they differ with respect to the motives ascribed to the USSR.

The interpretations matter because they ultimately concern Soviet goals and intentions. Some observers have raised doubts about the significance of Soviet BMD activities by suggesting that they simply respond to U.S. military programs or derive from the imperatives of isolated Soviet military-industrial factions. Such simplistic "arms race" and "bureaucratic politics" explanations of Soviet BMD activities are largely inadequate. Both types of interpretation can nonetheless provide some illuminating insights to temper and strengthen a composite hypothesis based on apparent Soviet policy preferences.

"Arms Race" Interactions

The phrase *arms race,* as various scholars have pointed out, has been used rather indiscriminately to refer to diverse models of competitive armament. The phrase is misleading if taken to imply a necessary symmetry in quantitative and qualitative weapons acquisitions, convergence in military doctrine, or similarity in political objectives and interests. Several motives can enter into arms race decisions simultaneously, and simple models of emulative reactions to foreign examples often prove on examination to be unsatisfactory.[1]

A standard Western assumption regarding Soviet-U.S. arms race interactions since the 1960s has nonetheless been that each side can be expected "to react in much the same way to any effort" by the other side "to reduce the effectiveness of their deterrent" capability: "This 'action-reaction' phenomenon is central to all strategic force planning issues as well as to any theory of an arms race."[2] The assumption holds, in other words, that each side can be expected to increase its offensive potential in response to the other side's improved defenses, to develop defenses to counter the opponent's offensive-force expansion, and to attempt to maintain a position of rough equivalence in relation to the adversary's offensive and defensive capabilities. This assumption has not been substantiated by the most detailed historical analyses of the post-1945 development of the U.S. and Soviet force postures. These studies have all found that "the interactive process is slower paced and more complex than usually assumed . . . no one consistent pattern of interaction exists . . . The hypothesis that the United States or Soviet Union develop their forces only or mainly in direct and immediate reaction to what the other does is at best difficult to maintain."[3]

The Soviet and U.S. force postures are obviously not mirror-image replicas of each other. The United States has, for example, maintained a larger intercontinental bomber force than the Soviet Union has since such aircraft (B-52s) were first introduced in the late 1950s. The Soviet Union has invested far more than the United States in high throwweight ICBMs since the late 1960s, with larger numbers of warheads. The USSR has for over two decades devoted far more attention to strategic defense measures than the United States.

Such broad differences in approach have long been obvious, for the introduction of new technologies for long-range offense and defense takes more time than is commonly supposed. The "friction" of development, testing, and large-scale production has enabled each side to monitor gross evolutions with at least some warning. Although the Soviets tested the world's first ICBM in 1957, they did not deploy ICBMs in large numbers until the late 1960s.[4] Similarly, although the United States began developing the technology for multiple independently targeted reentry vehicles (MIRVs) in the early 1960s, it took a decade to deploy such warheads on a limited number of operational ICBMs.[5]

New technologies and engineering improvements in existing systems appear to have been pursued along parallel lines in some cases. Some innovations have been logical modifications in established systems. Nikita Khrushchev contended, for example, that he thought of basing ballistic missiles in hardened silos (for better survivability) independently of the United States, owing to his experiences in coal mining and subway construction. According to his account, Soviet technical experts only agreed to follow through with the construction of silos when the Americans published plans to replace launching pads with silos. Khrushchev described this as a "coincidence" in U.S. and Soviet thinking, and regretted the loss of time occasioned by his deference to Soviet engineering specialists.[6]

Another difficulty with standard Western assumptions about the arms race is the stress placed on intercontinental strike forces or, as Americans call them, "strategic nuclear forces." This concept probably imposes an American category of analysis on the Soviets, for they do not appear to have ever separated their intercontinental forces from their shorter-range systems. Intercontinental and intermediate-range ballistic missiles have, of course, been attached to the USSR's Strategic Rocket Forces, and shorter-range missiles (such as the SS-21, SS-23, and Scaleboard) have been part of the Ground Forces. But both types of forces have been integrated into broad concepts of operations and political-military strategies preoccupied with the regions immediately contiguous to the USSR. Intercontinental strike forces are viewed as instruments in support of these regional missions.[7]

The priority placed on forces relevant to these contiguous regions may help to explain why the Soviets in the 1950s and early 1960s decided not to match the long-range bomber force of the United States but concentrated on producing medium-range bombers capable of attacking U.S. and allied forces on the Soviet periphery. Similarly, in the late 1950s and early 1960s, the true "missile gap" between the Soviet Union and the West turned out to involve medium- and intermediate-range missiles rather than the ICBM force the Soviets claimed to be then deploying. In actual Soviet missile deployments, capabilities relevant to Europe took priority over intercontinental strike systems. From a West European perspective, the U.S. preoccupation with Soviet and U.S. intercontinental strike systems has at times seemed to be a rather simplistic (if not self-centered) analytical framework.

The initial Soviet emphasis on intermediate-range strike capabilities was nonetheless probably a function of the USSR's technical capacities as well as its political-military priorities. Attempts to gain an ability to threaten the United States directly were hindered by difficulties in developing reliable intercontinental bombers and ICBMs. Setbacks in the ICBM and long-range bomber programs may well have contributed to the 1962 decision to deploy intermediate-range missiles to Cuba.

An interpretation that would explain the Soviet interest in active defenses by reference to U.S. arms race leadership must, in any case, be rejected as ill founded. In the case of Soviet BMD, for example, an "arms race" interpretation would be clearly insufficient if it attributed the strong and long-standing Soviet interest in BMD to imitative action-reaction arms race behavior. While such imitative interactions—based on seeking equivalent capabilities—have obviously taken place in some areas of military policy, this model fails to explain the origins of the Soviet BMD program. In this case, as Edward Warner observes, an internal dynamic appears to have been more important than reactions to U.S. initiatives: "Soviet ABM development, which began in the late 1940s, provides an example of self-generated weapons development with obvious arms race impact . . . The Soviet propensity to deploy air defense missile systems at the first possible opportunity has meant that they have often triggered American reactions rather than responding in an emulative manner."[8] Despite uncertainties about some achievements of Soviet BMD programs (discussed in Chapter 1), it is clear that Soviet BMD deployments in the 1960s preceded those of the United States.

Marked increases in Soviet efforts in all forms of strategic defense came in the mid-to-late 1970s, well before the March 1983 speech that launched the U.S. SDI. In most areas of strategic defense—air defenses, civil defense, hardened leadership command posts, and the like—the United States has not emulated Soviet initiatives. The Soviets have not been imitating U.S. strategic defense programs in these areas, for the U.S. programs have been, and remain, quite modest. Explanations for this contrast no doubt include historical and cultural factors, but the U.S. failure to imitate Soviet behavior by pursuing strategic defense measures of comparable dimensions stands out as a major arms race anomaly—"inaction" in the face of "action." The Soviets have plainly not been stimulated by U.S. programs in strategic defense in deciding to invest enormous resources in programs apparently intended to limit damage to the USSR in the event of war.

Indeed, air defenses offer examples of another type of possible action-reaction arms race behavior—interactions based on seeking effective countermeasures rather than parallel capabilities of the same kind. One may speculate that the Soviet decision in the late 1950s to cease large-scale bomber production and emphasize ballistic missile development was, at least in part, a tribute to the massive U.S. air defense network of the 1950s—a network developed, incidentally, after that of the Soviet Union. The Soviets may have decided to leapfrog U.S. air defenses with delivery means more certain to penetrate those defenses than bombers. Hence the Soviet test of the world's first ICBM in 1957.

In his memoirs, Nikita Khrushchev suggested that Soviet decision making followed this pattern. It became clear that the Soviet Union could not develop a bomber in the 1950s that was capable of reaching the United States and returning to the USSR and that could, moreover, "fly through dense antiaircraft fire." In Khrushchev's words, "manned aircraft is limited in speed and therefore vulnerable to antiaircraft fire . . . We realized that if we were to deter our adversaries from unleashing war against us, we needed to have some means more reliable than bombers of delivering our bombs to their targets. In short, we needed to develop guided missiles."[9] In the third (1968) edition of the authoritative treatise *Military Strategy*, Marshal V. D. Sokolovskiy described the Soviet decision to turn from long-range bomber plans to ICBMs in much the same fashion.[10]

U.S. air defenses also offer an example of what may have been an "inaction-reaction" sequence of events. The atrophy of U.S. air defenses during the late 1960s and early 1970s was almost certainly noticed by the Soviet military. Development of the Blackjack intercontinental bomber began in the early 1970s. The development of the Blackjack bomber (which is to be operational in 1988 or 1989), AS-15 air-launched cruise missiles (operational on newly produced Bear H bombers since 1984), and sea-launched cruise missiles (SS-NX-21s)[11] may have been partially encouraged by the relative paucity of U.S. (and allied) air defenses.[12]

Conversely, Soviet air defense efforts have been sustained at a high level during the entire post-1945 period. This may be attributed not only to Soviet experiences with German strategic bombing during World War II (and earlier experiences of war in Russian history) but also to the fact that the United States has maintained large bomber and (more recently) cruise missile fleets capable of attacking the USSR throughout this period—to say nothing of the other potentially hostile air forces on the Soviet periphery in Europe and Asia. U.S. and Canadian radar surveillance capabilities have been improved since the 1970s, and new interceptor aircraft such as U.S. F-15s and F-16s and Canadian CF-18s have been introduced. But neither the recent expansion of Soviet bomber and cruise missile capabilities nor the continued improvements in Soviet air defenses have so far provoked any U.S. efforts to develop air defenses as comprehensive as those of the USSR.[13]

U.S. efforts to devise means of penetrating Soviet air defenses have continued, however. Even though these efforts have included short-range attack missiles (SRAMs) to suppress defenses, electronic countermeasures to jam and deceive Soviet radars, and (prospectively) "stealth" technologies to reduce radar signatures, the Soviets have not abandoned their air defense efforts. A measure of the success of Soviet air defense efforts is the fact that the United States no longer even contemplates high-altitude flight profiles for its bombers and cruise missiles, while low-altitude missions may well be endangered by SAMs such as the SA-10 and SA-12 systems, by Soviet look-down/shoot-down fighters, and by Soviet naval SAMs (SA-N-6s) with performance characteristics comparable to the SA-10.[14]

This interpretation of Soviet air defense successes is not, of course, universally shared. Secretary of Defense Weinberger held that "our shift to low-level bomber penetration operations exploited the Soviet concern about homeland defense, and thus contributed to large Soviet resources being diverted into air defenses" instead of offensive forces.[15] This statement implied, perhaps inadvertently, that the United States could have easily continued to rely on higher-altitude attack tactics. Rather than citing this as an example of what Weinberger called an "intelligent and sensible use of competitive strategies," some observers would judge that Soviet air defenses forced the United States to shift to low-level bomber penetration operations and to invest heavily in "low observable" designs and other costly countermeasures. Soviet air defense investments might nonetheless appear inefficient and noncompetitive from a U.S. perspective if U.S. bombers and cruise missiles were significantly less costly than Soviet air defenses and could continue to penetrate Soviet defenses.

The apparent arms race interactions regarding ballistic missiles and BMD have been at least equally complex. The USSR tested the world's first ICBM in August 1957, followed in October of that year by *Sputnik*. These feats initiated Soviet claims, articulated by Khrushchev and Defense Minister Rodion Malinovsky, of an abundant supply of ICBMs and shorter-range ballistic missiles. In November 1959, for example, Khrushchev said, "We now have stockpiled so many rockets, so many atomic and hydrogen warheads, that, if we were attacked, we would wipe from the face of the earth all of our probable opponents."[16] The Soviet claims contributed to "missile gap" anxieties in the United States and thus probably played some role in promoting U.S. ICBM and SLBM deployments during the 1960s. The *Sputnik* launch and the Soviet ICBM tests evidently helped to convince the U.S. secretary of defense, Neil McElroy, in early 1958 to authorize the army to undertake development of the first U.S. BMD system, the Nike-Zeus.[17]

After U-2 flights in 1960 exposed the Soviet attempt at deception over Soviet ICBM numbers, the Soviets initiated a series of claims about their successes in BMD. Malinovsky, for example, announced in October 1961 that "the problem of destroying missiles in flight has been successfully solved." In July 1962 Khrushchev made his famous declaration that Soviet interceptor missiles could "hit a fly in outer space," and in December 1962 Marshal S. S. Biryuzov claimed that "the USSR has proved her superiority over the United States in the field of antimissile defenses." Soviet BMD claims continued in the same pattern as late as February 1967, when General P. A. Kurochkin asserted that, "if enemy missiles fly, they will not arrive in Moscow." Later that month, Marshal Andrei Grechko and other Soviet military leaders began to acknowledge that Soviet BMD could not intercept all enemy missiles. As Michael Mihalka notes, claims about Soviet BMD effectiveness "gave way to virtual silence and disclaimers as SALT approached."[18]

It may be hypothesized that these attempts to convince the United States that Soviet BMD was quite effective backfired on the Soviets. The Soviet claims had to be taken into account during the U.S. government's deliberations about the significance of the Griffon, the SA-5, and the Galosh, and may have reinforced analyses tending to attribute more rather than less BMD capability to the USSR.[19] The Soviets may have discovered, as Mihalka puts it, that they had "succeeded (certainly something they had not intended) in stimulating U.S. MIRV development."[20] According to Alton Frye, evidence of Soviet BMD activities in the mid-1960s "gave decisive impetus" to the U.S. MIRV development programs for Minuteman III ICBMs and Poseidon SLBMs.[21]

Indeed, convincing the United States of the importance of Soviet BMD potential probably encouraged two developments adverse to Soviet strategic interests, for U.S. BMD and offensive force programs were both accelerated. Lawrence Freedman argues that the weight of evidence in the early 1960s, including the Soviet pronouncements, made it "quite realistic to expect a major Soviet ABM effort." Freedman adds that "there was general agreement in the early 1960s that a Soviet ABM would 'matter.' U.S. policy had become almost hypersensitive to such a threat. But the military saw this in terms of an 'ABM race,' so that a Soviet ABM ought to accelerate U.S. ABM development, while the Administration saw it in terms of an offense-defense duel, so that a Soviet ABM ought to trigger an acceleration of U.S. offensive weapon programmes, such as MIRV, designed to degrade ABMs."[22]

Such counterproductive results may have contributed to the Soviet Union's willingness to experiment with arms control as a means of managing U.S. arms race behavior. It has been reliably reported that the prime objective of Soviet negotiators in SALT I was placing limitations on BMD, with ICBM and SLBM constraints of secondary urgency.[23]

Many American experts assumed at that time that Soviet motivations in seeking BMD limitations were similar to those of U.S. policymakers— that is, avoiding an action-reaction arms race in which offensive forces would be expanded to counter BMD capabilities. George Rathjens wrote in 1971 that, "with the right kind of ABM agreement, incentive for either side to expand its offensive missile forces or to put MIRVs on them would be much reduced since, in the absence of concern about adversary ABM deployment, each side could be confident that it had an adequate deterrent even if it believed that a large fraction of its strategic force might be destroyed by preemptive attack."[24]

These expectations were disappointed by Soviet behavior after the conclusion of the ABM Treaty. Soviet ICBM MIRV and hard-target counterforce programs have turned out to be more ambitious than those of the United States, and the absence of BMD (or mobility or deception) to protect U.S. ICBMs and most other land-based targets has assured the Soviets of high damage expectancies.[25] Although other considerations no doubt affected Soviet and U.S. behavior, this example might be seen as another "inaction-reaction" interaction, with U.S. inaction on BMD assured through a negotiated agreement and part of the Soviet reaction consisting of an expansion of Soviet counterforce capabilities. Another part of the apparent Soviet reaction, discussed in Chapter 1, has consisted of an expansion of treaty-permitted Soviet BMD activities and the development of a Soviet BMD deployment potential that is probably superior to that of the United States, at least with respect to near-term systems using ground-based interceptor missiles.

This brief survey suggests that imitative action-reaction models of arms race behavior are incapable of accounting for Soviet strategic defenses, including BMD. Countermeasure-oriented action-reaction models may help to explain the Soviet turn toward emphasis on ballistic missiles in the late 1950s, the continuing development of Soviet air defenses, and the ongoing expansion and improvement of Soviet hard-target counterforce capabilities. Contrary to U.S. expectations, U.S. inaction in BMD and air defenses did not lead to imitative Soviet inaction but to reactions that seem to be intended to capitalize on the U.S. lack of strategic defenses. In 1979 U.S. Secretary of Defense Harold Brown concluded that "we cannot afford to underestimate the Soviet dedication to the achievement of expanding military power, or overestimate the effectiveness of unilateral restraint on our part as a way of controlling or reversing the military competition . . . The Soviets appear not to have cultivated much of a taste either for great unilateral restraint in their defense decisions, or for reciprocity to U.S. and allied restraint."[26]

What inferences the Soviets may have drawn from these arms race interactions can only be a matter of speculation. On the one hand, Soviet commentaries have long portrayed the U.S. "imperialists" as principally responsible for the arms race; the USSR is depicted as defensive and reactive, with no responsibility for the continuing military competition.[27] On the other hand, the Soviets are generally credited with the world's first deployed MRBMs, IRBMs, ICBMs, ABMs, and ASAT systems.[28]

Until recently, Soviet military commentators claimed credit for certain Soviet innovations in the arms race. In 1978, for example, Major General Stepan Tyushkevich pointedly observed that the USSR's "strong scientific and technological base" enabled it to "make and test" a hydrogen bomb "in August 1953, before the U.S. did so."[29] According to David Holloway's authoritative study in 1983, "Soviet writers . . . consistently claim that the Soviet Union developed the thermonuclear bomb before the United States, and portray this as a great triumph for Soviet science and technology."[30] The Soviets contended, in other words, that although the Americans had exploded a thermonuclear device in 1952, this was not a practical air-portable and deliverable explosive mechanism such as the one the USSR exploded in 1953.[31]

The Soviet line appears, however, to have changed in recent years. In 1982 Marshal Nikolai Ogarkov, then chief of the General Staff, simply emphasized the U.S. test in 1952 preceding a Soviet test in 1953. He also omitted Soviet "firsts" in developing MRBMs, IRBMs, ICBMs, and ABMs and gave only examples of U.S. technology blazing the trail (SSBNs, MIRVs). Ogarkov claimed that "it is precisely the United States which has always been and continues to be the 'designer' of more and more new weaponry and the initiator of each new round of the unchecked arms race."[32] In 1983 a Soviet publication asserted that "the Soviet Union has on no occasion initiated the development of new types of weapons, and produced them only as a response to their appearance in the United States." The list of new types of weapons (SSBNs, MIRVs, nuclear aircraft carriers, and so on) did not include any examples of Soviet contributions.[33]

One can only conjecture about why the Soviets have sought in recent years to downplay their accomplishments in introducing new types of weapons, for they have offered no explanations. Although both the

Soviet Union and the United States have taken initiatives in military technology over the years, the Soviets seem at present to prefer to renounce the credit they previously demanded. Perhaps the Soviets have decided that the desire to claim technological achievements for Soviet socialism should yield to the potential opportunity to exploit widespread Western assumptions about the causative mechanisms of an apparent action-reaction arms race. If the Soviets could place all responsibility for the pace of innovation in arms competition on the United States, the Soviet Union might be perceived as blameless and Western self-restraint might be encouraged. Recent statements about the accomplishments of Soviet science and technology have, at any rate, avoided referring to military exploits.[34]

The recent shift in the Soviet line confirms a long-standing tendency. Soviet sources on the history of the USSR's behavior in the military competition have been disappointing because of the scarcity of detail about Soviet weapons and decision making. The Soviets have always placed all political responsibility for the "arms race" on capitalist and "imperialist" powers—the United States, above all, since 1945. The Soviet approach has, however, now become more uniform in portraying the USSR as always in the reactive mode—not only politically but also (in recent years) in terms of military technology. As Phillip Karber has observed, this approach means that Soviet accounts amount, even more than in the past, to history with "one hand clapping." As a result, Soviet sources throw little light on the contribution of Soviet-U.S. interactions to Soviet BMD activities.

The Soviets do not appear to have made public any analyses regarding the Western assumptions about arms race stability that led to the ABM Treaty. Although the Soviets did express, in approving the treaty, a desire to avoid head-to-head competition with the United States in developing BMD capabilities and offensive countermeasures,[35] they did not endorse the model of arms race stability through mutual societal vulnerability that many Americans attached to the ABM Treaty. Instead, Soviet military spokesmen of the early and mid-1970s continued to emphasize the counterforce missions of the Strategic Rocket Forces and the need to develop other means of damage limitation and strategic defense.[36]

Bureaucratic Politics

While "arms race" interpretations of Soviet strategic-force-procurement policy stress the role of external stimuli, "bureaucratic politics" has become a shorthand rubric for interpretations that emphasize the primacy of internal decision making. As with arms race models, some versions of bureaucratic-politics analysis are more illuminating than others. Just as the least satisfactory form of arms race model is that which would attempt to represent Soviet BMD activities as simply an imitative response to external example, the least persuasive version of bureaucratic-politics analysis is that which would dismiss Soviet BMD activities and their congruence with other elements of the Soviet force posture as only the result of internal political struggles, with no purposeful significance for the outside world.

Western observers are sometimes tempted to project their perceptions of Western governmental decision-making processes onto the Soviet Union. Because some U.S. force-procurement decisions appear to be less than entirely rational outcomes of internal struggles between separate and self-directed interest groups and institutions, some suppose that all such decisions must derive from equally incoherent processes—including those of the USSR. Rather than the purposeful and deliberate policy of an essentially unified national government, Soviet strategic force procurement (including BMD) would be, by this logic, only the sum total of ill-coordinated projects carried out by competing military services, research and design bureaus, industrial production complexes, and other bureaucracies. According to this reductionist viewpoint,

> it may be that the military on either side is engaged not so much in an arms race as in simply doing what it wants to do for its own institutional reasons. The other side is relevant only in that it serves as a convenient excuse for these unilateral activities . . . Just as names like General Dynamics, Lockheed, and McDonnell Douglas are synonymous with American warplanes and missiles, so too the Russians have big-name defense contractors. They are called design bureaus . . . the relationship of these "contractors" to their military customers and the manner in which the bureaus execute their contracts have many similarities with how American defense contractors conduct their business.[37]

In a bureaucratic-politics interpretation of this type, the activities of Soviet agencies would include elements of almost mindless inertia (organizational habits, standard operating procedures, routines) and elements of vigorous struggle (competition for resources, missions, and prestige, sometimes qualified by bargaining and compromise). But the outcome could be virtually benign in its import—bureaucracies in collision for their own institutional goals, with foreign phenomena only used as pretexts for internal competitions. From this perspective, the development of the new Moscow BMD system components, the potentially BMD-capable SA-X-12B/Giant, the new network of large phased-array radars, and so forth, might be the unconnected outputs of an internal political process, of no self-evident significance for the Western alliance. Nonrational "bureaucratic inertia" can, it has been argued, explain Soviet strategic-defense activities:

> In the final analysis, we can not conclusively know *why* the Soviets have been devoting so much money and effort to the Moscow ABM deployment, to high altitude air defence or to civil defence. No convincing rational argument has been provided, by either the Soviets themselves or by Western analysts . . . [T]his author sees reason to believe that while bureaucratic inertia was overcome in the cases of scrapped programs, it might have prevailed over rational considerations in others. This seems particularly probable in the case of programs which did seem to have a rational objective at the outset but later lost it because the threat changed qualitatively—e.g., the SA-5 high altitude air defense system—or grew to unmanageable proportions—e.g. civil defense.[38]

This perspective is sometimes associated with the view that "the desire for the new weapon or a longer production line comes first; only afterward is the threat discovered that the weapon is supposed to meet." It then seems reasonable to contend that Soviet (and U.S.) military doctrine "tends to evolve in response to demands from generals for an excuse to justify whatever they happen to be interested in spending money on."[39] As Matthew Evangelista has noted, with reference to such interpretations, "theories emphasizing bureaucratic politics or a military-industrial complex posit that weak political control over the military allows weapons to be produced that have no genuine strategic rationale."[40]

Here is where the parallel with the less satisfactory arms race models becomes apparent. In such models, a real and universal circumstance—the need for every government to monitor the military capabilities of potential adversaries and to prepare, as it deems fit and feasible, for possible contingencies—has been exaggerated into an assumption that the imitation or offsetting of the military behavior of the United States can explain Soviet strategic-force-procurement patterns. This assumption cannot survive empirical analysis. Similarly, extreme forms of the bureaucratic-politics paradigm would take an indisputable fact—that the policies of governments result from the interactions of various lesser institutions that have their own goals and behavorial patterns—and draw excessive and reductionist conclusions. One extreme overstates the primacy of specific external causative factors, whereas the other exaggerates the self-interested internal determinants of policy to the exclusion of conscious political and strategic purposes.

If the merit of arms race models resides in underlining the contribution of international interactive factors in the framing of Soviet strategic-force-procurement policies, the value of bureaucratic-politics analyses consists in qualifying portrayals of Soviet decision-making processes as simply unitary and uniformly rational. Bureaucratic-politics in the form of rivalry over resources and perquisites has no doubt been a continuing factor in Soviet decision making. For example, the creation of the Strategic Rocket Forces, its designation as the leading service of the Soviet armed forces, and the buildup of land-based ballistic missiles can be seen as a triumph for those favoring and benefiting from these policy priorities and as a setback for those (in and out of uniform) who would have preferred other policies.

Moreover, knowledge of Soviet bureaucratic politics is relevant, in that it may help to explain some features of Soviet strategic-force-procurement policy. Soviet practice differs from that of the United States, for example, in that the Soviets simultaneously procure several designs for the same item of equipment while making incremental improvements in deployed systems. This pattern may be at least partially explicable in terms of organizational politics: the Soviets may well value the maintenance of multiple design teams and production complexes, and modest innovations may be seen as less risky from a technological (and internal political) viewpoint than radical improvements in system designs.[41]

Institutional competition may also help to explain, though only to a secondary degree, the contrast in magnitude between Soviet active defenses—air defenses and BMD—and those of the United States. In the Soviet Union, such active defenses (and antisatellite capabilities) are the responsibility of a separate service of the Soviet armed forces — the Voyska Protivovozdushnoy Oborony Strany, or Troops of National Air Defense. This service was separated from the ground forces in 1948 and has been generally ranked third in precedence, after the strategic rocket forces and the ground forces, and ahead of the air forces and navy.[42] In contrast, the United States lacks a service dedicated solely to active defense against enemy aircraft, missiles, and satellites; BMD research and development has historically been an army responsibility, and air defense one of the many missions mainly fulfilled by the air force, under the North American Aerospace Defense Command. The Voyska PVO's unique organizational charter—active defense of Soviet territory—may also help to explain its remarkable success in obtaining budgetary support over the years.[43]

Institutional procedures and imperatives help to explain so many facets of force-procurement behavior in both the United States and the Soviet Union that Andrew Marshall has suggested that "both the Soviet and U.S military establishments are clusters of organizations, interconnected as regards perceptions and stimulation to adaptive changes. A picture of either side's adaptation process as rational centralized planning must be rejected, *except perhaps during a period of major adjustment.*"[44]

This concluding caveat would seem to apply to the decisions taken by the USSR in the period leading up to and including the SALT I negotiations and the ABM Treaty. It was presumably a "major adjustment" for the Soviets (1) to admit that their BMD efforts had been unsuccessful and had—in conjunction with their ICBM programs— helped to provoke both BMD and MIRV programs in the United States, and (2) to decide to experiment with arms control as a means of managing U.S. strategic-force procurements. This meant a decision to emphasize the counterforce role of the strategic rocket forces and the SLBM fleet for damage limitation and to shift BMD investments to research and development, because deployments beyond the partly completed Moscow system would be wasteful. Highly centralized top-level decision making would account for the change in direction and the defeat of any internal opposition. Institutionally, this shift may have been perceived as a setback by the service then known as the PVO Strany, which may have lobbied for an ABM Treaty permitting higher ceilings on BMD deployments and for assurances on the continued expansion and modernization of air defenses.[45]

Marshall's caveat would also seem relevant to any planning the Soviets may have done with respect to the preparation of an option for possible breakout from the ABM Treaty. (*Breakout* may mean either a relatively abrupt and large-scale violation of agreements legally in force or—less typically—an effective expansion of previously limited capabilities when treaty constraints cease to apply, owing to their expiration or legal abrogation.) As Abraham Becker has argued, "Is not Breakout likely to be a 'major adjustment' in Marshall's sense, thus implying probable deviation from the rule of adaptive change in a bureaucratic politics model? The departure from the rule would be more likely if the apparatus of Soviet military decisionmaking, relatively circumscribed under ordinary circumstances, should be further centralized and compressed for Breakout planning."[46]

If such high-level breakout planning received any concrete follow-up, one would expect institutional structures to yield, if necessary, to the requirements of rationalized command. One possibly relevant institutional change in recent years was the consolidation, clear by January 1981, of the Troops of Air Defense of the Ground Forces (PVO SV) with the PVO Strany. Some analysts have speculated that this consolidation might be related to new problems posed by overlapping strategic and theater BMD challenges, though the reorganization of air defenses could also be explained by other managerial aims.[47] During the early 1980s, it appeared that the Soviets intended to give military district commanders greater flexibility in their control of air defense aircraft, SAMs, and radars. But subsequent reorganizations have implied a shift away from control by local commanders toward greater centralization.[48] This may be related to the internetting of air surveillance radars and the development of interceptor missiles (such as the SA-X-12B/Giant) with some BMD potential.

The institutional changes in 1980 roughly coincided with the beginning of the modernization of the Moscow BMD system (1978–1980). This does not, however, indicate anything precise about the timing of a hypothetical Soviet decision to build an ABM Treaty breakout option, because the new large phased-array radars were reported to be under construction as early as 1978, and the other systems currently being tested and/or deployed (such as the improved Galosh and the SH-08) may also stem from development decisions in the late 1960s or early 1970s— or perhaps even earlier, in the case of some system components.

Bureaucratic politics interpretations based on U.S. or other Western governmental experiences must be made with caution, in any case, for two fundamental reasons. The first reason is a commonplace: the available evidence for attempting to explain Soviet defense decision making with a bureaucratic-politics paradigm is fragmentary at best, if not clearly insufficient, owing to Soviet secrecy. The second reason is that such interpretations sometimes fail to recognize the differences in political culture and organizational structure in the Soviet Union and the United States.

With respect to political culture, the distinctive contrasts between Russian traditions and those of Western countries such as the United States have been well known since the Marquis de Custine and Alexis de Tocqueville, to say nothing of earlier political observers. Traditional features of Russian political culture—for example, secretiveness and central controls over information channels—have persisted under Soviet rule and affect Soviet political decision making.[49] Matthew Evangelista has noted that it is not surprising that "bureaucratic forces" are "most important" in weapons-procurement decisions in the United States; for it is "a country with a relatively weak state apparatus and strong interest groups." The United States occupies "an extreme position in its relationship of weak state to strong society, and it seems likely that the Soviet Union represents the other extreme."[50]

More specifically, with regard to organizational structure, it should be recognized that all Soviet decision making takes place in a framework in which a single institution—the Communist party of the Soviet Union (CPSU)—has for many decades insisted on the commanding role designated in the 1977 Soviet Constitution. The Soviet decision-making structure lacks any "separation of powers" in the form of an independent legislature or judiciary. Policymakers who disagree with decisions cannot resign and take new positions with private industries, universities, or research institutions, for no such private organizations exist.[51]

The lack of institutional alternatives or private power bases tends to promote personal conformity and policy continuity, with the same persons maintained in key positions for many years. Marshal Sergei Sokolov, for example, who served as minister of defense in 1984–1987, after the death of Marshal Dmitri Ustinov, had been first deputy minister of defense since 1967. Admiral S. G. Gorshkov was deputy minister of defense and commander-in-chief of the navy from 1956 to 1985. All top-level Soviet military officers are full members of the Central Committee of the CPSU.[52] Only 7 percent of the Soviet population enjoys membership in the CPSU, but over three-fourths of the officer corps are members. Even higher proportions of the officer corps are party members in duties involving nuclear weapons delivery (for instance, the Strategic Rocket Forces, SSBN crews, and air force pilots and navigators).[53]

Continuity in office, highly centralized decision-making structures, and secrecy would seem to lend themselves to the planning and execution of long-range projects such as seeking an ABM Treaty in the hope that it would inhibit U.S. BMD efforts. If such a basic strategy was devised in the late 1960s, it would have been facilitated by institutional developments in the mid-1960s. According to Becker, "there was considerable centralization of Soviet weapons development in the mid-1960s, reflected in the revival of the Defense Council and the Military Industrial Commission. It is difficult to believe that bureaucratic inertia in a centralized decision-making environment was sufficiently powerful to sweep away considerations based on threat analysis and policy objectives."[54]

During the SALT negotiations, Thomas Wolfe reports, the Soviet decision-making structure "seemed to have a bias in defense policy decisions toward the preferences of the military professionals and their close allies in the defense-industrial ministries." As a result, the Soviet political leadership "tended to eschew agreements that, in the judgment of the military professionals, might adversely affect the Soviet military posture."[55] This was not surprising, given the shared interests of the party and the military, the prominence of high-level military figures in the upper reaches of the party, and the predilection of party leaders for military affairs and even military titles. (Marshal Ustinov, for example, was in fact a civilian but held various high-level military ranks after 1944, when he was made a general colonel.)[56]

In short, it is important to recognize that the Soviet state is not a simple unitary actor and that its decisions are not all made on the basis of rational advantage maximization; evidence regarding Soviet decision-making processes is so scarce that it must be highly prized and weighed with the utmost gravity. At the same time, it is apparent that the Soviet state may well be capable of highly focused decision making and policy implementation in matters of critical strategic importance. Even in areas of policy formulation of relatively secondary consequence, Soviet politics is characterized by "a high degree of centralized power, with policy initiative wholly reserved for the center."[57]

While bureaucratic-politics competitions regarding scarce resources, military roles and missions, and policy direction no doubt occur in the Soviet Union, this fact does not suffice as an explanation for purposeful behavior in a major program sustained over decades and closely tied to the requirements of Soviet military doctrine. The Soviet BMD effort seems like other principal developments in Soviet military policy—so important that they are "unlikely to have bubbled up as the result of bureaucratic momentum. They suggest 'top down' reforms, driven by a policy perception of military need."[58] As Stephen Meyer has pointed out, Soviet strategic-defense programs have to be assessed as the products of deliberate strategic choices:

> Soviet investment in strategic defence cannot be explained by simple-minded organizational politics. Too many big military programs have been cancelled or curtailed by the Soviet leadership— e.g., the SS-14 and SS-15 intermediate-range ballistic missiles, the M-50 strategic bomber, a multi-city ABM programme, and numerous major ship-building programmes—to be consistent with the notion that organizational inertia accounts for the tremendous Soviet investment in air defence, civil defence, strategic C^3 [command, control, and communications], and ballistic missile R & D [research and development].[59]

Soviet BMD capabilities and activities cannot, in short, be accounted for by a reassuringly benign bureaucratic-politics model. Although internal political struggles no doubt help to shape these programs, they are too costly and too coherently purposeful to be explained away as the uncoordinated outputs of quasi-independent bureaucracies pursuing their own policies without central direction. The CPSU, the General Staff, the Military-Industrial Commission, and the joint-service "combined-arms" military academies appear to be the principal mechanisms that ensure a coherence overriding the "administrative parochialism" of the armed forces.[60]

The assumption that improvements in the Soviet BMD potential could be regarded as less troubling because influenced by bureaucratic politics seems faulty in any case. Even if some Soviet factions or institutions were as inner directed and as lacking in broader purposes as some theorists would suggest, other agencies could more than make up for them. Increased capabilities at the command of the Soviet state would still be the result.

A Composite Hypothesis

Of the three standard interpretations of Soviet defense decision making, a composite hypothesis emphasizing "mission requirements" seems to offer most assistance in clarifying the pattern of Soviet BMD activity in the past and in furnishing a basis for what appears to be a reasonable working hypothesis about likely Soviet preferences regarding BMD in the future. A mission requirements explanation should, however, be qualified and enriched with the useful insights offered by the two other main categories of interpretation—those accenting external causes ("arms race") and internal factors ("bureaucratic politics").

The arms race and bureaucratic-politics explanations of Soviet behavior fall short, at least in their more extreme versions, because they overemphasize either external stimuli or internal decision-making dynamics. Both nonetheless receive due attention in what Stephen Meyer has called a "composite model" that recognizes the relevance of all the factors that may well affect Soviet defense decision making.[61] More specifically, Meyer suggests that a "mission model" may help to explain Soviet force-procurement behavior. Although this model does not resolve all anomalies in American eyes (Meyer gives as an example the USSR's seemingly gratuitous simultaneous acquisition of several types of ICBMs), it directly relates force procurement to military doctrine. In Meyer's words, this model "posits that decisions regarding Soviet weapons acquisition and force structuring logically follow from the designation of specific military missions devised by the Soviet military."[62]

This model, which might also be called a mission requirements interpretation of Soviet defense decision making, has three advantages. First, it throws light on specific force-procurement decisions by suggesting that they may have purposes other than imitating or offsetting foreign capabilities or satisfying internally generated institutional needs. Military requirements statements may well be used as instruments for institutional purposes in intragovernmental politics in the Soviet Union, but the capabilities acquired may nonetheless have political and strategic utility by Soviet criteria. Meyer notes that this interpretation would help to explain why the Soviets developed "silo-busting warheads" for their ICBMs "despite deliberate U.S. decisions not to build such systems in the late 1960s and early 1970s."[63]

In this case, the Soviets may not have believed that the Americans were in fact exercising restraint—or that the Americans would continue to do so indefinitely, even if U.S. decisions for restraint were sincerely taken at the time.[64] Indeed, the Soviets may not have cared about U.S. restraint, to the extent that they were more interested in developing their own counterforce capabilities than in trying to emulate U.S. self-restraint and thereby encourage the United States to prolong self-imposed restrictions on U.S. force improvements. By this logic, even if the United States had refrained from developing hard-target kill capabilities for a longer period, the Soviets would have gone forward with their own programs, for their own purposes, as soon as they became technically capable of doing so.[65]

Second, this mission requirements interpretation of Soviet force-development policy may be qualified to encompass the enlightening and useful elements of the arms race and bureaucratic-politics approaches. Meyer wisely submits that an appropriate inventory of "influences and constraints" on the "mission model" would include "Soviet and foreign military-technical developments, internal cognitive factors (for instance, historical experience, tradition, institutional biases and operational codes) and external analytic factors (for instance, the deployment changes in adversary weapons systems)."[66] If these factors are included, even seeming anomalies such as the simultaneous acquisition of multiple types of ICBMs can be accounted for: if the missiles do not have differing mission profiles that happen to have so far escaped Western detection, the variety of types may derive from the Soviet style of procurement—keeping competitive design bureaus and production industries in operation at a steady pace.

The regularity of internal production cycles may also help to explain the steady growth of the Soviet nuclear weapons stockpile. According to testimony by Richard L. Wagner, Jr., then assistant to the secretary of defense (atomic energy), the Soviet Union is believed to have surpassed the United States both in the total potential yield of its nuclear stockpile (in the late 1960s) and in total numbers of nuclear warheads (in the late 1970s). But, Wagner adds, the "growth pattern" of the Soviet stockpile has continued to be "constant and unaffected by Soviet economic difficulties, our effort toward rapprochement, successes or failures in the arms control arena, or even international crises."[67]

In other words, a composite hypothesis should encompass mission requirements and explain how external and internal constraints could significantly affect the practical implementation of Soviet political and doctrinal decisions in force development. It remains, of course, hard to determine which factors have been most significant in specific decisions. But a more thorough and complex multifactor framework of analysis should be more illuminating than one that would discount conscious Soviet purposes in order to place undue stress on either foreign or domestic political determinants of the Soviet force posture. As Andrew Marshall has noted, "it is probably both less biased and more perceptive to see military force postures of nations as evolving under the influence of many factors and to see the simultaneous evolution of the forces of potential adversaries as interactive in some ways and as autonomous in others."[68]

From this more comprehensive perspective, the activities of Western governments would usually function as "constraints, not causes." The decisive determinants of Soviet force development would reside in Soviet policy objectives and Soviet assessments of their economic constraints and of the military significance of new technologies. Although the Soviets would always monitor foreign military developments carefully and often attempt to offset them, they might set and pursue their own goals in some areas (in strategic defense, for example) with little regard for whether Western governments saw fit to seek similar capabilities.[69]

A third merit of a composite hypothesis featuring Soviet mission requirements is that it may help to explain the basic Soviet choices in BMD—that is, why the Soviets devoted so much effort to BMD prior to SALT, why they approved the ABM Treaty, why they have since built up a certain BMD breakout potential and why they may be conducting activities that could eventually amount to a creepout from certain treaty constraints. A plausible interpretation of this past and current behavior could supply a foundation for a working hypothesis about Soviet BMD preferences in the future.

A mission requirements interpretation would argue that Soviet military doctrine and associated strategic-force-posture trends offer the most illuminating explanation of Soviet BMD behavior. More precisely, Soviet behavior regarding BMD may be explained as an attempt to fulfill the demands of Soviet military doctrine within technological and political constraints—both external and internal. Western specialists generally agree that Soviet military doctrine reflects the policy prescriptions of the Communist party leadership. This is virtually axiomatic, because party reviewers in the Main Political Administration screen all military publications in order to ensure their consistency with the military policies of the party leadership.[70]

The USSR's "peace" policy reflects the preferences of the Soviet leadership: the CPSU would prefer to attain its foreign policy objectives without war; military doctrine supports the objective of war prevention and guides preparations for achieving Soviet goals in the unwanted but nonetheless genuinely possible contingency of war.[71] While Soviet military doctrine and crisis behavior suggest that the Soviets are well aware of the profound risks and uncertainties that would attend any major war,[72] Soviet military doctrine is intended to hold these risks and uncertainties to the lowest level possible.

In seeking maximum control over wartime risks and uncertainties, Soviet strategic thought places greater emphasis than American thinking "on unilateral, as opposed to cooperative, damage-limiting strategies . . . For a variety of reasons, *the preponderance of Soviet thought on this question has shown a preference for the unilateral approach to damage limitation by means of unrestrained counterforce strikes and, where technically feasible, active and passive defenses.* By contrast, U.S. thinking has increasingly moved toward the cooperative strategy of mutual restraint and intrawar deterrence."[73]

Although some Western commentators continue to maintain that the USSR has endorsed U.S.-Soviet mutual deterrence as a desirable condition,[74] specialists in the study of Soviet military affairs generally agree that the Soviets view deterrence as the product of capabilities for war fighting and war survival. No concept is more alien to Soviet thought than viewing Soviet vulnerability to enemy weapons as an advantageous situation to be perpetuated indefinitely. As Benjamin Lambeth notes, "Bolshevik ideology . . . is insistent on controlling the historic process to the fullest extent possible. In Soviet reasoning, the idea that a state should passively consign its fate to some autonomous, impersonal, self-equilibrating 'system' of deterrence based on mutual vulnerability is inadmissible."[75] France's Ecole Polytechnique group recently reached a similar conclusion: "The idea that national security could rest solely on mutual vulnerability to enemy attack is foreign to a Soviet mind . . . The entire history of the Soviet Union pleads in favor of the idea that its rulers place much more confidence in their own forces in order to safeguard what they define as their security interests, than in the presumed psychology of their adversaries."[76]

Approval of the ABM Treaty

If vulnerability to enemy attack is rejected as an undesirable condition, why did the Soviet Union sign the ABM Treaty? Some observers in the West have argued that Soviet acceptance of the ABM Treaty (and its 1974 protocol) implies tacit endorsement of the U.S. principle of strategic stability through mutual vulnerability. In their view, severe limitations on deployed BMD meant that both sides had implicitly chosen to leave their populations vulnerable to ballistic missile attack. The assumption of a similarity in Soviet and U.S. motives has even been expressed by high-level West European officials. According to Sir Geoffrey Howe, the British foreign secretary, "the ABM Treaty reflected the agreement that there could be no winner in a nuclear conflict and that it was a dangerous illusion to believe that we could get round this reality . . . The net effect was . . . to enhance the strategy of nuclear deterrence through the clear recognition of mutual vulnerability."[77]

Many Western experts consider this interpretation of Soviet motives superficial. They judge that the Soviet decision to approve the treaty may well have been motivated by strategic and political purposes quite at variance with endorsement of a principle of mutual vulnerability. To begin with, a primary political-military purpose of the USSR in the SALT I Interim Agreement, the ABM Treaty, and the simultaneous statement on Basic Principles of U.S.-Soviet Relations was probably to ratify Soviet superpower status and nuclear "parity," thus "closing the books" on the 1962 Cuban missile crisis and underlining the Soviet Union's reduced susceptibility to U.S. pressure and its greater political freedom of action.[78] During the session in the Supreme Soviet Presidium devoted to the ABM Treaty, high-level Soviet officials and party leaders declared repeatedly that the SALT treaties were "the result of the increase in the might of the Soviet Union and the change in the correlation of forces in the world arena to the advantage of socialism."[79]

In terms of Soviet planning with respect to the possible course of the U.S.-Soviet competition in intercontinental nuclear forces, the USSR may have entertained several additional motives in endorsing the ABM Treaty and the associated agreements: (1) obtaining ceilings on U.S. ICBM and SLBM launchers inferior to those allowed the USSR in the SALT I Interim Agreement on Strategic Offensive Arms; (2) leaving U.S. ICBMs and other hardened targets unprotected so that Soviet counterforce targeting objectives could be pursued, if necessary, with fewer impediments; (3) slowing down and hampering U.S. BMD research and development efforts; (4) gaining time for Soviet BMD technology to catch up with that of the United States; and (5) funding Soviet BMD activities at less cost than such efforts would require if the United States were competing on a more intensive basis.

The Soviets could obviously have no assurance that these consequences would follow the conclusion of the accords. They had presumably learned not to expect predictability from the United States from previous experiences. No analysis of probable political trends in the United States could be prescient enough to guarantee these results. But the U.S. government's eagerness to conclude an ABM treaty may have been recognized as an opportunity worth grasping, because the consequences might approximate the ones preferred by the Soviet Union.

The ABM Treaty was not a Soviet stratagem but a convention first favored by the United States. The Soviets seemed to be skeptical of or divided on the idea for some time. The subsequent Soviet decision to approve such a treaty was probably an informed wager, based on some study of the rather volatile political climate within the United States during the Vietnam War. The Soviets probably had no more than an expectation about the likely outcome.[80] According to William Hyland,

> the Soviets might have decided that, faced with a competition they might lose and saddled with a system that was far from being the best technically attainable, it was a prudent option to (a) continue exploring the technological possibilities of strategic defense on a broader foundation than the ABM alone, and (b) use the treaty period (at least for the five years of the interim agreement) to continue research and development. They might have calculated, correctly, that the United States would find it increasingly difficult to sustain a similar R & D program.[81]

The crucial consideration was probably the fact that Soviet BMD capabilities of that era were not likely to be as effective in protecting the USSR against U.S. multiple-warhead ICBMs as Soviet counterforce attacks against those missiles, rather than any approbation of mutual vulnerability as a desirable state of affairs.[82] The U.S. plan to deploy Safeguard to protect U.S. ICBMs and associated command centers threatened to blunt the effectiveness of Soviet preemptive strikes intended to cripple U.S. strategic control capabilities and to reduce the U.S. arsenal capable of threatening the USSR.[83]

An additional incentive for limiting the U.S. ability to improve and develop the Safeguard system was that this would constrain a major area of strategic defense—high-technology BMD—in which the United States had a clear competitive advantage. As Sayre Stevens notes, Safeguard "embodied substantially more sophisticated and powerful technology than the Moscow system."[84] Hans Rühle has suggested that the Soviet decision to approve the ABM Treaty was based "on the realization that American missile defense technology was so superior that it threatened to neutralize the Soviet Union's offensive options—and so inevitably compelled the Soviet Union to prevent this technology from being put into effect."[85] France's Ecole Polytechnique group has also concluded that the superiority of U.S. BMD technology was probably decisive in convincing the Soviets that the ABM Treaty offered them a double advantage: "the possibility of bringing a certain pressure to bear on the American programs; [and] the grant to Soviet engineers and technologists of additional time to develop effective ABM systems."[86]

Soviet decision making about the ABM Treaty probably also encompassed some assessment of likely developments in other types of capabilities. The United States had already essentially abandoned civil defense and had cut back its previously extensive air defense network.

The United States had indicated as well that it had no intention of developing a prompt counterforce potential as great as that of the Soviet Union. U.S. ICBM deployments had leveled off in 1967. The United States relied thereafter on ICBMs with smaller throwweights than those deployed and under development in the USSR. The United States had as a matter of policy refrained for many years from developing warheads of greater accuracy and effectiveness in order not to pose a counterforce threat to major elements of the Soviet force posture, for fear that it would be destabilizing to do so. U.S. Secretary of Defense Melvin Laird testified before the Senate Armed Services Committee in 1970 that the president had "made it perfectly clear that we do not intend to develop counterforce capabilities which the Soviets could construe as having a first-strike potential."[87] The most authoritative expressions of this policy were presented to the Soviets during the SALT I negotiations.[88]

The Soviets nonetheless rejected U.S. proposals for MIRV control in SALT I and set forth proposals for what Gerard Smith has characterized as "an unverifiable ban on MIRV production and deployment" that would have allowed them to test MIRVs; the Soviets seemed to prefer that the SALT I agreement not include MIRV controls.[89] As Alton Frye has pointed out, "the Soviet Union bears a heavy responsibility for avoiding direct negotiations on MIRV at a moment when the U.S. domestic political setting was uniquely favorable to restraining such weapons."[90]

Why the Soviets were so indifferent to the opportunity for MIRV control cannot be conclusively determined. Frye surmises that the Soviets may have felt that the United States should have taken even more of a lead in this subject area, since the U.S. had a technological edge in MIRV and the Soviet Union "could not initiate hard bargaining from a position of weakness." In addition, Frye notes, some Soviet decisionmakers may have judged that the development of MIRV technology had already gone too far to be controlled.[91]

Frye also points out a "less sanguine interpretation," one based on possible Soviet strategic purposes: "Moscow may have concluded that its payload advantage, with large boosters unmatched in the United States inventory, would be a decided asset when it ultimately developed a MIRV, and it may simply have chosen to keep open the option of a sizeable counterforce capability . . . the Russian military planners might well have been convinced that some counterforce damage-limiting capability . . . would be useful if war actually occurred."[92] Soviet counterforce strikes would have a greater probability of damage-limiting success if U.S. BMD deployments were limited to very low levels by the ABM Treaty.

The ABM Treaty could also have been perceived by the Soviets as likely to serve "arms race management" purposes to the extent that it might influence the perceptions of Western publics regarding the nature of their strategic situation and Soviet political-military intentions. In both the United States and Western Europe, it would seem, strategic ethnocentrism—a tendency to ascribe Western views on deterrence to the Soviet Union—may have been encouraged by the ABM Treaty. The fact that the USSR had agreed to the ABM Treaty's limitations was widely interpreted as a Soviet acceptance of mutual vulnerability equivalent to that of the West, a belated Soviet recognition of what many in the West believed to be the only possible strategic logic in the nuclear age. The assumption of a mutual recognition of permanent and equal vulnerability was associated with a belief, during these early years of "détente," in the stabilization and reduction of East-West tensions through dialogue intended to result ultimately in mutual accommodation and understanding.

If the Soviets had in fact approved the ABM Treaty for purposes of strategic expediency, the widespread Western assumptions about a Soviet-U.S. identity of views on stability through mutual vulnerability would amount to wishful thinking and self-deception, encouraged by Soviet discretion. This perceptual situation would facilitate the Soviet buildup of intercontinental capabilities as well as conventional and nuclear forces directed against Western Europe in the post-1972 period. The assumption of Soviet acceptance of mutual and equal vulnerability in strategic nuclear war could enable many in the West to dismiss the Soviet buildup as strategically irrelevant and perhaps the unintentional product of bureaucratic politics in the Soviet Union.

Another possible consideration in the Soviet calculus of interests in approving the ABM Treaty and its 1974 protocol may have been the fact that the USSR would be able to retain and modernize the BMD site around Moscow. This would furnish some protection—for a number of years at least—against possible ballistic missile attacks by China, the third party the Soviets may have perceived as most likely to threaten Soviet interests, and against other third parties with ballistic missiles (Britain and France above all). The system could not prevent the destruction of Moscow, but a preferential use of the defenses—depending in part on the scope of the attack—might grant the leadership additional minutes of time to hasten to deep underground command facilities.[93] While it would also provide some protection against small or accidental attacks, the Moscow BMD site would be perhaps even more important as a justification for continuing BMD research and development, as a base for operational experience with BMD deployments, and as the keystone of an option for more widespread deployments.

BMD-relevant research and development could also be continued through work on air defense radars and surface-to-air missiles (SAMs). Although the Americans insisted on treaty provisions intended to hinder the upgrading of air defense radars and SAMs to strategic BMD capability, the treaty placed no restrictions on defenses against shorter-range ballistic missiles and aircraft. Indeed, during the negotiations "the Soviet Union adamantly resisted all U.S. efforts to limit air defenses."[94] The head of the Soviet delegation "went so far as to state that it was 'impossible' to use air defense missiles against ballistic missile warheads."[95]

Finally, the Soviets refused to accept the restrictions on large phased-array radars (LPARs) that the United States proposed, and the United States was obliged to settle for more permissive provisions. The United States was concerned because the Hen House radars (the generation preceding the network of nine modern LPARs currently under construction) were "suitable for long-range acquisition and were comparable in this respect to our ABM system perimeter acquisition radar (PAR)." The United States recognized that LPARs are "inherently multipurpose systems," and that "the technology of space tracking or early warning radar was also useful for predicting missile trajectories for ABM purposes."[96] According to Gerard Smith,

> the Soviets took special exception to our proposal that numbers and types of ABM radars to be permitted be spelled out . . . One Soviet argued that it was inadvisable to limit the numbers of radars and their technology because a SALT agreement would be of long duration. Others said radars would be self-limiting because of their expense. Extra radars would only mean "extra trouble" . . . Asked if they thought Hen Houses should be left unlimited and deployable anywhere in the Soviet Union, they replied that there was no question of large numbers in view of their purpose and cost. They were needed only on the periphery of the country.[97]

Because of the Soviet insistence on minimizing constraints on LPARs, the ABM Treaty places no limits on the number, size, or power potential of LPARs for ballistic missile early warning, tracking objects in space, or use as national technical means of verification (NTM). LPARs for ballistic missile early warning are, however, to be oriented outward and located on the periphery of the national territory—the normal location and orientation of such radars. According to Agreed Statement F, neither party's phased-array radars may have "a potential (the product of mean emitted power in watts and antenna area in square meters) exceeding three million, except as provided for in Articles III, IV, and VI of the Treaty, or except for the purposes of tracking objects in outer space or for use as national technical means of verification." In other words, the exceptions to the power potential limit refer to one LPAR at the treaty-permitted operational BMD deployment area, the LPARs at agreed test ranges, and all LPARs for ballistic missile early warning, space tracking, and NTM. Because the intended purposes of potentially multi-purpose LPARs cannot be conclusively determined by external observation, the Soviets retained noteworthy freedom of action for LPAR construction.[98]

To sum up: It would appear that the Soviets established a requirement for BMD concurrently with their initial development of ballistic missiles. The BMD effort was carried forward covertly until the Soviets became aware that the United States had detected the Sary Shagan test range and the true dimensions of the Soviet ICBM force in 1960–61. Claims about the effectiveness of Soviet BMD were then made until it became apparent in the late 1960s that (1) Soviet BMD technology could not measure up to them and (2) they had helped to provoke BMD and MIRV programs in the United States. The preliminary U.S. plans for SALT in December 1966 and January 1967 heavily emphasized BMD limits, and the Soviets evidently perceived an opportunity to experiment with arms control as a means of constraining U.S. military programs.

It is not known when the Soviets perceived this opportunity, nor who in the Soviet leadership made the key decisions. In the first official exchange of notes in January 1967, the Soviets indicated that they would amend the U.S. proposal to examine mutual limits on BMD by adding offensive forces to the discussions. This had been the Soviet position in earlier conversations in 1966.[99] Some Soviet public statements nonetheless continued to imply a lack of interest in limiting BMD deployments. According to *Pravda,* Prime Minister Aleksei Kosygin asked reporters in London in February 1967:

> Which weapons should be regarded as a tension factor—offensive or defensive weapons? I think that a defensive system, which prevents attack, is not a cause of the arms race but represents a factor preventing the death of people. Some persons reason thus: Which is cheaper, to have offensive weapons that can destroy cities and entire states or to have defensive weapons that can prevent this destruction? . . . An antimissile system may cost more than an offensive one, but it is intended not for killing people but for saving human lives.[100]

Within days after this statement, another *Pravda* article reported that in London Kosygin had expressed the Soviet Union's readiness to negotiate about both offensive and defensive arms. This article was described as a "mistake" by a Soviet source, who asserted that the USSR was opposed to such talks, partly because of the prominence of strategic defense in Soviet military doctrine. Although Kosygin had apparently not expressed any Soviet willingness to negotiate in London, the *Pravda* article was an otherwise accurate reflection of the secret exchanges then under way.[101] These exchanges led to President Johnson's announcement in March 1967 that Kosygin had replied positively to his letter in January, and that the two governments intended to discuss limits on offensive and defensive nuclear weapons.[102]

The Soviets maintained their agreement in principle regarding talks on defensive and offensive arms limitations until July 1968, when they finally approved a specific date and place for the negotiations to begin. (In the event, of course, the negotiations were delayed until 1969 by the Soviet invasion of Czechoslovakia in August 1968.) During this period of delay, the Soviets continued to express views that implied reservations about constraints on BMD. At the June 1967 Soviet-U.S. summit in Glassboro, New Jersey, Kosygin conveyed the impression that the Soviets did not want to limit their ability to defend themselves against enemy missiles.[103] Moreover, Kosygin did not seem particularly concerned about U.S. BMD. He told the U.S. secretary of defense, Robert McNamara, "When I have trouble sleeping nights, it's because of your offensive missiles, not your defensive missiles."[104]

Several considerations may help to explain why the Soviets delayed the start of the SALT negotiations for well over a year. Raymond Garthoff suggests four possible reasons: (1) the Soviet interest in building their intercontinental offensive-force levels to numbers approximately equal to those of the United States prior to the initiation of the negotiations; (2) continuing disagreement within the Soviet leadership about the technological and doctrinal issues associated with BMD deployments and limitations; (3) a reluctance to negotiate on sensitive security matters when the United States was escalating its involvement in the Vietnam War; and (4) waiting until the Nonproliferation Treaty (NPT) had been concluded and signed by West Germany. As Garthoff puts it, the West German signature on the NPT "removed one possible requirement for an antimissile capability. It was, as the Russians like to say, not by accident that West Germany signed the NPT and the SALT talks began within the same 24-hour period."[105]

An additional and probably critically important factor was the Soviet assessment of the technological progress of U.S. BMD programs and of the likelihood that these programs could be sustained politically. Gerard Smith reports that the U.S. programs were making "good technical progress": "Of twenty-six test firings in 1969 (which the Soviets undoubtedly monitored), eighteen were totally successful, four partially successful, and only four were failures."[106]

The opportunity to negotiate limitations on U.S. BMD may have become more alluring to the Soviets when the U.S. administration was supported by the Congress in undertaking BMD programs in 1967–1969. As Alton Frye has noted,

> the Soviets may have felt no necessity to move toward joint arrangements on ABM until convinced that Congress would not kill the American program. Without intimate details from inside the Kremlin we are limited to speculating about the real Soviet attitudes and incentives in this matter. Nonetheless, the overt evidence fits the hypothesis that the Soviet appetite for the Strategic Arms Limitation Talks was whetted by the U.S. start on ABM, even if many American

experts considered the system a very poor beginning. After the tardy start of the SALT talks, the discussions uncovered unwonted Soviet interest in stopping the U.S. ABM deployment.[107]

In other words, one may hypothesize that the Soviet decision to approve constraints on BMD deployments evolved gradually as several considerations came into clearer focus: above all, the disappointing performance of Soviet BMD systems, the superior technical prospects of U.S. BMD programs, the continuing domestic political survival of U.S. BMD programs, and the sustained U.S. interest in an ABM treaty. The Soviets have not, of course, revealed how straightforward or groping their decision-making process was.[108]

It has been reported that General Colonel Anatoly A. Gryzlov, then the Defense Ministry/General Staff liaison with the Foreign Ministry, defended the Soviet BMD program in a September 1967 paper at a Pugwash conference. Gryzlov asked, "If the United States was so concerned about the Soviet ABM, why didn't it build its own ABM?" Soviet inquiries to this effect evidently stopped when Secretary of Defense McNamara announced the initiation of the Sentinel program later that month.[109]

It is clear, at any rate, that the Soviets had formulated definite goals about BMD constraints by the time the SALT negotiations began. Although they proposed three alternatives (a total ban, a light deployment, or a heavy defense of a large area), the way in which these alternatives were characterized made it obvious that "the Soviet preference was for limiting ABMs to a light deployment which would permit them to keep their Moscow system."[110] They argued that a large-scale deployment (such as the twelve sites envisaged in the U.S. Safeguard program) could be too easily transformed into an effective nationwide deployment. Conversely, a total ban would leave Moscow vulnerable to attacks by third parties. The Americans presumed that the Soviets were primarily concerned about China.[111]

Although the Soviets indicated they would be willing to consider a total ban on BMD if the United States made arrangements that could provide the USSR with equivalent protection against third parties,[112] it is doubtful that the Soviets genuinely expected the United States to cooperate in such a venture. It would have amounted to the United States aligning itself with the Soviet Union against China, and (hypothetically, at least) against U.S. allies—Britain and France. Moreover, the Soviets probably judged that the United States intended to follow through with the construction of at least one Safeguard site.[113]

The final outcome was consistent with the mission requirements interpretation of Soviet behavior. The ABM Treaty, as modified by the 1974 protocol, allowed the Soviet Union to maintain the Moscow site as a foundation for continuing BMD research and development and as a defense against third-party or small attacks. Restrictions on building new LPARs and upgrading air defense radars and SAMs were accepted, but they were less rigorous than those sought by the United States. The Soviet Union retained freedom of action for carrying forward BMD research and development and building an infrastructure (including LPARs) for potential deployments more extensive than the treaty-permitted Moscow system.

In addition to obtaining these provisions as a basis for future Soviet BMD activities, the Soviets gained the constraints on U.S. BMD they probably hoped for. With the treaty constraints, the U.S. Safeguard program could not interfere with Soviet counterforce targeting in any substantial way. Indeed, perhaps to the surprise of the Soviet Union, the United States closed down its sole Safeguard site (Grand Forks, North Dakota) soon after it was completed.

It is uncertain whether the Soviets in 1969–1972 attached a great deal of importance to restraining the development of systems "based on other physical principles." Gerard Smith's account of the negotiations suggests that the United States was much more interested than the Soviet Union in limiting BMD applications of lasers and other so-called futuristics. The Soviets expressed reservations about restricting undefined systems and considered the proposed provision unsuited for inclusion in the treaty. The result was Agreed Interpretation D.[114] (The controversy associated with this agreed interpretation and the U.S. "broad interpretation" of the ABM Treaty is discussed in Chapter 4.) The Soviets appear to have devoted far more attention during the negotiations to the formulation of restrictions that could affect their development of ground-based BMD systems of traditional types. The Soviets were nonetheless probably sensitive to the advantages of an interpretation that might restrict U.S. work on advanced technologies relevant to BMD, including space-based BMD. The successes of the U.S. space program during the 1960s, including the moon landing in 1969, had profoundly impressed them.

This mission requirements interpretation of Soviet BMD behavior acknowledges the external constraints (above all, U.S. BMD and MIRV programs and the U.S. interest in arms control) and the likelihood of internal struggle during the determination of Soviet policy. This interpretation would be even more plausible if Soviet military doctrine called for such strategic expediency and if Soviet force-posture trends were also consistent with the doctrine. The two bodies of evidence we must briefly survey are, therefore, Soviet military doctrine and Soviet force posture trends since 1972.

Military Doctrine

BMD AND STRATEGIC DEFENSE

Soviet military doctrine with respect to BMD and other forms of space warfare (notably, antisatellite systems, or ASATs) has exhibited a peculiarity that is representative of other areas of Soviet military policy but carried to an extreme degree for BMD and ASAT: the general absence of any admission that the USSR even has such capabilities. Chapter 1's discussion of Soviet BMD capabilities is based almost exclusively on U.S. and other Western sources because it is virtually impossible to locate any information on the subject in Soviet sources. As Michael Deane notes, Soviet military literature normally reveals "very little" about Soviet operational capabilities and weapons, but there is an "absolute void with regard to Soviet anti-missile and anti-space weaponry."[115]

This situation stands in contrast to the 1961–1968 period, when the Soviets made frequent and specific claims about their BMD capabilities and even alluded to the performance parameters of particular systems—for instance, a broad indication of the Galosh's range.[116] The Soviets in 1968 failed for the first time since 1963 to include media reference to any of their BMD missiles in the annual Bolshevik Revolution parade, and "there has never been such mention since then." With the principal exception of generals and other officers of the air defense forces, even Soviet allusions to the BMD mission "virtually disappeared from Soviet military writings" after the conclusion of the ABM Treaty.[117]

Soviet silence on the subject does not signify lack of interest, given the scope of observable Soviet BMD activities. Two factors probably explain the silence: the wish to assure as much secrecy as possible about Soviet capabilities and intentions, and the propaganda value of having said nothing about Soviet capabilities. The propagandistically motivated restrictions on discussing Soviet space activities evidently began in 1967, when the USSR signed the Treaty on Principles Governing the Activities of States in the Exploration and Use of Outer Space, including the Moon and Other Celestial Bodies (generally known as the Outer Space Treaty). Signing this treaty seems to have led the Soviet leadership to restrict all published discussions of possible Soviet military uses of space. For example, in the third edition of Marshal Sokolovskiy's *Military Strategy* (published in 1968), a section titled "The Problems of Using Outer Space for Military Purposes" previously located in chapter 6, "Methods of Conducting Warfare," was removed entirely from this chapter, with part of the material placed instead in chapter 2, "Military Strategy of Imperialist Countries and Their Preparation of New Wars."[118]

> This was obviously an attempt to buttress the Soviet claim that only the imperialists seek to exploit outer space for military purposes. Several key passages, which indicate a concern that the USSR not allow the West to gain superiority in outer space, were also omitted. . . , eliminating any indication that the Kremlin might be developing its own military space program.[119]

Nevertheless, the Soviets employ a technique enabling them to discuss BMD and the military uses of space: they attribute the concepts and systems discussed to "foreign military specialists." As the Defense Intelligence Agency observes, "use of the qualifier 'foreign' is particularly widespread in Soviet treatment of military space issues, largely because Soviet propaganda denies any Soviet military exploitation of outer space."[120] An example of the level of discussion this technique permits is the June 1982 article on BMD in the unclassified Soviet journal *Technology and Armaments*. The article's illustration (see the accompanying figure) and its caption show that the Soviets have a full understanding of multiple-layer BMD concepts, including ground-based missiles with non-nuclear kill mechanisms and space-based lasers for boost-phase intercepts.[121]

This article and its illustration suggest that the Soviets were considering the advantages of this type of strategic-defense architecture before President Reagan launched the SDI and before the Fletcher Commission recommended that the United States investigate the practicality of a comparable architecture. Soviet research on BMD has been so little known in the West that some West European critics of the SDI have mistakenly assumed that such complex defense architecture designs were unknown before the U.S. research launched in March 1983. Denis Healey, for example, has said that "both sides have been pursuing research in those areas, but neither had even conceived the possibility of developing the sort of system in which the Americans are now engaged."[122]

In the period from the 1972 ABM Treaty to President Reagan's Strategic Defense Initiative in 1983, there was apparently only a single public Soviet reference to the Soviet Union's having both BMD and ASAT capabilities. This came in the context of a Soviet criticism of the U.S. space shuttle in July 1982: "Some people in Washington do not hide their

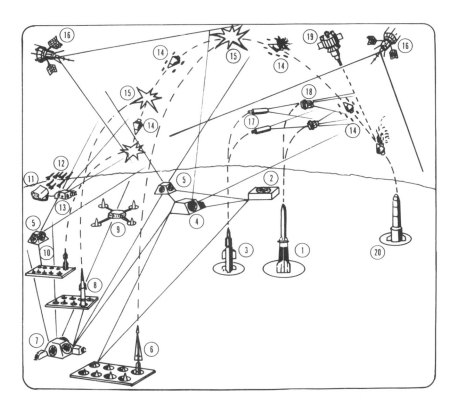

Diagram of Antimissile System

1. antimissile with maneuverable conventional warheads
2. central control point of ABM systems
3. missile equipped with optical sensors for detecting and tracking nuclear warheads
4. early-warning radar
5. ABM guidance radar
6. antimissile for destroying warheads in the portion of the flight path outside the atmosphere
7. tracking and target recognition radar
8. antimissile for destroying warheads on flight path within the atmosphere
9. defended object (launch silos)
10. antimissile for destroying warheads in immediate vicinity of ballistic missile launch silos
11. multiple launcher
12. unguided missiles
13. radar for tracking warheads and guiding missiles
14. attacking missile warhead
15. destruction of warhead
16. early-warning satellite
17. optical detection sensor
18. maneuverable conventional warhead (cluster)
19. satellite with laser device for destroying ballistic missile power plant during boost phase
20. ballistic missile with nuclear warhead

intentions of creating a military space potential that would enable them to knock out the Soviet antisatellite system ensuring the normal functioning of the Soviet Union's defensive forces, and also to make strikes against its air defense and ABM systems."[123]

This admission may have resulted from an oversight by Soviet censors, for no further acknowledgments of Soviet space-warfare capabilities were made until Soviet spokesmen began to participate in Western debates about the U.S. Strategic Defense Initiative and U.S. antisatellite research. It seems that the Soviets may have decided that their previous policy of saying nothing about any comparable Soviet capabilities was undermining their credibility because of the intrinsic implausibility of complete Soviet passivity. One of the first high-ranking Soviet officials to confirm publicly that the USSR has ASAT capabilities was Colonel General Nikolai Chervov, in a May 1985 interview:

> According to Chervov, this system consists of land-based missiles. He described as "nonsense" and "fantasies" assertions by the United States that the Soviet Union has "killer satellites" that can be put into orbit and then be maneuvered toward their target . . . According to Chervov, the Soviet Union started building its antisatellite system "in the late seventies." Since 1982 it has voluntarily renounced further testing of these missiles because it supports a ban by treaty of all space weapons.[124]

Although the Soviets have recently conceded that they do engage in some military uses of space, they deny any sinister intentions or violations of the ABM Treaty:

> Certainly, space research is also being done in the Soviet Union, and in the military field too. But none of it is aimed at developing strike weapons or "nation-wide" ABM space systems. It concerns improvement of space-based early warning, surveillance, communication, and navigation systems. The USSR is not developing any space strike weapons. And it has no intention of building a "nation-wide" missile defense system. The claim that the same sort of work as in America is being conducted in the Soviet Union is nothing but a lie. The USSR abides rigidly by the provisions of the permanent ABM Treaty signed in 1972.[125]

Owing to the scarcity of Soviet references to Soviet BMD capabilities since 1972, except for instances such as the above, it is necessary to look at Soviet military doctrine in historical perspective—that is, the missions for BMD articulated prior to the ABM Treaty. Virtually all Western authorities agree that Soviet military doctrine preceding the conclusion of the ABM Treaty was fully committed to principles of strategic defense, including BMD. "Indeed, to the extent that Soviet military doctrine had a bias, it was to emphasize the importance of strategic defense, rather than to rely upon a strategic offensive capability for deterrence as the United States has done. BMD was thus pressed by the Soviet leaders, just as strategic air defense had been ever since the 1950s."[126] Extraordinary claims about the effectiveness of Soviet BMD were made by Khrushchev and others during the early 1960s. The most celebrated statement of the Soviet doctrinal rationale for BMD was made in 1964 by Major General Nikolai Talensky: *"The creation of an effective anti-missile system enables the state to make its defenses dependent chiefly on its own possibilities, and not only on mutual deterrence, that is, on the goodwill of the other side . . .* History has taught the Soviet Union to depend mainly on itself in ensuring its security and that of its friends."[127]

Moreover, the Soviets published analytical models of the "correlation of forces" that made it clear they regarded relative superiority in war-survival capabilities as a key determinant of that correlation. In 1967, for example, the Soviet General Staff journal, *Military Thought*, featured an article in which Major General I. Anureyev argued that "a most important factor which makes it possible to accomplish the task of changing the correlation of forces in one's own favor is antiair defense (antimissile and antispace)." In the same article, however, Anureyev postulated that the BMD capabilities of both sides were then nil.[128]

This judgment was part of a general pattern in the Soviet military literature during the 1960s and the SALT negotiations in 1969–1972. Although no one questioned the desirability of BMD,[129] more and more doubts were voiced about the likely operational effectiveness of available Soviet BMD technology.[130] The minister of defense, Marshal Rodion Malinovsky, qualified previous Soviet claims as early as April 1966, when he said that Soviet defenses could cope with "many" ballistic missiles— a tacit acknowledgment that the earlier assertions about an impenetrable defense were inflated.[131] In 1968 the third edition of the most authoritative treatise, Marshal Sokolovskiy's *Military Strategy*, reaffirmed the importance of BMD and the judgment that "under present-day conditions the methods and means of nuclear attack unquestionably predominate over the methods and means of protection against them."[132]

At the same time, there was increasing recognition that counterforce strikes could perform damage-limiting missions through, in Marshal Sokolovskiy's words, the "destruction of strategic and operational means of enemy nuclear attack throughout his territory."[133] The pattern of doctrinal reasoning pointed toward preventing future U.S. BMD from hindering the execution of counterforce missions and gaining time for Soviet BMD research to advance. In other words, the Soviets may have accepted the ABM Treaty and the vulnerability it entailed in order to prevent the greater vulnerability asymmetry that a U.S. advantage in BMD (and protection of the U.S. ICBM force) would have produced.

Thomas Wolfe's analysis of Soviet military literature in the post-1972 period tends to confirm the supposition that in the ABM Treaty the Soviets sought to leave U.S. ICBMs undefended so that their counterforce objectives could be pursued, if necessary, with fewer hindrances:

> In Soviet discussions of strategic defense, the ABM Treaty for the most part was simply ignored . . . The main themes, as prior to the treaty, were that "it is essential to carry out complex measures" to protect the Soviet Union "against enemy strikes" and to ensure "the survivability of the country and the armed forces" . . . Soviet military leaders continued to allude to the specific counterforce role of the SRF [Strategic Rocket Forces] as the "chief strike force" to "destroy the enemy's main nuclear missile weapons and troop formations" . . . Indeed, if any effects of the [ABM] Treaty were to be read into Soviet strategic thinking as reflected in the available military literature, the most likely implication would seem to be that the treaty had given Soviet strategic planners fresh reason for counting upon counterforce systems as the most effective means of carrying out the damage-limitation missions traditionally close to their hearts.[134]

The BMD mission, as noted earlier, essentially disappeared from Soviet military writings in the post-1972 period. The principal exception has remained officers of the National Air Defense forces. In 1976, for example, Marshal G.V. Zimin, chief of the military academy of the PVO Strany, declared:

> Now victory or defeat in war has become dependent on how much the state is in a position to reliably defend the important objects on its territory from the destruction of strikes from air or space.
>
> The enormous destructive power of nuclear warheads raises the necessity of destroying *all targets without exception*, which accomplished a breakthrough into the interior of the country *from air or space*.
>
> All of these conditions put before the air defense complex and responsible tasks, the resolution of which will be determined by the ability to repulse strikes *not only of aerodynamic, but also of ballistic* means of attack.[135]

These requirements were stated without any acknowledgment, much less assessment, of actual Soviet means. As noted above, the Soviets generally avoided making any allusion to their own military space capabilities in the period from the late 1960s to the mid-1980s, when they acknowledged the Soviet Union's interest in certain military uses of space, but disclaimed any interest in "space strike weapons" or large-scale BMD deployments. A few Soviet military authors have, however, called attention to the potential advantages of preceding adversaries in deploying strategic defenses:

> If potential opponents possess weapons of mutual destruction, *decisive advantage goes to that side which first manages to create a defense from it.* The history of military arms development is full of examples in which weapons which seemed irresistible and frightening are, after some time, opposed by a sufficiently reliable means of defense. Thus, an absolute limit to the development of military power from the position of the internal development of military affairs and military-technical progress cannot exist.[136]

Some Western experts have suggested that these statements and the few more explicit discussions of the strategic advantages of BMD in Soviet military publications in the 1970s may have reflected disagreements within the Soviet military establishment, with champions of military research and development and BMD contending with the strategic rocket forces and other rivals for budgetary support.[137] Hints of high-level support for vigorous BMD research activities do not seem to have been more explicit than Marshal Ogarkov's remarks in 1978 and 1982 about the impossibility of halting the perennial struggle between means of offense and defense.[138] This interpretation seems quite plausible and not inconsistent with a mission requirements explanation of Soviet BMD activities. Continuing divisions about the exact degree of emphasis to place on BMD activities (and about whether and how to articulate BMD requirements) would appear likely. Such divisions would not rule out the continuation of large-scale BMD research and development programs.

Prominent Soviet military authorities have continued to describe strategic defense as one of the principal tasks of the Soviet armed forces. In 1982 and 1985, Lieutenant General M. M. Kir'yan indicated that the three "basic forms of strategic action" remain: "[1] actions by strategic forces; [2] military actions on continental and maritime (oceanic) theaters; and [3] repulsion of aerospace attacks of the enemy and defense of the territory of the country from strikes by mass-destruction weapons."[139] Use of the word *aerospace* is usually the only hint that the Soviet Union actually has BMD and ASAT capabilities. More typically, the Soviets refer only to the virtues of their air defense forces: "The Air Defense troops . . .

are in constant readiness, they possess modern means for warning of an air attack, [and] powerful airborne and antiaircraft missile equipment capable of destroying any airborne enemy targets under difficult situational conditions."[140]

Some date the doctrinal commitment to strategic defense to Stalin's five permanently operating factors, of which the first was protecting the stability of the "rear." Colonel General Alexander Altunin, then director of Soviet civil defense, was therefore not suggesting any innovations in doctrine in 1980, when he argued that "protecting the rear from aerial attack is becoming one of the most important tasks of war . . . The modern means and methods of armed conflict have produced an urgent need for creating a system which would insure protection of the rear from the air over our country's entire territory."[141]

The Soviet civil defense effort has been described as entirely praiseworthy and doctrinally correct by the same Soviet spokesmen who deplore the U.S. Strategic Defense Initiative. Lev Semeyko in 1984, for example, argued that "politically, to strengthen civil defense is to show concern about millions of Soviet lives. To save just 1 percent of the Soviet population would mean to save 3 million people. No one in this country would understand the government if it failed to strive for this. In military terms, civil defense is an important part of the Soviet military doctrine, which is defensive in nature."[142] The contrast with Western attitudes could not be more marked; in the West, strategic defensive measures are often regarded as discredited and pointless if even 1 percent of "leakage" could result from deficiencies in the defenses.

REQUIREMENTS FOR DAMAGE LIMITATION
Soviet doctrine regarding strategic defense fits within an overall concept of damage limitation. It appears in retrospect that, during the mid to late 1960s, the Soviets began to reassess their thinking about nuclear weapons as well as about BMD. As John Hines, Phillip Petersen, Notra Trulock, and other Western experts have noted, Soviet military planners started to move away from an excessive reliance on nuclear arms after Khrushchev's removal from power in 1964. As Major General Tyushkevich noted in 1978, "after the October (1964) plenary session of the CPSU Central Committee, action was taken to correct certain mistaken views held in military research circles as a result of overestimating the capabilities of nuclear weapons, their effect on the nature of warfare, and their role in the further organizational development of the Armed Forces."[143]

The Soviets seem to have paid increasing attention to the possibility that future major wars might be conducted with conventional means alone or that use of nuclear weapons might be limited to one or more theaters of military operations. While leading Soviet military strategists underline the need to be prepared for possible general nuclear war, even of a protracted nature, their references to the possibility of more limited conflicts amount to an implicit acknowledgment of the desirability of keeping war to more manageable levels. In 1968 Marshal Sokolovskiy and General Cherednichenko wrote:

> The consuming, unprecedentedly destructive nature of nuclear war forces us to maintain in constant readiness, even in peacetime, a structure of armed forces, with appropriate stores of combat and material means that would enable us to carry out the strategic missions of a general nuclear war in a short period of time and in the most complicated circumstances . . . Along with this, the possibility is not excluded of wars occurring with the use of conventional weapons, as well as the limited use of nuclear means in one or several theaters of military operations, or of a relatively protracted nuclear war using the capabilities of all types of armed forces.[144]

In 1972 the Soviet Union presented a draft proposal to the United States regarding prevention of nuclear war that was consistent with this trend of policy. Henry Kissinger remarked that "the [Soviet-] proposed agreement did not preclude the use of nuclear weapons in a war involving NATO and the Warsaw Pact; however, their use would have to be confined to the territory of allies; employment against the territory of the United States and the Soviet Union was proscribed."[145] Although Kissinger is no doubt correct in interpreting this Soviet proposal as having been a ploy "to promote European neutralism" and to undermine U.S. alliances and freedom of action throughout the world, it may also have been (as other Western authorities have suggested) another indicator of an understandable Soviet desire to avoid nuclear strikes against the USSR and to limit any nuclear employment to immediate war areas.

In pursuit of this aim, Soviet military doctrine appears to have articulated three main requirements. All three seem intended to expand the range of useful choices available to Soviet decisionmakers and to diminish those of Western governments. All three depend in part on strategic-defense capabilities.

The first requirement is an ability to discourage Western governments from using nuclear weapons or, if some nuclear weapons are used, from extending the geographical scope and intensity of nuclear operations. The Soviets appear to believe that their ability to wage nuclear war on any scale (including global operations, if necessary) might impose discipline on the decision making of their "imperialist" opponents and influence their choice of weapons. The Soviets may have drawn this inference from their observation of Western behavior in postwar conflicts: "Experience has shown that capitalist countries, when engaged in direct aggression, were often forced to limit the scale of utilization of their armed forces and weapons, in order not to provoke a major international outcry. In all these instances they were deterred by the political, economic, and military might of the socialist countries, and in the first place by the nuclear missile might of the Soviet Union."[146]

In 1985 Colonel General M. A. Gareyev, deputy chief of the General Staff, revealed that the Soviet leadership now considers that some propositions in the treatise prepared under Marshal Sokolovskiy in the 1960s are no longer valid. According to Gareyev,

> in the 1960s and 1970s, the authors of this and many other books proceeded primarily from the view that a war, under all circumstances, would be waged employing nuclear weapons and military operations employing solely conventional weapons were viewed as a brief episode at the start of a war. However, the improvement and stockpiling of nuclear missile weapons have reached such limits where the massed employment of these weapons in a war can entail catastrophic consequences for both sides.[147]

Gareyev, now the leading doctrinal spokesman of the Soviet military establishment,[148] does not conclude that this situation will rule out war. He attributes to the West an expectation of a comparatively long conventional war, in which new types of high-precision nonnuclear weapons will be of primary significance. Moreover, Gareyev notes, a Western initiation of nuclear weapons employment cannot be excluded. Gareyev appears, however, to expect that any Western use of nuclear weapons would be limited, owing perhaps to the USSR's capacity for retaliation and the West's own interest in escalation control.

As has been the case with Soviet military commentators for years, Gareyev refers in particular to the strategic rocket forces as "a sure means for restraining the imperialist aggressors; they are constantly ready for a devastating retaliatory strike." He envisions "a protracted, stubborn and fierce armed struggle" in which nuclear weapons may "have a decisive influence both on the course of the war as a whole and on the conduct of military operations." But Gareyev implies (as Hines, Petersen, and Trulock have noted) that any use of nuclear weapons might remain limited by referring to the possibility that Soviet victory could be derived from a sequence of "partial victories" by Soviet combined-arms operations.[149] Strategic defense capabilities could clearly help fulfill this doctrinal requirement—"restraining" Western governments from engaging in more than limited use of nuclear weapons, if any—by helping to assure the survivability of Soviet nuclear forces and associated means of command, control, and communications (C^3).[150]

Gareyev's recent revelations about the current standing of certain premises in the Sokolovskiy text confirm what has been suspected by some Western analysts for many years.[151] This brings us to the second main requirement of Soviet military doctrine. If Soviet nuclear war-waging capabilities could help to deter Western governments from employing nuclear weapons (or at least discourage them from engaging in any extensive use of such weapons), the Warsaw Pact might be able to improve its chances for deciding any eventual conflict on conventional terms, to the maximum extent possible.

The Soviet preference for winning any eventual war in Europe with conventional means alone goes back to the late 1960s. It has recently been disclosed that in 1966 a secret Frunze Military Academy textbook, edited by Major General V. G. Reznichenko, called for Warsaw Pact forces to fight "with the use of conventional means of attack, but under threat of the use of nuclear weapons on the part of the enemy."[152] This specific formulation "did not appear in Soviet unclassified military writings until the early 1980s."[153] Prior to 1982, public Soviet formulations were generally more ambiguous—that is, the use of nuclear weapons could derive from either Western or Soviet decisions. Since 1982, the Soviet interest in avoiding the use of nuclear weapons—and preventing Western use—has been more explicit. Soon after Soviet Foreign Minister Gromyko announced in June 1982 the Soviet Union's pledge not to be the first to use nuclear weapons, Defense Minister Dmitri Ustinov explained that the pledge meant that "during their training, the Armed Forces will now devote even greater attention to the tasks of preventing a military conflict from developing into a nuclear one."[154]

Although the no-first-use pledge was not made until 1982, many doctrinal studies in the late 1960s and early 1970s underlined the attraction of conducting operations "with the employment of only conventional means of destruction. "[155] Two of the most fundamental reasons for this Soviet preference stand out. First, as General Semen Ivanov pointed out in 1969, "there is too great a risk of the destruction of one's own country, and the responsibility to humanity for the fatal consequences of the nuclear war is too heavy for an aggressor to make an easy decision on the immediate employment of nuclear weapons from the very beginning of a war without having used all other means for the attainment of its objectives."[156] Second, nuclear weapons could disrupt command arrangements and operational plans and thus make it even more difficult for the Warsaw Pact to carry out successful combined-arms conventional offensives.[157]

To maximize their prospects of being able to win any conflict in Europe with conventional means alone, the Soviets would require not only an ability to deter Western governments from using nuclear weapons but also superior conventional forces and operational strategies. The Soviets have been building up their conventional forces since the late 1960s, with a view to making them capable of conducting "combat operations that involve either nuclear weapons or conventional weapons alone."[158] In order to reduce the West's capacity to use nuclear weapons (or to fight effectively with conventional forces), the Soviet Union has developed plans for destroying as many as possible of the West's nuclear weapons and control systems with conventional means, as rapidly as possible.[159] According to Gareyev, "of enormous significance is the primary hitting of enemy nuclear missile weapons and high precision weapons even before the moving up of the main grouping of one's troops into the jump-off areas for the offensive and for launching counterstrikes."[160]

Colonel General Gareyev, Marshal Ogarkov, and others have suggested that the West could pursue the same line of reasoning. Marshal Sergei Akhromeyev, chief of the General Staff and first deputy minister of defense, in 1985 wrote:

> Realizing the inevitability of a retaliatory nuclear strike and its catastrophic consequences, our probable adversaries have devoted special attention in recent years to developing systems of conventional weapons with higher effective power, range, and precision characteristics. At the same time, they are also improving the methods of unleashing military actions by using conventional strike weapons and, first and foremost, new types of automatically controlled high-precision weapons.[161]

The presumption that Western countries could engage in similar planning for strikes with "long-range high-accuracy terminally guided combat systems"[162] (to use Marshal Ogarkov's phrase) leads again to a requirement for strategic defense—that is, capabilities for intercepting Western nonnuclear means of attack and/or blunting their effects.

The third main requirement of Soviet military doctrine follows logically from the first two. Even though the Soviets would apparently prefer to achieve their goals without employing nuclear weapons, they might choose to engage in selective nuclear attacks if certain military targets had to be neutralized in that manner in order to assure the success of their conventional offensive. They might do so with greater assurance, even though they would still be concerned about risks of escalation to larger-scale use of nuclear weapons, if they had some confidence in their ability to dissuade Western governments from using such weapons.

Some of the reasons for Soviet restraint and selectivity in using nuclear weapons would be the same as those for preferring not to use nuclear weapons at all: the risk of escalation to strikes against the Soviet Union and the threat to the effectiveness of Warsaw Pact conventional offensives. Other justifications for selectivity could include an interest in shaking the political cohesion of the Western alliance, keeping the scope of military operations under Soviet control, and avoiding needless damage to a region the USSR would hope to dominate and exploit in the postwar period. Once again, early indications of this policy became apparent during the late 1960s. As long ago as 1966, Soviet authorities pointed out practical reasons for selectivity in their nuclear targeting:

> The objective is not to turn the large economic and industrial regions into a heap of ruins (although great destruction, apparently, is unavoidable), but to deliver strikes which will destroy strategic combat means, paralyze enemy military production, making it incapable of satisfying the priority needs of the front and rear areas, and sharply reduce the enemy capability to conduct strikes . . . it is very important to determine which targets and enemy economic regions should be left intact or rapidly reconstructed and used in the interests of strengthening the economic potential of our own country and/or supplying the troops.[163]

Soviet military sources have specified various constraints that the political leadership has approved regarding potential limited use of nuclear weapons.[164] These include the timing of any nuclear attacks; the quantities, yields, and types of nuclear weapons; and the geographic regions and target sets within these regions.[165] Once again, strategic defense capabilities are required, in order to assure the survivability of Soviet nuclear forces, C^3 networks, and command posts.

Force Posture Trends

Trends in the Soviet strategic force posture since 1972 have long been recognized as consistent with doctrinally articulated mission requirements. As long ago as 1979, the U.S. secretary of defense, Harold Brown, found this consistency "troublesome" and called attention to "the degree of emphasis in Soviet military doctrine on a war-winning nuclear capability, and the extent to which current Soviet programs are related to the doctrine."[166]

INTERCONTINENTAL OFFENSIVE FORCES

The widespread assumption on the U.S. side in 1972 was that essentially outlawing defenses against ICBMs and SLBMs (through the ABM Treaty) would ensure strategic stability by prolonging a situation of mutual vulnerability. Because each side could easily attack the other's cities, neither side would have any incentive to expand its ICBM and SLBM arsenals; reductions in these arsenals were therefore expected by many in the United States. Moreover, it was expected that the USSR would emulate the United States and reduce its civil and air defenses. The United States had decided that civil defenses were too costly and ineffective to be worth substantial investments, and that defenses against bombers were practically useless in the absence of BMD. (Although the Soviet long-range bomber force had not grown as had been anticipated during the 1950s, Soviet ICBM and SLBM deployments exceeded U.S. expectations.) As already noted, the United States even dismantled the sole active BMD installation it was allowed after the ABM Treaty's limitations were tightened in the 1974 protocol. Finally, the United States expected both sides to respect the principle of not threatening retaliatory forces, in the interests of stability through mutual vulnerability.

As the West German defense minister recently pointed out, however, "the American concept of mutual arms restraints, which underlay the SALT agreements of 1972, has not been realized in the meaningful limitation and reduction of strategic-offensive capabilities that had been anticipated by the United States and its allies. To the contrary: SALT I was followed by a large buildup in the strategic capabilities of the Soviet Union."[167]

The Soviet Union has, for example, developed capabilities to threaten major elements of U.S. retaliatory forces. In April 1983, the President's Commission on Strategic Forces (the Scowcroft Commission) noted that "only a portion" of the Soviet ICBM force would be required to destroy "almost all" of the U.S. ICBM force, whereas the entire U.S. ICBM force then deployed could not cause similar damage to the Soviet Union.[168] This judgment did not imply that such an attack was probable: the commission underlined that coordinating a simultaneous attack against other elements of the U.S. strategic force posture (notably, bomber bases) would be difficult, and the deployment of a new U.S. ICBM (the MX) was recommended. Furthermore, the premises of the commission's judgment have subsequently been qualified by a downward reassessment of the accuracy of the Soviet SS-19 ICBMs.[169] The counterforce potential of the Soviet ICBM force remains, however, much greater than that of the U.S. force, owing to the significantly greater throwweight of Soviet ICBMs.[170]

Soviet strategic-force expansion has stemmed from a level of spending on such forces that was in 1978 "about three times that of the United States."[171] The Soviet force acquisitions since 1971 include several new types of ICBMs (SS-17, SS-18, SS-19, SS-24, SS-25), improved versions of existing ICBMs, two new types of SSBNs (Delta and Typhoon), five new types of SLBMs (SS-N-8, SS-N-17, SS-N-18, SS-N-20, SS-N-23), five improved versions of existing SLBMs, long-range cruise missiles, and development of a new intercontinental bomber (the Blackjack). The United States did not deploy any new ballistic missile submarines between 1966 and 1981, when the first Ohio-class Trident SSBN entered service, and the U.S. SSBN fleet declined in that period from forty-one boats to thirty-one. During the same period, the USSR deployed sixty-two new SSBNs.[172]

Although the United States has in the interim greatly increased its SLBM warhead numbers and developed a new long-range bomber (the B-1B) and cruise missiles, the ICBM differences are striking. The United States has emphasized the modernization of its existing ICBM force and the development of the MX ICBM, whereas the Soviets have substantially expanded their ICBM warhead numbers. (The current totals are estimated at 2110 U.S. ICBM warheads and 6420 Soviet ICBM warheads on missiles in SALT-counted launchers. The SALT-counted SLBM warhead numbers are estimated at 6656 for the United States and 3216 for the Soviet Union.)[173] Indeed, since signing SALT I in 1972, the Soviets have quadrupled the number of warheads on their strategic ballistic missiles. The concomitant accuracy improvements mean that the capability of this missile force to attack hardened military targets has increased more than tenfold.[174]

Although the Soviets already have ample capabilities to attack all U.S. ICBM silos, SSBN bases, and launch control facilities (and additional military targets), the CIA projects an extensive modernization and expansion of Soviet offensive forces in the next decade. This may include mobile ICBMs (the road-mobile SS-25 and the rail-mobile SS-24) with more MIRVed warheads and improved accuracy, more and longer-range SLBMs, and more air-launched cruise missiles on the Bear H bombers and, beginning in 1988 or 1989, on the new Blackjack bombers.[175]

SHORTER-RANGE OFFENSIVE FORCES

The Soviet buildup of offensive-strike systems of less than intercontinental range has been a matter of concern to the Western alliance since the mid-1970s. Since the SS-20 intermediate-range ballistic missile (with a range of up to 5000 km) first appeared in test versions (SS-X-20) in 1975–76,[176] it must have been under development since the late 1960s. The Soviets have replaced all their SS-5 IRBMs with SS-20s, and it is expected that the remaining 120 SS-4s will gradually be phased out as well. The Soviets currently maintain 441 SS-20 launchers, each with at least one reload missile; over 270 of these systems are believed to be allocated to targets in Western Europe.[177] The SS-20s and SS-4s are all to be eliminated during the three years after the December 1987 INF treaty comes into force.

Although the Soviets could also threaten targets in Western Europe with variable-range ICBMs and SLBMs, shorter-range ballistic missiles (SRBMs) have been seen as a crucial element of the emerging threat. The SRBMs that have earned the most attention in recent years are the successors of the older Scaleboard, Scud, and Frog missiles—the SS-21, SS-22, and SS-23. The SS-21, with a range of 120 km, began to replace the 70 km-range Frog missiles with Soviet divisions in East Germany in 1981; the SS-21 is believed to have nuclear-, chemical-, and conventional-warhead options. The SS-22, which appears to be a more accurate version of the Scaleboard/SS-12 missile, has a range of 900 to 1000 km. The USSR has approximately 120 SS-12/22 units, with two missiles per launcher, of which about 50 units have been based in East Germany and Czechoslovakia since 1984. The SS-23, with a range of 500 km, has been replacing 300 km Scud missiles in Soviet armies and fronts since 1985.[178]

Although SRBMs with ranges exceeding 500km (including the SS-12/22s and the SS-23s) are to be eliminated under the terms of the December 1987 INF treaty, the new SRBMs have received a great deal of attention because they have appeared to represent a means of building on the Warsaw Pact's superiority in numbers of missile launchers with systems of increased range and accuracy, with nonnuclear-warhead options. The older-generation SRBMs were so inaccurate that they could not be used effectively with conventional warheads. Indeed, owing to probable "delivery errors of a kilometer or more," the Soviets have had rather large "tactical" nuclear warheads—even as high as 400 kilotons in yield—to compensate for delivery errors.[179] In the early 1980s, however, Soviet authorities began to refer to the provision of their troops with "highly precise and reliable tactical and battlefield missile complexes carrying conventional and nuclear warheads."[180] According to Soviet sources, the combination of improved inertial guidance with an in-flight update or terminal guidance is expected to cut a maximum circular error of "a few hundred meters" by a factor of ten—that is, to a few tens of meters.[181]

Such accuracies should be feasible for the Soviets in the foreseeable future. The U.S. Pershing II is attributed a "circular error probable" of 40 meters today.[182] Richard DeLauer's statement that the upgraded models of the SS-21, SS-22, and SS-23 could hit "within 30 meters of a target" is therefore a reasonable projection.[183] Western authorities disagree as to how soon the Soviets might be able to field a large force of highly accurate SRBMs; the estimates range "from the late 1980s to the mid-1990s,"[184] with some experts suggesting "the next 10 to 15 years."[185]

The distinctly improved accuracies of the SRBM force are expected to permit the Soviets to conduct effective attacks with conventional or chemical warheads. The Soviets have been publishing discussions of specialized conventional munitions for SRBM warheads since the late 1960s. These specialized munitions and submunitions include high-explosive charges, fragmentation and incendiary devices, and antiarmor "minelets." The Soviets have, however, shown particular interest in developing blast-enhanced fuel-air explosive munitions, apparently because these nonnuclear-warhead designs would have effects comparable to those of low-yield nuclear weapons.[186] Ogarkov, Gareyev, and other Soviet authorities have referred frequently to "the development of highly accurate, guided weapons which in terms of effectiveness are close to low-yield nuclear weapons."[187]

According to the International Institute for Strategic Studies (IISS), the new SRBMs with nonnuclear warheads could give the Soviets "a potent capability to suppress NATO air defenses and to strike deep against critical NATO nuclear forces and conventional reinforcements." As the IISS adds, such strikes would "appear to be consistent with the more recently expressed Soviet interest in fighting without resort to (but under the constant threat of) nuclear escalation."[188] The ability to attack targets with missile-delivered conventional warheads that would today require nuclear weapons or conventional aircraft sorties would, of course, be backed up by forces capable of selective nuclear strikes, if necessary. As on the level of intercontinental ballistic missile strike capabilities, NATO and Warsaw Pact SRBM assets differ. While the Western alliance has only 300 launchers for missiles in these range categories, the Warsaw Pact has over 1600 such launchers and has probably "accumulated substantial stocks of reload missiles."[189] The implementation of the December 1987 INF treaty may lead the Soviets to concentrate on the modernization of

SRBMs with ranges below 500 km (SS-21s and possible new systems) and potential theater applications of intercontinental missile systems.

The Soviets have also continued to modernize their nonballistic means of airborne attack in Europe. These include hundreds of medium-range bombers (Badgers and Blinders) and longer-range bombers well suited to regional missions (Backfires), and over 2000 fighter-bombers (Fitters, Fishbeds, Floggers, and Fencers). The more advanced versions of the Fitter, Flogger, and Fencer are capable of deep-strike operations and have been compared to the U.S. F-16 and West European Tornado.[190] The Fencer is especially threatening because of its range (3600 km), its speed (Mach 2.3), and its avionics for all-weather operations.[191]

As with the SRBMs, Soviet sources suggest that destroying NATO's nuclear weapons would be a high priority in Soviet air attacks.[192] Since the late 1960s, the Soviets have developed and deployed more effective ground-attack aircraft while continuing to modernize and expand their air defense assets—fighters, radars, and surface-to-air missile units. According to the West German Ministry of Defense, "the quantitative superiority of the Warsaw Pact air forces is gaining in weight," owing to the fact that Warsaw Pact aircraft have become "comparable" to those of the West in qualitative terms.[193] It is likely that a number of the 2000 to 3000 cruise missiles that the CIA expects the USSR to deploy over the next ten years will have targets in Europe.[194]

These developments are consistent with Soviet forecasts of future trends in military technology. Although the Soviet military has demonstrated an interest in more advanced nuclear systems (with improved survivability, accuracy, and command-and-control responsiveness), an even greater emphasis has been placed on new conventional weapons technologies. More effective nonnuclear munitions are to be delivered with highly accurate long-range strike systems, guided by new types of sensors and fire-control systems. These advanced weapons systems would support the doctrinal aim of achieving military objectives without the use of nuclear weapons. At the same time, given the basic Soviet forecast of future war—the threat of "global conventional war fought under the constant threat of escalation to the use of nuclear weapons," the Soviets have perceived an increasing requirement for defenses against long-range cruise missiles and highly accurate conventional-warhead ballistic and stand-off missiles.[195]

AIR DEFENSES
Trends in the Soviet defensive-force posture have been consistent with the thrust toward capabilities for damage limitation and discrimination in

the use of force in the Soviet offensive posture. Air defenses are the most obvious illustration of the Soviet unwillingness to abandon active defense of the USSR, despite the ABM Treaty. NATO's Central European air defenses are currently incapable of intercepting Soviet ballistic and cruise missiles, and highly placed NATO officials judge that Warsaw Pact helicopters and aircraft could saturate and break through the air defenses to attack NATO's command centers and other targets in Western Europe.[196] The contrast in U.S. and Soviet investments in radars, fighter aircraft, and surface-to-air missiles for defense against intercontinental air attack was reviewed in Chapter 1. Whatever counting rules are adopted, the USSR and its Warsaw Pact allies have built up an air defense posture that is numerically far stronger than that of the Western alliance.

It is hard to estimate how effective Soviet air defenses would be. The United States has been forced by Soviet air defenses to invest in expensive countermeasures, including aircraft capable of withstanding the rigors of low-altitude penetration tactics. Investments in advanced cruise missiles and other types of air-launched stand-off missiles are, to some extent, a direct result of U.S. reluctance to subject U.S. personnel (and expensive aircraft) to the hazards posed by Soviet air defenses. Developments in some West European air forces have shown a similar pattern—for example, the French decision to rely on a stand-off missile, the *air-sol moyenne portée* (ASMP), instead of trying to penetrate Soviet air defenses with a manned bomber.

Western governments would, it seems, have some basis for concern on quantitative grounds alone. The Warsaw Pact maintains over four times as many fighters and interceptors as does NATO in Europe.[197] The most modern Soviet interceptors (Flanker and Fulcrum) are, moreover, expected to close the gap with Western systems in terms of technological quality.[198] In addition to the fighters, Western aircraft would have to contend with the densest array of surface-to-air missiles in the world. The first 300 miles beyond the inter-German border are defended by 15,550 SAMs of various types.[199] The Soviet concentration on developing and deploying mobile SAMs, radars, and C^3 systems in recent years tends to invalidate assumptions that Soviet air defenses could be readily neutralized by a ballistic missile attack.

MOBILITY AND OTHER PASSIVE DEFENSES

The Soviets have in fact made extensive use of mobility for both their defensive capabilities and their offensive forces. Mobility is a form of "passive" defense, as opposed to the "active" defense potential of air defenses and BMD. As France's Ecole Polytechnique group has pointed out, however, "passive defense programs are the logical complement" of Soviet active defenses and "therefore provide additional light on Soviet intentions."[200] The active and passive defenses are both dedicated to protecting the key elements of Soviet war-waging potential—above all, the leadership, the forces, and the command, control, and communications systems.

The Soviets have made several types of military assets mobile and thus harder for adversaries to locate and target. As noted in Chapter 1, Soviet investments in mobile or transportable systems include components of the Moscow BMD system (the Flat Twin and Pawn Shop radars) and surface-to-air missiles and radars that may have BMD potential. The new shorter-range ballistic missiles (SS-21, SS-22, and SS-23) are designed with "improved mobility, faster reaction time and reduced support requirements" in order to pose "a much more difficult targeting problem for NATO."[201] Although the Soviet mobility program also includes "an extensive network of mobile command, control, and communications facilities,"[202] the Soviet development of mobile ICBMs deserves special attention.

Mobile ICBMs—road-mobile SS-25s and rail-mobile SS-24s—are today operationally deployed in the Soviet Union, whereas the United States has yet to make a production decision on the concept, for either a rail-garrison deployment of MX missiles or the "Midgetman" small ICBM under development. The Soviet rail-mobile SS-24 is approximately the same size as the U.S. MX; it became operational in 1987 and is expected to carry up to ten MIRVs. The CIA projects that mobile ICBMs will constitute approximately one-fifth of the Soviet ICBM force by the mid-1990s.[203]

The mobile ICBMs will, like the new SRBMs and the SS-20 intermediate-range ballistic missile force, enjoy various advantages in terms of survivability. The United States would have to locate the mobile ICBMs in order to target them, and make use of that information promptly, before the ICBMs moved again. As a result, to provide additional protection for the mobile ICBM force, the Soviets could attack or simply interfere with U.S. means of target acquisition, communications, or guidance—with antisatellite systems or electronic warfare, for example[204]— or simply conceal the ICBMs under forestlike camouflage or in hardened shelters (for instance, railheads dug into mountainsides). Even if the Soviets did not interfere with U.S. means of attack assessment, mobile ICBMs could make it more difficult for the United States to reach judgments on the results of counterforce strikes. U.S. officials testified in 1986 that "strategic relocatable targets" such as the new Soviet mobile

ICBMs are already "reducing the effectiveness of our present strategic weapons" by making it more difficult "to hold these offensive forces at risk."[205]

Among the many advantages that Soviet planners probably perceive in mobile ICBMs is some relief from incentives to engage in preemptive launches on warning of an attack. This is consistent with the Soviet interest in trying to avoid any use of nuclear weapons and to control the scope of any nuclear operations that become unavoidable. It could be argued that Soviet SLBMs already provide a hedge against such contingencies. Land-mobile ICBMs, however, may be expected to be superior to SLBMs in their endurance (because SSBNs must eventually expose their locations to replenish their supplies of food and other consumables); in their accuracy (because they could use presurveyed launch sites, although the importance of this consideration might be diminished in the future by in-flight satellite correction and terminal guidance systems on maneuverable reentry vehicles); and in their reliability (because communications could consist of hardened lines to the presurveyed launch sites, whereas SSBNs would remain vulnerable to the disruption or interception of radio contact). SSBNs might also be more subject to attrition during a conventional phase of war, because nuclear escalation might be seen as more likely to follow strikes against targets on Soviet territory than attacks on ships at sea.

Although the Soviets probably value their land-based systems highly because of their control advantages, they have not neglected SLBMs. In retrospect, it seems likely that the Soviets developed long-range SLBMs such as the 9100-km-range SS-N-8 (first deployed in 1973) and 8300-km-range SS-N-20 (first deployed in 1981)[206] before the United States developed such long-range SLBMs because they wanted to avoid exposing their SSBNs to superior U.S. antisubmarine warfare (ASW) capabilities. The range of these SLBMs is such that they could be launched from ports in the USSR and strike targets in the United States. The long SLBM range has enabled the Soviets to organize SSBN "bastions" in Arctic waters, near and beneath the polar ice, to protect their SSBNs from U.S. ASW capabilities with various Soviet naval forces—attack submarines, surface ships, aircraft, and land- and sea-based air defenses.

According to John Collins, "about 25% of Soviet SSBNs are at sea on any given day, compared with about 55% of our Poseidon boats and 65% of Tridents. Another 25% of Soviet SSBNs probably are on alert in port."[207] The high proportion of SSBNs estimated to be on alert in port—and capable of striking targets in the United States (and Western Europe) from that location—may offer another explanation for the Soviets' pioneering the development of long-range SLBMs: the relative ease of maintaining central control over SSBNs in port. At the same time, the long-range SLBMs at sea—notably those in protected "bastions"—could be rapidly joined by SSBNs kept on alert in port in order to constitute a large and survivable reserve force; this reserve force could compensate for possible attrition of the ICBM force and give the USSR leverage for intrawar deterrence and war-termination bargaining. The bastion approach offers the advantage of keeping the SSBNs near Soviet communications networks in Soviet-controlled waters. It has been estimated that "Soviet SSBNs could surge to on-station rates exceeding 50 percent," and that this "could approach 75 percent after several weeks."[208]

Hardening is another key form of passive defense and, like mobility, closely linked to protective tactics such as concealment, dispersal, and redundancy. Soviet civil defense programs have been expanded since 1972. The civil defense programs go far beyond those in any Western country; they reportedly include over 1500 hardened alternate leadership facilities with survivable communications for over 175,000 key personnel, plus shelters and other practical preparations (for example, stockpiles of raw materials) for economic mobilization and military production in war.[209] Soviet civil defense measures extend to general-purpose military forces, war-supporting industries, internal security forces, and the populace at large.[210]

The survivability of the Soviet leadership, political and military, and their means of command, control, and communications (C^3) must be a priority concern. This priority would come to the fore in any war. It would also be of supreme importance if the Soviets were trying to maximize their chances of deterring their adversaries from using nuclear weapons or (if nuclear weapons were used) from expanding the scope of nuclear operations.

In 1977 the chairman of the Joint Chiefs of Staff indicated that the Soviet program of hardening leadership and C^3 shelters began in the 1950s, and that hardened headquarters sites have been dispersed throughout the USSR, Eastern Europe, and Mongolia.[211] Prior to 1966, several Soviet sources described the construction of leadership shelters buried twenty to forty meters below the surface and possibly capable of withstanding an airburst nuclear explosion of one megaton.[212] The Moscow system reportedly includes tunnels running "60 km in two directions to give underground access to the High Level Command Posts."[213] The Strategic Rocket Forces, which command IRBMs such as the SS-20s and SS-4s in addition to the ICBM force, have about 300 hardened command centers.[214] According to Desmond Ball, in comparison with the United States, the USSR's "protection of the top political and military leadership is much more extensive, and Soviet communications links are much more dispersed and redundant."[215]

Dispersal, redundancy, and hardening are supplemented by concealment. In 1980 Secretary of Defense Harold Brown said that "the relatively few leadership shelters we have identified would be vulnerable to direct attack."[216] But, as the wording of his statement implied, "it is believed that many other facilities exist which have not been located and identified"—a point the administration had reported to the Congress in 1979.[217] As Amrom Katz once noted, the United States has "never found anything that the Soviets have successfully hidden."[218] Albert Wohlstetter has pointed out that, even if the location of a Soviet command structure 1000 feet deep was known within a radius of tens of miles, a "blind barrage using many thousands of [nuclear] weapons could harm the environment without stopping command."[219]

The hardening alone might enable most of the Soviet leadership to survive even in the improbable case of a large-scale U.S. attack, although significant uncertainties would remain.[220] The October 1985 report of the Department of State and Department of Defense indicated that "the USSR has hardened its ICBM silos, launch facilities, and key command and control centers to an unprecedented degree. Much of today's U.S. retaliatory force would be ineffective against those hardened targets."[221] According to the CIA, "with as little as a few hours' warning, a large percentage of the wartime management structure would survive the initial effects of a large-scale US nuclear attack . . . Deep underground facilities for the top national leadership might enable the top leadership to survive—a key objective of their wartime management plans."[222]

How effectively a surviving Soviet leadership might be able to command and control the remaining military assets of the USSR would be hard to judge, even for the Soviets themselves. High-level CIA officials testified in 1985 that the hardening of redundant means of communications has been so extensive that "it seems highly likely that the Soviets could maintain overall continuity of command and control, although it would probably be degraded and they could experience difficulty in maintaining endurance."[223] Skeptical observers have complained that phrases such as "overall continuity" and "difficulty in maintaining endurance" are hard to pin down or reconcile; but it is doubtful that anyone could responsibly offer more than broad judgments of probability regarding unprecedented circumstances. Desmond Ball reached a comparable conclusion in 1980: "It would probably not be possible to isolate the Soviet NCA [national command authority] completely from the strategic forces or completely to impair the Soviet strategic intelligence flow."[224] These judgments might be qualified if the United States could identify a greater proportion of the Soviet deep underground facilities and develop methods of effectively attacking them. Some officials have reportedly suggested that earth-penetrating nuclear weapons could be developed to attack such hardened targets, as well as other types of hardened targets in the Soviet Union.[225]

EAST-WEST DIFFERENCES IN STRATEGIC DEFENSE AND BMD
Non-BMD forms of strategic defense for the Soviet leadership, their means of command, control, and communications (C^3), and the forces help to explain why the target set that the Soviet Union represents for the United States and its NATO allies differs from the target set that the Western alliance offers to the Soviet Union. The Soviet target set includes more and harder hardened targets, more mobile targets (including ICBMs), and more concealed targets (camouflaged or buried). Elements of the Soviet target set could well become more dispersed in a crisis, whereas certain U.S. and allied targets might well become more lucrative (for example, troop concentration centers).

Although it is true that the USSR has more land and forests than the United States, it is probably mainly for social and political reasons that the United States and its allies have so far been unable to compete with the Soviets in passive means of defending land-based C^3 and forces—mobility, redundancy, extensive hardening, deception through concealment, and so forth. France's Ecole Polytechnique group attributes the Soviet lead in mobile ballistic missiles to the fact that the Soviets can act "without being constrained by any public opinion."[226]

Similarly, the United States and West European governments would find it difficult to develop constituencies for programs of redundant, deep underground leadership shelters and associated C^3 networks. Western governments have generally favored minimal preparations of this genre, apparently because of the cost and a conviction that such installations would soon become pointless in a large-scale nuclear war. Three underground command facilities were built in the United States in the 1950s and early 1960s—for the Strategic Air Command, the North American Aerospace Defense Command, and the Alternate National Military Command Center. These facilities were "hardened for the yield and accuracy combinations of the times, but the rapid improvement in warhead accuracy (even though accompanied by reductions in warhead yield) has made them vulnerable to complete destruction by missile attack."[227]

Whatever the reasons, the U.S. and allied target set is less dispersed, less hardened, and almost entirely without active defenses (no BMD and little air defense, except for Central Europe) in comparison with that under Soviet direction. Soviet investments in complementary passive defenses have already affected the U.S. ability to attack critical targets in the USSR. According to the under secretary of defense for research and engineering, "Soviet efforts toward surviving a nuclear exchange through mobility, hardening, and deep underground emplacement of key war-fighting assets make the U.S. strategic targeting problem increasingly difficult."[228]

Under some circumstances, Soviet passive defenses (hardening, mobility, concealment, and so forth) might be able, in conjunction with various forms of active defense (such as BMD, air defense, and attacks on U.S. satellites), significantly to reduce damage to the military and command, control, and communications assets most highly prized by the Soviet leadership. This would, of course, depend on the nature and scope of the attack. This might in turn depend on the effectiveness of Soviet preemptive attacks in degrading the capabilities of Western governments to attack, by destroying or disabling their forces and C^3 networks. The nature and scope of any attacks by Western governments would almost certainly also be influenced by their assessment of the likely residual "counterretaliation" capabilities of the Soviet Union. For this reason, the most probable attacks—those the Soviet Union is most likely to have to contend with—would be far more limited than the full-scale assaults considered in some assessments of the robustness and adequacy of Soviet strategic defenses.

Although this situation already encompasses a number of advantages for the Soviet Union, it could be made more favorable through BMD deployments of essentially traditional types. France's Ecole Polytechnique group has pointed out that, owing to Soviet investments in passive defenses such as mobility, "the Soviet Union has less of a need than the United States for an active ABM defense of its strategic sites."[229] Few estimates of what moderately effective BMD could offer the USSR under such assumptions have been made public. In 1983 John L. Gardner, then director of defense systems, Department of Defense, testified that, even in the presence of passive defense measures, Soviet air defenses could provide the Soviets only "a fairly modest payoff" if Soviet BMD capabilities were ineffective. He added, "If on the other hand, they can accompany their air defense deployment with a deployment of even moderately effective ballistic missile defenses, they can significantly reduce the damage to their military value structure."[230] In other words,

Soviet force-posture trends imply a commitment to operational effectiveness and war survival that logically requires BMD to place a "cap" or "roof" on a structure of counterforce capabilities and active and passive defenses that already place the Soviet Union at an overall advantage in certain specific types of nuclear war-fighting capabilities.

Western experts are not, however, in complete agreement on what the Soviets would choose to defend with expanded BMD capabilities. According to Sayre Stevens,

> in general, the Soviet Union will want to defend clusters of high-value leadership, communications, military, and economic targets, striving to limit damage and preserve those elements important to warfighting and reconstitution . . . The Soviet Union appears to have little interest in ICBM defense . . . Such defenses have not been a focus of Soviet BMD R & D. Moreover, other options are available to provide protection for these weapons: hardening, mobility, preemption, and launch on warning (or under attack).[231]

This judgment and similar ones expressed by other analysts—that mobility and other non-BMD forms of strategic defense could suffice to protect Soviet ICBMs[232] —may understate the future value to the Soviet Union of BMD for ICBM defense.[233] In the first place, as Andrew Marshall has remarked, the Soviet Union "has an especially strong commitment—bureaucratic and otherwise—to maintaining the Strategic Rocket Forces as the main element of her strategic forces," and may therefore seek "a variety of measures to increase the protection of the silo-based systems," including BMD site defense.[234] Indeed, it seems contrary to the Soviet approach to strategic defense—which is to build upon the cumulative effects of several types of measures—to disregard the potential contribution of BMD to the security of Soviet ICBMs.

Moreover, prudent Soviet military planners will have to assume that U.S. hard-target kill capabilities will increase in the years to come if the United States goes forward with programs for the MX ICBM, the Trident II D-5 SLBM, air-launched cruise missiles, and so forth. The Soviets may therefore perceive an increased need for BMD to help protect ICBMs, even in the context of investments in hardening, mobility, deception, and other measures for the same purpose. Even mobile ICBM and SRBM systems presumably involve some fixed sites where missiles are stockpiled, loaded, repaired, and so forth—main operating bases, as it were—that could benefit from BMD protection. Defenses for ICBMs could also help to protect other assets highly valued by the USSR, depending on the capabilities of the systems eventually deployed.[235]

Stevens' judgment must nonetheless be regarded as essentially correct with regard to Soviet priorities. The supreme priority is probably defense of the leadership, military command posts, and associated C^3 installations, for these capabilities would be critical to the Soviets' ability to retain control over the conduct of their military operations and their negotiations with adversaries. A preliminary indication of Soviet BMD priorities may, in any case, be discernible in the next few years as the SA-12 receives operational assignments. It is possible that the SA-12 may be given roles in addition to serving as an antitactical ballistic missile (ATBM) to protect Warsaw Pact ground and air forces in Europe.

Interpretations and Inferences

All explanatory hypotheses oversimplify historical contexts, which always remain more complex than the organizing constructs used to describe and analyze them. Some hypotheses are nonetheless more illuminating than others. A composite hypothesis emphasizing Soviet mission requirements in force-procurement and arms control behavior seems to throw the most light on Soviet BMD decision making, partly because it is supported by the evidence of Soviet military doctrine and force posture trends.

The mission requirements interpretation may, however, be usefully qualified by the insights available from the more illuminating versions of arms race and bureaucratic-politics explanations. The arms race models suggest that the Soviets are attentive to developments in the U.S. force posture and capable of capitalizing on at least some opportunities offered by U.S. inaction and policy preferences. The Soviets may therefore have perceived advantages in experimenting with arms control as a means of arms race management—specifically, accepting (for Soviet political and strategic purposes) the opportunity presented to them by the United States to limit U.S. BMD deployments and the further development of superior U.S. BMD technology. The bureaucratic-politics approach reminds us that, while Soviet policy-making processes are not uniformly rational and advantage maximizing, the Soviet leadership is capable of highly centralized decision making. The Soviet Union might therefore be able to implement policies of critical strategic importance with great continuity, even in the presence of continuing institutional conflicts and divisions over what degree of emphasis to attach to basic strategic priorities.

The mission requirements interpretation would suggest that Soviet acceptance of the ABM Treaty was a decision grounded in expediency.

The ABM Treaty was evidently approved because of limitations in Soviet technological capacities for BMD and because of the need to be able to perform the damage-limiting "defensive" mission of counterforce unhindered by U.S. BMD. This instrumental approach to the ABM Treaty implies that the Soviet Union would have no doctrinal motive for continued Soviet observance of the treaty if its technological capabilities advanced sufficiently—although self-imposed constraints by the United States on its own BMD research and development would logically be favored and actively encouraged by the Soviets. For the indefinite future, therefore, it would be to the advantage of the USSR to enhance its lead over the United States in promptly exploitable BMD capabilities without unambiguously violating provisions of the ABM Treaty, in order to encourage continued U.S. compliance with the treaty.

Sayre Stevens has suggested that the "apparent purposefulness and direction [of the Soviet BMD effort] in the presence of a treaty that precludes the ultimate payoff" can be explained by a Soviet judgment that such an agreement "cannot be expected to remain acceptable in changing circumstances for so long into the future as to obviate the need to press ahead with R & D."[236] Many factors in Soviet history, force posture trends, and military doctrine suggest that the Soviets would have multiple incentives to invest in large-scale BMD deployments if they had determined that effective technologies were within reach and that the costs—in terms of probable responses by the United States (and other Western countries)—were manageable.

This is a critical point. If our working hypothesis is correct, and the Soviets approved the ABM Treaty primarily in order to constrain the United States in an area of evident U.S. competitive advantage (high-technology BMD), the Soviets probably would not wish to legitimize U.S. BMD programs unless they were convinced that their technological capabilities had at last equaled or excelled those of the United States.

It seems doubtful that the Soviets hold this conviction, except perhaps with respect to traditional ground-based BMD interceptor missiles and radars; even in this regard, they might be more likely to rate their technological attainments as having lately become roughly equivalent to those of the United States and still inferior with respect to data processing, sensors, and other critical areas. The discretion with which the Soviets have developed and discussed antitactical ballistic missile (ATBM) systems for defense against shorter-range missiles, such as the SA-X-12B/Giant, suggests that they would not welcome a competition in this area either; they would probably prefer to continue improving these systems without facing competition from Western counterparts. Similarly, the Soviet lead in developing weapons based on lasers that some observers discern might amount to a temporary engineering and investment advantage. The Soviets might estimate that the United States could overcome this advantage fairly rapidly, with the application of concentrated effort. That is, truly practical laser weaponization could be too far in the future for the Soviets not to be concerned about potential U.S. accomplishments.

Such an assessment would help to explain the vigorous Soviet opposition to the U.S. Strategic Defense Initiative, which may seem all the more threatening to the extent that it appears to favor advanced-technology space-based BMD—potentially an area of U.S. technological advantage, and arguably the type of BMD the United States would require, given the magnitude of the Soviet ballistic missile threat and the vulnerability of the U.S. target set.

In other words, while the Soviets may well have a BMD breakout potential superior to that of the United States in terms of traditional ground-based BMD, the Soviets may also have incentives not to exploit it too visibly, given the risks of provoking serious U.S. competition in BMD. The balance of Soviet incentives (unilateral political and strategic advantages) and disincentives (risks of U.S. and allied responses) with respect to their BMD breakout potential is complex and probably not entirely clear-cut, in that tradeoffs are involved in trying to maximize certain critical advantages and minimize the risks of prompting the United States and its allies to engage in an earnest competition in BMD (and other forms of strategic defense) and offensive countermeasures.

Several of the incentives are explored in Chapter 3, which considers the implications for the Western alliance of an expansion of Soviet BMD capabilities. The disincentives are discussed in Chapter 4, which examines Soviet interests in arms race management. It appears that a current imperative of Soviet policy is to avoid an intense BMD competition with the United States, particularly in the area of space-based BMD and associated antisatellite capabilities. A Soviet policy shift in the foreseeable future seems plausible only with respect to ground-based BMD of traditional types.

3

Implications for the Western Alliance

Three doctrinal requirements, as noted in Chapter 2, help to explain Soviet force development. These requirements may be summed up as nuclear forces capable of discouraging Western governments from using nuclear weapons; conventional-force superiority and operational plans to enhance Soviet prospects for deciding any conflict on nonnuclear terms; and a capability for selective nuclear attacks, if necessary. These requirements support an overall concept of damage limitation in the event of war—intended, above all, to prevent nuclear strikes against the USSR, to limit any nuclear employment, and to blunt the effects of nuclear attacks.

Implementation of this damage-limitation concept should not be seen as the uncomplicated fulfillment of a hyperrational master plan. As suggested in Chapter 2, Soviet strategic thinking and the Soviet force posture are affected by external constraints (including interactions with foreign governments and unforeseen events) and internal decision-making processes (including organizational priorities) as well as by economic circumstances and technological limitations. The coherence and purposefulness of Soviet strategic thought and military-force development have nonetheless been impressive.

The changes in the conventional- and nuclear-force balances with the West over the past two decades have, moreover, been mainly positive from the Soviet perspective. The essential effect of these trends, taken together, has been to degrade and narrow the West's plausible force employment options while increasing and enhancing those available to the Soviet Union. The Soviets have built on their geographical and organizational advantages with respect to amassing and projecting conventional forces in Europe and have steadily continued to widen the gap between NATO and the Warsaw Pact in conventional combat power. This has heightened the West's dependence on nuclear threats. But the Soviets have attempted simultaneously to neutralize NATO's nuclear-deterrent posture by building up "counter-deterrent" nuclear capabilities in the form of short- and intermediate-range nuclear superiority and robust intercontinental capabilities.

The Soviets have, in other words, gradually deprived NATO's "flexible-response" strategy of much of its flexibility. The growth of Soviet conventional-force superiority has made the long-standing nuclear dilemmas of the Western alliance harder to manage politically. These dilemmas are intrinsic to the situation of West European dependence on U.S. nuclear guarantees. This situation stems from the West's unwillingness since the founding of NATO to erect a conventional defense posture that would lessen dependence on nuclear weapons. After the destruction of the intra-European balance of power during World War II and the Soviet entry into Central Europe, the Western allies (including the United States) found reliance on U.S. nuclear threats preferable to the exertions of matching the Soviet conventional force posture.

The Western dependence on U.S. nuclear threats has, however, become more uncomfortable as the Soviet capacity to retaliate in kind has increased. Until the late 1950s, when the Soviets developed ICBMs, they had few means to threaten direct nuclear retaliation against the United States if the Americans honored their nuclear guarantees to Western Europe. (As we have seen, the Soviets had relatively few intercontinental bombers, and these would have had to penetrate the formidable air defenses of North America in the 1950s.) Until the late 1960s, the United States enjoyed superiority in intercontinental nuclear strike systems. Since the late 1960s, however, the United States has faced increasingly survivable and potent Soviet intercontinental strike systems, with little in the way of active or passive defenses.

As Soviet strategic nuclear forces have become more numerous and survivable, Soviet military theorists appear to have reasoned that a situation could be created in which nuclear conflict at any level of intensity would seem unacceptable to many in the Western alliance. By matching and even exceeding U.S. nuclear capabilities in specific areas, these theorists seem to have judged, the USSR could hypothetically discourage the United States from initiating use of nuclear weapons during a limited conflict—or could at least attempt to dissuade the United States from striking targets in the USSR, for fear of Soviet retaliation against the U.S. homeland. These shifts in force balances have, at any rate, had an impact on the perceived credibility of the U.S. nuclear commitments at the heart of NATO's flexible-response strategy. As General Brent Scowcroft put it in 1979, one of the "stark realities of this new situation" is that NATO "can no longer improve war outcome by escalating, or threatening to escalate, the level of conflict."[1]

In other words, the adequacy of NATO's overall deterrent posture has for many years been growing increasingly problematic quite apart from potential improvements in Soviet ballistic missile defenses. A significant Soviet advantage in BMD capabilities would not intrude into an otherwise "stable" and satisfactory situation, but would help to worsen trends in nuclear- and conventional-force relationships that have already eroded the perceived reliability of U.S. nuclear guarantees. Expanded Soviet BMD capabilities would support other elements of the Soviet military posture—active and passive defenses, long-range nuclear and nonnuclear offensive strike forces, and conventional combat units. Depending on the circumstances (including possible Western countermeasures) and the specific systems deployed, enlarged Soviet BMD capabilities could further undermine Western security. Such capabilities would be consistent with the history of purposeful force-posture building in the USSR and could advance long-standing Soviet political objectives.

It is not clear, however, how the Soviets are most likely to improve their BMD systems. Although the Soviet Union is probably capable of expanding its existing traditional ground-based defenses more quickly than the United States could develop and deploy such systems, the Soviets have incentives—including the risk of Western countermeasures—not to engage in an explicit breakout from the constraints of the ABM Treaty. (These incentives and possible Soviet decision making about the SDI are discussed in Chapter 4.) A gradual creepout from the treaty's constraints (in conjunction with treaty-permitted infrastructure expansion and system modernization) may therefore be more probable than an overt breakout. Either case—an overt breakout or a more surreptitious creepout—could furnish the basis for a large unilateral advantage in BMD. Although such an advantage might not be sustained long (depending on Western responses), it could for a time augment existing Soviet capabilities—offensive and defensive—in significant ways.

Soviet Strategic Priorities

Before turning to what might be the consequences for the West of such a Soviet advantage, certain fundamental features of Soviet strategic policy should be clarified in order to throw light on Soviet priorities. It would, for example, be a misconception to suppose that the Soviets always pursue their military-force programs with specific political ends in view and intend to wage particular wars to achieve those ends. In fact, the

Soviets often appear to be inspired in their force building by what Herbert Goldhamer termed a "general contingency aim," owing in part to their history and their complex geostrategic situation, in addition to specific political objectives. Moreover, rather than planning to advance those objectives through war, the Soviets are well aware of the hazards of war—especially large-scale nuclear war—and are intensely interested in achieving desired political changes without war and, should war come, in keeping military operations and possible nuclear escalation under their control.

A GENERAL CONTINGENCY AIM

In the Soviet strategic culture, as suggested in Chapter 2's discussion of Soviet military doctrine, a high priority is placed on unilateral measures of assuring security. Russian and Soviet military-historical experiences suggest that peacetime military preparations can scarcely be excessive. To build military forces of the highest feasible quality and operational effectiveness and, if possible, in superior numbers is, in the Soviet calculus, simply common sense as well as the dictate of "scientific" study of Marxist-Leninist theory.[2] A position of strength and, if possible, of de facto military superiority is expected to provide the Soviet state with (1) insurance against both likely and unforeseeable risks and (2) instruments for use in the event of opportunities that may be equally unpredictable.

In contrast to the Soviet approach, U.S. military power has more often been "improvised against specific, perceived dangers"—threats identified with some precision and hence justifying a response.[3] As Herbert Goldhamer noted, the United States "tends to act in relation to power somewhat in the manner of a person who saves money only when a specific purchase is in view." As a result, American interpretations of Soviet military programs and activities, "while stressing that the Soviets have different objectives from us, often attribute to them the same specificity accorded to our own actions."[4]

This American tendency, a facet of the general strategic ethnocentrism of the West, inhibits understanding of the autonomous springs of Soviet power-seeking behavior. As Goldhamer pointed out,

> power may be pursued, not for specific ends now foreseen, but precisely because the contingencies of international life cannot in fact be anticipated. Uncertainties regarding the future, including uncertainties concerning one's own future objectives, make desirable increased room for maneuver, a greater number of options, and an increased ability to exercise control over the international environment . . . Only when power is viewed as being such an important

general asset that increments of it are sought without regard to any specific and foreseeable use to which they may be put, is a nation most fully committed to a "power struggle." It is in this sense that the United States has been less fully engaged than the Soviet Union in a power conflict.[5]

The Soviet approach seems incredible and irrational to many Americans and other Westerners, who take a very specific and instrumental approach to building military power.[6] Goldhamer concluded, however, that "being 'power hungry' may not be any less rational than preferring a larger to a smaller bank balance . . . Soviet attempts to extend their military-political power can be interpreted as having a general contingency aim in the sense described above and not, or not only, specific objectives or goals whose nature we may or may not correctly guess."[7]

This concept of a general contingency aim stands in opposition to attempts to infer a detailed Soviet master plan from observable evidence. As argued in Chapter 2, some Soviet military capabilities have probably been acquired for specific purposes to give the Soviet government certain options of critical strategic importance; but the utility of other capabilities may have been perceived dimly at the outset and may still be unclear. The value of the latter capabilities may nonetheless become more obvious as a function of developments in technology and/or in the opportunities offered by international political developments. It is useful to keep the general contingency aim in mind, because Soviet defense decision making seems to proceed in accordance with its own traditions and dynamics, not solely with reference to U.S. or general Western military policy.

Indeed, the various incentives the Soviet Union evidently perceives for continued expansion and improvement of its BMD potential no doubt derive from Soviet assessments of global strategic requirements. For example, whereas only the United States among NATO countries seems to have ever regarded Chinese ballistic missile capabilities as a potential threat, the Soviet Union has taken the possibility of Chinese attack (or retaliation) seriously enough to deploy SA-5s and other systems in order to defend against Chinese aircraft and missiles.[8] The broader international context in which the Soviets discern strategic defense requirements should not be forgotten.

CAUTION REGARDING WAR, ESPECIALLY NUCLEAR WAR
Western authorities on Soviet political-military affairs generally agree that the Soviets have always been cautious in deciding to initiate wars. Soviet military doctrine has consistently upheld the Leninist principle that

the political leadership, "from an evaluation of military and political factors, selects the most propitious moment to start a war, taking into account all the strategic considerations."[9] Peter Vigor has pointed out that, on all the occasions when the Soviet leadership has "deliberately embarked upon a war" (as opposed to having war thrust upon it, as in June 1941), the victims of Soviet aggression were far weaker than the USSR, and effective foreign intervention in support of the victims was either impossible or unlikely.[10]

Vigor's list, compiled in 1975, includes the subjugation of the independent republic of Georgia (1921), the attack in China (1929), the occupation of Eastern Poland (1939), the attack on Finland (1939), and the annexation of Latvia, Lithuania, and Estonia (1940). In the immediate post-1945 period, the Soviets were cautious in imposing "socialism" in Eastern Europe until they were confident that Western governments would not vigorously oppose their doing so. In subsequent decades, the Soviets have been relatively cautious in using force to maintain their control structures in the Warsaw Pact and have assured Western governments that Soviet-directed interventions (for example, Hungary in 1956 and Czechoslovakia in 1968) have not been directed against Western security interests.[11] The 1979 invasion of Afghanistan fits the established pattern. In Vigor's words, "the USSR has never started a war against another country which was not significantly smaller and weaker than itself."[12]

Nuclear weapons have almost certainly reinforced the Soviet Union's historically demonstrated caution about undertaking war. Attacking the United States with nuclear weapons would only increase the unprecedented risks that any Soviet nuclear operations directed against military targets in Europe would pose. Soviet policy appears far more likely to be oriented toward trying both to avoid Soviet use of nuclear weapons, unless it were to become unavoidably necessary for the fulfillment of Soviet aims, and to prevent enemy use of nuclear weapons. Any Soviet-initiated use of nuclear weapons in Europe would probably be as limited as possible, and the Soviets would be likely to go to great lengths to keep the course of nuclear operations under their control.

How then should Soviet investments in nuclear war-waging capabilities be understood? Although there is a widespread tendency in the West to assume a high degree of symmetry in the strategic nuclear-force postures and planning of two undifferentiated "superpowers," U.S. and Soviet doctrines and force postures are distinctly different. The United States and its NATO allies are almost exclusively dependent on offensive retaliatory forces, with little in the way of active and passive defenses.

Although U.S. hard-target kill capabilities may be expected to improve in the next decade (particularly as a result of projected deployments of MX ICBMs, Trident II D-5 SLBMS, and air-launched cruise missiles), current-force structure asymmetries and continuing Soviet force expansion will probably keep the United States well behind the Soviet Union in its ability to attack hardened military targets. The Soviet Union has devoted much more attention than the United States to obtaining capabilities suitable for actually fighting a nuclear war. The USSR has acquired prompt counter-force strike capabilities much greater than those of the United States, as well as notable advantages in active and passive defenses.[13]

These investments do not demonstrate a Soviet desire or intention to initiate a large-scale nuclear war, but attest to Soviet seriousness about the prospect of such a conflict. Precisely because the risks in an intercontinental nuclear war would be unprecedented, the Soviets appear to have concluded, they must try to avert it and be prepared to wage it effectively if it cannot be avoided. The Soviets know from experience that crises not expected to lead to war could do so, and apparently consider it irresponsible not to be as well prepared as possible. Situations could go out of control; a certain sense of "war-is-coming" inevitability could force decisions to act; and the Soviets evidently wish to be as well placed as possible to reassert a measure of control over events.

Soviet military theorists acknowledge that superiority confers no guarantees of success in an enterprise as hazardous and unpredictable as war: "Even a significant superiority is merely a favorable opportunity. Its conversion into actuality is a complex and contradictory process."[14] Major General Stepan Tyushkevich, a professor at the Institute of Military History of the Soviet Defense Ministry, has nonetheless argued:

> Success in a nuclear missile war on the whole will depend on that correlation of forces which is established prior to its beginning . . . In the process the advantage in principle accrues to that side which significantly surpasses the other in strength in the aggregate or in individual and the more essential components of combat might. Superiority accelerates the process of the physical and moral defeat of the enemy, makes it possible to operate more daringly and decisively, and to impose one's will on the enemy and to attack him more successfully.[15]

It must be underscored again that the Soviet doctrinal interest in achieving operational effectiveness in all relevant categories of combat potential does not imply an intention to initiate a nuclear war. Military prowess is intended to provide backing for Soviet peacetime diplomacy in diverse ways. Highly effective war-waging capabilities are seen as likely to deter the initiation of war by any adversary of the Soviet state, and such capabilities might enable the USSR to make political gains through intimidation. If war should nonetheless break out, the Soviets would probably try to limit it to the operations necessary to achieve their essential political objectives in specific contiguous theaters and to deter the United States and other nuclear-armed governments from using nuclear weapons or (if one or more opposing governments had initiated such use) from expanding the geographical extent of nuclear operations. As Soviet theorists have noted, "a serious restraining influence is exercised on the policies of the imperialist states by the masses, and particularly the peoples of the socialist nations, which possess modern weapons, including the nuclear weapons in the possession of the USSR."[16]

If the Soviets were persuaded that the consequences of not undertaking large-scale attacks against military targets in the United States (including, above all, U.S. strategic C^3I assets and the ICBM force) would be worse than the consequences of carrying out the attacks, they might decide to undertake such attacks. The Soviets evidently see value in preemptive offensive strikes that would limit potential damage to the USSR and reduce the burdens placed on active and passive defenses. As Stephen Meyer has observed,

> there is no taboo in Soviet political culture against pre-emption, in contrast to the clear sense of several American presidents (faced with the option) that the American people would never understand an American-initiated attack. Indeed, there is ample evidence that *the Soviet political leadership has authorized the military to pursue a damage limitation strategy, combining strategic offensive and both passive and active strategic defence, within set economic constraints.*[17]

Uncertainties about the reliability and effectiveness of active defenses could be assuaged if counterforce operations destroyed major elements of U.S. strategic forces, including command and control centers. Moreover, although the Scowcroft Commission pointed out that U.S. ICBM vulnerability should not be viewed in isolation because of the timing and operational difficulties the Soviets would face in mounting a coordinated attack on bombers and ICBMs, these difficulties would not necessarily prevent determined Soviet planners from trying to limit damage to the USSR. As Harold Brown noted in 1979, when he was secretary of defense, "it is equally important to acknowledge, however, that the coordination of a successful attack is not impossible, and that the 'rubbish heap of history' is filled with authorities who said something reckless could not or would not be done. Accordingly, we must take the prospective vulnerability of our ICBM force with the utmost seriousness for our planning purposes."[18]

Although the Soviets evidently see advantages in being prepared to conduct large-scale attacks against nuclear forces in the United States (and might actually carry them out in exceptional circumstances), they would probably regard such attacks as extraordinarily risky and therefore suitable only as a desperate, last-ditch expedient. The Soviets probably have at least three major reasons for preferring not to carry out such attacks.

First, the Soviets take many factors in addition to static force inventories into consideration. Uncertainties about the reliability and accuracy of their ICBMs and other intercontinental strike forces must concern them. They probably undertake comprehensive analyses that examine numerous factors that are often neglected in public discussions of intercontinental nuclear deterrence and operations in the West: command, control, and communications (C^3); active and passive defenses; operational tactics; deception and surprise; training; endurance; intelligence; maintenance and logistics; force reconstitution assets; and so forth.[19] Thorough analyses have presumably underlined the complexities of intercontinental attacks, for the Soviets do not appear to be afflicted with the sort of "technological hubris" that would minimize the practical uncertainties in, for example, an attack against the U.S. ICBM force.[20] On the contrary, the Soviets are so cautious in their approach to war planning that they may at times conservatively understate their own prospects.

Soviet analyses of the possible conduct of such operations are, furthermore, probably much more complex than the homeland-to-homeland intercontinental exchanges that are often the focus of Western discussions. It appears that the Soviets rarely, if ever, decouple planning about possible intercontinental operations from planning for simultaneous campaigns in Europe and, possibly, other theaters of strategic military action contiguous to the USSR. This means that Soviet planning for possible intercontinental strikes is linked to the complexities of planning the "combined-arms" offensives of Soviet conventional forces in Europe and other regions. Variables such as reconnaissance and the conduct of long-range nonnuclear strikes have therefore been included in Soviet planning analyses.[21]

The Soviet preoccupation with victory in adjacent theaters of strategic military action probably constitutes a second major reason for Soviet reluctance to initiate intercontinental nuclear attacks. Notra Trulock has pointed out, with respect to Soviet thinking about war in Europe, that

> Soviet military planners have enshrined the objectives of an early establishment and continued exercise of Soviet control over operational timelines and over the actions of both Soviet and enemy forces in an attempt to reduce uncertainty to an absolute minimum . . . These planners would probably conclude that there is no more sure method to increase uncertainty and allow such control to slip away than to engage in large intercontinental exchanges with the United States.[22]

The third reason for caution may be the most fundamental—the threat that large-scale intercontinental attacks would pose to the Soviet Union and to the world as a whole. Soviet attacks against U.S. land-based nuclear forces and associated command-and-control facilities could well result in "the deaths of millions of Americans,"[23] even though the Soviets might at some point in the future attempt to lessen U.S. fatality totals significantly by using highly accurate low-yield earth-penetrating weapons against hardened targets.[24] In either case, as the Office of Technology Assessment has noted, "the Soviets would be imprudent, to say the least, to believe that the United States would fail to retaliate."[25] The Soviets would probably hesitate to presume (1) that they could confidently hold U.S. fatalities down to low enough levels to be assured of U.S. restraint in retaliation or (2) that they could fully neutralize U.S. capabilities to command and control surviving U.S. nuclear forces. As David Holloway has observed, in an often-cited passage in *The Soviet Union and the Arms Race*, the Soviets "have tried to prepare for nuclear war, and they would try to win such a war if it came to that. But there is little evidence to suggest that they think victory in a global nuclear war would be anything other than catastrophic."[26]

Holloway's formulation could in fact be reworded in an affirmative sense: there is ample evidence that the Soviets think a general nuclear war would be catastrophic. This has been a theme of Soviet military doctrine since the late 1960s.[27] The potential results of such a conflict were outlined in the third edition (1968) of Sokolovskiy's treatise *Military Strategy*: "The losses in a world nuclear war will not only be suffered by the USA and their NATO allies, but also by the socialist countries. The logic of a world nuclear war is such that in the sphere of its effect would fall an overwhelming majority of the world's states. As a result of a war many hundreds of millions of people would perish, and most of the remaining alive, in one respect or another, would be subject to radioactive contamination."[28]

Similar assessments of the consequences of a general nuclear war for both East and West were presented in the authoritative General Staff journal *Military Thought* during the late 1960s.[29] The lecture materials from the Voroshilov General Staff Academy in the mid-1970s (previously classified and recently released by the U.S. government) portrayed the effects of large-scale nuclear war as follows: "Roads, industries, electric power stations and military targets would be destroyed, the government and military command and control would be disrupted, and large radioactive contaminated areas would be created, large fires would erupt, and large areas would be flooded in the territories of the belligerent countries. Normal living conditions would stop for prolonged periods in major countries participating in the war." These lecture materials indicated that, in such circumstances, victory would consist of inflicting even greater damage on the enemy, so that the USSR could more rapidly reconstitute its military and economic potential.[30] Long-standing Soviet apprehensions about the possible results of a large-scale nuclear war may have been reinforced in recent years by analyses of potential environmental consequences.[31]

Given their caution about war, and nuclear war in particular, it is reasonable to conclude that the Soviets would prefer to avoid any actual use of nuclear weapons. The Soviets appear, however, to see merits in being as well prepared as possible for large-scale nuclear war. Although these preparations could not prevent devastating damage to the USSR in a general nuclear war, they could serve to affect the risk assessments of other governments in crises and wars and thus help to confine military operations to lower levels of violence. The preferred use of the Soviet nuclear posture (including strategic defense) would, in other words, be entirely coercive—to restrict the capability of opposing powers to use nuclear weapons in support of their political-military objectives and (if possible) to discourage them from using nuclear weapons at all.[32]

The most likely targets of limited Soviet nuclear attacks in a contiguous region would be military installations that would make a critical difference in a conventional campaign. In Europe, these targets might well include selected airfields, nuclear and nonnuclear munitions stockpiles, logistics assets, and radar and C^3 sites. The Soviets would logically be interested in minimizing damage that could hinder their own military operations and in maximizing the probability that opposing governments would retain substantial stakes in demonstrating prudence in their responses. Selective nuclear use in Europe in the course of a nonnuclear offensive appears far more plausible than an intercontinental nuclear attack.

If intercontinental nuclear strikes were made, they might be directly related to operations in Europe—for example, U.S. conventional reinforcement capabilities.[33] But, although nuclear attacks against a few key reinforcement facilities in the United States could cripple the U.S. ability to support operations abroad, the Soviets might well choose to forgo even these attacks (especially if they could accomplish their aims without them) in order to avoid increasing the risks of U.S. nuclear retaliation against targets in the Soviet Union and a possible loss of whatever control over nuclear escalation the USSR had been able to achieve. The Soviet interest in long-range targeting in support of theater operations and concern about the risks of nuclear escalation probably help to account for the recent Soviet discussions of using nonnuclear weapons with effects comparable to those of nuclear weapons for such purposes.[34]

It should, moreover, be understood that Soviet discussions of possible limited nuclear operations have concerned theater wars rather than intercontinental war. According to Stephen Meyer, Soviet theorists have identified three levels of nuclear attacks: "hundreds of weapons for a massed attack, tens of weapons for a group attack, and single weapons for the individual attack. Such discussions, however, are invariably tied to theater nuclear war, not intercontinental war."[35] In discussing possible intercontinental operations, Soviet commentators have shown an interest in targeting U.S. strategic command, control, and communications assets as well as U.S. nuclear and other military forces that suggests Soviet attacks might be much more extensive than the more selective strikes the Soviets may well be hypothetically capable of carrying out.[36]

Selective strikes that did not essentially neutralize U.S. command- and-control capabilities might appear too risky to contemplate, especially because U.S. authorities might feel impelled to retaliate before these capabilities became too degraded to function. It appears, in short, that Soviet preferences for more limited nuclear operations could be overridden in some contingencies by doubts about the feasibility of exerting control over U.S. nuclear employment decisions. In such cases, it might seem that the only way to limit damage to the Soviet Union would be to cause "maximum damage" to the forces and military-industrial potential of its adversaries. To cause such damage, large-scale attacks against military targets in the United States and allied countries could be undertaken. These attacks might cut back the burdens on Soviet BMD and other strategic defenses and place the USSR in a better postwar power position.[37]

POLITICAL AIMS IN EUROPE

The Soviet Union has always regarded the configuration of power relationships affecting Europe as supremely important. Although Soviet political aspirations and activities extend to distant regions of the world, the principal bases of Soviet power have remained in Europe. The bulk of the USSR's economic and military might is west of the Urals, in the Soviet Union itself or based on the territory of Warsaw Pact allies. Soviet diplomatic activities and military deployments directed toward other regions of the world are therefore substantially affected by European considerations. One reason why the USSR works to maintain a favorable force balance against China is evidently to minimize the risks of a potential two-front war and consequent Soviet vulnerability in Europe.

The first priority of Soviet policy in Europe has been to safeguard the USSR's territorial and political gains in World War II. The USSR during 1939–1945 incorporated three independent countries into its frontiers (Latvia, Lithuania, and Estonia) and annexed portions of Finland, Poland, Romania, Germany, and Czechoslovakia, areas with a total population of roughly 25 million and a geographical extent over twice that of West Germany today. In the immediate postwar period (up to 1949), the Soviet Union established communist governments subservient to Soviet direction in most of Eastern Europe, including East Germany. The Soviet leadership considers continued control of these acquisitions imperative for several reasons: above all, to maintain dominion over the component nationalities of the USSR; to prevent Poland from resuming its traditional Western alignment; and to minimize the possibility that West Germany might challenge Soviet influence in Eastern Europe or become an autonomous power center.

Soviet aims in Europe extend beyond maintaining the status quo, however. The Soviets feel that the establishment of NATO and the U.S. presence in Europe have deprived the USSR of an ideological, geographical, and power-based "right" to dominate all of Europe.[38] During World War II, Stalin appears to have expected that the Soviet Union would have preponderant political and military power in Europe. Much of Eastern and Central Europe would be under direct Soviet control. Western Europe would be composed of militarily weak states, not joined by any effective alliance, and hence susceptible to decisive Soviet influence.[39]

Stalin regretted that the United States, Britain, and other Western countries liberated France, Italy, and the Western areas of Germany from Nazi control. Soviet sources describe the Western liberation of the Nazi-dominated portions of Western Europe in the final years of World War II as intended to deny the USSR the opportunity to bring "socialism" to the region. The USSR would not have sponsored the restoration of "bourgeois" democracy or the promotion of free-market capitalism in Western Europe; nor did the Soviet Union favor the creation of a European-American alliance.[40] In 1966 Soviet Foreign Minister Gromyko deplored the fact that President Roosevelt's statement at Yalta—that he did not expect U.S. forces to remain in Europe for more than two years after the war—had proved to be mistaken: "Ten times two years have elapsed since then, but the American army is still in Europe and, by all signs, claims permanent status here. But the peoples of Europe are having and will continue to have their say on this score."[41]

In the Soviet view, Western Europe is the most important geographical region in the historic struggle between "socialism" and "imperialism," because it represents the greatest concentration of advanced economic and industrial assets in Eurasia. Western Europe is seen by the Soviets as the main bridgehead of American power in Eurasia; and the democratic and free-market political and economic organization of Western Europe is deemed a threat to Soviet control over Eastern Europe. The Soviet Union has never been a "status quo" power in Europe, in that it has always tried to weaken the security ties between Western Europe and North America as well as the security ties among West European countries.

In order to achieve a position of dominance in an "all-European" order, the Soviet Union has sought gradually to neutralize U.S. security guarantees to Western Europe and to promote a reduction in the U.S. military and nuclear presence. The USSR has at the same time tried to discourage the defense efforts of West European countries in alliance either with the United States or with one another. The Soviet goals have, in other words, included promoting U.S.–West European disunity and preventing intra–West European cooperation from posing a threat to the USSR's preeminence. The long-term aim is to eliminate the U.S. presence while inhibiting the constitution of West European obstacles to Soviet dominance. Subsidiary goals of Soviet policy include winning recognition for existing political frontiers in Europe (that is, acceptance of Soviet territorial and political acquisitions in 1939–1945); obtaining access to Western trade, technology, and credits; supporting local Communist parties and other "progressive" and "peace-loving" social groups in Western Europe; and encouraging West European countries to show deference to Soviet security interests.[42]

Soviet incentives in pursuing these aims extend beyond achieving dominance in Europe. To excise the U.S. military and nuclear presence in Europe would reduce U.S. global power fundamentally. It would facilitate Soviet advances in other regions of the world and drastically undermine the postwar political and economic order.[43] The Soviet objective is to strengthen the Warsaw Pact's relative power position without war, in order to be better prepared for the contingency of war and to achieve maximum political gains without fighting.

The goal of establishing an "all-European" collective security system has long been central to the USSR's policy for favorable peaceful change in Europe. The Soviets have portrayed the United States and NATO as troublesome impediments to constructive all-European progress toward peace. Vadim Zagladin in 1981 told a West German audience: "Your security and ours are the same. Our common security is not being threatened by Moscow or by Bonn, but by Washington."[44] The all-European collective security theme has been readily linked to the U.S. "threat" to Europe and to demands for progress in arms control:

> Washington's idea is that the old continent should not be allowed to set an example in the field of disarmament, for this would inevitably entail a wind-down of the arms race on a global scale. After all, the global arms race would have no justification if Europe . . . took steps towards effective military detente . . . Hence the urge to strike a blow at the emerging model of European good-neighbourliness . . . Thus, profound changes in political thinking have occurred in Western Europe in the years of detente; a new attitude towards the future of Europe is taking shape on the strength of the recognition that this continent can and must be turned into a zone of lasting peace.[45]

The Soviets evidently envisage a protracted process of gradually changing the U.S. role in Europe. Certain types of arms control agreements could be an important element in this process in that they might, in conjunction with Soviet military programs, help to change the objective conditions of European security and erode (1) West European confidence in the reliability of U.S. protection and (2) U.S. willingness to continue to extend guarantees to Europe. The Soviets may intend to rely on the continuing U.S. presence to help discourage West European defense cooperation efforts while encouraging a long-term Western accommodation to Soviet political preferences. As Hannes Adomeit has suggested, current Soviet political strategy consists of an "abandonment of crude endeavors at either forcing the United States out of Europe or trying to settle matters unilaterally with Washington at the expense of Europe. It is, thus, an attempt at persuading the United States to consent to a reduction in its European role and encouraging an 'all-European' consciousness among the Europeans."[46]

The relationship between Soviet arms control initiatives and the all-European vision has been especially clear with respect to nuclear-weapons-free-zone (NWFZ) proposals. As long ago as 1959, Soviet authorities indicated that a Scandinavian NWFZ could lead to political neutrality for the region as a whole.[47] In 1981 Brezhnev claimed that the

Conference on Security and Cooperation in Europe was "in effect aimed at making all of Europe" a NWFZ, even though the Helsinki Final Act makes no reference to such zones.[48]

The Soviet preference for "progressive" political change without armed conflict is consistent with the USSR's approach to deterrence and force-posture development. The Soviet concept of deterrence differs from that dominant in Western thinking in that the Soviets are not guided by a concept of strategic stability based on rough parity in offensive-force capabilities and mutual societal vulnerability; instead, for the Soviets, deterrence is an ability to "restrain" or coerce their adversaries by marshaling a superior array of war-fighting and damage-limiting capabilities as part of an overall "correlation of forces" increasingly favorable to the USSR. The changing correlation of forces is expected to affect the decision making of "sober and realistic" political leaders abroad and help to promote favorable political change without war.

It should, moreover, be noted that the Western concept of "stable deterrence" is sometimes construed in a misleading fashion. Some Western observers have assumed that it signifies a mutual vulnerability that both sides have sought for similar reasons. But, whereas the Western objective is to deter Soviet aggression, the Soviet objective is to intimidate the West and improve Soviet prospects for gaining a position of dominance, preferably without war. Stable deterrence should therefore be understood as a Western capacity to contain the threat of Soviet coercion or aggression. As Robert Osgood and Henning Wegener have noted, the Soviet approach to nuclear deterrence places emphasis "on the danger of the use of nuclear weapons rather than on deterring a conventional attack, since this danger does not confront the Soviet Union in view of its overwhelming conventional superiority over any conceivable adversary and the clearly defensive posture of NATO. Thus, the overriding objective of nuclear deterrence, in the Soviet view, is to deter a Western nuclear response to an Eastern attack and, more broadly, to hold Western Europe hostage to Soviet political will under the gun of overwhelming conventional and nuclear power."[49]

In contrast to the Western emphasis on prewar deterrence, the Soviets consider how they might control the outcomes of campaigns in the key theaters of strategic military action if attempts to achieve political change without war were to fail. The "diplomatic struggle" would continue during the transition to war as well as during the war and its aftermath.

The Soviet analytical framework, in other words, does not divorce strategy from politics. Whereas Western (and especially U.S.) analysts of strategic affairs are inclined to take a depoliticized "hardware" and weapons-centered approach to developing strategies for deterrence and arms control, the Soviets focus on long-term political objectives.[50] Soviet strategic force planning appears to be embedded in—and practically inseparable from—comprehensive planning for the management of threats and the advancement of Soviet political aims without war, to the maximum extent possible. Soviet planning nonetheless involves preparing for contingencies of specific potential wars, especially on the Soviet periphery, with due attention to the risk that such conflicts might lead to the supreme challenge of intercontinental nuclear war.

In considering such contingencies, Soviet planning remains resolutely political and therefore focused on war outcomes—that is, on how the Soviet Union could gain political control in the specific contiguous regions of greatest interest for the Soviet power position in the postwar period. Of all the regions adjacent to the Soviet Union, none is more important than Western Europe. As Fritz Ermarth has remarked, "the U.S.S.R. tends to see intercontinental forces, and strategic forces more generally, as a means to help it win an all-out conflict in its most crucial theater, Europe."[51] The preferred contribution of Soviet intercontinental forces in the event of war would not be high-risk attacks on U.S. ICBMs—nor reckless (and politically and strategically senseless) attacks on U.S. cities. The preferred contribution would be dissuading the United States from attacking the Soviet Union with nuclear weapons during the course of nonnuclear campaigns in the theaters of strategic military action on the Soviet periphery.

Specific territorial and political objectives in a war in Europe would probably be scenario dependent. The objectives could well depend on the events that gave rise to the war, on the effectiveness of Soviet policies for "progressive" political change during the prewar period, on the impact of Soviet appeals to West European elites and governments for a "separate peace" that would permit a "special relationship" with the USSR in the postwar period,[52] on the military options retained by the Western governments disposed to resist the expansion of Soviet dominance, and so forth. In other words, the Soviets might choose not to attack all the allies directly, and Soviet war objectives might well not include the immediate conquest of all of Western Europe. The Soviets would probably try to simplify their military tasks by political means. The objectives and the instruments employed would probably be dictated in part by the opportunities of the situation.

Christopher Donnelly of the Royal Military Academy at Sandhurst has suggested that, because NATO's Central Region is seen by the Soviets as the main theater, "an invasion can stop at nothing less than the occupation of West Germany, the Low Countries, and the Baltic Littoral. It seems unlikely that the USSR would at this time willingly embark on an invasion of France or the United Kingdom."[53]

John Hines and Phillip Petersen have speculated, in contrast, that the Soviets might, in some circumstances, try to avoid fighting in Central Europe: "If a crisis in the Southwestern TSMA [theater of strategic military action] arose, and the Soviets could successfully avoid the outbreak of fighting in Central Europe, they might hope that the Greeks would not react to a Soviet strike against Western Turkey, thereby limiting Soviet operations in this event to a single strategic direction." Moreover, although Hines and Petersen agree that NATO's Central Region (the forward portion of the large zone the Soviets have designated their Western theater of strategic military action) is supremely important, they do not judge it likely that the Soviets would halt at the French border. In their view, in a prolonged conflict, the offensive into France would divide into two strategic directions aimed at the United Kingdom and Iberia.[54]

Peter Stratmann of West Germany's Stiftung Wissenschaft und Politik has underlined likely Soviet political aims in seeking rapid success in Central Europe: "The key objective is to penetrate NATO's forward defence and reach the Rhine and the North Sea ports within a few days. The rapid achievement of this intermediate strategic objective would—in the view of Soviet military leaders—lead to the political collapse of the Western Alliance, thus predetermining the final outcome of the war."[55]

Whatever the specific political objectives of the campaign, the Soviet leadership would in all probability attempt to cause as little damage as possible, especially with regard to the potential employment of nuclear weapons. Western Europe could well form a vital part of the USSR's postwar recovery base, and victory would be meaningful to the extent that the region could be kept intact and made to serve Soviet purposes. Soviet strategic planning accordingly places great emphasis on the results of "theater-strategic" campaigns, even in the context of possible intercontinental war.

Potential Consequences in War

A significant Soviet advantage in deployed BMD capabilities would supplement a Soviet military posture already keenly attuned to the risks of nuclear war. Paradoxical as it may seem, the extensive Soviet investments in active and passive defenses and in offensive forces probably testify to the seriousness with which the Soviets approach nuclear war and to their desire to avert and avoid it. In the event of war involving the Soviet armed forces, the Soviet leadership would presumably wish to prevent nuclear strikes on Soviet soil and, to the maximum extent possible, to keep any operational use of nuclear weapons under their control. The use of nuclear weapons would increase uncertainties about the outcome of a war. The development of Soviet nuclear war-waging capabilities appears therefore to be intended to degrade the credibility of NATO's nuclear threats and to give the USSR more discriminate and controllable nuclear strike options, in case such strikes are required to achieve victory.

Although the contingency of war cannot be ruled out, the preferred Soviet strategy appears to be one of winning without war by leading West Europeans (and, if possible, North Americans) to an accommodation to Soviet political goals in the face of unmistakably superior Soviet war-waging potential. This strategy is preferred for several reasons, including the uncertainties involved in attempting to control nuclear escalation and the likely losses in war, however effective Soviet active and passive defenses and capabilities for counterforce strikes become.

The potential significance for NATO of a large unilateral expansion of Soviet BMD capabilities should therefore be considered with respect to circumstances of both war and peace. The basic premise—that the Soviet Union could achieve a large unilateral advantage over NATO in deployed BMD of traditional types—is technically plausible (as discussed in Chapter 1), but it is not politically inevitable. On the one hand, the advantages the Soviets might achieve from a large unilateral breakout—or from a sustained creepout—from the ABM Treaty appear to be incentives for the Soviets to capitalize on their superior potential for large-scale deployments of ground-based BMD systems of essentially traditional types. On the other hand, the likely Western responses constitute disincentives for the Soviets to go too far, for fear of provoking and legitimizing an intense competition in BMD and BMD countermeasures that could be counterproductive in terms of Soviet interests in arms race management. Soviet interests in arms control are considered in Chapter 4.

This chapter's discussion of the implications of a large and unmatched Soviet advantage in BMD is intended to illustrate the stakes at issue for the Western alliance, and the incentives and opportunities the Soviets might perceive and be tempted to pursue, if they were confident that the West would not respond in a timely fashion. The principal implications discussed represent extreme and "pure" cases to the extent that they are not qualified by Western countermeasures. Possible Western countermeasures, including offensive-force improvements as well as strategic defenses, are considered in Chapter 5.

Published doctrine, force posture trends, and other external indicators (for example, exercises) cannot provide absolutely conclusive evidence as to how the Soviets would intend to use their capabilities or why they have chosen to build the capabilities they have. But a logical Soviet aim would be to develop positions of nuclear strength and likely war-waging effectiveness to establish a higher probability that the United States (and other nuclear powers) would be deterred from any use of nuclear weapons, even in the context of an East-West conventional war. It would be in Soviet interests to maximize the probability of escalation control, or stalemate, at the intercontinental level, and thus to confine war to more manageable levels of intensity, with more attainable and more politically meaningful results.

This interpretation of Soviet military strategy toward the Western alliance furnishes a basis for considering the implications of a large unilateral expansion of Soviet BMD capabilities. Such an expansion could make Soviet advantages in strategic defenses—active and passive— more pronounced. At least four major and closely interconnected consequences relating to Soviet prospects in a war in Europe could follow: (1) the credibility of NATO's strategy of flexible response could be reduced; (2) Soviet control over the escalation process could be enhanced; (3) Soviet prospects for victory in conventional operations could be improved; and (4) the credibility of the British and French independent nuclear deterrents could be diminished.

It should, however, be recognized that what improved Soviet BMD could mean for Soviet military prospects in a war with NATO is an extremely complex topic. The main variables in a comprehensive analysis would include not only the combat scenarios envisaged and the scope and effectiveness of Soviet BMD in reinforcing Soviet defensive and offensive capabilities but also whether and to what extent the United States and its allies had BMD as well. (At present, unlike the USSR, neither the United States nor any other NATO country has any deployed or readily deployable BMD capability, except for the modest capabilities that may be derived from upgrades of the Patriot air defense missile.)[56] As noted above, in order to highlight the implications for the Western alliance of a large expansion in Soviet BMD capabilities, this brief discussion will concentrate on a hypothetical and (it is hoped) improbable situation of a substantial unilateral Soviet BMD advantage.

NATO'S STRATEGY OF FLEXIBLE RESPONSE
The strategy of flexible response, which was adopted by the alliance in 1967, is not intended to guide NATO in winning a hypothetical NATO–Warsaw Pact war, but rather to deter aggression and, if necessary, to

obtain a cessation of hostilities and restore prewar boundaries. Although not an official statement on behalf of the alliance, a West German defense white paper in 1976 included a particularly concise description of the scenario envisaged by NATO:

> The initial tactical use of nuclear weapons must be timed as late as possible but as early as necessary, which is to say that the doctrine of Forward Defense must retain its validity, the conventional forces of the defender must not be exhausted, and incalculability must be sustained so far as the attacker is concerned. The initial use of nuclear weapons is not intended so much to bring about a military decision as to achieve a political effect. The intent is to persuade the attacker to reconsider his intention, to desist in his aggression, and to withdraw. At the same time, it will be impressed upon him that he risks still further escalation if he continues to attack. Such further escalation would mean that [U.S.] strategic nuclear weapons would be used against the attacker's own territory. Such weapons would initially be used selectively against military targets.[57]

The guidelines worked out by NATO's Nuclear Planning Group since its establishment in 1967 have concurred with these principles for any initial as well as follow-on use of U.S. nuclear weapons that Soviet aggression might force on NATO.[58] Selective use is envisaged at every intermediate stage of escalation because of the desire to limit damage and leave the Soviets grounds for restraint. The threat of selective employment of nuclear weapons against targets in the Soviet Union and elsewhere in the Warsaw Pact could, however, be directly countered by Soviet BMD. To the extent that NATO's selective nuclear strike options depend on U.S. ICBMs and SLBMs, and on shorter-range ballistic missiles such as the Pershing II and the Lance, Soviet BMD could erode the credibility of NATO strategy. As noted in Chapter 1, the Department of Defense judges that the SA-10 and the SA-12 may have capability against tactical ballistic missiles as well as against some types of strategic ballistic missiles.[59]

The degree to which U.S. "extended-deterrence" guarantees would be eroded would depend in part on the level of effectiveness of Soviet BMD, in combination with other active defenses, in denying U.S. ballistic missiles and other nuclear and nonnuclear delivery means access to the Soviet Union and the Warsaw Pact as a whole. If the Soviets deployed systems capable of exoatmospheric midcourse and boost-phase intercepts of MIRVed ballistic missiles, the USSR could well achieve great leverage in its attempts to nullify U.S. guarantees.

The more likely Soviet deployments in the next decade and perhaps the only ones seriously contemplated for that period would, as noted in Chapter 1, consist of ground-based interceptors of essentially traditional types. These would probably have to depend on (1) counterforce strikes to reduce the size of the U.S. arsenal and (2) the synergism of the other strategic defenses—active and passive—working in combination, if it were a question of defending the USSR against major U.S. strategic attacks. If the attacks were of the relatively limited and selective sort envisaged in NATO strategy, however, even traditional ground-based BMD could significantly degrade the credibility of U.S. guarantees. Indeed, traditional ground-based BMD deployments of this sort could have an appreciable probability of effectiveness against the types of nuclear retaliation NATO would be most likely to mount—selective and restrained strikes. Kevin Lewis has suggested that

> since ICBMs probably will remain the instrument of choice for limited strategic attacks over the near term, it could very well be the case that *even a fairly modest new Soviet ABM deployment could jeopardize our limited employment capability.* Unfortunately, constraints on the azimuth of the ICBM threat to the USSR, the extended flight times of U.S. land-based missiles (compared with some INF and SLBMs), and other factors would combine to render U.S. land-based missiles incapable of some, perhaps many, limited employment missions should new Soviet ABM deployments take place.[60]

The value of U.S. ballistic missiles as a deterrent to Soviet aggression and as a lever to enforce intrawar restraint on the USSR could thus be reduced, depending on the scope and effectiveness of expanded Soviet BMD deployments. Air-breathing systems (aircraft and cruise missiles), perhaps equipped with "stealth" technology to reduce signatures visible to Soviet radars, could still be used to attack targets in the Soviet Union; but they would have to penetrate the extremely dense and sophisticated air defenses (SAMs and fighter-interceptors) of the USSR. The "thicker" and more effective the combination of Soviet BMD and air defenses, the higher the level of weapons attrition per target for NATO would be—and the harder it would be for the United States to honor the flexible-response guarantees.

If Soviet BMD and air defense programs resulted in the at least partial neutralization of U.S. extended deterrence guarantees to NATO Europe, Western Europe would be more vulnerable to Soviet attack or intimidation, because it would be harder for the United States to threaten retaliation for Soviet aggression.

Three alternatives to trying to penetrate Soviet BMD and air defenses with limited strikes can be imagined. One would be to attack relatively peripheral targets in areas not covered by defenses of the Warsaw Pact and the Soviet zone of interior—for example, Soviet naval forces at sea (such as SSBNs) or Soviet forces in Vietnam or Cuba. This threat would, however, probably not offer as much value in deterring the Soviets as threatening targets in the USSR proper.

A second alternative would be for the United States to use much larger commitments of ballistic missiles, aircraft, and/or cruise missiles to try to overwhelm Soviet BMD and air defenses. If the United States was determined to undertake a massive attack, Soviet active and passive defenses could probably be overwhelmed. Paul Warnke, then director of the U.S. Arms Control and Disarmament Agency, stated in 1978, "The fact of the matter is that our more than 9000 nuclear warheads could totally saturate any civil defense effort and wreak totally unacceptable havoc on the Soviet Union."[61]

Such a threat lacks political and strategic credibility, however. If an attack against U.S. ICBMs would be a high-risk proposition for the Soviet Union, an attack against Soviet population centers would be an even more reckless enterprise for the United States to contemplate, given Soviet retaliatory capabilities. Even if the United States were not vulnerable to retaliation in kind, it is hard to see how carrying out such an attack could serve any rational political or strategic purpose.[62] In recent years, the U.S. government has held that such threats are "neither moral nor prudent" and hardly likely to deter nuclear, much less conventional, aggression against U.S. allies.[63]

A variation of this second alternative would be to try to deliver the selective strikes envisaged in NATO strategy by undertaking large-scale but nonetheless limited attacks in order to overwhelm Soviet BMD and air defenses (and passive defenses such as hardening and mobility) protecting certain targets. Soviet strategic defenses might indeed prove inadequate in the face of larger-scale U.S. attacks. This alternative would, however, be less than entirely satisfactory or plausible, because it would be much harder for the United States to communicate restraint in intent with larger-scale attacks. Although the controllability of nuclear escalation is unknown and scenario dependent, U.S. and allied officials have long regarded restraint and selectivity as essential to controlling escalation. The goal in NATO planning has been to maximize the probability that any use of nuclear weapons necessitated by Soviet aggression would remain as limited as possible. Selective use should therefore be recognizable, even though no guarantees or confident predictions about the results of selective use can be made. As Konrad Seitz, the head of the

Planning Department in the West German Foreign Ministry, has pointed out, "if two warheads cannot be sure to destroy the target, twenty may be able to do so. However, such a method could lead away from the present NATO strategy, which is to ensure that the selective options are clearly recognizable as limited options . . . Although it is improbable that such a defense would fully block NATO's selective nuclear options, it is clear that these options, and with them the flexibility of flexible response, could be seriously impaired."[64]

Soviet BMD could also complicate any plans to use ballistic missiles to facilitate bomber attacks. Although some observers have claimed that "Soviet air defenses could be easily crippled by destroying the main radar systems and command posts" with a "few" nuclear-armed ballistic missiles,[65] mounting such attacks for selective and limited purposes would in practice not be easy. As Walter Slocombe has observed, "the need to keep the attack limited in size and duration poses special operational problems. For example, the number of weapons used for air defense suppression must be limited, which reduces the suitability of bombers that must penetrate deep into Soviet territory. Deployment of even partially effective ballistic missile defenses could have a similar impact."[66]

A third alternative would be to attack poorly defended targets in the USSR. These targets would be, by definition, of lesser value to the Soviets, and such a choice of targets by the United States might fail to impress the Soviets with the imperative of early war termination on terms acceptable to the Western alliance. Although some Western observers have argued that the Soviets would have to defend large numbers of targets to degrade U.S. selective attack options fundamentally, others have pointed out that BMD would supplement other active and passive defenses in the USSR and that the "footprint," or area coverage, of Soviet BMD systems could be as difficult to assess as their likely effectiveness. The Soviets could, moreover, choose to defend certain types of targets preferentially. Cautious and conservative U.S. and NATO officials might be inclined to hedge against these uncertainties by attributing a higher degree of effectiveness to the Soviet BMD capabilities than might the Soviets themselves. In other words, it might be difficult to choose targets that would be poorly defended enough to assure NATO a high likelihood of attack success and nonetheless allow NATO to achieve the intended consequences with respect to Soviet decision making.

Soviet ground-based BMD deployments could therefore raise serious problems for the selective nuclear strikes envisaged in NATO's flexible-response strategy. This result would depend, of course, on the extent to which existing Soviet BMD deployments were expanded, how effective they seemed likely to be, and several other factors. The West German defense minister, Manfred Wörner, has suggested that even capabilities of modest potency could have grave effects: "If the Soviets were able to put around the European part of Russia an anti-ballistic defense system of even limited effectiveness, NATO's capacity for exercising even its limited nuclear options could be substantially compromised—and the credibility of the Alliance's nuclear deterrent would thereby be seriously weakened."[67]

It is reasonable to conclude that Soviet BMD could constrain NATO's targeting flexibility. Damage expectancies could become even more unpredictable, weapons requirements could be increased, and escalation control prospects could be made even more uncertain. Given the difficulties and dilemmas Soviet BMD would clearly pose for NATO strategy, and the corresponding strategic advantages for the Soviet Union, it seems plausible that the Soviets long ago recognized these potential advantages. Soviet BMD programs are probably partly motivated by a desire to erode the credibility and effectiveness of NATO's flexible-response strategy.

The effective neutralization of key elements of NATO's ability to threaten selective nuclear strikes must have a certain attraction for the Soviets, because NATO needs such limited options more than does the USSR. The Soviet Union has built up the Warsaw Pact's conventional capabilities to such a degree that NATO is heavily dependent on threats of escalation to limited nuclear strikes for deterrence and, if necessary, for conflict management—on the assumption that the Soviets would eventually desist rather than face further nuclear escalation. The Soviets have already narrowed the flexibility of U.S. nuclear choices by building the "counter-deterrent" retaliatory capabilities discussed in Chapter 2. Moderately effective ground-based BMD in the USSR could further constrain this flexibility.

This result would be consistent with the interpretation of Soviet military policy outlined in Chapter 2. The apparent Soviet preference for conducting only conventional and, if need be, limited nuclear operations does not imply any Soviet willingness to conform to the scenario postulated in NATO's strategy of flexible response. (The intent of the alliance's strategy in planning for initial and follow-on use of nuclear weapons is, it may be recalled, "to persuade the attacker to reconsider his intention, to desist in his aggression, and to withdraw.")[68] It is rather the reverse: Soviet strategy is intended to convince NATO governments to desist in their resistance by being better prepared than NATO to prevail at higher levels of violence. The "objective conditions" of existing force balances and capabilities—including Soviet superiority in strategic defenses, and survivable Soviet nuclear forces and operational C³I—might persuade NATO governments not to initiate nuclear use or not to engage in more extensive use after the failure of initial selective strikes.

It could in fact be argued that the Soviets have taken the Western concept of flexible response and recast it in accordance with Soviet political-military objectives. Soviet force procurements since the mid-1960s could be interpreted as intended, inter alia, to deny the West plausible nuclear and conventional response options. Soviet interests reside in depriving NATO's flexible response of its flexibility and increasing the range of usable force employment options—conventional, chemical, and nuclear—available to the USSR.

PROSPECTS FOR ESCALATION CONTROL

Some Western observers have argued for several years that the Soviets may already enjoy a degree of "escalation dominance," owing to the virtually complete vulnerability of the U.S. homeland and land-based U.S. strategic forces to Soviet ballistic missile attack. Manfred Wörner, for example, prior to becoming West Germany's minister of defense, argued that "the ability by the United States to control the process of escalation in the event of a conflict in Europe" was critically dependent on the U.S. ICBM force: "For the foreseeable future, land-based ICBMs represent the most reliable, quickly reactive and accurate strategic weapons, especially in terms of systems applicable to a conflict in Europe. Only survivable ICBMs fill the NATO requirement of keeping open the options of first and selective use of [intercontinental] nuclear weapons."[69] The assumption has been that the United States would be less likely to use part of its ICBM force for selective strikes if the remainder of the ICBM force were vulnerable to Soviet retaliation. Since U.S. ICBM vulnerability has now been widely acknowledged to be far more serious than Soviet ICBM vulnerability (though the significance of this situation is still debated), it can be argued that the Soviets could already be at an advantage in exerting escalation control in a crisis or war.

This does not necessarily mean that the Soviets would conduct an actual attack against all or part of the U.S. ICBM force. Indeed, as noted earlier, the Soviets would probably prefer not to conduct such an attack, because of the high risks involved. Although a Soviet first strike against U.S. ICBMs and other vulnerable U.S. nuclear forces would dramatically shift the "correlation of forces" and make Soviet escalation dominance more concrete, the issue here is possible Soviet escalation dominance in crises and more limited conflicts, owing in part to Western as well as Soviet assessments of Soviet operational prowess and relative Soviet and Western vulnerabilities.

The distinction matters because of the apparent Soviet preference for avoiding any use of nuclear weapons and, if nuclear weapons employment is nonetheless necessary, for confining it to the minimum number of selective strikes required to assure victory in Europe. Escalation dominance implies maintaining nuclear forces capable of decisively discouraging enemy decisions to "escalate" the level of violence either to nuclear weapons use or, if nuclear weapons have been used, to more destructive levels of nuclear war; it suggests an ability to coerce the adversary into accepting restraints in his conduct of operations and his overall political goals. The object would be to influence the adversary's decisions by affecting his risk perceptions.

Most definitions of escalation dominance stress the need for superior military capabilities in order to exert influence over enemy decision making.[70] A capability comparison should include relative vulnerabilities in light of the potential effectiveness of active and passive defenses as a matter of course. Another important element in theories of escalation dominance is what has been termed the "balance of perceived interests"—that is, the importance each side seems to attach to certain interests, and each side's apparent willingness to suffer in order to protect or advance these interests.[71]

Theories of escalation dominance are speculative, owing to the dearth of positive empirical knowledge and the unpredictability of behavior in complex and, in some ways, unprecedented situations. Some commentators deny the theories any practical relevance and contend that the Soviets could not convert an apparent superiority in nuclear capabilities into a usable advantage if NATO was determined to raise the risks of large-scale nuclear war facing the USSR. Michael Legge, a British Ministry of Defence official, has argued as follows:

> When MC 14/3 [the strategy of flexible response] was formally adopted by NATO in 1967, the Alliance could not claim that it possessed escalation dominance either at the strategic or theater nuclear level. And although the balance of forces has moved further in favor of the Warsaw Pact since then, it has not done so to such an extent as to undermine the credibility of the deterrent: Despite its ambiguities, flexible response remains as valid now as it was when it was introduced.[72]

By this logic, Soviet numerical and operational superiority in certain categories of nuclear capabilities would not in practice be as significant in Soviet decision making as the risk that escalation could go out of control. Selective U.S. use of nuclear weapons would be intended to confront the Soviets with unacceptable escalatory risks so they would decide to stop their offensive and withdraw. Legge notes that NATO studies of planning guidelines for follow-on use of nuclear weapons have concluded that, "if the initial signal had failed adequately to convey the twin messages of NATO's determination to resist and the risks thereby involved in continuing the conflict, then the signal would have to be repeated in a more peremptory manner."[73]

The implicit assumption is that the Soviets would be more likely than the West to yield in such a contest of wills, and that the incalculable uncertainties of nuclear escalation would deter the Soviets from attempting aggression in the first place.[74] Numerous Western observers have agreed with McGeorge Bundy in endorsing Michael Howard's formulation of Healey's Theorem: "if there is one chance in a hundred of nuclear weapons being used, the odds would be enough to deter an aggressor even if they were not enough to reassure an ally." As Bundy put it, the credibility of U.S. nuclear guarantees "rests not on numbers of warheads but on an engagement that poses a wholly unacceptable and innately unpredictable risk to the other side."[75]

Although judgments differ on how escalation dominance assessments might affect the behavior of governments in various concrete situations, the concept cannot be dismissed as abstruse and therefore irrelevant to Western security. It derives from familiar considerations of vulnerability and blackmail. Soviet and Western assessments of comparative strengths and vulnerabilities could have an undeniable influence on decisions in specific circumstances. In a practical sense, escalation dominance effects could be present if government officials perceived them to be operative, owing to their appraisals of the military balance and other elements of the particular case—such as the interests and resolve of the contending governments.

In recent years, U.S. officials have publicly suggested that a generally shared assessment of Soviet nuclear strength could grant the USSR a measure of self-assurance in risk taking.[76] In 1983, for example, Secretary of State George Shultz testified as follows to the Senate Armed Services Committee:

> We no longer possess the strategic advantage we once had, and, indeed, we face significant weaknesses in several areas of strategic weaponry . . . My concern is that the growth of Soviet strategic power can, therefore, have an important effect on the Soviets' willingness to run risks in a regional conflict or crisis. Correspondingly, it makes our response more difficult. In the Cuban missile crisis in 1962, and in the Middle East alert in 1973, American strategic power was an important element in denying the Soviet Union any

credible option to escalate beyond the local level . . . If the Soviets can strike effectively at our land-based ICBMs while our land-based deterrent does not have comparable capability, the Soviets might believe that they have a significant advantage in a crucial dimension of the strategic balance; they could seek to gain political leverage by a threat of nuclear blackmail.[77]

In 1985 Hans Rühle, head of the planning staff in the West German Ministry of Defense, presented an even more sobering assessment:

The previous clear-cut superiority of the U.S. in the realm of strategic nuclear weapons has been replaced by an approximate parity . . . In the sphere of intermediate-range nuclear systems the Soviet Union has come to enjoy a clear superiority—even when all the NATO states will have implemented the dual-track decision of 1979. The nuclear escalation dominance of the U.S. has thus been lost, while escalation control has become extremely difficult [for the United States]. The effectiveness of extended deterrence has thereby neces- sarily been diminished . . . This implies on the other hand that the Soviet Union's ability to threaten Western Europe militarily and intimidate it politically has increased considerably.[78]

Comparable statements by other U.S. and West European officials demonstrate that the basic concept of escalation dominance has had political effects, even though some reject it as irrelevant in the face of the incalculabilities associated with nuclear war.[79]

Soviet officials have, moreover, revealed over the years certain expec- tations regarding the impact of their nuclear strike capabilities on the decision making and risk assessments of Western governments. In his memoirs, Khrushchev described the rationale for the Soviet acquisition of ICBMs as follows: "We wanted to exert pressure on American militarists—and also influence the minds of more reasonable politicians— so that the United States would start treating us better."[80] This was hardly escalation dominance, if only because the Soviet Union was still quite inferior to the United States in nuclear capabilities; but Khrushchev described it in 1956 as an ability to prevent war: ". . . war is not fatalistically inevitable. Today there are mighty social and political forces possessing formidable means to prevent the imperialists from unleashing war, and if they actually try to start it, to give a smashing rebuff to the aggressors and frustrate their adventurist plans."[81]

The Soviets in the late 1960s and early 1970s attributed key changes in U.S. and NATO strategy to the growth of Soviet nuclear forces, which deprived previous U.S. nuclear threats of credibility. In 1970 General

Lieutenant I. G. Zav'yalov wrote as follows: "The successes achieved in the Soviet Union in the [nuclear] sphere had a sobering effect on the reactionary circles of imperialist states, became a restraining factor in the path of their aggressive aspirations, and compelled them to change their strategic concepts. As a result, the 'strategy of flexible response' emerged first in the United States, and later was also adopted by the aggressive NATO Bloc."[82]

Soviet officials have also indicated that they attach great significance to the Soviet acquisition of "parity" in intercontinental nuclear forces with the United States during the period of the first Strategic Arms Limitation Talks (SALT), 1969–1972. This has been evident in the appraisals of the overall "correlation of forces" set forth by Soviet analysts. The correlation of forces is an analytical construct that Soviet experts employ in evaluating competitive situations. Its most general application is found in broad assessments of what Marxist-Leninist ideology defines as a historically inevitable struggle between "socialism" (the USSR and its allies) and "imperialism" (in Soviet parlance, the United States and its allies). In 1982, for example, a Soviet analysis of world politics edited by Vadim Zagladin, the first deputy chief of the International Department of the Central Committee of the Communist party of the Soviet Union, indicated that

> the active struggle of the main forces of the world revolutionary process and also the deepening of the general crisis of capitalism . . . led on the eve and at the outset of the 1960s to an appreciable change in the world arena in favor of socialism. By the start of the 1970s this change in the correlation of forces in favor of socialism had essentially assumed an irreversible nature. *The turning point in the correlation of forces between the two systems was the elimination of imperialism's superiority in the military sphere.*[83]

In recent years, although Soviet authorities have underlined the doctrinal advantages of superiority, if only to "force" the enemy "to fight under disadvantageous conditions,"[84] they have refrained from claiming an ability to dominate—that is, decisively influence—Western nuclear employment decisions through their superiority in certain categories of nuclear capability. Rather than referring to any areas of Soviet nuclear superiority, they emphasize Western vulnerability to Soviet nuclear attack. In February 1985, for example, Marshal Sergei Akhromeyev indicated that "the opposing sides have now accumulated such a quantity of nuclear weapons that their use can lead to catastrophic and irremediable consequences . . . the aggressor is no longer able to inflict a disarming strike and act with impunity, something about which those on the other side of the ocean have entertained illusions until now."[85]

This statement and others imply that the Soviets perceive a new U.S. awareness of vulnerability to Soviet nuclear retaliation, should the United States threaten to "escalate" the level of violence in a conflict by resorting to nuclear weapons. Although Soviet military doctrine acknowledges the desirability of operational superiority in nuclear war-waging capabilities, the Soviets appear to reason that an essential and primary task is deterring Western governments from using nuclear weapons. If Western use of nuclear weapons could be prevented, the Soviets could hope to confine conflicts to the conventional level. As Paul K. Davis and Peter J. E. Stan have remarked, increased Soviet confidence in "their ability to fight and win a conventional war that might well not escalate" may stem not from an assessment of Soviet escalation dominance, but from a judgment that *"neither* side has such dominance."[86]

In other words, the Soviets might seek to turn against NATO the threat that nuclear escalation risks could go out of control. An ability to neutralize U.S. threats of intercontinental nuclear strikes with counter-threats could serve the highest priority of the Soviet state—the security of the USSR—and promote the increase of Soviet influence in contiguous regions. If U.S. intercontinental nuclear threats could be effectively vitiated, Soviet regional advantages—nuclear and nonnuclear—could have a more conclusive role in the theaters of strategic military action contiguous to the USSR. If Western Europe was already a "hostage" to Soviet regional military superiority in the face of U.S. intercontinental nuclear superiority prior to the late 1960s, Western Europe's position would be much more vulnerable if U.S. nuclear guarantees were thwarted by Soviet counterdeterrent capabilities.

Although the Soviets have refrained from claiming that they have attained the superiority that some theories of escalation dominance call for, they have underlined the U.S. loss of nuclear superiority. Moreover, as discussed in Chapter 2, they have suggested in various ways that they regard the prospects for confining military operations to the nonnuclear level as improved. Their discussions of selective nuclear strikes also suggest a judgment that it may be possible to control the scope of nuclear escalation, although for reasons of deterrence and peacetime diplomacy (to be discussed shortly) the Soviets apparently see no advantage in publicly highlighting these assessments. Finally, as noted earlier, some high-level Western officials have suggested that Soviet nuclear capabilities have already achieved a "counter-deterrent" potential vis-à-vis those of the United States that might enhance Soviet confidence in risk taking and make U.S. responses more difficult.

It is in this context that an expansion of existing Soviet BMD capabilities could make a critical difference. Soviet strategic defensive measures today certainly fall short of the standards of effectiveness that Western governments would set, but they could nonetheless contribute to meeting Soviet requirements. The USSR has been seriously investing in such defensive measures for decades and Soviet analysts include the probable impact of such defenses in their attempts to calculate the strategic correlation of forces. As Sayre Stevens has pointed out, "what might appear useless to the United States with its much more demanding expectations of ballistic missile defense might have significant incremental value in Soviet military eyes. A system that is not fully effective but can be made more effective over time would not be so ridiculous an investment as it might appear to the United States."[87]

The Soviets could, in other words, intend to limit the damage that might be caused by enemy attacks by relying on the cumulative effects of several types of defensive measures, active and passive. Nonnuclear (and, possibly, selective nuclear) strikes against enemy nuclear weapons within and, if necessary, beyond Europe might decrease substantially the size of the most plausible enemy attacks that Soviet defenses would have to counter. Moreover, Soviet criteria of effectiveness differ from those typical in Western analyses. Whereas Western observers often consider defenses discredited if even a small percentage of the population would remain vulnerable, Soviet commentators underscore the value of defenses capable of protecting only a small percentage of the Soviet public. Soviet investments in strategic defense are, at any rate, concentrated in protecting more plausible and defensible targets than cities—for example, hardened and mobile forces and command and control assets.

If the Soviet Union were to gain an operational BMD advantage significantly larger than that at present, the resulting asymmetry in relative U.S. and Soviet vulnerabilities could endow the USSR with a more clear-cut ability to try to influence U.S. nuclear employment decisions—that is, to control escalation by "deterring the U.S. deterrent." This might occur because a BMD "cap" composed of ground-based interceptors could complement the USSR's other active defenses (above all, air defenses) and passive defenses (especially command and control and force-protection measures based on hardening, redundancy, concealment, dispersion, and mobility) to reduce further the relative vulnerability of the USSR's military assets in war.

Uncertainties about the operational reliability and effectiveness of Soviet BMD systems would persist, as suggested in Chapter 1. John Gardner, then director of defense systems, Department of Defense, nonetheless testified in 1983 that, despite uncertainties about the likely effectiveness of Soviet BMD, air defenses, and passive defenses, a large-scale expansion of Soviet BMD capabilities could have a substantial impact on the U.S. ability to attack targets in the USSR: ". . . if we fail to be able to contain the Soviet Union from providing active ballistic missile defenses, then of course we put ourselves in some serious jeopardy with respect to our ability to retain a significant damage capability against them."[88]

The practical effects of this assessment of a reduction in vulnerability could be manifested in various ways. On the one hand, it is probable that the Soviets would still prefer to achieve their political objectives without war and would still be highly conscious of the risks and uncertainties of war in the nuclear age. On the other hand, the situation would be changed to the extent that the Soviet leadership and Western governments believed the USSR capable of countering at least some types of ballistic missile attacks. Although the consequences that might follow from such an assessment are neither predictable nor measurable, the perceived reduction in Soviet vulnerability could lead to (1) fewer Soviet inhibitions in contemplating aggression; (2) increased Soviet advantages in intrawar bargaining and war-termination negotiations; and (3) most important, an improved Soviet ability to control directly the scope of nuclear escalation, owing to an enhanced ability to counter and absorb selective U.S. nuclear attacks against the Soviet Union, with the United States less prepared to defend against possible Soviet attacks.

The last effect would be among the most important for Western Europe in war, because it would imply an improved Soviet ability to carry theater offensives forward. As Konrad Seitz has remarked, "the situation in Europe would be totally unfavorable to NATO if only the Soviet Union and its allies had an anti-missile defense and Western Europe did not, for then escalation dominance would be fully on the side of the Soviet Union."[89]

The Soviets might, in other words, be able to project military power into Western Europe with less fear of (or hindrance from) U.S. long-range strike forces based on ballistic missiles. This could in turn increase the operational and political importance of Soviet conventional and shorter-range nuclear-force advantages. Prominent U.S. experts on Soviet military affairs have suggested that strategic defense, including BMD, is vital to the Soviet Union, largely because "it is imperative as a backdrop for managing theatre warfare of the kind she is preparing for."[90]

Although there are significant asymmetries in U.S. and Soviet capabilities for intercontinental nuclear war, the more likely cases of crisis and limited conflict would involve the threats of selective nuclear employment foreseen in NATO doctrine. In such cases, the relative vulnerabilities of the Soviet Union and the Western alliance could affect decision making on escalatory options. The Soviet leadership would have a logical incentive to maintain strategic nuclear war-waging capabilities that could act as a counter-deterrent to dissuade the United States from "escalating" any eventual war to the intercontinental level, and that could thus work to confine wars to levels of violence short of nuclear strikes against Soviet territory. At the same time, the Soviets could aim to be as well prepared as possible for the extension of war to greater regional depth and higher levels of destructiveness, including intercontinental nuclear exchanges. Rather than forcing the United States to consider massive attack options, as some have alleged, reinforced Soviet strategic defenses might degrade the credibility of the more plausible NATO strikes. This would enhance Soviet prospects for exerting escalation control and holding down the level of violence, and might therefore enable the USSR to terminate conflicts on Soviet terms.

In other words, improved unilateral BMD capabilities could enable the Soviets to improve their prospects for confining future wars to Europe and other contiguous theaters and for avoiding any intercontinental nuclear operations. General Wolfgang Altenburg, then the inspector general of the West German armed forces, remarked in early 1986 that, if the Soviets developed defenses like those foreseen in the U.S. SDI that were effective against short- and medium-range weapons as well as intercontinental systems, "we could come to a situation, in which a limited, regionalized conventional war in Central Europe would again become possible. For then the threat of nuclear escalation in the current strategy, with which we hinder the outbreak of a conventional conflict, would become ineffective; then the nuclear weapon would no longer be at our disposal as a signal to enforce the end of the war."[91]

The Soviets may also foresee that increasing the significance of their conventional and shorter-range nuclear force advantages could logically lead NATO governments to recognize increased requirements for similar forces in the West. The Soviets could anticipate that this would exacerbate already divisive intra-NATO debates on burden sharing with respect to conventional-force efforts and on requirements for modernizing shorter-range nuclear forces—at a time when some political trends in NATO favor withdrawing such nuclear forces, and when the Soviets are increasing their nuclear artillery and short-range missile capabilities. Further the-ater-force expansion might then be attractive to the Soviets, permitting them to capitalize on this situation, even in the context of new Soviet proposals for nuclear and conventional arms control in Europe. (The apparent Soviet calculus of interests regarding arms control is discussed in Chapter 4.)

The Soviets could well speculate that another effect of heavy unilateral BMD and air defenses in the Warsaw Pact could be the virtual reduction of NATO military options to short-range nuclear and nonnuclear weapons. This would imply a war limited to Central Europe—a concept that would be more welcome to the Soviets than a war involving the Soviet homeland; but this concept is unlikely to be approved by West European governments. For many West Europeans, a threat to use a large number of battlefield nuclear weapons would be no solution; for, even if that threat could deter the Soviets (and defeat a Warsaw Pact offensive), the prospective cost to West Germany and Western Europe as a whole would be too high to be sustained before public opinion.

It would be all too clear that NATO's options had become limited if possible long-range U.S. strikes were virtually neutralized by Soviet BMD and air defenses (and by Soviet "counter-deterrent" threats) and if NATO as a whole proved politically incapable of generating sufficient conventional forces to deter and counter Warsaw Pact aggression. The cohesion of the Western alliance could therefore be severely undermined. If any eventual war seemed virtually certain to be confined to Central Europe and likely to be intense and protracted, some West Europeans might find surrender preferable to war. According to the West German expert Peter Stratmann, "a termination of [U.S.] extended strategic deterrence would pin NATO down to an untenable doctrine of regional conventional and nuclear defense against an opponent whose territory . . . would remain unendangered and which, in the shade of regional strategic superiority, could bring into action stronger conventional and nuclear offensive potentials. In West European eyes, such a strategy would necessarily have a primarily self-deterring effect."[92]

CONVENTIONAL OPERATIONS

Prospective improvements in Soviet escalation control capabilities are clearly closely related to the declining credibility of the selective nuclear strike threats intrinsic to NATO's flexible-response strategy. The improvements in Soviet offensive nuclear capabilities over the past two decades may have already had the effect of creating a certain "counter-deterrent" to U.S. threats to use nuclear weapons in defense of Western Europe. If Soviet BMD led to the direct neutralization of the most plausible U.S. ballistic missile–dependent nuclear threats and enhanced Soviet prospects for escalation control, this would increase the probability that any future war in Europe might remain at the conventional level of operations. The USSR has actively sought this development, because it would bolster the importance of Soviet conventional-force superiority. NATO strategy has since the outset countered Soviet conventional superiority with nuclear threats, and the Soviets have steadily worked to degrade the credibility and utility of these threats.

The Soviet interest in keeping any eventual war in Europe at the conventional level of operations has been more clearly recognized in recent years. The expansion and modernization of all types of Soviet nuclear forces may be partly explained by an aspiration to undermine the credibility of potential U.S. nuclear responses to Warsaw Pact conventional aggression. At the same time, Warsaw Pact conventional forces, particularly those of the USSR, have become increasingly capable of conducting rapid air and ground offensives with short and ambiguous warning that might well be intended to neutralize promptly most NATO nuclear capabilities in Europe by nonnuclear means. This is obviously not the only Soviet option, nor even necessarily the most likely one in certain specific contingencies; but it is a particularly troubling one, because it implies reduced risks for the USSR.

Soviet military authorities have argued in the recent past that the Soviet armed forces must be thoroughly prepared for "combined-arms" operations involving both conventional and nuclear forces, and for operations with conventional forces alone. In 1982 Lieutenant General Kir'yan stated that "the ability to conduct combat operations that involve either nuclear weapons or conventional weapons alone has been made basic to the structure of military formations. As a result, a well-balanced organization of the army and navy has been created, one that makes it possible to carry out missions on any scale and under various conditions."[93]

Although Soviet nuclear capabilities would of course be protected to the maximum extent possible and kept ready for operational employment, if necessary, the Soviet Union might well hope to win a war in Europe by conventional means. As John Hines and Phillip Petersen have described this possibility, Warsaw Pact conventional "forces would strive to quickly fragment NATO's forward defense and occupy key political and economic centers in an effort to induce the perception among NATO allies that continued resistance or nuclear escalation would be futile."[94] The Soviets would probably employ deception, threats, and political appeals to aggravate the fear and confusion that would attend the outbreak of war and thus complicate and delay NATO decisions to use nuclear weapons. The rapid seizure of some West European territory could make it even more difficult for NATO governments to authorize the use of nuclear weapons.

The roles that Soviet BMD could play in such a Soviet strategy for conventional victory in Europe could include, as suggested above, helping to protect Soviet nuclear and nonnuclear means of attack and helping to convince NATO governments that further combat or nuclear escalation would be pointless.

Less obvious and more operational implications would stem from the functions ATBM (antitactical ballistic missile) forms of BMD could perform in support of Soviet tactical air defenses. Soviet tactical air defenses are already the most comprehensive in the world, with over 4600 SAM launchers and 12,000 antiaircraft artillery pieces deployed at regimental through front levels.[95] The U.S.-Soviet gap in battlefield air defense systems was already assessed at "approximately three-to-one in favor of the U.S.S.R. . . . and likely to widen further," with a Soviet "technological edge," in 1979.[96]

The importance the Soviets attach to tactical air defense in Europe is evident in the fact that the "largest concentration of SAM launchers and AAA [antiaircraft artillery] pieces—over 8100—is found opposite European NATO."[97] The relationship to BMD is evident in the fact that the SA-12A is replacing the SA-4, the "standard weapon at army and front level."[98] The apparent decision to equip operational ground force units with the SA-12A, a mobile system potentially capable of intercepting cruise missiles as well as some types of ballistic missiles, implies that the Soviets attach a high priority to the success of any offensive they may eventually conduct in Europe.

The Soviets have undoubtedly noticed that several NATO "emerging technologies" programs and concepts—for example, Counter-Air 90, Follow-on-Forces Attack (FOFA), and the Army Tactical Missile System (Army TACMS)—propose to employ precision-guided ballistic missiles such as Lance or Pershing II (or entirely new missiles) to deliver advanced conventional submunitions against Warsaw Pact airfields and other military targets.[99] While U.S. ground-based SRBMs with ranges over 500 km will be eliminated, in accordance with the December 1987 INF treaty, SRBMs of shorter ranges (such as the possible Lance follow-on) could be effective in delivering nonnuclear munitions. But ATBM-equipped Soviet ground forces could, depending on the effectiveness of their BMD systems and NATO offensive countermeasures, directly counter such ballistic missile threats and reduce their credibility and utility. BMD at this level of operations could therefore be most valuable to the USSR in trying to gain and hold air superiority—an indispensable key to victory.

A central element of the Soviet campaign for conventional victory would be an offensive air operation conducted with various types of fighter and bomber aircraft, helicopters, artillery, and missiles, and by airborne and special-purpose troops. Western analysts have judged that shorter-range advanced Soviet ballistic missiles (above all, SS-21s, SS-22s, and SS-23s) of high accuracy and responsiveness, equipped with conventional warheads, could play a notable role in such an air offensive. The more accurate ballistic missiles "have allowed the Soviets to obtain a greater potential for suppressing NATO's air and nuclear assets without nuclear means, while still having the ability to complete the task with nuclear means if that should be necessary."[100] It should, however, be noted that the SS-22s and SS-23s are to be eliminated under the terms of the December 1987 INF treaty; this could make the Soviets dependent on SRBMs with ranges below 500 km (notably SS-21s) and on possible theater use of missiles capable of ranges exceeding 5,500 km.

If the Soviets used nuclear warheads, these might be weapons of low yield with confined effects. A relatively small number of accurate nuclear strikes might be able to accomplish decisive political-military objectives without causing much collateral damage. Western governments would therefore retain many grounds for restraint in contemplating nuclear escalation in response.

Chemical weapons (CW) delivered by accurate shorter-range ballistic missiles (SRBMs) might also offer useful strike options to the Soviets. Richard DeLauer, until recently the U.S. under secretary of defense for research and engineering, has revealed that "all their tactical surface-to-surface missiles are configured to carry cw payloads."[101] European experts such as François Heisbourg have noted that Britain, France, and the United States might find it difficult to justify nuclear retaliation "if chemical strikes were limited to narrow targets with little or no collateral damage."[102]

Advanced conventional-warhead designs could nonetheless offer the Soviets the best prospects for containing risks of nuclear escalation. Soviet sources have indicated that the targets of Warsaw Pact SRBM strikes would include airfields, air defenses, command and control centers, nuclear systems, troop concentrations, logistic sites, and so forth.[103] Most of the highest-value military installations of these types are located within 500 km of the inter-German border and could be attacked from Eastern Europe with conventionally armed SRBMs. An extensive conventional SRBM attack could, as suggested above, function as the leading edge of an offensive air operation and simplify large-scale follow-on attacks with aircraft and other forces, including operational maneuver groups.

Such an SRBM attack could minimize requirements for nuclear weapons employment, reduce the warning time available to NATO, free Warsaw Pact aircraft for other missions, hamper and delay numerous NATO mobilization and deployment activities during the initial phase of war, and degrade NATO's nuclear response capabilities. A successful attack along these lines might, moreover, compensate for inflexibilities in the Warsaw Pact command-and-control structure and for the uncertain reliability of some non-Soviet Warsaw Pact allies. Minimizing casualties in Western Europe might also help to make the risks of nuclear retaliation by Western governments appear more manageable.[104]

The Soviets themselves have underlined the challenges that must be addressed to make such an SRBM attack practical. In addition to survivable and highly accurate SRBMs with advanced nonnuclear munitions in large numbers (for some targets would require several warheads), the Soviets would require substantial improvements in what Marshal Ogarkov has described as "automated reconnaissance-and-strike complexes . . . and qualitatively new electronic control systems."[105] Accuracy improvements could be useless in the presence of errors in locating targets or delays in transmitting data about mobile targets. The "friction" of wartime conditions would also apply: operational performance in combat could fall short of that achieved on test ranges in peacetime. There is nonetheless wide agreement with the judgment of the West German minister of defense, Manfred Wörner: "The Soviet Union is in the process of adding a new component to its offensive capabilities which has the potential of decisively shifting the military balance in Europe in Moscow's favor: namely, a massive threat exercised by nonnuclear missiles."[106]

These new ballistic missile options—with conventional, nuclear, and/ or chemical warheads—are to be coupled with ATBM in the form of the SA-10 and SA-12 to defend Soviet strike capabilities against any NATO attempt to use ballistic missiles to interfere with a Soviet offensive air operation or other elements of Warsaw Pact combined-arms attacks. The Soviets appear to have developed an ATBM concurrently with their development of improved shorter-range ballistic missile strike options, just as they seem to have initiated strategic BMD development work in the late 1940s and early 1950s concurrently with their work on the world's first ICBMs and IRBMs.

The Soviets evidently anticipated the threat of NATO's employing conventionally armed ballistic missiles by developing the SA-12. This system may have been originally designed for defense against nuclear-armed ballistic missiles. As noted in Chapter 1, both the SA-12 and the SA-10 may also be effective against cruise missiles and aircraft. Even if NATO elected to develop and deploy such defensive systems (that is, capabilities more robust than those expected from upgrades of the Patriot air defense missile), it would be several years away from having a comparable ATBM. Indeed, NATO is almost as far away from having conventional-warhead ballistic missile strike capabilities comparable to those of the USSR.

BRITISH AND FRENCH FORCES

The foreseeable emergence of Soviet options for precise and discriminate nonnuclear missile attacks also threatens to undermine the credibility of the British and French nuclear forces. It has long been agreed that these forces enjoy far greater political and strategic credibility as deterrents to Soviet nuclear attack against Britain and France than as instruments to protect nonnuclear allies in Western Europe. The long-standing assumption has been that the Soviets could not substantially disable either country's nuclear forces and command centers without using nuclear weapons and causing widespread civilian fatalities—losses that might provoke the British or the French to implement their threats to use their surviving submarine-based ballistic missiles to deliver nuclear weapons against key elements of the Soviet state, including economic and administrative centers.

Soviet capabilities for controlled and limited nonnuclear attacks promise to alter this situation and to make it even more difficult for Britain and France to pose a politically credible threat of massive strikes that would cause large-scale fatalities in the Soviet Union. As General Jeannou Lacaze, then chief of staff of the French armed forces, pointed out in 1985, "the [possible] attack of our fixed installations—[the IRBMs at] Albion, strategic bases, pre-strategic missile depots, command posts, communications centers—by ballistic or cruise missiles with conventional warheads represents a new threat which we must take into account, all the more since an aggressor could be led to think that their use would not be considered a major attack and would not give rise to massive reprisals."[107] Jacques Baumel has described this threat even more starkly. In his view, a highly accurate nonnuclear missile attack, "causing limited collateral effects, could have paralyzing effects on our nuclear deterrent potential."[108]

Soviet BMD improvements beyond the ABM Treaty's limitations, depending on their scope and effectiveness, could also undermine the credibility of the British and French deterrents. Some observers have suggested that the Soviets might choose not to defend themselves effectively against British or French attacks in order to reserve Soviet BMD capabilities for use against possible U.S. attacks: "Soviet strategists would probably consider any European attack as a precursor to an American one, and they would be reluctant to exhaust their defensive potential against the first and less powerful attacker."[109] The British and French governments seem likely, however, to assume that the Soviets would choose to defend themselves as ably as possible against attacks from any quarter. If capable of making such interceptions, the Soviets would probably perceive incentives to destroy the attacking nuclear warheads immediately at hand, if only because their effects might degrade Soviet war-waging capabilities in unpredictable (and potentially significant) ways—to say nothing of the other losses that might result from their detonation.[110]

The Soviets have almost certainly recognized that non-U.S. ballistic missile delivery systems pose discrimination and interception challenges distinct from those raised by U.S. systems. The Polaris SLBMs currently in the British fleet were, it is true, built by the United States; but Polaris SLBMs are no longer in service in the U.S. Navy, and the British have equipped the missiles with a British-made reentry package known as Chevaline. Although the third-country forces are numerically much smaller than those of the United States, there is reason to presume that the Soviets have devoted attention to understanding whatever is unique about their likely attack corridors and their "signatures" for sensor discrimination.

Given the probability that expanded Soviet BMD deployments would be intended to defend as capably as possible against potential British and French attacks (in addition to possible U.S. and Chinese attacks), the possibility that these deployments could erode the credibility of the British and French deterrents must be considered. If the Department of Defense is correct regarding the SA-10 and SA-X-12B/Giant systems' possibly having "the potential to intercept some types of strategic ballistic missiles,"[111] the Soviets may expect to have supplementary capabilities against the British SLBMs and the French SLBMs and IRBMs. Because Britain and France have only a certain number of SSBNs at sea at any time (those in port are less likely to be available for use and far more vulnerable to Soviet attack), an appreciable expansion of Soviet BMD capabilities would have some impact on their penetration prospects.

If this capability against the British and French forces became impressive, it would be an important bonus for the Soviets on top of the other strategic advantages in BMD sketched above. Once again, Soviet risks of sustaining damage in war could be reduced. This result would be even more likely if Britain and France contemplated limited and selective strikes and if the USSR could benefit from other means of active and passive defense. The Soviets could also gain greater control over the possibility that British or French (or, for that matter, Chinese) use of nuclear weapons could function as a "trigger" or catalyst for nuclear escalation by the United States or another government. Effective BMD could make the "trigger" threat inherent in a situation of multiple centers of independent nuclear decision making more manageable for the Soviet Union, and related Soviet risk calculations could be simplified.

The British and French governments have been aware of these possibilities for over twenty years. Even after the United States and the Soviet Union concluded the ABM Treaty, it was noted that, as a French expert put it, "the signatories reserve the possibility of modifying the treaty in a sense unfavorable to our interests."[112]

The main British precaution against improved Soviet BMD has been the Chevaline system for Britain's Polaris SLBMs. Chevaline has been described as "two maneuvering clusters of real warheads and decoys."[113] The costly Chevaline program (conducted mainly during the 1973–1980 period) has been justified by improvements in Soviet BMD. According to official testimony, "had we not modified our system to produce Chevaline, Polaris would have become ineffective. So in that sense even a simple defence has a considerable effect."[114] In testimony before the House of Commons Defence Committee in 1985, a British official could not offer any firm judgments on how long Chevaline might remain capable of penetrating Soviet BMD: ". . . our view is that the Chevaline system has at present a very good capability against the present ABM defenses. There are known research and developments by the Soviets which are allowed within the ABM Treaty———[deleted] . . . we ought to aim to replace Polaris/Chevaline in the mid-1990s. I think it would in a way be giving false precision in one sense if we tried to say that come a given date Chevaline would be of no effect."[115]

According to British officials, the planned replacement for the Polaris-Chevaline combination, the U.S.-built Trident II (D-5) SLBM, is expected to "provide the best possible means of ensuring the continued effectiveness of our national nuclear deterrent well into the future, regardless of Soviet ABM programmes."[116] Few British sources acknowledge that, even with Trident, large-scale Soviet BMD deployments "might threaten the integrity of the British deterrent."[117] Most official statements go no further than remarking, "From what we know of the advancement of the Russian system, Trident does seem to be a sensible answer, but that does not mean you do not have to keep looking."[118]

British scholars such as John Roper have, however, noted that an enhanced Moscow BMD system "could at some point present a challenge to Britain's capability."[119] Lawrence Freedman has pointed out that British aspirations to hold Moscow at risk "would be most threatened by a Soviet move to an endoatmospheric ABM system, which might be better able to discriminate between real warheads and decoys."[120] Ian Bellany has added that "gradual upgrading of the SA-12 ATBM . . . could present a problem . . . for Pershing II and the comparatively short range (and hence comparatively low re-entry speed) offensive missiles that currently form the core of the British and French *strategic* nuclear forces."[121]

Possible British countermeasures to expanded Soviet BMD capabilities do not appear to have been discussed in public official sources. British scholars have mentioned some of the basic technical possibilities—building more SSBNs, buying more Trident SLBMs from the United States, increasing the number of warheads per missile, adopting de-pressed-trajectory launch tactics, developing more advanced decoys and other penetration aids, and pursuing an ability to attack Soviet radars or at least to disable the performance of Soviet sensors with "blackout" and "redout" effects.[122] But official sources seem to have refrained from public speculation. The British government has so far maintained that it plans no increase in warheads on the prospective Trident II D-5 SLBMs beyond what had been planned for Trident I C-4 SLBMs—that is, 8 warheads per missile, or 128 warheads per SSBN.[123] The goal is to keep the Trident force at "the minimum size compatible with cost-effectiveness and credibility"[124] during its lifetime—usually described as 1990 to 2020.[125] The 1987 defense white paper nonetheless suggests a principle that might justify increased numbers of warheads—the need to keep up with improvements in Soviet BMD such as the modernization and expansion of the Moscow system:

> This means that, if the Soviet Union is to be denied any possible sanctuary from which to prosecute aggression without fear of direct reprisal, we shall need to carry more warheads in the future to pose the same threat as in the early days of Polaris . . . The increased payload of D5 offers the best prospect of being able to penetrate Soviet ABM defenses in the face of possible improvements during the life of the system . . . The essential capability for us is to be able to continue to hold at risk key aspects of Soviet state power, not to threaten the maximum possible number of individual targets. Our Trident forces will deploy with the minimum number of warheads consistent with this requirement.[126]

In contrast to the British government's reticence, official French sources have provided extensive discussions of potential Soviet BMD improvements and possible French countermeasures. French officials regard an expansion of Soviet ground-based "terminal" defenses of traditional types as the most likely development in the period up to the year 2000;[127] but the French government has also commissioned studies, such as the January 1986 Delpech report, to examine possible Soviet deployments of space-based directed-energy BMD systems in the more distant future.[128]

In November 1985, the French defense minister, Paul Quilès, announced an intention to develop miniaturized warheads "almost invisible to radars" to overcome "the most immediate and serious threat" of an expansion of improved Soviet terminal defenses.[129] Quilès also suggested "increasing the number of attacking objects," implying that France might add lightweight decoys or additional warheads, perhaps with more advantageous yield-to-weight ratios.[130] Although General Lacaze mentioned the possibility of maneuvering warheads,[131] the references to other "very elaborate penetration aids under development"[132] have not included details on their precise nature. French officials have, however, referred repeatedly to the need to develop "third-generation" nuclear warheads with "specialized effects"—emphasizing electromagnetic pulse, x-rays, infrared radiation, or blast effects—to blind or destroy Soviet radars and sensors and disable Soviet communications.[133] The minister of defense in office since March 1986, André Giraud, has indicated that the *Hélios* reconnaissance satellite will be equipped with an ability to gather electronic intelligence in order to determine "the characteristics of the radars and the nature of the defenses" that French ballistic missiles will face.[134]

Attack tactics designed to complicate the challenges facing Soviet BMD have also been mentioned: depressed-trajectory ballistic missile launches, coordinated attacks launched from various types of platforms, and salvos of shortened duration.[135] Such tactics might maximize France's chances of defeating Soviet defenses in specific areas. If French warheads were hardened and so widely separated in their reentry trajectories that the Soviets would have to expend at least one interceptor missile to intercept each French warhead, as some French authorities maintain,[136] the prospects for successful penetration would be enhanced. This type of cost ratio would probably apply to nonnuclear kills. But, depending on variables such as the RV separation distance and the radius of specific types of nuclear effects, large-yield Soviet nuclear warheads might succeed in neutralizing more than one French reentry vehicle—at the cost, of course, of self-inflicted nuclear effects.

As far as space-based directed-energy systems capable of boost-phase interceptions are concerned, the Delpech report stated that the "most plausible" hypothesis is that only chemical laser technology will have advanced sufficiently to permit effective space-based deployments as early as 2010—and even this would "suppose extremely rapid technical progress, and therefore considerable efforts, with no guarantee of success possible today." Such a space-based laser "would permit protection against British and French ballistic weapons," but only if their missiles were not hardened and launch tactics remained unchanged. Because such countermeasures are feasible, the report concluded, "the French deterrent capacity would remain sufficient, at the price of a limited increase in the number of ballistic missiles as well as hardening measures whose cost would be difficult to estimate, but probably within our reach."[137]

Additional possible countermeasures to space-based directed-energy systems might include further changes in the missiles. French sources have referred to fast-burn boosters, spinning boosters, and "independent submissiles" that might separate from the ascending booster.[138] French officials have also called attention to "the great fragility of a space defense system."[139] Soviet defenses could, in other words, be directly attacked with "electromagnetic jammers, laser reflectors, [and] nuclear explosions that would neutralize an enemy space defense for a limited time by blinding its means of detection and pointing."[140] The logical next step, if necessary, would be "to forge the sword that will pass through the shield"[141]—that is, French antisatellite (ASAT) capabilities to "open breaches" in the Soviet defenses and thus maintain the deterrent credibility of French nuclear forces.[142]

French officials maintain that France will be able to afford all the necessary countermeasures: "The cost of this adaptation will be marginal vis-à-vis that of [Soviet] anti-ballistic [missile] spending and will remain within our reach."[143] The preponderant theme of high-level official commentary has been that France's deterrent will remain credible for decades to come, because France will be able to act to keep Soviet cities at risk. Few officials have publicly voiced judgments similar to those of General Lacaze:

Unfortunately, the efforts that such a diversification [of deterrent means] would impose risk not being within our reach, and choices will therefore be inevitable. Everything will depend ultimately on the evolution of defenses, whether ground-based or space-based . . . The latter [that is, space-based defenses] could gravely destabilize strategic relations, by provoking an intensification of the arms race, but even more, they could place medium nuclear powers in a situation of particular vulnerability.[144]

Lacaze did not specify the reasons for this judgment, but one may speculate that his thinking may have been influenced by the difficult choices that France is already facing in the modernization of her strategic nuclear forces. The Socialist government in office prior to the March 1986 elections qualified its own previous commitment to build a mobile land-based IRBM, the SX, partly on the grounds that France's SSBN force at sea was likely to remain invulnerable to Soviet detection and, more important, partly because Soviet BMD capabilities were judged likely to expand. Quilès and other officials of that government indicated that the decision on SX and alternative means of penetrating Soviet active defenses (for example, cruise missiles) would be postponed until the probable evolution of Soviet defenses could be more clearly understood.[145]

The RPR-UDF government in office since March 1986 has maintained that France cannot become too exclusively dependent on its SSBN force, because its future invulnerability to Soviet antisubmarine warfare capabilities cannot be guaranteed.[146] The new government originally proposed building thirty single-warhead mobile IRBMs, now designated S-4 instead of SX, to replace the eighteen fixed S-3 IRBMs on the Albion plateau and the obsolescent Mirage IV bombers by 1996. The S-4 project has been relatively controversial, partly because of its cost (25 billion francs), but mainly because of reports that it might result in delaying the introduction of the M-5 SLBM (expected to have about twelve warheads) from 1994 (the date previously presumed) to 2002 or even 2009.[147] The military program law for 1987-1991 specified simply that the S-4 will be "a light ballistic missile capable of depressed trajectories and equipped with a penetration capability permitting it to reach defended targets."[148] The question of whether the S-4 will be fixed or mobile has been left open for the present, and the cruise missile possibility seems to have been abandoned for the time being.[149] The law also indicates that the M-5 SLBM will have "sufficient penetration characteristics" to cope with improved defenses.[150] A new warhead for the M-4 SLBM, the TN-75, will be equipped with "remarkable stealthiness" and deployed "as soon as possible."[151]

In this context of costly tradeoffs about ballistic missile choices, it is not clear that France will be able to afford the long-term options mentioned by some officials, of building cruise missiles with low-observable technology ("almost invisible to enemy radars")[152] and/or capable of "supersonic" attacks "in sufficient numbers to saturate [Soviet] air defenses."[153] The French are, however, concerned about becoming excessively reliant on ballistic missiles, given prospective Soviet BMD improvements, and may reconsider the possibility of developing cruise missiles. If they do so, French cruise missiles may not have the range, fuel efficiency, or accuracy of U.S. or Soviet ones. They might be more likely to resemble longer-range advanced versions of the ASMP stand-off missile.[154]

The British situation is simpler, at least as far as the Conservative government is concerned, for it has not implied that it is considering any major alternatives or supplements to the Trident program. The opposition parties have been united in rejecting Trident. The Labour and Liberal parties favor abandoning Britain's nuclear deterrent, whereas the Social Democrats seek a less costly replacement (so far unspecified) for Polaris.

Some of the countermeasures to Soviet BMD discussed in Britain and France may not be effective. As noted in Chapter 1, lightweight penetration aids such as chaff travel at the same speed as real warheads outside the atmosphere and are therefore hard to identify, except with exotic techniques such as infrared sensors; but once they enter the atmosphere, their trajectories are radically altered. Soviet missiles capable of interceptions within the atmosphere, such as the SH-08 Gazelle, should then be able to attack the real warheads. Electronic countermeasures and maneuvering warheads might constitute more effective penetration aids, but the weight and cost penalties might prohibit their acquisition in large numbers.[155]

Nor would it be simple for either Britain or France to attack Soviet BMD radars. As suggested in Chapter 1, the Soviets would almost certainly intend to defend these radars and to invest in redundant coverage, as a hedge against direct attacks and against blackout and other nuclear effects. The Soviets could attack British and/or French forces and command-and-control assets before either government was prepared to attack the Soviet radars, a circumstance that could make it difficult for either to carry out a tailored attack against the radars. Moreover, as James C. Wendt has pointed out, neither government is likely to be able to afford to spend its surviving SLBMs at sea on remotely situated targets:

> The smallest attack that could be directed against a particular radar would be the full complement of warheads contained on one missile . . . The attack is too large because the DE [damage expectancy] to one soft radar from six to eight attacking warheads would be much higher than would be required. Perhaps one or two warheads would suffice. However, each British D-5 will contain eight and each French M-4 will contain six MIRVed warheads, most of which would not be effectively used because many of the Soviet radars would be located in isolated areas on the periphery of the Soviet Union . . . Yet, this attack is too small because . . . there is a

reasonably high probability that the entire missile might malfunction. Then, none of the warheads would reach the target. To guard against this possibility, radars could be cross-targeted from different missiles. But this would introduce even greater inefficiencies in the employment of the force . . . A small attacker may not be able to afford this luxury.[156]

An even more serious problem is that expanded Soviet BMD deployments could aggravate each country's dependence on countercity threats, because it could be much more difficult for either to undertake limited and selective attacks against military targets with any assurance of success. The French case may serve as an informative example, because the French are far less inhibited in discussing their policies. The French government has long maintained that "France will always have the means for a deterrence by the weak of the strong,"[157] on the grounds that "the extreme case of a virtually leak-proof screen, which would practically block our anti-cities strategy, would seem to be excluded."[158] The implicit assumption is that this strategy of "avoiding war through the threat . . . of a massive retaliation inflicting intolerable damage on the aggressor"[159] is credible.

French experts acknowledge that Soviet BMD could "block or at least reduce the effectiveness of certain options for limited counter-force nuclear strikes."[160] But they hold that assuring "the technical credibility of our anti-cities strategy of deterrence" will guarantee French security, "even if the adversary were to obtain a sufficiently effective ABM system to render a counter-force first strike very problematical."[161]

These declarations evade the possibility that a technically credible capacity to attack Soviet cities might prove an inadequate means of assuring national security. If one considers challenges more stressful than deterring the Soviets from doing what they probably have little or no interest in doing anyway (that is, attacking British or French cities with nuclear weapons), it is apparent that a Soviet ability to lessen the feasibility and utility of limited attacks could degrade the political and strategic credibility of the British and French forces.

Although neither government has revealed much information about its capabilities and plans for possible limited strikes, it must be assumed that responsible officials have given the matter careful consideration. In a real case of Soviet aggression, each country would be likely to have an interest in more strategically and politically purposeful plans than attacking Soviet population centers. Both governments have indicated that their targets could include economic and administrative infrastructure assets in the USSR.[162] It would seem that only selective and discriminate strikes could offer either country a chance of achieving useful results and controlling escalation.[163] Actually implementing threats to attack Soviet cities could guarantee a more nearly total defeat through Soviet nuclear retaliation, a harsher Soviet occupation regime, or both.

No guarantees could be offered on the consequences of more flexible targeting. British and French inferiority in nuclear war-waging capabilities could rapidly become as obvious with threats of limited strikes as with threats of causing massive destruction in the USSR. Depending on Soviet aims and risk assessments, however, more limited strikes might lead to politically constructive results.

Expanded BMD deployments could therefore reinforce the Soviet force posture by providing additional means of discouraging Soviet adversaries from using or expanding their use of nuclear weapons. If British and French capabilities were confined to the far less credible options of large-scale attacks against Soviet cities, Soviet risks in undertaking aggression would be reduced. To some extent, Soviet passive defenses (hardening, deception, mobility, and so forth) are probably already narrowing British and French options for militarily meaningful limited strikes. Although some official French spokesmen have contended that Soviet BMD could not degrade the credibility of the French deterrent unless the Soviets had "a real shield" so effective that "not one missile" could get through,[164] others have acknowledged that the Soviets do not set such unreasonable standards. As the Ecole Polytechnique group noted, "it is unlikely that these [Soviet] ground-to-space systems could ever reach 100% effectiveness. But the Soviets have always had a perspective oriented toward *warfighting* and therefore toward *damage limitation*. Such a perspective permits them to be satisfied with less than 100% effectiveness."[165]

Another hypothetical solution that some British and French experts have suggested should be noted in this regard. This solution would be to aim at "targets other than protected sites."[166] As Ian Bellany has pointed out, "a British targeting policy which avoided the most heavily defended Soviet targets could maintain the total casualties threatened close to the level that has been customarily thought to be necessary for a British minimum deterrent."[167] This suggestion overlooks three difficulties. First, both governments have tacitly acknowledged the political and strategic shortcomings of a policy based on threatening simply to kill large numbers of people. Second, it might be hard to determine which targets were in fact undefended, given the large "footprints" of more advanced BMD systems and the possibility of preferential defenses. Third, undefended or poorly defended targets would presumably be those least valued by the Soviet leadership, so threatening to attack them might contribute little more to deterrence than threatening to attack defended targets and achieve some penetration against highly valued assets.

The political consequences of a perceived lowering of the deterrent credibility of the British and French forces are not entirely predictable. In the French case, as Pierre Hassner has suggested, increased Soviet BMD deployments might cause "paralysis" before the Soviet Union, "to the extent to which the weak would risk becoming too weak and the strong too strong for the deterrence by the weak of the strong to keep its minimum declaratory value (for lack of operational value), which is indispensable for maintaining political consensus."[168] In order to protect the national consensus based on independence and nuclear deterrence, the French are likely to invest in countermeasures to Soviet BMD, to make the technical potential of their systems as convincing as possible.

In Britain, in contrast, no national consensus in favor of an autonomous nuclear deterrent prevails. French-style reservations about dependence on U.S. nuclear guarantees and NATO policy have less resonance in Britain. Although the prospect of Soviet BMD improvements may convince many Conservatives of the value of Trident over any less costly alternatives, the Labour and Liberal parties may well see such developments as another argument for abandoning any attempt to retain nuclear forces.[169] Such an abandonment would, one may conjecture, gratify the Soviets; the disappearance of an independent center of nuclear decision making would ease their risk calculations to some extent.

If Britain and France made reductions in spending on conventional forces in order to increase their numbers of ballistic missiles, warheads, and penetration aids—and to enhance their nonballistic nuclear delivery means—the reduced level of conventional capability in Western Europe could facilitate the realization of Soviet plans for conventional victory in the event of war. If London withdrew the British Army of the Rhine (BAOR) and RAF Germany from the Federal Republic as a cost-saving measure, it could stimulate similar withdrawals by other allies maintaining forces in West Germany.

In the French case, increased nuclear investments at the expense of conventional forces could reverse recent positive trends toward enhanced Franco–West German defense cooperation and reconfirm French allegiance to nationalistic nuclear "sanctuary" concepts. French conventional force levels have been cut back repeatedly since the early 1960s, just as French conventional-equipment procurement has been neglected because of the emphasis on nuclear forces. For example, during the Giscard d'Estaing presidency (1974–1981), the French army was reduced by some 20,000 troops, and the Socialist government of 1981–1986 reduced the army by another 22,000. These reductions took place in the context of efforts to streamline the army and facilitate improvements in its firepower and mobility.[170] Although the Defense Ministry of the RPR-UDF government announced an intention to hold further personnel cutbacks to a minimum,[171] some Gaullists are reported to favor cutting the army by 100,000 to 150,000 men to free funds for nuclear forces.[172]

The West European allies of Britain and France might respond with criticisms if such proposals were implemented and trends toward reduced spending on conventional forces became predominant.[173] While the British and French are naturally most concerned about the potential effects of Soviet BMD on their penetration capabilities, West European defense experts outside of Britain and France have often voiced support for the arguments that additional centers of nuclear decision making complicate Soviet risk assessments, could help to prevent U.S. strategic nuclear decoupling in a crisis or war, and provide Western Europe with long-term options for effective defense cooperation in an uncertain future. There is a risk, however, that many Europeans in nonnuclear countries could conclude that Britain and France are spending too much on forces that serve only national purposes, with little deterrent benefit for their allies. This could even be the case with the British forces, despite their nominal assignment to NATO purposes since 1962.[174]

West German experts, however, have expressed concern about the risk that "a Soviet limited area defense would weaken the penetration credibility of the British and French nuclear forces" and thereby "undermine the credibility of nuclear deterrence in Europe."[175] As one West German has noted, Soviet BMD could "pre-empt the evolution" of British and French policy toward the more flexible targeting that "would be required for any extension of the sanctuary protected by the national deterrents from the UK and French homelands to all [of] Western Europe."[176] Doubts about the credibility of U.S. nuclear guarantees could persuade West Europeans in some nonnuclear countries to offer political support to the British and French nuclear programs in order to gain additional indirect nuclear insurance. Informed Europeans are well aware of the Soviet interest in eliminating the British and French nuclear forces. As Peter Stratmann has observed,

> it is important to prevent the USSR from becoming the sole nuclear power in Europe. The material prerequisites for developing a sufficient politico-strategic counterweight in Western Europe must be preserved in order to obviate potential difficulties that could result

from a total dependence on the American readiness to maintain extended strategic deterrence in the long run ... [S]tatements by conservative voices in the Federal Republic appear short-sighted in seeing an advantage in [the Soviets] building strategic missile defense systems such that the French "force de dissuasion," the most visible symbol of the Gaullist pretense of independence and status discrimination over the neighbor across the Rhine, would become obsolete.[177]

Many obstacles, however, stand in the way of any aspiration to devise a nuclear deterrent for a West European defense entity on the basis of the British and French forces. The political barriers to building such a capability may be even more intractable than the economic and technical requirements. These barriers include the uncertain credibility of extending British and French deterrent guarantees to nonnuclear allies, understandable British and French reluctance to dilute national control mechanisms, the credibility uncertainties associated with any system of multiple "keys" and vetoes, the sensitivities attached to any West German involvement in control over nuclear weapons, possible Soviet attempts to exploit the Nonproliferation Treaty to oppose the constitution of a West European nuclear deterrent, and widespread West European concerns that such a joint deterrent could somehow become a pretext for a reduction in the U.S. military presence in Europe.

Even the coordination of British and French SLBM targeting, in order "to swamp the Soviet defenses," as some West Europeans have suggested,[178] would encompass great technical and political challenges. The technical challenges would include developing multiple target sets and retargeting capabilities for each SLBM on each SSBN, because the number of SSBNs surviving Soviet attacks could not be predicted. Each government's system of command, control, communications, and intelligence (C^3I) would have to survive sufficiently well to permit useful communications with the remaining SSBNs and with the other national command authority. The political challenge would reside in agreeing on the appropriate combined response, in a situation in which Britain or France (or both) might be unsure about how to assess the situation and unwilling to share information that might be critical to its own national survival.[179]

It is possible that an expansion of Soviet BMD capabilities could exacerbate the political obstacles to effective defense cooperation in Western Europe by making these obstacles more obvious. The Soviets, however, may well fear the contrary effect—an advance in meaningful cooperation oriented toward the building of a West European "power center" on the basis of the British and French nuclear forces.[180] This may constitute an incentive, along with others, to avoid a conspicuous breakout from the ABM Treaty's constraints and to maintain a certain discretion about their BMD activities. For the long term, however, there can be no doubt about the Soviet interest in lessening the credibility of these independent nuclear forces. A significant expansion of Soviet BMD capabilities could restrict Britain and France to the most politically implausible of nuclear strike options, confront them with costly nuclear choices, and encourage them to divert spending away from conventional forces; it might also aggravate political tensions within the Western alliance.

Potential Consequences in Peace

The discussion above naturally included some observations about the implications of Soviet BMD for Western security in situations short of war, because peacetime perceptions are affected by opinions about likely events in war. Improved unilateral BMD capabilities could be of great value to the Soviets in advancing their aim of hegemony without war, precisely because of the effects that would be anticipated from Soviet BMD in war. If the Soviet Union achieved a large unilateral advantage in BMD, Western vulnerability to Soviet military power would be increased, because Soviet vulnerability to retaliation would be decreased. By reducing the credibility of British and French as well as U.S. ballistic missile means of attack, the Soviets could hope to persuade West Europeans that they have no reliable nuclear deterrent options, either in alliance with the United States or through West European capabilities.

Enhanced BMD capabilities could reinforce other Soviet military strengths, offensive and defensive. As suggested in Chapter 2, the Soviets have been investing for decades in other forms of strategic defense, in offensive strike forces, and in nonnuclear forces suitable for missions in regional theaters of strategic military action. BMD should not (and indeed cannot) be isolated from other elements of the Soviet force posture as a whole—and long-term Soviet political-military aspirations—without distorting its significance. In potential operations in Europe, for example, it is clear that Soviet theater BMD capabilities (the SA-10 and SA-12) would offer protection to the Soviet conventional offensive, that this offensive would include air operations intended to achieve air superiority for the Warsaw Pact, and that a key role in the air offensive would probably be played by highly accurate nonnuclear shorter-range ballistic missiles (SRBMs).

These capabilities could have consequences in peacetime by affecting Western perceptions. As François Heisbourg has noted, the highly accurate nonnuclear SRBMs alone could constitute an unprecedented "surprise attack capability." This capability would represent a means of "slipping under the nuclear threshold" and therefore "a major political component of the global correlation of forces." If the foreseeable Soviet capabilities were not effectively countered, "Western Europe could be subjected to a regime of permanent intimidation."[181] West German Defense Minister Manfred Wörner has also pointed out that the aggregate effect of emerging and foreseeable Soviet capabilities could undermine the foundations of Western security in Europe:

> In combination, these looming developments on the Soviet side—offensive options augmented by conventional missiles, and defenses against ballistic missiles—portend decisive advantages for Soviet strategy in Europe. These advantages could lead planners in Moscow to the calculation that a successful conventional attack can be launched in Europe, while any NATO measures of nuclear escalation would be prevented or minimized. In light of the approximate parity between the superpowers at the strategic nuclear level, the Soviets could thus transform their nuclear superiority in Europe into nuclear dominance.[182]

Western students of Soviet political-military affairs have long recognized that the Soviets would prefer to achieve political hegemony in Europe without war, by demoralizing public opinion with the display of superior military power and by making it increasingly more difficult for Western governments to maintain adequate defense capabilities. As Hannes Adomeit has pointed out, one of the principal purposes of the Soviet military buildup is "to influence Western perceptions . . . to convey the impression that Western Europe *cannot* and therefore, *will not* be defended."[183] To fulfill this purpose, the Soviet Union must maintain military forces visibly capable of effective employment in war.

Soviet hegemonial aspirations, the buildup of Soviet military power, and the narrowing of Western defense options are entirely compatible with Soviet "peace" policies oriented toward improved Soviet–West European relations. The USSR would prefer that Western Europe's accommodation to Soviet political dominance take place without war and be described as a process of establishing an "all-European system of security and co-operation," "safeguarding peace," building a "common European home," and "deepening the European detente." This appears to be a Soviet aim in the Conference on Security and Cooperation in Europe and in related negotiations.[184]

Improved unilateral BMD capabilities could be useful in this endeavor because they could underline and enhance West European insecurity. Although Soviet inhibitions in contemplating visible coercion would be reduced, the Soviets would probably prefer to use more subtle methods to convince West Europeans that, as far as Moscow is concerned, security cannot be obtained in an anti-Soviet alliance framework and there is no alternative to pursuing security in cooperation with the USSR.

If it were not countered by the Western alliance, a large unilateral Soviet advantage in BMD could enhance the prospects for success of the apparent Soviet "option denial" strategy. It can be argued that the Soviets have for decades been increasing NATO's dependence on nuclear weapons (by widening the gap in conventional capabilities) while attempting to neutralize NATO's nuclear options with a nuclear "counter-deterrent." General Bernard Rogers, the supreme allied commander, Europe (SACEUR), until June 1987, has repeatedly pointed out in recent years that NATO's fundamental military "problem was and is Soviet–Warsaw Pact conventional nonnuclear military superiority."[185]

> Through the constant amassing of military might, the Soviet Union continues to widen the gap between Warsaw Pact and NATO force capabilities . . . The major menace we face is that the Soviet Union will continue to widen and manipulate this gap until the military situation, even for a defensive alliance, gets beyond restoration; then it will be able to achieve its major objective in Western Europe: intimidation, coercion and blackmail without having to fire a shot.[186]

Expanded BMD capabilities could be of critical importance to the Soviet Union in this endeavor. The objective operational value of such capabilities might be magnified by the high political visibility that BMD matters have earned since the debates of the late 1960s, the 1972 ABM Treaty, and the U.S. pursuit of the SDI research program. Even if the reliability and effectiveness of Soviet BMD were in fact debatable, Western perceptions of narrowed and denied options could have debilitating effects useful to Soviet peacetime diplomacy. The possibility that the Soviets might try to use BMD deployments of doubtful technical effectiveness for peacetime political effects should be recognized. As the January 1986 report to the French minister of defense noted,

> aside from these purely technical considerations, it is essential not to forget the psychological aspects that govern public opinion: the mere mention of space-based weapons has already produced a profound effect, as has been apparent for some time. It is even more serious that the demonstration by the USSR of a powerful laser in space

seems perfectly conceivable to us in the next few years, given the working methods of the Soviets: it would of course only be a simple experimental device, of perhaps debatable utility, and not a practical basis for a possible deployment; but this could be a skillful political *coup*, for such an experiment could seem to undermine very seriously our concept of deterrence in the eyes of the public. It would be very difficult to make understood the considerable differences between scientific feasibility, technical capacity, and effective deployment.[187]

The Soviets are, however, more likely to be interested in affecting the long-term assessments performed by Western governments than in achieving a short-term impact on Western public opinion. They would in fact probably prefer to bring about enduring effects on the perceptions of both governments and publics. Western governments are constrained by public opinion, whereas Western publics may be gradually influenced by the messages of confidence or caution transmitted by the behavior of their governments. If Western governments assessed expanded Soviet BMD deployments as likely to be reasonably effective in war, the Soviet option denial strategy would be all the more likely to work without war. As Harold Brown once observed, when he was secretary of defense, "if both sides perceive an imbalance on the strategic side, then the side that both sides believe is stronger has a political edge [and] may even use it for intimidation purposes."[188]

The Soviet Union's cautiousness about war, discussed at the outset of this chapter, is only one of several factors that help to explain the Soviet preference for a policy of peaceful political change. This general cautiousness, based on a sober recognition of the uncertainties and dangers of any war that might involve nuclear weapons, is buttressed by concerns about the potential impact of war on the Soviet Union's domestic development and its system of relations with allies in Europe—to say nothing of the broader consequences of the potential devastation of Europe, from the Soviet perspective.

This situation confirms the importance of Soviet efforts to work for peaceful political change. The continuing buildup of superior conventional forces and of nuclear counter-deterrent capabilities provides the Soviet Union with usable options in the unwanted event of war; but the buildup also provides instruments for intimidation and coercion without war. As the statements by Western officials such as Shultz, Wörner, Rühle, and Rogers suggest, the Soviets have empirical grounds—aside from force balance assessments—for some satisfaction with established trends in the overall "correlation of forces." These trends point toward increasingly constricted military choices for Western governments in the event of a crisis or conflict, with correspondingly greater choices for the USSR.

Although the Soviets would, for example, probably be loath to take the risks involved in undertaking a large-scale conventional offensive in Europe, their continually improving capacity to do so aggravates the West's nuclear dilemmas. The Soviets have gained increasingly credible nonnuclear-force employment options, an improving capacity for selective nuclear attacks, and more survivable intercontinental counter-deterrent nuclear forces. As the Soviets build on their geographical and organizational advantages for the massing of conventional military power in Europe, they may make it more difficult for the West to muster credible nonnuclear responses—and the potential nuclear responses may appear to be checkmated by Soviet nuclear capabilities.

In other words, these trends aggravate the Western dependence on threats to use nuclear weapons. These trends, largely the result of Soviet (and Western) military investment choices, are intrinsically problematic for the Western alliance. Soviet public diplomacy suggests, however, that the Soviets have an interest in exacerbating the political effects of these trends in order to sap the cohesion of the West.

Since the mid-1970s, and especially since Brezhnev's speech at Tula in January 1977, Western analysts of Soviet political-military policy have had to contend with the anomalies stemming from what some experts call the "Tula line." The Tula line is at variance with the vast bulk of Soviet military literature, but it has received great prominence in the West because its message is so reassuring in terms of widespread Western assumptions and preferences. The Tula line has been articulated by the top leaders of the Soviet Union since 1977 and, in the West, by highly visible Soviet spokesmen such as Georgi Arbatov and Vadim Zagladin.

The essence of the Tula line is the following message: The Soviet Union does not seek superiority in nuclear weapons or in any other form of military power—only equality and equal security.[189] Nuclear war cannot be a reliable instrument of policy, because such war cannot be limited. Escalation to all-out nuclear war would be inevitable.

Several Western experts on Soviet military affairs suspect that the Tula line is intended to give Soviet nuclear policy a less threatening image in Western perceptions, as certain past Soviet views are denied and the Soviets claim to accept mutual vulnerability and to favor Western-style concepts of strategic stability. They note that the Tula line has been articulated with a high degree of consistency during a period in which significant Soviet public statements on military doctrine have become relatively scarce. The period since the late 1970s has also seen an increase in Soviet investments (discussed in Chapters 1–2) in capabilities oriented toward damage limitation and escalation control—not only counter-force strike systems but also various forms of strategic defense, including ICBM mobility, deep underground shelters, and BMD infrastructure expansion and system modernization. It is clear that the International Information Department (IID) of the CPSU Central Committee, under the leadership of Leonid Zamyatin and Valentin Falin, played an especially important role in promoting this portrayal of Soviet policy during its existence in 1978–1986.[190] (In May 1986, the CPSU abolished the IID and merged its functions with Aleksandr Yakovlev's Propaganda Department.)

How could the Tula line simultaneously endow Soviet policy with a less threatening image and exacerbate the political-military dilemmas of the Western alliance? The issue of the controllability of nuclear escalation provides perhaps the clearest example of how this effect might be promoted. As noted in Chapter 2, a great deal of evidence supports the judgment that, although the Soviets would, in the event of war, prefer to avoid any use of nuclear weapons, they are prepared to undertake selective and discriminate nuclear attacks, if necessary. The physical characteristics of the Soviet force posture imply an interest in limiting damage if the controlled and purposeful employment of nuclear weapons is determined to be necessary. Similarly, although Soviet military author-ities never discount the dangers of nuclear escalation, their doctrinal writings have reflected "a guarded confidence in the ability of Soviet forces to fight and prevail in a nuclear war limited to the theater level. Soviet views on the feasibility of limited nuclear warfare at the intercon-tinental level were more ambiguous, but a similar set of concerns, and especially the threatened loss of control over the course of the conflict, probably conditioned Soviet military thinking at this level as well."[191]

This does not mean, of course, that the Soviets have adopted the concepts of tit-for-tat bargaining with "demonstrative" nuclear ex-changes that some Western theorists have speculated about; Soviet targeting would involve militarily consequential objectives. The Soviets have, however, made it clear that they perceive practical incentives for limiting nuclear employment, including the need to avoid degrading the effectiveness of their conventional operations. Moreover, in major crises such as the 1962 Cuban affair, the Soviets have shown great concern about retaining control over risks of nuclear escalation.[192] But improve-ments in the Soviet conventional-force posture make nuclear employ-ment increasingly less likely to be necessary.

The Western alliance, in contrast, finds its dependence on threats of nuclear escalation increased in tandem with the widening of the gap in

NATO and Warsaw Pact conventional combat capability. In practice, for most West Europeans (and for the British and French as well, to some extent), this means dependence on U.S. threats to use nuclear weapons in the limited and selective fashion prescribed in NATO's flexible-response strategy. Although the Soviets have already materially degraded the credibility of these selective strike threats by building nuclear counter-deterrent capabilities and active and passive defenses (and might further degrade them with BMD deployments), they have apparently also been attempting to lessen the political acceptability of these threats in the West by misrepresenting Soviet policy.

The misrepresentation for Western consumption resides in the declarations that nuclear escalation cannot be controlled, that any use of nuclear weapons would inevitably lead to massive attacks expending all available weapons, and so forth. In the words of Leonid Brezhnev, "there can be in general no 'limited' nuclear war. If a nuclear war breaks out, . . . it would inevitably and unavoidably assume a worldwide character."[193] According to Marshal Ogarkov, "any attempt to use nuclear weapons will inevitably result in a catastrophe which may put into question the fate of life itself in the world as a whole."[194] Ogarkov has also placed the responsibility for NATO selective strike plans squarely on the United States: "The calculation of the strategists across the ocean, based on the possibility of waging a so-called 'limited' nuclear war, now has no foundation whatever. It is utopian: Any so-called limited use of nuclear facilities will inevitably lead to the immediate use of the whole of the [two] sides' nuclear arsenal."[195]

The actual probabilities are, of course, more prosaic. The controllability of nuclear escalation is unknown and scenario dependent, but nuclear-armed governments would have the highest incentives to keep escalation under control. The Soviets have invested heavily in capabilities intended to maximize the prospects for keeping nuclear escalation under their control; and they have outlined, especially in documents for restricted circulation within the Soviet military, rationales for the controlled and purposeful use of nuclear weapons.[196] Some of the less extreme statements of the Tula line genre may reflect genuine doubts and uncertainties about the feasibility of controlling escalation and could help to explain the Soviet interest in avoiding nuclear war, if possible. But the statements for Western consumption omit Soviet doctrinal judgments about the potential feasibility and utility of limited nuclear employment and say nothing about Soviet capabilities for selective strikes and the Soviet determination to keep any unavoidable nuclear operations under Soviet control, to the maximum extent possible.

The Tula line articulations would appear to serve multiple purposes. To begin with, the theme of rapid and inevitable escalation to extremes may well serve Soviet deterrence objectives. As Nathan Leites has noted, this theme "expresses a desire to maximize deterrence more than a forecast— not to speak of a resolve."

> It is perhaps just because the Soviets are so interested in the distinction between deterrence and war-fighting that they have kept silent about it. The war not being yet begun, this is the hour of deterrence: deterrence by the prospect of a maximum initial strike, of preemption, and of the none-or-all character of nuclear war. Once the war is on, the Authorities may adopt that "controlled" conduct about which the West (in a possible Soviet estimate) is now so prematurely chattering.[197]

It is in the interests of the USSR to call attention to U.S. nuclear vulnerabilities and to try to convince the United States that the Soviet Union would not cooperate in any U.S. attempts to control the scope of nuclear escalation, so that the likelihood of any selective U.S. nuclear strikes in support of allies in Western Europe (or elsewhere) may be diminished. Indeed, it would be surprising, given the USSR's geopolitical aspirations and interests in "restraining" U.S. nuclear-employment decisions, if the Soviets conceded that the United States might be able to use nuclear weapons in Eurasia and avoid escalation to North America.

Another major purpose of the theme of uncontrollable escalation and universal destruction may well be to promote demoralization in the West and to encourage indigenous political trends that point toward a delegitimization of NATO's nuclear strategy. Demoralization—including feelings of futility, hopelessness, and desperation—could obviously be useful in undercutting the political will of the Western alliance. The uncontrollable-escalation theme seems intended, as Albert Wohlstetter has noted, "either to frighten us into believing that it is futile to prepare to use nuclear weapons, even in response to their use of nuclear weapons, or to lull us into believing that they would never use them. Or both."[198] Both sentiments could serve as justifications for Western passivity and could lessen resistance to the expansion of Soviet political influence.

The uncontrollable-escalation theme may, moreover, be seen as congruent with the Soviet no-first-use pledge made in 1982. The USSR's renunciation of "first-use" options appears logical and responsible in the context established by the Soviet declarations that nuclear weapons employment cannot be controlled. As John Hines, Phillip Petersen, and

Notra Trulock have pointed out, "The Soviets have clearly intended the NATO public to interpret Soviet unilateral renunciation of nuclear use as an indication of their peaceful intentions rather than as a manifestation of Soviet confidence in both their nuclear and conventional strengths."[199] Making a no-first-use pledge and challenging NATO governments to do likewise is evidently a way to undermine the consensus behind NATO strategy in the West. However, while the Soviets have strong incentives to avoid nuclear weapons employment (and to deter Western governments from using nuclear weapons), the Soviets might in practice not feel obliged to comply with their no-first-use pledge if their assessment of military requirements in a specific operational situation dictated the controlled and selective use of nuclear weapons.

The theme of inevitable escalation may also be useful to the Soviets because it may exacerbate public doubts about the validity of NATO's flexible-response strategy. NATO strategy foresees deliberate and controlled nuclear escalation by the West in the event that Soviet aggression cannot be contained by conventional means; but Soviet threats to cause apocalyptic devastation in response could make NATO strategy seem reckless and suicidal. The delegitimization of a strategy dependent on nuclear threats could in turn make it more difficult for the West to undertake necessary nuclear modernization programs or simply to sustain public support for existing capabilities. The delegitimization effect could also promote U.S.–West European divisions. The Soviets regularly accuse the United States of recklessly planning to wage a limited nuclear war in Europe, and warn West Europeans that their best hope of escaping war is political cooperation with the USSR. As Robert Osgood and Henning Wegener have noted, "the single-minded preoccupation with uncontrollable apocalyptic scenarios in Soviet public doctrinal statements is best explained as an example of the political and psychological exploitation of terror, intended, particularly, to play on European nuclear anxieties and to loosen Europe's strategic bond to the United States."[200]

Finally, the theme of unavoidable escalation might help to advance the Soviet objective of "progressive" peaceful change. If West Europeans could be persuaded that the flexible-response strategy is bankrupt and doomed to fail in a real crisis or conflict, they might be interested in alternative approaches to security. They might well become more convinced of the merits of the argument supported by the Soviet Union, that Western Europe would be safer without a U.S. nuclear presence. They could find the concept of nuclear-weapons-free zones in Western Europe more attractive. The long-term Soviet policy for Europe, building an "all-European system of collective security," could gain in appeal if Western military policies no longer seemed tenable. The USSR's aim of gradually transforming the character of its relations with Western Europe might then succeed; the security links between Western Europe and the United States might be progressively undone, and West European governments might accept a certain Soviet *droit de regard* over their foreign and defense policies.

This protracted process of nonviolent change might be more likely than abrupt developments if expanded unilateral BMD deployments bolstered the existing strengths of the Soviet military posture, partly because of Soviet cautiousness about the risks of war. It must be recognized, however, that an accentuation of preexisting NATO–Warsaw Pact imbalances in vulnerabilities and in military options might lead the USSR to less cautious behavior. The United States and its allies might perceive narrower options and less freedom of action; the Soviets might, at least, expect this result, and Soviet expectations about the willingness of the U.S. and allied governments to take risks in order to counter Soviet expansionism could be affected.

As was noted at the beginning, however, some concerns about the consequences of a large unilateral expansion of Soviet BMD capabilities are premature. This chapter has reviewed the possible consequences of extreme cases in order to highlight the stakes at issue for the Western alliance. The future depends in part on the Soviet calculus of interests (Chapter 4) and Western response options (Chapter 5).

4

Soviet Arms Control Diplomacy and the Unlikely Prospect of Breakout

Few Western experts question the assessment discussed in Chapter 1: the Soviet Union has built a potential superior to that of the United States for relatively rapid deployments of traditional ground-based BMD interceptors beyond the ABM Treaty's limitations. This potential offers the Soviets a hypothetical option to break out of the ABM Treaty's constraints. Although it is not clear that Soviet leaders have made any decision to exercise this option, they have supported the expense of developing many of the requisite capabilities. As James Schear has remarked,

> there is little dispute that components of the ABM-X-3 system, which is essentially ready to deploy, could be proliferated nationwide fairly rapidly—perhaps over a period of one to three years—if the Soviets (for whatever reason) decided to take the step. From the strategic standpoint, a greater capacity for rapid deployment of ABM components—even within the confines of the treaty—does confer some break-out advantage . . . [S]uch a capacity would become especially significant in the context of other developments, such as the mass production and stockpiling of components, the further construction of LPARs, or the preparation of possible deployment sites at priority target areas.[1]

As suggested in Chapter 1, the term *breakout* may refer to (1) a relatively sudden and large-scale violation of arms control agreements legally in force or (2) the expansion of previously limited military capabilities when treaty constraints no longer apply, owing to their expiration or legal abrogation.[2] The ABM Treaty is of indefinite duration, but each party has the right to withdraw, with six months' notice, "if it decides that extraordinary events related to the subject matter of this

Treaty have jeopardized its supreme interests" (article XV). The latter meaning of breakout potential—a capacity to benefit from the legal termination of treaty limitations—has rarely been considered in this context, however. It has usually been assumed—and probably correctly —that in the foreseeable future the Soviets would prefer not to exercise their right of abrogation, because such an abrogation would free the United States from its ABM Treaty commitments.

It has also been widely presumed that a true breakout from the ABM Treaty would involve illegal deployments of a much greater scale than the Krasnoyarsk radar (the only major Soviet system component the U.S. government has declared to be unambiguously in violation of the ABM Treaty)—that is, deployments that would substantially exceed the capabilities allowed by the ABM Treaty. In defining breakout, some U.S. officials have drawn a distinction between overt and covert activities: "An overt 'break-out' of the ABM Treaty would involve the *overt* deployment of ABM missiles and radars at levels above those allowed by the treaty . . . and in areas not permitted by the treaty . . . *Covert* deployments would involve the same thing but might also involve the upgrade of SAM missiles into ABMs. A 'break-out' would involve the deployment of regional or nationwide defenses."[3]

Incentives and Inhibitions regarding Breakout

A number of the possible Soviet incentives for exercising a breakout option were reviewed in Chapter 3: namely, the advantages that would redound to the Soviet Union in war and peace from such a reduction in Soviet vulnerabilities, assuming that Western governments failed to take timely countermeasures. Sayre Stevens has suggested:

> One possibility is that the Soviet Union might conclude that the situation is ripe—because of the vulnerability of U.S. ICBMs, the hiatus before new U.S. forces come on line, and a significant Soviet advantage in lead time to BMD deployment—to effect a dramatic shift in the strategic balance that would produce great political leverage. That initiative might consist of a nationwide deployment of several thousand interceptors. Although such a move might trigger a U.S. response, it could not be a rapid one.[4]

This judgment about the infeasibility of a "rapid" U.S. response should probably be qualified. Unmistakable evidence of a Soviet breakout from the ABM Treaty might well convince the U.S. administration and Congress of the need to respond with accelerated strategic-force programs—offensive and defensive.

On the one hand, it would probably be difficult for the United States to increase significantly the numbers of warheads and penetration aids on its existing ICBMs and SLBMs, because the reentry packages on most of these missiles have already been designed to make the most efficient use possible of their limited throwweight. (U.S. ICBM throwweight is significantly smaller than Soviet ICBM throwweight.) Nor would it be easy for the United States (or Britain or France) to proliferate SLBM numbers, owing to the lengthy construction times for additional SSBNs. On the other hand, the MX ICBM production line might still be open, and the only obstacles to proliferating U.S. ICBM numbers on an accelerated schedule would be political will and resources, including supplies of special nuclear materials for warheads. Additional nonballistic offensive forces—for example, air- and sea-launched cruise missiles—might also be produced fairly expeditiously. Britain and France might also be able to increase their offensive forces relatively promptly in some ways—with air-delivered stand-off missiles, for example.

U.S. and allied responses in strategic defense could not, however, be as rapid as in the offensive domain. The investments over decades in hardening, mobility, deception, and so forth in the USSR have made the Soviet military "target set" more defensible than that of the Western alliance, and no crash program of a few years' duration could achieve equivalent protection. The West also lacks an infrastructure for BMD comparable to that which the Soviets have built up, from their air defense establishment and large phased-array radar network to their operational Moscow BMD system. Unlike the USSR, the United States and its allies have not been developing and testing ground-based BMD systems of traditional types with a view toward early deployments.

The disparity in deployed and promptly deployable BMD capabilities favoring the Soviet Union argues against any suggestion that Soviet BMD programs are simply a hedge against possible future U.S. BMD deployments. Hedge interpretations are on more solid ground when they argue that the Soviets may have prepared a breakout option in case it might turn out to be valuable in unpredictable circumstances. One of several Soviet motives may, in other words, be one of simple prudence: seeing that the USSR is as well positioned as possible for unforeseeable events, including a potential breakdown of the ABM Treaty regime or a change in Soviet military requirements.

This would be consistent with the "general contingency aim" that appears to be characteristic of the Soviet approach to developing military power. If, for instance, the climate of East-West relations should turn markedly sour, the risk of war could seem more significant. It might then seem advantageous to deploy capabilities that could (1) accentuate the relative vulnerabilities of the United States and its allies and (2) make the effectiveness of the more plausible U.S. (or British or French) retaliatory strikes appear dubious. This might deter such U.S. strikes entirely or provide a measure of protection for key assets of the Soviet state. This reasoning appears to support Michael Mihalka's interpretation: "The bulk of the evidence suggests that the Soviets are developing a 'surge' ABM capability. Soviet notions regarding the likelihood of nuclear conflict presuppose that a period of tensions would precede nuclear war. If the Soviets viewed a nuclear war as a likely occurrence, they would feel no need to honor the ABM Treaty. Moreover, the deployment of even a partially effective nationwide ABM system may deter a US attack."[5]

Whatever the Soviet incentives for exercising a breakout option might be in unpredictable and extreme circumstances, a clear-cut decision for breakout seems improbable in normal peacetime conditions. If the working hypothesis about Soviet decision making and motives advanced in Chapter 2 is sound, the same calculus of risks and benefits that led the Soviet Union to approve the ABM Treaty in 1972 is probably still operative.

If the Soviets approved the ABM Treaty to constrain U.S. competition in a critical area of high-technology strategic defense, they would probably still prefer to avoid such competition. The Soviet Union could not obtain the theoretically maximum advantages of a large unilateral BMD deployment without raising high risks of eventual responses by the United States and its allies. Western defensive responses could not, however, be as rapid as a full-scale Soviet breakout, given the West's current BMD capabilities. This could endow the USSR with potentially great advantages in a future crisis or conflict.

But, unless the outcome of that crisis or conflict somehow dramatically altered international political configurations and/or basic technological and industrial strengths, the West would be likely to respond to a Soviet breakout in order to prevent or moderate consequences such as those discussed in Chapter 3. CIA officials have testified that, although the Soviets "could undertake rapidly paced ABM deployments to strengthen the defenses at Moscow and cover key targets in the western USSR, and to extend protection to key targets east of the Urals, by the early 1990s," they will "have to weigh the military advantages they would see in such defenses, against the disadvantages of such a move, particularly the responses by the United States and its Allies."[6]

As in 1972, when the ABM Treaty was concluded, one of the principal disadvantages for the Soviet Union could be the alleviation of U.S. ICBM vulnerability, for this application is often at the top of U.S. BMD priorities.

Reduced U.S. ICBM vulnerability would probably be viewed by the Soviet Union "as an undesirable threat to its preemptive counterforce capabilities."[7] Keeping U.S. BMD under control through the ABM Treaty simplifies the attainment of Soviet targeting objectives, whereas U.S. and allied BMD deployments (depending on their scope and effectiveness) could dramatically increase Soviet offensive-force requirements and create uncertainties with potentially severe practical consequences for Soviet attack planners.[8]

This would be particularly true of the multilayer BMD arrangements, including space-based elements for midcourse and boost-phase intercepts, that have been envisaged in the SDI. The large Soviet ICBM force, with its substantial throwweight and warhead advantages over the U.S. ICBM force, could possibly enable the Soviets to overwhelm a U.S. BMD system consisting solely of ground-based terminal defenses, depending on the scope and effectiveness of the U.S. system. If a revision of the ABM Treaty limited the United States to such defenses and allowed the Soviets to expand their network of ground-based terminal defenses, the outcome might well be to the net advantage of the USSR—given the more defensible character of Soviet strategic forces and the USSR's other military assets, the superior Soviet potential for a relatively rapid and extensive deployment of such traditional BMD systems, and the Soviet advantage in prompt counterforce capabilities.

But the Soviets would probably prefer to retain the ABM Treaty regime for the time being, even if the traditional ground-based BMD fallback position might be to their net advantage, partly because even ground-based U.S. defenses could pose substantial uncertainties for Soviet attack planners. As noted in Chapter 2, the Soviets may rate the technological potential of the United States in sensors and data processing more highly than their own: they might be more conscious of the uncertain reliability and effectiveness of their own BMD systems than of the possible deficiencies of future U.S. BMD systems. Moreover, the Soviets might not discount the risk that the United States could not be kept limited to ground-based systems of traditional types. A shift to a position favoring a revision of the ABM Treaty to permit more extensive deployments of ground-based BMD of traditional types, perhaps for ICBM defense or other limited purposes, could nonetheless be plausible if, for example, Soviet assessments of likely U.S. behavior accorded greater probability to actual U.S. BMD deployments.[9]

The likelihood of a clear-cut Soviet breakout decision in prevailing political circumstances may, at any rate, be considered low. If the hypothetical breakout advantages did not lead to decisive events favoring the Soviet Union, a breakout could raise risks of energizing unpredictable Western responses, including a high degree of U.S. and allied unity on crash programs—offensive and defensive—to counter the effects of the Soviet breakout.

The political impact of an unmistakable Soviet breakout would probably be counterproductive, from the Soviet viewpoint. As David Schwartz has noted, "the Soviet Union's ability to portray itself as a champion of disarmament would be seriously weakened by such a move."[10] A more fundamental risk is that crash Western countermeasures, offensive and defensive, could be transformed into well-sustained programs that would ultimately place the USSR at a disadvantage. Because of the risks that a highly visible breakout would entail, the Soviets may choose not to pursue the possibility raised in the January 1986 Delpech report to the French minister of defense—that is, the deployment of spectacular space-based systems of dubious technical effectiveness in order to evoke intimidating psychological effects.[11]

Another major Soviet incentive for maintaining the ABM Treaty—and hence an inhibition with respect to the breakout option—is the fact that the USSR has been able to do a great deal to improve its BMD potential under the ABM Treaty. It has, for example, been able to expand its BMD infrastructure by enlarging and upgrading its air defense network and developing potentially BMD-capable SAMs. While upgrading SAMs to BMD capability by testing them in "an ABM mode" is forbidden by the ABM Treaty, the SA-12 has reportedly demonstrated its ability to perform in an ATBM role—a capability that is not explicitly limited by the ABM Treaty. The Soviets have thus been able to profit from the blurring of distinctions between air defense and tactical and strategic BMD. Stevens suggests that the Soviets could use mobile ATBM systems such as the SA-12 to gain strategic BMD capabilities:

> [T]heir rapid deployment in large numbers (possibly from covert storage) would constitute another means whereby the Soviet Union could extend its defensive forces, very possibly within the provisions of the ABM Treaty. Although the treaty does prohibit giving non-ABM systems the capability to intercept strategic ballistic missiles, it would be extremely difficult to make an airtight case that it had occurred if the Soviet Union denied the allegation.[12]

Soviet spokesmen have not only denied that the SA-12 could be capable of intercepting strategic ballistic missiles. They also deny that it is capable of serving as an ATBM and maintain that it is simply an air defense missile.[13] These denials are consistent with their position that developing U.S. ATBM systems for deployment in defense of Western Europe would be a violation of the ABM Treaty[14] and an attempt by the United States to circumvent the commitment in article IX "not to transfer to other States, and not to deploy outside its national territory, ABM systems or their components limited by this Treaty."[15]

In addition to making progress on SAM upgrades, the USSR has been able to develop transportable components for the Moscow system that could be proliferated fairly rapidly. Both the upgraded SAMs and the transportable radars and other Moscow system components could be supported by the extensive new large phased-array radar network under construction. Finally, the USSR has been able to conduct research on advanced "exotic" technologies for possible operational applications in the 1990s and beyond. The ABM Treaty has been advantageous for the Soviets in that, despite its constraints, it has allowed them to work on developing capabilities that might at some future point outweigh the advantages of keeping the United States in compliance with the ABM Treaty.[16]

Some West European observers have concluded that the Soviets have chosen a course of keeping their BMD options open through a mix of treaty-permitted deployments and intensive research and development programs. François Heisbourg has referred to the modernization of the Moscow system, the new large phased-array radar network, and the SA-12 as developments that "allow one to think that the USSR is reserving the possibility of leaving the treaty or making it evolve in a direction more favorable to the extension of ABM systems."[17] The British minister of defense, George Younger, has reached a comparable verdict:

> The Soviet Union wishes to explore the scope that new technologies might offer for an effective, active defence of the Soviet homeland against nuclear attack—defence against ballistic missiles which would complement the substantial effort which—unlike the West—the Soviet Union has already been putting into civil defence and defence against aircraft . . . I am not arguing that the Soviet Union is about to deploy such a defence or that there is an intention at this time to do so in the future. It is, perhaps, simply a question of it keeping its options open. What is incontrovertible is that the Soviet Union has not accepted for all time the existing relationship between offensive and defensive forces at the nuclear level.[18]

Soviet BMD activities under the ABM Treaty regime have been so extensive, in conjunction with other offensive and defensive investments, that they have raised questions in the West about their intended purposes and about the risks that might be posed for Western security. According to David Schwartz, "the most difficult situation is not one of a clear Soviet breakout, but one of a more ambiguous nature, wherein Soviet activities are difficult to interpret but suggest that Moscow may intend to achieve the capability for a breakout, not in order to use this capability but to keep it in reserve for a crisis."[19] An even more difficult situation than crisis-breakout capability would perhaps be posed by Soviet "creepout" from the ABM Treaty during normal peacetime conditions.

In contrast to a breakout, which would consist of actions plainly in violation of treaty commitments, a creepout would amount to an evasion of treaty obligations through a complex array of seemingly secondary and/or ambiguous activities. A creepout could, in principle, be under way for years while U.S. and allied intelligence services disputed the significance of fragmentary pieces of evidence. If the Soviet authorities declined to acknowledge the BMD potential of certain systems (for instance, the SA-12) and refused to be forthcoming in sessions of the Soviet-U.S. Standing Consultative Commission, the residual ambiguities could place a U.S. administration at a disadvantage in trying to generate congressional and allied support for a response. The ABM Treaty might in effect be used as a "cover" to disguise a gradual buildup of BMD potential. The judgment of the Office of Technology Assessment should be recalled in this regard: even while feigning compliance with the treaty, the Soviets might "gain a significant unilateral ballistic missile defense capability through treaty violations and through technical advances in systems (e.g., theater ballistic missile defenses) nominally permitted by the treaty."[20]

The creepout possibility cannot be dismissed as implausible. Some U.S. experts on Soviet military affairs consider Soviet creepout from the ABM Treaty "probably a much greater threat" than breakout.[21] As the January 1986 report to the French minister of defense pointed out, "the evolution of technology . . . can be extremely discreet in a closed society such as the USSR."[22] The head of the Planning Department in the West German Ministry of Defense has added that, "in the West . . . the necessity of both individual weapons and complete weapons systems must be explained and justified to a critical public. In the closed system of the Soviet Union, however, it was—and is—relatively easy to deploy the elements of weapons systems in such a way that each element seems of little significance, and sometimes even pointless, whereas when they are eventually brought together they represent a qualitative advance."[23]

On the one hand, the risks for the Soviet Union in an undisguised breakout probably make such a breakout unlikely in any situation other than a war-threatening crisis. On the other hand, the advantages of deliberate ambiguity in a creepout could make this an inviting, low-risk course of action. One may speculate that Soviet policy has been calculated to develop as much breakout potential as possible and perhaps even to creepout to some extent (via SAM upgrades, among other activities), as long as this may be done without provoking the United States and its allies into a vigorous BMD competition and/or the pursuit of substantial offensive force countermeasures. The Soviets may see it as a sensible objective to enhance their lead over the United States in promptly exploitable BMD capabilities without endangering U.S. compliance with the ABM Treaty by engaging in violations or ambiguous activities that the United States would find intolerable. Soviet BMD activities may therefore be calibrated to "a scale designed to minimize U.S. objections and claims of SALT violations."[24] An actual Soviet BMD breakout would be risky to the extent that the United States and its allies would respond with countermeasures.

Since signing the ABM Treaty, the USSR has invested heavily in a broad spectrum of BMD technologies while building up other forms of active and passive defense, as discussed in Chapters 1 and 2. The "mission requirements" interpretation of Soviet motives would explain these activities by alluding, above all, to the need to be able to fulfill military requirements in the event of war. Other incentives, including the "general contingency aim" that seems typical of the Soviet approach to military power, probably also apply: for example, developing advanced-technology systems that might give the USSR a unilateral advantage or, at least, prevent it from falling far behind in a highly visible and politically significant area of competition, should the United States at some point choose to invest seriously in the military applications of such technologies; and cultivating Soviet deployment options that might give the United States incentives to agree in arms control negotiations to limit U.S. BMD deployments that the Soviet Union would find especially disadvantageous in terms of Soviet strategic requirements.

The ABM Treaty has, in short, been valuable for the Soviet Union because it "has left it running virtually alone in the pursuit of effective BMD systems, as the United States has allowed its own efforts to diminish and be buffeted by changes in direction . . . Certainly this is a better arrangement than having to compete."[25] The benefits of noncompetition and the risks of genuine competition probably combine to dispose the Soviets to favor maintaining the ABM Treaty.

The U.S. Strategic Defense Initiative in Soviet Eyes

Given what appears to have been the long-standing Soviet calculus of interests regarding BMD, the U.S. Strategic Defense Initiative (SDI) launched in March 1983 must have come as an unsettling development for the USSR. An eventual increase in U.S. interest in BMD was predictable, given the views of various U.S. officials and the mounting evidence of Soviet BMD activities and of the Soviet ballistic missile threat to U.S. ICBMs and other military assets. But the exact shape of the SDI—a program dedicated by President Reagan to "rendering these nuclear weapons impotent and obsolete"[26] and widely perceived as likely to depend heavily on advanced space-based systems—may have come as a surprise.

This judgment is speculative, of course. The secretive traditions of Soviet statecraft hinder any outside analyst attempting to understand Soviet assessments of U.S. BMD decision making. It is, moreover, often hard to determine whether specific anti-SDI arguments developed by Soviet spokesmen are sincerely held or set forth for a manipulative purpose, with certain audiences in mind. Soviet planning regarding the USSR's long-term political-military strategy is hardly an open book, and BMD is probably one of a number of highly sensitive topics in Soviet strategic analyses.

The SDI would nonetheless seem to be disturbing to the Soviets on at least three grounds: (1) the threat of competition in areas of expensive high-technology where the United States is at a comparative advantage; (2) the risk that certain BMD deployments could erode or even negate established Soviet force advantages in Europe and at the level of the U.S.-Soviet intercontinental balance, and that the SDI could lead to other strategic challenges; and (3) the possibility that the SDI could lead to a fundamental shift in Western attitudes regarding the value of strategic defense.

The Soviets would appear to have several economic incentives to try to avoid a costly high-technology BMD competition, even though they have demonstrated an impressive capacity to invest in strategic systems. The CIA estimated in June 1985 that the growth rate in Soviet strategic force expenditures (offensive and defensive) would be "between 5 and 7 percent a year over the next five years," with a rate of "7 to 10 percent if widespread ABM defenses were deployed." The Soviets might be able to afford this, given the fact that, despite "serious economic problems since the mid-1970s," they have continued to acquire large numbers of new strategic systems and have even increased investments in enhancing force survivability—for instance, through mobile SRBMs, IRBMs, and ICBMs. Moreover, there are "no signs that the Soviets feel compelled to forego important strategic programs or that they will make substantial concessions in arms control in order to relieve economic pressures . . . [S]trategic forces will continue to command the highest resource priorities and therefore will be affected less by economic problems than any other element of the Soviet military."[27] In March 1987, the CIA and DIA estimated that overall Soviet defense spending in constant prices increased in 1986 by about 3 percent, and outlays for SA-10 and SA-12 surface-to-air missiles helped to account for the increase in procurement expenditures.[28]

Economic realities, however, could force the rate of Soviet strategic-force modernization to be stretched out more than in the past. The economic difficulties since the late 1970s and the "sluggish" prospects for growth in the next few years could pose truly constraining choices for the Soviets: "Increasing the share of the GNP devoted to defense will confront the Soviets with the difficult choice of reducing the growth in investment, which is critical to modernizing the industrial base, or curtailing growth in consumption, which is an important factor in the Soviet drive to improve labor productivity."[29]

Soviet leaders have accused the United States of wishing to use the SDI "to exhaust the Soviet Union economically," and have insisted that no such aspirations could succeed: "The Soviet Union has something to respond with to whatever challenge is brought to bear."[30] There is nonetheless probably an element of truth in the concerns about economic implications that the Soviets have conveyed to West European observers. In the words of Hubert Védrine, "the Soviets really do want to save and do without this new stage" of military competition.[31] If the United States pursued the SDI intensively, the costs of Soviet offensive and defensive military programs would be even higher than in the absence of U.S. competition. These costs could hinder modernization of the Soviet economy, particularly in the nonmilitary sectors.

The Soviets have, it appears, been debating for several years the pace at which they should attempt to introduce new nonnuclear weapons such as long-range high-accuracy delivery systems, as well as how to prepare "for the emergence in the very near future of even more destructive and previously unknown types of weapons based on new physical principles."[32] Some Western analysts have speculated that the removal of Marshal Ogarkov from his position as chief of the General Staff in September 1984 was related to his insistence that such weapons should be developed soon, and that "it would be a serious mistake not to consider it right now."[33]

The disagreement probably concerned not the desirability of the USSR's developing such capabilities, but the opportunity costs in pressing ahead rapidly. While due allowance must be made for other factors that no doubt helped to complicate the calculus (considerations of productivity, consumer goods incentives, agricultural investments, and so forth), the ultimate choice may have been between (1) spending more now for greater military power in the near term and (2) recapitalizing the industrial sector to be able to develop military power more effectively in the future.[34]

The trend under Gorbachev seems to favor the latter course. According to CIA and DIA judgments, the military appears to have endorsed this course of action as one likely to "accelerate the introduction of new technology, thus setting the stage for more rapid military modernization in the 1990s. In particular, weapons to be introduced in the mid-1990s will use more sophisticated guidance, sensor, computer, and communication subsystems, which in turn will require advanced microelectronics, design, fabrication, and testing capabilities."[35] The assessment that "Gorbachev has told military leaders that . . . they will have to use resources more effectively"[36] may be related to the concept of "sufficiency" that has become prominent under his leadership.[37]

If the party leadership would prefer to invest more in industrial modernization for long-term military strength, the Soviets must be especially concerned about the challenge of competing in the near term in the areas of costly high technology that have been envisaged for the SDI. In a number of these technologies—high-speed data processing, microelectronics, sensors, guidance—the United States retains an edge that might be widened under the impulse of large investments. The SDI may therefore look to the Soviets like a threat by the United States to capitalize on the comparative weaknesses of the Soviet technological base.

The Soviets may, of course, overestimate U.S. technological prospects. But U.S. and West European experts have concluded that the Soviets probably fear that the SDI and other high-technology U.S. military programs could leave the Soviet Union far behind in space warfare capabilities and in the fundamental technologies of the future, including computers.[38] Previous Soviet military investments could be devalued and rendered less useful if the United States persisted with such a course.[39] The Soviets may also fear that these technologies could threaten their long-standing advantage in conventional military forces in Europe—with battlefield applications of lasers and rail-guns against Soviet armor; defenses against Soviet aircraft and missiles; new means of command, control, communications, and intelligence (C^3I); and so forth.[40]

The Soviet interest in advanced nonnuclear technologies has, as suggested in Chapter 2, grown in conjunction with concern about the undesirable side effects of nuclear weapons and the uncertain controllability of large-scale nuclear operations. An increasing recognition of the limited operational utility of nuclear weapons in regional contingencies—unless specifically designed for confined effects and/or used with some discrimination—may tend simultaneously to lower the probability of Soviet nuclear weapons employment and to enhance Soviet incentives to devise nonnuclear offensive systems and defenses against such systems. The Soviets usually contend that any Western plans to use SDI-related nonnuclear technologies to place the USSR at a disadvantage will be thwarted. According to Mikhail Gorbachev, "Right now, by venturing into an arms race in space, they [the Americans] intend to outpace us in electronics and computers. But, as has been the case many times in the past, we will find a response. It will be an effective response, sufficiently quick and quite likely cheaper than the U.S. program."[41]

In contrast to the "countermeasures" theme of Soviet public diplomacy (that is, that SDI systems could be easily defeated by Soviet offensive-force improvements), "Soviet military discussions of the feasibility of the US SDI reveal a belief that neither the technological hurdles nor the financial cost are insurmountable for the US."[42] General Sergei Lebedev of the General Staff has cited the statements about "remarkable progress" by the director of the Strategic Defense Initiative Organization, Lieutenant General James Abrahamson: "We have to believe him, in order to be on the safe side . . . Even if S.D.I. doesn't look feasible now, we are afraid it will reach the stage where it can't be stopped."[43] Both the impression of a deliberate U.S. decision to build on areas of U.S. technological strength and fear that the United States may succeed in doing so are perhaps enhanced by a U.S. attitude the Soviets may perceive as "patronizing"—that is, the U.S. suggestions that the United States would be prepared to share its SDI research findings with those "less capable" of developing such BMD systems.[44]

In Soviet eyes, one of the strategic risks posed by the SDI is that it might lead to actual BMD deployments in the United States and allied countries that could threaten laboriously established Soviet force advantages. In Europe, Western ATBM capabilities might directly counter new and increasingly accurate Soviet ballistic missiles equipped with nonnuclear warheads and evidently intended to help clear the way for Soviet ground and air offensives. At the intercontinental level, U.S. BMD might in the long term erode or even negate the Soviet advantage in ICBM-based counterforce by threatening to intercept Soviet ICBMs in boost and midcourse flight phases and by protecting U.S. ICBMs and other targets with terminal defenses. U.S. BMD might also degrade the effectiveness of the SLBMs that the Soviets could target against U.S. command and control centers, airbases, naval ports, and other installations.

This risk may appear all the more worrisome for the Soviets in that the SDI has been chartered to investigate space- as well as ground-based defenses, and even to emphasize the former. This could well appear entirely logical to the Soviets, because the United States might require space-based boost-phase and midcourse-intercept capabilities to obtain leverage against the high numbers of Soviet ballistic missiles and warheads and to compensate for U.S. deficiencies in passive defenses. A dramatic lessening of U.S. and allied vulnerability to Soviet military power would be such a great political and strategic setback for the Soviet Union that some Soviet spokesmen may be sincere in claiming to believe that the U.S. goal is to use the SDI to gain strategic superiority.

Moreover, the Soviets have linked space-based SDI systems to anti-satellite systems (ASATS) with their term *space strike weapons.* The Soviet definition of space strike weapons currently includes all space-based systems that could attack targets in space or on earth (including targets at sea and in the atmosphere) and all earth-based systems that could attack satellites in space. (Previous Soviet definitions of space strike weapons are to be reviewed shortly, in conjunction with Soviet arms control proposals.)

U.S. officials seem to be divided on whether the professed Soviet concern about possible U.S. space strike weapons that could attack targets on earth is sincere. Paul Nitze has expressed "skepticism about Soviet seriousness on this point." In his view, "the Soviets know what kinds of systems are being researched in the SDI program. They know that systems effective in an SDI ballistic missile defense would be highly optimized for this purpose and would be unsuitable for attacks on ground targets. They also realize that the United States is developing new offensive systems in its strategic modernization program which are optimized for attacks on ground targets."[45]

Richard Perle has, in contrast, advanced the following hypothesis: "They have . . . discovered a potential for offensive uses of space that we haven't yet discovered. But they seem concerned that we might somehow, in the course of the SDI program, stumble upon offensive technologies, and they're trying to stop that. My guess is that they have already stumbled upon such technologies."[46]

As Perle notes, "the Soviet argument isn't a very logical one," because it would be "far more effective to proceed directly" to the development of offensive weapons.[47] At any rate, in planning for potential military contingencies in the next several years, the Soviets are probably more concerned about possible deployments of ground-based BMD systems to protect military targets in the West than about hypothetical space strike systems for ground-attack purposes. Interceptors capable of neutralizing warheads within the atmosphere would be especially worrisome to the Soviets, because atmospheric drag would facilitate the identification of most low-cost penetration aids. According to Lieutenant General William Odom,

> endoatmospheric systems are feasible and probably well within NATO's capability to deploy in the 1990s. These systems would therefore worry the Soviet planner most . . . A NATO effort to defend cities or other broad area targets would not likely disturb the Soviet planner deeply. Carefully selected military capabilities that are critical to NATO military operations, however, would galvanize his attention . . . [H]e does not have the stockpiles of warheads to overwhelm even a terminal defense system except in limited points. To concentrate on some targets will mean he must give up others.[48]

The more plausible Soviet attacks would probably not, of course, consist of reckless assaults with large numbers of nuclear warheads. As noted in Chapter 2, the Soviet leadership's interest in keeping any unavoidable nuclear operations under its control means that Soviet nuclear attacks—particularly in Europe—would be more likely to be limited and selective. Even ground-based systems of traditional types (depending on their scope and effectiveness) in the Western alliance could therefore diminish the confidence of Soviet military planners.

The countermeasures to BMD in the Western alliance that the Soviets have discussed—attacking components of the defensive systems, overwhelming them with increased numbers of warheads, circumventing them with nonballistic means of attack, and so forth—are hardly cost free. Some of the projected countermeasures (such as "fast-boost" missiles and "hardened" missiles) would involve cost, weight, and performance penalties pointing toward a reduction in the number of Soviet warheads that could be reliably delivered to their targets. Countermeasures adapted to one layer of defense would leave less throwweight for countermeasures against other elements of the defense, even in a relatively simple two-layer system of ground-based terminal defenses.[49]

Some Western analysts have speculated that the Soviets might suspect the SDI is in fact secretly intended to provide defenses for the military targets that they would like to be able to threaten, or that it will ultimately be reoriented toward this purpose, because such defenses would be far more feasible than the population defenses emphasized by the Reagan administration. To the Soviets, the practical utility of defenses of military targets—including means of command and control—may seem so self-evident that they may be tempted to suspect that the U.S. administration's stress on comprehensive population defenses is a strategic deception, intended to mislead the USSR.

"Mirror-imaging" may also lead the Soviets to magnify the significance of the SDI. The Soviets tend to attribute to the United States and the West as a whole the comprehensiveness and continuity that characterize their own approach to strategic planning. The Soviets therefore integrate the SDI into an array of U.S. and allied programs that they see as forming a coherent whole—"emerging technologies" initiatives for ground and air forces in Europe, improvements in C^3I survivability, offensive force modernization (MX ICBMs, B-1 and "stealth" bombers, cruise missiles, Trident SLBMs in the United States and Britain, M-4 SLBMs in France), and so forth. The SDI is seen not in isolation but in combination with a large number of foreseeable and/or potential Western capabilities.[50]

It is also possible that the Soviets think that vigorous U.S. programs in military space systems could give the United States dominance in the "high ground" of the future, an area that the United States has tended to neglect since the 1960s, in comparison to the pace of Soviet military space programs. The Soviets probably recall that in the *Sputnik*-provoked "space race" of 1957–1969, the achievements of the United States revealed overall U.S. technological superiority. From the political standpoint, this was extremely damaging to the Soviet Union, even though the military utility of men on the moon was negligible. Similarly, the Soviets may today fear the political consequences of U.S. BMD and antisatellite capabilities, even if they understand that the military consequences would not be demonstrable short of war, and that the United States might regard these systems' cost effectiveness (narrowly conceived) as unimpressive.[51]

The Soviets may, in other words, fear that the SDI might somehow catalyze the United States into taking military space operations more seriously than in the recent past. The Soviet military space program has emphasized some areas (as noted in Chapter 1) neglected in the United States—for example, heavy-lift transportation, long-endurance manned platforms, and the maintenance of a robust and reliable system of launch capabilities. This suggests an interest in developing the infrastructure (including the logistics and command-and-control capabilities) that would be required for the likely Soviet approach to certain space warfare missions (building on the unique advantages of man-in-the-loop systems). The Soviets are probably concerned about the potential consequences of the United States applying its technological advantages (such as microelectronics and reliable long-lived space components) to the development of military space systems.

Finally, the Soviets may well be concerned about the possibility that the SDI could presage a shift in Western attitudes regarding the value of strategic defense. If the United States and its allies found their vulnerability to Soviet means of long-range attack less acceptable, the Soviets may reason, this could threaten the virtual Soviet monopoly on strategic defenses—active and passive—across the board. It could imply a different psychological attitude in the West. "The concept of mutual vulnerability, upon which Soviet negotiators and planners have traded without accepting for their own planning, could no longer be expected to constrain Western force development."[52] This could lead to the West's competing in areas where the Soviet Union has had the field to itself and has been able to proceed at its own pace. The technological and economic challenge could appear enormous to the Soviets, who may overestimate the likelihood of the West's (1) making such a shift in strategic paradigms (for the Soviets, the value of active and passive defenses seems like self-evident common sense) and (2) following through with the requisite investments.

It should be noted in this regard that the SDI's long-term aim—promoting the obsolescence of ballistic missiles—represents a political challenge to the USSR. If these delivery means were rendered "impotent and obsolete," to use President Reagan's phrase, the forces that have symbolized the Soviet Union's attainment of superpower status would be useless. Such a fundamental change in the "rules of the game" would endanger the Soviet Union's military counter-deterrent. In the Soviet view, it would represent a "trump" move in the military competition even more far-reaching than the Soviet move in the 1950s to leapfrog U.S. bombers and air defenses with ballistic missiles. Although the Soviets may doubt the feasibility of the SDI's maximum goals, they may well be concerned that more modest objectives—BMD deployments in the West of reasonable effectiveness to defend critical military targets—could impose unwelcome costs and raise the risk of a long-term shift in Western attitudes regarding strategic defense.

Soviet Arms Control Policy

The Soviet inhibitions about breakout from the ABM Treaty have probably been confirmed by the emergence of the U.S. SDI, which may have had a certain deterrent effect. A clear-cut Soviet breakout from the treaty could entrench the SDI and enlarge support for it in North America and Western Europe. This could in turn lead to the realization of some of the consequences the Soviets appear to fear in the SDI.

Because the Soviet calculus of interests probably favors maintaining the

ABM Treaty as a constraint on U.S. BMD activities, it would be logical for the Soviets to rely heavily on the ABM Treaty in a political campaign against the SDI. The campaign would be oriented toward returning to the pre-SDI situation, to the maximum extent possible. This would mean reaffirming the ABM Treaty and adding new arms control constraints on U.S. research and development activities, especially those relevant to BMD or ASAT missions.[53]

The Soviets might at some point, as noted earlier, be attracted by the idea of revising the ABM Treaty to prohibit space warfare systems and to confine the BMD competition to traditional ground-based interceptor technologies. For the present, however, the Soviets would probably prefer constraints that would preserve Soviet advantages in BMD break-out potential based on ground-based interceptors of traditional types and that would encourage the United States and its allies to return to their previous low level of interest in pursuing strategic defenses of their own. The USSR could then continue to develop the BMD infrastructure most appropriate for protecting its military assets and conduct research on advanced military technologies at a more deliberate and affordable pace.

An arms control approach with these goals seems much more likely than a force deployment response specifically tailored to the SDI on top of ongoing force-expansion programs, at least in the next few years. For one thing, the Soviets probably know from experience that U.S. force-procurement behavior is so "uncertain and erratic" that responsive military programs could be wasteful if initiated too soon.[54] The SDI is scheduled to be only a research program for the next several years, and such high standards of effectiveness have been established as its goals that its prospects for winning development approval in the early 1990s are uncertain; deployment decisions are even more remote. Indeed, the SDI may proceed at a slower pace than originally envisaged, since funding patterns have fallen short of the figures announced at the outset.[55]

This situation suggests that the Soviets have ample time to monitor the SDI's direction and prospects and to try to achieve a public diplomacy and/or arms control solution before they implement possible military responses. France's Ecole Polytechnique group has suggested that Soviet threats to increase the USSR's arsenal of ballistic missiles to counter any eventual SDI deployments are "perfectly logical, while waiting for precise information on the effective performance of the American ABM systems likely to be deployed, and on the will of the Americans to deploy them."[56]

Another argument against any near-term military solution to the SDI is the relatively inflexible nature of the Soviet force-acquisition process, discussed in Chapter 2. While the process is capable of developing and producing weapons with incremental improvements, it exhibits a certain "stickiness" that "argues against rapid, tailored responses."[57] No hasty responses are likely to be necessary, anyway, given the long lead-times the Soviets will be allowed by the SDI research schedule.

A final argument in favor of using arms control as a means of constraining U.S. BMD activities is that it has been so successful in the past. The Soviets may well recall that their claims about Soviet BMD accomplishments in the 1960s helped to provoke a U.S. BMD program that overtook theirs in funding and in technological quality, whereas the ABM Treaty was followed by a decline in U.S. BMD efforts in the 1970s. Diminished U.S. attention to BMD then allowed the Soviet Union to move forward at its own pace, under the relatively permissive ABM Treaty regime.

Arms control could have other attractions for the Soviets, aside from offering a potential means to limit or delay the SDI. The Soviets often compare the "détente" of the period 1969–1979 with the post-1979 period in ways that suggest a desire to see Western governments return to détente policies. These policies could entail a shift in the climate of opinion in the West that could have the effect of relaxing Western competitive efforts. While this could make SDI research in particular seem less necessary and less worthy of funding, it could also ease Soviet competitive pressures in general. In a period of détente, Western credits and technology become more readily available to the Soviet Union and enrich its technological base and productivity. During the 1969–1979 period of détente, the Soviet Union demonstrated its ability to afford increasing investments in military power, whereas Western governments were less inclined to take full advantage of their technological and economic superiority by developing its military potential.[58] The Soviets might anticipate that this situation could recur if similar political conditions were established.[59]

A broad arms control and détente policy could therefore have multiple purposes in addition to hampering U.S. pursuit of the SDI. Gorbachev's numerous arms control initiatives appear to be aimed at making headway in several domains simultaneously, from chemical and conventional weapons to nuclear and "space strike" systems. Gorbachev has emphasized his wish to manage the military, economic, and technological competition with the West by political means: "To ensure security is increasingly seen as a political problem, and it can only be resolved by political means."[60] It is not clear whether the Soviets truly have a new and comprehensive design for what Gorbachev has called "an all-embracing system of international security"[61] or whether his policies amount to adroit tactical reworkings of traditional themes of Soviet diplomacy.

It is evident, however, that an important and not incidental effect of fostering the emergence of a new détente could be the creation of an inhospitable climate for the SDI. This climate could also promote pressures for an arms control solution on so-called space strike weapons that would be compatible with Soviet preferences. The Soviets are attempting to make the SDI seem the obstacle to large-scale nuclear arms reductions and to a rebirth of détente, an unwelcome hindrance to a relaxation of East-West tensions. In Mikhail Gorbachev's words, "The stubborn desire of the U.S. side to go on with the creation of space weapons has only one end result—the blocking of the opportunity of ending the nuclear arms race . . . The Soviet Union proposes an all-embracing complex of measures which would block all the roads of the arms race whether in space or on earth; whether in nuclear, chemical, or conventional weapons."[62] If this climate of opinion could be successfully cultivated, the SDI's political sustainability could become increasingly uncertain.

If the Soviets had chosen an arms control approach to restrain the SDI and to seek a return to some approximation of the pre-SDI situation, one would expect to discover considerable consistency in Soviet public argumentation about the SDI and in formal Soviet positions in the negotiations and with respect to compliance questions. These activities are closely coordinated in the Soviet government and subject to direction from the Defense Council—a body chaired by the general secretary of the CPSU and composed of top party, military, and government officials. Paul Nitze has reported on the existence of a subordinate committee that handles the implementation of arms control directives:

> The chief of the Soviet negotiating team [Yuli Kvitsinsky] at the negotiations on intermediate-range nuclear forces (INF) told me that there is also [in addition to the Defense Council] a subordinate body, chaired by Foreign Minister Andrei Gromyko, which deals with the day-to-day operations concerned with arms control. On that committee are members of the military establishment; Leonid Zamyatin, who chairs the Central Committee section dealing with the media and propaganda; Vadim Zagladin, who chairs the Central Committee section dealing with relations with other Communist parties and with what they call "political action"; and representatives from the Ministry of Foreign Affairs and the KGB. He left me with the impression that it was this group that formulated his instructions and

coordinated with the political action, propaganda, and other operations which were related to the objectives that their arms control
positions and statements were designed to support.[63]

While institutional and personnel adjustments have been made since
this description was composed,[64] it is reasonable to assume that Soviet
policy regarding SDI and related arms control issues has been as
thoroughly coordinated as was the case with INF. The main elements of
Soviet arms control policy in this domain may be organized under three
headings: ABM Treaty compliance issues, proposals at the Geneva
negotiations, and arguments against U.S. BMD research in Soviet public
diplomacy.

ABM TREATY COMPLIANCE ISSUES
Soviet policy on ABM Treaty compliance issues may be summed up
concisely: the USSR denies having in any way violated the treaty and
accuses the United States of various violations.

The Soviet denials concern, above all, the six issues discussed in
President Reagan's March 1987 report to the Congress on Soviet noncompliance with arms control agreements: the Krasnoyarsk radar, mobile
land-based ABM systems or components, concurrent testing of ABM and
SAM components, ABM capability of modern SAM systems, rapid reload
of ABM launchers, and ABM territorial defense. As was noted in Chapter
1, the Krasnoyarsk radar has been found by the United States to be a
violation of the ABM Treaty, the development of transportable components a "potential violation," the concurrent testing a "highly probable"
violation in "several cases," and the rapid-reload launchers "an ambiguous situation" and a "serious concern." The evidence on SAM upgrade
was found "insufficient to assess compliance" with ABM Treaty obligations. Finally, with respect to territorial defense, the report indicated that
"the U.S. government reaffirms the judgment of the December 1985
report that the aggregate of the Soviet Union's ABM and ABM-related
actions . . . suggests that the USSR may be preparing an ABM defense of
its national territory."[65]

If the working hypothesis outlined in Chapter 2 is correct, the Soviet
construction of the Krasnoyarsk radar calls for some explanation. An
unambiguous violation of the ABM Treaty would be inconsistent with
Soviet interests in maintaining the treaty regime to constrain U.S. BMD
activities. As Bruce Parrott has noted, it is not plausible that the decision
resulted from "a bureaucratic oversight" in which the ABM Treaty's
provisions were overlooked, given the radar's cost and the identity of

those responsible for it. More persuasive interpretations might focus on (1) Soviet doubts in the early 1980s about U.S. plans to comply with the ABM Treaty and other SALT agreements; (2) a Soviet interest in economizing on construction costs by selecting a more optimal location for the radar than on the USSR's periphery; or (3) a Soviet belief that it might be possible to induce the United States to accept the radar, perhaps by comparing it with the modernization of U.S. early-warning radars. These possible explanations are not mutually exclusive.[66]

One may speculate that the Soviets did not expect the United States to react to the Krasnoyarsk radar by accusing the USSR of an unambiguous violation of the ABM Treaty; they may have thought the United States would accept their "space tracker" explanation. They may be chagrined by this development, because widespread perceptions of Soviet ABM Treaty violations in the West could make it easier for the United States to build a case for the SDI or even for abrogation of the ABM Treaty.

No solution to the Krasnoyarsk radar issue was discernible in early 1988. In October 1985, it was reported that the Soviet Union had offered to halt the construction at Krasnoyarsk in return for the United States forgoing plans to modernize its radars at Thule, Greenland, and Fylingdales, England, a proposal rejected by the United States.[67] In February 1987, Georgi Arbatov said that work on the radar had been "deliberately halted," whereas some U.S. analysts reportedly indicated that the site's exterior construction was "fundamentally" finished anyway.[68] In April 1987, General Mikhail Milshtein repeated the argument that the radar was intended to serve space-tracking purposes, but said that his government had offered to "destroy" it. Another Soviet general, Boris Surikov, said that the radar was "not suitable" for BMD and not inconsistent with "the spirit of the ABM Treaty." He added that, "in territorial terms, its location is not quite adequate."[69]

In September 1987, the Soviets followed through with a suggestion made in April 1985 by Anatoly Dobrynin, then Soviet ambassador to the United States, and permitted an inspection of the Krasnoyarsk radar by a small U.S. congressional delegation. As noted in Chapter 1, this visit does not appear to have supplied any significant new evidence bearing on the treaty compliance issue, because early-warning and battle management functions would both violate the treaty, given the radar's location and orientation. Large phased-array radars may, at any rate, be applied to multiple purposes, depending on their design.[70]

Given the sensitive context created by the treaty violation charges and the SDI, it is possible that the Soviets will try to avoid further activities that might be seen as additional unambiguous violations of the ABM

Treaty in the foreseeable future. Rather than provoking an acceleration of Soviet BMD activities, the SDI may be in some ways persuading the Soviets to slow down their BMD activities or at least lower their profile, for fear of providing evidence of ambiguous activities that could help the United States make a stronger case for the SDI within the Western alliance. The Soviet decisions to permit an on-site inspection of the Krasnoyarsk radar and to offer to allow such inspections of additional radars detected at Gomel are consistent with this judgment, because such inspections may persuade some Western observers to accept Soviet assurances regarding the character of the USSR's BMD activities.[71] The Soviets may reason that slowing down the visible pace of Soviet BMD infrastructure expansion and related testing programs would be a small price to pay if it helped weaken the case for U.S. BMD research programs.

Soviet complaints about alleged U.S. treaty violations may be intended to deflect blame and promote a certain equating of the two "superpowers" in public perceptions. The three specific Soviet accusations that have received the most attention concern the June 1984 Homing Overlay Experiment, the construction of early-warning radars in Georgia and Texas, and the modernization of early-warning radars at Thule and Fylingdales. In the Homing Overlay Experiment, a modified Minuteman ICBM was used to attack a target, and the Soviets claim that this violated article VI's commitment not to test non-ABM missiles in an ABM mode; the U.S. response is that the Minuteman was modified so extensively for the test that it was not a non-ABM missile.[72] The early-warning radars in Georgia and Texas are in fact located along the periphery of the United States and oriented outward, as required by the treaty. Finally, the United States has held that the radars at Thule and Fylingdales were in existence when the treaty went into force and were therefore exempted.

The Soviets have also complained that a number of the SDI program's publicly announced test plans may go beyond what is permissible under the treaty and that the SDI research program represents an intention to deploy large-scale defenses that is tantamount to a violation of the ABM Treaty. The Reagan administration, however, has made it clear that SDI research will be conducted within a restrictive interpretation of the ABM Treaty's provisions, even though a broader interpretation would, in its judgment, be justified. Various SDI tests and experiments have been reviewed and modified to ensure full compliance with a restrictive interpretation of the ABM Treaty.[73]

Since October 1985, the Reagan administration has maintained that a broad interpretation of the ABM Treaty would allow the development and testing of space-based BMD systems "based on other physical principles." The administration has based this position on several grounds: above all, its interpretation of the historical record's evidence of Soviet views during the negotiations, apparent ambiguities in certain treaty definitions, and the fact that Agreed Statement D of the ABM Treaty states that limitations on deployments of "such systems and their components would be subject to discussion" and "agreement" in accordance with treaty-specified procedures.[74]

The administration's interpretation has been criticized by a number of experts and congressmen. The Reagan administration and key legislators such as Senator Sam Nunn have disagreed on the meaning of the Senate ratification record, subsequent U.S. declaratory policy, and the negotiating record. Reagan administration officials have interpreted the negotiating record as permitting the development and testing of BMD systems and components based on other physical principles in all basing modes, with any deployments subject to discussion.[75] Senator Nunn has, in contrast, concluded that the negotiating record shows that the Soviets agreed to an interpretation that would prohibit the testing and development of mobile "exotic" BMD systems and components while permitting such testing and development for fixed, land-based systems; but, in his judgment, the deployment of fixed, land-based (and/or mobile) "exotic" BMD systems is banned.[76]

The Soviets have denounced the Reagan administration's broad interpretation as "deliberate deceit."[77] Some Soviet statements, however, have implied that the deployment of fixed, land-based BMD systems based on other physical principles might be permitted, if approved through the consultation and amendment procedures described in Articles XIII and XIV of the treaty. According to an article in *Pravda*, "the possibility of the appearance of such 'exotic' means as replacements for those that previously existed is admitted by the statement in question [Agreed Statement D] only with regard to the limited ABM areas authorized by Article III of the treaty and only with regard to stationary land systems."[78] This position has been upheld in Soviet legal journals as well.[79] The Soviets may, in other words, be suggesting that a ground-based BMD laser could at some point, in accordance with treaty-prescribed procedures, legally replace elements of the Moscow system.[80]

Some Soviet legal judgments about the permissibility of BMD infrastructure development may differ from U.S. interpretations:

> The undertaking not to provide a base for a territorial ABM defense is of fundamental significance . . . It should be taken into account that certain stages of "providing a base" for a territorial ABM defense

can take place even without directly violating the undertaking not to develop, test, or deploy corresponding systems or components of ABM defense. These stages include, for example, the preparation of the necessary infrastructure, communications system, and so forth.[81]

U.S. officials have noted that any future deployments exceeding the ABM Treaty's ceilings would require modifications to the treaty.[82] The treaty, however, provides for amendments, regular joint reviews at five-year intervals, and a Standing Consultative Commission to discuss possible amendments and to consider "possible changes in the strategic situation which have a bearing on the provisions of this Treaty." The U.S. position, as set forth by Paul Nitze, is that

> the treaty was intended to be adaptable to new circumstances, not to lock the United States and the Soviet Union into a strategic relationship that might be less stable and less desirable than other possibilities that might emerge in the future . . . should new defenses be feasible and offer the potential of making a contribution to stability, we and the Soviets should move forward jointly in an agreed manner. To lay the foundation for such an approach, we have offered, even now, to discuss with the Soviets in Geneva the implications of new defense technologies for strategic stability and arms control . . . We urge the Soviets to cease bluntly rejecting this offer and, instead, to take us up on it.[83]

The Soviets have not ceased rejecting this offer and have so far shown no signs of being likely to accept it. In Marshal Akhromeyev's words, the ABM Treaty is "the basis on which strategic stability and international security rest. We are convinced that everybody, including the United States, will stand to lose from a violation of this treaty. The USSR is strictly observing all commitments under the treaty and is not doing anything that would contradict its provisions."[84]

The Soviet stand on ABM Treaty compliance—that the USSR has not violated the treaty in any way, that the United States has violated specific treaty provisions, and that the SDI endangers the treaty as a whole—is closely related to the Soviet position at the Geneva negotiations.

PROPOSALS AT THE GENEVA NEGOTIATIONS

When President Reagan first proposed his Strategic Defense Initiative in March 1983, Soviet attention was focused on the negotiations on intermediate-range nuclear forces (INF) in Geneva and the prospective initial deployments of U.S. Pershing II ballistic missiles and ground-launched cruise missiles in Western Europe. Since no arms control agreement that would make these deployments unnecessary was reached in the two years of negotiations from November 1981 to November 1983, NATO governments followed through with their plan of December 1979 and deployed U.S. INF missiles in Britain, Italy, and West Germany. Part of the Soviet response was to suspend the USSR's participation in both the INF negotiations and the Strategic Arms Reduction Talks (START).[85]

For most of 1984, the Soviet Union refused to return to the Geneva negotiations on nuclear arms control. In June 1984, the Soviets proposed that negotiations begin in September 1984 in Vienna regarding space warfare capabilities—ASATS and BMD. The United States agreed to this proposal, subject to the proviso that the new Vienna negotiations also cover strategic and intermediate-range nuclear forces. The Soviets found this condition unacceptable, and the proposal for negotiations beginning in September 1984 was aborted. As late as November 1984, Soviet spokesmen insisted that "space is an independent problem, and to link the question of preventing its militarization to the question of nuclear armaments is a red herring and a waste of time."[86]

It was not until January 1985 that the Soviets agreed, at the Shultz-Gromyko summit in Geneva, with the U.S. position that offensive nuclear capabilities should be considered at the same time. The Soviets, however, insisted that these would be "entirely new" negotiations (they had previously maintained that they would not return to the INF and START negotiations until the new NATO INF missiles were withdrawn), and that the subject matter was not offensive nuclear forces and defenses against them but "space and nuclear arms." In contrast to their previous insistence on isolating the "militarization of space" issue, when they were not willing to discuss offensive nuclear forces, the Soviets argued that "it was only as a result of persistent, hard work by the Soviet side that the U.S. delegation finally had to adopt the viewpoint that questions relating to space and nuclear armaments are inseparable and must be discussed and solved together."[87]

The change in Soviet policy was perhaps intended to render the SDI more vulnerable by making it appear the obstacle to nuclear arms control. If this was the Soviet intention, the language of the January 1985 communiqué that chartered the negotiations initiated in March 1985 might be read as helpful to this end:

> The sides agree that the subject of the negotiations will be a complex of questions concerning space and nuclear arms, both strategic and intermediate range, with all the questions considered and resolved in their interrelationship. The objective of the negotiations will be to

work out effective agreements aimed at preventing an arms race in space and terminating it on earth, at limiting and reducing nuclear arms and at strengthening strategic stability.[83]

The Soviets have placed particular emphasis on the phrases about the "interrelationship" of "space and nuclear arms" and "preventing an arms race in space."

Prior to the October 1986 Reykjavik summit, the principal Soviet initiative regarding BMD was to ask the United States to pledge not to withdraw from the ABM Treaty for fifteen to twenty years and to conform to a definition of permissible research that the U.S. government considered more constraining "than the strictest American interpretations" of the treaty's provisions.[89] Apparently the only change in Soviet policy before Reykjavik was to suggest that the USSR might be willing to accept an ABM Treaty nonwithdrawal pledge of "up to" fifteen years instead of fifteen to twenty years.[90] The July 1986 U.S. proposal—to delay BMD deployments beyond treaty-permitted ceilings for seven and a half years, and to discuss plans to eliminate all ballistic missiles and to manage mutual BMD deployments and possible BMD benefit-sharing arrangements[91]—was criticized as an invitation to participate in "the legitimizing of the 'Star Wars' program."[92] Soviet spokesmen said that the United States was conceding "absolutely nothing" because "the United States is technologically unable to commence the SDI deployment" until the 1990s.[93] The proposed delay would therefore amount to "impotence being passed as virtue."[94]

At the Reykjavik summit in October 1986, the two sides agreed to the principle of a mutual pledge not to withdraw from the ABM Treaty for ten years. They did not agree, however, on the extent of allowable research, development, and testing or on the permissibility of deployments at the end of the ten-year nonwithdrawal period. The United States proposed that during a ten-year period of nuclear arms reductions, both sides would continue "research, development and testing, which are permitted by the ABM Treaty . . . At the end of the 10-year period, either side could deploy defenses if it so chose unless the parties agree otherwise."[95] Secretary of State Shultz added that, in view of the U.S.-proposed elimination of all ballistic missiles, U.S. BMD deployment plans "would be substantially altered in what was needed and would be in the nature of an insurance policy—insurance against cheating, insurance against somebody getting hold of these weapons."[96]

The Soviet-proposed text at Reykjavik stipulated that "all testing of space-based elements of a ballistic missile defense in outer space will be prohibited except research and testing in laboratories." In contrast to the U.S. view that both sides should be free to deploy defenses at the end of the ten-year period, the Soviets suggested that the sides "must find mutually acceptable solutions."[97] This implied that the USSR would gain a veto right over U.S. BMD deployments after the ten-year period. The Soviets held that no "insurance policy" BMD capabilities would be needed if there were no longer any ballistic missiles.[98] Gorbachev described the idea of approving SDI deployments after ten years as unacceptable: "To eliminate the nuclear weapons as a means of deterring American aggression, and to get the threat from outer space in return— only politically naive people can accept that."[99] The Soviet-proposed text excluded the Moscow system and the other principal elements of the near-term Soviet BMD potential: "That will not require a ban on tests allowed by the ABM Treaty—of fixed land-based systems and their components."[100]

Since the October 1986 Reykjavik summit, the main issues in the defense and space area of the Geneva negotiations have been (1) the duration of the period of mutual commitment to nonwithdrawal from the ABM Treaty; (2) the freedom of the parties to deploy BMD after the period of nonwithdrawal; and (3) the definition of treaty-permitted research. Until the December 1987 summit, the Soviets held that the nonwithdrawal period should be ten years and that subsequent deployment decisions would have to be mutually acceptable. The United States had three proposals on the table, with possible nonwithdrawal periods expiring in 1991, 1994, and 1996. All three proposals would have left either side free to deploy BMD at the end of the nonwithdrawal period, unless both parties agreed otherwise.[101]

At the December 1987 summit, Reagan and Gorbachev agreed to instruct their negotiators "to work out an agreement that would commit the sides to observe the ABM Treaty as signed in 1972, while conducting their research, development, and testing as required, which are permitted by the ABM Treaty, and not to withdraw from the ABM Treaty, for a specified period of time. Intensive discussions of strategic stability shall begin not later than three years before the end of the specified period, after which, in the event the sides have not agreed otherwise, each side will be free to decide its course of action."[102] This formulation did not resolve the definitional questions concerning treaty-permitted research.

Definitions of Permitted Research. The Soviet proposals since 1985 regarding treaty-permitted research have thrown some light on Soviet aspirations. The Soviet proposals have included concepts such as banning "space strike" weapons, prohibiting "purposeful research," and circumscribing permitted research to the "laboratory."

The January 1985 communiqué's phrase about "preventing an arms race in space" seems to have been less favored by the Soviets over time than stopping the "militarization of space" and, more recently, banning "space strike" weapons. The initial Soviet definitions of space strike arms included all space-based systems that could attack targets in space or on earth (including the sea and the atmosphere) and all earth-based systems that could attack targets in space. One of the early Soviet definitions, for example, indicated that the banning of space strike arms would mean "preventing weapons from being placed in space, and banning the use of force in space or from space against the earth. and also from the earth against targets in space. Space strike armaments, based on whatever principles of operation and whatever basing modes, must not be created, tested or deployed either for use in space, or for use from space against targets on earth, in the air, or at sea."[103]

The Soviets subsequently revised this definition, apparently because it was too comprehensive for their own plans. After all, if weapons usable "from the earth against targets in space" were to be outlawed, the ABM Treaty would have to be revised to rule out the only operational ground-based strategic BMD system on earth—the Moscow system. Later Soviet definitions have stressed what they depict as the especially reprehensible character of potential space-based weapons. In 1985, for example, Soviet Defense Minister Sergei Sokolov contended that the United States planned "to create an antimissile shield over the United States, [and] to simultaneously deploy strategic first-strike offensive armaments, new strategic space-based forces intended to hit targets on earth, in the sea, in the atmosphere and in outer space."[104]

From a U.S. viewpoint, the Soviet demand for a ban on so-called space strike weapons implies the establishment of constraints "far beyond the limits of the 1967 Outer Space Treaty and the 1972 ABM Treaty" for these pacts do not, for example, rule out all antisatellite (ASAT) weapons, and the Soviets have already tested ASAT systems.[105] Moreover, some BMD systems may be applied to ASAT missions: the Galosh interceptor, especially in its modified form, could be used against low-orbit satellites. It seems that the Soviet definition would probably exclude space-based elements of ground-based systems (for example, the Soviet satellites that would provide early warning of ballistic missile attack and perhaps some pointing and tracking data). It might also be noted that some space-based elements of advanced-technology concepts might be virtually inert (such as laser mirrors or information relay stations in space) yet indispensable to a weapons system as a whole. The Soviet meaning has yet to be fully clarified.

It is clear, however, that the Soviet-proposed ban on what they term space strike weapons would constrain research on such systems. During the negotiations at Geneva in 1985, the Soviet negotiators argued that even "scientific research" in support of developing "space strike arms" should be forbidden.[106] According to Paul Nitze,

> the Soviets are already positioning themselves, however, to avoid having such a ban apply equally to the research of both sides. They currently deny that any of their efforts fall within their definition of research "designed to create space-strike arms," while asserting that all of the U.S. SDI program fits within that definition. Moreover, even were a research ban to be applied equally to the sides, given its inherent unverifiability and the closed nature of the Soviet Union— and particularly its scientific community compared to ours—the Soviets very well might be able unilaterally to continue their research on a clandestine basis.[107]

Some suggestions of movement in late 1985, however, implied that the demand for a blanket prohibition of all research was simply an opening bargaining position. In September 1985, Mikhail Gorbachev said that

> what we have in mind is not research in fundamental science. Such research concerning space is going on and it will continue. What we mean [to ban] is the designing stage, when certain orders are given, contracts are signed, for specific elements of the systems. And when they start building models or mockups or test samples, when they hold field tests, now that is something—when it goes over to the designing stage—that is something that can be verified.[108]

Similarly, in October 1985, Marshal Akhromeyev indicated that "the USSR views as impermissible any out-of-laboratory work connected with the development and testing of models, pilot samples, separate assemblies and components. Everything that is done for the subsequent designing and production of space strike systems should be banned."[109]

These Soviet definitions of permitted research were consistent with the apparent Soviet aim of blocking both the SDI and the development of associated U.S. ASAT capabilities. In January 1986, a new Soviet distinction was reported by U.S. officials: "purposeful" and "nonpurposeful" research, with only the latter to be permitted.[110] In response, U.S. negotiators pointed out that the concept of purposeful research does not figure in the ABM Treaty; nor does the treaty even include the word *research,* because neither the U.S. nor the Soviet delegations to the SALT I negotiations believed it feasible to monitor limits on research.[111] According to Paul Nitze, "Soviet work in these areas is clearly in applied research and development, not merely in basic research as they would have us believe ... The Soviet concept of 'purposeful research' is an artificial distinction designed to exploit the fact that the United States openly states the goals of its research and, therefore, that it is 'purposeful.' The Soviet claim that their research is 'fundamental' and has no purpose is not credible."[112]

In mid-to-late 1986, the Soviets offered several indications that their previous position—in the words of General Nikolai Chervov, that "everything was to be banned, including research"—would be abandoned in order "to stimulate discussion" and promote offensive-force reductions.[113] Soviet officials said that, as "a concession to Ronald Reagan," they would authorize laboratory tests in SDI research.[114]

The text proposed by the Soviets at Reykjavik, as noted earlier, would have prohibited all testing in space of space-based elements of BMD systems. According to Gorbachev,

the president insisted until the end that the United States retained the right to test, have experiments and to test things relating to SDI not only in the laboratories but also out of the laboratories, including in space. So who was going to accept that? It would have taken a madman to accept that. But madmen normally are in hospitals. I don't see madmen in important positions running governments.[115]

Gorbachev's insistence that "development of this program should not be put in space but should remain within laboratory walls"[116] has since been qualified by other Soviet statements. Some have suggested that the United States recognize that "a laboratory is not [necessarily] a four-walled building."[117] On the one hand, most Soviet statements have underlined that "the main thing is that no testing whatsoever in space can be permitted."[118] On the other hand, a Soviet scientist, Roald Sagdeyev, has stated that "some tests could be carried on in space," because "we scientists consider manned space stations as orbital laboratories." In Sagdeyev's view, assessments on the permissibility of specific experiments under the ABM Treaty—for example, whether a particular laser test would be "modest" or "destabilizing"—"should be done by experts in Geneva or in the Standing Consultative Commission."[119]

Sagdeyev's concept, which could grant the USSR a certain oversight role over the conduct of the SDI program, does not appear to have been adopted as official Soviet policy at this point. Foreign Minister Eduard

Shevardnadze has stressed that the research limitations proposed by the USSR would include "the testing of the cosmic elements of the ABM defense in outer space . . . Laboratory research, including the building of ready samples, prototypes of corresponding defensive systems, will be allowed for 10 years."[120] The November 1986 Soviet text outlining a future course for the negotiations repeated the Soviet stipulation that the ban on the testing in space of space-based BMD system components "would not entail a ban on the testing of fixed landbased systems permitted under the ABM Treaty, or their components."[121] Some Western diplomats have speculated that this might mean Soviet approval of ground-based lasers in addition to ground-based interceptor missiles and radars, but it is not clear whether the Soviets intend to foster such an interpretation.[122]

Secretary of State Shultz has drawn a contrary interpretation—that the Soviets seek "a prohibition on all testing outside laboratories—except testing of the sort of ABM system the Soviets now have around Moscow." In Shultz's view, the Soviet position would, in effect, "amend" the ABM Treaty.[123] According to Paul Nitze, the Soviet-proposed constraints would be "far more severe than those imposed even by the 'narrower' interpretation of the ABM Treaty." Even under the restrictive interpretation of the ABM Treaty that the United States has observed, Nitze has added, both parties have been free to use the distinction between "research" and "development" outlined by Harold Brown in a statement to the Soviet SALT I delegation in 1971: "Research includes conceptual design and testing, conducted both inside and outside the laboratory. Development follows research and precedes full-scale testing of systems and components designed for actual deployment."[124] Moreover, the Soviet-proposed restrictions on the testing of space-based systems in space would contradict (1) Soviet practice and (2) agreed interpretations in the U.S.-Soviet Standing Consultative Commission about permissible testing.[125]

The U.S. government's view has been that the Soviets are attempting "to amend the ABM Treaty indirectly by reopening questions of permitted and prohibited activities under the Treaty."[126] According to Shultz, the Soviet object is "to restrict research in such a way as to cripple the American S.D.I. program."[127] This impression has been confirmed by Soviet statements. Soviet officials have reportedly indicated that their definitions of permitted research would block SDI tests that the United States regards as consistent with a restrictive interpretation of the ABM Treaty—for example, the Airborne Optical System, a sensor mounted on a Boeing 767 and intended to aid in the detection of incoming warheads.[128] The Soviet negotiator Viktor Karpov has said that the Soviets have proposed a ten-year prohibition of "the testing of space ABM elements in outer space" in order to pose "an obstacle for the deployment of such systems right after the 10-year period expires."[129]

The December 1987 summit formula of "research, development, and testing as required, which are permitted by the ABM Treaty," has been interpreted differently by the USSR and the United States. The Soviets have continued to reject the U.S. "broad interpretation" and hold that U.S. BMD activities contrary to the traditional interpretation (as viewed by the Soviets) would be grounds for a Soviet withdrawal from negotiated limits on strategic nuclear forces. Soviet proposals since mid-1987 for negotiations on a list of treaty-permitted activities—types of possible space-based devices to be barred from testing in space by mutual agreement—have raised questions in the United States about verification and the risk that overly restrictive limits could amount to amendments to the ABM Treaty. The Soviets seem to be interested in devising constraints that would make potential SDI developments more predictable and manageable for the USSR. While the Soviets have reportedly indicated that some types of system components could be tested in space, they have suggested limits on the brightness of space-based lasers, the size of space-based mirrors, the speed of kinetic interceptors, and so forth.[130]

From a Soviet perspective, it appears, neither the broad nor the restrictive U.S. interpretation of the ABM Treaty is satisfactory. The Soviets have not, moreover, been pleased with U.S. proposals for an "open laboratories" arrangement, whereby "both sides would provide information on each other's strategic defense research programs and provide reciprocal opportunities for visiting associated research facilities and laboratories."[131] The proposals have formed part of the U.S. invitations to the Soviets to pursue strategic defense improvements jointly. In Soviet eyes, such proposals probably seem intended to help legitimize the SDI and the U.S. "strategic concept" for a "cooperative transition" to a defense-dominant relationship between the United States and the Soviet Union.

Cooperative Transition Concepts. The U.S. strategic concept for relating the SDI to nuclear arms control was devised by U.S. officials in preparing for the January 1985 Shultz-Gromyko summit. As noted in the Introduction, this concept calls for radical reductions in offensive nuclear weapons over a ten-year period, to be followed by a transition phase in which defenses become dominant. As the defenses become more and more dominant, the concept suggests, the transition could lead to the elimination of all nuclear weapons. The U.S. concept, in other words, favors Soviet-U.S. cooperation in introducing defenses in tandem with offensive force reductions.[132] In the U.S. view, the United States could accept the phrase proposed for the January 1985 communiqué—the goal of "preventing an arms race in space"—because "the SDI concept we are pursuing is, in fact, the opposite of an 'arms race.' SDI envisions a jointly managed approach designed to maintain proper control, at all times, over the mix of offensive and defensive systems of both sides."[133]

The highest-level Soviet response has come from Gorbachev:

> We cannot take in earnest the assertions that the SDI would guarantee invulnerability from nuclear weapons, thus leading to the elimination of nuclear weapons. In the opinion of our experts (and, to my knowledge, of many of yours), this is sheer fantasy. However, even on a much more modest scale, in which the Strategic Defense Initiative can be implemented as an antimissile defense system of limited capabilities, the SDI is very dangerous. This project will, no doubt, whip up the arms race in all areas, which means that the threat of war will increase.[134]

Gorbachev's choice of words about the U.S. strategic concept ("sheer fantasy" and "very dangerous") is restrained in comparison with the formulations employed by less prominent Soviet spokesmen. Marshal Akhromeyev, for example, has described it as a means for U.S leaders "to cover up their aggressive designs" with "deceiving" and "manipulations." Akhromeyev argues that "propaganda aside, the essence of the American Star Wars program boils down to the treacherous aim of giving the United States the potential to make a first nuclear strike at the Soviet Union with impunity and deprive it, by creating a national antimissile defense, of the opportunity to make a retaliatory strike."[135]

The Soviets have made four key points in rejecting the U.S. strategic concept for a cooperative transition to a defense-dominant U.S.-Soviet relationship. First, the idea of a cooperative arrangement whereby BMD systems would be phased in during reductions in offensive missile forces contradicts the Soviet understanding of the competitive relationship between the "two world systems" and their strategic armaments. In the Soviet perspective, the relationship is a struggle for advantage largely dependent on self-help (moderated by arms control agreements) for whatever stability it exhibits. The Soviets therefore argue that the SDI "destabilizes the strategic situation, impels the other side to restore the situation either by the buildup of its strategic offensive armaments, or by supplementing them with anti-missile systems, or, most likely, both."[136] The Soviets, in other words, tend to interpret the SDI as an American attempt to undermine the effectiveness of Soviet nuclear strike forces, not as an opportunity for both sides to reduce their vulnerability to ballistic missile attack.

Second, because the Soviets see the relationship as profoundly competitive, they are not inclined to favor U.S. arms control propositions calling for "agreed schedules for introducing the defensive systems of both sides, and associated schedules for reductions in ballistic missiles and other nuclear forces."[137] The Soviets evidently judge that their BMD-relevant technologies are on the whole inferior to those of the United States, and therefore fear that the United States could readily surge ahead of the Soviet Union if they legitimized the SDI by agreeing to more expansive definitions of permissible research and approved the idea of large-scale BMD deployments.

The Soviets do not trust the United States to share technology in the interests of stability, despite President Reagan's offers. Soviet spokesmen have contended that, "essentially, all this talk about 'readiness to share technology' is pure demagoguery and nothing more."[138] Gorbachev has said that he told the president at Reykjavik, "I cannot take this idea of yours seriously, the idea that you will share results on S.D.I. with us. You don't want to share with us even equipment for dairy plants at this point, and now you're promising us that you're going to share results on S.D.I. development?"[139] Rather than expressing confidence in U.S. technology-sharing promises, Soviet commentators have repeatedly articulated a fear that, if the United States deployed the systems envisaged in the SDI, "Washington's strategists may have the temptation, under the cover of the space anti-missile shield, to risk the use of nuclear and space weapons for dealing a strike on the Soviet Union and its allies, counting to go off with impunity."[140]

A related point with respect to technological asymmetries is the fact that the Soviet approach to large-scale BMD deployments would almost certainly differ from the space-based emphasis the United States has given to the SDI. As noted in Chapter 1, current Soviet BMD deployments and the systems likely to be used in any large-scale expansion in the next decade consist of ground-based defenses of essentially traditional types. The Soviet Union would, moreover, have different BMD requirements, owing to its substantial investments in passive defenses and the specific missions assigned to its armed forces in the event of war. While the hypothesis of Soviet agreement to a schedule for simultaneous BMD deployments of the advanced sort favored in the SDI seems to be of remote probability in any case, the technological asymmetries imply that, if the United States pursued the SDI program intensively, the Soviets might have either the humiliation of publicly accepting U.S. technology or that of being visibly inferior in their actual deployments. Any attempt to establish comparability and parity in BMD capabilities for a schedule of simultaneous deployments would require a degree of open information sharing that would probably be rejected by the Soviets.

Third, the U.S. strategic concept is illegitimate in Soviet eyes because it would aim to establish a form of enduring deterrence based on superior defensive technologies. All concepts of enduring, stable deterrence—whether brought about through a cooperative transition to defense dominance or as the de facto result of unilaterally devised military postures—are ideologically unacceptable to the USSR, to the extent that they imply freezing the political status quo. In the Soviet view, it is a fact that the USSR shares certain practical "common interests" with the West (above all, avoiding catastrophic nuclear war); but this fact does not mean that the Soviets believe that East and West have common interests in maintaining the current political situation.[141] The Soviets have argued that mutual U.S.-Soviet deterrence cannot last in the long run, and that enduring peace can be established only by "rebuilding the entire structure of international relations" along Soviet-proposed lines.[142]

Even a revival of détente in East-West relations would not be sufficient, in the Soviet view. In the words of Mikhail Gorbachev, "detente is not the end goal of politics. It is needed but only as a transitional stage from a world cluttered with arms, to a reliable and all-embracing international security system."[143] According to Georgi Arbatov,

> we have reached the point at which deterrence has proved to be a temporary solution, which we can leave behind by moving only in two directions. The first is to display the ability to fight and win a war, with all the known concepts of the limited nuclear war . . . One instance of such an approach is that of Star Wars. The second way is the quest for collective security not directed against anybody, because security is indivisible.[144]

What the Soviets mean by "collective security" and "indivisible" security as a permanent solution that should replace the "temporary solution" of mutual deterrence is rarely made clear in remarks directed to Western audiences. Vadim Zagladin in 1983 told a group at a Stockholm International Peace Research Institute conference that "the security of one country cannot be achieved by creating a threat to other countries, or by undermining the security of other countries and peoples . . . The only acceptable principle of security in our time is the parity and equal security of all countries . . . Security in our time can only be ensured by the efforts of all members of the world community, acting together."[145] In a book he edited in the Soviet Union in 1982, in contrast, Zagladin included lengthy chapters about "man's revolutionary transition from capitalism . . . to socialism and communism"; the book analyzed in detail the objective utility of the détente of the 1970s in weakening the West and helping to shift the overall "correlation of forces" in a direction favorable to Soviet interests and ultimate Soviet victory in the long-term competition with "imperialism."[146]

As John Van Oudenaren has suggested, an advantage of vague formulations such as "collective security" in Soviet statements for Western consumption is that they obscure the fact that "no Soviet official can . . . concede the right of 'bourgeois' societies to exist and to defend themselves from external threat."[147] Soviet analyses intended for domestic audiences have long held that permanent and universal peace can be established only by the elimination of the sources of war (above all, "imperialism") and the triumph of Soviet-style socialism. Soviet spokesmen therefore reject (as in the above statement by Arbatov) any concept of an enduring "armed peace" based on an equilibrium of military capabilities, for a lasting arrangement of that type would be seen as delaying the progressive establishment of perpetual and indivisible peace.[148] At the same time, the Soviets regularly affirm their preference for a nonviolent victory over "imperialism." Indeed, according to Mikhail Gorbachev, "the outcome of the historical competition between the two systems cannot be determined by military means. Our commitment to the policy of peaceful coexistence is evidence of the strength of the new social system, of its faith in its historical possibilities."[149]

A fourth and final reason reinforces the other grounds for rejecting the U.S. strategic concept. If the Soviet Union endorsed the idea of cooperating with the United States in jointly managing a safe transition to a defense-dominant world, it would "legitimize" the SDI. In Mikhail Gorbachev's words, "If the laboratories are to be opened, then it is only for purposes of verification of compliance with the ban on the creation of offensive space weapons, and certainly not to legitimize them."[150] Giving the Soviet stamp of approval to the strategic concept associated with the SDI would help clear the way to its pursuit; and this would be contrary to Soviet interests in seeking unilateral strategic advantage.[151] While the Soviets assert (and may sincerely believe) that the concept of a mutually beneficial defense-dominant world is simply an "imperialist" ruse, they are probably more concerned about the risk of an intense BMD competition with the United States. The Soviet Union therefore appears unlikely to endorse the U.S. strategic concept of substantially reducing offensive forces while expanding active defenses to create a defense-dominant strategic relationship.

The current Soviet reactions may nonetheless not be the USSR's last word on the subject. A version of the strategic concept now favored by the United States was once urged by the Soviet Union. In the early 1960s, the USSR argued for what was known as the Gromyko plan. This Soviet proposal "called for the two nations to reduce their offensive missile forces to extremely low levels under an ABM screen that would protect populations and forces."[152] This proposal was, of course, made in a different strategic context—one in which the USSR was concerned about a U.S. lead in ballistic missile forces. It appears to have been defeated by political factors and by technological realities. Both the USSR and the United States were then beginning to perform research on multiple independently targeted reentry vehicles (MIRVs), and the available BMD technology was assessed as incapable of countering foreseeable MIRV expansion. But the Gromyko plan shows at least a precedent in Soviet policy for the concept of defense dominance in the context of drastic nuclear arms reductions.

The main argument that has been advanced for a possible change in Soviet policy in the long term is not the precedent of the Gromyko plan, however, but the fact that the Soviet Union has long been dedicated to the strategic goal of damage limitation. If BMD systems of sufficient effectiveness eventually became feasible (in conjunction with highly capable air defenses and other forms of strategic defense), it has been argued, the Soviets might no longer be able to hope to achieve damage-limiting goals through counterforce strike capabilities or through "counterdeterrent" nuclear threats "restraining" their adversaries. If further offensive force expansion then appeared futile and ineffective, the Soviets might see some attraction in cooperating in the establishment of a defense-dominant arms control regime, for such a regime could offer some promise for the fulfillment of Soviet damage-limiting goals. Radical offensive-force reductions might assure both sides that neither could seek strategic superiority or make a significant "first strike"; this would address at least one of the Soviet arguments against the U.S. strategic concept.[153] As the Office of Technology Assessment has noted, however, "the argument that sufficiently great U.S. technical success would force the Soviets to cooperate in their own security interests is logically compelling, but there can be no assurance that the Soviets would actually behave as we think they should."[154]

Another argument for possible eventual Soviet acceptance of the defense-dominant concept has been suggested by some West European observers in private interviews. They note that a Soviet-U.S. relationship of defense-dominance would neutralize U.S. capabilities to threaten the USSR with long-range strike systems and would therefore provide what the Soviets have sought since their 1972 proposal to the Nixon administration: an effective end to U.S. extended deterrence guarantees, through an agreement not to threaten U.S. or Soviet territory with nuclear weapons. The defense-dominance arrangement would, however, have the disadvantage in Soviet eyes of eliminating U.S. vulnerability to Soviet long-range strikes; and the Soviets seem far more likely to prefer to continue to seek unilateral advantages in strategic-offense and -defense capabilities. From the Soviet perspective, it probably appears preferable to degrade the credibility of U.S. extended deterrence guarantees through unilateral means, including nuclear counter-deterrent and strategic-defense capabilities, than to legitimize the SDI and the associated U.S. strategic concept.

Prospects for fundamental change in the Soviet attitude toward the SDI and the U.S. strategic concept for defense dominance seem quite speculative at this point. The Soviets appear to judge that their interests reside in keeping U.S. strategic-defense efforts politically constrained while continuing to develop Soviet strategic defenses of all types, active and passive, and continuing to expand and improve Soviet offensive forces. As Paul Nitze has acknowledged, the Soviets "see little advantage in moving cooperatively to a more defense-reliant regime under which their current advantages in both offense and defense would be reduced or balanced."[155]

In other words, the calculus of interests that evidently led to Soviet approval of the ABM Treaty will probably continue to guide the Soviet approach to the Geneva negotiations. The Soviets are committed to investing in all forms of strategic defenses, but space warfare capabilities (BMD and ASAT) constitute an area of likely U.S. technological advantage they would prefer to see limited. To help keep such U.S. capabilities limited, the ABM Treaty must be reaffirmed and the SDI portrayed as an unprecedented threat to international security.

If the SDI could be defeated politically, the Soviets may reason, it might be possible to restore an approximation of the pre-SDI situation: an ABM Treaty regime under which the Soviet Union could quietly continue to deploy systems with some BMD potential on a large scale (such as the SA-12) and develop an infrastructure and missiles and radars suitable for a fairly rapid breakout, should exercising that option seem advisable at some point. Moreover, an ambiguous creepout with respect to certain ABM Treaty provisions might proceed as well. The creepout course of action would probably be, as noted earlier, more attractive than an explicit breakout.

The key point is that Soviet BMD activities could be carried forward for greater unilateral advantage if competition from the United States in the form of the SDI could be prevented. This assessment helps to explain why the Soviets reject the U.S. strategic concept for an arms control agreement that could aid the United States in pursuing the SDI. As Defense Minister Sokolov put it in 1985, "the United States should give up attempts to impose upon the Soviet Union an agreement, unacceptable to it, an agreement that would open the door wide for realisation of Washington-planned military programs."[156]

A compromise agreement—one permitting BMD deployments on a smaller scale than in the defense-dominant world envisaged in the U.S. strategic concept but beyond those allowed in the ABM Treaty—is more likely to be acceptable to the Soviets than one authorizing the United States to pursue the development of what the Soviets call "space strike weapons." Some Americans have speculated about possibly revising the treaty to allow the United States to defend its vulnerable ICBMs and other critical targets, such as key command, control, and communications (C^3) sites. Although the Soviet Union is unlikely to see many advantages in alleviating a vulnerability it has worked so hard to create for Soviet damage-limiting and escalation control purposes, it is possible that the Soviets might at some point see a net benefit to the USSR in revising the ABM Treaty to permit a proliferation of ground-based BMD interceptors of traditional types. The Soviets might benefit asymmetrically from an expansion of such ground-based BMD systems owing to the more defensible nature of the Soviet target set, Soviet advantages in active and passive defenses, and Soviet quantitative superiority in ICBM throw-weight and warhead numbers (to penetrate U.S. terminal defenses).[157] Yet the Soviets may fear that any deviation from the ABM Treaty's constraints on U.S. BMD efforts could lead to an unregulated momentum of expansion, and that improved U.S. military space capabilities might unavoidably follow the ground-based interceptor deployments.

Nuclear Arms Control. The relationships between these possible assessments and recent U.S. and Soviet nuclear arms control proposals have yet to be fully clarified. The possibility, for example, that the Soviets might benefit from the licensing of an expansion in permitted ground-based BMD deployments of traditional types depends in part on the assumption that the USSR would retain a substantial advantage in ICBM throw-weight and warhead numbers. But U.S. proposals have called for severe reductions in this Soviet-U.S. disparity, and the Soviets have agreed that the envisaged strategic arms reductions should include "a significant number of heavy missiles." At the same time, however, the Soviets expect reductions to take into account "the historically formed features" of each side's strategic posture.[158] While this implies continuing relative advantages in ICBM throwweight and warhead numbers for the Soviet Union, whether those advantages would be sufficient for Soviet purposes would depend on the scope of U.S. BMD deployments.

Soviet interest in tightening the ABM Treaty's constraints on U.S. BMD research and in establishing new limitations on related U.S. research and development activities (for example, ASAT) has been apparent since the Geneva negotiations began in 1985. The Soviets appear to be looking beyond the uncertain fate of the SDI to the likelihood that SDI-related research could spur technological advances in various types of military equipment, including C^3I systems. For example, confining SDI tests to the laboratory could hinder the West's development of detection and guidance technologies and associated applications of information processing for nonnuclear long-range offensive and defensive systems. New limits on nuclear tests could inhibit the development of means of hardening these new technologies against nuclear effects. In other words, the Soviets may see bringing about a slowdown in the development of SDI-related technologies as a means (1) to make the SDI itself more vulnerable to political and arms control interdiction and (2) to circumscribe U.S. research and development in key areas of advanced technology relevant to both nonnuclear and nuclear military operations.[159]

It is possible that the Soviets are more interested in perpetuating and strengthening the existing constraints on U.S. BMD activities and related areas of high technology than in achieving their declared goal of total nuclear disarmament. The most practical Soviet priority is probably an explicit U.S. agreement to a multiyear pledge (ten years in current proposals) not to withdraw from the ABM Treaty. The Soviets may judge that such a pledge (which would represent a noteworthy change from the six months' notice currently required by the treaty) could have the effects of (1) reducing congressional support for near-term BMD deployments and (2) limiting research and engineering development work for both near-term and advanced deployment options.

In 1986 and 1987 the Soviets seem to have experimented with linking and delinking INF agreements to their SDI-related proposals. They appear, for example, to have made a formal agreement on an INF "zero option" dependent on new restrictions on U.S. SDI-related research at the October 1986 Reykjavik summit because they hoped to translate West European support for such an agreement into pressure on the SDI. When it became clear that this strategy would not work, the Soviets decided in early 1987 to follow through with the INF zero option, thereby advancing several aims: to create a climate of arms control progress unfavorable to the SDI, to remove all U.S. missiles capable of striking the USSR from European soil, to provoke doubts in Western Europe about the reliability of U.S. deterrence commitments, to promote a process of denucleariza- tion in Western Europe, and so forth. The Soviets have in recent years made it clear they expect that a new phase of détente in East-West relations would result in a general slowdown in Western defense efforts and an increase in Western loans and technology transfers to the Warsaw Pact.

In October 1987, Gorbachev conditioned the holding of a summit devoted to the signing of an INF accord to agreement on "key provisions" regarding START and the future of the ABM Treaty, but dropped the condition within a week when it was apparent that it would not produce immediate U.S. concessions regarding the SDI.[160] The December 1987 INF accord was apparently seen as sufficiently useful for Soviet interests to be concluded without any linkage to the SDI. It consists of a "double zero" eliminating all U.S. and Soviet land-based missiles with ranges between 1000 and 5500 km (long-range INF such as Soviet SS-4s and SS-20s and U.S. Pershing IIs and ground-launched cruise missiles) and between 500 and 1000 km (short-range INF such as Soviet SS-12/22s and SS-23s). This accord could simplify the challenges facing Soviet offensive attack planning (and Soviet ATBM and air defense systems) by removing U.S. INF missiles from Europe and barring future U.S. deployments of land-based missiles—with nuclear or nonnuclear warheads—with ranges of 500 km to 5500 km. The Soviet Union could retain a large numerical advantage over NATO in SRBMs (such as SS-21s) with ranges below 500 km; but the accord could make NATO pursuit of ATBM capabilities less likely, because of the planned elimination of missiles with ranges between 500 and 5500 km. By creating an apparent gap in the range capabilities of Soviet ballistic missiles (SS-21s in Europe as opposed to ICBMs such as the SS-25), the accord could also make U.S.–West European cooperation in devising a BMD architecture for the Western alliance as a whole seem less plausible and necessary.

The Soviets may, however, be willing to negotiate reductions in their residual advantages in SRBM capabilities in return for greater political-military benefits that might be derived through further arms control agreements. The Soviet negotiator Viktor Karpov has described the INF accord as "a first step toward a denuclearized Europe."[161] Pressures for a "triple zero" diminishing the U.S. nuclear presence in Europe may be stimulated by the December 1987 double-zero accord, especially in socialist and social democratic circles in Western Europe. Such pressures could make the modernization of remaining U.S. nuclear forces in Europe more difficult.

The priority that the Soviets attach to nuclear disarmament measures is partly explained by their desire to make the Warsaw Pact's conventional-force superiority more useful politically and to reduce risks of nuclear employment in the event of war. The denuclearization of Western Europe could dramatically reduce NATO's capacity to create nuclear contingencies that could threaten Soviet control over the course of military operations and hinder Soviet attempts at coercion short of war. The credibility of U.S. nuclear guarantees could be fundamentally compromised.

In the context of Reykjavik and other Soviet proposals to reduce and otherwise restrain Western nuclear options, the Soviet initiatives for conventional-arms control in an Atlantic-to-the-Urals framework appear to be intended to advance the Soviet Union's denuclearization aims in Europe by neutralizing Western recognition of the Warsaw Pact's conventional force superiority. While the U.S. nuclear presence in Western Europe historically has been justified by various considerations (the risk of Soviet aggression or coercion, the deterrent effect of nuclear arms, and so forth), the need to counter the conventional preponderance in Europe of the Soviet Union has been an important factor in Western security policy. If the Soviets could use a new arms control forum to persuade Western publics that the existing conventional-force relationship in Europe is one of overall parity (as they have asserted for years in their public diplomacy), they could deprive the U.S. nuclear presence in Europe of one of its main political-military rationales. The Soviets appear to favor the establishment of a new conventional arms control forum to promote a negotiated withdrawal of the U.S. military presence in Europe while pursuing a *droit de regard* over Western Europe's conventional-defense arrangements.[162]

Beyond Europe, however, the possibility that the Soviet campaign for complete nuclear disarmament is disingenuous cannot be excluded. The Soviet Union has invested a great deal in its nuclear strike capabilities. These forces constitute (together with the rest of the Soviet military posture) the USSR's main claim to superpower status—more important, in some ways, than the Soviet Union's collection of clients and allies around the world, and one of the guarantors of the subservience of Soviet clients and allies. The Soviet leadership almost certainly regards its nuclear assets as relevant to Soviet security in contexts other than East-West relations in Europe—with respect to China, above all.

It is possible, therefore, that the extraordinary ambitions declared in Soviet arms control policy (for instance, global nuclear disarmament by the year 2000) are intended to serve purposes other than concluding treaties for implementation. The broad purposes might include encouraging a certain "delegitimization" of nuclear weapons in Western societies and putting the United States and other Western governments on the defensive by underlining their dependence on nuclear threats that Western public opinion seems to find less acceptable. One of the more specific purposes might be reinforcing the Soviet public diplomacy campaign against the SDI.

ARGUMENTS AGAINST U.S. BMD RESEARCH

Many of the arguments raised by Soviet commentators have already been reviewed, because ABM Treaty compliance issues and the Geneva negotiations have been central to the Soviet campaign against the SDI. The long-standing emphasis in Soviet anti-SDI commentary on the Soviet Union's capacity to counter the SDI with offensive and defensive systems has been supplemented with an increasing stress on the need for an arms control solution interdicting the SDI.[163]

The "countermeasures" theme persists, however. It has been somewhat self-contradictory in that the Soviets have maintained simultaneously (1) that the USSR has not done any research on "space strike" weapons nor engaged in any activities inconsistent with the ABM Treaty;[164] (2) that the USSR could readily match any U.S. space warfare systems;[165] and (3) that space warfare systems could be easily foiled by a variety of relatively inexpensive offensive countermeasures.[166] It is not clear how the Soviets could match prospective U.S. BMD developments without a comparable research base[167] or why they would want to do so if the systems could be so easily defeated with cheap offensive countermeasures or through an expansion of existing offensive forces.

As noted earlier in this chapter, with respect to probable Soviet perceptions of the SDI (to the extent that genuine views may be distinguished from public diplomacy), the Soviets tend in their public argumentation to exaggerate the ease with which countermeasures to BMD systems can be devised—especially countermeasures to the complex, multilayer defenses under investigation in the SDI. The Soviets logically have no interest in acknowledging that countermeasures might be difficult and costly and obvious interests in discouraging the United States from pursuing the SDI.

In their attempts to discredit the SDI, the Soviets have sometimes been careless in framing their arguments. In 1984, for example, a panel of the

Committee of Soviet Scientists for Peace, Against Nuclear Threat, headed by Roald Sagdeyev, director of the Institute of Space Research of the USSR Academy of Sciences, and Andrei Kokoshin. deputy director of the Institute of the USA and Canada, released a study of the implications of space-based BMD systems. According to this study,

> even a high level of operational reliability is no absolute guarantee against failure. Let us consider the case of a three-"layer" SBAMS [space-based antimissile system], with the operational reliability of each of them equal to 90%. In the launch of 1,000 ICBM[s] 100 missiles pass the first layer intact (let us assume that each carries 10 warheads). So even after passing the two subsequent layers at least 10 warheads will be able to close in on the target.[168]

This example suggests, in other words, that the attacker would have to launch 1000 ICBMs carrying a total of 10,000 warheads in order to deliver 10 warheads on a single target area. Because the Soviet Union today is attributed only 1398 ICBMs with 6420 warheads[169] (not counting reload ICBMs), a system with this level of "operational reliability" might come remarkably close to President Reagan's goal of rendering nuclear weapons "impotent and obsolete"—at least with respect to Soviet ICBM warheads. If such a defense were feasible, the costs of expanding the Soviet ICBM force to be able to attack a significantly larger number of targets would probably be prohibitive. This hypothetical example, rather than discrediting the SDI concept, tended (no doubt inadvertently) to support it.

Another example of unconvincing "countermeasures" argumentation is the suggestion that the USSR could establish missile bases on the moon;[170] this would hardly be a low-cost or simple enterprise. Probably the least persuasive countermeasure is that advanced by the former Soviet ambassador to the Federal Republic of Germany, Valentin Falin. Falin has suggested that the Soviet leadership might simply cause great devastation to the USSR while damaging the ecology of the entire planet: "Finally, no ABM options will change the fact that a precisely known quantity of nuclear devices detonated simultaneously on one's own territory would have irreversible global consequences."[171]

Some of the Soviet Union's most prominent scientists and technical experts have joined in the countermeasures aspect of the anti-SDI campaign. It is, in a sense, understandable that a number of the Soviet scientists who have concentrated on this theme in presentations in the West have been leading figures in the Soviet development of traditional and advanced BMD technologies, for they are well versed in the technical literature and the current state of both Western and Soviet BMD research. But their prominent participation in framing the countermeasures commentary against the SDI has struck some U.S. and allied observers as disingenuous.[172]

The apparent shift away from a strident emphasis on the countermeasures theme may be partly explained by a Soviet discovery that it may be more effective simply to posit the infeasibility of building a highly effective strategic defense as an established fact. In October 1986, for example, President Reagan asked, "Why are the Soviets so adamant that America remain forever vulnerable to Soviet rocket attack?"[173] Gorbachev responded as follows in a televised speech:

> I'm surprised by such questions . . . They have the air of indicating that the American President has an opportunity to make his country invulnerable, to give it secure protection against a nuclear strike. As long as there exist nuclear weapons and the arms race is continuing, he does not have such an opportunity. The same, naturally, applies to ourselves. If the President counts on S.D.I. in this respect, it is vain.[174]

Indeed, the Soviets may have discovered that it was in fact counterproductive to place so much emphasis on their anxieties regarding SDI because this tended to endow the SDI with a higher degree of technical and political credibility than it might enjoy if they treated it with relative complacency. The calmer tone may also have stemmed from revised Soviet judgments about the political and budgetary sustainability of the SDI in the United States. In November 1987 Gorbachev emphasized the Soviet Union's interest in reaching arms control agreements and acknowledged the Soviet Union's efforts in BMD-relevant technologies in the following terms:

> Practically, the Soviet Union is doing all that the United States is doing, and I guess we are engaged in research, basic research, which relates to these aspects which are covered by the S.D.I. of the United States. But we will not build an S.D.I., we will not deploy S.D.I., and we call upon the United States to act likewise.[175]

In other words, if there has been a shift in Soviet anti-SDI argumentation away from the countermeasures theme, it may stem in part from a Soviet wish to deemphasize the USSR's capacity to engage in an arms race and to stress instead the Soviet Union's dedication to peace and arms control. In the words of Foreign Minister Shevardnadze, "to counter the sinister plans of 'Star Wars,' the U.S.S.R. is putting before the international community a concept of 'Star Peace.' "[176] Soviet spokesmen have dismissed the statements by Kosygin and other Soviet officials of the 1960s as irrelevant to the current strategic situation of mutual vulnerability to nuclear attack.[177]

The "threat-to-peace" theme has had two aspects—the specific culpability of the United States and the general dangers that might be posed by expanded BMD deployments. The U.S.-specific themes include broad accusations (for example, that the SDI is intended to enable the United States to gain a first-strike capability against the USSR; that the SDI threatens the ABM Treaty; and so forth) and more particular indictments. Some of the latter amount to relatively secondary exaggerations (for example, Gorbachev's assertion in 1985 that the United States has earmarked $70 billion for SDI research "for the next few years,"[178] and Shevardnadze's claim in 1986 that the United States plans to deploy SDI systems "precisely in seven years"[179]).

The other aspect of the threat-to-peace theme portrays the SDI as the nemesis of arms control and the source of increased dangers of deliberate and accidental war. Soviet spokesmen have argued that "the deployment of the antimissile system would lead to an increase in the danger of a deliberate unleashing of a nuclear war"[180] and that "the probability of erroneous decisions in crisis situations will grow considerably."[181] According to *Izvestia*,

the development of such [advanced BMD] systems would affect the correlation of the [two] sides' strategic forces even more tangibly and would render it extremely unsteady and unstable. Furthermore, the danger of a nuclear war being unleashed . . . would increase sharply. Expert calculations indicate that, even if both sides possessed approximately equivalent large-scale ABM systems, even the most insignificant differences in their efficiency would be likely to substantially undermine strategic parity and destabilize the entire situation. In addition to this, sober-minded scientists in the United States itself correctly point out that the actual work on implementing the program Washington announced is in itself of a provocative and destabilizing nature, regardless of its ultimate results.[182]

By evoking general dangers, the Soviets can portray the SDI as a "sore spot in everybody's eyes, as a thorn, as a stumbling block, which does not allow us to find a way out of the [nuclear] threat that hangs over the heads of mankind."[183] By making nuclear arms reduction agreements such as the December 1987 INF treaty and opening up a prospect of further nuclear-force reductions, the Soviets may promote the impression that an ambitious U.S. BMD research program such as the SDI is unnecessary and potentially an obstacle to concluding additional arms control agreements. Although Gorbachev has described the SDI as "a question of the security of our country and the security of all peoples, all nations and all continents,"[184] the Soviets have devoted special attention to Western Europe in their anti-SDI campaign.

The "destabilization" theme has, for example, been given special prominence in anti-SDI commentary in Western Europe, where it is frequently linked to a long-standing Soviet argument—that the United States intends to use Western Europe in plans to launch an aggressive war against the Soviet Union, a nuclear war that would be confined to Europe. This concept provides one of several links to the INF affair of the early 1980s. According to a Tass broadcast in 1984, the United States regards the West Europeans

> as its nuclear hostages who could be sacrificed in the name of achieving the goal, proclaimed by Reagan, of eliminating socialism as a socio-political system . . . The Pentagon's plans for militarizing outer space are further confirmation that American leaders meant what they said . . . about the admissibility of fighting a "limited" nuclear war . . . This is indicated also by the crash deployment of American first-strike weapons, Pershing 2 and cruise missiles, in Western Europe. The Pentagon is clearly bent on unleashing such a war in Europe in the hope of riding it out behind the space-based anti-missile "umbrella."[185]

The Soviets warned West Europeans that their participation in the SDI could make destabilization all the more likely. In November 1985, it was reported that Mikhail Gorbachev had written to the West German chancellor, Helmut Kohl, to underline his concern that West German corporations might participate in "American programs which have as their goal the creation of space strike systems." Gorbachev added that the West German government would have to choose "whether it [will] allow the material, scientific and technological potential of its country to be used for the realization of the most dangerous military plans in space, or whether it will assert its reputation and influence in order to contribute to bringing about mutually acceptable agreements."[186] The Soviet anti-SDI campaign did not in fact prevent Britain, Italy, and the Federal Republic of Germany from making SDI participation agreements with the United States in 1985 and 1986, but it may have contributed to raising the level of controversy associated with the SDI in Western Europe.[187]

Some West European experts have suggested that the Soviets may have discovered unanticipated propaganda advantages in the Reagan administration's public presentation policy. For many, the U.S. emphasis on the SDI as a U.S. initiative placed arms race responsibility on the United States. The vision of an infallible shield protecting populations could be easily attacked as technically implausible, and it reinforced the widespread impression that BMD must be essentially perfect to be useful; this may hinder the United States in pursuing BMD for more limited and strategically relevant tasks in the future. Finally, the U.S. administration's attacks on nuclear deterrence as dangerous and immoral have been broadly consistent with the Soviet Union's own antinuclear campaigns and may have contributed to a certain delegitimization of the Western alliance's deterrent posture in public perceptions.[188]

5

Alliance Reactions:
Arms Control and Deterrence

Soviet actions have posed a challenge for the Western alliance. A continuing buildup of the Soviet BMD potential—whether in ABM Treaty-compliant infrastructure expansion and system modernization, in an ambiguous creepout from the ABM Treaty, or (a less likely prospect) in an explicit and relatively rapid breakout—could have serious implications for the security of the alliance, given other elements of the Soviet force posture. (The gravity of the implications would depend in part on the scope and effectiveness of the defenses deployed, and in part on the manner of deployment—for instance, a protracted creepout could affect the West's ability to respond in a timely fashion.) At the same time, the Soviet arms control and public diplomacy campaign seems intended to hinder the pursuit of current U.S. and allied BMD research programs (NATO ATBM studies as well as the SDI), even though these programs have respected the constraints of the ABM Treaty, and U.S. and allied investments in BMD activities and in other types of strategic defense remain inferior to those of the USSR.

The responses of Western governments to these Soviet actions are still being formulated, but it is clear that the Western alliance will persevere in its long-standing search for balanced arms control agreements while maintaining a reliable deterrent posture, in order to be able to contain the threat of Soviet coercion or aggression. Both elements of this policy—the ongoing quest for balanced arms control agreements with the Soviet Union and the conduct of force-improvement programs to stabilize deterrence—will be difficult. Significant problems complicate each aspect of Western policy, the arms control efforts as well as the necessary programs to improve offensive and defensive capabilities. These problems stem in part from the dimensions of the Soviet challenge and the manner in which the Soviets have structured their political-military policies. But the way forward is also encumbered by disagreements within the alliance about the precise nature of the Soviet challenge and the requirements for deterrence and arms control.

Grounds for Western Consensus

The Western alliance has been founded on shared security interests and values—above all, peace and freedom. To protect these values and interests, it has been generally agreed, the West must be capable of deterring Soviet aggression and neutralizing any Soviet attempts at coercion. In the event of war, the Western allies have also agreed, their aim would be to restore the security and integrity of the NATO area as promptly as possible, while containing the scope of violence to the minimum. To make war even less likely, and to promote the achievement of nonmilitary solutions to East-West differences, the Western allies have promoted and participated in dialogues and negotiations with the Soviet Union and its Warsaw Pact allies.

Apart from basic principles, consensus within the alliance has often been problematic. The disagreements have no doubt derived from multiple causes, including (despite shared values and interests) important objective differences in vulnerabilities and capabilities. The West European allies are, for example, far more vulnerable to conventional Soviet aggression than the allies in North America, whereas the United States controls most of the West's nuclear retaliatory means. Recurrent conflicts about the sharing of risks and responsibilities in the alliance have naturally followed. Divergent assessments of security interests have sometimes become evident—for example, in planning for the specific contingencies that could arise in the event of Soviet aggression. The issues include matters as fundamental as how to conduct military operations and achieve timely war termination on acceptable terms.

Discord has also frequently stemmed from differences in judgment about the practical requirements of the alliance's basic peacetime policies: What capabilities are truly necessary and prudent in order to deter Soviet aggression and neutralize Soviet blackmail pressures? Do the uncertainties about the controllability of nuclear escalation mean that the task of deterrence is easily accomplished? Or do these uncertainties imply high risks of Western self-deterrence and effective Soviet counter-deterrence in a crisis or war, leading logically to a requirement for alternatives to the West's high degree of dependence on nuclear threats? To what extent can Western governments expect to make their military problems more predictable and manageable through arms control negotiations?

The ethic of the Western alliance has always been one of problem solving or, at least, facade preserving. Irreconcilable differences of judgment about specific policies have been accepted, when necessary, to preserve the alliance, for the sake of larger, long-term purposes. The alliance's "self-correcting mechanisms" remain rooted in shared security interests and political values.

The current and prospective strategic defense capabilities of the USSR, in combination with other Soviet programs and policies, nonetheless pose unusually severe problems for consensus in the Western alliance. This is partly because of the intrinsic magnitude of their strategic and arms control implications, and partly because of three key contextual factors. First, intra-Western disagreements about the merits of strategic-defense capabilities, especially BMD, have been marked since the late 1960s. Assessments of the ABM Treaty have become closely linked to beliefs about the mechanisms of strategic stability and the future prospects of East-West arms control negotiations.

Second, since the late 1970s, views on Western security requirements and assessments of the Soviet Union have, in several Western countries, tended to polarize into what Peter Stratmann has aptly labeled "dramatizing and minimizing political interpretations." For the former, only military capabilities that are "in practice unattainable for the Western alliance" might address the Soviet threat. For supporters of the latter interpretation, the Soviet military buildup since the 1960s has "little strategic, military and political relevance," and Western security may be readily assured through arms control negotiations.[1] This political polarization (evident in Britain, West Germany, and the United States, among other countries) has been accompanied by a certain perceived "delegitimization" of the alliance's nuclear policies during the same period, together with an increase in "equidistancing" perceptions of the "superpowers" in Western Europe.[2]

Third, assessments of Soviet BMD have been complicated by the peculiarities of the Reagan administration's campaign for the SDI, including arguments about Soviet BMD prospects that have been seen as inconsistent and unpersuasive. West European officials and experts have probably been most repelled by the arguments (1) perceived as exaggerating the threat posed by Soviet BMD and (2) asserting the potentially benign or even beneficial character of Soviet BMD.

Perhaps the best-known example of overstatement appeared in the January 1985 White House pamphlet *The President's Strategic Defense Initiative*: "The Soviets are also engaged in research and development on a rapidly deployable ABM system that raises concerns about their potential ability to break out of the ABM Treaty and deploy a nationwide ABM defense system within the next ten years should they choose to do so. Were they to do so, as they could, deterrence would collapse, and we would have no choices between surrender and suicide."[3] As noted in Chapter 4, the West could respond with offensive force improvements to counter—to some significant degree, at least—an explicit breakout in a relatively timely fashion. Substantial Soviet BMD activities in violation of treaty commitments would probably—despite Soviet efforts at camouflage and deception—eventually include enough unambiguous indications to justify improved offensive-force countermeasures. The judgment of the Office of Technology Assessment on this point appears to be more widely shared than that expressed in the White House pamphlet: "Although any defense deployable by the Soviets in the next 10 years would certainly complicate U.S. targeting, the available offensive countermeasures technologies make it extremely unlikely that we could be forced to choose between 'surrender and suicide.' "[4]

The declarations implying that improved Soviet BMD capabilities could be beneficial in some circumstances include the president's technology-sharing offers and the U.S. "strategic concept" for a cooperative transition to a defense-dominant Soviet-U.S. relationship. West Europeans have been skeptical, it seems, about the feasibility of persuading the Soviets to "legitimize" the SDI by endorsing the strategic concept of a jointly managed transition toward greater reliance on defenses. This outcome would be plausible, it has been argued, only if unrealistic assumptions were made about cooperative behavior in moving toward a defense-dominant relationship; and, if that degree of mutual understanding could be attained, would such BMD capabilities be necessary?

Nor have many West Europeans been convinced that highly effective Soviet BMD capabilities would have essentially beneficial effects for their own security interests. A number of West Europeans have concluded that, on a Soviet-U.S. cooperative basis, such capabilities might represent a major structural element in a great-power "condominium" of joint hegemony. Such capabilities might increase Western Europe's dependence on U.S.-Soviet relations for security.[5] In the event of conflict, the Soviets might attempt to use such capabilities to confine future military operations to regions on the Soviet periphery. Except for the obvious advantage of a protected "rear area" for the Western alliance in North America, it is far from clear that a defense-dominant Soviet-U.S. relationship would offer benefits over the current situation for Western Europe. The theoretical advantage of more credible U.S. guarantees—owing to radically decreased U.S. vulnerability—would be canceled out by the similar reduction in Soviet vulnerability to long-range attack that is posited in the defense-dominance vision. It is not evident that Western Europe or the United States would benefit from a Soviet ability to counter U.S. deterrent forces with high effectiveness. The theoretical possibility of a universal invulnerability to ballistic missile attack through ubiquitous SDI deployments (raised implicitly in the president's statement that "we will make available to everyone this weapon")[6] has been taken less seriously than the strategic concept for a bilateral Soviet-U.S. transition to defense dominance and has in any case not been as central to the administration's SDI advocacy.

The technical and financial feasibility of hypothetical defense-dominance arrangements remains, of course, to be demonstrated—especially as concerns "responsive" offensive-force countermeasures, as opposed to concepts calling for prior nuclear or delivery-vehicle disarmament. Moreover, the technological possibilities and their costs will remain uncertain for several years to come. Indeed, given the announced SDI research and decision schedule and generally agreed assessments of Soviet BMD prospects, a situation of defense dominance is not likely to be a matter of practical concern for at least two decades. For the foreseeable future, the Western alliance is far more likely to be concerned with imperfect defenses than with systems of such high effectiveness that a defense-dominant situation could be established.

Rather than focusing on grand designs for defense dominance, pragmatic Western analysts have increasingly turned their attention to more immediate and practical issues. Although some reports suggest that initial SDI deployments might include a number of first-generation space-based nonnuclear kinetic interceptors, the most likely BMD deployments in the next decade would consist of ground-based interceptors with nuclear and/or nonnuclear kill mechanisms. While the operational reliability and effectiveness of such systems would be relatively uncertain (as discussed in Chapter 1), they would be based on known technologies. At present, according to the Office of Technology Assessment and other authorities,[7] the Soviet Union appears to be better placed than the West to engage in large-scale deployments of such systems. Because this is a much more plausible medium-term challenge for Western strategy than a situation of Soviet-U.S. defense dominance, it deserves more sustained attention than do hypothetical and distant conditions.

It is essential to strive for a reasonably rigorous assessment of this challenge if Western response options are to be based on sound premises. It should be possible to pursue a consensus on the principle that the most plausible threats merit primary attention and action. The most plausible long-range offensive threats that the Soviet Union is likely to pose to the Western alliance, particularly in Europe, would consist of relatively limited and discriminate strike options, with nuclear and/or nonnuclear warheads. The all-out Soviet attacks against cities in North America and Western Europe posited by some Western commentators are much less likely because of the reckless and potentially suicidal risks they would entail. The Soviets are more likely to be interested in using force in ways that would leave Western governments an enormous stake in caution and moderation. Similarly, the defenses that the Soviet Union is most likely to build in the medium term—an expanded array of traditional ground-based interceptors—might be relatively effective against the selective attacks envisioned in NATO's flexible response strategy. The common view that only nearly "leakproof" defenses could benefit the USSR is therefore ill-founded; it is often based on a prior assumption that the United States (or other Western governments) would be likely to undertake massive attacks, despite Soviet retaliatory capabilities.

It would, moreover, almost certainly be a mistake to assume that the Soviet Union is essentially passive in its BMD decision making—that is, that Soviet programs are imitative of U.S. examples. The historical development of Soviet BMD capabilities suggests that there are purposeful rationales behind Soviet programs. These rationales become apparent in the light of Soviet military doctrine and force-posture trends (Chapter 2), and even clearer in view of the strategic advantages that BMD could offer the USSR in Europe (Chapter 3). The strategic advantages that could be derived from a unilateral edge in active and passive defenses (and not only in Europe) help to account for the long-standing Soviet commitment to developing such capabilities.

Continued development of the Soviet BMD potential appears virtually certain, whatever the fate of U.S. BMD research projects. Even if the SDI were to be limited to the narrow definitions of allowable research proposed by the USSR (or entirely abandoned), the Soviet Union would still be interested in degrading the credibility of the U.S. nuclear guarantees outlined in NATO's flexible-response strategy. The improvement of the Soviet potential for expanded BMD deployments cannot therefore be prevented by Western restraint. As General Wolfgang Altenburg noted in 1986, "the Soviet Union already has an operational missile defense system. It will carry forward its current research and development. This must naturally have consequences."[8]

As argued in Chapter 4, however, a clear-cut Soviet breakout from the ABM Treaty—an explicit abrogation or large-scale violations—remains improbable. A breakout would raise large risks, with uncertain long-term rewards. It seems more likely that the Soviets will continue to build up their breakout potential within the permissive constraints of the ABM Treaty (regarding, for example, LPAR construction and the development and testing of traditional ground-based interceptor systems). They may also engage in an ambiguous creepout, to the extent that this seems prudent in light of Western political attitudes and intelligence capabilities. The Soviets do not appear likely in the foreseeable future to cooperate in a comprehensive review of their suspected ABM Treaty violations or to endorse any U.S. strategic concept that would legitimize the SDI. Soviet interests reside in trying to interdict the SDI politically while carrying their own BMD activities forward as discreetly as possible.

The principal Soviet interest appears, in other words, to be strengthening the USSR's strategic position in relation to the Western alliance. This does not imply any interest in reckless and strategically pointless enterprises such as attacking U.S. or West European cities with nuclear weapons.[9] Instead, the objective seems to be a long-term one of dominating the Soviet periphery, especially in Europe, and preferably without war.

As suggested in Chapters 2 and 3, the basic Soviet strategy seems to be one of narrowing Western military options. Soviet nuclear counter-deterrent capabilities tend to undercut the credibility of U.S. nuclear threats, while Western dependence on these nuclear threats is increased through the continued expansion of the Warsaw Pact's conventional-force superiority. This process places the Soviet Union in an advantageous position for the contingency of war. If Western confidence in the cogency and credibility of NATO strategy could be sufficiently eroded, Soviet prospects for political gains without war—what the Soviets view as positive peaceful change—could be advanced.

This assessment of Soviet objectives and prospects is, of course, not universally shared in the Western alliance. Disagreements about how to interpret and deal with Soviet behavior have long burdened the formulation of alliance policies, and differences in judgment have been especially acute since the late 1970s. This survey of some of the principal problems of alliance consensus with respect to the arms control and deterrence issues posed by Soviet strategic defense is, moreover, illustrative rather than comprehensive.

Continuing Arms Control Efforts

As noted in Chapter 4, the Soviet public diplomacy campaign against the SDI has placed particular stress on "threat-to-peace" themes—above all, the idea that the SDI endangers arms control. Soviet anti-SDI arguments have probably had less impact in Western Europe, however, than well-established skeptical attitudes about BMD in elite circles. These attitudes have probably been reinforced to some extent by various features of U.S. declaratory policy. The surprise U.S. announcement of the SDI in March 1983 cast the United States into a role susceptible of being perceived as initiating a new round of the arms race and thus forcing the USSR to intensify its own BMD activities and to prepare improved countermeasures to penetrate and overcome projected U.S. BMD capabilities. In addition, as the Delpech report pointed out in January 1986, "the announcement of the SDI has had the drawback of permitting Soviet propaganda to accuse the United States of militarizing space and giving credibility to the idea that this research could be a currency for the Geneva negotiations, with the USSR retaining total discretion about its own work in this domain."[10]

U.S. references to Soviet BMD activities as a justification for the SDI have sometimes been greeted with suspicion, despite the public evidence (discussed in Chapter 1) that the United States has been monitoring Soviet progress and has been concerned about the growth of the Soviet BMD potential since the mid-1970s. Some West Europeans argue that the SDI has tended to legitimize Soviet BMD activities because of the widespread and persistent impression, conveyed through the SDI, that the United States has taken the "first step" in a new cycle of the arms race. High officials of the Reagan administration have, furthermore, asserted the desirability of heavy Soviet BMD capabilities in the future— declarations that also appear to legitimize the Soviet programs.

West European skepticism about the SDI for reasons specific to U.S. declaratory policy (the vision of making nuclear weapons "impotent and obsolete," the denigration of retaliatory deterrence capabilities as morally inferior to strategic defenses, the strategic concept for future nuclear arms control, and so forth) may have been bolstered to some degree by the Soviet anti-SDI campaign, which has stressed the risk of "destabilization." Concern about destabilization through changes in the existing strategic order is profound in Western Europe, and the SDI has made the United States appear to be the principal agent of change— despite the earlier initiation and still superior magnitude of Soviet BMD programs.

This does not mean, however, that the Soviets have had great success in purveying an image of Soviet inactivity in strategic defense. In November 1985, for example, the West German newsweekly *Der Spiegel* published several articles about strategic defense. Although *Der Spiegel* has been quite critical of the SDI, it included a lengthy and detailed discussion of Soviet BMD programs. On December 6, 1985, *Pravda* published a translation of almost all of the main *Der Spiegel* article about the SDI, under the title "Creation of Arms Monopoly," and omitted the article describing Soviet BMD activities. The West German magazine's editors informed their readers, "The report published in the same issue of *Der Spiegel* about the Soviet efforts to build a defense similar to the SDI was evidently not found worthy of reprinting by the central organ of the CPSU."[11]

Nor have the Soviets succeeded in convincing key West European opinion leaders that they have definitively renounced their doctrinal views of the 1960s, even though some Soviet spokesmen have implied that the USSR has adopted Western-style concepts of strategic stability through mutual vulnerability. Some of the best-informed West European experts have examined the Tula line with a certain skepticism. Michel Tatu of *Le Monde*, for example, has written, "Today's campaign against the SDI leads them to take up without much modification the arguments of the MAD [mutual assured destruction] partisans; but it is nonetheless not certain that the conceptions expressed by General Talensky [in 1964] have been definitively abandoned."[12]

The Soviet Union's policy of silence and denial with respect to its BMD and ASAT activities has not, moreover, always played to its advantage. When General Nikolai Chervov in May 1985 admitted that the USSR had an operational ASAT system, he asserted that it was based on direct-ascent ballistic missiles tested from the late 1970s to 1982. As Nicholas Johnson notes, "the continued Soviet refusal to admit to the presence of the co-orbital ASAT system cast doubt on the veracity of the entire statement . . . the Soviet Union was now telling the world that she had been lying for at least the past half-dozen years."[13] The Soviets did not admit until December 1985 that they had tested a co-orbital ASAT device between 1969 and 1982.[14]

West European governments have been fully aware that Soviet public diplomacy efforts and arms control initiatives have been intended, at least in part, in the words of West German Chancellor Helmut Kohl, "to prevent the U.S. space program and to influence West European public opinion."[15] But they have not been particularly impressed or influenced by the excessive and one-sided features of the Soviet anti-SDI campaign. George Younger, the British secretary of state for defense, has observed: "The Soviet Union has mounted a major campaign to try to cast doubt on the motivation behind the SDI, notwithstanding its own research activities in related fields, and to foster alarm in the West about the consequences of pursuing it. We have seen these scare tactics before, over cruise missiles prior to their deployment in 1983 . . . We will continue to take a more balanced view, and will encourage the Soviet Union to do the same."[16]

Similarly, even though all Western societies are quite sympathetic to the basic concept of arms control (negotiated accords to lower the costs and, above all, the risks in existing international security arrangements), West European governments have evaluated Soviet proposals since 1985 regarding nuclear weapons and strategic defense with caution. The governing elites of Western Europe have generally regarded proposals such as the Soviet design for a nonnuclear world by the year 2000 as utopian and reminiscent of the calls for general and complete disarmament in the late 1950s and early 1960s. The reactions of West European governments have therefore been restrained and unenthusiastic. For example, Sir Geoffrey Howe stated in March 1986: "To call for instant nuclear disarmament is propaganda. Much as we might wish it otherwise—I profoundly wish it were—nuclear weapons will continue for the foreseeable future to make an essential contribution to preserving peace. Simply making Europe safe for conventional war is no way to preserve our children's future."[17]

West European experts are well aware of the broader purpose behind contemporary Soviet arms control policy—the Soviet interest in promoting the emergence of a new détente in East-West relations. Gorbachev's program for resolving security problems by "political means" (discussed in Chapter 4) evidently includes an expectation that a more relaxed international political climate would enable the Soviet Union to increase its investments in industrial modernization, to obtain loans and technology transfers from the West, and to encourage a slowdown in Western defense efforts. The challenge for Western policy is maintaining an adequate military posture and making the right hedges in military research and development in a situation in which the reassuring "atmospherics" may obscure the continuing security challenges posed by the USSR.

West European caution regarding Soviet arms control proposals has not, however, led to an enthusiastic endorsement of the U.S. approach to the negotiations about long-range nuclear forces and strategic defense. Continuing reservations about the SDI have affected assessments of the U.S. arms control proposals linked to the SDI.

NUCLEAR FORCES

West European concerns about the U.S. approach to nuclear arms control have been especially apparent since the October 1986 Reykjavik summit.[18] The reservations have concerned INF, intercontinental nuclear forces, the relationship between nuclear and conventional forces, and the British and French nuclear forces.

The December 1987 U.S.-Soviet treaty regarding a "double zero" for INF missiles with ranges between 500 and 5500 km has, for example, raised concerns in Western Europe because, by the terms of this agreement, the United States will no longer retain any missiles on European soil capable of striking the USSR, whereas the Soviet Union will retain shorter-range missiles and other systems capable of attacking from Warsaw Pact territory all the militarily significant targets in Western Europe. Because of the elimination of a key part of the U.S. nuclear presence in Europe, it has been argued, Western Europe may become more vulnerable to Soviet intimidation. While the treaty has been widely approved by West European publics, such reservations have been evident in expert circles, especially in France.[19]

West European reservations about U.S. intercontinental-force proposals have been most evident with respect to the concept of eliminating all ballistic missiles in ten years. In mid-November 1986, Prime Minister Margaret Thatcher reported that she had persuaded the president not to pursue that goal, partly because of the need to modernize the West's nuclear deterrent capabilities, including Britain's planned Trident force.[20] The British defense minister had already said that "we would certainly not recommend" the elimination of ballistic missiles "unless it left conventional, chemical and biological weapons on the ground and sea in Western Europe at a more or less reasonable balance, with no side certain of an easy victory."[21]

The U.S. approach to the relationship between conventional and nuclear forces since Reykjavik has also given West Europeans some cause for concern. Secretary of State Shultz has, for example, said that, although "deterrence based on conventional forces is sharply more expensive" than nuclear deterrence, "it's a safer form of deterrence."[22] Many experts and officials in Western Europe would disagree with this judgment. Since the 1950s, West European strategists have rejected nuclear-or-conventional formulations in favor of a deterrent posture based on both types of capabilities. They have, moreover, emphasized the necessity of nuclear threats for reliable deterrence. West German Chancellor Helmut Kohl's statement was similar to those by high-level French and British officials: "Disarmament agreements must . . . increase and not diminish the security of the allies. In no case must a conventional war in Europe again become feasible and more probable . . . as nuclear weapons are progressively reduced, growing importance will attach to the question of an equilibrium in conventional weapons on account of the linkage between the two and the conclusions this must imply."[23]

Finally, the U.S. attitude toward the British and French nuclear forces has evoked concern in London and Paris. Immediately after Reykjavik, Secretary of State Shultz commented as follows about the U.S. proposal to abolish all ballistic missiles: "You would, if you agreed to a program like this, obviously, you would then have to go to the British and the French and the Chinese and persuade them to join you in ending these particular kinds of weapons . . . We and the Soviets aren't going to get rid of all of our ballistic missiles and leave some other countries with them."[24] This statement and similar ones by other U.S. officials irritated British and French strategists and officials, who have long been concerned about the risk of their forces (1) being portrayed as the obstacle to arms control agreements and (2) being somehow "taken into account" in a U.S.-Soviet bargain without their participation.

West European reservations about far-reaching arms control proposals have been received with a certain disappointment in Moscow. Some observers have even detected scorn and sarcasm in Soviet comments about the analyses of the Reykjavik summit in Western Europe. According to Shevardnadze, "the position of some European leaders on nuclear disarmament is illogical. Now that a real opportunity has finally emerged to rid the continent of missiles, they have begun to talk of the need to retain U.S. nuclear weapons in Europe and to protect their own alleged privileges as nuclear states."[25] In Gorbachev's words: "What was being thoroughly disguised previously is now becoming more clear: among U.S. and West European ruling circles, there are powerful forces which seek to frustrate the process of nuclear disarmament. Some people began to assert again that nuclear weapons are almost a boon."[26]

STRATEGIC DEFENSES

West European reservations about the Reagan administration's approach to strategic defense and arms control have been perhaps even more profound than their misgivings about the arms control policies relating to nuclear forces.

Five main areas of disagreement stand out: the value attributed to the ABM Treaty; how to interpret the treaty's constraints on research and development activities; allegations of Soviet noncompliance with the treaty; the importance of the treaty for the credibility of the British and French nuclear forces; and the prospect of a transition—cooperative or noncooperative—to large-scale U.S. and Soviet BMD deployments.

The merits of the ABM Treaty in West European eyes can scarcely be overstated. The assumption that U.S. and Soviet motives in endorsing the ABM Treaty were essentially similar is widespread, and relatively few West Europeans have examined the possibility that the Soviets were actuated by purposes such as constraining U.S. investments in an area of strategic defense in which the United States had an evident competitive advantage. The treaty is widely considered a bulwark against the "destabilization" of a tolerable situation of mutual vulnerability. This situation is viewed as one of the bases for long-term East-West political accommodation and cooperation. Without the ABM Treaty, it is feared, an offense-defense arms race would endanger prospects for arms control and détente and increase the risks of war. Many West Europeans have accordingly been displeased by indications that the United States might subordinate the ABM Treaty to the realization of the SDI.

This position directly concerns, of course, the definition of allowable research and development activities that might be observed during the proposed period of a mutual commitment to nonwithdrawal from the treaty. The Soviets have proposed definitions of permitted research that the United States has regarded as even more confining than the restrictive U.S. interpretation of the ABM Treaty. The U.S. side has not indicated whether the United States would observe its restrictive interpretation of the treaty during the period of nonwithdrawal or whether it might at some point adopt the broader interpretation that the Reagan administration regards as legally correct.

Adopting the broader interpretation would place the United States at odds with the reported policies of its allies. It was easy for West European governments to take issue with the "indefensible" Soviet position, as Sir Geoffrey Howe described it, that "their research is legitimate but that the SDI must stop."[27] The Soviet shift to the position that SDI research is permissible if confined to "laboratories" has highlighted the interpretive controversy. Various West European governments have reportedly underlined their support for a restrictive interpretation.[28] Shirley Williams, the president of Britain's Social Democratic party, has written: "Under the ABM Treaty, narrowly interpreted—and no Western European government would accept the broad interpretation floated by some members of the U.S. administration—SDI is effectively consigned to the laboratory."[29] West German Chancellor Kohl has said that the United States and the USSR should both conform to "an agreed interpretation . . . until such time as a new agreement is concluded between them."[30]

U.S. allegations of Soviet noncompliance with the ABM Treaty represent a third broad area of U.S.–West European disagreement. From an American perspective, Soviet behavior under the ABM Treaty has been discouraging and has undermined the confidence essential to an effective arms control process. As President Reagan has noted, evidence of noncompliance "increases doubts about the reliability of the USSR as a negotiating partner," especially when the Soviets have thus far failed to provide satisfactory explanations or to take corrective actions to alleviate U.S. concerns.[31]

West European governments have shown that they perceive several grounds for caution in broaching this subject, as noted in the Introduction. Their comments have usually been limited to the Krasnoyarsk radar and to broad statements of principle, as in the October 1986 NPG communiqué: "We renewed our call on the Soviet leadership to take the steps necessary to ensure full compliance with its arms control commitments. We noted in this connection that a double standard of compliance with arms control agreements would be unacceptable and would undermine the security of the alliance."[32] The essential difference between the Reagan administration and the West European governments seems to be one of degree: the West Europeans generally display higher confidence that arms control regimes such as the ABM Treaty can be used to prevent a situation of one-sided advantage from developing.

A fourth area of disagreement concerns the future of the British and French nuclear forces. The 1986 British defense white paper repeated London's long-standing conditions for nuclear-force reductions: "If Soviet and U.S. strategic arsenals were to be very substantially reduced, and if no significant changes occurred in Soviet defensive capabilities, we would want to review our position and to consider how best we could contribute to arms control in the light of the reduced threat."[33] The French government has outlined a more complex and precise set of conditions.[34] But, like Britain, France has recently reemphasized the central importance of "the potential defensive systems that might in the future be opposed to these nuclear forces."[35]

This condition means that long-established British and French policy is inconsistent with the U.S. strategic concept for relating the SDI to arms control. The U.S. strategic concept holds, it will be recalled, that radical reductions in offensive nuclear forces should take place in tandem with substantial increases in U.S. and Soviet defenses against such weapons. The British and French reject the idea that they could be expected to reduce their offensive forces in the face of dramatically improved Soviet defenses; indeed, they would probably have to increase their forces in order to maintain the technical credibility of their deterrent threats.

Finally, the fundamental "transition" issues show no sign of resolution. The U.S. strategic concept for a cooperative transition is one that the Soviets may seek to exploit for their own purposes, and the concept of a noncooperative transition raises even greater anxieties in Western Europe. The ultimate goal of both concepts—a Soviet-U.S. relationship of defense dominance—holds little appeal for Western Europe.

The U.S. concept calls for, in the words of Paul Nitze, "a cooperative approach to the deployment of defensive systems—as opposed to a 'race' —were our research, or theirs, to demonstrate that such systems could help the world get rid of the threat of mutual destruction."[36] It is possible that the continuing U.S. efforts to highlight the American preference for a cooperative transition, regulated by arms control, to a strategic relationship in which defenses play a much greater role could be used by the Soviets to buttress their own anti-SDI position. The idea that SDI deployments should be made with Soviet concurrence to avoid an arms race could be seen as linked to the announced U.S. intention to conform to the ABM Treaty's provisions for joint agreement on revising that arms control regime. The Soviets may therefore argue that the U.S. strategic concept and the declared U.S. intention to pursue the SDI within the ABM Treaty's constraints together establish a decision framework in which the USSR has an effective veto right regarding the future of the SDI. The Soviets are well embarked on this course already in that, aside from their avowed rejection of the U.S. strategic concept, they have repeatedly asserted that they are the true supporters of the ABM Treaty and that the U.S. SDI threatens that treaty and arms control and international security in general.

In other words, the Soviets may attempt to convert the U.S. strategic concept for the SDI—with its explicit preference for Soviet offensive-force reductions and Soviet cooperation in a transition to defense dominance[37]—into an instrument that could be used against the SDI. Some attitudes prominent in the West may encourage them in this course. The United States has, for example, accepted Margaret Thatcher's December 1984 suggestion that the United States stipulate that "SDI-related deployment would, in view of treaty obligations, have to be a matter for negotiations" with the Soviet Union.[38] This declaration and others in support of the ABM Treaty have confirmed U.S. obligations to conform to ABM Treaty provisions in making decisions about possible BMD deployments.

These confirmations of U.S. obligations have been underscored by West European governments. Horst Teltschik, the West German chancellor's national security adviser, has said, "Mutual research into new anti-missile and anti-satellite systems must lead to cooperative solutions so as to prevent instability in the transitional phase, should strategic defense systems be deployed."[39] The stated requirement of Soviet cooperation logically implies that a Soviet decision not to cooperate would give the Soviets a veto over the SDI's future, but West German government spokesmen have denied that this would be the case.[40] Some prominent Europeans have, however, deplored U.S. statements indicating that the

United States could eventually choose to deploy SDI systems even if the USSR refused to amend the ABM Treaty to permit such deployments. According to Denis Healey, "there is no chance of progress on strategic nuclear disarmament unless the United States is prepared to negotiate about the abandonment of the strategic defense initiative."[41]

Rather than agreeing to negotiate the abandonment of the SDI, since 1985 several U.S. officials have affirmed that the United States has retained its sovereign rights, even while adhering to agreements such as the ABM Treaty. They have accordingly indicated that "we would not under any circumstances give the Soviets a veto over our future defensive deployments."[42] Moreover, since early 1986 Paul Nitze's statements have acknowledged that "the Soviets have given absolutely no encouragement" to the U.S. concept for a cooperative transition:

> Indeed, the Soviets give every programmatic indication of pursuing their own noncooperative transition to an offense-defense mix by deploying an illegal radar system and apparently developing other capabilities in violation of the ABM Treaty. President Reagan has determined and reported to Congress that the USSR may be preparing the base for a prohibited territorial defense; the Soviets, thus far, have failed meaningfully to address our concerns about these activities or otherwise correct their noncompliance. As of now, there is no evidence that they will do other than continue to acquire defensive capabilities—including those envisioned for SDI—on a noncooperative basis. This being the case, we must be ready, if necessary, to act on our own. Paradoxically, our being prepared for a noncooperative transition could ultimately provide the Soviets with a powerful incentive to cooperate in the future.[43]

This analysis of the situation has not won widespread acceptance in Western Europe. Although awareness of Soviet BMD activities and their significance in relation to other Soviet military capabilities has grown in government and expert circles, the prevailing impression is that reported Soviet treaty infractions have not been serious enough to justify steps that would imply U.S. abandonment of the treaty. Moreover, the United States is still generally perceived as the principal initiator of competition in this area, owing in part to the impressions established with the surprise announcement of the SDI in March 1983.

If the U.S. preparations for a possible "noncooperative transition" involved SDI development tests that were perceived in Western Europe as contraventions of the ABM Treaty, the United States might well be harshly criticized for sabotaging prospects for arms control and stability— even if the tests were in fact legal elements of a treaty-permitted research and development program, and no decisions on SDI deployments had in fact yet been made. The Soviets might attempt to use the U.S. SDI activities to create an atmosphere of tension in East-West relations. In this context, with renewed fears of war, it is possible that "a new wave of nuclear angst" could sweep over West Germany and the other countries of northern Europe where antinuclear protest movements were strongly represented in the anti-INF campaigns of the early 1980s.[44]

The U.S. strategic concept for a cooperative transition is, in any case, flawed from a West European perspective because of the strategic implications of radically diminished Soviet vulnerability. Aside from the rather theoretical and remote possibility of Soviet-U.S. hegemony, West European strategists who have examined the concept are concerned that other means of competition could well become more prominent if the credibility of long-range nuclear threats were diminished by technical advances in active defenses against air and missile forms of attack. An arms control regime of defense dominance would not necessarily extend to other means of nuclear attack (such as Soviet nuclear artillery) or Soviet conventional and chemical weapons advantages. Given that the Soviet Union would probably continue to seek political advantage in the contiguous regions of Eurasia, the United States and its allies would have to increase substantially their local defense and deterrence capabilities to compensate for the decreased credibility of U.S. "extended-deterrence" guarantees based on long-range nuclear strike assets. Some have argued that Western Europe would have less security (because of its increased relative vulnerability) at higher cost.

EMERGING CHALLENGES

The intra-alliance disagreements about recent U.S. arms control proposals (and about the goals to pursue in negotiations with the Soviet Union) underline the need to relearn some long-established principles about arms control. Three principles are especially relevant: (1) the goal in negotiations should be security, and not necessarily force reductions or the elimination of broad categories of weapons, including nuclear weapons; (2) for security, numbers of forces may be less significant than their characteristics, such as their survivability and potency in relation to opposing capabilities, including strategic defenses; and (3) the relationship between conventional and nuclear forces must be recognized.

The first principle is especially pertinent to the security of Western Europe. Some critical West European observers of U.S. arms control policy believe that it has been overly focused on utopian and politically counterproductive goals since at least January 1977, when the United

States declared its "ultimate goal" to be "the elimination of all nuclear weapons from this earth."[45] They note that the SDI and the INF "zero option" have both been presented by high-level American officials as contributions to the realization of this goal. Both have been publicly championed by some U.S. officials, West European critics have remarked, as if the principal threat to Western security were the existence of nuclear weapons, rather than Soviet political aspirations.

From the perspective of critical West European strategists, the U.S. long-term vision of a world without nuclear weapons, which has been endorsed by many in Western Europe. has helped the Soviet Union to promote the perceptual delegitimization of nuclear weapons in Western societies. The previous Western defense consensus on the need for a reliable nuclear deterrent has been undermined; and, it is argued, the West's own arms control policies have abetted this development. As Peter Stratmann has noted, the INF zero option goal illustrates "a fundamental contradiction of perspectives between the thrust and direction of East-West security talks on nuclear arms control and the task of politically stabilizing and thus in the long term assuring the structure of the accepted NATO strategy."[46]

In other words, Western security planning should recognize that credible nuclear response options have to be maintained as long as they have a useful role to play in balancing Soviet capabilities and making the West less vulnerable to Soviet blackmail or aggression. Nuclear weapons are instruments that help to keep the risks of political and military aggression incalculable for the USSR. Rather than focusing on these instruments of Western security and war prevention, which will remain indispensable for the foreseeable future. Western diplomacy should focus on the political roots of East-West antagonism. The availability of an alternative to nuclear deterrent threats through strategic-defense measures or other means has yet to be demonstrated. As a result, the West needs "a progressive and measured approach to disarmament: to know what is possible but also to recognize what remains out of reach for a long time to come."[47]

It would be useful in this respect to cultivate public awareness of the limits of arms control. Western arms control theorists often approach deeply rooted political conflicts as if technical agreements modifying some of the external symptoms of antagonism—certain types and levels of weapons deployments—could in themselves resolve Western security problems. The political and strategic implications of specific accords are sometimes neglected because the changes in weapons levels and characteristics are analyzed solely according to technical "crisis stability" criteria devised by Western theorists. The differences in the political and strategic objectives of the antagonists tend to be ignored in such analyses. Deficient awareness of Soviet political and strategic objectives leads in turn to a neglect of the possibility that unwise agreements with nominally equal terms (but unequal effects) could work to advance Soviet aims. Carefully devised arms control measures may usefully complement unilateral means of assuring Western security, but they cannot substitute for necessary force modernization programs.

The second principle suggests that goals such as 50 percent reductions in strategic nuclear forces are not necessarily constructive. Security and stability are more important than numerical reductions. Although strategic stability may be more a product of political factors than of force characteristics and balances, some types of reductions could be dangerous and destabilizing. The 50 percent reductions under negotiation by the United States and the Soviet Union might produce a more dangerous situation if the specific reductions were not carefully formulated because attacks against a large portion of the remaining U.S. forces could become a more practical and attractive proposition than in the current situation. The Soviets have made their intention to retain ICBM throwweight and prompt counterforce superiority explicit, as noted in Chapter 4. U.S. inferiority in this respect is not likely to be altered by equal or proportionate cuts in force levels. Alexander Haig pointed out in 1979, "When you have imbalances that exist and you recreate them at lower levels, it makes them more dangerous than at higher levels, where you have greater flexibility and there is some synergism."[48]

Because what matters operationally is capability relative to an opponent, strategically balanced negotiations would focus on damage-limiting capabilities as well as offensive strike forces. As suggested in Chapter 2, the Soviet Union's extensive damage-limiting investments include passive means of force survivability (mobility, deception, hardening, redundancy, and so forth) and active defenses (above all, air defenses) that have never been subject to negotiated constraints. The inclusion of strategic defenses in arms control negotiations would be beneficial, in that it would oblige Western policymakers to devote greater attention to East-West asymmetries and to the implications for security and stability of specific accords. Large-scale nuclear force reductions might, for example, increase requirements for BMD, in order to enhance U.S. force survivability prospects and strategic stability.

The third principle—the need to recognize the relationship between conventional and nuclear forces—has been implicit since the origins of the Western alliance. But the Western alliance appears to lack an agreed frame of reference for relating its nuclear arms control goals to conventional arms control and conventional-force-development planning. One of the fundamental challenges to Western security from the outset has been Soviet conventional force superiority in Europe.

This conventional-force superiority places the Soviet Union in a strong negotiating position with respect to both nuclear and conventional arms control in Europe. The Soviet Union derives "maneuverability" for nuclear arms control through its steadily enhanced conventional-force advantages. At the same time, of course, the USSR generally declines to acknowledge that it enjoys geographical and numerical advantages in conventional military deployments in Europe. The Western alliance should logically make reductions in its nuclear forces at least partially dependent on reductions in Soviet capabilities for conducting conventional offensives in Europe.[49] Nuclear forces are linked to conventional forces in NATO's military strategy of flexible response, and Western arms control policy should recognize this linkage.[50]

With these three principles, it is clear that the West needs to undertake a comprehensive analysis of its security requirements and the possible contributions of arms control. The analysis should be more explicit and complete than has been evident in the past. The result should be a "package" including nuclear forces, strategic defenses, and conventional forces at least as comprehensive as the current Soviet proposals. Such a package should be designed, if only to guide the Western alliance in the framing and evaluation of specific and more limited agreements.[51]

The design of the package should, of course, be informed by an awareness of the uniquely Soviet approach to arms control, including Soviet behavior under the ABM Treaty and the Soviet buildup of strategic defenses and offensive strike options since the mid-1960s. It is uncertain whether arms control efforts alone will be able to address these challenges. To begin with, as noted in Chapter 1, the ABM Treaty has not prevented the Soviet Union from making substantial progress toward BMD capabilities beyond those allowed by the treaty. Some infrastructure expansion is legal, and the results of certain Soviet BMD activities appear impressive. Some prominent experts judge that the Soviet potential for fairly rapid deployments of ground-based BMD interceptors of essentially traditional types may be as much as five years in advance of that of the United States.[52]

It appears that it would be difficult to use the ABM Treaty to prevent the Soviets from pursuing the course the Office of Technology Assessment has labeled "creepout"—that is, simulating adherence to the treaty, but gaining "a significant unilateral ballistic missile defense capability" through ambiguous or seemingly minor treaty violations and through improvements in systems (for example, ATBM) evidently permitted by the treaty.[53] It seems that it would be imprudent to count on the hypothetical option of strengthening the ABM Treaty, with improved cooperative verification and tighter constraints on the ambiguities and latitude it contains regarding permitted activities (especially with respect to LPARs and other elements of the traditional ground-based systems favored by the Soviets). The Soviets have so far shown relatively little willingness to address U.S. concerns about ABM Treaty compliance, have accused the United States of violating the treaty, and have proposed that the United States reaffirm the treaty by accepting limitations on SDI research even more constraining than those in the restrictive U.S. interpretation.

This Soviet reaction may be explained in part by a Soviet desire to protect the advantages earned through their massive investments in offensive forces and in passive and active forms of strategic defense, including BMD. As Paul Nitze has suggested, "it is not unreasonable to conclude that they would like to continue to be the only ones pressing forward in this field . . . The Soviets hope to foster a situation in which we would unilaterally restrain our research effort, even though it is fully consistent with existing treaties. This would leave them with a virtual monopoly in advanced strategic defense research; they see this as the most desirable outcome."[54]

This does not mean that the Soviets are not interested in arms control. The Soviets are in all likelihood sincere in trying to minimize the costs of competing in BMD and ASAT capabilities. They would almost certainly prefer to carry their programs forward at less cost and at a more convenient pace, with minimal Western competition, in order to be better able to afford industrial modernization investments for the long-term competition with the West. The Soviets would therefore probably prefer to persuade the United States to comply with a highly restrictive interpretation of the ABM Treaty, to add constraints on U.S. ASAT research as well, and to discourage other Western countries from investigating their own BMD and ASAT options. As suggested in Chapter 4, the Soviets may intend to propose nominally equal restrictions on BMD development and testing that could well have unequal effects on U.S. and Soviet BMD research and potential capabilities.

Further grounds for doubt about the feasibility of using negotiated constraints to control Soviet BMD reside in the purposeful rationale that seems to explain Soviet BMD activities most persuasively. As noted in Chapter 2, "arms race" and "bureaucratic politics" explanations of Soviet

BMD activities fail (at least in their more simplistic forms) to account for the historical record. The preponderance of the evidence suggests that Soviet BMD and other strategic defense efforts represent an attempt to fulfill the demands of Soviet military doctrine within prevailing economic, technological and political constraints. Soviet approval of the ABM Treaty seems to have been based on various grounds of expediency: above all, the need to prevent the United States from competing in an area of apparent U.S. technological advantage.

The ABM Treaty is such a valued instrument for keeping U.S. BMD efforts under control that it is unlikely that the Soviet Union will endorse any deviation from the ABM Treaty's constraints on the United States for defenses of ICBMs or for more ambitious purposes. If the Soviets were to decide to endorse a revision of the ABM Treaty at some future point, they would be more likely to favor an expansion of allowed levels of ground-based BMD of traditional types (an area of competition in which the USSR may well have some comparative advantages, owing to the nature of the Soviet target set and other Soviet offensive and defensive capabilities) than approval of the space-based capabilities featured prominently in SDI research. As noted in Chapter 4, the apparent incentives that led the Soviets to approve the ABM Treaty will probably remain operative for the indefinite future, barring an unanticipated Soviet technological breakthrough or an unpredictable decision to capitalize on their near-term breakout potential or a possible decision to propose treaty revisions authorizing more ground-based BMD deployments of traditional types.

The Western alliance should be prepared for such contingencies. It is not clear, for example, whether the United States should approve a possible future Soviet proposal to revise the ABM Treaty to authorize more extensive deployments of ground-based BMD interceptors of traditional types and to prohibit space-based BMD and associated anti-satellite capabilities. Under such a regime, the United States might reduce the vulnerability of its ICBMs at the cost of magnifying other asymmetries. Because of the more defensible nature of Soviet military assets (owing mainly to enormous Soviet investments in hardening, dispersal, mobility, deception, and so forth), the superior Soviet ability to proliferate such terminal defenses relatively rapidly, and the substantial Soviet lead in prompt counterforce capabilities (which could be used in attempts to defeat U.S. terminal defenses), such an arms control arrangement could well be to the net advantage of the Soviet Union.

It is doubtful that the Soviets would propose (or agree to) such a revision of the ABM Treaty's constraints unless they had calculated that it would result in certain advantages for themselves. Since the Soviets have not historically revealed any interest in assuring the survivability of U.S. nuclear forces by making the challenges facing Soviet strategic forces more complex, they would probably not approve such a treaty revision because of a desire to bolster the deterrent credibility of U.S. retaliatory forces. It appears more likely that the Soviets would have calculated that they would benefit asymmetrically from such a regime, depending on its specific terms. An expansion of permitted ground-based BMD deployments in the United States and the Soviet Union could, for example, benefit the Soviets if it degraded the credibility of the selective strike capabilities of the United States, Britain, and France. A treaty-compliant expansion of ground-based BMD capabilities could also facilitate the pursuit of a "creepout" from remaining ABM Treaty constraints, since the level of ambiguity in assessing potential treaty violations could rise in conjunction with the magnitude of treaty-approved deployments.

Active defenses could also be used in combination with passive defenses to achieve synergistic effects. A preferential defense of the escape paths of the USSR's mobile command-and-control centers could, for example, achieve great leverage against any U.S. attempts to barrage a wide area.[55] Similar location-uncertainty principles could apply to the defense of deeply buried command centers. Because the Soviets have a substantial advantage in such passive defenses, they might be able to make more effective use of an increase in permitted land-based BMD deployments than could the United States.

In theory, at least some space-based BMD systems and components might have to be allowed in ABM Treaty revisions to avoid an outcome asymmetrically favorable to the Soviet Union. Deployable and effective space-based BMD systems will, however, probably remain distant and hypothetical possibilities for several years to come in comparison with ground-based interceptors of traditional types. Moreover, because space-based BMD technologies overlap significantly with certain ASAT technologies, decisions about whether to pursue ASAT arms control would have to be addressed simultaneously.

It can be argued that antisatellite capabilities should not be restricted in any way that would hinder the United States in protecting space-based BMD assets; ensuring the survivability of such systems would be essential for strategic stability. The counterargument, that U.S. and Western security interests would be better served by comprehensive ASAT limitations that would protect space-based BMD systems from attack, assumes a degree of Soviet-U.S. cooperation that may be unrealistic. Some Western analysts have speculated, however, that it might be possible to devise balanced ASAT arms control arrangements that would benefit from unilateral enforcement mechanisms—for instance, "keep-out" zones protected by treaty-permitted ASAT capabilities. Space-based BMD systems and other critical space-based assets could theoretically be lodged within such zones.

A more near-term issue concerns the possibility of arms control constraints on antitactical ballistic missiles (ATBM). Some arms control arrangements could, of course, significantly limit requirements for such capabilities—for example, the U.S. proposal at Reykjavik to abolish all ballistic missiles or the December 1987 "double-zero" treaty that is to eliminate U.S. and Soviet ground-based missiles with ranges between 500 and 5500 km. The issue at hand, however, is whether ATBM development and deployment programs should be constrained.

The Soviet position, as noted in Chapter 4, is that U.S. ATBM systems for deployment in defense of Western Europe would contravene article IX of the ABM Treaty, which states that "each Party undertakes not to transfer to other States, and not to deploy outside its national territory, ABM systems or their components limited by this Treaty." Agreed Interpretation G indicates that article IX "includes the obligation of the US and the USSR not to provide to other States technical descriptions or blueprints specially worked out for the construction of ABM systems and their components limited by the Treaty."

In contrast, the United States has noted that the ABM Treaty defines an ABM system as "a system to counter strategic ballistic missiles or their elements in flight trajectory" (article II). Because the Soviet Union has long held, in arms control negotiations, that its intermediate-range missiles are incapable of threatening the continental United States and are therefore not "strategic,"[56] defenses against such missiles should be seen as legal, even by Soviet definitions. As noted in Chapter 1, the Reagan administration has maintained that the Soviet SA-12 is an entirely legal system as long as its capabilities are limited to the interception of non-"strategic" ballistic missiles. On similar grounds, the Office of Technology Assessment of the U.S. Congress has concluded that ATBM systems are "not prohibited" by the ABM Treaty, although ATBM systems capable of intercepting SLBMs and ICBMs could "undercut" its provisions.[57]

ATBM in Western Europe would therefore not contradict the ABM Treaty, unless the systems and components deployed were originally designed by the United States for defense against Soviet "strategic ballistic missiles" or were capable of such performance levels. West Europeans are legally at liberty to develop their own ATBM systems, and to cooperate with the United States in doing so, as long as the systems at issue in this cooperation were not originally developed for defense of the United States or capable of intercepting "strategic" missiles.[58] The United States is likewise legally free to deploy ATBM defenses to protect U.S. and allied forces and other assets in Western Europe. This interpretation has also been accepted by some West European officials. For example, Manfred Wörner, the West German defense minister, has written, "The provisions of the ABM Treaty, a bilateral agreement in which the United States and the Soviet Union agreed in 1972 to limit systems to counter strategic ballistic missiles, do not impose any constraints on the deployment of a European antimissile system, even if interpreted in a restrictive manner."[59]

It seems likely that the Soviet position on ATBM—which includes a denial that Soviet SAM systems have any ATBM or strategic BMD capability—has been devised with some care. Some West European analysts have speculated that the Soviets would like to use the ABM Treaty to create friction in U.S.–West European relations and to hinder the Western development of ATBM capabilities comparable to those in the USSR. If this tactic failed, the Soviets (and Western opponents of ATBM) might at some point propose that the ABM Treaty be amended to constrain ATBM deployments. Although a well-devised and verifiable ATBM accord might have some theoretical attractions,[60] Soviet behavior with respect to BMD and other forms of strategic and theater defense has made an equitable agreement on ATBM appear improbable.

As on the intercontinental level, the Soviet Union has deployed far more ballistic missiles and warheads capable of being directed against Western Europe than the United States has deployed for the defense of Western Europe. Similarly, the military assets of the United States and its allies in Western Europe, the targets the Soviet Union would threaten, are more vulnerable than the corresponding target set in the Warsaw Pact, owing to superior Soviet investments in various forms of active and passive defense. Above all—to complete the parallel with the intercontinental situation—the Western alliance currently lacks any ATBM capability and has not yet decided to develop and deploy ATBM systems (except for the modest Patriot upgrades), whereas the Soviet Union has been deploying SA-10s since 1980. (While both the SA-10 and SA-X-12B/Giant are judged to have some ATBM and strategic BMD potential, the latter is considered more advanced and potent.)

An ATBM agreement providing for equal numbers of ATBM systems would therefore not favor the Western alliance. Unless extensive programs of active and passive defense (hardening, mobility, and so forth) were accomplished, the West's military assets would require more ATBM protection for "parity" in defense, assuming that the reliability and effectiveness of Soviet and Western ATBM systems were roughly similar. Soviet superiority in missile and warhead numbers would at the same time place asymmetrical burdens on Western ATBM. The December 1987 "double-zero" INF treaty may, moreover, eliminate U.S. INF missiles and promote a climate of opinion in which the modernization of U.S. ground-based missiles with ranges below 500 km would be politically difficult to pursue, even in the face of Soviet numerical superiority in SS-21s and other missile delivery systems with ranges below 500 km.

Qualitative restrictions on ATBM development and deployment might also be proposed by the Soviets and could entail equally problematic implications for Western security. The net result of such qualitative constraints, given prevailing verification uncertainties and compliance practices, might well be to exacerbate East-West asymmetries in active and passive defenses. To guard against this possibility, the Western alliance should retain its freedom to deploy ATBM in Western Europe and avoid subjecting ATBM to quantitative or qualitative restrictions that would asymmetrically favor the Soviet Union.

Force Posture Improvements

Although the Western alliance will continue to seek arms control solutions in negotiations with the Soviet Union, the uncertain prospects of such arrangements will necessitate the maintenance and improvement of the West's military posture. The principle of force modernization to maintain deterrence has not historically been controversial. But chronic intra-alliance disagreements about the specific improvements that are required seem to have grown more intense in recent years.

Differences about the value of strategic defenses have been especially profound. Judgments also differ, however, with respect to nuclear-force requirements and the proper relationship between conventional and nuclear capabilities. The issues have been more sharply argued because of economic constraints in all Western countries, coupled with the increased costs of all types of military capabilities. As with the intra-Western disagreements about arms control, this overview is not comprehensive; it seeks rather to identify some of the most salient issues and possible points of consensus.

NUCLEAR FORCES

Consensus about the need for the West to maintain a reliable nuclear-deterrent posture is reasonably solid. Although nuclear-force modernization issues remain sensitive in countries such as Britain and West

Germany, the SDI has had the paradoxical effect of helping—at least in some quarters—to "relegitimize" nuclear deterrence. West European politicians have found that the message that nuclear deterrence will remain necessary for many years to come has been welcomed by those alarmed by the prospect of "destabilization" through BMD.

When the threat that Soviet defenses might pose for NATO's flexible-response strategy is assessed, offensive countermeasures receive primary attention. Many West European experts and officials would agree with the Office of Technology Assessment: "Offensive countermeasures probably contribute more than defensive actions towards our ability to deter or respond to [a] Soviet defensive breakout."[61]

There is no question that the adverse implications of additional Soviet BMD deployments could be partially addressed through improved U.S. abilities to penetrate Soviet BMD. As was pointed out by the President's Commission on Strategic Forces (the Scowcroft Commission) in April 1983, it is particularly important

> to counter any improvement in Soviet ABM capability by being able to maintain the effectiveness of our offensive systems. The possibility of either a sudden breakthrough in ABM technology, a rapid Soviet breakout from the ABM treaty by a quick further deployment of their current ABM systems, or the deployment of air defense systems also having some capability against strategic ballistic missiles all point to the need for us to be able to penetrate some level of ABM defense. This dictates continued attention to having sufficient throwweight for adequate numbers of warheads and of decoys and other penetration aids.[62]

Improved U.S. abilities to penetrate Soviet air and ballistic missile defenses against U.S. delivery systems (bombers, cruise missiles, and ballistic missiles) would help to prevent the Soviets from gaining a great advantage in escalation control capabilities. Improved penetration means could also hinder Soviet efforts to undermine the credibility of NATO's flexible-response strategy and to defeat NATO's "emerging technologies" programs. There is wide agreement within the Western alliance that the West must be able to respond promptly to a Soviet BMD breakout that could endanger the deterrent credibility of U.S. and allied nuclear forces. These forces must continue to be able to penetrate Soviet defenses and to hold at risk targets highly valued by the Soviet leadership.

There is little agreement, however, on how challenging the offensive-countermeasures tasks may be. From one perspective, more prominent in the United States than in Western Europe, it seems plain that developing and maintaining adequate penetration capabilities will not be easy or inexpensive. To begin with, the United States is already at a disadvantage with respect to numbers of intercontinental missiles (ICBMs and SLBMs) and in terms of total ballistic missile throwweight. This asymmetry means that U.S. prospects for multiplying numbers of warheads and penetration aids are more limited than Soviet options. The MX experience since the late 1970s has shown that it is politically difficult for the United States to deploy large ICBMs comparable to those in the Soviet ICBM force. Soviet SS-18 ICBMs have over twice the throwweight of U.S. MX ICBMs, and Soviet SS-19 ICBMs have slightly more throwweight than the MX ICBMs. While the USSR maintains 308 SS-18 and 360 SS-19 launchers, the U.S. Congress has so far approved the deployment of 50 MX ICBMs. The small ICBM, or "Midgetman," may provide little additional throwweight for warheads and penetration aids. As noted in Chapter 2, Soviet passive defenses such as mobility, deceptive basing, and hardening are already posing significant challenges to U.S. target acquisition capabilities and raising the possibility that the United States may require earth-penetrating weapons to hold deeply buried targets at risk. Moreover, some types of penetration aids, such as MaRVs (maneuvering reentry vehicles), are politically controversial because they imply high accuracy in addition to an ability to evade Soviet defenses.[63]

The challenge appears formidable, in other words, to those inclined to accept analyses comparable to the one outlined in Chapter 3. It is assumed that the West requires survivable and controllable nuclear strike forces in order to maintain the credibility of the flexible-response strategy. Indeed, in order to enhance its prospects for successful crisis management, escalation control, and war termination, the West needs to improve its capacity to carry out discriminate strikes against key military targets in the Warsaw Pact, including the USSR. The West's ability to develop a more credible nuclear posture—one that might be used in a politically responsible and nonsuicidal fashion—could therefore be challenged rather fundamentally by the requirement to penetrate significantly improved Soviet defenses, active and passive.

From another perspective, shared perhaps more widely in Western Europe than in the United States, the utility (and possible negation) of specific limited options is less significant than the ability to pose a risk of nuclear escalation that might go out of control and cause unacceptable damage. It is sometimes assumed that this risk is sufficient to deter the Soviet leadership from contemplating aggression or attempting coercion, that no likely Soviet defenses could cancel out this risk, and that affordable improvements in offensive nuclear capabilities can readily be accomplished. Sir Geoffrey Howe has underlined the British govern-ment's confidence in the long-term stability of what Thomas Schelling once called the "balance of prudence" by citing with approval Schelling's highway metaphor for the operation of nuclear deterrence: "People regularly stand at the curb watching trucks, buses and cars hurtle past at speeds that guarantee injury and threaten death if they so much as attempt to cross against the traffic. They are absolutely deterred. But there is no fear. They just know better."[64]

This perspective on deterrence requirements has helped to persuade a number of British and French strategists that the political and strategic credibility of their national nuclear forces could be maintained, even if the Soviet Union deployed large numbers of ground-based BMD interceptors of plausible reliability and effectiveness. The negation of their potential limited strike options that might follow, as sketched in Chapter 3, might not undermine the credibility of declaratory targeting policies based on a "Moscow criterion" or "enlarged anti-cities" strikes. It nonetheless remains true (as some British and French statements have tacitly ac-knowledged) that these forces would enjoy greater political and strategic credibility if their capacity to penetrate Soviet defenses was robust enough to allow for greater selectivity.

Although some American analysts have suggested that the loss of the credibility of the British and French forces would not change the East-West strategic balance fundamentally,[65] the future credibility of these forces is in the overall interest of the West—for purposes of European-American alliance cohesion and for deterrence. As Phil Wil-liams has noted, "given a choice, Moscow would probably prefer the United Kingdom to abandon Trident, rather than simply cut conventional forces."[66] The Soviets have an interest in simplifying the risks that would attend an invasion of Europe and/or an attempt at coercion. The Western allies have a countervailing interest in complicating Soviet risk calcula-tions, and the British and French forces contribute substantially to this purpose. It is important to persuade the Soviets that the risks in miscalculating the consequences of aggression could be intolerable, and that they cannot gain any usable superiority in means of escalation control.

The soundest solutions to any reduction in the credibility of the British and French forces owing to Soviet BMD might well be found in greater intra-European cooperation within a strengthened European-U.S. part-nership. Such cooperation and partnership could offer the means to develop improved retaliatory forces as well as defenses, including BMD. Whether such cooperation would be of interest to France is an open question. The French take understandable pride in the fact that they have built their strategic nuclear forces, including their modern SSBN fleet, without anyone's help. The total independence of France's nuclear strategy and decision making is believed to be one of the foundations of its foreign policy autonomy. Some influential Frenchmen might prefer an intra-European BMD project excluding the United States to one in cooperation with the United States. Stimulating West European support for such a project would represent an enormous challenge for French diplomacy, especially if it were to be a truly autonomous European enterprise, rather than one carried out in association with the United States.

Strategic necessity may nonetheless require more intensive European-U.S. cooperation in the long term, and it would not necessarily diminish the autonomy of France's nuclear decision making if France and its allies shared more information and worked together on BMD matters. No one considers France's freedom of decision in nuclear matters to have been diminished through the purchase from the United States of KC-135 tankers (for in-flight refueling of its Mirage IV bombers) and very low frequency transmitters (for command and control of its strategic nuclear forces).[67] Britain has, in contrast, a long tradition of working closely with the United States in the maintenance and improvement of its strategic nuclear forces.

Expanding such cooperation would involve tradeoffs for the United States. Some U.S. officials were notably hostile to the French nuclear program during the 1960s, with Secretary of Defense Robert S. McNamara the most prominent critic. The principal U.S. objections were that the expense needlessly diverted resources from conventional forces and that the French might somehow trigger U.S. involvement in a nuclear war. U.S. attitudes changed with the Nixon administration. NATO's 1974 Ottawa communiqué referred to Britain and France possessing "nuclear forces capable of playing a deterrent role of their own contributing to the overall strengthening of the deterrence of the alliance."[68] The trigger risk has been seen in subsequent years as less significant than the advantage of maintaining additional centers of nuclear decision-making that could multiply Soviet risks in undertaking aggression.

Other advantages for the United States in working with Britain and France to preserve the credibility of their nuclear forces could be maintaining alliance cohesion, facilitating the development of common infrastructure programs for BMD systems in Europe, promoting the progress of long-term efforts toward greater West European defense unity and reduced dependence on U.S. guarantees, and lessening the impact of the increased cost of penetration aids and other BMD countermeasures on British and French conventional forces. Robert Komer, who was under secretary of defense for policy in 1980, when the United States decided to sell Trident SLBMs to the United Kingdom, reports that this decision was made "essentially because we saw the UK as determined to modernize anyway, and hence calculated that we might as well help it do so less expensively in order to minimize the impact on its conventional NATO contribution."[69] It is understandable that some Americans would prefer that the United States monopolize direct control over nuclear escalation decisions in the West, but the alliance advantages of collaborating with Britain and France should be judged as outweighing the disadvantages of perpetuating a sort of trigger situation and furnishing new evidence of allied cooperation that the USSR could use in trying to convince the credulous that British and French nuclear forces should be counted with U.S. totals in arms control negotiations.

Public attitudes skeptical about offensive nuclear force improvements will (in Britain and the United States, at least) restrict spending on such forces, as will financial constraints—limits on national budgets as well as defense budgets. Modernizing offensive forces in order to be able to overcome projected improvements in Soviet BMD and other active and passive Soviet defenses may not win great support during a time of budgetary stringency. Public attitudes and financial constraints, together with arms control, will condition the extent to which the United States and its allies can develop improved nuclear strike capabilities.

Even if Britain, France, and the United States succeed in building more discriminate and controllable nuclear options (ones capable, moreover, of penetrating Soviet defenses), the West will need stronger conventional forces to ensure the security of Western Europe. Although NATO's conventional forces have been improved, the gap between the conventional capabilities of NATO and those of the Warsaw Pact has continued to widen, owing to the high investments of the USSR in conventional military strength.[70] As suggested in Chapters 2 and 3, one of the effects of the widening disparity in conventional force capabilities has been to accentuate Western dependence on nuclear threats. These threats have in turn been neutralized, to some unmeasurable degree, by Soviet "counter-deterrent" nuclear capabilities. The result, according to General Bernard Rogers, has been to reinstate the significance of the conventional-force balance: "Although nuclear weapons contribute to deterrence of all forms of aggression, given the changes that have occurred in the nuclear balance since 1967, the conventional leg of the triad has become more important to our efforts at maintaining the credibility of our deterrent."[71]

The conventional-force balance is extremely important because of the Soviet military doctrines and force-development policies reviewed in Chapters 2 and 3. Even though significant uncertainties remain with respect to the controllability of nuclear escalation, the Soviets have devoted a great deal of effort to developing forces apparently intended to be capable of discouraging Western governments from employing nuclear weapons; operational plans and forces to decide conflicts on nonnuclear terms, if possible; and doctrines and systems for selective nuclear attacks, if necessary.

In view of these developments on the Soviet side, the continued improvement of Western nuclear capabilities should be supplemented with enhanced capacities for conventional defense. The West could most effectively deny the Soviets confidence in their ability to achieve rapid successes on the nonnuclear level by building conventional forces that would pose the risk of a relatively prolonged conventional campaign. This risk would in turn probably augment the dangers (in Soviet assessments, at least) of increased instability in Eastern Europe and more deliberate and purposeful decision making about nuclear force employment in the Western alliance. In short, the West's ability to defend Western Europe by conventional means—to frustrate Soviet attack plans for the opening phase of war—could be of decisive importance in deterring Soviet aggression in a crisis.

This prescription—to rely less on nuclear weapons to deter conventional aggression—has been a commonplace since the late 1950s. It has taken on new relevance, however, owing to changes in both the conventional and the nuclear balances. Soviet conventional capabilities have been significantly improved, and Soviet nuclear forces have complicated Western reliance on nuclear threats. Long-term trends in West European public opinion appear to have also made Western dependence on nuclear responses to Soviet aggression problematic; several opinion surveys have suggested that majorities would not support the use of nuclear weapons in defense of Western Europe, even if the Warsaw Pact was winning the war by conventional means.[72] Western threats to use nuclear weapons in a serious crisis or war might therefore lack credibility, and actual force-employment options could be severely limited for lack of conventional capabilities.

The logical inferences have been drawn by key West European officials. General Wolfgang Altenburg, chairman of NATO's Military Committee since October 1986, has called attention to the need for conventional forces with greater sustainability.[73] The West German defense minister, Manfred Wörner, has written, "A Soviet capability in effect to preempt nuclear escalation with a conventional offensive can be offset by the Alliance only through necessary improvements in NATO's conventional forces."[74]

The problem, even more than with nuclear force modernization, is one of resources. Given the demographic and financial constraints of the four principal countries in the Western alliance (that is, the four main contributors of defense resources) and the national nuclear and out-of-area power-projection commitments of three of them (Britain, France, and the United States), it will probably be difficult for the Western alliance to improve its conventional capabilities in Europe in a more than marginal fashion for several years to come. Indeed, these capabilities might actually deteriorate in relation to those of the Warsaw Pact. According to Peter Stratmann, "unless current national priorities are realigned, NATO's conventional defense will be even less assured in the 1990s than today."[75] This is the stringent context in which the Western alliance will assess possible costly improvements in its active defenses—air defenses and, potentially, BMD—in the years to come.[76]

STRATEGIC DEFENSES
The most politically sensitive form of strategic defense is BMD. Except for isolated instances of local concern, air defenses and passive defenses (hardening, mobility, and so forth) have never evoked as much controversy as BMD.

As noted earlier, the problems that might be posed by a hypothetical Soviet-U.S. relationship of defense dominance are probably at least two decades in the future. In November 1986, Max Kampelman, the head of the U.S. delegation to the Geneva negotiations on nuclear, space, and defense systems, said:

> A decision on whether to move ahead with the deployment of strategic defenses is probably years away; it might be made by President Reagan's successor, but it will not likely be made by President Reagan himself. Nor is the decision foreordained. There are ample examples of weapons systems for which research was completed but which were not deployed or maintained . . . We will not decide on SDI [deployment] without additional thorough discussions and consultations with our allies.[77]

The three practical issues that are likely to concern the alliance in the foreseeable future are (1) the proper dimensions of a research and technology program as a "prudent hedge" against Soviet BMD activities; (2) possible near-term deployments of strategic BMD interceptors by the

United States; and (3) possible deployments of theater BMD systems in Western Europe, also known as antitactical ballistic missiles (ATBM).

Research as a "Prudent Hedge." The basic principle of a U.S. research and technology program in BMD is not controversial in Western Europe. No one disputes the fact that the ABM Treaty allows research and development activities in support of permitted BMD deployments. Such activities are generally seen as sensible and desirable, within ABM Treaty constraints, if only to advance Western understanding of Soviet BMD activities. In the words of Sir Geoffrey Howe, "common prudence dictates that the massive Soviet research programmes into the new technologies should be matched."[78]

West Europeans agree that BMD research will probably be carried forward by the next administration, whether Republican or Democratic. According to the January 1986 report to the French minister of defense, "whatever the political evolution in the U.S. might be, a pure and simple abandonment of the SDI program seems improbable during its research phase, although delays or inflections always remain possible."[79] In November 1986, German Chancellor Helmut Kohl said: "Like the Soviet Union, Washington will also carry out its research program. Recent statements, even by prominent American critics of SDI such as Robert McNamara, prove that the United States regards the research program as a necessary guarantee and insurance against possible abuse during the intended disarmament process. An administration under the Democrats will also adhere to SDI research."[80]

In support of his judgment, Kohl referred to a recent Democratic party document prepared in anticipation of the 1988 elections. It is worth noting in this regard that the Democratic Leadership Council in September 1986 published a report on defense policy prepared under the direction of Senator Sam Nunn, Representative Les Aspin, and Senator Albert Gore, Jr. This report concluded that the Krasnoyarsk radar is "definitely a violation" of the ABM Treaty and recommended that U.S. BMD research be continued: "In view of the size and scope of Soviet research programs (and considering the magnitude of Soviet investment in actual defenses, including the missile defense of Moscow), a comprehensive U.S. program of SDI research is necessary to hedge against a possible Soviet breakthrough."[81]

Such prudent-hedge arguments are similar to those advanced by the Reagan administration, and West European governments generally endorse such an approach. West European elites can also accept a feasibility-study rationale for BMD research. Yet many object to the a priori assumption of some Americans that the defense-dominance vision is necessarily desirable, that its realization will prove technically feasible, and that it will then be pursued, even to the point of transferring the requisite technology to the Soviet Union. At an important conference of U.S., British, French, and West German experts in strategic affairs in 1985, "European support for [BMD] R & D applied to research to determine *whether* defenses were feasible, on the assumption that their contribution to Western deterrence would then be assessed, not to research to determine *how* the West could proceed down a road to a strategy of defensive deterrence."[82]

If the prudent-hedge and feasibility-study approaches constitute the most solid foundation for alliance consensus, it is important to consider the specific Soviet possibilities that merit precautionary insurance. As noted in Chapter 4, the two basic possibilities are creepout and breakout (either illegal or legal, upon treaty abrogation).[83]

The circumstances in which the Soviets might exercise the option of exploiting their apparently superior ability at present to proliferate traditional ground-based BMD interceptors in an unambiguous large-scale breakout from the ABM Treaty are not entirely predictable. As indicated in Chapter 4, the balance of evidence would suggest that the Soviets would probably prefer not to engage in a breakout that could well energize U.S. BMD efforts and seriously complicate Soviet ballistic missile targeting. Moreover, the Soviets may also be concerned that an intensive and sustained U.S. BMD program might ultimately place the Soviet Union at a disadvantage with respect to possible future space-based systems that might be more effective against Soviet ICBM throwweight advantages and might also partially compensate for U.S. deficiencies in other forms of strategic defense (hardening, mobility, deception, and so forth).

But Soviet decision making is not entirely predictable. There is a tendency to assume that, even if the USSR is better positioned for a post–ABM Treaty breakout situation than the United States, the Soviets are not likely to exercise their breakout option unless provoked by the U.S. SDI. A recent British analysis, for example, stated, "Should this [ABM] Treaty collapse as a result of the Strategic Defense Initiative, given that the Soviet Union is best placed to take advantage of such a collapse, the credibility of the UK deterrent may be called into question."[84]

There are two difficulties with this assumption. The first is that a great deal of BMD progress has been made by the Soviets since the ABM Treaty came into force. Although significant uncertainties persist about the likely operational reliability and effectiveness of the Soviet BMD systems (discussed in Chapter 1), the Soviet Union has modernized the Moscow system with missiles and radars suitable for relatively rapid proliferation, developed potentially BMD-capable mobile SAMs (for instance, the SA-X-12B/Giant), and constructed an extensive network of large phased-array radars that may well be capable of contributing to early warning, attack assessment, and battle management for a large-scale BMD deployment. Further improvements in this BMD potential can be expected, and relative Soviet superiority in rapidly exploitable BMD options could therefore increase.

This leads to the second difficulty with the assumption of Soviet inaction. It would be unwise and imprudent to allow the Soviet BMD breakout potential to continue to improve without taking compensatory steps. For, however improbable it seems, the Soviets could at some point calculate that they could gain a meaningful strategic advantage by exercising a breakout option that had grown tempting, owing in part to their counterforce superiority and investments in active and passive defenses. As the Office of Technology Assessment has noted, "there can be no assurance that the Soviets would actually behave as we think they should."[85]

However remote the contingency may seem, the strategic advantages the Soviets could gain vis-à-vis the Western alliance through a large unilateral expansion of their BMD capabilities make it clear that the United States and its allies should prepare for this contingency by conducting their own research and development programs on BMD. Vigorous research and development efforts in BMD technologies are necessary to be better prepared to respond to the contingency of an expansion of existing Soviet BMD capabilities in a timely fashion. Such research efforts could also help to deter the Soviets from more extensive breaches of the ABM Treaty and/or from undertaking a clear-cut breakout from its constraints. The President's Commission on Strategic Forces (the Scowcroft Commission) noted: "Vigorous research and development on ABM technologies—including, in particular, ways to sharpen the effectiveness of treaty-limited ABM systems with new types of nuclear systems and also ways to use non-nuclear systems—are imperative to avoid technological surprise from the Soviets. Such a vigorous program on our part also decreases any Soviet incentive—based on an attempt to achieve unilateral advantage—to abrogate the ABM treaty."[86]

The creepout possibility constitutes a far more difficult case, because it would mean that Western governments would have to make their decisions on the basis of ambiguous evidence. As suggested in Chapters 1, 2, and 4, the Soviets have evidently seen advantages in maintaining a high degree of discretion about their BMD and space warfare activities since the late 1960s. The available evidence on Soviet ABM Treaty compliance is apparently burdened with significant ambiguities. An ambiguous situation—a buildup of breakout potential coupled to possible creepout activities—would be much harder for the West to deal with, because the arguments for restraint could appear overwhelming, even though the growth in the Soviet potential could become quite threatening over time. The creepout course would probably be preferred by the Soviets, given the risks in an unambiguous breakout.

Near-Term Strategic BMD Deployments. The January 1986 report to the French minister of defense noted that, although the principle of research on BMD is supported by a large consensus in the United States, "the very principle of an ABM defense (with or without space-based components) remains very controversial."[87] One of the principal disputes has concerned the purpose of the SDI: Is the program intended solely to investigate the means of comprehensive defense dominance, or are more near-term strategic BMD deployments desirable?

American proponents of relatively near-term strategic BMD deployments have included figures as diverse as Zbigniew Brzezinski, President Carter's national security adviser; Alexander Haig, a former secretary of state; Jeane Kirkpatrick, a former U.S. ambassador to the United Nations; Eugene Rostow, a former director of the U.S. Arms Control and Disarmament Agency; Senators Gordon Humphrey, Richard Lugar, Dan Quayle, Malcolm Wallop, and Pete Wilson; Representatives Jim Courter and Jack Kemp; and experts such as Fred Hoffman and Albert Wohlstetter.[88] Their opinions are, of course, not identical, and no composite summary could adequately represent the views of individuals.

As a broad generalization, however, the case for near-term strategic BMD deployments might include the following three points:

1. The SDI has been biased against early-deployment options and has devoted resources primarily to high-leverage concepts such as space-based boost-phase intercept capabilities using directed-energy systems that will probably not be available for deployment until the next century. The emphasis on building a comprehensive defense of the U.S. population against an all-out Soviet nuclear attack has made the entire research effort appear dedicated to technically questionable aims. This aim misrepresents Soviet (and, incidentally, U.S.) strategy by implying that cities are prime targets. The emphasis on defense against the least plausible form of attack has meant a neglect of more strategically significant threats—for instance, selective Soviet attacks against key military targets in the Western alliance. These threats could mature in the foreseeable future, with improvements in Soviet missile accuracy and advanced

nuclear and nonnuclear munitions, and BMD could form part of the response. But the all-or-nothing approach to SDI deployments—the lack of concrete results in developing specific near-term deployment plans—has made the SDI vulnerable to cutbacks in congressional appropriations. An SDI destined to remain in research-only status for many years cannot expect to win sustained public support and may be more subject to asymmetrical arms control constraints than one that involves actual deployments.

2. The United States should at least take steps permitted even under a restrictive interpretation of the ABM Treaty. The United States could, for example, reactivate the treaty-permitted site at Grand Forks, North Dakota, and use it—as the Soviets use their Moscow site—as a basis for practical experience with BMD deployments. (Its actual operational value would, of course, differ from that of the Moscow site, owing to the vital Soviet command-and-control assets and other military facilities near Moscow.) The United States should build a treaty-compliant large phased-array radar network more extensive than that currently envisaged and take other measures to reduce the Soviet-U.S. disparity in rapidly deployable BMD capabilities. Studies of the potential utility of nonnuclear as well as nuclear-tipped ground-based BMD interceptors (and associated radars and battle management capabilities) should receive more urgent attention. When the ABM Treaty was approved in 1972, the United States specified that continued compliance with the treaty would depend on the status of limitations on offensive forces.[89] Since SALT I and SALT II failed to prevent the Soviet Union from gaining a potential ability to attack U.S. land-based forces and command-and-control capabilities, the United States should seriously consider whether BMD deployments more extensive than those permitted by the treaty and its protocol might eventually be needed. Such a decision could be deferred during work on near-term deployments, pending the results of further arms control negotiations.

3. Near-term strategic BMD deployments could fulfill several important missions: bolstering deterrence by substantially "raising the ante" for Soviet attacks against such key targets as national command authorities and associated command, control, communications, and intelligence (C^3I) sites; providing a prudent measure of protection against the highly unlikely but potentially catastrophic prospect of accidental or unauthorized launches; defending at least part of the U.S. retaliatory force; establishing a functioning production base as a hedge against the risk of Soviet breakout or creepout; and furnishing a basis for more extensive BMD deployments in the future, if such deployments then seem advis-

able. Because the more plausible Soviet attacks would be selective, limited strategic BMD deployments could seriously affect Soviet calculations of likely attack outcomes. Active defenses of the most probable targets of Soviet attacks could reinforce deterrence by causing uncertainties for Soviet attack planners, could help to protect the U.S. population from collateral damage, and could supplement the improved passive defense measures that the United States also requires. The United States should have means of damage limitation other than relying on Soviet restraint in the face of U.S. retaliatory threats. The lack of strategic defenses could result in self-deterrence in a crisis, while a less vulnerable United States would be more capable of fulfilling its guarantees to allies.

President Reagan has given three reasons for rejecting such proposals: (1) "Our research is aimed at finding a way of protecting people, not missiles." (2) "To deploy systems of limited effectiveness now would divert limited funds and delay our main research. It could well erode support for the program before it's permitted to reach its potential."[90] (3) An end to the ABM Treaty's constraints would favor the Soviets, because "they are much more prepared to take advantage of such a thing than we are. In other words, they could suddenly expand their military might to a far greater degree than we could if that treaty didn't exist."[91]

The president's continuing emphasis on the comprehensive goal of making nuclear weapons "obsolete" has differed from the policy articulations of some lower-level U.S. officials who have foreseen the possibility of incremental deployments of limited BMD capabilities for various military purposes. Lieutenant General James Abrahamson, the director of the SDI organization, said in July 1986, however, that initial SDI deployments could not begin until "after the mid-1990s," assuming that basic development decisions were made by 1992. In November 1987, it was reported that these decisions might be delayed, owing to cuts in the SDI budget.[92]

Supporters of the president's approach hold that near-term deployments "would sacrifice the larger design" and deflect attention from the ultimate goal.[93] The president's approach is consistent with the U.S. approach to active defense of the continental United States since the 1960s. Imperfect defenses incapable of complete damage denial have not enjoyed sustained support. The United States has never maintained BMD systems capable of defending only selected targets on a long-term basis; the Safeguard system at Grand Forks, North Dakota, was operational for only a period of months in 1975-1976.[94]

The most sensitive point in U.S. discussions of possible near-term BMD deployments remains the future of the ABM Treaty. Relatively few proponents of such deployments recommend that the United States exercise its right of withdrawing from the treaty with six months' notice. Even Congressman Kemp, who has written that it is "a strategic and moral imperative that we commit to the earliest possible deployment, step by step, of SDI, and that we modify—or withdraw from—the ABM Treaty as necessary," has recommended first steps that could be treaty compliant—above all, "building an operational BMD facility in North Dakota, which could be integrated into a future defense network."[95]

Although no substantial political constituency for near-term abrogation of the ABM Treaty is evident, some prominent politicians have noted that the combination of arms control and U.S. strategic-offensive-force improvements may eventually prove inadequate, necessitating a U.S. reconsideration of strategic defenses and the ABM Treaty. In March 1987, Senator Nunn remarked, "Certainly a U.S. decision to withdraw from the ABM Treaty would be enormously controversial at home and abroad. I am not counseling this course at this time. Nonetheless, the American public and our allies need to understand that if we cannot solve current strategic vulnerabilities through arms control or our own [offensive] strategic programs, we may have no recourse but to consider deploying some form of strategic defense, in the future."[96]

Proposals for near-term BMD deployments have been more controversial than suggestions that could achieve some of the same ends, especially in terms of preparing a responsive hedge against possible Soviet creepout or breakout from the ABM Treaty. William J. Perry, Brent Scowcroft, Joseph S. Nye, Jr., and James A. Schear recently recommended that, in view of the Soviet "comparative advantage" in BMD systems of essentially traditional types, the United States should establish "a fully functional prototype test complex." In their view, "such a facility would help to close the 'lead time' that the Soviets now enjoy in deployable BMD technologies, and it could serve as the test bed for more advanced technologies for tracking and intercept of sophisticated maneuvering warheads. Above all, we need to know much more about the prospects and limits of mounting a cost-effective terminal BMD defense."[97]

The concept of prototype development and testing has won support on diverse grounds. Above all, it could keep long-term options open, while improving the U.S. ability to react promptly to an expansion of Soviet BMD deployments. Moreover, as William A. Davis, Jr., notes, it concerns the development of "a response option, not a unilateral decision to deploy a BMD system."[98]

West European reactions to proposals in the United States for near-term strategic BMD deployments to protect selected targets have been mixed. The favorable reactions fall into two categories. First, some West European experts have been concerned that the apparent Soviet advantage in capabilities to proliferate traditional ground-based BMD systems could become greater and pose risks for Western security. They have not been entirely reassured by the Office of Technology Assessment's report that, in order to deal with the contingency of a Soviet breakout from the ABM Treaty, "the SDI approach relies on a combination of U.S. ability to penetrate Soviet defenses and an ability to deploy as-yet-untested non-nuclear defense options; it has largely discontinued investigation of the 'traditional' ballistic missile defenses of the sort once deployed by ourselves and now deployed by the Soviets."[99]

In their view, the evident Soviet advantage in rapidly deployable traditional BMD capabilities will continue to grow if the United States abstains from competing in this area. If the Soviets made use of an enhanced advantage in this area, the additional BMD deployments could supplement other Soviet means of strategic defense and enlarge important vulnerability asymmetries favoring the USSR; stable deterrence and Western security might be jeopardized. The general principle has been noted by the West German Ministry of Defense: "Unilateral advantages of the Soviet Union in antimissile systems could result in a considerable destabilization of the balance of forces between the East and the West."[100] The concept of improving the U.S. ability to undertake large-scale BMD deployments in a timely fashion, if necessary, has therefore been welcomed by some West European strategists, and this could include actual BMD deployments, within ABM Treaty limits. Prototype development and testing could, however, satisfy some of the same objectives with less political controversy.

The second type of favorable reaction is an extension of the first. Some high-level West European political figures (for instance, Manfred Wörner) have indicated support for BMD deployment concepts that would be intended to stabilize existing deterrence arrangements by creating uncertainties for Soviet attack planners and protecting retaliatory capabilities.[101] A number of West European experts expect that, if the United States does eventually deploy BMD capabilities, these will serve mainly to defend offensive retaliatory forces and associated C³I systems. From this perspective, the SDI has made a positive contribution to Western security in that it has advanced knowledge about how to bring practical defense measures with military value closer to concrete realization.

West European critics of possible near-term BMD deployments in the United States have made five points. (1) ICBM vulnerability is not, in their view, a serious enough problem to justify BMD deployments that could lead to an erosion of the ABM Treaty regime. (2) Offensive-force countermeasures could suffice to defeat expanded Soviet BMD deployments. The purpose of U.S. BMD research and technology programs should be to understand how to counter Soviet BMD deployments, not how to undertake comparable deployments. (3) BMD-protected targets could attract large-scale attacks, and passive defenses such as mobility and concealment could protect retaliatory forces without jeopardizing the ABM Treaty.[102] (4) BMD deployments of an appreciable scale could promote dangerous misperceptions: "in his 1983 address, President Reagan himself acknowledged that a mix of offensive and defensive systems could be 'viewed as fostering an aggressive policy.' "[103]

The fifth West European criticism of possible near-term strategic BMD deployments in the United States is the most complex—the possible arms race responses that might be provoked in the Soviet Union. Some have expressed concern that U.S. investments in near-term deployments, even within ABM Treaty limits, could prompt the Soviets to respond by rapidly expanding their own BMD capabilities. The result might be increased tensions and strategic disadvantages for the West along the lines discussed in Chapter 3, at least until the Western alliance could take countermeasures. Sir Geoffrey Howe raised this issue as follows:

> Other things being equal, we welcome any cost effective enhancement of deterrence to meet palpable weaknesses on the Western side. But we also have to consider what might be the offsetting developments on the Soviet side, if unconstrained competition in ballistic missile defenses beyond the ABM Treaty limits were to be provoked. In terms of NATO's policy of forward defense and flexible response, would we lose on the swings whatever might be gained on the roundabouts?[104]

This criticism is the most complex because different estimates of probable arms race interactions have been derived from divergent assumptions about U.S. and Soviet intentions and likely behavior. In interviews in Western Europe, four distinct and yet rather impressionistic judgments were expressed: (1) the Soviets probably would have improved their BMD capabilities even if the SDI had never been launched, and they will continue to go forward, whatever the fate of the SDI; (2) the Soviets will expand their BMD activities and capabilities only if the United States goes forward with the SDI, because the Soviet Union would prefer not to take the risk of a BMD competition with the United States; (3) U.S. pursuit of the SDI would make an expansion of Soviet BMD capabilities more certain, because it would justify greater funding and commitment for Soviet strategic defenses; and (4) the SDI may have already had a "dialectical" effect in accelerating both Soviet BMD and Soviet offensive-force investments.

Of these views, only the first assumes that Soviet BMD decision making is completely autonomous; it is usually associated with a forecast of a likely Soviet breakout from the ABM Treaty and a recommendation that the United States prepare for possible deployment contingencies as vigorously as possible. It may be deficient in failing to give enough attention to the possibility that the SDI could affect Soviet BMD deployment policies. The latter three views share an assumption that the pace of Soviet BMD activities is at least partially dependent on U.S. choices.

View (2) would seem to be flawed to the extent that it neglects the probability that Soviet BMD capabilities may be improved anyway, at least in terms of treaty-permitted infrastructure expansion and system modernization and possibly on a creepout basis, because of the various incentives the USSR has to improve its strategic defense posture. As indicated in Chapter 2, the historical development of Soviet BMD programs suggests that they may be understood in terms of purposeful strategic rationales, not imitative arms race behavior. The Soviet Union began modernizing key elements of the Moscow system, developing potentially BMD-capable SAMs, and building new LPARs in the 1970s, without any stimulus in the form of the SDI. There nonetheless remains a tendency to see Soviet BMD as a threat only if the United States implements the SDI with actual deployment decisions, with a corresponding recommendation that the United States curtail or abandon the SDI.[105]

View (3) is one of the most pervasive, especially with respect to actual SDI deployments. In November 1985, for example, French Defense Minister Paul Quilès said, "If the SDI is actually put into effect, the adversary's defense systems will be reinforced, and it will be necessary for our nuclear missiles to be more effective."[106] It would be comparable to view (4) if it were not for the doubts some West Europeans express about the long-term sustainability of the SDI in the United States. In other words, the USSR's BMD programs may be pursued with greater consistency than those of the United States. No arms race would take place because the United States would scale back its interest in BMD, as in the past, after having stimulated Soviet efforts. As the Delpech report informed the French minister of defense, "the risk is real, for the United States, of having unleashed, in the USSR . . . a reflex analogous (but in the reverse direction) to that which the 'Sputnik gap' of the 1960s provoked."[107]

View (4) may be excessive to the extent that, as suggested in Chapter 4, the SDI may have had a certain deterrent effect with respect to any Soviet inclinations to capitalize on their currently superior capability to deploy relatively rapidly a widespread network of traditional ground-based BMD interceptors. Moreover, Soviet offensive-force responses specifically tailored to the SDI will probably await a clearer definition of any eventual U.S. BMD deployment choices. It is nonetheless possible that the SDI has strengthened the standing of Soviet programs concerning weapons "based on other physical principles." Sayre Stevens has speculated that the SDI has "given credibility to these Soviet programs, has undoubtedly increased their funding, and has lent impetus to the effort."[108]

The most deep-seated West European apprehension appears to concern the risk that SDI deployments could convert the possibility of expanded Soviet BMD deployments into a certainty. In other words, many West Europeans fear that large-scale U.S. BMD deployments could provoke the Soviets into making use of their own substantial BMD deployment potential. In their view, the United States should carefully consider the possibility that BMD deployments beyond mutually agreed levels could result in an extraordinarily demanding and risky unregulated BMD competition. They conclude that U.S. BMD decisions should be made deliberately, with a full recognition of the potential arms race risks of specific choices.

Although it is important to avoid turning the possibility of more extensive Soviet BMD deployments into a virtual certainty, it would be wise to recognize that the probability of continued improvements in the Soviet BMD deployment potential will remain. The ABM Treaty has not prevented the upgrading of Soviet BMD systems, and the Soviets appear to perceive numerous political and military incentives to press forward, as long as these activities do not endanger U.S. compliance with the ABM Treaty. Soviet BMD decision making is, moreover, less than entirely predictable. U.S. restraint cannot ensure that the probability of continued Soviet BMD infrastructure improvement will not eventually result in extensive deployments or an even greater unilateral advantage in near-term deployment potential in the Soviet Union. The United States should therefore pursue prudent precautionary measures with respect to defensive as well as offensive capabilities. It is especially important to narrow the gap in capabilities to deploy and benefit from traditional ground-based BMD systems while vigorously conducting research in advanced technologies and reconstructing U.S. military space assets.

It would be prudent in this regard to exercise caution with respect to widespread assumptions about trade-offs in the arms race. The term *tradeoffs* might be construed to imply that Western choices could be based on confidence in the West's ability to influence the development of the Soviet force posture—for example, that a Western decision to pursue certain types of BMD capabilities (and gain certain benefits from such defenses) would provoke certain specific Soviet responses (and thus entail certain predictable disadvantages for the West), and that, in making a decision to refrain from investing in BMD (or in other military capabilities), the West could count on corresponding Soviet inaction. By this logic, forgoing the potential benefits of a BMD research program (or eventual BMD deployments) might be worthwhile, because the tradeoff or compensation would be an avoidance of the anticipated disadvantages for the West in an expansion of Soviet BMD and ballistic missile strike capabilities. Similarly, the term *arms race* is sometimes understood to imply that the West may choose not to compete in specific areas of military technology and may be assured of parallel Soviet restraint.

The implicit theories about arms competitions and Soviet behavior behind such assumptions appear to be flawed on at least two basic grounds. First, the theories oversimplify the origins of arms competition behavior by suggesting that external stimuli constitute the principal determinants of force posture development. As noted in Chapter 2, military force postures are the product of many factors, some interactive and some internal and relatively autonomous. East-West (and U.S.-Soviet) arms competition interactions are far more complex than generally assumed.

Second, simplistic theories of bilateral arms competitions would tend to equate the strategic objectives and force posture development patterns of the Western alliance and the Warsaw Pact. Soviet strategic objectives, however, differ profoundly from those of the Western alliance, and this has been reflected in contrasting military posture investments. In virtually all areas of strategic defense—BMD, air defense, hardening, mobility, deception, civil defense, and so forth—the West's restraint has not been matched by imitative Soviet forbearance. On the contrary, Soviet efforts in these domains have been marked by steady expansion and modernization, reinforced by complementary offensive-force programs.

Antitactical Missiles. The expression *antitactical missiles* (ATM) has some advantages over *antitactical ballistic missiles* (ATBM) because it implies a capability against cruise missiles and aircraft-delivered stand-off weapons as well as shorter-range ballistic missiles (SRBMs). The development of active defenses against these missile systems has been under study in the alliance since 1979.[109] Some modest upgrades to the Patriot air defense missile deployed with U.S. and West German forces in the Federal

Republic of Germany are under way, in order to provide the Patriot with some limited self-defense capability against ballistic missiles with nonnuclear warheads. In April 1986 the NATO Council directed that all the work within the alliance on "tactical missile defense capabilities" be coordinated by the NATO Air Defense Committee. NATO's defense ministers have described potential defenses against tactical missiles as an important element of the Conventional Defense Improvement (CDI) effort.[110]

There are some uncertainties about how soon in the next decade Soviet SRBMs may have the accuracies that would permit effective use of conventional warheads, as noted in Chapter 2. But, as the International Institute for Strategic Studies has pointed out, "there is little debate about the nature and potential effectiveness of the new Soviet short-range missiles."[111] Highly accurate conventionally armed SRBMs promise to be a critical component of Warsaw Pact capabilities for an air offensive that would consist mainly of aircraft and other nonballistic means of attack, including cruise and stand-off missiles, helicopters, artillery, special forces, and so forth. The SRBMs would be of critical importance because of their speed, accuracy, reliability, and high-confidence ability to penetrate NATO defenses and attack NATO's nuclear forces, airfields, command centers, and so forth. Building an effective ATM defense against these SRBMs and advanced cruise and stand-off weapons—sometimes called a medium surface-to-air missile (MSAM)—would probably take more than a decade.[112]

The effort to develop ATM defenses—or ATBM defenses dedicated specifically to countering SRBMs—has been less controversial than the SDI. The ATBM concept has nonetheless attracted criticism on five grounds. First, Social Democratic party spokesmen in West Germany and others have accused the U.S. administration of trying to use ATBM projects for purposes distinct from meeting the SRBM threat—to persuade West Europeans to support the SDI.[113]

Second, there is some concern that, even though the ABM Treaty does not specifically exclude ATBM deployments, the pursuit of ATBM capabilities could undermine the ABM Treaty by expanding the "gray area" of overlap between air defense and BMD capabilities. The situation is complicated further by (1) the Soviet refusal to admit that certain Soviet SAM systems have tested ATBM capability and may also have some strategic BMD potential and (2) the Soviet insistence that even modest ATBM developments such as the Patriot upgrade would violate the ABM Treaty. The Soviets may attempt to avoid the foreign deployment and technology-transfer issues if the SA-X-12B/Giant is deployed in Eastern Europe by asserting that it is simply an air defense system.

Third, as some observers have properly pointed out, it would be preferable to seek arms control solutions. The Western development of ATBM capabilities might, they argue, encourage the Soviets to increase their short-range missile forces and might make negotiated reductions more difficult to achieve. The Western alliance will undoubtedly pursue available arms control opportunities. The December 1987 "double-zero" accord may eliminate land-based INF missiles with ranges between 500 and 5500 km. But uncertainties about the results of the arms control process—and the large Soviet superiority in SRBMs, including systems below 500 km in range—will probably dictate prudent ATBM programs, for deterrence and as a safeguard for arms control accords.

Fourth, some critics are concerned that a NATO–Warsaw Pact competition in tactical ballistic missiles and ATBM capabilities could be "destabilizing." In their view, the existing situation of mutual vulnerability could be upset by ATBM and offensive missile deployments on both sides that could create anxieties and incentives for preemption during crises. NATO could, some have contended, be secure without ATBM defenses because, if the Soviets used conventionally armed SRBMs to attack nuclear forces in Western Europe, the attack could be regarded as equivalent to a nuclear attack; it would therefore justify a Western nuclear response, so—they conclude—the Soviets would not dare to undertake such attacks. This line of argument may overestimate both the instability that would be fostered by ATBM deployments and the reliability of the West's existing retaliatory threats, given Soviet nuclear "counter-deterrent" capabilities. According to the International Institute for Strategic Studies, "the deployment of ATBM defenses could enhance stability by enhancing the survivability of the forces on both sides."[114]

The fifth main criticism of ATBM is the most serious: cost. When NATO's air defenses are already inadequate and the alliance has many other deficiencies to address (including the need to strengthen conventional ground forces and build up stockpiles of munitions and other "consumables" for sustainability), how can the expenditure of scarce resources on ATBM be justified? This important question leads directly to the search for less costly alternatives.

There are three basic types of countermeasures to the Soviet SRBM threat: (1) passive defenses such as hardening, mobility, deception, and redundancy; (2) offensive counterforce strikes to destroy the missiles and/or associated control capabilities before they can be used; and (3) active defense in the form of ATBM.

Few question the desirability of improving the alliance's passive defenses in Europe. Specific measures might include building additional runways at air bases and more hardened munitions bunkers and aircraft shelters, and improving runway repair capabilities and crisis dispersal preparations for aircraft and nuclear forces. There are limits to what can be accomplished with passive defenses, however. Space for additional runways is scarce at some airfields. Hardening programs for aircraft shelters and munitions bunkers would have to involve the construction of barriers of exceptional thickness to withstand foreseeable threats; current above-ground concrete structures (including aircraft shelters) could be destroyed by accurately delivered nonnuclear SRBM warheads with blast effects comparable to low-yield nuclear weapons.[115] It seems unlikely that the Western alliance will invest in hardening measures as extensive as those of the USSR. It is, moreover, probable that some Western politicians would oppose the implementation of dispersal measures in an actual crisis for fear this could appear provocative and could therefore aggravate the situation. Nuclear dispersal procedures are in any case time-consuming and would be subject to disruption by SRBM attacks.

The potential contribution of offensive counterforce strikes is more controversial. As noted in Chapter 3, the United States is developing nonnuclear strike systems such as the Army Tactical Missile System and the joint surveillance and target attack radar system (JSTARS). These systems might be able to strike some Soviet SRBM launchers before they could be reloaded for follow-on strikes. The performance of Western counterbattery fire might, however, be degraded by Soviet ATBM systems such as the SA-10 and SA-X-12B/Giant.

The controversy associated with offensive counterforce is twofold: first, a nuclear retaliatory strategy might be disproportionate and counterproductive in terms of escalation control; second, any conventional preemption by NATO would obviously be "politically unacceptable,"[116] for it would contradict the alliance's fundamentally defensive character. As Manfred Wörner has noted, "the alliance has renounced initial use of all weapons and will therefore have to absorb the 'first strike' in [the] case of the missile threat as well."[117] While a "capability to seek out and destroy TBM [theater ballistic missile] launchers subsequently would have obvious benefit in disrupting further attacks,"[118] the use of counterforce strikes during a conflict would be complicated by the difficulties of target acquisition. The new Soviet SRBMs (as discussed in Chapter 2) are endowed with increased range and improved mobility and are therefore hard to locate.

Many Western officials and strategists have concluded that passive defenses and offensive strike capabilities should be complemented with active defenses—improved air defenses and ATM capabilities, with some dedicated ATBM potential. In their view, active defenses would be more consistent with NATO's defensive posture than reliance on counterforce capabilities in retaliatory operations and more stabilizing than a high level of dependence on dispersal arrangements. Active defenses could reduce Soviet confidence in the ability of the USSR to gain victory in a fast-paced conventional offensive in two ways: (1) by protecting NATO's key conventional defense assets, and (2) by helping to assure the survival of NATO's nuclear assets and associated command facilities, in that time would be gained to allow for dispersal. Active defenses could also offer some protection against limited Soviet nuclear attacks. If effective and deployed in sufficient numbers, active defenses could make a rapid victory on Soviet terms infeasible and increase the sustainability of NATO's defense capabilities; active defenses could thus bolster deterrence.

West European proponents of ATM-capable active defenses, such as Wörner, have pointed out that studies regarding NATO's "extended air defense" preceded the SDI. Moreover, in Wörner's words, "it is imperative to proceed with the building blocks of an anti-missile defense in Europe irrespective of the ultimate decisions that may be made in the United States with respect to SDI."[119]

Wörner's caution may stem from the widespread reservations about the SDI in Western Europe. One West German defense analyst has stated: "There is strong opposition to SDI in West Germany, so there is a need to separate the two. We could not successfully conduct the antitactical missile discussion unless we get away from SDI."[120] Rather than a U.S. SDI-dominated "top-down" approach, a number of West Europeans favor a European-led "bottom-up" approach intended to improve existing air defenses. In their view, it would be wiser to keep this effort separate from the SDI and pursue it in a nonpoliticized and deliberate fashion within the standard NATO channels.

Certain links with the SDI are, however, unavoidable. Some U.S officials would like to portray West European support for ATM as equivalent to endorsement of the SDI. Some West Europeans have been gratified that defenses against Soviet theater missiles will, in Wörner's words, "be an integral part of the conceptual overall architecture of any SDI system."[121] Moreover, ATM capabilities in Europe would help to meet one of Western Europe's strategic reservations about the SDI. As General Altenburg put it, "it must be established that not only intercontinental range missiles, but [missiles of] all ranges would be protected against. Otherwise it would be a question of zones [within the alliance] with differing security risks."[122]

In the long term, furthermore, active defenses in Western Europe could benefit from space-based support assets. Wörner has said, with respect to extended air defense, "There is no discernible requirement for stationing weapons systems or components in space, such as may eventuate in SDI."[123] A prestigious private West German study group, under the auspices of the Deutsche Gesellschaft für Auswärtige Politik (German Society for Foreign Policy) in Bonn, has pointed out, however, that space-based sensors and surveillance systems could be quite useful.[124] Mobile missiles in Poland, for example, might be beyond the range of airborne radars, which would in any case be quite vulnerable to Soviet surface-to-air missiles and fighter aircraft. Space-based surveillance systems might make it possible to monitor the locations of Soviet missiles, to track flight trajectories, to achieve earlier interceptions, and so forth. Even if the December 1987 "double-zero" INF agreement eliminates Soviet land-based missiles with ranges between 500 and 5500 km, Western Europe will remain vulnerable to land-based missiles of greater and lesser ranges, including mobile ICBMs (SS-24s and SS-25s) and mobile SRBMs (such as SS-21s)—to say nothing of Soviet sea-based and air-delivered missiles. There is a certain practical and technical logic to integrating any future defenses against ballistic missiles in Western Europe and North America, even if political factors sometimes argue against linkage.

Maintaining Stable Deterrence and Alliance Security

Soviet strategic defense capabilities promise to sharpen some of the most fundamental dilemmas facing Western security policy. These dilemmas —highlighted to some degree during the alliance debates regarding INF modernization and arms control (1979-1983) and the SDI (since 1983) —could be regarded as tolerable during the eras of U.S. nuclear superiority (roughly 1949-1969) and nominal U.S.-Soviet détente (approximately 1969–1979).

These dilemmas stem from the tensions involved in trying to maintain the credibility of U.S. nuclear deterrent guarantees to allies (in effect, U.S. threats to strike the Soviet Union with nuclear weapons, if necessary, to dissuade the Soviets from undertaking coercion or aggression) in the face of Soviet nuclear "counter-deterrent" capabilities (that is, Soviet threats to retaliate against the United States). The credibility of U.S. guarantees was believed to be based on U.S. nuclear superiority until the late 1960s, when U.S. leadership elites accepted the Soviet acquisition of strategic nuclear parity and endorsed the goal of stable U.S.-Soviet mutual nuclear deterrence. U.S. commitments were not reassessed in the light of parity, and a latent contradiction emerged between U.S. guarantees to allies and the goal of stability based on U.S.-Soviet mutual vulnerability.

This contradiction could be discounted if (1) U.S. and allied interests were regarded as closely linked and virtually identical; (2) the United States was presumed to be willing to carry out its threats to attack the Soviet Union with nuclear weapons, if necessary; and (3) the allies on both sides of the Atlantic were prepared to carry out programs to improve NATO's capabilities for nonnuclear direct defense in Europe. One of the chief goals of Soviet policy has been to divide the United States from its allies by degrading the credibility of U.S. nuclear threats and highlighting differences in U.S. and West European interests. The credibility of the U.S. nuclear threats formalized in NATO strategy depends on the perceived willingness and capability of the United States to undertake nuclear strikes against the USSR. The plausibility of U.S. willingness to undertake such strikes has been repeatedly questioned since the advent of U.S. vulnerability to prompt Soviet nuclear retaliation (the late 1950s) and, even more frequently, since the Soviet acquisition of nuclear parity (the late 1960s).

The tendency in the West has been to stress the uncertainties and risks of nuclear escalation as a compensation for the apparently decreased credibility of U.S. nuclear threats. As Pierre Hassner put it in 1973, "the risk of escalation is today the central element of deterrence in Europe . . . The basis of deterrence is less the credibility of a deliberate [U.S.] decision than the unpredictability of a process; the substitute for American strategic *superiority*, which gave its plausibility to the former concept, is *continuity* between the two American-led systems of deterrence"—that is, U.S. capabilities for protection of the United States itself, and NATO's capabilities to prevent Soviet aggression or coercion in Europe.[125] As noted in Chapter 3, for a number of West Europeans, the decisive element in deterrence remains the U.S. capacity to undertake selective nuclear strikes—against the Soviet Union itself, if necessary—and thereby make it clear to the Soviet leadership that it could not hope to confine a war to Europe.

Although the reliability and effectiveness of more extensive Soviet strategic defense capabilities (including BMD) might well be questioned, few would dispute the judgment that—in order to hedge against the potential effectiveness of Soviet defenses—the United States would have to threaten to undertake larger nuclear strikes in the actual implementation of its commitments to carry out nuclear retaliation, if necessary, in response to Soviet aggression. In other words, as suggested in Chapter 3, one of the effects of improved Soviet strategic-defense capabilities could be to accentuate and underline the West's dependence on nuclear threats and to increase the risks of a loss of escalation control—risks that would be involved in undertaking any nuclear attacks. One result might be effective Soviet nuclear "counter-deterrence"—that is, confining any eventual conflict to nonnuclear operations in Europe; or, if that could not be achieved, limiting nuclear operations to isolated areas outside the USSR; or (the Soviet preference) promoting the circumstances for what the USSR would regard as positive peaceful change without war. Another result—relatively large-scale U.S. nuclear attacks against targets within the Soviet Union—would still, however, be hypothetically possible. Such attacks could be catastrophic for the USSR. U.S. nuclear guarantees will therefore probably retain some residual credibility in Soviet eyes, especially when significant numbers of U.S. troops and nuclear weapons remain deployed in Western Europe.

The strategic options of the Western alliance could, however, be narrowed eventually to extreme choices, owing to the West's high degree of dependence on nuclear threats. The questions raised with remarkable foresight by Dean Acheson in 1949, when the alliance was founded, would become even more relevant. One of Acheson's fundamental questions concerned the prospect that Soviet nuclear forces could eventually function "effectively to neutralize" U.S. nuclear guarantees: "If this is so, would we be better off addressing ourselves now to finding substitutes for the defensive shield our atomic weapons are now giving our allies?"[126]

If some continued Western reliance on nuclear threats is unavoidable, the question becomes one not of *substitutes* but of *supplements* that might diminish an excessive dependence on nuclear threats. One alternative, of course, that has been pursued since the 1960s is to prepare more limited nuclear employment options—forces capable of carrying out operational plans for selective, discriminate, and (one hopes) controllable strikes in order to achieve constructive political effects in the event that Soviet aggression cannot be contained by nonnuclear means. Capabilities for such strikes deserve more attention and continued development, partly in order to be able to deter the more plausible Soviet nuclear attacks. But if such capabilities are viewed as (1) increasingly problematic, owing to Soviet strategic defenses and retaliatory capabilities and (2) politically less than satisfactory, owing to public attitudes, the Western alliance will have to devote more attention to supplements to threats of nuclear retaliation.

The two main possible courses are obvious if the problem is formulated as one of overdependence on threats of offensive nuclear retaliation:

stronger conventional forces and *strategic defenses* to reduce vulnerabilities to long-range strike systems. Strategic-defense capabilities of various types, active and passive, could help to counter Soviet investments in offensive strike forces and balance Soviet investments in strategic defense. Stronger conventional forces—including units equipped with long-range precision-guided munitions—could (barring Soviet decisions to use nuclear weapons) deal with some nonnuclear contingencies and gain time for possibly unavoidable nuclear employment choices by Western governments.

If the geopolitical structure of the Western alliance were taken into account, the problem might be formulated as one of West European overdependence on U.S. threats of offensive nuclear retaliation. The logical solutions for Western Europe would then reside in some combination of increased West European conventional and nuclear forces and strategic defenses.

Inferences of this sort have been drawn, especially in France. High-level French officials and strategists have in recent years deplored what they see as an underlying trend of U.S. policy—a tendency to disengage from past U.S. nuclear commitments to Western Europe by emphasizing conventional-force improvements (such as the "emerging technologies" initiatives), nonnuclear strategic defenses (the SDI), and visions of a U.S.-Soviet defense-dominance relationship that might eliminate the nuclear vulnerabilities of the United States.[127] Because Western Europe is judged incapable of making more than marginal additional investments in conventional forces or of competing with the USSR in strategic defenses (except perhaps for limited defenses of nuclear forces), some have concluded that the principal states of Western Europe—above all, France and West Germany—should work together to build a more credible deterrent posture. In order to counter the potential growth in Soviet BMD capabilities (and because of the conviction that nuclear threats are decisive in affecting Soviet risk calculations), some have recommended that French nuclear forces be substantially strengthened.[128]

West European reservations about the reliability of U.S. nuclear guarantees could lead to three outcomes: steps toward greater accommodation with the USSR; greater West European self-reliance; or attempts to recast the terms of consensus within the alliance and, to the maximum extent possible, restore the credibility of U.S. commitments. The latter two outcomes are not mutually exclusive. Some West European officials and experts have for years advocated greater autonomy for Western Europe within the alliance. This could be attained only through substantially enhanced military capabilities, based on increased defense efforts and improved security cooperation, in order to reduce Western Europe's dependence on the United States. As François Heisbourg and others have noted, the factors working against the maintenance of the U.S.–West European strategic consensus —Soviet-U.S. nuclear parity, U.S. perceptions of inadequate West European burden-sharing, and the perceived delegitimization of nuclear deterrence—"can probably be mastered" if the West Europeans demonstrate "more coherence and will than they have shown in the past . . . Indifference will only kill the alliance if the more vulnerable states of the coalition show their incapacity to take their own security seriously."[129]

It might be noted in this regard that some Americans have discounted a number of the West European criticisms of the SDI as irrelevant attacks against easy targets—above all, the President's vision of a world in which nuclear weapons have been rendered "impotent and obsolete" by strategic defenses. An excessive focus on this vision has, they maintain, diverted attention from the truly serious issues posed by Soviet military capabilities, offensive and defensive. Moreover, many of the West European objections to the SDI recapitulate long-standing complaints about allied dependence on the United States—from fears of the United States not negotiating with the USSR to fears of the United States abandoning Western Europe or even participating in a condominium with the Soviet Union. These fears would naturally be less salient if West Europeans cooperated in building military capabilities that would diminish their dependence on the United States.

It is also important for West Europeans to counter the impression that some Americans have derived of West European policy preferences. Too often, it seems, Americans receive the impression that West Europeans are unwilling to improve the alliance's conventional-defense posture substantially, because they would prefer to place the burden of deterrence on U.S. nuclear retaliatory threats—not simply because they deem these threats highly effective in deterring Soviet coercion and aggression, but also because they are unwilling to accept the costs and responsibilities of helping to strengthen NATO's capacities for nonnuclear direct defense. An apparent West European preference for a high level of dependence on U.S. nuclear forces naturally implies a risk of prompt escalation to nuclear employment, potentially including intercontinental attacks. When this impression is combined with another—that Western Europe also objects to the U.S. pursuit of strategic-defense research that might eventually help to lessen U.S. nuclear vulnerabilities—the overall picture conveyed to some Americans is one of Western Europe helping to maintain the United States in a posture of unnecessarily high nuclear vulnerability.

Many West Europeans might object that this impression is a caricature of their true policy preferences, and that in their view, in a long-term historical perspective, the United States itself bears a great deal of responsibility for the West's high degree of dependence on nuclear retaliatory threats—from the condition of the alliance's conventional-defense posture to the paucity of U.S. investments in all forms of strategic defense, active and passive. But the impression exists in the United States as a political reality, and it is more widespread than is healthy for alliance cohesion. West Europeans should therefore take additional steps to demonstrate to the United States that they understand (1) that allied dependence on U.S. nuclear capabilities should be diminished, whenever possible, through efforts to strengthen the alliance's conventional-defense posture, including enhanced intra–West European cooperation; (2) that it would be irresponsible—in the interests of allied as well as U.S. national security—for the United States not to investigate damage-limiting capabilities; and (3) that the United States—and NATO as a whole—may well have to invest substantial resources in strategic defenses, especially if Soviet long-range strike forces cannot be adequately countered through arms control regimes and U.S. retaliatory forces.

The long-standing conviction of many West European observers is that reduced U.S. vulnerability could not be obtained through BMD without provoking parallel Soviet BMD deployments that would reduce the credibility of U.S. nuclear guarantees (and the credibility of the British and French nuclear forces) and have other harmful consequences for Western security. The latent risk for alliance cohesion in the mutual-vulnerability model of strategic stability—apparent West European opposition to a reduction in U.S. nuclear vulnerability—may be managed if the West Europeans make clear their recognition that strategic policies and defensive force posture improvements that could in fact diminish U.S. vulnerabilities are intrinsically desirable and may well be required, depending on the effectiveness of arms control regimes and (above all) the development of the Soviet intercontinental force posture and Soviet attack options.

The renewed U.S. interest in strategic defense has been beneficial for Western security in various ways: above all, despite the SDI's stress on longer-term comprehensive defenses, the research undertaken in the SDI has probably helped to improve the West's ability to build defenses with military value (for instance, defenses of retaliatory forces and command and control capabilities). For an alliance policy to be sustainable and relevant to the strategic challenges at hand, however, it must be capable of winning support in Western Europe as well as North America. In retrospect, it is clear that some of the central concepts associated with the SDI have not been well calculated to gain allied support. The counterproductive features of the rationale set forth for the SDI have detracted attention from the serious strategic challenges facing the alliance and may have undermined prospects for a more balanced and sustainable policy.

Two of the most unfortunate features of the SDI are interrelated: it is a U.S. initiative for highly effective ballistic missile defenses, and it includes a concept of U.S.-Soviet cooperation in establishing a relationship of defense-dominance.

From an alliance perspective, it would have been far more effective to build up a consensus on the need for increased Western investments in BMD activities on the basis of shared assessments of the Soviet ballistic missile threat and Soviet BMD activities, including possible violations of arms control treaties. Because of the defensive orientation of NATO, Western military preparations can be justified only as reponses to specific external challenges. The need for a U.S. and allied reply to Soviet capability improvements—a Strategic Defense Response—should have been established in a deliberate and sustainable fashion. If alliance cohesion is to be maintained, the emphasis should be on the need to ensure the continued credibility of the West's deterrent capabilities while pursuing reliable arms control agreements. Soviet strategic defenses could, for example, gravely undermine the credibility of NATO's flexible-response strategy. The need to prevent Soviet BMD from having such a "decoupling" effect could have been—and could still be—one of the strongest bases for alliance consensus in strategic policy.

But the U.S. *initiative* in BMD has made the United States appear to many as the wellspring of arms race activity in this domain and hence the principal threat to arms control and the ABM Treaty. It has encouraged assumptions, at least in some quarters, about Soviet passivity and reactiveness. Some West Europeans have even blamed the United States for the possible degradation of U.S. nuclear guarantees by Soviet BMD because, they reason, the Soviet Union has been forced to increase its BMD investments by the SDI. Existing Soviet BMD deployments, long-standing Soviet activities in BMD and other forms of strategic defense, and Soviet offensive strike capabilities—and the Soviet interest in degrading the credibility of U.S. guarantees—have often received less consideration than the U.S. initiative.

The related problem for alliance consensus is that the final goal in the U.S. strategic concept for the SDI—a cooperative transition to a situation of U.S.-Soviet defense dominance—is not generally regarded as technically credible or as politically or strategically desirable. The Reagan administration's argument that progress toward the realization of the SDI cooperative vision is being frustrated by the USSR fails to alarm West Europeans who do not regard the vision as intrinsically attractive. West Europeans do not on the whole care for the concept of U.S.-Soviet defense dominance, whether attained by cooperative or noncooperative means. For many, U.S.-Soviet defense dominance implies a negation of NATO's flexible-response strategy, the obsolescence of the British and French nuclear forces, the potential subordination of Western Europe to a U.S.-Soviet condominium, and increased West European vulnerability to Soviet coercion and aggression. In their view, the U.S. advocacy of vigorous Soviet BMD research programs tends to legitimize Soviet efforts that have detrimental effects on Western security.

At the same time, some West European critics have added, the defense-dominance concept associated with the SDI may have contributed to the delegitimization of nuclear deterrence policies in the West, because it implies that the alliance's security problems are rooted not in politics but in the characteristics of specific weapons—nuclear warheads and/or ballistic missiles. The stigmatization of nuclear weapons and certain types of delivery systems implies that security depends mainly on achieving particular technical force characteristics and force ratios in the East-West military balance. This narrow and depoliticized conception of security overlooks East-West differences in political and strategic objectives and promotes a disorienting impression that nuclear weapons are in themselves a factor of insecurity, quite aside from the policies and purposes of the governments that maintain them.[130] This outlook delegitimizes the West's deterrent posture while distracting attention from Soviet political aims. As the French foreign minister has noted, it is a "paradox" that the United States has adopted "what has been, since the fifties, the stated objective of the Soviets, namely, the abolition of all nuclear weapons." In his view, the West should "break out of the Soviet logic of denuclearization," because it is aimed at eliminating the U.S. nuclear presence in Western Europe and placing the alliance in a more vulnerable position.[131]

What concepts might address the true strategic challenges and have a better prospect of gaining the support of a substantial alliance consensus? In criticizing the SDI concept of defense dominance, some West Europeans have called attention to "a strongly idealistic approach rooted in massive criticism against nuclear deterrence" and have noted that "a technologically determined finality of European history is being suggested, which is contrary to all previous historical experience."[132] General Franz-Joseph Schulze, a former Commander of Allied Forces

Central Europe, testified to the Bundestag in 1985 as follows: "No perfect, unbeatable defense is required. 'Strategic invulnerability' will hardly come in the foreseeable future, if it is not in any case a quality not meant ever to be granted to men. Speculation about conflict scenarios, in which the invulnerability of both great powers is foreseen, is unrealistic. Equally unrealistic, however, is the argument that an imperfect strategic defense system is meaningless."[133]

It would seem that responsible West European strategists would generally prefer pragmatic policies intended to stabilize deterrence in response to developments in Soviet forces and doctrine. For many, a U.S.-initiated project for essentially perfect BMD capabilities in both the United States and the Soviet Union, plus U.S.-Soviet cooperation in ridding the world of nuclear weapons, is less attractive than a policy that accepts—for the indefinite future—the realities of nuclear vulnerability and East-West political antagonism. From this perspective, it would be wiser to accept the infeasibility of a permanent solution to the West's security dilemmas. As Lieutenant General William Odom has pointed out,

> No single strategy or weapons system will provide security indefinitely. Security is maintained through continuous efforts, frequent reviews, periodic changes in doctrine and strategies, and rhythmic acquisition of weapons and forces using new technologies. Security cannot be bought cheaply, and there are no panaceas to be had, not even in nuclear force capabilities. There are, however, more effective and less effective approaches to building security for the West . . . the competition [should] be shaped into "a substitute for war," rather than "a prelude to war." The West cannot escape the military competition, but it can compete in ways that make war less likely.[134]

If the challenges posed by Soviet strategic defense were addressed from this more pragmatic perspective (rather than the ultimate SDI vision), a constructive alliance consensus might emerge. Elements of that consensus might include the following six points:

1. Nuclear deterrence contributes substantially to international stability and war prevention. It would not be sensible to reduce nuclear deterrent forces to low levels, either through defense dominance or through disarmament (or a combination of these methods), unless key conditions were first met: for example, an elimination of conventional and chemical weapons imbalances, a durable reduction in East-West political antagonism, and an assurance of the robust survivability of the remaining nuclear forces.[135]

2. The West could usefully qualify its continuing dependence on nuclear deterrence by developing a more balanced mix of offensive and defensive capabilities, plus stronger conventional forces. The West must prevent dangerous Soviet assessments regarding simplified risks and thus avert Western susceptibility to coercion. This can be done through a balanced program of improved options for offensive and defensive deployments, to be implemented as necessary for the maintenance of stable deterrence. It would be imprudent and destabilizing to leave Soviet offensive and defensive investments unanswered. To leave the field of strategic defense to the Soviet Union alone would be a prescription for strategic instability and Western vulnerability to Soviet military power.

3. In addressing the challenges raised by Soviet strategic defenses and Soviet offensive strike capabilities, primary attention should be given not to the most implausible and unlikely cases (such as nuclear attacks against the major cities of NATO countries) but to the most plausible cases from the political-military standpoint of Soviet policy (such as nonnuclear and selective nuclear attacks against key NATO military assets relevant to the outcome of a conflict in Europe). In order to defend against—and respond to—such attacks, the West may require effective active defenses of key military targets (including command-and-control centers) and long-range strike forces capable of precise and discriminate attacks. More credible capabilities for controlled response and damage limitation might deter aggression more effectively.

4. Arms control efforts should be pursued as intensively as possible, but with a full awareness of the objective limits to any quest for technical solutions to fundamentally political antagonisms. Given the character of Soviet political and strategic objectives, Western policymakers must look beyond the technical criteria of Western theories of stability and consider the political and military implications of specific proposals and agreements. As James A. Thomson has noted, "firm links between the implementation of arms programs and the success of arms control negotiations should be avoided," in order to maintain the principle that arms control arrangements cannot substitute for unilateral defense capabilities.[136] A serious approach to arms control should, moreover, encompass a firm commitment to reciprocity in arms control compliance and remedies for noncompliance.

5. If decisions for relatively large-scale BMD deployments in the Western alliance are eventually made, these deployments should be undertaken with precautions about potential Soviet responses. It would be important to devise deployment designs and procedures that would maximize prospects for affecting Soviet strategic planning in ways helpful

to deterrence and strategic stability. The Soviets have to date been able to size their offensive forces against a Western alliance without active defenses, except for limited air defenses, and with little passive defense. This has enabled them to develop capabilities that appear oriented toward seizing Western Europe in a matter of weeks through ground and air offensives supported by selective long-range targeting of assets critical to the defense of NATO Europe. BMD capabilities and stronger air defenses in NATO should be pursued in ways that could significantly affect Soviet calculations of prospects for victory. The price of successful attacks should be raised with a combination of active and passive defenses. The higher likelihood of survival of critical Western military assets should enhance deterrence and make potential Soviet attempts at coercion (or aggression) more improbable. The West should enhance the credibility of its deterrent posture by affecting Soviet assessments of its will to reduce its vulnerabilities and to resist the expansion of Soviet power.

6. Such Western responses to Soviet force posture developments would represent practical and necessary adjustments in established policy, not a doctrinal upheaval or the pursuit of a panacea. As François Heisbourg has noted, the possible deployment of ATBM systems to defend key targets against Soviet SRBMs "carries with it no doctrinal revolution: such an adaptation to a changing threat has little to do with a Star Wars–like pretense of decimating swarms of nuclear warheads. Conventional air and missile defense is certainly something that the Europeans need militarily, know how to do technically, and can bear politically."[137] Except for isolated groups, there is little support in Western Europe for building comprehensive population defenses and little confidence that such a goal could be attained, at any cost. Nor do many regard such defenses as strategically necessary.

Manfred Wörner has written that ATBM deployments "would mark a continuing evolution in the Alliance's deterrent strategy away from the concept of deterrence based on the threat of nuclear retaliation to a concept based on the credible ability to convince the Soviets that a conventional attack in Europe has no chances of success—in other words, the concept of 'deterrence by denial.' "[138] But Wörner has also pointed out, "To be strategically effective, the defense system need be neither impenetrable nor cover the entire European region."[139] The same principle applies to possible future strategic BMD deployments in the United States. Useful defenses could be built to make plausible attacks— strikes against military targets—less feasible.

The six points above might be more likely to gain reasonably broad and sustainable support in the Western alliance than would a vision of

Soviet-U.S. defense dominance. From a West European perspective, the SDI vision of Soviet-U.S. defense dominance has entailed a perplexing endorsement of ongoing Soviet strategic defense programs in the context of parallel BMD development by both the United States and the Soviet Union. Although many West Europeans would be pleased to see a reduction in U.S. strategic vulnerabilities (some have argued, quite persuasively, that U.S. deterrent guarantees would then become more credible), the advantages for the West in a lessening of Soviet vulnerability to Western retaliation are not obvious.[140]

A one-sided lessening of Soviet vulnerability to Western retaliation is, of course, the principal goal of Soviet strategic defense programs. These programs involve, as noted in Chapter 2, far more than the Soviet BMD capabilities and activities discussed in Chapter 1. Except for BMD, none of these programs is currently subject to arms control constraints, and continuing investments may be expected in all of them. In the BMD area as well, there is reason to expect Soviet investments to proceed. Treaty-permitted infrastructure expansion and system modernization are probable, while activities that may eventually constitute an ambiguous creepout from the ABM Treaty may continue as well. Soviet capabilities to benefit from a breakout from the ABM Treaty—either through illegal violations or a legal abrogation—may therefore improve. Even though a breakout appears unlikely, for the reasons reviewed in Chapter 4, it would be imprudent to discount completely the possibility. Soviet force-posture decisions derive from autonomous Soviet purposes as well as from interactions with the policies of foreign governments. A long-term trend toward increased—and potentially more effective and reliable—strategic-defense capabilities in the Soviet Union probably cannot be altered by Western decisions.[141]

It is clear that a unilateral Soviet advantage in BMD would have harmful consequences for the security of Western Europe. As the Union pour la Démocratie Française pointed out in 1985, "it is a Soviet superiority and, all the more so, monopoly in ABM defense that would create the danger of decoupling that Europeans fear."[142] These potential consequences, as reviewed in Chapter 3, need not depend on the achievement of systems of exceptionally high effectiveness and reliability. A capability for the virtual negation of the more plausible selective attacks by Western governments could have a substantial impact in advancing Soviet ambitions for political gains without war.

Some of the consequences of a unilateral Soviet advantage in BMD and other forms of strategic defense could also arise in an environment of mutual imperfect defenses. While many variables (including the scope and effectiveness of each side's active and passive defenses, the specific types of attacks in question, and the strategic and political objectives of the adversaries in the particular circumstances) would have to be included in a comprehensive analysis, some of the same difficulties could arise for the West, even if the Western alliance had BMD capabilities—and other strategic defenses—comparable to those that may eventually be acquired by the Soviet Union. In both cases, for example, it could be more costly and difficult for Western governments to assure the penetration credibility of their forces and to conduct selective and discriminate attacks. As suggested in Chapter 3, there are no easy solutions to this problem. The prospective reduction in targeting flexibility could, however, be at least partially addressed through offensive-force countermeasures, including nonballistic means of attack.

A situation of imperfect and limited strategic defenses on both sides would at any rate be more advantageous for the West than one of clear Soviet superiority. Within Europe, enhanced air defenses—including ATBM capabilities—could hinder the implementation of Soviet SRBM strikes. The fact that Soviet BMD could reduce the variety and credibility of some U.S. limited strike options should be set against the fact that the virtually complete vulnerability of the U.S. homeland and land-based U.S. strategic forces to Soviet ballistic missile attack has already eroded the credibility of those options. The greater the effectiveness of active defenses (BMD plus defenses against aircraft and cruise missiles) in the United States, the smaller the degree of U.S. vulnerability and the higher the level of U.S. deterrent credibility could be in threatening implementation of the selective strike options in NATO's flexible response strategy. (Actual implementation could, however, be significantly complicated by the requirement to overcome or evade Soviet air defenses and BMD.) A reduction in the vulnerability of U.S. ICBMs could in particular bolster the credibility of U.S. guarantees. In both Western Europe and North America, active defenses could cause uncertainties for Soviet attack planners, help to protect retaliatory capabilities, and reduce the utility of preemptive strikes.

Challenges such as those outlined in an extreme and pure form in Chapter 3 may be unavoidable in the long term, in view of the Soviet programs—offensive as well as defensive—that have tended to erode the ABM Treaty regime and in view of the continuing improvement of the Soviet BMD deployment potential within the treaty's limitations and the array of ambiguous Soviet BMD activities that may eventually constitute a creepout from its constraints. A situation of mutual limited BMD deployments instead of the current situation—one of noteworthy

Soviet advantages in air and passive defenses, but little BMD, and the West with essentially no BMD and inferior air and passive defenses—would be more balanced in some ways, but it would not necessarily be a more stable arrangement.[143] Even if the BMD capabilities in the Western alliance and the Warsaw Pact were essentially equal in their scope and effectiveness, numerous variables would have to enter into any reasonably complete assessment of the prospects for stability under various conditions. While it would not be prudent to generalize in a hasty or summary manner, it is important to note that stability would depend on factors in addition to technical force characteristics and military balances.

It must be acknowledged in this regard that there are significant uncertainties about how large-scale BMD deployments would affect prospects for strategic stability.[144] Theories about reciprocal fears of "first-strike" intentions are plentiful, but they have been challenged by analyses contending that greater stability could result from a situation in which both sides would face increased uncertainties about the effectiveness of countermilitary attacks. Discussions about "crisis stability" theories have not reached any definitive resolution because, as David Schwartz has noted, there is "little empirical evidence to back up claims on either side of the argument; this lack of data is perhaps one reason why strategic debates of this sort take on a theological tone."[145] The historical record suggests that stability in the nuclear age has, at least in some cases, been affected more by political factors than by the presence or absence of the theoretical stability derived from the technical characteristics of the force postures of the potential belligerents.[146]

Certain structural and force characteristics could, however, continue to favor the Soviet Union. It would be difficult, for example, for the West to overcome the USSR's geographical and peacetime organizational advantages in amassing conventional combat power in Europe.[147] Warsaw Pact conventional-force superiority would mean that the USSR would be less dependent on nuclear threats in a severe crisis or war. In other words, the burden of nuclear escalation, the requirement to implement selective strike options, could continue to fall initially on the West. Limited BMD deployments of equal scope and effectiveness in the United States and the USSR could therefore be of greater political and strategic value to the Soviet Union in the sort of war the Soviets would probably prefer to wage, if war could not be avoided—one limited to Europe, with a minimization or avoidance of intercontinental operations. Other Soviet advantages could include the USSR's superior investments in passive defenses (hardening, deception, mobility, and so forth), the Soviet lead in ICBM and SRBM warheads and throwweight, and the flexibility of

Soviet decision making in at least some critical areas (for example, building large throwweight mobile ICBMs).

As these East-West asymmetries suggest, the issue at hand may not be deciding what configuration of BMD capabilities and other strategic defenses would best satisfy the requirements of a preferred theoretical model of technical "crisis stability." Given the pace of Soviet investments in various forms of strategic defense and in advanced types of offensive strike systems, nuclear and nonnuclear, the true issue may become one of redefining the practical necessities for assuring the security of the Western alliance. Meeting the challenge posed by Soviet strategic defenses, in combination with other Soviet capabilities, could require a comprehensive set of investments in offensive force modernization, strategic defenses (including improved BMD deployment options). and increased conventional forces. Extraordinary and enduring successes in arms control negotiations—accords that would genuinely enhance Western security— might avert or qualify these requirements, but such successes can scarcely be taken for granted.

Pending such arms control achievements, the only prudent course for the West would be to address the Soviet force-posture improvements that have already had the effect of narrowing the West's strategic options. If the Western alliance failed to demonstrate the clarity of political vision and determination required to pay the price of the necessary countermeasures, its strategic options could become more constrained. Properly directed Western countermeasures might, in contrast, promote Soviet restraint and have stabilizing effects. Such countermeasures would be less dangerous than inaction in the face of Soviet offensive-force expansion and modernization and the complementary improvements in Soviet strategic defenses.

Notes

Index

Notes

Introduction

1. Sir Geoffrey Howe, "Defence and Security in the Nuclear Age," *RUSI Journal*, 130 (June 1985), 5. This is the text of the widely remarked speech of March 15, 1985.
2. Ballistic missiles also represent a significant area of arms proliferation in the Third World, based on indigenous missile production capabilities and exports from industrialized countries. For background, see Aaron Karp, "Ballistic Missiles in the Third World," *International Security*, 9 (Winter 1984–85), 166–195, and Arthur F. Manfredi et al., *Ballistic Missile Proliferation Potential in the Third World* (Washington, D.C.: Congressional Research Service, April 23, 1986). In April 1987, seven Western nations (Canada, Britain, France, Italy, Japan, West Germany, and the United States) agreed to control exports of large ballistic missiles and related technologies. John H. Cushman, Jr., "7 Nations Agree to Limit Export of Big Rockets," *New York Times*, April 17, 1987, pp. A1, A6.
3. An exception might be the measures taken to protect the USSR's party, military, and administrative leadership, including deep underground shelters and hardened and redundant communications networks. Protection for the general Soviet population in nuclear attacks would be more questionable.
4. For background, see David S. Yost, "Ballistic Missile Defense and the Atlantic Alliance," *International Security*, 7 (Fall 1982), 143–174.
5. For an overview of initial reactions, see David S. Yost, "European Anxieties about Ballistic Missile Defense," *Washington Quarterly*, 7 (Fall 1984), 112–129. For useful surveys of the three principal countries, see Trevor Taylor, "Britain's Response to the Strategic Defense Initiative," John Fenske, "France and the Strategic Defense Initiative: Speeding Up or Putting on the Brakes?" and Christoph Bluth, "SDI: The Challenge to West Germany," *International Affairs* (London), 62 (Spring 1986), 217–264.
6. Stephen M. Meyer, "Soviet Strategic Programmes and the US SDI," *Survival*, 27 (November/December 1985), 288.

7. This possible Soviet fallback position was first suggested to me by Joseph Pilat.

8. Hans Rühle, "Gorbachev's 'Star Wars,' " *NATO Review*, 33 (August 1985), 26–32.

9. Ministry of Defence paper, "The Soviet Ballistic Missile Defence Programme," presented to the House of Commons by John Stanley, minister of state for the armed forces, in Great Britain, Parliament, *Parliamentary Debates* (House of Commons), November 26, 1985, cols. 562–564.

10. Commission d'Etudes sur les Armes Spatiales, *Rapport de synthèse présenté au ministre de la défense*, January 30, 1986.

11. Groupe X-Défense, *Les défenses anti-missiles, la France et l'Europe* (Paris: Fondation pour les Etudes de Défense Nationale, 1986). It should be noted that *X* is a French abbreviation for the Ecole Polytechnique, one of the *grandes écoles* maintained by the French government.

12. Department of Defense and Department of State, *Soviet Strategic Defense Programs* (Washington, D.C.: Government Printing Office, October 1985).

13. President Reagan, "Address to the Nation on Defense and National Security," March 23, 1983, in *Public Papers of the Presidents of the United States, Ronald Reagan 1983*, bk. I (Washington, D.C.: Government Printing Office, 1984), pp. 442–443.

14. Reagan interview with *New York Times* correspondents, February 11, 1985, in *Weekly Compilation of Presidential Documents*, 21 (February 18, 1985), 174.

15. Reagan interview with the BBC, October 29, 1985, in *Weekly Compilation of Presidential Documents*, 21 (November 4, 1985), 1320.

16. The president has repeated this offer on various occasions, including his debate with Walter Mondale on October 21, 1984, and his interview with the BBC, October 29, 1985. See *Weekly Compilation of Presidential Documents*, 20 (October 29, 1984), 1604, and 21 (November 4, 1985), 1319.

17. Defense and State, *Soviet Strategic Defense Programs*, p. 22.

18. *National Security Strategy of the United States* (Washington, D.C.: White House, January 1987), pp. 22–23. Part of the confusion in this respect stems from a failure to distinguish between the specific operational applications of military technologies and the political and strategic goals of governments. BMD capabilities (like other military capabilities) could be used in support of various policies (self-defense, deterrence, aggression, and so forth), depending on the political and strategic intentions of a particular government. For an illuminating discussion of valid and misleading distinctions between "offense" and "defense" in terms of weapons and military technologies, military capabilities, military strategy, and political goals, see Samuel P. Huntington, "U.S. Defense Strategy: The Strategic Innovations of the Reagan Years," in *1987–1988 American Defense Annual*, ed. Joseph Kruzel (Lexington, Mass.: D.C. Heath/Lexington Books, 1987), pp. 35–37.

19. Weinberger cited in *Wall Street Journal*, December 7, 1983, p. 60.

20. Weinberger on NBC's "Meet the Press," March 27, 1983, p. 5 of transcript.

21. Reagan, radio address to the nation, October 12, 1985, in *Weekly Compilation of Presidential Documents*, 21 (October 21, 1985), 1247.

22. J. Robert Oppenheimer, "Atomic Weapons and American Policy," *Foreign Affairs*, 31 (July 1953), 533–535.

23. See the address by the Soviet foreign minister, Andrei Gromyko, to the U.N. General Assembly, September 21, 1962, in U.S. Arms Control and Disarmament Agency, *Documents on Disarmament 1962*, II, July–December (Washington, D.C.: Government Printing Office, 1963), pp. 904–905.

24. Paul Nitze, *On the Road to a More Stable Peace*, Current Policy no. 657 (Washington, D.C.: Bureau of Public Affairs, U.S. Department of State, February 20, 1985), p. 1.

25. Weinberger cited in *Washington Times*, April 12, 1983, p. 4.

26. As one West German said in an interview in May 1985: "We don't want to base deterrence on conventional means alone; the Soviet Union can't be deterred by the thought of losing a conventional battle in North Rhine–Westphalia—but the threat of an intercontinental nuclear war is deterring." This view is consistent with long-standing West German views on the need to avoid any "decoupling" of U.S. strategic nuclear guarantees from European security. See David S. Yost and Thomas C. Glad, "West German Party Politics and Theater Nuclear Modernization since 1977," *Armed Forces and Society*, 8 (Summer 1982), 525–560, esp. pp. 547–549.

27. Weinberger testimony in U.S. Senate, Committee on Armed Services, *Department of Defense Authorization for Appropriations for Fiscal Year 1985*, hearings, 98th Cong., 2nd sess., February 1, 1984 (Washington, D.C.: Government Printing Office, 1984), p. 89.

28. Some critics have referred to statements by U.S. officials regarding the desirability of superior BMD capabilities in certain circumstances without considering the need to take Soviet-U.S. asymmetries in various forms of strategic offense and defense into account. Differences in the U.S. and Soviet "target sets" that might benefit from BMD deployments are discussed in Chapter 2.

29. Howe, "Defence and Security," p. 6.

30. According to François Heisbourg, the responding-to-the-Soviets justification for the SDI would have been more persuasive if the scope of Soviet BMD efforts had been emphasized prior to the March 1983 speech and if the SDI had been joined to an arms control effort aimed at strengthening the ABM Treaty and the 1967 Outer Space Treaty. Heisbourg, "L'Europe face à la politique militaire américaine," *Politique Etrangère*, 49 (Autumn 1984), 581.

31. Paul Quilès, "L'avenir de notre concept de défense face aux progrès technologiques," *Défense Nationale*, January 1986, p. 17.

32. This issue is reminiscent of the 1979–1983 INF affair, when some West Europeans repeatedly (and unsuccessfully) urged the U.S. government to make public a photograph of the Soviet SS-20 missile. The United States finally released photographs of the SS-20 in 1986. (U.S. Department of Defense, *Soviet Military Power 1986*, Washington, D.C.: Government Printing

Office, 1986, pp. 16–17.) There is a certain East-West asymmetry at work in this domain in that the United States makes vast quantities of photographs of U.S. military equipment freely available to the public, and the Soviet Union can draw on these to illustrate *Whence the Threat to Peace*, the Soviet Defense Ministry's retort to *Soviet Military Power*. Determined skeptics can, of course, question the authenticity of photographs as well as drawings.

33. Department of Defense, *Soviet Military Power 1987* (Washington, D.C.: Government Printing Office, 1987), p. 49.

34. Mark Daly, "Krasnoyarsk: First Picture Suggests Treaty Violation," *Jane's Defence Weekly*, April 11, 1987, pp. 620–621.

35. Stephen F. Szabo, "European Opinion after the Missiles," *Survival*, 27 (November/December 1985), 270.

36. David M. North, "U.S. Using Disinformation Policy to Impede Technical Data Flow," *Aviation Week and Space Technology*, March 17, 1986, pp. 16–17. See also "Washington Roundup," *Aviation Week and Space Technology*, July 28, 1986, p. 15.

37. Department of Defense, *Soviet Military Power* (Washington, D.C.: Government Printing Office, 1981), pp. 28 and 31; *Soviet Military Power 1983*, p. 38; and *Soviet Military Power 1984*, p. 53.

38. Department of Defense, *Soviet Military Power 1985* (Washington, D.C.: Government Printing Office, 1985), p. 38; *Soviet Military Power 1986*, p. 37; and *Soviet Military Power 1987*, p. 41.

39. *The Military Balance, 1985–1986* (London: International Institute for Strategic Studies, 1985), p. 162.

40. See, for example, Alexander M. Haig, Jr., "Judging SALT II," *Strategic Review*, 8 (Winter 1980), 13, and Harold Brown, *Department of Defense Annual Report for Fiscal Year 1980* (Washington, D.C.: Government Printing Office, 1979), p. 81.

41. *Report of the President's Commission on Strategic Forces*, April 1983, pp. 7–8.

42. According to the president: "We seek to render obsolete the balance of terror—or mutual assured destruction, as it's called—and replace it with a system incapable of initiating armed conflict or causing mass destruction, yet effective in preventing war. Now, this is not and should never be misconstrued as just another method of protecting missile silos." Remarks at National Space Club, Washington, March 29, 1985, in *Weekly Compilation of Presidential Documents*, 21 (April 1, 1985), 380. The president's science adviser in 1981–1986, George Keyworth, echoed this sentiment in several statements—for example: "Protecting weapons represents no change in present policy. It simply strengthens—entrenches—the doctrine of mutual assured destruction. Protecting people, on the other hand, holds out the promise of dramatic change." (Keyworth cited in *Aviation Week and Space Technology*, April 29, 1985, p. 225.) In the same vein, Secretary of Defense Weinberger indicated that "the defense that might evolve from the research program will not be intended to defend our strategic weapons systems." Caspar W. Weinberger, *Department of Defense Annual Report for Fiscal Year 1987* (Washington, D.C.: Government Printing Office, 1986), p. 287. On the

other hand, Weinberger also said that the SDI "does not preclude, of course, any intermediate deployment that could provide, among other things, defense of the offensive deterrent forces, which of course we still have to maintain." Remarks at the National Press Club, Washington, D.C., May 1, 1984, p. 4 of transcript.

43. Joint Chiefs of Staff. *Statement to the Congress on the Defense Posture of the United States for FY 1979* (Washington, D.C.: Government Printing Office, 1978), p. 31.

44. Department of State, *SALT II Agreement*, Selected Documents no. 12B (Washington, D.C.: Government Printing Office, 1979), p. 58.

45. Defense, *Soviet Military Power*, 1981, p. 54.

46. Defense, *Soviet Military Power 1983*, p. 24.

47. Defense, *Soviet Military Power 1984*, p. 28.

48. Defense, *Soviet Military Power 1985*, p. 34.

49. Defense, *Soviet Military Power 1986*, p. 32.

50. Defense, *Soviet Military Power 1987*, p. 37. In early 1988 the Joint Staff indicated that, "Although considered primarily theater and maritime weapons, BACKFIRE bombers are estimated to have the technical capability to reach CONUS [the continental United States]. depending on operational procedures." *United States Military Posture for FY 1989* (Washington, D.C.: Government Printing Office. 1988), p. 41.

51. The frequently reported disagreements between the Central Intelligence Agency and the Defense Intelligence Agency (about, for example, Soviet defense spending trends) are routinely noted by West European experts.

52. See Albert Wohlstetter. "Is There a Strategic Arms Race?" *Foreign Policy*, 15 (Summer 1974), 3–20; idem, "Rivals, But No 'Race,' " *Foreign Policy*, 16 (Fall 1974), 48–81; and idem, *Legends of the Strategic Arms Race* (Washington, D.C.: U.S. Strategic Institute, 1975).

53. Groupe X-Défense, *Les défenses anti-missiles*, p. 27.

54. Schmidt interview in Michael Charlton, *The Star Wars History, from Deterrence to Defence: The American Strategic Debate* (London: BBC Publications, 1986), p. 136.

55. A comment by a senior British Ministry of Defence official, reported in John Newhouse, "The Diplomatic Round," *The New Yorker*, July 22, 1985, p. 52.

56. *Intervention de Claude Cheysson devant la seconde session extraordinaire de l'Assemblée Générale consacrée au désarmement, New York: le 11 juin 1982* (New York: French Permanent Mission to the United Nations, 1982), p. 15.

57. "Discours prononcé par le Président Giscard d'Estaing à l'Assemblée Générale extraordinaire (New York, 25 mai 1978)," *Documents d'Actualité Internationale*, 25 (1978), 492.

58. Jacques Isnard, "Le satellite militaire français Hélios pourra espionner des radars adverses," *Le Monde*, March 25, 1987, p. 10.

59. Quilès, "L'avenir de notre concept." p. 23.

60. *Le Monde*, March 27–28, 1988, p. 8.

61. Egon Bahr cited in Hamburg DPA despatch, January 15, 1985, in *Foreign Broadcast Information Service—Western Europe*, daily report, January 16,

1985, p. J2; Helmut Schmidt, "Deutsch-französische Zusammenarbeit in der Sicherheitspolitik," *Europa-Archiv*, 42 (June 10, 1987), 310; and Michael Feazel, "German Panel \Urges Autonomy for European Space Program," *Aviation Week and Space Technology*, June 30, 1986, p. 25.

62. François Heisbourg, "Coopération en matière d'armements: rien n'est jamais acquis," in *Le couple franco-allemand et la défense de l'Europe*, ed. Karl Kaiser and Pierre Lellouche (Paris: Institut Français des Relations Internationales, 1986), p. 122.

63. Jurgen Kronig, "England: Spionagesatellit und Pressefreiheit," *Die Zeit*, February 6, 1987.

64. Sir Frank Cooper cited in Duncan Campbell, "The Parliamentary Bypass Operation," *New Statesman*, 113 (January 23, 1987), 9.

65. François Heisbourg, "Défense française: l'impossible statu quo," *Politique Internationale*, 36 (Summer 1987), 151.

66. For background, see David S. Yost, "Western Europe and the U.S. Strategic Defense Initiative," *Journal of International Affairs*, 41, no. 2 (Summer 1988).

67. Para. 5 of the final communiqué of the NATO Nuclear Planning Group, March 27, 1985.

68. NPG communiqué of October 22, 1986, para. 7.

69. Younger in Great Britain, Parliament, *Parliamentary Debates* (House of Commons), February 19, 1986, col. 337.

70. *Redresser la défense de la France* (Paris: Union pour la Démocratie Française, November 1985), p. 53.

71. Groupe X-Défense, *Les défenses anti-missiles*, p. 28.

1. Soviet BMD Capabilities and Activities

1. Sayre Stevens, "The Soviet BMD Program," in *Ballistic Missile Defense*, ed. Ashton B. Carter and David N. Schwartz (Washington, D.C.: Brookings Institution, 1984), p. 183.

2. It has been reported that the information the United States provided to the USSR in the SALT I negotiations "enhanced the Soviets' ability to jam American electronic equipment used to monitor Soviet antiballistic missile tests, upgraded surface-to-air missile tests, and radar tests." Rebecca V. Strode, "Strategic Issues and Soviet Foreign Policy," in Gerrit W. Gong, Angela E. Stent, and Rebecca V. Strode, *Areas of Challenge for Soviet Foreign Policy in the 1980s* (Bloomington: Indiana University Press, 1984), p. 97.

3. Malcolm Wallop, "Soviet Violations of Arms Control Agreements: So What?" *Strategic Review*, 11 (Summer 1983), 18.

4. Testimony by John L. Gardner, then director of defense systems, Department of Defense, in U.S. House of Representatives, Committee on Armed Services, *Defense Department Authorization and Oversight*, Hearings, 98th Cong., 1st sess. (Washington, D.C.: U.S. Government Printing Office, 1983), pt. 5, p. 270. Richard Perle, assistant secretary of defense for international security policy, has added, "There will always be uncertainties about the ultimate effectiveness and vulnerability of any defensive system." Testi-

mony in U.S. House of Representatives, Committee on Armed Services, Research and Development Subcommittee and Investigations Subcommittee, *Hearing on H.R. 3073, People Protection Act*, 98th Cong., 1st sess., November 10, 1983 (Washington, D.C.: Government Printing Office, 1984), p. 30.

5. Ashton B. Carter, "Introduction to the BMD Question," in *Ballistic Missile Defense*, ed. Carter and Schwartz, p. 7.

6. Stevens, "The Soviet BMD Program," pp. 189, 191.

7. John Prados, *The Soviet Estimate: U.S. Intelligence Analysis and Soviet Strategic Forces* (Princeton, N.J.: Princeton University Press, 1986), p. 152.

8. Stevens, "The Soviet BMD Program," pp. 191–192.

9. Sidney Graybeal and Daniel Gouré, "Soviet Ballistic Missile Defense (BMD) Objectives: Past, Present, and Future," in *U.S. Arms Control Objectives and the Implications for Ballistic Missile Defense*, proceedings of a symposium held at the Center for Science and International Affairs, Harvard University, November 1–2, 1979 (Cambridge, Mass.: Puritan Press, 1980), p. 70. Although the Russians trace their interest in rockets to the remarkable work of Konstantin E. Tsiolkovsky (1857–1935) and others, the capture of German scientists and technology during World War II seems to have provided the foundation for postwar Soviet programs. Soviet sources indicate that development work on "the first Soviet rocket, the R-1" was completed in 1947, that "more powerful liquid-fuel rocket engines" were developed and tested in 1947–1949, and that "next to be designed were ballistic missiles." Major General Stepan A. Tyushkevich, *The Soviet Armed Forces: A History of Their Organizational Development*, originally published by the Soviet Ministry of Defense, 1978, translated by the CIS Multilingual Section Translation Bureau, Secretary of State Department, Ottawa, Canada, and published under the auspices of the United States Air Force (Washington, D.C.: Government Printing Office, 1984), p. 380. No precise date for the origins of Soviet BMD research seems to be available. In 1961, Khrushchev said, "I can only tell you that at the same time we told our scientists and engineers to develop intercontinental rockets we told another group to work out means to combat such rockets." C. L. Sulzberger, "Khrushchev Says in Interview He Is Ready to Meet Kennedy," *New York Times*, September 8, 1961, pp. 1, 10.

10. Johan J. Holst, "Missile Defense: The Soviet Union and the Arms Race," in *Why ABM? Policy Issues in the Missile Defense Controversy*, ed. Johan J. Holst and William Schneider, Jr. (New York: Pergamon Press, 1969), pp. 146–148.

11. McNamara testimony in U.S. Senate, Committee on Armed Services and the Subcommittee on Department of Defense of the Committee on Appropriations, *Military Procurement Authorizations for Fiscal Year 1968*, hearings, 90th Cong., 1st sess. (Washington, D.C.: Government Printing Office, 1967), p. 303.

12. Laird press conference of February 28, 1969, cited in Holst, "Missile Defense," p. 148.

13. Hans Rühle, "Gorbachev's 'Star Wars,' " *NATO Review*, 33 (August 1985), 26.

14. Michael Mihalka, "Soviet Strategic Deception, 1955–1981," *Journal of Strategic Studies*, 5 (March 1982), 52.

15. Stevens, "The Soviet BMD Program," pp. 193, 195. Some experts argue, however, that the contrast between the U.S. and Soviet approaches during this period should not be overdrawn, since the U.S. also performed BMD-relevant high-altitude nuclear tests.

16. Benson D. Adams, *Ballistic Missile Defense* (New York: American Elsevier, 1971), pp. 79, 81. Lawrence Freedman points out that, although a number of these tests were BMD-related, reports that the tests included firing a nuclear interceptor warhead were rejected in 1963 by Harold Brown, then director of defense research and engineering. Brown said that the tests had not involved firing a nuclear interceptor or efforts to intercept a real ICBM. Lawrence Freedman, *U.S. Intelligence and the Soviet Strategic Threat* (Boulder, Colo.: Westview Press, 1977), p. 87.

17. Sayre Stevens, "Ballistic Missile Defense in the Soviet Union," *Current History*, 84 (October 1985), 314.

18. Robert P. Berman and John C. Baker, *Soviet Strategic Forces: Requirements and Responses* (Washington, D.C.: Brookings Institution, 1982), p. 147.

19. As suggested earlier, it does not seem possible to identify even the year in which the Soviets first initiated research on BMD, though circumstantial evidence points to the late 1940s. In contrast, the first U.S. BMD research projects (Thumper and Wizard) began in 1946; but no engineering development decision was taken until 1958 (Nike-Zeus), and no U.S. administration proposed actual BMD deployments until 1967. Nor is it possible to specify when the Soviets decided to pursue BMD deployments. There is uncertainty about whether the Griffon, for example, was intended to serve as a means of BMD, and the Soviets do not appear to have revealed when they decided to produce and deploy the Galosh.

20. Stevens, "The Soviet BMD Program," p. 196.

21. Edward L. Warner, III, *The Military in Contemporary Soviet Politics: An Institutional Analysis* (New York: Praeger, 1977), p. 206.

22. Mark E. Miller, *Soviet Strategic Power and Doctrine: The Quest for Superiority* (Bethesda, Md.: Advanced International Studies Institute, 1982), p. 100.

23. Stevens, "The Soviet BMD Program," p. 196.

24. Berman and Baker, *Soviet Strategic Forces*, p. 148.

25. Miller, *Soviet Strategic Power*, p. 100.

26. Stevens, "The Soviet BMD Program," p. 205. Freedman summarizes the U.S. debate in the 1960s over the significance of the Tallinn Line in *U.S. Intelligence*, pp. 90–96, 207n.

27. Warner, *Military in Contemporary Soviet Politics*, p. 207.

28. Prados, *The Soviet Estimate*, p. 164.

29. Stevens, "The Soviet BMD Program," pp. 198–199.

30. Miller, *Soviet Strategic Power*, p. 101.

31. Stevens, "The Soviet BMD Program," p. 199.

32. Ibid., pp. 199–200.

33. Rühle, "Gorbachev's 'Star Wars,' " p. 28.

34. Miller, *Soviet Strategic Power*, p. 173.

35. Rühle, "Gorbachev's 'Star Wars,' " pp. 28–29.

36. Stevens, "The Soviet BMD Program," pp. 199, 201. Only 64 Galosh ABM-1B missiles were deployed in the period prior to the beginning of the modernization of the Moscow system (1978–1980), although "about 150" of the missiles were built. *Jane's Weapon Systems, 1987–1988* (London: Jane's Yearbooks, 1987), p. 16. A useful summary of official U.S. views on Galosh during the 1960s is provided in Freedman, *U.S. Intelligence*, pp. 87–90, 96. Additional details on U.S. interpretations of the Leningrad (Griffon) system, the SA-5, and the Galosh in the pre–ABM Treaty period are supplied in Prados, *The Soviet Estimate*, pp. 151–171.

37. Stephen M. Meyer, "Soviet Nuclear Operations," in *Managing Nuclear Operations*, ed. Ashton B. Carter, John D. Steinbruner, and Charles A. Zraket (Washington, D.C.: Brookings Institution, 1987), p. 482.

38. *Pravda*, September 30, 1972, p. 2.

39. Stevens, "The Soviet BMD Program," p. 211.

40. Berman and Baker, *Soviet Strategic Forces*, p. 149.

41. Currie news conference of February 20, 1976, cited in Graybeal and Gouré, "Soviet Ballistic Missile Defense," p. 78.

42. William Perry's testimony in U.S. House of Representatives, Committee on Appropriations, *Department of Defense Appropriations for 1979*, hearings, 95th Cong., 2nd sess. (Washington, D.C.: Government Printing Office, 1978), pt. 3, p. 622.

43. E. C. Aldridge, Jr., and Robert L. Maust, Jr., "SALT Implications of BMD Options," in *U.S. Arms Control Objectives and the Implications for Ballistic Missile Defense*, proceedings of a symposium held at the Center for Science and International Affairs, Harvard University, November 1–2, 1979 (Cambridge, Mass.: Puritan Press, 1980), pp. 55–56. Another source suggests a total of $240.7 million in U.S. BMD research and development in FY 1980 and provides details on how U.S. BMD spending declined after the termination of the Safeguard site and was held to a low level during the late 1970s. David N. Schwartz, "Past and Present: The Historical Legacy," in *Ballistic Missile Defense*, ed. Carter and Schwartz, p. 344.

44. Aldridge and Maust also offered conclusions: "Two summary responses seem in order: (1) While the SALT process has seriously eroded funding support for the U.S. BMD programs, Soviet BMD programs appear to have remained reasonably stable, and (2) the 5- to 10-year BMD technological lead-time advantage that the United States enjoyed in the late 1960s has eroded substantially. It is conceivable that the Soviet Union today has the advantage in some aspects of BMD system technology."

45. Vorona testimony in U.S. Senate, Committee on Armed Services, Subcommittee on General Procurement, *Soviet Defense Expenditures and Related Programs*, hearings, 96th Cong., 1st and 2nd sess., November 1, 8, 1979,

and February 4, 1980. (Washington, D.C.: Government Printing Office, 1980), p. 84. (Emphasis added.)

46. Graybeal and Gouré, "Soviet Ballistic Missile Defense," pp. 78–79.

47. Organization of the Joint Chiefs of Staff, *United States Military Posture for FY 1987* (Washington, D.C.: Government Printing Office, 1986), p. 28. Another source attributes "nearly 12,000" SAM launchers to the USSR and notes that 2800 fighter-interceptor aircraft in addition to the 1200 dedicated fighters "would also be used in strategic defense missions." (This source also differs from the OJCS statement by attributing 118 strategic air defense radars to the United States.) U.S. Under Secretary of Defense for Research and Engineering, *The FY 1987 Department of Defense Program for Research and Development* (Washington, D.C.: Government Printing Office, 1986), p. III–15.

48. *The Military Balance, 1986–1987* (London: International Institute for Strategic Studies, 1986), p. 38.

49. *The FY 1986 Department of Defense Program for Research, Development and Acquisition*, statement by the under secretary of defense for research and engineering to the 99th Cong., 1st Sess., 1985 (Washington, D.C.: Government Printing Office, 1985), p. II–7. It should, however, be noted that this figure includes SAMs manufactured for export. A breakdown regarding SAMs retained for Soviet internal purposes and SAMs exported does not seem to be available. In 1983 the Defense Intelligence Agency indicated that the USSR had produced approximately 53,000 SAMs a year in the period 1978–1982, but that "very limited data is available on exports or specific quantities exported. Therefore total output is shown." Testimony by Major General Schuyler Bissell in U.S. Congress, Joint Economic Committee, Subcommittee on International Trade, Finance, and Security Economics, *Allocation of Resources in the Soviet Union and China—1983*, hearings, 98th Cong., 1st sess., June 28 and September 20, 1983 (Washington, D.C.: Government Printing Office, 1984), p. 191.

50. *The FY 1986 Department of Defense Program*, p. IV–7.

51. Weinberger speech to the Foreign Press Center, December 19, 1984, OASD (PA) News Release no. 648–84, p. 4.

52. Department of Defense, *Soviet Military Power 1987* (Washington, D.C.: Government Printing Office, 1987), p. 45.

53. Robert M. Gates, deputy director of the CIA, "The Soviets and SDI," address to the World Affairs Council of Northern California, November 25, 1986, text furnished by the U.S. Information Service, London, p. 2.

54. Fred Charles Iklé, "Nuclear Strategy: Can There Be a Happy Ending?" *Foreign Affairs*, 63 (Spring 1985), 814.

55. Paul Nitze, *SDI: The Soviet Program*, Current Policy no. 717 (Washington, D.C.: Bureau of Public Affairs, U.S. Department of State, June 28, 1985), p. 1.

56. "Strategic offensive and defensive forces account for about one-fifth of total defense spending—about one-tenth each." *Soviet Strategic Force Developments*, testimony before a joint session of the Subcommittee on Strategic and

Theater Nuclear Forces of the Senate Armed Services Committee and the Defense Subcommittee of the Senate Committee on Appropriations, June 26, 1985, by Robert M. Gates, chairman, National Intelligence Council, and deputy director for intelligence, Central Intelligence Agency, and Lawrence K. Gershwin, national intelligence officer for strategic programs, National Intelligence Council, pp. 5–6, 9.

57. Caspar W. Weinberger, *Department of Defense Annual Report for Fiscal Year 1987* (Washington, D.C.: Government Printing Office, 1986), pp. 59–60.

58. Caspar W. Weinberger, *Department of Defense Annual Report for Fiscal Year 1988* (Washington, D.C.: Government Printing Office, 1987), p. 27.

59. Weinberger, *Defense Annual Report FY 1987*, pp. 59–60, 75.

60. Gates, "The Soviets and SDI," p. 2.

61. Weinberger, *Defense Annual Report FY 1987*, p. 60.

62. Perry, testimony in *Department of Defense Appropriations for 1979*, p. 623.

63. Henry S. Bradsher, "Soviet ABM Efforts Have Pentagon Worried," *Washington Star*, February 16, 1978, p. 11.

64. Vorona, testimony in *Soviet Defense Expenditures*, p. 75.

65. Harold Brown, *Department of Defense Annual Report for Fiscal Year 1980* (Washington, D.C.: Government Printing Office, 1979), p. 73.

66. Harold Brown, *Department of Defense Annual Report for Fiscal Year 1981* (Washington, D.C.: Government Printing Office, 1980), p. 82.

67. Official sources differ on when this upgrading began. In 1981 the Department of Defense used the same phrase as the previous administration ("developing a rapidly deployable ABM system") but did not imply that changes in the Moscow system were already under way: "When development of this system is completed, its main elements could be deployed in the Moscow area to replace or supplement the existing system." Defense, *Soviet Military Power* (Washington, D.C.: Government Printing Office, 1981), p. 68. In 1983 the Department of Defense stated that the Soviets were "building additional ABM sites and . . . retrofitting sites with new silo launchers." Defense, *Soviet Military Power 1983*, p. 28. In both 1984 and 1985, the Defense Department stated that "since 1980, the Soviets have been upgrading and expanding this system." Defense, *Soviet Military Power 1984*, p. 33, and *Soviet Military Power 1985*, p. 47. In 1986, however, the Department of Defense indicated that "in 1978, the Soviets began to upgrade and expand that system." *Soviet Military Power 1986*, pp. 42–43.

68. Defense, *Soviet Military Power 1986*, p. 43.

69. Stevens, "The Soviet BMD Program," p. 212.

70. Admiral William J. Crowe, Jr., has, for example, referred to the Soviet "development of components . . . suitable for use in an extensive deployment to protect key military, industrial, and urban population centers. These components include a transportable engagement radar, an endo-atmospheric interceptor, and a missile guidance radar." "Report to the Congress on Military Impact Statement by the Chairman of the Joint Chiefs of Staff on U.S. Noncompliance with Existing Strategic Offensive Arms Agreements," October 17, 1986 (typescript), p. 7.

71. Prados, *The Soviet Estimate*, p. 170.
72. The date foreseen in *Soviet Military Power 1986* (p. 43) was 1987. This became "the late 1980s" in *Soviet Military Power 1987* (p. 47). Gates suggests 1988 in "The Soviets and SDI," p. 2.
73. Miller, *Soviet Strategic Power*, p. 242. Prados notes that Soviet development work on an ABM missile with a restarting engine capability was first mentioned by Secretary of Defense Melvin Laird in 1969, and that it was then described as the ABM-2. Prados, *The Soviet Estimate*, pp. 167–168.
74. Berman and Baker, *Soviet Strategic Forces*, p. 148. See also Miller, *Soviet Strategic Power*, p. 242, and Michael J. Deane, "Soviet Military Doctrine and Defensive Deployment Concepts: Implications for Soviet Ballistic Missile Defense," in Jacquelyn K. Davis et al., *The Soviet Union and Ballistic Missile Defense* (Cambridge, Mass.: Institute for Foreign Policy Analysis, 1980), p. 56.
75. Groupe X-Défense, *Les défenses anti-missiles, la France et l'Europe* (Paris: Fondation pour les Etudes de Défense Nationale, 1986), pp. 157, 161. See also *Defense Daily*, October 27, 1986, p. 297.
76. Jacques Baumel, *Avis présenté au nom de la Commission de la Défense Nationale et des Forces Armées sur le projet de loi des finances pour 1987, (no. 363), tome V, Défense, espace et forces nucléaires*, no. 398 (Paris: Assemblée Nationale, October 1986), p. 33.
77. Jake Garn, "The Suppression of Information concerning Soviet SALT Violations by the U.S. Government," *Policy Review*, 9 (Summer 1979), 27n.
78. Ministry of Defence paper, "The Soviet Ballistic Missile Defence Programme," presented to the House of Commons by John Stanley, minister of state for the armed forces, in Great Britain, Parliament, *Parliamentary Debates* (House of Commons), November 26, 1985, col. 562.
79. *Aviation Week and Space Technology*, August 29, 1983, p. 19. See also *International Defense Review*, 16 (September 1983), 1193.
80. Thomas K. Longstreth, John E. Pike, and John B. Rhinelander, *The Impact of U.S. and Soviet Ballistic Missile Defense Programs on the ABM Treaty*, 3rd ed. (Washington, D.C.: National Campaign to Save the ABM Treaty, March 1985), p. 57.
81. Wallop, "Soviet Violations," p. 18.
82. *The President's Unclassified Report on Soviet Noncompliance with Arms Control Agreements* (White House, Office of the Press Secretary, December 23, 1985), p. 8. These judgments were repeated in *The President's Unclassified Report on Soviet Noncompliance with Arms Control Agreements* (White House, Office of the Press Secretary, March 10, 1987), p. 10.
83. Longstreth, Pike, and Rhinelander, *Impact of BMD Programs*, p. 57. The statement evidently assumes that U.S. SLBMs would be fired from launch points relatively close to the USSR. The United States has, however, developed long-range SLBMs with comparatively lengthy flight times. Long-range SLBMs permit an enlarged ocean patrol space and thus enhance submarine survivability prospects.
84. *Jane's Weapon Systems, 1987–1988*, p. 17.

85. Groupe X-Défense, *Les défenses anti-missiles*, p. 158.

86. François Heisbourg, "La France face aux nouvelles données stratégiques," *Défense Nationale*, April 1986, p. 37.

87. *Aviation Week and Space Technology*, September 15, 1986, p. 21.

88. For additional details on the Moscow system's radars, see "Major Improvements to Moscow's ABM Network," *Jane's Defence Weekly*, February 7, 1987, pp. 182–183. The Pill Box designation was introduced in *Soviet Military Power 1987*, p. 47.

89. Groupe X-Défense, *Les défenses anti-missiles*, p. 158.

90. Longstreth, Pike, and Rhinelander, *Impact of BMD Programs*, pp. 57–58.

91. U.S. Department of State, *SALT One. Compliance, SALT Two: Verification*, Selected Documents no. 7 (Washington, D.C.: Bureau of Public Affairs, Office of Public Communications, March 1978). p. 10. (Emphasis added.)

92. *A Quarter Century of Soviet Compliance Practices under Arms Control Commitments: 1958–1983* (Washington, D.C.: General Advisory Committee on Arms Control and Disarmament, October 1984), pp. 9–10.

93. *The President's Unclassified Report to the Congress on Soviet Noncompliance with Arms Control Agreements* (White House, Office of the Press Secretary, February 1, 1985), p. 8. The December 1985 report (p. 7) reached a similar conclusion but referred to "development and testing" rather than development alone and alluded to "sites requiring relatively limited site preparation." The March 1987 report (p. 9) repeated these formulations, except for further qualifying the latter phrase: "relatively limited special-purpose site preparation." In December 1987, the administration charged the Soviets with violating the prohibition against deploying BMD engagement radars outside the treaty-permitted BMD deployment area and test ranges, owing to the discovery that Pawn Shop and Flat Twin radars had been moved from Sary Shagan to Gomel. See Michael R. Gordon, "U.S. Says Kremlin Broke '72 Treaty Covering the ABM," *New York Times*, December 3, 1987, pp. 1, 7.

94. Longstreth, Pike, and Rhinelander, *Impact of BMD Programs*, p. 58.

95. Wallop, "Soviet Violations," p. 18.

96. Rebecca V. Strode, "Space-Based Lasers for Ballistic Missile Defense: Soviet Policy Options," in *Laser Weapons in Space: Policy and Doctrine*, ed. Keith B. Payne, (Boulder, Colo.: Westview Press, 1983), p. 118.

97. Stevens, "The Soviet BMD Program," pp. 212, 214.

98. Groupe X-Défense, *Les défenses anti-missiles*, p. 161.

99. *Military Balance, 1986–1987*, p. 38.

100. See, for example, the testimony of John S. Foster, Jr., director of defense research and engineering, in U.S. House of Representatives, Committee on Foreign Affairs, *Diplomatic and Strategic Impact of Multiple Warhead Missiles*, hearings before the Subcommittee on National Security Policy and Scientific Developments, 91st Cong., 1st sess. (Washington, D.C.: Government Printing Office, 1969), pp. 248, 276–278; General Bruce Holloway, commander of the Strategic Air Command, in U.S. House of Representatives, Committee on Armed Services, *Hearings on Military Posture* (Washington, D.C.: Gov-

ernment Printing Office, 1971), p. 2909; and General Holloway in U.S. Senate, Committee on Armed Services, pt. 1, *Fiscal Year 1972 Authorization for Military Procurement, Research and Development, Construction and Real Estate Acquisition for the Safeguard ABM, and Reserve Strengths,* hearings (Washington, D.C.: Government Printing Office, 1971), pt. 2, p. 1693.

101. The date is provided in Department of State, *SALT One: Compliance, SALT Two: Verification* (p. 6), and the reference to "some 50" violations in such SA-5 tests is made by Admiral Elmo Zumwalt (chief of naval operations at the time of the tests), who adds that "the Soviets should have gotten all the information they need from those tests." Zumwalt testimony in U.S. Senate, Committee on Appropriations, *SALT II Violations,* hearing before a subcommittee, 98th Cong., 2nd sess., March 28, 1984 (Washington, D.C.: Government Printing Office, 1984), pp. 68–69.

102. Richard Perle, testimony in U.S. Senate, Committee on Armed Services, *Soviet Treaty Violations,* hearing, March 14, 1984 (Washington, D.C.: Government Printing Office, 1984), pp. 18–19.

103. Department of State, *SALT One: Compliance, SALT Two: Verification,* pp. 5–6, 10.

104. "Soviets' S-200 [SA-5] SAM system," *Jane's Defence Weekly,* October 12, 1985, p. 793. Some sources maintain that the Gammon designation for the SA-5 replaced the term *Griffon* (for example, Prados, *The Soviet Estimate,* p. 169). Others, however, indicate that the Griffon system was distinct from the SA-5 (for example, Miller, *Soviet Strategic Power,* p. 100).

105. Joint Chiefs of Staff, *Military Posture for FY 1987,* p. 28.

106. *Jane's Weapon Systems, 1987–1988,* p. 172.

107. Defense, *Soviet Military Power,* 1981, p. 67.

108. Stevens, "The Soviet BMD Program," p. 205.

109. Miller, *Soviet Strategic Power,* p. 243.

110. Strode, "Space-Based Lasers," p. 119. See also Stevens, "The Soviet BMD Program," p. 205, and Miller, *Soviet Strategic Power,* p. 243.

111. *Jane's Weapon Systems, 1984–1985* (London: Jane's Yearbooks, 1984), pp. 95–96.

112. Defense, *Soviet Military Power 1984,* p. 37.

113. Defense, *Soviet Military Power 1985,* p. 50.

114. Defense, *Soviet Military Power 1987,* p. 61.

115. Ibid., p. 61.

116. Senator John Warner in U.S. Senate, Committee on Armed Services, *Department of Defense Authorization for Appropriations for Fiscal Year 1981,* hearings, pt. 5, Research and Development, March 13, 1980 (Washington, D.C.: Government Printing Office, 1980), p. 3013. Warner's comment was preceded by an unofficial report in 1978 of a mobile Soviet antitactical ballistic missile under development (Bradsher, "Soviet ABM Efforts," p. 11).

117. Caspar W. Weinberger, *Department of Defense Annual Report for Fiscal Year 1983* (Washington, D.C.: U.S. Government Printing Office, 1982), p. III–72.

118. William J. Perry, then under secretary of defense for research and engineering, in Senate hearings, *Appropriations for Fiscal Year 1981*, p. 3018.

119. Defense, *Soviet Military Power*, 1981, pp. 29, 67, and *Soviet Military Power 1983*, pp. 29, 38.

120. *Report of the President's Commission on Strategic Forces*, April 1983, p. 5.

121. Defense, *Soviet Military Power 1984*, p. 34. (Emphasis added.)

122. Defense, *Soviet Military Power 1985*, p. 48. The fact that the SA-10 was attributed strategic BMD potential but no ATBM capability was consistent with a comment by an unnamed U.S. official in November 1982; he described the Pershing II as likely to "stress" the SA-10, because the SA-10 was designed "against ballistic missiles for a 30-min. reaction time — computational capability, signal processing—and that system is standardized and rigid. And now it must be improved to react to the threat of Pershing 2 . . . within 8–10 minutes." See *Aviation Week and Space Technology*, November 8, 1982, p. 18.

123. Defense, *Soviet Military Power 1987*, pp. 60, 61.

124. Groupe X-Défense, *Les défenses anti-missiles*, p. 160.

125. Defense, *Soviet Military Power 1987*, p. 61.

126. Cooper cited in *Washington Times*, March 9, 1984, p. 3A.

127. *The FY 1987 Department of Defense Program*, p. III–6.

128. Defense, *Soviet Military Power 1986*, p. 57.

129. Groupe X-Défense, *Les défenses anti-missiles*, p. 26. It has been reported that "the Soviets are continuing to deploy improved air surveillance data systems that can rapidly pass data from outlying radars through the air surveillance network to ground-controlled intercept sites and SAM command posts." Defense, *Soviet Military Power 1985*, p. 46.

130. Defense, *Soviet Military Power 1987*, p. 60.

131. Hubertus G. Hoffmann, "A Missile Defense for Europe?" *Strategic Review*, 12 (Summer 1984), 53.

132. Longstreth, Pike, and Rhinelander, *Impact of BMD Programs*, p. 55.

133. Michael R. Gordon, "CIA Is Skeptical that New Soviet Radar Is Part of an ABM Defense System," *National Journal*, March 9, 1985, p. 524. See also Pierre Lellouche, *L'avenir de la guerre* (Paris: Editions Mazarine, 1985), p. 235.

134. The Scud test is reported in *Jane's Weapon Systems, 1987–1988*, p. 17. For the SS-4, see "New Soviet Missile Defenses," *Foreign Report*, April 14, 1983, p. 3-E, cited in George Schneiter, "The ABM Treaty Today," in *Ballistic Missile Defense*, ed. Carter and Schwartz, p. 239.

135. Jack Anderson in *Washington Post*, April 5, 1983, p. C15. See also *Aviation Week and Space Technology*, November 14, 1983, p. 23.

136. Michael R. Gordon, "Defense Dept. Is Rebuffed on Soviet ABM Threat," *New York Times*, March 5, 1987, p. A10.

137. Gordon, "CIA Is Skeptical," and Longstreth, Pike, and Rhinelander, *Impact of BMD Programs*, p. 56.

138. Stevens, "The Soviet BMD Program," pp. 215-216. (Emphasis added.)

139. Garn, "Suppression of Information," p. 27n.

140. *Military Balance, 1986–1987*, p. 200. The number of Poseidon SLBMs will decline as Trident I (and, eventually, Trident II) SLBM deployments increase.

141. The ideal in reentry vehicle design is an RV with low radar return and high "beta." An RV's beta, or ballistic coefficient, is principally a function of its weight, base area, and drag coefficient ($B = W/C_D A$). If the RV was shaped and weighted in order to increase its beta (that is, if the RV was heavy, long, and thin), its drag effects would be reduced, it would not lose much velocity in reentering the atmosphere, and it would not give BMD radars much time to detect it or much radar return. Although progress has been made in designing SLBM RVs of higher beta, SLBM RVs generally still weigh less than ICBM RVs and (for all the progress in engineering RVs of higher beta) some older SLBM RVs still offer greater radar cross sections. For background, see C. W. Besserer, *Missile Engineering Handbook* (Princeton, N.J.: Van Nostrand, 1958), pp. 323–325, and Frank J. Regan, *Re-Entry Vehicle Dynamics* (New York: American Institute of Aeronautics and Astronautics, 1984), p. 100.

142. Wayne R. Winton, "Applications of BMD Other than ICBM Defense," in *U.S. Arms Control Objectives and the Implications for Ballistic Missile Defense*, proceedings of a symposium held at the Center for Science and International Affairs, Harvard University, November 1–2, 1979 (Cambridge, Mass.: Puritan Press, 1980), p. 96. For a similar judgment, see Stephen Weiner, "Systems and Technology," in *Ballistic Missile Defense*, ed. Carter and Schwartz, p. 73.

143. Groupe X-Défense, *Les défenses anti-missiles*, p. 160.

144. Ibid., pp. 26, 160.

145. General Jeannou Lacaze, "L'avenir de la défense française," *Défense Nationale*, July 1985, p. 23.

146. Groupe X-Défense, *Les défenses anti-missiles*, p. 160.

147. Defense, *Soviet Military Power 1986*, p. 57.

148. Tom Diaz, "U.S. Detects New Breach of Arms Treaty by Soviets," *Washington Times*, November 12, 1985, p. 1, and Peter Samuel, "Signals May Reveal New ABMs," *Defense Week*, November 18, 1985, p. 3.

149. Defense, *Soviet Military Power 1987*, p. 50.

150. "SA-12 SAMs Deployed to South-western TVD," *Jane's Defence Weekly*, March 7, 1987, p. 359.

151. Gates and Gershwin, *Soviet Strategic Force Developments*, p. 5.

152. Jones testimony in U.S. House of Representatives, Committee on Armed Services, *Department of Defense Authorization and Oversight*, hearings, 98th Cong., 1st sess. (Washington, D.C.: Government Printing Office, 1983), pt. 5, p. 242.

153. Testimony of Richard Perle, assistant secretary of defense for international security policy, in *SALT II Violations*, p. 5.

154. "Summary of Miscellaneous Agreements Relating to the Standing Consultative Commission," in U.S. Senate, Committee on Foreign Relations, *SALT II Treaty: Background Documents*, committee print, 96th Cong., 1st sess.,

November 1979 (Washington, D.C.: Government Printing Office, 1979), p. 80.

155. Longstreth, Pike, and Rhinelander, *Impact of BMD Programs*, pp. 58–59.

156. President, *Report to the Congress on Soviet Noncompliance* (February 1985), p. 9. (Emphasis added.) According to another U.S. government statement, "for these activities not to be violations one must accept that on each and every occasion SAM radar operation was for defense or safety of the range or as instrumentation equipment for permitted purposes. We have strong circumstantial evidence of improper Soviet concurrent testing of SAM and ABM radars." U.S. Arms Control and Disarmament Agency, *Soviet Noncompliance* (Washington, D.C.: Government Printing Office, February 1, 1986), p. 4.

157. President Reagan, *Report to the Congress on Soviet Noncompliance* (December 1985), pp. 7–8. Both of these conclusions were repeated in the March 1987 report (pp. 9–10).

158. U.S. Arms Control and Disarmament Agency, press release, June 14, 1985.

159. R. Jeffrey Smith, "Arms Agreement Breathes New Life into SCC," *Science*, August 9, 1985, p. 535.

160. Wallop, "Soviet Violations," p. 18.

161. Phased-array radars differ from mechanically steered dish radars in that they are able to track a number of targets simultaneously. The radar antenna consists of an array of thousands of small antennas called elements, each of which receives electronic signals in a phased pattern. As Stephen Weiner has noted, "the new development of the last twenty years has been electronic beam steering, which can be computer controlled in a very small fraction of a second and which makes it possible for one radar to conduct the entire BMD engagement. It can simultaneously cover the search volume at a given rate, perform tracking and discrimination on all targets that are detected, and guide interceptors to objects identified as threatening RVs [reentry vehicles, including the warhead]." Weiner, "Systems and Technology," pp. 68–69.

162. Defense, *Soviet Military Power 1987*, p. 47. For a valuable discussion of Soviet strategic radars, see Meyer, "Soviet Nuclear Operations," pp. 478–482, 509.

163. Henry S. Bradsher, "Soviet ABM Efforts," p. 11.

164. Perry testimony in *Department of Defense Appropriations for FY 1979*, p. 622.

165. Brown, *Defense Annual Report FY 1980*, p. 73, and *Defense Annual Report FY 1981*, p. 82.

166. U.S. Joint Chiefs of Staff, *United States Military Posture for FY 1982* (Washington, D.C.: Government Printing Office, 1981), p. 101.

167. In the 1981 and 1983 editions of *Soviet Military Power*, the Department of Defense referred to the construction of new LPARs but offered no indication as to their number. *Soviet Military Power 1984* (p. 33) revealed the existence of six new LPARs, counting the one at Krasnoyarsk. In August 1986, the existence of two more LPARs under construction was made public. See John Walcott, "U.S. Analysts Find New Soviet Radars, Possibly Complicating Arms-Pact Effort," *Wall Street Journal*, August 15, 1986, p. 2. In

December 1986, an additional LPAR was mentioned. George C. Wilson, "U.S. Says Soviet Erects 3 Radars, Apparently for Anti-Missile Use," *International Herald Tribune*, December 13–14, 1986, p. 6.

168. *The President's Report to the Congress on Soviet Noncompliance with Arms Control Agreements* (White House, Office of the Press Secretary, January 23, 1984), p. 4.

169. Department of Defense and Department of State, *Soviet Strategic Defense Programs* (Washington, D.C.: Government Printing Office, October 1985), pp. 10–11.

170. Richard Perle, testimony in *Soviet Treaty Violations*, p. 43.

171. Peter Samuel, "Why Soviet Radar Worries U.S.," *Defense Week*, September 16, 1985, pp. 15–16.

172. See the various judgments reported in Gordon, "CIA Is Skeptical," pp. 523–526. The September 1987 visit to Krasnoyarsk by three U.S. congressmen and other Americans does not appear to have provided any significant new evidence bearing on the treaty compliance issue. Several participants in this visit concluded that the radar's orientation and frequency suggest a function as an early-warning radar, and that it is probably not suited for a battle management role. Department of Defense and DIA officials replied that the expected frequency is suitable across the entire spectrum of potential LPAR roles, including battle management, and that the radar could provide hand-over data for other radars. Either function—battle management or early warning—would represent a treaty violation, given the radar's location and orientation. Among other sources, see Paul Mann, "Administration Disputes Findings of U.S. Visit to Soviet Radar," *Aviation Week and Space Technology*, September 14, 1987, pp. 26–28.

173. Buchheim cited in R. Jeffrey Smith, "U.S. Experts Condemn Soviet Radar," *Science*, March 22, 1985, p. 1443.

174. President Reagan, *Report to the Congress on Soviet Noncompliance* (February 1985), p. 8.

175. President Reagan, *Report to the Congress on Soviet Noncompliance* (December 1985), pp. 6–7, and *Report to the Congress on Soviet Noncompliance* (March 1987), pp. 3–4, 8–9.

176. For the Senate, see Helen Dewar, "Senate Backs Reagan's Treaty Efforts," *Washington Post*, February 18, 1987, p. A7; for the House, see *Congressional Quarterly Weekly Report*, May 9, 1987, p. 948. It might be noted, however, that some congressmen have adopted the view that, although the radar "may constitute a technical violation of the ABM Treaty when fully deployed," it "poses no *military* threat to the U.S." This is the judgment of U.S. Representative Jim Moody (D-Wisc.) in his article "A Visit to Krasnoyarsk," *Christian Science Monitor*, October 5, 1987, p. 14 (emphasis in original). The president's science advisor, William Graham, remarked that this approach would imply that "the Soviets can evidently construct LPARs in unspecified numbers, at unspecified locations, and, so long as they claim their mission is space-track, and we can inspect them periodically, they will not be regarded as violations until the day they are 'turned on' and

demonstrated to be operationally connected with engagement radars, interceptors and launchers." Graham, "The big show at Krasnoyarsk," *Washington Times,* October 7, 1987, p. F1.

177. Howe, "Defence, Deterrence and Arms Control," speech to the Foreign Press Association in London, March 17, 1986, in *Arms Control and Disarmament,* 1 (April 1986), 3, a publication of the Foreign and Commonwealth Office, London.

178. Lord Trefgarne in Great Britain, Parliament, *Parliamentary Debates* (House of Lords), June 6, 1986, col. 1202.

179. Reported in Gordon, "CIA Is Skeptical," pp. 523–526.

180. Final communiqué of the Nuclear Planning Group. October 30, 1985, para. 5. (NATO Press Service Communiqué M-NPG-2[85]21.)

181. Policy statement by Chancellor Helmut Kohl to the Bundestag in Bonn on the Strategic Defense Initiative, April 18, 1985, in *Statements and Speeches,* 7, no. 10 (April 19, 1985), 2, issued by the German Information Center, New York.

182. Groupe X-Défense, *Les défenses anti-missiles,* pp. 158–159.

183. The Soviet satellite-based launch detection system has long covered U.S. ICBM fields. According to a 1985 statement by the British Ministry of Defence, however, it is not capable of detecting SLBM launches at present, and the Soviets have "a strong research programme to improve capabilities in this field," including an experimental geostationary satellite. (British Ministry of Defence, "The Soviet Ballistic Missile Defence Programme," col. 563.) In 1987 the U.S. Department of Defense indicated that the Soviets "probably have the technical capability to deploy" a geosynchronous SLBM launch-detection satellite system "by the end of the decade." *Soviet Military Power 1987,* p. 54. While the current LPAR network and other Soviet radars could detect and track incoming SLBMs, a geosynchronous satellite launch-detection system might substantially increase warning time.

184. Longstreth, Pike, and Rhinelander, *Impact of BMD Programs,* p. 53.

185. Zumwalt testimony in *SALT II Violations,* p. 52. Soviet officials at Krasnoyarsk during the September 1987 U.S. visit indicated that the radar's computer capacity was comparable to that of a Cray supercomputer, which they specified as " 'millions' of instructions per second." See *Aviation Week and Space Technology,* September 14, 1987, p. 27. Some observers have raised doubts about the possibility that the Soviets could use the Krasnoyarsk radar to defend nearby ICBM fields (and/or other military assets), on the grounds that the radar's orientation is unsuitable for dealing with the more likely flight paths of U.S. SLBMs and ICBMs. But this argument discounts the apparent Soviet interest in comprehensive radar coverage, not only for early warning purposes but possibly also for defense—even against potential threats that may seem remote from a Western standpoint.

186. Defense, *Soviet Military Power 1987,* pp. 47–48. *Soviet Military Power 1985* (p. 46) indicated that a network consisting of six new LPARs (including Krasnoyarsk) "probably will be operational by the late 1980s." The estimated operational date appears to have been pushed forward because of the recent discovery of three additional LPARs under construction. Accord-

ing to the map in *Soviet Military Power 1987* (p. 48), the three new radars are located at Skrunda, Baranovichi, and Mukachevo.

187. Groupe X-Défense, *Les défenses anti-missiles*, p. 26.

188. Gates and Gershwin, *Soviet Strategic Force Developments*, p. 5.

189. Gates's response to question from Senator Proxmire, reported in Michael R. Gordon, "C.I.A., Evaluating Soviet Threat, Often Is Not So Grim as Pentagon," *New York Times*, July 16, 1986, p. D24.

190. Stevens, "The Soviet BMD Program," p. 200. As long ago as 1973, Soviet experts noted that "the general trend in using the radar station bands is in developing the higher frequencies for protection against 'blinding' by a nuclear explosion." Colonel General N. A. Lomov, ed., *Scientific-Technical Progress and the Revolution in Military Affairs*, originally published in Moscow by the Ministry of Defense in 1973, translated and published under the auspices of the U.S. Air Force (Washington, D.C.: U.S. Government Printing Office, 1974), p. 66.

191. Charles M. Herzfeld has explained blackout as follows: "A nuclear explosion above the ground produces a 'cloud' consisting of fragments of the nuclear weapon and ionized air. This cloud may absorb, reflect, or deflect radar waves, making it difficult or impossible for the radar to see behind the cloud. The area coverage and duration of the cloud depends on the altitude of the nuclear burst, its yield, the radar operating frequency (and related technical characteristics), and the object observed. How much these clouds interfere with the defense depends on their timing and spacing in relation to the location of the defense, and the timing and spacing of the attack. The attack levels at which blackout is a problem can be estimated reasonably well (based on pre-1963 atmosphere tests and later related experiments) to assess the minimum defense capability." Herzfeld, "Missile Defense: Can It Work?" in *Why ABM? Policy Issues in the Missile Defense Controversy*, ed. Johan J. Holst and William Schneider, Jr. (New York: Pergamon Press, 1969), p. 40. Stephen Weiner has noted that the ionization "within a kilometer or two of the burst . . . persists for tens of seconds." Weiner, "Systems and Technology," p. 65. Ashton Carter has pointed out, however, that bursts at or above 60 to 80 km can produce "a region of ionization tens of kilometers or wider in extent, and disruption can persist for minutes at moderate frequencies." Carter, "BMD Applications: Performance and Limitations," in *Ballistic Missile Defense*, ed. Carter and Schwartz, p. 107.

192. Defense, *Soviet Military Power 1987*, p. 49.

193. Weiner, "Systems and Technology," pp. 65–66. Analyses discounting the utility of Soviet LPARs on the grounds of their reported low frequencies may be premature. Low frequencies may be useful for search functions, and the LPARs could provide hand-over data to other radars for tracking, discrimination, and engagement. While low frequencies are less suited for tracking functions, the Soviets may not have revealed all the frequencies their radars are capable of, and the West does not have access to test data that might indicate precisely what the radars could do. As Weiner notes, the performance of sensor discrimination algorithms is "not observable," and "ter-

minal BMD radars used in the past have ranged over a factor of ten in wavelength." (Ibid., pp. 62, 70-71.)

194. Diaz, "U.S. Detects New Breach of Arms Treaty by Soviets," and Samuel, "Signals May Reveal New ABMs."

195. Paul Bracken, *The Command and Control of Nuclear Forces* (New Haven: Yale University Press, 1983), p. 112.

196. Stevens, "Ballistic Missile Defense in the Soviet Union," p. 316.

197. Michael M. May and John R. Harvey, "Nuclear Operations and Arms Control," in *Managing Nuclear Operations*, ed. Carter, Steinbruner, and Zraket, pp. 721–722.

198. Stevens, "The Soviet BMD Program," pp. 212–213.

199. Weiner, "Systems and Technology," pp. 64–65.

200. Richard Perle, in commenting on the Krasnoyarsk radar, once noted that "space track radars . . . unlike radars that may become part of a system of anti-ballistic missile defense, are not surrounded by thousands of tons of concrete and hardened to resist the blast overpressures of a nuclear war." Perle, "The Soviet Record on Arms Control," *The National Interest*, 1 (Fall 1985), 99. On the other hand, participants in the September 1987 U.S. visit to Krasnoyarsk were impressed by the shoddiness of the radar's construction, the lack of EMP hardening, the apparent absence of an independent power-generation capability, and the inclusion of features in the complex—windows, for instance—that could scarcely withstand nuclear blasts in the proximity. Defense Department and DIA officials noted in response that no BMD radars can be hardened against a direct attack; that even the radars in the Moscow area such as Pushkino are militarily significant without such hardening; that the apparent deficiencies of the Krasnoyarsk radar could be remedied in the course of construction; and that the Soviet LPARs could be defended. See, among other sources, Paul Mann. "Administration Disputes Findings of U.S. Visit to Soviet Radar," *Aviation Week and Space Technology,* September 14, 1987, pp. 26–28.

201. Major General Aloysius G. Casey. USAF, commander of the air force's Ballistic Missile Office, cited in Edgar Ulsamer, "Countering the Soviet Strategic Shield," *Air Force Magazine*, 67 (October 1984), 73.

202. Weiner, "Systems and Technology," pp. 59, 79; Carter, "BMD Applications," p. 107.

203. Defense, *Soviet Military Power 1986*, p. 45.

204. Most U.S. sources agree in dating the initiation of these Soviet research efforts in the 1960s. The Department of Defense in the 1981 edition of *Soviet Military Power* (p. 75) said that the Soviets have been interested in particle beam weapons concepts "since the early 1950s." but did not speculate on when the Soviets may have linked this interest to BMD.

205. Stevens, "The Soviet BMD Program," p. 214.

206. U.S. Congress, Office of Technology Assessment, *Ballistic Missile Defense Technologies*, OTA-ISC-254 (Washington, D.C.: Government Printing Office, September 1985), p. 244. (Emphasis in original.)

207. Wallop, "Soviet Violations," p. 19.

208. U.S. Senate, Committee on Armed Services, *Department of Defense, Strategic Defense Initiative, Authorization for Appropriations for Fiscal Year 1985*, hearings, 98th Cong., 2nd sess. (Washington, D.C.: Government Printing Office, 1984), pt. 6, p. 2929.

209. Currie, cited in U.S. Senate, Committee on Commerce, Science, and Transportation, *Soviet Space Programs: 1976–1980* (Washington, D.C.: Government Printing Office, 1982), pt. 1, p. 185.

210. Brown, *Defense Annual Report FY 1980*, p. 73. Brown repeated this assessment, using almost exactly the same words, the following year, in *Defense Annual Report FY 1981*, p. 82. It has been reported that U.S. Air Force intelligence officials in the late 1970s contended that Soviet BMD activities in such advanced technologies were more extensive than other U.S. intelligence agencies suggested. Prados, *The Soviet Estimate*, pp. 286–287.

211. *The FY 1981 Department of Defense Program for Research, Development and Acquisition*, statement by the under secretary of defense for research and engineering, to the 96th Cong., 2nd sess., 1980 (Washington, D.C.: Government Printing Office, 1980), p. II–9, cited in Strode, "Space-Based Lasers," p. 122.

212. Perry cited in Miller, *Soviet Strategic Power*, p. 244.

213. Paul Nitze cited in Hedrick Smith, "Nitze Details U.S. Charges Soviet Has Own 'Star Wars,' " *New York Times*, July 12, 1985, p. 6; and Lieutenant General James Abrahamson cited in *Aviation Week and Space Technology*, October 21, 1985, p. 18. This *New York Times* article describes Nitze as believing the Soviets are ahead in high-energy lasers, but roughly on "the same timeframe" in research on both particle beam and kinetic energy weapons. In contrast, the CIA is reported to believe there is "essential equivalence" in U.S. and Soviet laser technologies, except for a Soviet advantage in metal-vapor lasers, and that the Soviets "may have the edge over the U.S. in some important areas" of particle beam and microwave weapon design. (Peter Samuel, "CIA Sees Dead Heat in Star Wars," *Defense Week*, July 15, 1985, p. 14.) The CIA is also reported to have rejected the Department of Energy's view that the Soviet Union might be so far ahead of the United States in developing x-ray lasers that it might be able to deploy such weapons without additional nuclear explosive tests. (William J. Broad, "C.I.A. Disputes White House on Soviet Antimissile Gains," *New York Times*, May 29, 1986, p. B5.) In 1986 the under secretary of defense for research and engineering rated the United States and USSR as "equal" in laser technologies and in the associated areas of optics and mobile power sources. (*FY 1987 Department of Defense Program*, p. II–11.)

214. Clarence A. Robinson, Jr., "Soviets Accelerate Missile Defense Efforts," *Aviation Week and Space Technology*, January 16, 1984, p. 16.

215. Defense, *Soviet Military Power 1987*, p. 51.

216. Gates and Gershwin, *Soviet Strategic Force Developments*, p. 8.

217. Joint Chiefs of Staff, *Military Posture for FY 1987*, p. 26.

218. Defense, *Soviet Military Power 1986*, p. 47.

219. "White House Assesses Reports of Soviet Asat Laser Facilities," *Aviation*

Week and Space Technology, September 15, 1986, p. 21. See also William J. Broad, "New Clues on a Soviet Laser Complex," *New York Times,* October 23, 1987, p. A14.

220. Nitze, *SDI: The Soviet Program,* p. 2.
221. Defense and State, *Soviet Strategic Defense Programs,* p. 13.
222. Abrahamson cited in *Aviation Week and Space Technology,* October 21, 1985, p. 18.
223. Ministry of Defence, "The Soviet Ballistic Missile Defence Programme," col. 563.
224. Piotrowski cited in Richard Holloran, "General Describes Soviet Laser Threat," *New York Times,* October 24, 1987, p. 62.
225. Defense, *Soviet Military Power 1985,* p. 44.
226. Commission d'Etudes sur les Armes Spatiales, *Rapport de synthèse présenté au ministre de la défénse,* January 30, 1986, pp. 11–13.
227. Rühle, "Gorbachev's 'Star Wars,' " pp. 31–32.
228. The Soviet high-energy laser effort was described as "three-to-five times" that of the United States in the *Soviet Military Power* surveys of 1981 (p. 76) and 1983 (p. 75). The Soviet effort was "considerably larger" in the survey for 1984 (p. 106) and simply "much larger" in the surveys for 1985 (p. 44) and 1986 (p. 46). The CIA reportedly holds that it is not possible to make a reliable estimate of the ratio, although the Soviet program is "larger" than that of the United States. Samuel, "CIA Sees Dead Heat in Star Wars," p. 14.
229. Defense, *Soviet Military Power 1985,* p. 44.
230. Nitze, *SDI: The Soviet Program,* p. 2.
231. Defense, *Soviet Military Power 1986,* pp. 46–47.
232. Roger P. Main, "The USSR and Laser Weaponry The View from Outside," *Defense Systems Review,* 3, no. 3 (1985), 77.
233. Ibid., pp. 67–68, 71, 74, 76–77.
234. Charged particle beams are more readily generated and steered than neutral particle beams, but are subject to deflection by the earth's magnetic field. For background, see Weiner, "Systems and Technology," p. 96.
235. See the statements by Currie in U.S. Senate, *Soviet Space Programs,* p. 185, and Clarence A. Robinson, Jr., "Soviets Push for Beam Weapon," *Aviation Week and Space Technology,* May 2, 1977, pp. 16–23. This article initiated a prolonged discussion in the Western defense community.
236. *Aviation Week and Space Technology,* May 7, 1979, p. 9, cited in Deane, "Soviet Military Doctrine," p. 58.
237. Current statements by official U.S. sources disagree on when the Soviets initiated research to explore the feasibility of space-based particle beam weapons, with Paul Nitze (*SDI: The Soviet Program,* p. 2) referring to the "early 1970s" and a recent joint publication of the Department of Defense and Department of State (*Soviet Strategic Defense Programs,* p. 14) placing this in the "late 1960s."
238. Defense and State, *Soviet Strategic Defense Programs,* p. 15.
239. Main, "USSR and Laser Weaponry," p. 70.
240. Albert Carnesale, "Special Supplement: The Strategic Defense Initiative," in

1985–1986 American Defense Annual, ed. George E. Hudson and Joseph Kruzel (Lexington, Mass.: D.C. Heath /Lexington Books, 1985), p. 196.

241. Nitze, *SDI: The Soviet Program,* p. 2.
242. Defense and State, *Soviet Strategic Defense Programs,* pp. 14–15.
243. Gates and Gershwin, *Soviet Strategic Force Developments,* p. 8.
244. Ministry of Defence, "The Soviet Ballistic Missile Defence Programme," col. 653.
245. Meyer has pointed out that the Soviet pattern of military research and development has often involved the deployment of "what the United States would have considered an immature technology, which had little or no capability to accomplish its task. The Soviet goal, however, was to get the basic weapon into the field and then work on developing its performance capabilities. Thus it will not be surprising if the forecast Soviet directed energy weapons enter service with no military utility. Standard operating procedures within the military industries suggest that at least a decade of in situ modification and innovation will be required before a functional weapon finally emerges." Stephen M. Meyer, "Space and Soviet Military Planning," in *National Interests and the Military Use of Space,* ed. William J. Durch (Cambridge, Mass.: Ballinger, 1984), p. 81.
246. Vorona, testimony in U.S. Senate, *Soviet Defense Expenditures,* pp. 78, 83.
247. Defense, *Soviet Military Power,* 1981, p. 75.
248. Defense, *Soviet Military Power 1984,* p. 106.
249. Defense, *Soviet Military Power 1985,* p. 45.
250. Ministry of Defence, "The Soviet Ballistic Missile Defence Programme," col. 563.
251. Nitze, *SDI: The Soviet Programme,* p. 2.
252. Gates and Gershwin, *Soviet Strategic Force Developments,* p. 8.
253. Gates, "The Soviets and SDI," p. 6.
254. Nitze, *SDI: The Soviet Programme,* p. 2, and Defense and State, *Soviet Strategic Defense Programs,* p. 16.
255. Defense and State, *Soviet Strategic Defense Programs,* p. 16.
256. Ministry of Defence, "The Soviet Ballistic Missile Defence Programme," col. 563.
257. Commission d'Etudes, *Rapport de synthèse,* pp. 5, 15.
258. U.S. Senate, *Soviet Space Programs,* p. 13.
259. Defense, *Soviet Military Power 1985,* pp. 58–59.
260. Defense, *Soviet Military Power 1986,* p. 52.
261. Ministry of Defence, "The Soviet Ballistic Missile Defence Programme," col. 563.
262. Felicity Barringer, "Soviet Launches Mightiest Rocket on a Test Mission," *New York Times,* May 17, 1987, pp. 1, 29.
263. Ministry of Defence, "The Soviet Ballistic Missile Defence Programme," col. 563.
264. Defense, *Soviet Military Power 1986,* pp. 52–53.
265. Warren Strobel, "Soviet Space Platform Beams 'Star Wars' Test," *Washington Times,* July 21, 1987, p. 1.

266. In April 1983, the Soviet academician Vasily Mishin suggested that, with the use of "film mirror energy concentrators and thermoelectric transformers, . . . systems generating a power equivalent to that produced by all hydraulic power plants of the USSR in 1985 may be placed in orbit with 12 to 15 rockets carrying a useful load of 120–150 tons. Such systems would prove to be immeasurably more efficient when interacting with space thermonuclear power systems." Vasily P. Mishin, "Terrestrial Cosmonautics Program," *Kommunist*, April 1983, in JPRS USSR Report 83684, p. 95.

267. Peter E. Glaser cited in William J. Broad, "Soviet Plans Big Satellites to Make Electricity for Cities and Industry," *New York Times*, June 14, 1987, pp. 1, 30.

268. DeLauer testimony in U.S. Senate, Committee on Armed Services, *Department of Defense Authorization for Appropriations for Fiscal Year 1985*, pt. 6, *Strategic Defense Initiative*, hearings, 98th Cong., 2nd sess., March 8, 22, and April 24, 1984 (Washington, D.C.: Government Printing Office, 1984), pp. 2929–30.

269. Office of Technology Assessment, *Ballistic Missile Defense Technologies*, p. 12.

270. *The FY 1987 Department of Defense Program*, p. II–11.

271. Harold Brown, *Department of Defense Annual Report for Fiscal Year 1979* (Washington, D.C.: Government Printing Office, 1978), p. 124.

272. Stevens, "The Soviet BMD Program," p. 217.

273. *The FY 1986 Department of Defense Program*, p. II–5.

274. Defense and State, *Soviet Strategic Defense Programs*, p. 16.

275. Edwy Plenel in *Le Monde*, April 2, 1985; David Buchan, "Beam of Light on Soviet Star Wars Research," *Financial Times*, October 16, 1986.

276. D. J. Fewtrell, director of nuclear policy and security, Ministry of Defence, testimony in Great Britain, House of Commons, *Third Report from the Defence Committee, Defence Commitments and Resources and the Defence Estimates 1985–1986*, vol. 2 (London: Her Majesty's Stationery Office, 1983), p. 275.

277. Ministry of Defence, "The Soviet Ballistic Missile Defence Programme," col. 563.

278. Groupe X-Défense, *Les défenses anti-missiles*, p. 164.

279. Donald R. Cotter, "Peacetime Operations: Safety and Security," in *Managing Nuclear Operations*, ed. Carter, Steinbruner, and Zraket, p. 33.

280. A new BMD radar was installed in October 1975 at the Kamchatka impact area of the Soviet ICBM test range. In response to U.S. inquiries, the USSR confirmed that Kamchatka was a BMD test range that Soviet negotiators had not mentioned during the negotiation of the ABM Treaty in 1972. See Department of State, *SALT One: Compliance, SALT Two: Verification*, pp. 6–7. Some observers view this Soviet omission as inconsistent with the ABM Treaty's Common Understanding C. This understanding concerns current ABM test ranges and includes a mutual commitment that "ABM components will not be located at any other test ranges without prior agreement between our Governments that there will be such additional ABM test ranges."

281. Brown, *Defense Annual Report FY 1980*, p. 82.

282. *Report of the President's Commission*, p. 5.
283. The possibility that the Soviets might develop multiple-warhead interceptor missiles does not seem to have received much attention. But this concept could be advantageous, and it would be surprising if Soviet BMD researchers had not given it consideration. According to Agreed Statement E of the ABM Treaty, the parties are obliged "not to develop, test or deploy ABM interceptor missiles for the delivery by each ABM interceptor missile of more than one independently guided warhead." Improvements in guidance, target acquisition, and data-processing capabilities may nonetheless make this an increasingly attractive and cost-effective possibility. For recent discussions of the concept, see William J. Perry, "Advanced Technology and Arms Control," *Orbis*, 26 (Summer 1982), 357, and William A. Davis, Jr., *Asymmetries in U.S. and Soviet Strategic Defense Programs: Implications for Near-Term American Deployment Options* (Washington, D.C.: Pergamon Brassey's, 1987), pp. 26–27.
284. Defense, *Soviet Military Power 1985*, p. 48. (Emphasis added.) A similar judgment was included in the president's December 1985 report to the Congress (p. 8): "The US Government judges that the aggregate of the Soviet Union's ABM and ABM-related actions (e.g., radar construction, concurrent testing, SAM upgrade, ABM rapid reload and ABM mobility) suggests that the USSR may be preparing an ABM defense of its national territory." This conclusion was reaffirmed in the president's March 1987 report (p. 10).
285. Gates and Gershwin, *Soviet Strategic Force Developments*, pp. 5–6. The Joint Chiefs of Staff have also referred to Soviet work on "a rapidly deployable ABM system that raises concerns about their potential ability to deploy a nationwide ABM system within the next decade in violation of the ABM Treaty." *Military Posture for FY 1987*, p. 28.
286. Office of Technology Assessment, *Ballistic Missile Defense Technologies*, p. 9. Ashton Carter has likewise noted, "It is generally accepted that if either side abrogated the treaty today, the Soviets would be the first in the field with a working BMD deployment." Carter, "Introduction to the BMD Question," p. 20.
287. See for example, Paul Quilès, "L'avenir de notre concept de défense face aux progrès technologiques," *Défense Nationale*, January 1986, p. 17, and the statement by Jacques Chirac on April 9, 1986, in *Le Monde*, April 11, 1986, p. 7.
288. Groupe X-Défense, *Les défénses anti-missiles*, pp. 26, 161, 163–164.
289. Manfred Wörner, "A Missile Defense for NATO Europe," *Strategic Review*, 14 (Winter 1986), 16.
290. Rühle, "Gorbachev's 'Star Wars,' " pp. 30–31.
291. Harald Müller, *Strategic Defences: The End of Alliance Strategy?* CEPS Paper no. 32 (Brussels: Centre for European Policy Studies, 1987), p. 20.
292. Stevens, "Ballistic Missile Defence in the Soviet Union," p. 316.
293. Perry, testimony in *Defense Appropriations for 1979*, p. 623.
294. *The FY 1987 Department of Defense Program*, p. III–12. See also the statements

by Major General Casey, reported in Ulsamer, "Countering the Soviet Strategic Shield," p. 73.

295. Defense and State, *Soviet Strategic Defense Programs*, p. 8. *Soviet Military Power 1987* indicates that the Gazelle is "probably nuclear-armed" (p. 47).

296. See Lacaze, "L'avenir." p. 23, and Groupe X-Défense, *Les defénses anti-missiles*, pp. 64, 85–86.

297. Groupe X-Défense, *Les défenses anti-missiles*, pp. 157, 160.

298. *Jane's Weapon Systems, 1987–1988*, p. 17.

299. As Donald Cotter recently noted, the U.S. Sprint BMD interceptor missile used "an enhanced-radiation, reduced-blast 'neutron bomb' warhead to ensure destruction of incoming enemy warheads." Cotter, "Peacetime Operations: Safety and Security," in *Managing Nuclear Operations*, ed. Carter, Steinbruner, and Zraket, p. 32. Unclassified information on Soviet warhead designs appears to be nonexistent. In November 1978, however, Leonid Brezhnev told a group of U.S. senators: "Our designers tested a neutron bomb but we gave it up. We never started production." Brezhnev cited in *International Herald Tribune*, November 18–19, 1978, p. 2.

300. According to Herzfeld, "It is not true . . . that the explosion of a defensive warhead, when used according to plan, produces damage in the defended area. Nor would such an explosion produce radioactive fall-out locally." Herzfeld, "Missile Defense," p. 18.

301. Salvage fusing is a mechanism whereby the warhead will detonate unless the interceptor physically destroys it. Some contact fuses might be detonated by the impact of the interceptor's kill mechanism. The purpose would be to degrade the quality of the defender's radar and communications and cause other damage that would "salvage" something from an attack frustrated in its original purpose by the defender's interception of the warhead. Nonnuclear kill mechanisms, if sufficiently reliable and effective, would in principle be preferable to nuclear warheads. But salvage fusing could mean that the nuclear effects from NNK intercepts could be greater than what might be caused by low-yield nuclear intercepts that would destroy the warhead before it could salvage-fuse. This has led to speculation about tactics that might be adopted—for instance, using NNK warheads for high-level intercepts, where salvage fusing would be less damaging, and using low-yield nuclear warheads at lower altitudes, as a last resort, to attempt to neutralize salvage-fused warheads.

302. Main, "USSR and Laser Weaponry," p. 72.

303. Office of Technology Assessment, *Ballistic Missile Defense Technologies*, p. 61.

2. Interpretations of Soviet Behavior

1. See, among other works, Thomas A. Brown, *What Is an Arms Race?* (Santa Monica, Calif.: California Arms Control and Foreign Policy Seminar, 1973), and Colin Gray, "The Urge to Compete: Rationales for Arms Racing," *World Politics*, 26 (January 1974), 207–233.

2. Alain C. Enthoven and K. Wayne Smith, *How Much Is Enough? Shaping the*

Defense Program, 1961–1969 (New York: Harper and Row, 1971), pp. 175–176.

3. Andrew W. Marshall, "Arms Competitions: The Status of Analysis," in *The Western Panacea: Constraining Soviet Power through Negotiation,* ed. Uwe Nerlich, vol. 2 of *Soviet Power and Western Negotiating Policies* (Cambridge, Mass.: Ballinger, 1983), p. 7.

4. According to the data compiled by Robert P. Berman and John C. Baker, in 1960 the Soviet Union had 4 ICBMs; in 1965, 224 ICBMs; and in 1970, 1220 ICBMs. See Berman and Baker, *Soviet Strategic Forces: Requirements and Responses* (Washington, D.C.: Brookings Institution, 1982), p. 42.

5. For a useful discussion of the pace of arms race interactions and technological stability, see Stephen Peter Rosen, "Foreign Policy and Nuclear Weapons: The Case for Strategic Defenses," in *The Strategic Imperative: New Policies for American Security,* ed. Samuel P. Huntington (Cambridge, Mass.: Ballinger, 1982), pp. 142–146.

6. Nikita Khrushchev, *Khrushchev Remembers: The Last Testament,* trans. and ed. Strobe Talbott (Boston: Little, Brown, 1974), pp. 48–49. The SS-6 ICBM was in any case ill suited for silo deployment, owing in part to "the awkwardness and volatility of the missile's nonstorable liquid fuel." See Berman and Baker, *Soviet Strategic Forces,* p. 91.

7. Marshall, "Arms Competitions," pp. 8–9.

8. Edward L. Warner, III, *The Military in Contemporary Soviet Politics: An Institutional Analysis* (New York: Praeger, 1977), p. 208.

9. Khrushchev, *Khrushchev Remembers,* pp. 39, 43.

10. Marshal V. D. Sokolovskiy, *Soviet Military Strategy,* 3rd ed., ed. Harriet Fast Scott (New York: Crane, Russak, 1975), pp. 252–253.

11. *Soviet Strategic Force Developments,* testimony before a joint session of the Subcommittee on Strategic and Theater Nuclear Forces of the Senate Armed Services Committee and the Defense Subcommittee of the Senate Committee on Appropriations, June 26, 1985, by Robert M. Gates, chairman, National Intelligence Council, and deputy director for intelligence, Central Intelligence Agency, and Lawrence K. Gershwin, national intelligence officer for strategic programs, National Intelligence Council, pp. 3–4. The information on the initial development work on the Blackjack is found in "Gorbachev's Modernization Program: A Status Report," a paper prepared by the Central Intelligence Agency and the Defense Intelligence Agency for submission to the Subcommittee on National Security Economics of the Joint Economic Committee, U.S. Congress, March 19, 1987, p. 16.

12. Although some observers might speculate that the Backfire (first deployed in 1974) represents a Soviet response to the opportunity offered by inadequate U.S. air defenses, this thesis has been undermined by reassessments of the Backfire's intercontinental strike potential and by the aircraft's assignment to naval and contiguous theater commands. The International Institute for Strategic Studies attributes the Backfire a range of 11,000 km, which exceeds the 5500-km range that the Soviet Union and the United States agreed to define as "strategic" in the SALT negotiations. This is

comparable to the ranges attributed to the U.S. B-52G, B-52H, and B-1B (12,000 km) and the Soviet Bear (12,800 km) and Bison (11,200 km). *The Military Balance, 1986-1987* (London: International Institute for Strategic Studies, 1985), pp. 201, 206. Although Arctic basing, in-flight refueling, plans to land in Cuba, and other measures could enable the Backfire to perform missions against the United States, the tendency in recent years in public U.S. government assessments (as noted in the Introduction) has been to downplay the Backfire's intercontinental potential. Some Western observers doubt that the Soviets require the Backfire for intercontinental strike missions, given other Soviet capabilities, and argue that the Backfire would probably be more effectively employed in naval and regional missions.

13. Joint Staff, *United States Military Posture FY 1988* (Washington, D.C.: Government Printing Office, 1987), pp. 43–45.
14. Soviet naval groups—including Kirov cruisers equipped with SA-N-6 SAMs—appear to have been formed to protect SSBN "bastions" near the USSR, but they have also effectively extended the Soviet air defense envelope at sea. See *Jane's Weapon Systems, 1987–1988* (London: Jane's Yearbooks, 1987), p. 502. The recent Soviet interest in aircraft carriers may be attributable not only to aspirations regarding power projection in regional contingencies but also to the desire to extend Soviet air defenses.
15. Caspar W. Weinberger, *Department of Defense Annual Report for Fiscal Year 1987* (Washington, D.C.: U.S. Government Printing Office, 1986), p. 86.
16. This statement and others are discussed in Michael Mihalka, "Soviet Strategic Deception, 1955–1981," *Journal of Strategic Studies*, 5 (March 1982), 46–49.
17. David N. Schwartz, "Past and Present: The Historical Legacy," in *Ballistic Missile Defense*, ed. Ashton B. Carter and David N. Schwartz (Washington, D.C.: Brookings Institution, 1984), p. 332.
18. These BMD declarations and others are cited in Mihalka, "Soviet Strategic Deception," pp. 51–57.
19. The Soviets apparently intended to achieve this effect, perhaps without foreseeing the consequences. Khrushchev conceded the deceptive intent in his memoirs: "I used to say sometimes in my speeches that we had developed an antimissile missile that could hit a fly, but of course that was just rhetoric to make our adversaries think twice." Khrushchev, *Khrushchev Remembers*, p. 533.
20. Mihalka, "Soviet Strategic Deception," p. 56.
21. Alton Frye, *A Responsible Congress: The Politics of National Security* (New York: McGraw-Hill, 1975), pp. 49–51.
22. Lawrence Freedman, *U.S. Intelligence and the Soviet Strategic Threat* (Boulder, Colo.: Westview Press, 1977), pp. 95, 191.
23. Raymond L. Garthoff, *Detente and Confrontation: American-Soviet Relations from Nixon to Reagan* (Washington, D.C.: Brookings Institution, 1985), pp. 133, 142–143, 148.
24. George Rathjens, "A Breakthrough in Arms Control?" *Bulletin of the Atomic Scientists*, 27 (June 1971), 5.

25. Alton Frye has pointed out, however, that the Soviets may rate the relative counterforce capabilities of the United States more highly than do U.S. authorities. The Soviets may, in other words, conservatively overestimate U.S. capabilities. They may attribute higher reliability to U.S. ICBMs and control and guidance mechanisms than to their own. They may even judge the United States capable of exercising launch-on-warning or launch-under-attack options, even though some U.S. authorities have underlined the grave political and strategic drawbacks of seeking such remedies for ICBM vulnerability.

26. Harold Brown, *Department of Defense Annual Report for Fiscal Year 1980* (Washington, D.C.: Government Printing Office, 1979), pp. 35, 38.

27. Roger W. Barnett, "Trans-SALT: Soviet Strategic Doctrine," *Orbis*, 19 (Summer 1975), 554–555, 558.

28. Brown, *Defense Annual Report FY 1980*, p. 35; Marshall, "Arms Competitions," p. 8, and Stephen M. Meyer, "Space and Soviet Military Planning," in *National Interests and the Military Use of Space*, ed. William J. Durch (Cambridge, Mass.: Ballinger, 1984), p. 81.

29. Major General Stepan A. Tyushkevich, *The Soviet Armed Forces: A History of Their Organizational Development*, originally published by the Soviet Ministry of Defense, 1978, translated by the CIS Multilingual Section Translation Bureau, Ottawa, Canada, and published under the auspices of the U.S. Air Force (Washington, D.C.: Government Printing Office, 1984), p. 379.

30. David Holloway, *The Soviet Union and the Arms Race* (New Haven and London: Yale University Press, 1983), p. 24.

31. Holloway notes that the Soviet claim was misleading because the bomb exploded by the USSR in August 1953 was a boosted fission weapon with a yield of 200 to 400 kilotons rather than a megaton-range "superbomb" consisting of a relatively small fission "trigger" and a large amount of fusion fuel. The Soviets did not test a true superbomb until November 1955. See Holloway, *Soviet Union and the Arms Race*, pp. 24–25.

32. Marshal of the Soviet Union Nikolai Vasil'yevich Ogarkov, *Vsegda v Gotovnosti k Zashchite Otechestva* (Always in readiness to defend the homeland) (Moscow: Voyenizdat, 1982), p. 13.

33. The Soviet Committee for European Security and Cooperation, Scientific Research Council on Peace and Disarmament, *How to Avert the Threat to Europe* (Moscow: Progress Publishers, 1983), p. 25.

34. For example, in his speech in honor of "the 40th anniversary of the Soviet people's victory in the great Patriotic War" (that is, World War II), on May 8, 1985, a suitable occasion for referring to the postwar accomplishments and current military strength of the USSR, Mikhail Gorbachev chose only civil accomplishments as proofs that "in the postwar period Soviet science and technological thought have achieved more than one impressive success in major areas of world science and technology. The Soviet Union built the first atomic power station and the first atomic-powered ice-breaker and launched the first satellite." See *Foreign Broadcast Information Service—Soviet Union* (hereafter, *FBIS-SU*), daily report, May 9, 1985, p. R10.

35. According to V. V. Kuznetsov, first deputy foreign minister, "the alternative to the conclusion of the ABM systems limitation treaty with the United States would in essence have been an unending race in the development by both sides of expensive ABM systems with a simultaneous increase in the intensiveness of the buildup of strategic offensive arms." Kuznetsov's statement at the meeting of the Presidium of the Supreme Soviet on September 29, 1972, reported in *Pravda*, September 30, 1972, available in *FBIS-SU*, daily report, October 3, 1972, p. H–2.

36. Barnett, "Trans-SALT," pp. 546–549. See also Thomas W. Wolfe, *The SALT Experience* (Cambridge, Mass.: Ballinger, 1979), p. 112.

37. Andrew Cockburn, *The Threat: Inside the Soviet Military Machine* (New York: Random House, 1983), pp. 12, 79.

38. Marco Carnovale, "Strategic Defences and the Warsaw Pact," *The International Spectator*, October/December 1986, p. 39. (Emphasis in original.)

39. Cockburn, *The Threat*, pp. 14, 239.

40. Matthew A. Evangelista, "Why the Soviets Buy the Weapons They Do," *World Politics*, 36 (July 1984), 601.

41. Stephen M. Meyer, "Soviet National Security Decisionmaking: What Do We Know and What Do We Understand?" in *Soviet Decisionmaking for National Security*, ed. Jiri Valenta and William Potter (London: George Allen and Unwin, 1984), p. 264.

42. Harriet Fast Scott and William F. Scott, *The Armed Forces of the USSR* (Boulder, Colo.: Westview Press, 1979), p. 147.

43. Sayre Stevens, "Ballistic Missile Defense in the Soviet Union," *Current History*, 84 (October 1985), pp. 313–314. Bruce Parrott notes, however, that the CIA has estimated that the budget of the Voyska PVO began to drop in absolute terms after 1977. Parrott, *The Soviet Union and Ballistic Missile Defense* (Boulder, Colo.: Westview Press, 1987), p. 35.

44. Andrew W. Marshall, *Bureaucratic Behavior and the Strategic Arms Competition*, (Santa Monica, Calif.: Southern California Arms Control and Foreign Policy Seminar, October 1971), p. 7. (Emphasis added.)

45. Raymond Garthoff, "The Soviet Military and SALT," in *Soviet Decisionmaking*, ed. Valenta and Potter, pp. 149, 151.

46. Abraham S. Becker, *Strategic Breakout as a Soviet Policy Option*, R-2097-ACDA (Santa Monica, Calif.: Rand Corporation, March 1977), p. 17.

47. Harriet Fast Scott and William F. Scott cited in Henry S. Bradsher, "Soviets Alter Air Defense Network to Counter U.S. Missiles, Bombers," *Washington Star*, July 16, 1981, p. 10. Prior to January 1981 the Troops of National Air Defense were referred to as the PVO Strany. After the transfer of the ground troops air defense units to the Troops of National Air Defense, this service of the Soviet armed forces became known as Voyska PVO instead of PVO Strany. For further background on this air defense reorganization, see Cynthia A. Roberts, "Soviet Military Policy in Transition," *Current History*, 83 (October 1984), 334.

48. U.S. Department of Defense, *Soviet Military Power 1987* (Washington, D.C.: Government Printing Office, 1987), p. 59.

49. Other long-standing attributes of Russian and Soviet political culture include xenophobia, conformity, insecurity, deference to established authority, fear of anarchy, aversion to public debate, and hierarchical rather than decentralized decision making. For a useful recent discussion, see John M. Joyce, "The Old Russian Legacy," *Foreign Policy*, 55 (Summer 1984), 132–153.

50. Evangelista, "Why the Soviets Buy," p. 613.

51. James B. Bruce and Robert W. Clawson, "A Zonal Analysis Model for Comparative Politics: A Partial Soviet Application," *World Politics*, 29 (January 1977), 182–183.

52. Scott and Scott, *Armed Forces of the USSR*, pp. 120–122, 124.

53. Stephen M. Meyer, "Soviet Nuclear Operations," in *Managing Nuclear Operations*, ed. Ashton B. Carter, John D. Steinbruner, and Charles A. Zraket (Washington, D.C.: Brookings Institution, 1987), pp. 492–493.

54. Becker, *Strategic Breakout*, p. 22.

55. Wolfe, *SALT Experience*, pp. 74, 76.

56. Scott and Scott, *Armed Forces of the USSR*, p. 120.

57. William E. Odom, "A Dissenting View on the Group Approach to Soviet Politics," *World Politics*, 28 (July 1976), 567.

58. Major General William E. Odom, "Trends in the Balance of Military Power between East and West," in *The Conduct of East-West Relations in the 1980s, Part III*, Adelphi Paper no. 191 (London: International Institute for Strategic Studies, 1984), p. 17.

59. Stephen M. Meyer, "Soviet Strategic Programmes and the US SDI," *Survival*, 27 (November/December 1985), 279.

60. John G. Hines and George F. Kraus, "Soviet Strategies for Military Competition," *Parameters*, 16 (Autumn 1986), 31.

61. Meyer, "Soviet National Security Decisionmaking," pp. 280–281.

62. Ibid., p. 266.

63. Ibid., p. 267.

64. Alton Frye has pointed out that the Soviets may not have believed the Nixon administration's assurances, because the chief of staff of the air force, General John Ryan, gave testimony to the Congress in favor of developing hard-target kill capabilities in October 1969, months after the adoption of the policy of restraint. Even though President Nixon disavowed Ryan's statements and denied funding to the development of hard-target kill MIRV capabilities, the Soviets may not have trusted the Americans to continue with the policy of restraint. Frye notes that the Soviet tests of MIRVs on four new ICBMs in 1973 raised the "prospect of an eventual Soviet advantage in counterforce-capable systems" and "provoked the United States" to reactions, including Secretary of Defense James Schlesinger's decision to call for the development of a MIRV system of improved accuracy and higher yield for the Minuteman III ICBM. See Frye, *A Responsible Congress*, pp. 69–71, 91–92.

65. Richard Perle has raised this possibility with respect to the Nixon administration's attempts to control MIRV technology: "We made the effort, and it

was unsuccessful. I would be delighted if the Soviets did not have MIRVs today, but I fail to see how a unilateral decision by the United States not to proceed with MIRV would have produced a similar decision on the part of the Soviet Union, and indeed all of our historic experience suggests that the Soviets will deploy any weapon of which they are capable independently of the attitude of the United States." Testimony in U.S. Senate, Committee on Foreign Relations, *Strategic Defense and Anti-Satellite Weapons,* hearing, April 25, 1984, 98th Cong., 2nd sess. (Washington, D.C.: U.S. Government Printing Office, 1984), p. 29.

66. Meyer, "Soviet National Security Decisionmaking," p. 268.

67. Wagner testimony (including charts) in U.S. House of Representatives, Committee on Armed Forces, *Hearings on H.R. 5263, Department of Energy National Security and Military Applications of Nuclear Energy Authorization Act of 1985,* before the Procurement and Military Nuclear Systems Subcommittee, 98th Cong., 2nd sess. (Washington, D.C.: U.S. Government Printing Office, 1984), pp. 32–33. For more recent charts comparing estimates of the total number and yield (and average yield) of U.S. and Soviet nuclear weapons, see *Discriminate Deterrence,* the Report of the Commission on Integrated Long-Term Strategy, co-chaired by Fred C. Iklé and Albert Wohlstetter (Washington, D.C.: Government Printing Office, January 1988), p. 39.

68. Marshall, "Arms Competitions," p. 3.

69. Lieutenant General William E. Odom applies this interpretation to the history of Soviet force-posture development since the 1920s in his article "Soviet Force Posture: Dilemmas and Directions," *Problems of Communism,* 34 (July/August 1985), 1–14.

70. Scott and Scott, *Armed Forces of the USSR,* p. 263.

71. This is obviously a very summary statement about a vast and complex subject. The best discussion of these basic concepts remains Peter H. Vigor, *The Soviet View of War, Peace and Neutrality* (London and Boston: Routledge and Kegan Paul, 1975). It should also be noted that the Soviets attach precise definitions to terms such as *military doctrine, military science, military art, operational art,* and so forth. These definitions are not widely used in the West, and the present work uses the terms *doctrine* and *strategy* in a more general sense. For background on the Soviet terminology, see Scott and Scott, *Armed Forces of the USSR,* pp. 69–94.

72. Two of the most useful works on this topic are Peter H. Vigor, "Doubts and Difficulties Confronting a Would-Be Soviet Attacker," *RUSI Journal,* 125 (June 1980), and Benjamin S. Lambeth, *Risk and Uncertainty in Soviet Deliberations about War,* R-2687-AF (Santa Monica, Calif.: Rand Corporation, October 1981).

73. Jack L. Snyder, *The Soviet Strategic Culture: Implications for Limited Nuclear Operations,* R-2154-AF (Santa Monica, Calif.: Rand Corporation, September 1977), p. 29. (Emphasis added.)

74. The best known proponent of this interpretation is Raymond Garthoff. See Garthoff, "BMD and East-West Relations," in *Ballistic Missile Defense,* ed.

Carter and Schwartz, pp. 286, 298n, 301–302, and Garthoff, "Mutual Deterrence, Parity, and Strategic Arms Limitation in Soviet Policy," in *Soviet Military Thinking*, ed. Derek Leebaert (London: Allen and Unwin, 1981), p. 104. See also the valuable critical analysis of Garthoff's interpretation in Benjamin S. Lambeth, *The State of Western Research on Soviet Military Strategy and Policy*, N-2230-AF (Santa Monica, Calif.: Rand Corporation, October 1984), pp. 23–25.

75. Lambeth, *State of Western Research*, p. 23.
76. Groupe X-Défense, *Les défenses anti-missiles, la France et l'Europe* (Paris: Fondation pour les Etudes de Défense Nationale, 1986), pp. 27, 156.
77. Sir Geoffrey Howe, "Defence and Security in the Nuclear Age," *RUSI Journal*, 130 (June 1985), 4.
78. Students of Soviet strategic decision making have called attention to the statement of the Soviet deputy foreign minister, V. V. Kuznetsov, to John McCloy soon after the resolution of the Cuban missile crisis: "Never will we be caught like this again." (See the description of this incident in John Newhouse, *Cold Dawn: The Story of SALT*, New York: Holt, Rinehart and Winston, 1973, p. 68.)
79. Statement by Politburo member M. A. Suslov, reported in *Pravda*, September 30, 1972, in *FBIS-SU*, daily report, October 3, 1972, p. H–4. See also the statements by Kuznetsov and Grishin during the same session.
80. Benson D. Adams, *Ballistic Missile Defense* (New York: American Elsevier, 1971), p. 156.
81. William G. Hyland, "The ABM Treaty and Options for Ballistic Missile Defense," in Leon Gouré, William G. Hyland, and Colin S. Gray, *The Emerging Strategic Environment: Implications for Ballistic Missile Defense* (Cambridge, Mass.: Institute for Foreign Policy Analysis, 1979), p. 38.
82. Wolfe, *SALT Experience*, pp. 110–113, 130–131. For similar judgments, see Fritz W. Ermarth, "Contrasts in American and Soviet Strategic Thought," *International Security*, 3 (Fall 1978), 146; Robert Legvold, "Strategic 'Doctrine' and SALT: Soviet and American Views," *Survival*, 21 (January/February 1979), 11; and Sayre Stevens, "Ballistic Missile Defense in the Soviet Union," p. 315.
83. Hyland, "ABM Treaty and Options," p. 37.
84. Stevens, "Ballistic Missile Defense in the Soviet Union," p. 315.
85. Hans Rühle, "Gorbachev's 'Star Wars,'" *NATO Review*, 33 (August 1985), 29.
86. Groupe X-Défense, *Les défenses anti-missiles*, pp. 27, 156.
87. Laird cited in Frye, *A Responsible Congress*, p. 76.
88. According to Raymond Garthoff, who was a member of the U.S. SALT I delegation, in 1971 President Nixon's letter to Senator Brooke "reaffirming that the United States did not intend to develop those counterforce accuracies was cited to the Soviet delegation." Garthoff, *Detente and Confrontation*, p. 418.
89. Gerard Smith, *Doubletalk: The Story of the First Strategic Arms Limitation Talks* (New York: Doubleday, 1980), pp. 173–175.

90. Frye, *A Responsible Congress,* pp. 65–66; see also pp. 64–65, 81.
91. Ibid., p. 65.
92. Ibid.
93. Meyer, "Soviet Nuclear Operations," p. 487.
94. George Schneiter, "The ABM Treaty Today," in *Ballistic Missile Defense,* ed. Carter and Schwartz, p. 247. See also Garthoff, "BMD and East-West Relations," p. 305.
95. Smith, *Doubletalk,* p. 132.
96. Ibid., pp. 309–310 and 302, 310.
97. Ibid., pp. 309–310.
98. Article III authorizes two BMD deployment areas (reduced to one by the 1974 protocol) and indicates that a deployment area may have two LPARs. Agreed Statement B specifies that the smaller of these two LPARs is limited to a power potential of 3 million. Article IV authorizes test ranges and exempts them from the radar limitations of article III. Article VI (b) authorizes LPARs for ballistic missile early warning, but stipulates that they must be located on the country's periphery and oriented outward. As Gerard Smith notes, "an agreement permitting only a small number of ABM launchers and interceptors would be less meaningful in the long term if a nation could build as many and as large radars as it wished." Smith, ibid., pp. 302–303.
99. Garthoff, "BMD and East-West Relations," pp. 294–295.
100. A translation of the complete text of Kosygin's remarks on BMD in *Pravda* (February 11, 1967) is available in U.S. Arms Control and Disarmament Agency, *Documents on Disarmament 1967* (Washington, D.C.: Government Printing Office, 1968), p. 60. Raymond Garthoff has consulted a recording and determined that Kosygin's remarks were in fact incorrectly translated into English, and that *Pravda* based its report in Russian on the mistranslation by a British interpreter. According to Garthoff, Kosygin really said that a defensive system was "not a *factor in*," rather than "not a *cause of*," the arms race, and did not refer to "saving lives" at all, simply declaring that the costs of offensive and defensive systems "are not related to each other." But the version of Kosygin's remarks reported at the time in *Pravda* and in the Western press was widely viewed as an oblique rejection of the U.S. initiative in favor of negotiations on ABM limitations, owing to the Soviet commitment to BMD. See Garthoff, "BMD and East-West Relations," pp. 295–296.
101. Garthoff, ibid., pp. 296–297.
102. Johnson's remarks on March 2, 1967, are available in *Documents on Disarmament 1967*, pp. 108–110.
103. Dean Rusk said that Kosygin's position at Glassboro was, in effect, "How can you expect me to tell the Russian people they can't defend themselves against your rockets?" Newhouse, *Cold Dawn,* p. 94.
104. Kosygin cited in Fred Kaplan, *The Wizards of Armageddon* (New York: Simon and Schuster, 1983), p. 346. Alton Frye speculates that "perhaps the Premier was feigning indifference in order to extract some diplomatic

advantage from what he may have considered a Soviet lead in ABM. Only later—one must acknowledge, after the United States began to deploy an ABM—did Soviet writers and officials come to stress the dangers of a contest in missile defenses." Frye, *A Responsible Congress*, p. 18.

105. Garthoff, "BMD and East-West Relations," pp. 297–301. With regard to West Germany and the NPT-SALT linkage, see also Kosygin's remarks in *Pravda*, February 11, 1967, in *Documents on Disarmament 1967*, p. 61, and Newhouse, *Cold Dawn*, p. 104.

106. Smith, *Doubletalk*, p. 95.

107. Frye, *A Responsible Congress*, p. 38.

108. Holloway suggests that the Soviets may have been influenced by their experience with ICBMs. The USSR had preceded the United States in developing and testing ICBMs, but the United States soon attained a quantitative and technological superiority that cost the USSR a great deal to overcome. Holloway, *Soviet Union and the Arms Race*, p. 46.

109. Gryzlov cited in indirect discourse in Garthoff, "BMD and East-West Relations," pp. 293–294n.

110. Smith, *Doubletalk*, p. 94.

111. Ibid., pp. 94–96.

112. The third-party proviso was included when the Soviets initially mentioned the possibility of a complete ABM ban. When the possibility of such a ban was raised by the United States at a later point, after the two sides had agreed to permit defenses of national capitals, the Soviets again indicated that they would be willing to consider it. The U.S. government then decided not to seek such a ban, however; and it cannot be known whether the Soviets would have repeated their previous conditions regarding third-country capabilities, though it appears probable that they would have done so. See Garthoff, "BMD and East-West Relations," pp. 302–305.

113. By 1970, the Soviet interest in achieving an ABM treaty was so pronounced that the USSR proposed that the search for a combined offensive-defensive set of arrangements be abandoned, so that a separate ABM treaty could be concluded first. See Smith, *Doubletalk*, p. 147.

114. Ibid., pp. 263–265, 343–344.

115. Michael J. Deane, "Soviet Military Doctrine and Defensive Deployment Concepts: Implications for Soviet Ballistic Missile Defense," in Jacquelyn K. Davis et al., *The Soviet Union and Ballistic Missile Defense* (Cambridge, Mass.: Institute for Foreign Policy Analysis, 1980), pp. 42, 50.

116. Sayre Stevens, "The Soviet BMD Program," in *Ballistic Missile Defense*, ed. Carter and Schwartz, pp. 198–199.

117. Garthoff, "BMD and East-West Relations," pp. 300, 313.

118. Sokolovskiy, *Soviet Military Strategy*, pp. 84, 409–411, 455–460.

119. U.S. Defense Intelligence Agency, *Soviet Military Space Doctrine*, DDB-1400-16-84 (Washington, D.C.: Defense Intelligence Agency, August 1, 1984), p. 11.

120. Ibid., p. 9.

121. Colonel Engineer L. Migunov, "Borba s Ballisticheskymi Raketami" (Com-

batting ballistic missiles), *Technika i Vooruzhenie* (Technology and armaments), no. 6 (June 1982), 6–8. Soviet secrecy and the technique of attributing military-technical ideas to foreigners make it difficult to prepare a history of BMD concepts that might reflect accurately parallel thinking and borrowings of ideas. In 1973, for example, Soviet experts attributed the concept of space-based kinetic kill vehicles for BMD to American specialists. While U.S. research on space-based BMD concepts such as BAMBI (Ballistic Missile Boost Intercept) has been public knowledge since at least the early 1960s, it is not clear when the Soviets first became interested in the idea or whether Soviet defense scientists reached it independently. Colonel General N. A. Lomov, ed., *Scientific-Technical Progress and the Revolution in Military Affairs*, originally published in Moscow by the Ministry of Defense in 1973, translated and published under the auspices of the U.S. Air Force (Washington, D. C.: U.S. Government Printing Office, 1974), p. 58.

122. Healey in Great Britain, Parliament, *Parliamentary Debates* (House of Commons), February 19, 1986, col. 337. Healey's speech on this occasion was not, incidentally, directed against President Reagan's vision of a defense so effective that it would make "nuclear weapons impotent and obsolete." Healey called this "a noble vision, which has been endorsed by the Campaign for Nuclear Disarmament." Speaking for the Labour Party, Healey regretted the Conservative government's support for the SDI research program and called attention to what he saw as a redirection of the SDI, a shift from the vision of abolishing nuclear deterrence toward the defense of U.S. land-based missiles. (Ibid., cols. 327-328).

123. Aleksey Sitnikov, "International Review—Space Ambitions," *Sovietskaya Rossiya*, July 23, 1982, p. 1, cited in William F. Scott, *Soviet Policies and Perceptions of the Military Use of Space* (Wright-Patterson Air Force Base, Ohio: Foreign Technology Division, July 1984), pp. 102–103.

124. Pierre Simonitsch, "USSR Has Antisatellite System," *Frankfurter Rundschau*, May 30, 1985, p. 1, in *FBIS-SU*, daily report, May 30, 1985, p. AA5. The inaccuracies in General Chervov's assertions are discussed in Chapter 5.

125. *"Star Wars" Delusions and Dangers* (Moscow: Military Publishing House, 1985), p. 39.

126. Garthoff, "BMD and East-West Relations," p. 239.

127. Dr. Sc. (Mil.) N. Talensky, "Anti-Missile Systems and Disarmament," *International Affairs* (Moscow), 10 (October 1964), 18. (Emphasis in original.)

128. Major General I. Anureyev, "Determining the Correlation of Forces in Terms of Nuclear Weapons," *Voyennaya mysl'* (Military thought), 6 (June 1967), trans. no. FDP 0112/68, August 11, 1968, in *Selected Readings from Military Thought, 1963–1973*, Studies in Communist Affairs, vol. 5, pt. 1 (Washington, D.C.: Government Printing Office, 1982), pp. 164–165, 171.

129. General Semen P. Ivanov, for example, wrote that "tremendous significance is attached to the development of the national air defense troops for the purpose of making them capable of repulsing enemy nuclear attacks carried out with the use of air-space means." Ivanov, "Soviet Military Doctrine and

Strategy," *Voyennaya mysl'* 5 (May 1969), trans. no. FPD 0117/69, December 18, 1969, in *Selected Readings from Military Thought, 1963–1973*, Studies in Communist Affairs, vol. 5, pt. 2 (Washington, D.C.: Government Printing Office, 1982), p. 29.

130. Warner, *Military in Contemporary Soviet Politics*, pp. 152, 208, and Thomas Wolfe, *Soviet Power and Europe, 1945–1970* (Baltimore and London: Johns Hopkins Press, 1970), pp. 439–441.

131. Malinovsky in *Pravda*, April 3, 1966, cited in Garthoff, "BMD and East-West Relations," p. 298.

132. Sokolovskiy, *Soviet Military Strategy*, pp. 199, 204.

133. Ibid., p. 246.

134. Wolfe, *SALT Experience*, p. 112.

135. G. V. Zimin, ed., *Razvitiye protivorozdushnoy obornoy* (Moscow: Voyenizdat, 1976), pp. 191, 192, 100 (emphasis added), cited in Deane, "Soviet Military Doctrine," pp. 39, 41. For additional sources on Soviet military doctrine on strategic defense in the post-1972 period, see Michael J. Deane, *The Role of Strategic Defense in Soviet Strategy* (Washington, D.C.: Advanced International Studies Institute, 1980), pp. 77-94.

136. Colonel V. M. Bondarenko, *Sovremennaia nauka i razvitie voennogo dela* (Modern science and the development of military affairs) (Moscow, 1976), p. 132 (emphasis added), cited in Rebecca V. Strode, "Space-Based Lasers for Ballistic Missile Defense: Soviet Policy Options," in *Laser Weapons in Space: Policy and Doctrine*, ed. Keith B. Payne (Boulder, Colo.: Westview Press, 1983), p. 145.

137. Parrott, *Soviet Union and Ballistic Missile Defense*, pp. 32–35.

138. Ibid., pp. 39–41, 107.

139. Lieutenant General M. M. Kir'yan, *Problemi Voyennoi Teorii v Sovietskich Nauchno-sprabochnikh Tzdaniyakh* (Problems of military theory in Soviet scientific reference publications) (Moscow: Nauka, 1985), p. 61. See also Kir'yan, *Voyenno-technichesky Progress i Vooruznennyye Sily SSSR* (Progress in military technology and the armed forces of the USSR) (Moscow: Voyenizdat, 1982), p. 315, and M. I. Cherenchenko, "Strategischeskaya Operatsiya" (Strategic operation), *Sovietskaya Voyennaya Entsiklopediya* (Soviet military encyclopaedia) (Moscow: Voyenizdat, 1979), VII, 550–551.

140. Colonel General M. A. Gareyev, *M. V. Frunze—Voyennyy Teoretik: Vzglady M. V. Frunze i Sovremennaya Voyennaya Teoriya* (M. V. Frunze—Military theoretician: the views of M. V. Frunze and modern military theory) (Moscow: Voyenizdat, 1985), p. 305.

141. A. Altunin, "The Goals Are Humane and the Tasks Important," *Agitator Armii i Flota*, 1980, no. 3, JPRS 75618, May 2, 1980, p. 3.

142. Radio Moscow in English, April 24, 1984, in *FBIS-SU*, daily report, April 24, 1984, p. V–1.

143. Tyushkevich, *Soviet Armed Forces*, p. 471.

144. Marshal of the Soviet Union V. Sokolovskiy and Major General M. Cherednichenko, "Military Strategy and Its Problems," *Voyennaya mysl'*, 10 (October 1968), trans. no. FPD 0084/69, September 4, 1969, in *Selected*

Readings from Military Thought, 1963-1973, Studies in Communist Affairs, vol. 5, pt. 2 (Washington, D.C.: Government Printing office, 1982), pp. 8–9.

145. Henry Kissinger, *Years of Upheaval* (London: Weidenfeld and Nicolson and Michael Joseph, 1982), p. 277.

146. General I. Y. Shavrov, *Lokalnie Voini* (Local wars) (Moscow: Voyenizdat, 1981), p. 229.

147. Gareyev, *M. V. Frunze,* p. 240.

148. Gareyev was chief of the Military Science Directorate of the General Staff prior to his appointment as deputy chief of the General Staff. According to Lieutenant General Odom, Gareyev's recent book (*M. V. Frunze*) "can be taken as representing the present official line of military doctrine." (Odom, "Soviet Force Posture," p. 9).

149. Gareyev, *M. V. Frunze,* pp. 240–241, 305.

150. It is worth noting that the Soviets do not equate their concepts of deterrence—influencing enemy decisions for purposes of war prevention and conflict limitation—with those in use in the West. The word *sderzhivanie* can be used to denote "containment" as well as "deterrence" or "keeping out" or "restraining," whereas the word *ustrashenie* has a more offensive connotation. As David Holloway notes, "of these two terms it is *sderzhivanie,* restraining or holding back, that is used to describe Soviet policy; when *ustrashenie,* intimidation, is used it is applied to Western policy." Holloway, *Soviet Union and the Arms Race,* p. 33.

151. As long ago as 1969, General Ivanov wrote that "theoretically it can be assumed that for the purpose of scaring one another the belligerents will limit themselves to inflicting some selected nuclear attacks on secondary objectives, but will not dare to expand the nuclear conflict any further." See Ivanov, "Soviet Military Doctrine," p. 29.

152. V. G. Reznichenko, chief editor, *General Tactics* (Moscow: 1966), p. ii, cited in John G. Hines, Phillip A. Petersen, and Notra Trulock III, "Soviet Military Theory from 1945-2000: Implications for NATO," *Washington Quarterly,* 9 (Fall 1986), 122.

153. Hines, Petersen, and Trulock, ibid., p. 122. This interpretation of Soviet military doctrine is indebted to this article and other works by these authors.

154. Ustinov in *Pravda,* July 12, 1982, in *Current Digest of the Soviet Press,* 34, no. 28 (1982), p. 6.

155. Ivanov, "Soviet Military Doctrine," p. 28.

156. Ibid., p. 28.

157. According to General Lieutenant I. G. Zav'yalov, the following disadvantages could result from using nuclear weapons: "Whole subdivisions, units, and even formations can lose their combat capacity within a few minutes. Large territories will become useless for immediate continuation of the operation. Combat actions along many axes will become isolated and local in nature, troop control will be interrupted, and because of the break in the originally outlined plans for combat actions, new decisions will have to be made within restricted time limits." Zav'yalov, "The New Weapon and Military Art," *Red Star,* October 30, 1970, in *Selected Soviet Military Writings,*

1970–1975, translated and published under the auspices of the U.S. Air Force (Washington, D.C.: Government Printing Office, 1977), p. 209.

158. Kir'yan, *Voyenno-technichesky Progress*, p. 326. As long ago as 1970, Zav-'yalov wrote that "the constant threat of the employment of nuclear weapons . . . gives rise to a most important task, namely to teach the troops how to operate both with and without the use of nuclear weapons and how to make a swift transition from one mode of operations to another—from combat with conventional weapons to combat with nuclear weapons." Zav'yalov, "New Weapon," p. 211.

159. See Phillip A. Petersen and John G. Hines, "The Conventional Offensive in Soviet Theater Strategy," *Orbis*, 27 (Fall 1983), 695–739.

160. Gareyev, *M. V. Frunze*, p. 245.

161. Akhromeyev, "Prevoskhodstvo Sovietskoi Voennoi Nauki i Sovietskogo Voyennogo Iskusstva—Odin iz Vazhneishikh Faktorov Pobedi v Belikoi Otechestvennoi Voine" (Superiority of Soviet military science and Soviet military art—one of the most important factors of victory in the great patriotic war), *Kommunist*, February 1985, p. 62.

162. Marshal Nikolai Ogarkov, then chief of the General Staff, interview in *Red Star*, May 9, 1984, in *FBIS-SU*, May 9, 1984, p. R19.

163. Colonel M. Shirokov, "Military Geography at the Present Stage," *Voyennaya mysl'*, 11 (November 1966), trans. no. FPD 0730/67, July 27, 1967, in *Selected Readings from Military Thought, 1963-1973*, Studies in Communist Affairs, vol. 5, pt.1 (Washington, D.C.: Government Printing Office, 1982), pp. 135–136.

164. As Colonel M. P. Skirdo has noted, "It is primarily the political, not the military leaders who determine the necessity of employing weapons of mass destruction, who specify the principal targets and when they are to be hit." Skirdo, *The People, the Army, the Commander*, originally published by the Soviet Ministry of Defense, 1970, translated by the DGIS Multilingual Section, Translation Bureau, Secretary of State Department, Ottawa, Canada, and published under the auspices of the U.S. Air Force (Washington, D.C.: Government Printing Office, 1978), p. 97.

165. For details, see Notra Trulock III, "Soviet Perspectives on Limited Nuclear Warfare," in *Swords and Shields: NATO, the USSR, and New Choices for Long-Range Offense and Defense*, ed. Fred S. Hoffman, Albert Wohlstetter, and David S. Yost (Lexington, Mass.: Lexington Books, 1987), pp. 53–85.

166. Harold Brown, *Department of Defense Annual Report for Fiscal Year 1980* (Washington, D.C.: Government Printing Office, 1979), p. 80.

167. Manfred Wörner, "A Missile Defense for NATO Europe," *Strategic Review*, 14 (Winter 1986), 13–14.

168. *Report of the President's Commission on Strategic Forces*, April 1983, p. 4.

169. This reassessment was reported in 1985 and officially confirmed in the following statement: "The SS-19 Mod 3 ICBM, while less accurate than the SS-18, has significant capability against all but hardened silos." Department of Defense, *Soviet Military Power 1987* (Washington, D.C.: Government Printing Office, 1987), p. 29. For background, see John Prados, *The Soviet*

Estimate: U.S. Intelligence Analysis and Soviet Strategic Forces (Princeton, N.J.: Princeton University Press, 1986), pp. 304–305.

170. Important performance parameters besides warhead yield and accuracy affect counterforce potential. For single-shot-kill probability alone, aside from dynamic scenarios involving numerous warheads (with the risk of fratricide and other complex interactive effects), interrelated parameters such as height of burst, weapon radius, target hardness, and overpressure pulse duration are also involved. There are additional uncertainties about the reliability of guidance mechanisms (for example, neither the United States nor the USSR has tested missiles over polar flight paths). Some practical uncertainties may be less burdensome for the USSR than for the United States, because the Soviets (unlike the Americans) have repeatedly tested missile launches from operational silos. Attack outcome estimates should nonetheless be examined with caution. For a useful source on problems in ICBM vulnerability assessments, see Bruce W. Bennett, *Uncertainty in ICBM Survivability*, P-6394 (Santa Monica, Calif.: Rand Corporation, 1979).

171. National Foreign Assessment Center, *A Dollar Cost Comparison of Soviet and US Defense Activities, 1968-1978*, SR 79-10004 (Washington, D.C.: Central Intelligence Agency, January 1979), p. 5.

172. Statement by Richard N. Perle, assistant secretary of defense for international security policy, before the Senate Foreign Relations Committee, February 25, 1985, mimeo, pp. 4–5.

173. *The Military Balance, 1986–1987*, p. 222.

174. Paul Nitze, *SDI and the ABM Treaty*, Current Policy no. 711 (Washington, D.C.: Bureau of Public Affairs, U.S. Department of State, May 30, 1985), p. 2.

175. Gates and Gershwin, *Soviet Strategic Force Developments*, pp. 1–4. This testimony indicates that the single-warhead SS-25 currently being deployed may be followed by a new version with a MIRVed payload option.

176. See the discussion of the SS-X-20 in Donald H. Rumsfeld, *Department of Defense Annual Report for Fiscal Year 1977* (Washington, D.C.: Government Printing Office, 1976), p. 53.

177. *The Military Balance, 1986–1987*, pp. 204, 207.

178. These details are drawn from Kerry L. Hines, "Soviet Short-Range Ballistic Missiles: Now a Conventional Deep-Strike Mission," *International Defense Review*, 18 (December 1985), 1909–14, and *Strategic Survey 1985-1986* (London: International Institute for Strategic Studies, 1986), pp. 44–45.

179. Hines, "Soviet Short-Range Ballistic Missiles," pp. 1910, 1914.

180. Colonel General Vladimir Mikhalkin, "The Homeland's Fire Shield," *Soviet Military Review*, no. 11 (November 1984), 19, cited in Hines, "Soviet Short-Range Ballistic Missiles," p. 1910.

181. A. Starostin, "Takticheskiye Rakety" (Tactical rockets), *Technika i Vooruzhenie* (Technology and armaments), November 1981, pp. 8–9, cited in Hines, "Soviet Short-Range Ballistic Missiles," p. 1910.

182. *The Military Balance, 1986-1987*, p. 200. Accuracy is usually expressed in

terms of "circular error probable" (CEP), defined as the radius of a circle around the target point, within which half the missiles may be statistically expected to fall.

183. DeLauer cited in Walter Andrews, "Allies' Weapons Said to Be Inadequate to Threat of New Soviet Missile Power," *Washington Times*, November 1, 1984, p. 3.

184. *Strategic Survey 1985–1986*, p. 45.

185. François Heisbourg, "Conventional Defense: Europe's Constraints and Opportunities," in *The Conventional Defense of Europe: New Technologies and New Strategies*, ed. Andrew J. Pierre (New York: Council on Foreign Relations, 1986), p. 90.

186. For details, see Hines, "Soviet Short-Range Ballistic Missiles."

187. Gareyev, *M. V. Frunze*, p. 240.

188. *Strategic Survey 1985–1986*, p. 44.

189. Hines, "Soviet Short-Range Ballistic Missiles," p. 1913. According to Hines, the estimated annual production rate is 300 to 350 SRBMs.

190. Thomas Enders, *Missile Defense as Part of an Extended NATO Air Defense* (Sankt Augustin bei Bonn, West Germany: Social Science Research Institute of the Konrad Adenauer Foundation, May 1986), p. 30.

191. *The Military Balance, 1986–1987*, p. 206.

192. James H. Hansen, "Countering NATO's New Weapons: Soviet Concepts for War in Europe," *International Defense Review*, 17 (November 1984), 1619.

193. *White Paper 1985: The Situation and Development of the Federal Armed Forces* (Bonn: Federal Minister of Defense, 1985), p. 58.

194. Gates and Gershwin, *Soviet Strategic Force Developments*, p. 4.

195. Defense, *Soviet Military Power 1987*, pp. 45–46. For background, see Carl H. Builder, *The Prospects and Implications of Non-nuclear Means of Strategic Conflict*, Adelphi Paper no. 200 (London: International Institute for Strategic Studies, 1985).

196. Major General Jörg Bahnemann, "Air Defense in Central Europe," *NATO'S Sixteen Nations*, 30 (December 1985), 42.

197. See *The Military Balance 1987–1988* (London: International Institute for Strategic Studies, 1987), p. 31. Role categorizations are problematic because many aircraft may be applied to multiple purposes, and assumptions may vary regarding intentions, readiness and mobilization capability, possible use of training aircraft, and so on. See also Reimar Scherz, *Land- und Luftstreitkräfte in Europa. Ein militärischer Kräftevergleich*, SWP-S 318 (Ebenhausen, West Germany: Stiftung Wissenschaft und Politik, August 1985), p. 58.

198. Scherz, *Land- und Luftstreitkräfte*, p. 71.

199. Enders, *Missile Defense*, p. 33.

200. Groupe X-Défense, *Les défenses anti-missiles*, p. 155.

201. Hines, "Soviet Short-Range Ballistic Missiles," p. 1914.

202. Department of Defense and Department of State, *Soviet Strategic Defense Programs* (Washington, D.C.: Government Printing Office, October 1985), p. 21.

203. Gates and Gershwin, *Soviet Strategic Force Developments*, pp. 2, 11.

204. See the statements by Donald Latham, assistant secretary of defense for command, control, communications and intelligence, in "Military Satellite Jamming Threat Cited," *Aviation Week and Space Technology*, September 15, 1986, p. 26.

205. Richard L. Wagner, Jr. in March 1986 testimony, reported in Walter Pincus, "New Weapon Sought against Mobile ICBMs," *Washington Post*, July 14, 1986, p. A15.

206. *The Military Balance, 1986–1987*, p. 205.

207. John Collins, *U.S.-Soviet Military Balance, 1980–1985* (Washington, D.C.: Pergamon-Brassey's, 1985), p. 54.

208. Meyer, "Soviet Nuclear Operations," pp. 507–8.

209. For details, see Department of Defense, *Soviet Military Power 1985* (Washington, D.C.: Government Printing Office, 1985), pp. 51–53.

210. Two of the most useful studies on Soviet civil defense are Central Intelligence Agency, *Soviet Civil Defense*, Special Report no. 47 (Washington, D.C.: Bureau of Public Affairs, Department of State, September 1978), and Harriet Fast Scott and William F. Scott, *The Soviet Control Structure: Capabilities for Wartime Survival* (New York: Crane, Russak, 1983).

211. Letter from the Joint Chiefs of Staff to Senator Proxmire, February 3, 1977, in *Survival*, 19 (March/April 1977), 77.

212. For the Soviet sources and an analysis, see Leon Gouré, *Shelters in Soviet War Survival Strategy* (Washington, D.C.: Advanced International Studies Institute, 1978), pp. 5–10. According to Gouré, Soviet references to these shelters "ceased abruptly after 1966" (p. 9). This date roughly coincides with the cessation of Soviet discussions of their activities in ballistic missile defense and antisatellite warfare.

213. Richard D. Delauer, "Emerging Technologies and Their Impact on the Conventional Deterrent," in *The Conventional Defense of Europe: New Technologies and New Strategies*, ed. Andrew J. Pierre (New York: Council on Foreign Relations, 1986), p. 56.

214. Meyer, "Soviet Nuclear Operations," p. 507n.

215. Desmond Ball, *Can Nuclear War Be Controlled?* Adelphi Paper no. 161 (London: International Institute for Strategic Studies, 1981), p. 45.

216. Harold Brown, *Department of Defense Annual Report for Fiscal Year 1981* (Washington, D.C.: Government Printing Office, 1980), p. 78.

217. U.S. Congress, *Fiscal Year 1980 Arms Control Impact Statements*, joint committee print, 96th Cong., 1st sess. (Washington, D.C.: Government Printing Office, 1979), p. 87.

218. Amrom H. Katz, *Verification and SALT: The State of the Art and the Art of the State* (Washington, D.C.: Heritage Foundation, 1979), p. 42.

219. Albert Wohlstetter, "Between an Unfree World and None: Increasing Our Choices," *Foreign Affairs*, 63 (Summer 1985), 988. One of the implications of Wohlstetter's point is that, if imprecisely located targets in the Soviet Union—such as mobile ICBMs and deep underground shelters—could only

be attacked with barrages of high-yield weapons, the United States might be deterred from undertaking such attacks.

220. At least one Soviet leader acknowledged such uncertainties: "I know all about bomb shelters and command posts and emergency communications and so on. But listen here: in a single thermonuclear flash, a bunker can be turned into a burial vault for a country's leaders and military commanders." Khrushchev, *Khrushchev Remembers*, p. 542.

221. Defense and State, *Soviet Strategic Defense Programs*, p. 21.

222. Gates and Gershwin, *Soviet Strategic Force Developments*, p. 6. Although the Department of Defense refers to "more than 1,500 hardened alternate facilities" (*Soviet Military Power 1987*, p. 52), the CIA in this statement estimates that "there are at least 800, perhaps as many as 1,500, relocation facilities." The overall CIA assessment on survival prospects is, at any rate, similar to that made in 1977 by Admiral Stansfield Turner, then director of the CIA: "We believe that with reasonable warning a large percentage of the key military and civilian leadership probably would survive a retaliatory attack." Turner testimony in U.S. Congress, Joint Economic Committee, *Allocation of Resources in the Soviet Union and China—1977* (Washington, D.C.: Government Printing Office, 1977), pt. 3, p. 41.

223. Gates and Gershwin, *Soviet Strategic Force Developments*, p. 7.

224. Ball, *Can Nuclear War Be Controlled?*, p. 45.

225. For background, see John D. Morrocco, "Defense Department Plans to Study Earth-Penetrating Nuclear Weapons," *Aviation Week and Space Technology*, June 8, 1987, p. 28; Charles W. Corddry, " 'Earth Penetrator' Missile Proposed for Deep Strikes," *Baltimore Sun*, June 11, 1987, p. 3.

226. Groupe X-Défense, *Les défenses anti-missiles*, p. 30.

227. Theodore Jarvis, "Nuclear Operations and Strategic Defense," in *Managing Nuclear Operations*, ed. Carter, Steinbruner, and Zraket, p. 662.

228. *The FY 1987 Department of Defense Program for Research, Development and Acquisition*, statement by the under secretary of defense, research and engineering to the 99th Cong., 2nd sess., 1986 (Washington, D.C.: Government Printing Office, 1986), p. III–12.

229. Groupe X-Défense, *Les défenses anti-missiles*, p. 30.

230. Gardner testimony in U.S. House of Representatives, Committee on Armed Services, *Defense Department Authorization and Oversight*, hearings, 98th Cong., 1st sess. (Washington, D.C.: U.S. Government Printing Office, 1983), pt. 5, p. 270.

231. Stevens, "The Soviet BMD Program," p. 219.

232. Kevin N. Lewis, "BMD and US Limited Strategic Employment Policy," *Journal of Strategic Studies*, 8 (June 1985), 138.

233. During the SALT I negotiations, however, "at no point . . . did the Soviets show much interest in protecting their own missile fields." Hyland, "ABM Treaty and Options," p. 36.

234. Andrew Marshall, "Sources of Soviet Power: The Military Potential in the 1980s," *Prospects of Soviet Power in the 1980s, Part II*, Adelphi Paper no. 152 (London: International Institute for Strategic Studies, 1979), p. 13.

235. Whether defenses of ICBMs could also protect other valued assets depends on a large number of factors—what the BMD systems were originally designed to be able to defend, their siting, the coverage of their target acquisition and battle management "footprint," the hardness and other characteristics of the additional valued assets, and so forth.
236. Stevens, "The Soviet BMD Program," p. 210.

3. Implications for the Western Alliance

1. Scowcroft speech to the Atlantic Treaty Association, cited in *Daily Telegraph*, October 10, 1979.
2. A great deal of Soviet military literature combines Clausewitzian pragmatism and traditional principles of war with Marxist-Leninist interpretations of historical causation, as in the following example: "Military-technical superiority originates in economics, in the economic system, which develops according to its own specific laws . . . The military-technical superiority over the U.S. achieved by the Soviet Union is an impressive factor in containing imperialist aggression and an important condition for the achievement of victory in war, if the imperialists should start one . . . The favorable prerequisites being created by the socialist system do not in themselves automatically solve the problems of maintaining military-technical superiority . . . After science and industry have produced combat equipment excelling in quantity and quality over that of the enemy, and this has become part of the armament of our forces, the decisive role in establishing and maintaining military-technical superiority throughout the war and making it a real factor in the achievement of victory belongs to the military organization of the state, to military science, to combat training, and to the readiness, morale, and military spirit of the armed forces." Captain 1st Rank V. M. Kulakov, "Problems of Military-Technical Superiority," *Voyennaya mysl'*, (Military thought), 1 (January 1964), FPD 939, August 4, 1964, in *Selected Readings from Military Thought, 1963-1973*, Studies in Communist Affairs, vol. 5, pt. 1 (Washington, D.C.: Government Printing Office, 1982), p. 24.
3. Herbert Goldhamer, *The Soviet Union in a Period of Strategic Parity*, R-889-PR (Santa Monica, Calif.: Rand Corporation, November 1971), p. 4.
4. Ibid., pp. 6, 5.
5. Ibid., p. 5.
6. Conversely, the U.S. approach to military power may seem incredible to the Soviets, who may well attribute to the United States a "general contingency aim" and greater coherence and purposefulness in its strategic planning than actually exists.
7. Goldhamer, *Soviet Union in a Period of Strategic Parity*, p. 6.
8. *Aviation Week and Space Technology*, February 27, 1984, p. 18. See also the map of Soviet air defense concentrations in U.S. Department of Defense, *Soviet Military Power 1985* (Washington, D.C.: Government Printing Office, 1985), p. 51.

9. Marshal V. D. Sokolovskiy, *Soviet Military Strategy*, 3rd ed., trans. and ed. Harriet Fast Scott (New York: Crane, Russak, 1975), p. 21. In this translation, *politics* selects the most propitious moment. As Peter Vigor's discussion suggests, however, the *policy* of the political leadership might more fully convey the meaning of the Russian text. It should nonetheless be understood that Soviet ideology holds that the USSR is incapable of undertaking aggression or any sort of unjust war. For background, see Peter H. Vigor, *The Soviet View of War, Peace and Neutrality* (London and Boston: Routledge and Kegan Paul, 1975), pp. 58–89, esp. p. 87.

10. Vigor, ibid., p. 197.

11. Ibid., pp. 197–212.

12. Peter H. Vigor, "Lessons for NATO from the Soviet Invasion of Afghanistan," in *NATO's Strategic Options: Arms Control and Defense*, ed. David S. Yost (New York: Pergamon Press, 1981), p. 15.

13. Some Western observers judge that the Soviet Union's intercontinental nuclear forces may be asymmetrically vulnerable in the long term because a high proportion of Soviet warhead totals are currently based in fixed ICBMs, whereas the United States maintains a larger number of its warheads at sea on SLBMs. According to this reasoning, if the United States were capable of destroying the Soviet ICBM force, the United States would have an advantage in "surviving warheads." Moreover, the Soviet ICBM force would constitute an asymmetrically lucrative target, because of the high yields and large numbers of warheads on Soviet missiles. This speculation is likely to remain of purely academic interest. As Michael Nacht notes, "theoretically this asymmetry is a disadvantage for the Soviet Union, although operationally it would be of questionable significance if the Soviets perfected a substantial capability to destroy U.S. missile silos and the United States failed to develop a similar capability." Nacht, *The Age of Vulnerability: Threats to the Nuclear Stalemate* (Washington, D.C.: Brookings Institution, 1985), pp. 140–141. The United States in fact lacks the ICBM forces necessary to hold the entire Soviet ICBM force at risk and has no programs or plans that would provide such a capability. The Soviet ICBM force is becoming harder to attack, in any case, as more mobile ICBMs are deployed.

14. Major General Stepan Tyushkevich, "The Methodology for the Correlation of Forces in War," *Voyennaya Mysl'*, 6, (June 1969), trans. no. FDP 0008170, January 30, 1970, in *Selected Readings from Military Thought, 1963–1973*, Studies in Communist Affairs, vol. 5, pt. 2 (Washington, D.C.: Government Printing Office, 1982), p. 64.

15. Ibid., pp. 63–64.

16. Colonel A. A. Shirman, "Social Activity of the Masses and the Defense of Socialism," in *The Philosophical Heritage of V. I. Lenin and Problems of Contemporary War*, ed. General Major A. S. Milovidov and Colonel V. G. Kozlov, trans. U.S. Air Force, Soviet Military Thought, vol. 5 (Washington, D.C.: Government Printing Office, 1975), p. 127.

17. Stephen M. Meyer, "Soviet Strategic Programmes and the US SDI,"

Survival, 27 (November/December 1985), p. 278. (Emphasis in original.)

18. Harold Brown, *Department of Defense Annual Report for Fiscal Year 1980* (Washington, D.C.: Government Printing Office, 1979), p. 81.

19. Some of the likely differences between U.S. and Soviet assessments are discussed in Andrew W. Marshall, "A Program to Improve Analytic Methods Related to Strategic Forces," *Policy Sciences*, 15 (Fall 1982), 47–50.

20. David Holloway, *The Soviet Union and the Arms Race* (New Haven: Yale University Press, 1983), p. 50.

21. Lieutenant General William E. Odom, "The Implications of Active Defense of NATO for Soviet Military Strategy," in *Swords and Shields: NATO, the USSR, and New Choices for Long-Range Offense and Defense*, ed. Fred S. Hoffman, Albert Wohlstetter, and David S. Yost, (Lexington, Mass.: D. C. Heath/Lexington Books, 1987), pp. 169–173.

22. Notra Trulock III, "Soviet Perspectives on Limited Nuclear Warfare," in *Swords and Shields*, ed. Hoffman, Wohlstetter, and Yost, p. 77.

23. U.S. Congress, Office of Technology Assessment, *Ballistic Missile Defense Technologies*, OTA-ISC-254 (Washington, D.C.: Government Printing Office, September 1985), p. 72.

24. Albert Wohlstetter and Richard Brody, "Continuing Control as a Requirement for Deterring," in *Managing Nuclear Operations*, ed. Ashton B. Carter, John D. Steinbruner, and Charles A. Zraket (Washington, D.C.: Brookings Institution, 1987), pp. 162–163.

25. Office of Technology Assessment, *Ballistic Missile Defense Technologies*, p. 72.

26. Holloway, *Soviet Union and the Arms Race*, p. 179.

27. The best-known early expression of this view in the USSR was Malenkov's statement in 1954 that a nuclear war would mean the "destruction of world civilization." Malenkov's viewpoint became an element in the leadership contest, however. After Malenkov's removal, the Soviets usually stressed their conviction that "socialism" would triumph and "imperialism" would perish in the event of a nuclear war. After Khrushchev's removal, Soviet sources devoted more attention to the consequences of nuclear war for the USSR. For background, see Holloway, *Soviet Union and the Arms Race*, pp. 31–32, and Trulock, "Soviet Perspectives."

28. Sokolovskiy, *Soviet Military Strategy*, p. 197.

29. See, for example, the statement in *Military Thought* by General Ivanov in 1969 about the "risk of the destruction of one's own country and the responsibility to humanity for the fatal consequences of the nuclear war," cited in Chapter 2.

30. Only a few Western experts on Soviet military affairs have examined the Voroshilov General Staff Academy materials. For the sources of these statements, see Trulock, "Soviet Perspectives," pp. 65–66.

31. For an analysis relating "nuclear winter" studies to Soviet military planning, see Albert Wohlstetter, "Between an Unfree World and None: Increasing Our Choices," *Foreign Affairs*, 63 (Summer 1985), 962–994.

32. Soviet writers have indicated that, in their judgment, such restrictive effects can be discerned with respect to the United States; it has been noted that the

United States has been less inclined to alert its strategic nuclear forces during crises since the USSR gained parity. See Holloway, *Soviet Union and the Arms Race*, p. 50.

33. See Wohlstetter, "Between an Unfree World and None," p. 985, and Odom, "Implications of Active Defense of NATO," p. 172.

34. Ogarkov has, for example, noted that improvements in accuracy, range, target acquisition, command-and-control mechanisms, and so forth, "make many types of weapons global and make it possible to sharply increase (by at least an order of magnitude) the destructive potential of conventional weapons, bringing them closer, so to speak, to weapons of mass destruction in terms of effectiveness. The sharply increased range of conventional weapons makes it possible to immediately extend active combat operations not just to the border regions, but to the whole country's territory, which was not possible in past wars." Interview with Marshal N. V. Ogarkov, then chief of the General Staff, in *Red Star*, May 9, 1984, in *Foreign Broadcast Information Service—Soviet Union*, (hereafter, *FBIS-SU*), daily report, May 9, 1984, p. R19.

35. Stephen M. Meyer, "Soviet Nuclear Operations," in *Managing Nuclear Operations*, ed. Carter, Steinbruner, and Zraket, p. 511n.

36. Ibid., pp. 511–512.

37. Ibid., pp. 526–531.

38. As Malcolm Mackintosh has noted, "the Russians feel themselves to be not only the most numerous but also the greatest of all European peoples. They believe, on these grounds and on ideological grounds, that the Soviet Union has the right to greater influence in all European affairs than she has now." Mackintosh, "Moscow's View of the Balance of Power," *The World Today*, 29 (March 1973), 111.

39. The U.S. diplomat Charles E. Bohlen reported that Stalin envisaged a Europe consisting of weak and divided states: "The result would be that the Soviet Union would be the only important military and political force on the continent of Europe. The rest of Europe would be reduced to military and political impotence." *Foreign Relations of the United States: The Conferences at Cairo and Tehran* (Washington, D.C.: U.S. Government Printing Office, 1961), p. 845, cited in Jean Laloy, "Western Europe in the Soviet Perspective," in *Prospects of Soviet Power in the 1980s*, ed. Christoph Bertram (London: Macmillan, 1980), pp. 41–42. For a detailed analysis, see Vojtech Mastny, *Russia's Road to the Cold War: Diplomacy, Warfare, and the Politics of Communism, 1941–1945* (New York: Columbia University Press, 1979).

40. See the documentation and analysis in Vigor, *The Soviet View of War, Peace and Neutrality*, pp. 205–206.

41. Gromyko in *Pravda*, April 3, 1966, cited in Hannes Adomeit, "Soviet Policy toward the West: Costs and Benefits of Using 'Imperialist Contradictions,' " in *The Soviet Problem in American-German Relations*, ed. Uwe Nerlich and James A. Thomson (New York: Crane, Russak, 1985), p. 203.

42. For similar assessments of Soviet aims in Europe, see Adomeit, ibid., pp. 197–198; Angela E. Stent, "Accommodation: The U.S.S.R. and Western

Europe," *Washington Quarterly*, 5 (Autumn 1982), 93–95; and John Van Oudenaren, *Soviet Policy toward Western Europe: Objectives, Instruments, Results*, R-3310-AF (Santa Monica, Calif.: Rand Corporation, February 1986), pp. 4–22.

43. John Van Oudenaren, "Political Change and Detente in Europe: Soviet Policy, 1969–1976," Ph.D. diss., Massachusetts Institute of Technology, 1983, pp. 65–70.

44. Zagladin in *Frankfurter Rundschau*, June 1, 1981, cited in John Van Oudenaren, *Interviews by Soviet Officials in the Western Media: Two Case Studies*, R-3328-FF/RC (Santa Monica, Calif.: Rand Corporation, October 1985), p. 47.

45. N. Polyanov, "Europe at the Turn of the Decade," *International Affairs* (Moscow), April 1980, pp. 89, 91, 96.

46. Hannes Adomeit, "Capitalist Contradictions and Soviet Policy," *Problems of Communism*, 33 (May/June 1984), 8.

47. *Izvestia*, August 14, 1959, p. 6, cited in Robert K. German, "Nuclear-Free Zones: Norwegian Interest, Soviet Encouragement," *Orbis*, 26 (Summer 1982), 452.

48. *Pravda*, February 24, 1981, cited in Van Oudenaren, "Political Change and Detente in Europe," p. 180.

49. Robert Osgood and Henning Wegener, *Deterrence: The Western Approach* (Brussels: NATO Information Service, 1987), p. 8.

50. For a valuable discussion, see John G. Hines and George F. Kraus, "Soviet Strategies for Military Competition," *Parameters*, 16 (Autumn 1986), 26–31.

51. Fritz Ermarth, "Contrasts in American and Soviet Strategic Thought," *International Security*, 3 (Fall 1978), 147. Paul K. Davis and Peter J. E. Stan have offered a similar judgment: "U.S. nuclear-war scenarios in Europe are usually a mere trigger for the intercontinental 'exchange,' with little detail about events in the theater, especially after general war begins." Davis and Stan, *Concepts and Models of Escalation*, R-3235 (Santa Monica, Calif.: Rand Corporation, May 1984), p. 35.

52. With respect to the Soviet interest in coalition warfare (including means of disrupting opposing coalitions), see Vigor, *The Soviet View of War, Peace and Neutrality*, pp. 141–142, and John J. Yurechko, "Coalitional Warfare: The Soviet Approach," *Aussenpolitik*, 38, no. 1 (1987), 23–39.

53. Christopher N. Donnelly, "Soviet Operational Concepts in the 1980s," in *Strengthening Conventional Deterrence in Europe: Proposals for the 1980s*, Report of the European Security Study (London: Macmillan, 1983), p. 116.

54. John G. Hines and Phillip A. Petersen, "Changing the Soviet System of Control: Focus on Theatre Warfare," *International Defense Review*, 19 (March 1986), 281–289. Major General N. N. Kuznetsov has recently written in some detail on flexibility in the choice of limited strategic objectives in specific theaters of strategic military action. See Kuznetsov, "On the Categories and Principles of Soviet Military Science," *Voyenna mysl'*, no. 1, January 1984, as translated in the Vietnamese journal *Quan Doi Nhan Dan*, no. 6, June 1984, cited in Phillip A. Petersen and Notra Trulock III, "The

Changing Strategic Context: The Soviet View," paper presented at a conference sponsored by the London School of Economics and the Center for Strategic Concepts, September 24–25, 1987.

55. Peter Stratmann, "NATO Doctrine and National Operational Priorities: The Central Front and the Flanks: Part II," in *Power and Policy: Doctrine, the Alliance and Arms Control, Part III,* Adelphi Paper no. 207 (London: International Institute for Strategic Studies, 1986), p. 37.

56. Published reports suggest that the upgraded Patriot will be inferior to the SA-X-12B/Giant in acceleration, range, and other performance parameters. The upgraded Patriot may be capable of intercepting the slowest of the modern Soviet shorter-range ballistic missiles, the SS-21 and SS-23, but its capability against the SS-22 or SS-20 is regarded as doubtful. The SA-X-12B/Giant has, in contrast, been attributed capability against some types of U.S. strategic missiles. According to the International Institute for Strategic Studies, "the upgraded Patriot will only be successful against conventionally-armed short-range missiles, since it will lack the acceleration to intercept a nuclear or chemical warhead high enough to ensure destruction without collateral damage. Moreover, it will only protect itself or a narrow area around it." *Strategic Survey, 1985–1986* (London: International Institute for Strategic Studies, 1986), p. 47. Sir Ronald Mason, a former British official, has testified that "the anti-tactical ballistic missile capability of improved Patriot is negligible." Mason testimony in Great Britain, House of Commons, *Second Report from the Defence Committee, The Implications for the United Kingdom of Ballistic Missile Defence* (London: Her Majesty's Stationery Office, 1987), p. 71.

57. *White Paper 1975/1976: The Security of the Federal Republic of Germany and the Development of the Federal Armed Forces* (Bonn: Federal Minister of Defense, 1976), pp. 20–21.

58. J. Michael Legge, *Theater Nuclear Weapons and the NATO Strategy of Flexible Response,* R-2964 (Santa Monica, Calif.: Rand Corporation, April 1983), p. 27. This study was an expression of personal views and not an official statement.

59. U.S. Department of Defense, *Soviet Military Power 1987* (Washington, D.C.: Government Printing Office, 1987), pp. 60–61. The Pershing II ballistic missiles are to be eliminated as a consequence of the December 1987 INF treaty.

60. Kevin Lewis, "BMD and US Limited Strategic Employment Policy," *Journal of Strategic Studies,* 8 (June 1985), 140. (Emphasis added.)

61. Paul C. Warnke, "Arms Control: SALT II—The Home Stretch," *Department of State Bulletin,* 78 (October 1978), 21.

62. Nathan Leites provides a valuable discussion of the shortcomings of such counterpopulation threats in *Once More about What We Should Not Do Even in the Worst Case: The Assured Destruction Attack* (Santa Monica, Calif.: California Arms Control and Foreign Policy Seminar, June 1974). See also Nathan Leites, "Weaken...g the Belief in General War: Schelling on Strikes," *World Politics,* 19 (July 1967), 710–719.

63. Caspar Weinberger, *Department of Defense Annual Report for Fiscal Year 1984* (Washington, D.C.: Government Printing Office, 1983), p. 55.

64. Konrad Seitz, "Die Zukunft von Sicherheit und Abrüstung in Europa," *Europa-Archiv*, 41 (March 10, 1986), 122. This article is an expression of personal views, not a government policy statement.

65. Kosta Tsipis, *Understanding Nuclear Weapons* (London: Wildwood House, 1983), p. 164.

66. Walter Slocombe, "Preplanned Operations," in *Managing Nuclear Operations*, ed. Carter, Steinbruner, and Zraket, p. 125.

67. Manfred Wörner, "A Missile Defense for NATO Europe," *Strategic Review*, 14 (Winter 1986), 16.

68. *White Paper 1975/1976*, p. 20.

69. Manfred Wörner, "SALT II: A European Perspective," *Strategic Review*, 7 (Summer 1979), 13.

70. Herman Kahn, for example, defined escalation dominance as "a capacity, other things being equal, to enable the side possessing it to enjoy marked advantages in a given region of the escalation ladder . . . It depends on the net effect of the competing capabilities on the rung being occupied, the estimate by each side of what would happen if the confrontation moved to other rungs, and the means each side has to shift the confrontation to these other rungs." Kahn, *On Escalation: Metaphors and Scenarios* (New York: Praeger, 1965), p. 290.

71. Edward Luttwak, "The Problems of Extending Deterrence," in *The Future of Strategic Deterrence, Part I*, Adelphi Paper no. 160 (London: International Institute for Strategic Studies, 1980), pp. 33–34. See also Lawrence Freedman, *The Evolution of Nuclear Strategy* (London: Macmillan, 1983), pp. 218–219.

72. Legge, *Theater Nuclear Weapons*, p. 73.

73. Ibid., p. 27.

74. As Lawrence Freedman has pointed out, one of the difficulties with the assumption that the Soviets would stop their campaign and withdraw is the fact that the Soviets might have gained control over large sectors of Western territory in the meantime. In Freedman's view, Thomas Schelling's theory of "the threat that leaves something to chance" approximates the de facto policy of the Western alliance; but this theory fails, he notes, "to explain the mechanisms by which putting the onus on the enemy to escalate to higher levels of violence would compel him not to settle for the status quo but to relinquish the gains he had already made." Lawrence Freedman, "The First Two Generations of Nuclear Strategists," in *Makers of Modern Strategy from Machiavelli to the Nuclear Age*, ed. Peter Paret (Princeton, N.J.: Princeton University Press, 1986), pp. 766, 777–778. This essay develops the contrast in Freedman's *Evolution of Nuclear Strategy* between Schelling's theory of a "threat that leaves something to chance" and Kahn's theory of "escalation dominance." The contrast is instructive but artificial, in that Western officials responsible for controlling risks of nuclear escalation in the event of war find that far more is left to chance than they would prefer.

75. McGeorge Bundy, "The Future of Strategic Deterrence," *Survival*, 21 (November/December 1979), 271–272. Bundy was alluding to Michael Howard's article "The Relevance of Traditional Strategy," *Foreign Affairs*, 51 (January 1973), 262. For a similar viewpoint, see Freedman, *Evolution of Nuclear Strategy*, pp. 396–400. Bundy has subsequently espoused the view that the alliance should adopt a "no first use" policy regarding nuclear weapons. See McGeorge Bundy, George Kennan, Robert McNamara, and Gerard Smith, "Nuclear Weapons and the Atlantic Alliance," *Foreign Affairs*, 60 (Spring 1982).

76. For a concise analysis, see Paul H. Nitze, "The Relationship of Strategic and Theater Nuclear Forces," *International Security*, 2 (Fall 1977), 122–132.

77. George Shultz, *Modernizing U.S. Strategic Forces*, Current Policy no. 480 (Washington, D.C.: Bureau of Public Affairs, U.S. Department of State, April 20, 1983), p. 2.

78. Hans Rühle, "Die Zukunft der NATO," in *Die Kampagne gegen den NATO-Doppelbeschluss: Eine Bilanz*, ed. Gunther Wagenlehner (Koblenz: Bernard und Graefe Verlag, 1985), pp. 197–198.

79. According to Secretary of Defense Weinberger, "the Soviets could envision a potential nuclear confrontation in which they would threaten to destroy a very large part of our force in a first strike, while retaining overwhelming nuclear force to deter any retaliation we could carry out." Weinberger, *Defense Annual Report FY 1984*, p. 53.

80. Nikita Khrushchev, *Khrushchev Remembers: The Last Testament*, trans. and ed. Strobe Talbott (Boston: Little, Brown, 1974), p. 53.

81. N. S. Khrushchev, *Report of the Central Committee to the 20th Congress of the CPSU* (London: Soviet News Booklet, 1956), p. 28, cited in Holloway, *Soviet Union and the Arms Race*, p. 32.

82. General Lieutenant I. G. Zav'yalov, "The New Weapon and Military Art," *Red Star*, October 30, 1970, in *Selected Soviet Military Writings, 1970–1975*, translated and published under the auspices of the U.S. Air Force (Washington, D.C.: Government Printing Office, 1977), p. 207.

83. Vadim Zagladin, ed., *Mirovoye Kommunisticheskoye Dvizheniye* (The world Communist movement) (Moscow: Izdatel'stvo Politicheskoy Literatury, 1982), p. 19. (Emphasis added.)

84. Lieutenant General M. M. Kir'yan, *Voyenno-tekhnicheskiy Progress i Voorzhennyye Sily SSSR* (Progress in military technology and the armed forces of the USSR) (Moscow: Voyenizdat, 1982), p. 324.

85. Akhromeyev, "Prevoskhodstvo Sovetskoi Voennoi Nauki i Sovetskogo Voyennogo Iskusstva—Odin iz Vazhneishikh Faktorov Pobedi v Belikoi Otechestvennoi Voine" (Superiority of Soviet military science and Soviet military art—one of the most important factors of victory in the great patriotic war), *Kommunist*, February 1985, p. 60.

86. Davis and Stan, *Concepts and Models of Escalation*, p. 25. (Emphasis in original.)

87. Sayre Stevens, "Ballistic Missile Defense in the Soviet Union," *Current History*, 84 (October 1985), 345.

88. Gardner testimony in U.S. House of Representatives. Committee on Armed Services, *Defense Department Authorization and Oversight*, hearings, 98th Cong., 1st sess. (Washington, D.C.: U.S. Government Printing Office, 1983), pt. 5, p. 269.

89. Seitz, "Die Zukunft," p. 123.

90. Major General William E. Odom, "Trends in the Balance of Military Power between East and West," in *The Conduct of East-West Relations in the 1980s, Part III*, Adelphi Paper no. 191 (London: International Institute for Strategic Studies, 1984), p. 21.

91. Interview with General Wolfgang Altenburg in *Der Spiegel*, February 10, 1986, p. 69.

92. Peter Stratmann, *Aspekte der Sicherheitspolitischen und Militärstrategischen Entwicklung in den 90er Jahren*, AP 2474 (Ebenhausen, West Germany: Stiftung Wissenschaft und Politik. June 1986), p. 27.

93. Kir'yan, *Voyenno-tekhnicheski Progress*, p. 326.

94. Phillip A. Petersen and John G. Hines, *The Soviet Conventional Offensive in Europe*, DDB-2622-4-83 (Washington, D.C.: Defense Intelligence Agency, May 1983), p. vii. More readily accessible studies by Hines and Petersen, setting forth the same interpretation, are "The Conventional Offensive in Soviet Theater Strategy," *Orbis*, 27 (Fall 1983), and "Military Power in Soviet Strategy against NATO," *RUSI Journal*, 128 (December 1983).

95. Department of Defense, *Soviet Military Power 1985* (Washington, D.C.: Government Printing Office, 1985), p. 68.

96. Major Tyrus W. Cobb, "Tactical Air Defense: A Soviet-U.S. Net Assessment," *Air University Review*, 30 (March/April 1979), 35.

97. Defense, *Soviet Military Power 1985*, p. 50.

98. Ibid., p. 69.

99. See the discussion of FOFA and JTACMS by General Bernard Rogers in *Air Force Magazine*, February 1985, pp. 20, 23; Donald R. Cotter, "Potential Future Roles for Conventional and Nuclear Forces in Defense of Western Europe," in *Strengthening Conventional Deterrence in Europe: Proposals for the 1980s*, Report of the European Security Study (London: Macmillan, 1983), pp. 224, 238; and General Andrew J. Goodpaster, General Franz-Joseph Schulze, Air Chief Marshal Sir Alasdair Steedman, and William J. Perry, *Strengthening Conventional Deterrence in Europe: A Program for the 1980s*, European Security Study, Report of the Special Panel (Boulder, Colo.: Westview Press, 1985), pp. 57–64, 130.

100. Phillip A. Petersen and Major John R. Clark, "Soviet Air and Antiair Operations," *Air University Review*, 36 (March/April 1985), 51.

101. Richard D. DeLauer, "Emerging Technologies and Their Impact on the Conventional Deterrent," in *The Conventional Defense of Europe: New Technologies and New Strategies*, ed. Andrew J. Pierre (New York: Council on Foreign Relations, 1986), p. 59.

102. François Heisbourg, "Conventional Defense: Europe's Constraints and Opportunities," in *Conventional Defense of Europe*, ed. Pierre, p. 92. Heisbourg adds that, "since U.S. stocks of chemical weapons in West Germany

will apparently cease to be useful within a few years, the adversary might consider that he will be able to launch chemical attacks without risking similar retaliation and, consequently, without even having to adopt highly penalizing chemical defense measures."

103. See the sources cited in Kerry L. Hines, "Soviet Short-Range Ballistic Missiles: Now a Conventional Deep-Strike Mission," *International Defense Review*, 18 (December 1985), 1911. This discussion is indebted to Hines.

104. Ibid., pp. 1909–14; Heisbourg, "Conventional Defense," pp. 90–91; and Dennis M. Gormley, "A New Dimension to Soviet Theater Strategy," *Orbis*, 29 (Fall 1985), 537–569.

105. Ogarkov, *Red Star*, May 9, 1984, p. R19 of *FBIS* translation.

106. Wörner, "Missile Defense for NATO Europe," p. 14.

107. Jeannou Lacaze, "L'avenir de la défense française," *Défense Nationale*, July 1985, pp. 21–22.

108. Jacques Baumel, *Avis présenté au nom de la Commission de la Défense Nationale et des Forces Armées sur le projet de loi de finances pour 1987 (no. 363), tome V, Défense, espace et forces nucléaires*, no. 398 (Paris: Assemblée Nationale, October 1986), p. 38.

109. John Prados, Joel S. Wit, and Michael J. Zagurek, Jr., "The Strategic Nuclear Forces of Britain and France," *Scientific American*, August 1986, p. 39.

110. The Soviets would be even more likely to attempt to defend themselves if the British and/or French attacks were as unrestrained as those discussed in the above article. If British and/or French attacks consisted of the selective strikes that are far more plausible on political and strategic grounds, Soviet defenses designed primarily with U.S. limited attacks in mind would be more likely to be effective.

111. Defense, *Soviet Military Power 1987*, p. 50.

112. François Heisbourg, "La France face aux nouvelles données stratégiques," *Défense Nationale*, April 1986, p. 37.

113. Lawrence Freedman, "British Nuclear Targeting," in *Strategic Nuclear Targeting*, ed. Desmond Ball and Jeffrey Richelson (Ithaca, N. Y.: Cornell University Press, 1986), p. 122.

114. Stanley Orman, Director General of the SDI Participation Office, Ministry of Defence, in *Implications for the United Kingdom of Ballistic Missile Defence*, p. 47.

115. Testimony by Rear Admiral J. S. Grove, chief, strategic systems executive, in Great Britain, House of Commons, *Third Report from the Defense Committee, Defence Commitments and Resources and the Defence Estimates, 1985–86*, vol. 2 (London: Her Majesty's Stationery Office, 1985), pp. 274–275.

116. Lord Trefgarne, parliamentary under secretary of state for the armed forces, in Great Britain, Parliament, *Parliamentary Debates* (House of Lords), January 30, 1985, col. 719.

117. Great Britain, House of Commons, *Third Report from the Defence Committee, Defence Commitments and Resources and the Defence Estimates, 1985–1986*, vol. 1 (London: Her Majesty's Stationery Office, 1985), p. x.

118. Orman in *Implications for the United Kingdom of Ballistic Missile Defence*, p. 48.
119. John Roper, "The British Nuclear Deterrent and New Developments in Ballistic Missile Defense," *The World Today*, 41 (May 1985), 93.
120. Freedman, "British Nuclear Targeting," p. 123.
121. Bellany in *Implications for the United Kingdom of Ballistic Missile Defence*, p. 160. (Emphasis in original.)
122. Roper, "British Nuclear Deterrent," p. 93, and Freedman, "British Nuclear Targeting," pp. 122, 125.
123. D. J. Fewtrell, director of nuclear policy and security, Ministry of Defence, testimony in United Kingdom, House of Commons, *Sixth Report from the Defence Committee, Session 1984–85, the Trident Programme* (London: Her Majesty's Stationery Office, 1985), p. 49.
124. *Statement on the Defence Estimates 1985*, Cmnd. 9430–I (London: Her Majesty's Stationery Office, 1985), p. 7.
125. Roper, "British Nuclear Deterrent," p. 93.
126. *Statement on the Defence Estimates 1987*, Cm. 101–1 (London: Her Majesty's Stationery Office, 1987), pp. 40–41.
127. Jean-Yves Leloup and Pierre Cazalas, "Les options spatiales françaises," *Défense Nationale*, February 1986, p. 136. Leloup was the director of the Groupe de Planification et d'Etudes Stratégiques in the Ministry of Defense at the time of this article's publication.
128. Commission d'Etudes sur les Armes Spatiales, *Rapport de synthèse présenté au ministre de la défense*, January 30, 1986.
129. Quilès cited in *Le Monde*, November 13, 1985, p. 12.
130. Quilès interview in *Le Monde*, December 18, 1985, p. 6.
131. Lacaze, "L'avenir," p. 23.
132. Leloup and Cazalas, "Les options spatiales," p. 136. Several types of penetration aids (electromagnetic and infrared decoys, and so forth) are discussed in the Delpech report (Commission d'Etudes, *Rapport de synthèse*, p. 20), but in the context of countering space-based directed-energy systems.
133. General Jean Fleury, "L'évolution des armes nucléaires," *Défense Nationale*, March 1986, pp. 13–14. General Fleury, the commander of France's strategic air forces, provides the most detailed description of these ideas. See also the Delpech report (Commission d'Etudes, *Rapport de synthèse*, pp. 18, 20), and Paul Quilès, "L'avenir de notre concept de défense face aux progrès technologiques," *Défense Nationale*, January 1986, p. 18.
134. Giraud testimony in François Fillon, *Rapport fait au nom de la Commission de la Défense Nationale et des Forces Armées sur le projet de loi de programme (no. 432) relatif à l'équipement militaire pour les années 1987–1991*, no. 622 (Paris: Assemblée Nationale, April 1987), p. 288.
135. Fleury, "L'évolution," p. 13; Commission d'Etudes, *Rapport de synthèse*, p. 20; and Paul-Ivan de Saint Germain, "L'initiative de défense stratégique: quel défi pour la France?" *Défense Nationale*, June 1986, p. 136. M. de Saint Germain is the deputy director of the Direction des Recherches, Etudes et Techniques in the Ministry of Defense.

136. de Saint Germain, "L'initiative de défense," p. 124.
137. Commission d'Etudes, *Rapport de synthèse*, p. 11.
138. Ibid., p. 19; de Saint Germain, "L'initiative de défense," p. 127; and Quilès, "L'avenir de notre concept," p. 18.
139. Quilès interview in *Le Monde*, December 18, 1985, p. 6.
140. Commission d'Etudes, *Rapport de synthèse*, p. 20.
141. Fleury, "L'évolution," p. 12.
142. de Saint Germain, "L'initiative de défense," p. 127. Among other references to possible French ASAT capabilities, see Lacaze, "L'avenir," pp. 23, 27; Leloup and Cazalas, "Les options spatiales," p. 137; and Commission d'Etudes, *Rapport de synthèse*, p. 11. A longer discussion may be found in Groupe X-Défense, *Les défenses anti-missiles, la France et l'Europe* (Paris: Fondation pour les Etudes de Défense Nationale, 1986), pp. 88–89, 167–169.
143. Leloup and Cazalas, "Les options spatiales," p. 136.
144. Lacaze, "L'avenir," pp. 24, 26.
145. Quilès, "Au-delà des fausses querelles," *Le Monde*, March 7, 1986, p. 23.
146. Interview with Defense Minister André Giraud, *L'Express*, May 30, 1986, p. 25.
147. See the articles by Jacques Isnard in *Le Monde*, September 27, 1986, p. 15, and October 15, 1986, pp. 1, 8. Giraud has already indicated that, contrary to previous plans, France's seventh SSBN, scheduled to enter service in 1994, will receive the M-4 SLBM at first, with the M-5 to follow at an unspecified later date. (Giraud cited in *Le Monde*, October 11, 1986, p. 10.)
148. "Loi de programmation no. 87–342 du 22 mai 1987 relative à l'équipement militaire pour les années 1987–1991," *Journal Officiel de la République Française*, May 23, 1987, p. 5649.
149. Fillon, *Rapport*, p. 160.
150. "Loi de programmation," p. 5649.
151. Giraud testimony in Fillon, *Rapport*, p. 288.
152. Leloup and Cazalas, "Les options spatiales," p. 137.
153. Lacaze, "L'avenir," pp. 23–24.
154. For background about French policy on cruise missiles, see David S. Yost, *France's Deterrent Posture and Security in Europe, Part I: Capabilities and Doctrine*, Adelphi Paper no. 194 (London: International Institute for Strategic Studies, 1984/85), pp. 20–21, 28–29. For a useful discussion of the technical challenges and financial disincentives that would complicate any British or French efforts to shift to cruise missiles, see James C. Wendt, *British and French Nuclear Forces: Response Options to Soviet Ballistic Missile Defense*, P-7188 (Santa Monica, Calif.: Rand Corporation, March 1986), pp. 18–22.
155. Wendt, *British and French Nuclear Forces*, pp. 28–31.
156. Ibid., pp. 27–28.
157. Quilès interview in *Le Monde*, December 18, 1985, p. 6.
158. Commission d'Etudes, *Rapport de synthèse*, p. 12.
159. Leloup and Cazalas, "Les options spatiales," p. 138.

160. Ibid.

161. Jean-François Delpech, "De l'ABM à l'IDS: défenses antimissiles balistiques et initiative de défense stratégique," *Armées d'Aujourd'hui*, 109 (April 1986), 44.

162. In an uncharacteristically explicit policy statement, the British government in 1973 acknowledged that its targeting list of "key aspects of Soviet state power" may include targets outside Moscow "such as major dams and waterways, major oil refineries, major naval shipyards, major iron and steelworks, and major nuclear reactor establishments." Official evidence in the *Twelfth Report from the Expenditure Committee,* cited in Lawrence Freedman, *Britain and Nuclear Weapons* (London: Macmillan, 1980), p. 47.

163. One of the few official British statements on targeting flexibility indicated simply that Britain's "concept of deterrence is concerned essentially with posing a potential threat to key aspects of Soviet state power. There might with changing conditions be more than one way of doing this, and some flexibility in contingency planning is appropriate. It would not be helpful to deterrence to define particular options further." (*The Future United Kingdom Strategic Nuclear Deterrent Force*, London: Ministry of Defence, July 1980, p. 6.) The issue of targeting flexibility is relatively controversial in France for various reasons. Some Frenchmen are concerned that revealing limited-strike options could diminish the threat faced by the USSR and thus undermine deterrence. Others contend that the Soviets have recognized that France's capabilities to conduct limited strikes are improving, and that the consequent deterrent effects should be pursued without starting a debate that could disturb the national consensus on France's nuclear-deterrent policy. In a noteworthy statement, Jacques Chirac recently suggested that accurate S-4 IRBMs, to be deployed after 1996, could be used to deliver an "ultimate warning" against the "sanctuary" of the adversary. Chirac cited in *Le Monde*, March 9, 1988, p. 14. For background, see David S. Yost, "French Nuclear Targeting," in *Strategic Nuclear Targeting*, ed. Desmond Ball and Jeffrey Richelson (Ithaca, N.Y.: Cornell University Press, 1986), pp. 127–156.

164. Hubert Védrine, diplomatic adviser to President Mitterrand, interview broadcast on January 30, 1985, in *Foreign Broadcast Information Service—Western Europe*, daily report, February 1, 1985, p. K5.

165. Groupe X-Défense, *Les défenses anti-missiles*, p. 164. (The italicized words appeared in English in the original.)

166. Jean-Michel Boucheron cited in Jean-Pierre Bechter and Pierre André Wiltzer, *Rapport d'information déposé en application de l'article 145 du règlement par la Commission de la Défense Nationale et des Forces Armées sur la nouvelle composante des forces nucléaires stratégiques*, no. 368 (Paris: Assemblée Nationale, October 1986), p. 104.

167. Ian Bellany in *Implications for the United Kingdom of Ballistic Missile Defence*, p. 161.

168. Pierre Hassner, "Critique de la stratégie pure," *Commentaire*, 25 (Spring 1984), 65.

169. Roper, "British nuclear deterrent," p. 94.
170. See David S. Yost, *France and Conventional Defense in Central Europe* (Boulder, Colo.: Westview Press, 1985), pp. 29–39, 77–86.
171. The 1987 defense budget announces an intention to reduce the number employed by the Ministry of Defense by 4200. *Le Monde*, September 24, 1986, p. 22.
172. Jean-Yves Boulic, "Les choix difficiles de l'an 2000," *Le Point*, October 13, 1986, p. 32.
173. Further adverse trends in the conventional-force balance are not inevitable, of course; the past pattern could be reversed with sufficient political will.
174. The uncertainties in the relationship between British and NATO nuclear planning are discussed in Freedman, "British Nuclear Targeting," pp. 119–120, 125–126. The British could theoretically expand their warhead numbers fairly cheaply by increasing the number of reentry vehicles on the Trident II D-5 SLBMs. But this might create arms control penalties for the United States. All U.S. D-5 SLBMs would then be counted, according to past SALT rules, as having the largest number of warheads tested on the missile. See Roper, "British Nuclear Deterrent," p. 93, and Wendt, *British and French Nuclear Forces*, p. 5.
175. Seitz, "Die Zukunft," p. 123.
176. Harald Müller, *Strategic Defences: The End of Alliance Strategy?* CEPS Papers no. 32 (Brussels: Centre for European Policy Studies, 1987), p. 24.
177. Stratmann, *Sicherheitspolitischen und Militärstrategischen Entwicklung*, p. 30.
178. Roper, "British Nuclear Deterrent," p. 94.
179. Wendt, *British and French Nuclear Forces*, pp. 22–26.
180. For an informative discussion of Soviet commentary on this issue, see Robbin F. Laird, *France, the Soviet Union, and the Nuclear Weapons Issue* (Boulder, Colo.: Westview Press, 1985), pp. 112–120. John Van Oudenaren, however, judged that the Soviets may be confident, based on their observations of the postwar policies of major governments, that "Western Europe will not unite to form a West European counterweight to Soviet power, or even a strong European 'pillar' within the Atlantic alliance." Van Oudenaren, *Soviet Policy Toward Western Europe*, p. 108.
181. Heisbourg, "Conventional Defense," p. 90.
182. Wörner, "Missile Defense for NATO Europe," p. 16.
183. Hannes Adomeit, "The Political Rationale of Soviet Military Capabilities and Doctrine," in *Strengthening Conventional Deterrence in Europe: Proposals for the 1980s*, Report of the European Security Study (London: Macmillan, 1983), p. 95. (Emphasis in original.)
184. A revealing Soviet source is D. M. Proekter, ed., *European Security and Co-operation: Premises, Problems, Prospects* (Moscow: Progress Publishers, 1978). For a valuable discussion of Soviet political strategy in Western Europe, see Pierre Hassner, "Moscow and the Western Alliance," *Problems of Communism*, 30 (May/June 1981), 37–54. The basic continuity since the 1950s of Soviet policy themes regarding the future of Europe is evident in

Mikhail Gorbachev, *Perestroika: New Thinking for Our Country and the World* (New York: Harper and Row, 1987), pp. 190–209.

185. General Bernard W. Rogers, interview in *U.S. News and World Report*, January 20, 1986, p. 29.

186. General Bernard W. Rogers, "NATO's Strategy: An Undervalued Currency," in *Power and Policy: Doctrine, the Alliance and Arms Control*, Adelphi Paper no. 205 (London: International Institute for Strategic Studies, 1986), p. 4.

187. Commission d'Etudes, *Rapport de synthèse*, pp. 12–13.

188. Farewell news conference by Secretary of Defense Harold Brown, January 16, 1981, p. 5.

189. As David Holloway notes, the *Soviet Military Encyclopaedia* volumes published in the late 1970s affirmed themes of "military-technical superiority over the armed forces of probable enemies" and called for victory in the event of nuclear war. (Holloway, *Soviet Union and the Arms Race*, pp. 54–55, 191.) Indeed, high level officials such as Marshal Ogarkov have continued to call for capabilities suitable for achieving "total victory over the enemy" in the event of world war. (Ogarkov, *Istoriya Uchit Bditel'nost'* [History teaches vigilance], Moscow: Military Publishing House, 1985, excerpts published in "The Soviet Strategic View," *Strategic Review*, 13 (Fall 1985), 99.) In contrast, Mikhail Gorbachev and his immediate predecessors have made statements such as the following: "We . . . would not want to change the strategic balance in our favor. We would not want this because this kind of situation will increase the suspicion of the other side and increase the instability of the overall situation . . . both our countries will have to get used to strategic parity as the natural state." (Mikhail Gorbachev's address to the Supreme Soviet, November 27, 1985, in *FBIS-SU*, November 29, 1985, p. R24.)

190. For discussions of the Tula line, see Michael Mihalka, "Soviet Strategic Deception, 1955–1981," *Journal of Strategic Studies*, 5 (March 1982), 85–90, and Benjamin S. Lambeth, *The State of Western Research on Soviet Military Strategy and Policy*, N-2230-AF (Santa Monica, Calif.: Rand Corporation, October 1984), pp. 49–57. The recent Soviet innovations in references to arms race history and responsibility (discussed in Chapter 2) may be related to the themes of the Tula line.

191. Trulock, "Soviet Perspectives," pp. 72–73.

192. See the statements by Khrushchev cited in Wohlstetter, "Between an Unfree World and None," p. 986.

193. Brezhnev interview in *Der Spiegel*, November 2, 1981, in *Survival*, 24 (January/February 1982), 32.

194. Ogarkov, *Istoriya Uchit Bditel'nost'*, p. 99.

195. Ogarkov, *Red Star*, May 9, 1984, p. R19 of *FBIS* translation.

196. Examples include the Voroshilov General Staff Academy materials (see Trulock, "Soviet Perspectives") and articles in *Military Thought*, the classified journal of the Soviet General Staff. Selected English translations by the

U.S. government from *Military Thought* have been declassified for the period 1963–1973.

197. Nathan Leites, *Soviet Style in War* (New York: Crane, Russak, 1982), pp. 377, 379. The point made by Leites may help to resolve the apparent contradiction between the judgments of Stephen Meyer and Notra Trulock. Meyer finds Soviet discussions of limited operations "invariably tied to theater nuclear war, not intercontinental war." Notra Trulock judges that, while Soviet views on the feasibility of limited intercontinental nuclear operations are "more ambiguous" than their views on prospects for escalation control at the theater level, "a similar set of concerns"—including fear of a "loss of control over the course of the conflict" as a whole—has probably conditioned Soviet thinking. If Soviet concepts for intercontinental operations involved only large-scale preemptive attacks oriented toward limiting damage to the USSR by causing maximum damage to U.S. nuclear forces, C^3I capabilities, and military-industrial potential, U.S. plans for selective strikes with intercontinental forces would appear potentially irrelevant and likely to be ineffective. The dearth of Soviet commentary on the feasibility of limited intercontinental operations therefore may, as Leites suggests, amount to a discretion rooted in a calculation as to likely deterrent effects. But it may also reflect qualitatively greater Soviet doubts about the controllability of intercontinental, as opposed to theater, nuclear operations and a judgment that, in some circumstances, large-scale attacks might be considered necessary. Such attacks might nonetheless be viewed as much less plausible than limited attacks because of the higher risks of a loss of control and unacceptable devastation to the USSR.

198. Wohlstetter, "Between an Unfree World and None," p. 981.

199. John Hines, Phillip Petersen, and Notra Trulock, "Soviet Military Theory from 1945–2000: Implication for NATO," *Washington Quarterly*, 9 (Fall 1986), 134.

200. Osgood and Wegener, *Deterrence*, p. 9.

4. Soviet Arms Control Diplomacy and the Unlikely Prospect of Breakout

1. James A. Schear, "Arms Control Treaty Compliance: Buildup to a Breakdown?" *International Security*, 10 (Fall 1985), 160.

2. In 1974, for example, Henry Kissinger defined "the break-out period" as the time that would follow the expiration of the SALT I Interim Agreement in 1977. See Kissinger's Vladivostok press conference in U.S. Arms Control and Disarmament Agency, *Documents on Disarmament 1974* (Washington, D.C.: Government Printing Office, 1976), p. 756.

3. Richard Perle, assistant secretary of defense for international security policy, testimony in U.S. Senate, Committee on Armed Services, *Soviet Treaty Violations*, hearing, 98th Cong., 2nd sess. (Washington, D.C.: Government Printing Office, 1984), p. 40. (Emphasis in original.)

4. Sayre Stevens, "The Soviet BMD Program," in *Ballistic Missile Defense*, ed.

Ashton B. Carter and David N. Schwartz (Washington, D.C.: Brookings Institution, 1984), pp. 217–218.

5. Michael Mihalka, "Soviet Strategic Deception, 1955–1981," *Journal of Strategic Studies*, 5 (March 1982), 84.

6. *Soviet Strategic Force Developments*, testimony before a joint session of the Subcommittee on Strategic and Theater Nuclear Forces of the Senate Armed Services Committee and the Defense Subcommittee of the Senate Committee on Appropriations, June 26, 1985, by Robert M. Gates, chairman, National Intelligence Council, and deputy director for intelligence, Central Intelligence Agency, and Lawrence K. Gershwin, national intelligence officer for strategic programs, National Intelligence Council, p. 6.

7. Stevens, "The Soviet BMD Program," p. 217.

8. Lieutenant General William E. Odom, "The Implications of Active Defense of NATO for Soviet Military Strategy," in *Swords and Shields: NATO, the USSR, and New Choices for Long-Range Offense and Defense*, ed. Fred S. Hoffman, Albert Wohlstetter, and David S. Yost (Lexington, Mass.: D. C. Heath/Lexington Books, 1987), pp. 164–173.

9. William Beecher, "Soviet Change on Arms Hinted," *Boston Globe*, December 4, 1985, p. 1.

10. David N. Schwartz, "Assessing Future Prospects," *Ballistic Missile Defense*, ed. Carter and Schwartz, p. 355.

11. Commission d'Etudes sur les Armes Spatiales, *Rapport de synthèse présenté au ministre de la défense*, January 30, 1986, pp. 12–13.

12. Stevens, "The Soviet BMD Program," p. 216.

13. According to an *Izvestia* editorial, "it is also clear to every unbiased person that the Soviet Union's air defense system bears no relation to ABM defense." *Izvestia* of January 25, 1985, in *Foreign Broadcast Information Service—Soviet Union* (hereafter, *FBIS-SU*), daily report, January 25, 1985, p. AA5. In May 1985, Soviet spokesman Wjatscheslaw Daschitschew described the SA-X-12 as simply an "air defense missile." In an unusual exception to the standard Soviet position, however, Daschitschew acknowledged (1) that the Soviets are "building and perfecting" antitactical missile systems and (2) that ATBM defenses are permitted by the ABM Treaty. See Daschitschew, "Der sowjetische Standpunkte zu SDI," in *Standpunkte zu SDI in West und Ost*, ed. Hans-Joachim Veen and Peter R. Weilemann (Sankt Augustin bei Bonn, West Germany: Konrad-Adenauer-Stiftung, 1985), pp. 34, 39.

14. Even if the Soviets agreed that ATBM systems are allowed under the ABM Treaty, geographical asymmetries would favor the Soviet Union. A Soviet ATBM, whether capable of ICBM and SLBM RV interceptions or not, could defend Soviet as well as allied territory. U.S. ATBM systems in Western Europe could defend U.S. forces and allies, but not the U.S. homeland.

15. See the Tass dispatch of March 15, 1983, by Vladimir Bogachev, "The ABM Treaty and Stability," in *FBIS-SU*, daily report, March 16, 1983, pp. AA4–AA5.

16. Stevens, "The Soviet BMD Program," p. 218.

17. François Heisbourg, "La France face aux nouvelles données stratégiques," *Défense Nationale*, April 1986, p. 37.

18. Younger in Great Britain, Parliament, *Parliamentary Debates* (House of Commons), February 19, 1986, col. 338.

19. Schwartz, "Assessing Future Prospects," p. 359.

20. U.S. Congress, Office of Technology Assessment, *Ballistic Missile Defense Technologies*, OTA-ISC-254 (Washington, D.C.: Government Printing Office, September 1985), p. 61.

21. Odom, "Implications of Active Defense," p. 164.

22. Commission d'Etudes, *Rapport de synthèse*, p. 5.

23. Hans Rühle, "Gorbachev's 'Star Wars,' " *NATO Review*, 33 (August 1985), 31.

24. Roger P. Main, "The USSR and Laser Weaponry: The View from Outside," *Defense Systems Review*, 3, no. 3 (1985), 75.

25. Stevens, "The Soviet BMD Program," p. 217.

26. President Reagan, "Address to the Nation on Defense and National Security," March 23, 1983, in *Public Papers of the Presidents of the United States, Ronald Reagan 1983*, bk. 1 (Washington, D.C.: Government Printing Office, 1984), pp. 442–443.

27. Gates and Gershwin, *Soviet Strategic Force Developments*, p. 9. Robert Schmidt, deputy director of the Defense Intelligence Agency, has offered a comparable conclusion: "If economic progress does not proceed as planned, Soviet leaders are likely to return to larger investments in the military sector rather than in the economic infrastructure." Schmidt cited in Stephen Engelberg, "U.S. Reports Deny Soviet Is Pressed," *New York Times*, September 16, 1986, p. A7.

28. "Gorbachev's Modernization Program: A Status Report," paper presented by the Central Intelligence Agency and the Defense Intelligence Agency for submission to the Subcommittee on National Security Economics of the Joint Economic Committee, U.S. Congress, March 19, 1987, pp. 14, 16.

29. Gates and Gershwin, *Soviet Strategic Force Developments*, p. 9.

30. Mikhail Gorbachev, "Excerpts from Speech by Gorbachev about Iceland Meeting," *New York Times*, October 15, 1986, p. A12.

31. Védrine interview broadcast on January 30, 1985, in *Foreign Broadcast Information Service—Western Europe*, daily report, February 1, 1985, p. K8. See also Mitterrand's comments about Gorbachev and the SDI, reported in *New York Times*, July 4, 1986, p. A4.

32. Interview with Marshal Nikolai Ogarkov in *Krasnaya Zvezda* (Red star), May 9, 1984, in *FBIS-SU*, daily report, May 9, 1984, p. R19.

33. Ibid., p. R20. It should be noted that Ogarkov's new assignment is commander-in-chief of forces in the western theater of strategic military action (TMSA). (TMSA is an accepted translation of the Russian *TVD*, or *teatr voyennykh deystviy*.) As John Hines and Phillip Petersen have noted, this command is "essentially a forward deployed component of the Headquarters of the Supreme High Command . . . in the *main* TMSA in overall Soviet military strategy." This command is so important that Ogarkov's reassign-

ment may be seen as "lateral," and he may still ultimately become defense minister. Hines and Petersen, "Changing the Soviet System of Control: Focus on Theatre Warfare," *International Defense Review*, 19 (March 1986), 282–283.

34. For a useful background discussion, see Bruce Parrott, *The Soviet Union and Ballistic Missile Defense* (Boulder, Colo.: Westview Press, 1987), pp. 45–49.

35. See "The Soviet Economy under a New Leader," report presented to the Subcommittee on Economic Resources, Competitiveness, and Security Economics of the Joint Economic Committee, U.S. Congress, by the Central Intelligence Agency and the Defense Intelligence Agency, March 19, 1986, p. 20.

36. CIA and DIA, "Gorbachev's Modernization Program," p. 16.

37. For an articulation of the "defense sufficiency" concept, see the article by Defense Minister Dmitri Yazov in *Pravda*, July 27, 1987, p. 5, in *FBIS-SU*, daily report, July 27, 1987, p. BB3.

38. Groupe X-Défense, *Les défenses anti-missiles, la France et l'Europe* (Paris: Fondation pour les Etudes de Défense Nationale, 1986), p. 30.

39. Lieutenant General William E. Odom, "Soviet Force Posture: Dilemmas and Directions," *Problems of Communism*, 34 (July/August 1985), 1–2, 6–14.

40. See, for example, the statement by Aleksei Podberiozkin of the Soviet Institute on World Economics, cited in Flora Lewis, "Soviet S.D.I. Fears," *New York Times*, March 6, 1986, p. A27. One might consider in this context as well the comment made by Mikhail Gorbachev at the conclusion of the Reykjavik summit: "The SDI can lead to new types of weapons . . . It can lead to an entirely new stage of the arms race with serious, unpredictable consequences." Gorbachev cited in *Washington Post*, October 23, 1986, p. A22.

41. Mikhail Gorbachev's address to the Supreme Soviet, November 27, 1985, in *FBIS-SU*, November 29, 1985, p. R24.

42. Stephen M. Meyer, "Soviet Strategic Programmes and the US SDI," *Survival*, 27 (November/December 1985), 275

43. Lebedev cited in Lewis, "Soviet S.D.I. Fears," p. A27.

44. Sayre Stevens, "Ballistic Missile Defense in the Soviet Union," *Current History*, 84 (October 1985), 346.

45. Paul H. Nitze, *The Impact of SDI on U.S.-Soviet Relations*, Current Policy no. 830 (Washington, D.C.: Bureau of Public Affairs, U.S. Department of State, April 29, 1986), pp. 3–4.

46. Richard Perle, news briefing at the Pentagon, October 14, 1986, in *Defense Issues*, 70 (October 23, 1986), 7.

47. Ibid.

48. Odom, "Implications of Active Defense," pp. 165, 170.

49. For a concise discussion, see Daniel Gouré, "Soviet Counters to SDI," *NATO's Sixteen Nations*, 31 (April 1986), 34–37.

50. John G. Hines, Phillip A. Petersen, and Notra Trulock III, "Soviet Military Theory from 1945-2000: Implications for NATO," *Washington Quarterly*, 9 (Fall 1986), 128.

51. I am indebted to Thomas A. Brown for this reflection.

52. Odom, "Implications of Active Defense," p. 173.

53. This judgment is consistent with the findings of a recent analysis: "In the negotiating process the Soviets seek to constrain us where we appear to have a technological advantage (ballistic missile defense, ASW, ASAT) and maintain their freedom of action in areas where they can do well (land mobility, hardening, manned space)." John G. Hines and George F. Kraus, "Soviet Strategies for Military Competition," *Parameters*, 16 (Autumn 1986), 30.

54. Stevens, "Ballistic Missile Defense in the Soviet Union," p. 346.

55. Some news reports in early 1987 suggested that Secretary of Defense Weinberger favored making a decision on SDI initial deployments. But Secretary of State Shultz announced that no decision on whether to start SDI deployments would be made during the Reagan administration. Michael R. Gordon, "Shultz Rules Out 'Star Wars' Move within Two Years," *New York Times*, February 9, 1987, pp. A1, A11.

56. Groupe X-Défense, *Les défenses anti-missiles*, p. 30.

57. Stevens, "Ballistic Missile Defense in the Soviet Union," p. 30.

58. Cf. Odom, "Soviet Force Posture," pp. 11–13.

59. Douglas MacEachin, director of Soviet analysis at the CIA, has testified that Gorbachev's arms control proposals might be intended to promote reduced defense spending in the West: "To the extent that his policies can create an atmosphere that undermines Western willingness to sustain its major defense programs, if these things are questioned, it gives him, in effect, breathing space." MacEachin cited in Engelberg, "U.S. Reports," p. A27.

60. Mikhail Gorbachev, "Political Report of the CPSU Central Committee to the 27th Congress of the Communist Party of the Soviet Union," February 25, 1986, in *New Times*, March 10, 1986, p. 36.

61. Ibid., p. 39.

62. Gorbachev, address to the Supreme Soviet, November 27, 1985, pp. R28–R29.

63. Paul Nitze, "Living with the Soviets," *Foreign Affairs*, 63 (Winter 1984/85), 362.

64. Gromyko has been named president of the Soviet state, and Eduard Shevardnadze has become foreign minister. Zamyatin's International Information Department of the Central Committee has been disestablished, and Zamyatin has been appointed ambassador to Britain. The Central Committee's International Department is now headed by Anatoli Dobrynin, and its Propaganda Department is led by Alexander Yakovlev.

65. *The President's Unclassified Report on Soviet Noncompliance with Arms Control Agreements* (White House, Office of the Press Secretary, March 10, 1987), p. 10. The Soviets also deny the U.S. charges in December 1987 regarding the radars discovered at Gomel, outside the treaty-permitted BMD deployment area and test ranges. See Michael R. Gordon, "U.S. Says Kremlin Broke '72 Treaty Covering the ABM," *New York Times*, December 3, 1987, pp. 1, 7.

66. Parrott, *Soviet Union and Ballistic Missile Defense*, pp. 42–43, 108. In Decem-

ber 1987, Soviet officials told an American journalist that the Defense Ministry planned the network of nine LPARs during the late 1960s, and "chose the Krasnoyarsk site to save money . . . The Politburo approved construction of the network in the early 1970s, about the time the [ABM] treaty was being signed . . . [Defense Minister] Ustinov did not tell the Politburo that Krasnoyarsk potentially violated the treaty, but . . . Andrei A. Gromyko, then the foreign minister and a Politburo member, must have known . . . The Soviet Defense Ministry . . . expected the violation to be discovered by U.S. satellites, but counted on containing Washington's protests for years in the U.S.–Soviet committee set up by the ABM treaty. The Soviets hoped to be allowed to continue construction in exchange for dropping objections to what they would charge were U.S. violations." Walter Pincus, "U.S. Says ABM Extension Depends on Soviet Radar," *International Herald Tribune*, December 15, 1987, pp. 1, 6.

67. Leslie H. Gelb, "Moscow Proposes to End a Dispute on Siberia Radar," *New York Times*, October 29, 1985, p. 1.

68. Arbatov cited in R. Jeffrey Smith, "Soviet Radars of Concern to U.S. Removed," *Washington Post*, February 25, 1987, p. A20.

69. Milshtein and Surikov cited in Bill Gertz, "Soviet General Admits Radar Treaty Violation," *Washington Times*, April 29, 1987, p. 5B.

70. Dobrynin's suggestion was reported in the *Washington Post*, April 14, 1985, p. 8. Among other sources on the September 1987 inspection, see Paul Mann, "Administration Disputes Findings of U.S. Visit to Soviet Radar," *Aviation Week and Space Technology*, September 14, 1987, pp. 26–28.

71. The radars at Gomel reportedly consist of one Pawn Shop and one Flat Twin. See Michael R. Gordon, "Soviet Is Offering to Let U.S. Inspect Site of 2 More Radars," *New York Times*, October 28, 1987, p. 6, and "U.S., After a Debate, Accepts Soviet Offer to Examine Radars," *New York Times*, November 16, 1987, pp. 1, 4.

72. It might be added that, in current circumstances, it is hardly plausible that the United States would convert its ICBM force to BMD purposes. The ICBM boosters would need new "front ends"—preferably nonnuclear kill mechanisms—and suitable radar and battle management support. This would probably not be an attractive proposition for the United States unless a large portion of its ICBM force became redundant, perhaps as a result of some fundamental change in the U.S. force structure. In contrast, the upgrading of comparatively inexpensive SAMs to BMD purposes could be an attractive proposition for the USSR.

73. For a comprehensive review of the Soviet allegations and U.S. responses, see *Adherence to and Compliance with Agreements* (Washington, D.C.: Office of Public Affairs, U.S. Arms Control and Disarmament Agency, February 11, 1987). See also, among other sources, Department of Defense, *Report to the Congress on the Strategic Defense Initiative*, June 1986, pp. C-1–C-15, and the letter by Thomas Graham, Jr., general counsel, Arms Control and Disarmament Agency, in *Washington Post*, October 8, 1986, p. A26.

74. Paul Nitze and Abraham Sofaer, *The ABM Treaty and the SDI Program*,

Current Policy no. 755 (Washington, D.C.: Bureau of Public Affairs, U.S. Department of State, October 22, 1985), pp. 1–3.

75. Abraham Sofaer, "The ABM Treaty and the Strategic Defense Initiative," *Harvard Law Review*, 99 (June 1986), 1979.

76. Senator Sam Nunn, "Interpretation of the ABM Treaty, Part Four: An Examination of Judge Sofaer's Analysis of the Negotiating Record," *Congressional Record*, May 20, 1987, p. 12 of reprint furnished by Senator Nunn's office.

77. Akhromeyev's *Pravda* article of October 19, 1985, reprinted in full in *Washington Post*, October 25, 1985, p. A24.

78. K. Georgiyev, "Contrary to Facts and Logic," *Pravda*, October 18, 1986, p. 4, in JPRS-TAC-86-088, November 7, 1986, p. 46. Cf. Akhromeyev, ibid.

79. A. Natalin, "Protivopravnost 'strategicheskoi oboronnoi initsiativi' SSHA" (The illegality of the U.S. 'Strategic Defense Initiative'), *Sovietskoye Gosudarstvo i Pravo*, November 1985, p. 117. I am indebted to Stanley Kober for these references on the Soviet interpretation of Agreed Statement D.

80. Another directed-energy system concern has been raised by Paul Nitze, who has called attention to Soviet plans to develop a space probe with both laser and particle beam devices for testing against Phobos, one of the moons of Mars. In Nitze's view, "it would be difficult to prove that the power, brightness, and tracking and aiming characteristics of these devices" were not sufficient to serve as components of a weapon system. In other words, the Soviet plans could violate the interpretation of the ABM Treaty that the USSR has recently proposed in order to constrain the SDI. Nitze cited in Robert C. Toth, "Soviet Beam Devices to Aim at Mars Moon," *Los Angeles Times*, April 2, 1987, pt. 1, p. 28.

81. Natalin, "Protivopravnost," p. 115.

82. Nitze and Sofaer, *The ABM Treaty and the SDI Program*, pp. 1–3.

83. Paul Nitze, *SDI and the ABM Treaty*, Current Policy no. 711 (Washington, D.C.: Bureau of Public Affairs, U.S. Department of State, May 30, 1985), p. 3.

84. Akhromeyev, *Pravda*, October 19, 1985.

85. For background, see David S. Yost, "European-American Relations and NATO's Initial Missile Deployments," *Current History*, 83 (April 1984). Belgium decided to accept its share of ground-launched cruise missiles in March 1985, followed by the Netherlands in November 1985.

86. L. Semeyko, "Illusory Expectations," *Krasnaya zvezda* (Red star), November 3, 1984, in *FBIS-SU*, November 8, 1984, p. AA5.

87. Gennadiy Shishkin, "The Command of the Times," *Selskaya zhizn* (Rural life), March 2, 1985, in *FBIS-SU*, March 5, 1985, p. AA3.

88. The full text is reproduced in *New York Times*, January 9, 1985, p. A11.

89. For details, see Michael R. Gordon, " 'Star Wars' Debate," *New York Times*, July 3, 1986, p. A8, and Serge Schmemann, "Gorbachev Says West Fails to Reply on Arms," *New York Times*, July 16, 1986, p. 8.

90. Michael R. Gordon, "Gorbachev Yields on '72 ABM Treaty, U.S. Officials Say," *New York Times*, September 25, 1986, pp. A1, A6.

91. President Reagan described the letter of July 25, 1986, in his speech to the United Nations, *Prospects for World Peace*, Current Policy no. 867 (Washington, D.C., Bureau of Public Affairs, U.S. Department of State, September 22, 1986), pp. 1–2.
92. Deputy Foreign Minister Vladimir Petrovsky cited in John M. Goshko, "Soviet 'Disappointed' at Reagan Speech," *Washington Post*, September 23, 1986, p. A17.
93. Tass commentator Vladimir Chernyshev cited in Walter Pincus and Don Oberdorfer, "Principal U.S. Arms Negotiator Warns against 'Great Expectations,' " *Washington Post*, August 8, 1986, p. A26.
94. Foreign Ministry spokesman Gennadi Gerasimov cited in Celestine Bohlen, "Arms Talks Expected to Continue in U.S.," *Washington Post*, August 13, 1986, p. A19.
95. The initial and revised U.S. proposals were made public by the State Department and published in *New York Times*, October 18, 1986, p. 5.
96. Excerpts from George P. Shultz news conference in Reykjavik, in *New York Times*, October 13, 1986, p. A8.
97. For the full text of Gorbachev's proposal at Reykjavik, see Don Oberdorfer, "At Reykjavik, Soviets Were Prepared and U.S. Improvised," *Washington Post*, February 16, 1987, pp. A1, A28. This article offers an unusually detailed account of the events at the summit.
98. David Hoffman, "Iceland Talks: One Word Chills Hope," *Washington Post*, October 19, 1986, pp. A1, A42.
99. Mikhail Gorbachev, "Excerpts from Gorbachev Speech on the Reykjavik Talks and 'Star Wars,' " *New York Times*, October 23, 1986, p. A12.
100. See the text in Oberdorfer, "At Reykjavik," p. A28.
101. The 1991 expiration date was proposed in President Reagan's letter to General Secretary Gorbachev on July 25, 1986. The 1994 date was proposed by Secretary of State Shultz after his visit to Moscow in April 1987. The 1996 date was proposed by the president at the October 1986 Reykjavik summit. (According to the July 1986 U.S. proposal, after the termination of the nonwithdrawal period at the end of 1991, either side wishing to deploy BMD would be obliged to present a plan for sharing the benefits of strategic defense and eliminating ballistic missiles. Such plans would be subject to negotiation for two years. If no agreement could be reached during these two years, either side would be free to deploy BMD beyond ABM Treaty limits after giving six months' notice. The July 1986 proposal would have therefore in practice delayed large-scale BMD deployments for seven and a half years, until mid-1994.)
102. Joint statement by Ronald Reagan and Mikhail Gorbachev, December 10, 1987, in *Weekly Compilation of Presidential Documents*, 23 (December 14, 1987), pp. 1495–6.
103. A. Kokoshin, "Space and Security," *Pravda*, January 29, 1985, in *FBIS-SU*, January 30, 1985, p. AA14.
104. Marshal Sergei Sokolov, interview with Tass, May 4, 1985, in *FBIS-SU*, May 6, 1985, p. AA3.

105. Nitze, *The Impact of SDI on U.S.-Soviet Relations*, p. 2.
106. Nitze, *The Soviet Arms Control Counterproposal*, Current Policy no. 830 (Washington, D.C.: Bureau of Public Affairs, U.S. Department of State, April 29, 1986), p. 2.
107. Paul H. Nitze, *SDI: The Soviet Program*, Current Policy no. 717 (Washington, D.C.: Bureau of Public Affairs, U.S. Department of State, June 28, 1985), pp. 3–4.
108. Gorbachev interview in *Time*, September 9, 1985, p. 28.
109. Akhromeyev, *Pravda*, October 19, 1985.
110. John Tagliabue, "U.S. Aide Says Soviet Stance on 'Star Wars' Hasn't Shifted," *New York Times*, January 25, 1986, p. 5.
111. Paul Nitze, in *A Discussion on U.S.-Soviet Relations*, Current Policy no. 865 (Washington, D.C.: Bureau of Public Affairs, U.S. Department of State, June 16, 1986), p. 3, and Nitze, "Examining Restricted and Prohibited Activities under the ABM Treaty," remarks to the International Law Weekend group, New York, October 31, 1986, text furnished by ACDA, p. 2.
112. Paul Nitze, *The Promise of SDI*, Current Policy no. 810 (Washington, D.C.: Bureau of Public Affairs, U.S. Department of State, March 18, 1986), p. 2.
113. Chervov cited in Karen DeYoung, "Soviet General Cites 'Compromise' on SDI," *Washington Post*, July 8, 1986, p. A9.
114. Valentin Falin cited in Tatu, "Les ambiguités de l'après-Reykjavik," *Le Monde*, November 6, 1986, pp. 1, 3.
115. Gorbachev press conference at Reykjavik, October 12, 1986, excerpts in *Washington Post*, October 13, 1986, p. A28.
116. Gorbachev, "Excerpts from Speech," *New York Times*, October 15, 1986.
117. Anonymous Soviet officials cited in Michael R. Gordon, "U.S. to Send Top Team to Vienna Talks," *New York Times*, November 1, 1986, p. 4.
118. Deputy Foreign Minister Aleksander Bessmertnykh, cited in Gary Lee, "Soviets Cite Reagan on A-Arm Ban," *Washington Post*, October 26, 1986, pp. A1, A36.
119. Sagdeyev cited in Walter Pincus, " 'Modest' SDI Testing Called Compatible with ABM Pact," *Washington Post*, October 30, 1986, p. A4.
120. Shevardnadze cited in Philip Taubman, "Shevardnadze Specifies Limit on 'Star Wars' Test," *New York Times*, November 11, 1986, p. A8.
121. "Text of Soviet Proposal on How to Proceed in Arms Talks," *New York Times*, November 7, 1986, p. A11.
122. Michael R. Gordon, "U.S. Says Moscow May Be Flexible over 'Star Wars,' " *New York Times*, October 19, 1986, pp. 1, 12.
123. Secretary of State George Shultz, *Reykjavik: A Watershed in U.S.-Soviet Relations*, Current Policy no. 883 (Washington, D.C.: Bureau of Public Affairs, U.S. Department of State, October 31, 1986), p. 2.
124. Nitze, "Examining Restricted and Prohibited Activities," pp. 2, 9.
125. According to Nitze (ibid., p. 6), "the Treaty permits tests that are not in an ABM mode (e.g., against satellites) of experimental devices that do not have an ABM capability . . . an interceptor missile is considered to be 'tested in an ABM mode' if it has attempted to intercept a strategic ballistic missile or

its elements in flight trajectory . . . In practice, neither the U.S. nor the Soviet Union considers 'flight trajectory' to include an orbit in space, or 'tested in an ABM mode' to encompass tests against targets in space that do not follow a ballistic missile flight trajectory. The Soviet Union conducted tests against objects in earth orbit in the 1970s both prior to and after deploying their anti-satellite weapon (ASAT)."

126. Nitze, "Examining Restricted and Prohibited Activities," p. 10.

127. George P. Shultz, "Excerpts from Speech by Shultz in Vienna," *New York Times*, November 6, 1986, p. A16.

128. Anonymous Soviet negotiators, cited in Michael R. Gordon, " 'Star Wars' Semantics," *New York Times*, October 21, 1986, pp. A1, A12.

129. Karpov cited in Walter Pincus and David B. Ottaway, "Shultz Calls Soviet Statements since Summit 'Encouraging,' " *Washington Post*, October 18, 1986, p. A16.

130. R. Jeffrey Smith, "Soviets Offer Detailed Plan to Bar Space Arms Tests," *Washington Post*, July 30, 1987, p. A26; and Michael R. Gordon, "U.S. Spurns Talks on 'Star Wars,' " *New York Times*, October 17, 1987, pp. 1, 5; Philip Taubman, "Soviet Indicates It Might Accept 'Star Wars' Test," *New York Times*, February 26, 1988, p. 1; Michael R. Gordon, "Reversal on 'Star Wars,' " *New York Times*, March 25, 1988, pp. 1, 5.

131. Paul H. Nitze, *Negotiations on Nuclear and Space Arms*, Current Policy no. 807 (Washington, D.C.: Bureau of Public Affairs, U.S. Department of State, March 13, 1986), p. 2.

132. The concept was first outlined publicly by the then deputy secretary of state, Kenneth Dam, in New York on January 14, 1985. The best-known presentation, cited in the Introduction, is Paul Nitze, *On The Road to a More Stable Peace*, Current Policy no. 657 (Washington, D.C.: Bureau of Public Affairs, U.S. Department of State, February 20, 1985), p. 1. Fred Iklé, the under secretary of defense for policy, noted that "it's hard to talk to the Soviets about something we ourselves haven't thought through completely. We could discuss the transition only in the broadest terms." Iklé cited in *New York Times*, December 15, 1985.

133. Nitze, *Impact of SDI on U.S.-Soviet Relations*, p. 3.

134. Gorbachev, interview in *Time*, September 9, 1985, p. 24.

135. Akhromeyev, *Pravda*. October 19. 1985.

136. Sokolov, interview with Tass, May 4, 1985, p. AA4 of *FBIS* translation.

137. *Defense against Ballistic Missiles: An Assessment of Technologies and Policy Implications* (Washington, D.C.: Department of Defense, April 1984), p. 6.

138. G. A. Trofimenko, "Defense in Reverse," *Komsomol'skaya Pravda*, February 16, 1985, in *FBIS-SU*, February 20, 1985, p. AA4.

139. Gorbachev, "Excerpts from Speech," *New York Times*, October 15, 1986.

140. Sokolov, interview with Tass, May 4, 1985, p. AA3 of *FBIS* translation.

141. For a recent popular exposition of the view that Western security policies should be changed in fundamental ways, see Mikhail Gorbachev, *Perestroika: New Thinking for Our Country and the World* (New York: Harper and Row, 1987), pp. 210–254.

142. Georgi Arbatov on Moscow television, August 10, 1983, *FBIS-SU*, August 12, 1983, cited in John Van Oudenaren, *Interviews by Soviet Officials in the Western Media: Two Case Studies*, R-3328-FF/RC (Santa Monica, Calif.: Rand Corporation, October 1985), p. 52n. See also David Holloway, *The Soviet Union and the Arms Race* (New Haven: Yale University Press, 1983), pp. 33–35.

143. Mikhail Gorbachev, "The Soviet People's Immortal Exploit," report broadcast on Moscow television, May 8, 1985, in *FBIS-SU*, daily report, May 9, 1985, p. R16.

144. Arbatov interview in *La Repubblica*, January 24, 1984, cited in Van Oudenaren, *Interviews by Soviet Officials*, p. 52n.

145. V. V. Zagladin, "The Soviet Concept of Security," in *Policies for Common Security* (London: Taylor and Francis for the Stockholm International Peace Research Institute, 1985), pp. 66–67.

146. V. V. Zagladin, ed., *Mirovoye Kommunisticheskoye Dvizheniye* (The world Communist movement) (Moscow: Izdatelstvo politicheskoy literatury, 1982). Zagladin's own chapters (2 and 5) concern "the world revolutionary process" and means of carrying out "the socialist revolution."

147. Van Oudenaren, *Interviews by Soviet Officials*, p. 52.

148. A. S. Milovidov and Ye. A. Zhdanov, "Sotzialno-filosofskye problemi voini i mira" (Social-philosophical problems of war and peace), *Voprosy Filosofii* (Questions of philosophy), no. 10, (1980), 32–51.

149. Gorbachev, "The Soviet People's Immortal Exploit," p. R17 of *FBIS* translation.

150. Gorbachev, address to the Supreme Soviet, November 27, 1985, p. R23 of *FBIS* translation.

151. Some parallels may be drawn with the Soviet approach to NATO's decisions for modernization and arms control for intermediate-range nuclear forces (INF). During the 1981–1983 negotiations, the Soviets refused to accept any agreement that would permit deployments of U.S. ground-launched cruise missiles or Pershing II ballistic missiles, even though such an agreement could have dramatically reduced NATO's INF deployments in Europe. The Soviets appeared to prefer to campaign against the INF program vis-à-vis Western public opinion, particularly in West Germany, in the hope of preventing any NATO INF deployments without having to accept an arms control accord limiting Soviet INF. An agreement allowing some NATO INF deployments would have "legitimized" them by implying Soviet acceptance; this would have facilitated NATO INF deployments politically while undermining the Soviet public diplomacy campaign against them. For background, see David S. Yost, "The Soviet Campaign against INF in West Germany," in *Soviet Strategic Deception*, ed. Brian Dailey and Patrick Parker (Lexington, Mass.: D. C. Heath/Lexington Books, 1987), pp. 343–374.

152. Jerome H. Kahan, *Security in the Nuclear Age: Developing U.S. Strategic Arms Policy* (Washington, D.C.: Brookings Institution, 1975), p. 120. An example of various formulations of this plan may be found in the address by Soviet Foreign Minister Andrei Gromyko to the U.N. General Assembly, Septem-

ber 21, 1962, in U.S. Arms Control and Disarmament Agency, *Documents on Disarmament 1962*, vol. 2, July–December (Washington, D.C.: Government Printing Office, 1963), pp. 904–905.

153. A case for such a possible long-term change in Soviet policy is made by Keith Payne in *Strategic Defense: "Star Wars" in Perspective* (Lanham, Md.: Hamilton Press, 1986), pp. 156–159, 173–176.

154. Office of Technology Assessment, *Ballistic Missile Defense Technologies*, p. 34.

155. Nitze, *Impact of SDI on U.S.-Soviet Relations*, p. 3.

156. Sokolov, interview with Tass, May 4, 1985, p. AA5 of *FBIS* translation.

157. Although the Soviets enjoy certain geographical advantages (above all, in relation to the United States, fewer coastal targets vulnerable to sea-based firepower projection), the Soviet target set is more defensible mainly as a result of costly exertion. The Soviets have made their military assets—the most likely targets of attack—more defensible through investments over decades in hardening, mobility, deceptive basing, and so forth. These investments in passive defenses would facilitate an active BMD defense—"leakage" would be more tolerable, preferential defense tactics would be more effective, and so forth.

158. "Text of Soviet Proposal," *New York Times*, November 7, 1986, p. A11.

159. François Gorand, "Piège pour le high tech militaire," *Le Figaro*, January 31–February 1, 1987, p. 22.

160. Philip Taubman, "Soviet, in Switch, Will Seek Summit, Officials Report," *New York Times*, October 28, 1987, pp. 1, 6.

161. Karpov cited in Lionel Barber, "NATO Seeks United Response to Soviet Arms Cut Proposals," *Financial Times*, April 21, 1987, p. 1.

162. For background, see David S. Yost, "Beyond MBFR: The Atlantic to the Urals Gambit," *Orbis*, 31 (Spring 1987), 99–134; and Yost, "Soviet Aims in Europe," *Society*, 24 (July/August 1987), 72–79.

163. This is an impressionistic judgment based on reading a large quantity of the Soviet commentary. It has not been tested with formal content analysis methodology. For a more detailed survey, see U.S. Arms Control and Disarmament Agency, *The Soviet Propaganda Campaign against the U.S. Strategic Defense Initiative*, ACDA Publication 122 (Washington, D.C.: ACDA, August 1986). Alexander Alexiev of the Rand Corporation will soon publish a systematic analysis of Soviet commentary on the SDI, tentatively titled *The Soviet Political Campaign against SDI*.

164. "The Soviet Union has not and is not conducting any research or experimental and design work that would not fit within the framework of the ABM Treaty. It is not creating attack space weapons." Editorial in *Pravda*, May 27, 1985, in *FBIS-SU*, May 28, 1985, p. AA3.

165. "Nobel prize winning Soviet physicist Nikolay Basov said today that Moscow would have no technological difficulty in matching the U.S. 'star wars' program . . . He said the Soviet Union had not begun development of space weapons but would have 'no scientific problems in developing lasers capable of intercepting missiles in space.' " Agence France-Presse dispatch in *FBIS-SU*, January 29, 1985, p. AA7.

166. "There is absolutely no need to double or treble the number of strategic delivery vehicles of the present type to make the 'strategic shield' lose credibility. Scientists calculate that this would be achieved at a fraction of the expenditure, using heat shields, making missiles rotate, coating them with wave- and light-absorbing materials and so forth." Valentin Falin, "Fact and Fancy," *Izvestia*, April 10, 1985, in *FBIS-SU*, April 15, 1985, p. AA4.

167. This may explain why a Soviet spokesman in November 1985 admitted for the first time that the Soviet Union conducts "experiments and tests" with lasers against orbiting satellites, but maintained that the purpose of these tests is "to locate and detect [satellites] orbiting in our direction." General Nikolay Chervov denied, however, that these tests could be seen as violations of the ABM Treaty or in any way relevant to the development of "space strike weapons." Chervov cited in *Los Angeles Times*, November 18, 1985, p. 5. Similarly, Gennadi Gerasimov has dismissed as "pure invention" U.S. reports of Soviet tests of laser space weapons at Sary Shagan. Gerasimov cited in Serge Schmemann, "Soviet Trying to Explain Arms Linkage Issue," *New York Times*, October 17, 1986, p. A8.

168. "Space-Based Defenses: A Soviet Study" (excerpts), *Survival*, 27 (March/April 1985), 87.

169. *The Military Balance, 1986–1987* (London: International Institute for Strategic Studies, 1986), p. 222.

170. "But it is not difficult to imagine something a little more complex. Rocket bases on the moon, for example. Our natural satellite is a 3-day flight away. If the Americans, sheltering behind a space umbrella, decided to use their first-strike weapons—naturally, as a deterrent—3 days later they would be visited by gifts from the moon." Valentin Falin, "Problems and Judgments: Space—The Moment of Truth," *Izvestia*, December 14, 1984, in *FBIS-SU*, December 18, 1984, p. AA3.

171. Falin, ibid., p. AA4.

172. The official duties of several of the signatories of the "Soviet Scientists Appeal to All Scientists of the World" (*New York Times*, April 22, 1983, p. A10) are discussed in Department of Defense and Department of State, *Soviet Strategic Defense Programs* (Washington, D.C.: Government Printing Office, October 1985), p. 22.

173. President Reagan, *Report on Reykjavik*, Current Policy no. 875 (Washington, D.C.: Bureau of Public Affairs, Department of State, October 13, 1986), p. 3.

174. Gorbachev, "Excerpts from Gorbachev Speech," *New York Times*, October 23, 1986, p. A12.

175. Mikhail Gorbachev, "Gorbachev Interview: The Arms Agreement, Nicaragua and Human Rights," *New York Times*, December 1, 1987, p. 6. This is the text of Gorbachev's interview on NBC news on November 30, 1987.

176. Shevardnadze cited in Norman Kempster, "Shevardnadze Proposes a World 'Star Peace' Program," *Los Angeles Times*, September 25, 1985, p. 9.

177. "At the time Kosygin made his remark, there was neither strategic parity

nor the principle of mutually guaranteed destruction. There was no missile defense system or any agreement on the limitation of strategic arms. Things are quite different today." Aleksey Arbatov, interview in *Der Spiegel*, March 11, 1985, in *FBIS-SU*, March 14, 1985, p. AA8. As noted in Chapter 2, Raymond Garthoff has determined that the famous statements by Kosygin were in fact incorrectly reported, even in the Soviet press. But the Soviets usually describe the Kosygin statements (and similar statements of that era) as simply outdated.

178. Gorbachev interview in *Time*, September 9, 1985, p. 24. The Reagan administration proposed a sum of $26 billion for the period 1985–1989, and congressional appropriations have fallen substantially short of that.

179. Shevardnadze speech at the United Nations, September 23, 1986, excerpts in *New York Times*, September 24, 1986, p. A10. Even if one assumed that the administration had such plans, political and budgetary factors could obviously invalidate a specific timetable for deployment.

180. Vladimir Chernyshev in Tass dispatch, March 15, 1985, in *FBIS-SU*, March 18, 1985, p. AA3.

181. Boris Raushenbakh in Tass dispatch, February 1, 1985, in *FBIS-SU*, February 1, 1985, p. AA8.

182. *Izvestia* editorial of January 25, 1985, in *FBIS-SU*, January 25, 1985, p. AA3.

183. Gorbachev, "Excerpts from Speech," *New York Times*, October 15, 1986, p. A12.

184. Ibid.

185. Tass broadcast of December 26, 1984, in *FBIS-SU*, December 27, 1984, p. G9.

186. Gorbachev cited in William Drozdiak, "Moscow Warns Bonn on SDI," *Washington Post*, November 14, 1985, p. 33.

187. For background, see David S. Yost, "Western Europe and the U.S. Strategic Defense Initiative," *Journal of International Affairs*, 41, no. 2, Summer 1988.

188. French observers—official and unofficial—have outlined particularly incisive critical analyses of these features of U.S. SDI rhetoric. For examples, see Georges-Eric Touchard, "Désinformation et initiative de défense stratégique," *Défense Nationale*, May 1987, pp. 27–41; N. Pidec, "Est-Ouest: qui change quoi?" *Politique Etrangère*, Autumn 1987, pp. 671–681.

5. Alliance Reactions: Arms Control and Deterrence

1. K.-Peter Stratmann, *Aspekte der Sicherheitspolitischen und Militärstrategischen Entwicklung in den 90er Jahren*, SWP-AP 2474 (Ebenhausen, West Germany: Stiftung Wissenschaft und Politik, June 1986), p. 28.

2. Stephen F. Szabo, "European Opinion after the Missiles," *Survival*, 27 (November/December 1985), 269–270.

3. *The President's Strategic Defense Initiative* (Washington, D.C.: Government Printing Office, January 1985), p. 4.

4. U.S. Congress, Office of Technology Assessment, *Ballistic Missile Defense*

Technologies, OTA-ISC-254 (Washington, D.C.: U.S. Government Printing Office, September 1985), p. 242n.

5. Pierre Hassner, "L'Europe entre les Etats-Unis et l'Union soviétique," *Commentaire*, 33 (Spring 1986), 10.

6. Reagan interview with foreign broadcasters, November 12, 1985, in *Weekly Compilation of Presidential Documents*, 21 (November 18, 1985), 1387.

7. Office of Technology Assessment, *Ballistic Missile Defense Technologies*, p. 243. See Chapter 1 for details.

8. Altenburg interview in *Der Spiegel*, February 10, 1986, p. 68.

9. Lieutenant General William Odom, "The Implications of Active Defense of NATO for Soviet Military Strategy," in *Swords and Shields: NATO, the USSR, and New Choices for Long-Range Offense and Defense*, ed. Fred S. Hoffman, Albert Wohlstetter, and David S. Yost (Lexington, Mass.: D. C. Heath/Lexington Books, 1987), p. 173.

10. Commission d'Etudes sur les Armes Spatiales, *Rapport de synthèse présenté au ministre de la défense*, January 30, 1986, p. 6.

11. The set of articles was published in *Der Spiegel*, November 25, 1985, pp. 138–159; the editorial comment about *Pravda* appeared in *Der Spiegel*, December 16, 1985, p. 3.

12. Michel Tatu, "L'initiative de défense stratégique ou la 'guerre des étoiles,' " *1986 Universalis* (Paris: Encyclopaedia Universalis France, 1986), p. 135.

13. Nicholas L. Johnson, *Soviet Military Strategy in Space* (London: Jane's, 1987), p. 188. See Chapter 2 for further details about Chervov's May 1985 statement.

14. Roald Sagdayev, *Frankfurter Rundschau*, December 5, 1985, p. 8, cited in ibid.

15. Kohl speech at the Wehrkunde meeting in Munich, cited in DPA despatch, February 8, 1985, in *Foreign Broadcast Information Service—Western Europe* (hereafter, *FBIS-WE*), daily report, February 8, 1985, p. J1.

16. Younger in Great Britain, Parliament, *Parliamentary Debates* (House of Commons), February 19, 1986, col. 340.

17. Howe, "Defense, Deterrence and Arms Control," speech to the Foreign Press Association, London, March 17, 1986, in *Arms Control and Disarmament*, 1, (April 1986), 6–7, a publication of the Foreign and Commonwealth Office.

18. For a detailed discussion, see David S. Yost, "The Reykjavik Summit and European Security," *SAIS Review*, 7 (Summer/Fall 1987), 1–22.

19. See e.g. Pierre Lellouche, " 'Double zéro,' double péril," *Le Monde*, October 1, 1987, pp. 1, 6; Jean Villars, "Un parapluie en dentelle," *Politique Internationale*, no. 37 (Autumn 1987), pp. 123–133. Villars is the pseudonym of an official of the French Foreign Ministry.

20. Bernard Gwertzman, "Thatcher Reports Reagan Agreement on A-Arms Issues," *New York Times*, November 16, 1986, pp. 1, 17.

21. Younger cited in Steven Erlanger, "British Defense Chief Criticizes Elements of US Arms Stance," *Boston Globe*, October 29, 1986, p. 11.

22. Shultz cited in Bernard Gwertzman, "Shultz Details Reagan's Arms Bid at

Iceland to Clarify U.S. Position," *New York Times*, October 18, 1986, pp. 1, 5.

23. Address by Chancellor Kohl to the Bundestag, November 6, 1986, in *Statements and Speeches*, 9, no. 19 (November 7, 1986), 4, issued by the German Information Center, New York.

24. Shultz interview with the *Washington Post*, October 15, 1986, p. A24.

25. Shevardnadze address in Vienna on November 5, 1986, excerpts in *New York Times*, November 6, 1986, p. A16.

26. Mikhail Gorbachev, "Excerpts from Gorbachev Speech on the Reykjavik Talks and 'Star Wars,'" *New York Times*, October 23, 1986, p. A12.

27. Howe, "Defense, Deterrence and Arms Control," p. 7.

28. For examples, see the views of British Prime Minister Margaret Thatcher, reported in David Fairhall and Michael White, "Thatcher Gets US Reassurance on Star Wars," *Guardian*, February 26, 1987, and Belgian Foreign Minister Leo Tindemans, reported in Stewart Fleming, "Europeans Fear Acceleration of SDI Deployment," *Financial Times*, February 7, 1987.

29. Shirley Williams, "To Allies Who Yearn for an Agreement," *Washington Post*, October 24, 1986, p. A27.

30. Kohl cited in David B. Ottaway, "Kohl Points to Soviet Superiority in Conventional Forces," *Washington Post*, October 23, 1986, p. A36. In November 1987, the Reagan administration and congressional leaders agreed that all SDI testing in the 1988 fiscal year would conform to the restrictive interpretation of the ABM Treaty. Michael R. Gordon, "A Compromise on Arms Reached in Washington," *New York Times*, November 8, 1987, p. 10.

31. *The President's Unclassified Report to the Congress on Soviet Noncompliance with Arms Control Agreements* (White House, Office of the Press Secretary, February 1, 1985), pp. 1, 7–9.

32. Para. 8 of the Communiqué of the NATO Nuclear Planning Group, October 22, 1986.

33. *Statement on the Defense Estimates 1986*, Cmnd. 9763-I (London: Her Majesty's Stationery Office, 1986), p. 11.

34. The French conditions for agreeing to negotiate about limitations on French nuclear forces include substantial reductions in U.S. and Soviet nuclear arsenals; comprehensive limitations on BMD, ASAT, and antisubmarine warfare capabilities; significant reductions in the conventional-force imbalance in Europe; and the elimination of all chemical and biological weapons. For details, see David S. Yost, *France's Deterrent Posture and Security in Europe, Part II: Strategic and Arms Control Implications*, Adelphi Paper no. 195 (London: International Institute for Strategic Studies, 1984/85), pp. 52–54.

35. Jean-Bernard Raimond, the French foreign minister, cited in *Le Monde*, October 17, 1986, p. 4.

36. Paul H. Nitze, *The Nuclear and Space Arms Talks: Where We Are after the Summit*, Current Policy no. 770 (Washington, D.C.: Bureau of Public Affairs, Department of State, December 5, 1985), p. 3.

37. Fred Iklé, under secretary of defense for policy, has suggested that the

sequence of events outlined in the Nitze "strategic concept" of February 1985 (including the idea of radical offensive-force reductions preceding the transition to defense dominance) need not necessarily constrict U.S. decisions: "The more the offensive armaments can be reduced by agreement, the easier and cheaper the job of providing effective defenses. Yet, to be realistic about Soviet motivations, we must seek to develop and deploy systems that can provide effective defenses even without such reductions." Iklé, "Nuclear Strategy: Can There Be a Happy Ending?" *Foreign Affairs*, 63 (Spring 1985), 825.

38. *The Strategic Defense Initiative*, Special Report no. 129 (Washington, D.C.: Bureau of Public Affairs, Department of State, June 1985), p. 3.

39. Statement by Horst Teltschik at the Thirteenth German-American Conference jointly sponsored by the Atlantik Brücke and the American Council on Germany, Dallas, March 29, 1985, *Statements and Speeches*, 7, no. 9 (April 1, 1985), 5, issued by the German Information Center, New York.

40. West German government spokesman Friedhelm Ost in DPA despatch, October 14, 1985, in *FBIS-WE*, daily report, October 15, 1985, p. J2.

41. Healey in *Parliamentary Debates*, February 19, 1986, col. 330.

42. Caspar Weinberger, *Department of Defense Annual Report for Fiscal Year 1987* (Washington, D.C.: Government Printing Office, 1986), p. 292. See also the statement by Richard Burt in Don Oberdorfer, "ABM Pact Can't Be Used against SDI, Burt Says," *Washington Post*, March 7, 1985, p. 16, and Department of Defense and Department of State, *Soviet Strategic Defense Programs* (Washington, D.C.: Government Printing Office, October 1985), p. 23.

43. Paul Nitze, *U.S. Strategic Force Structures: The Challenge Ahead*, Current Policy no. 794 (Washington, D.C.: Bureau of Public Affairs, U.S. Department of State, February 4, 1986), p. 2.

44. Elizabeth Pond, "The Security Debate in West Germany," *Survival*, 28 (July/August, 1986), p. 334.

45. Inaugural address of January 20, 1977, in Jimmy Carter, *Keeping Faith: Memoirs of a President* (New York: Bantam Books, 1982), p. 20. Denuclearization goals have, of course, been expressed by U.S. presidents since President Truman. West European criticisms center on the style and content of U.S. proposals since the late 1970s and their impact on public perceptions of the Western alliance's nuclear deterrence policies.

46. Stratmann, *Aspekte der Sicherheitspolitischen*, pp. 4–5.

47. Jean-Bernard Raimond cited in *Le Monde*, November 6, 1986, p. 3.

48. Haig testimony in U.S. Senate, Committee on Foreign Relations, *The SALT II Treaty*, hearings, 96th Cong., 1st sess. (Washington, D.C.: Government Printing Office, 1979), pt. 3, p. 298.

49. Stratmann, *Aspekte der Sicherheitspolitischen*, p. 29.

50. Senator Nunn once proposed that the INF treaty might include a "supreme national interest clause" that would permit the United States not to withdraw 20 to 25 percent of its INF missiles until satisfied with the chemical and conventional force balance in Europe. Don Irwin, "Soviets

Urged to Cut Non-Nuclear Arms," *Los Angeles Times*, March 9, 1987, p. 15.

51. Formulating such a package would be quite difficult, owing in part to differences in interests and assessments in the Western alliance and the disjointed nature of the policy-making process in a coalition of democracies. It might be noted, however, that congressmen such as Senators John Warner and Sam Nunn have sponsored legislation in support of national strategic planning efforts. The Reagan administration has published two documents titled *National Security Strategy of the United States* (Washington, D.C.: White House, January 1987 and January 1988), with brief sections on arms control.

52. Sayre Stevens, "Ballistic Missile Defense in the Soviet Union," *Current History*, 84 (October 1985), 316.

53. Office of Technology Assessment, *Ballistic Missile Defense Technologies*, p. 61.

54. Paul Nitze, *SDI: The Soviet Program*, Current Policy no. 717 (Washington D.C.: Bureau of Public Affairs, U.S. Department of State, June 28, 1985), p. 3.

55. Albert Wohlstetter and Richard Brody, "Continuing Control as a Requirement for Deterring," in *Managing Nuclear Operations*, ed. Ashton B. Carter, John D. Steinbruner, and Charles A. Zraket (Washington, D.C.: Brookings Institution, 1987), p. 184.

56. For background on this point, see Gerard Smith, *Doubletalk: The Story of the First Strategic Arms Limitation Talks* (New York: Doubleday, 1980), pp. 91–93.

57. Office of Technology Assessment, *Ballistic Missile Defense Technologies*, p. 270.

58. Strategic missiles are, of course, directly relevant to West European security in that Soviet ICBMs and SLBMs could be aimed at targets in Europe. It appears that no proposals for ATBM systems capable of intercepting strategic missiles have been made in NATO. The December 1987 INF treaty implies, however, that the USSR may place more emphasis on ICBMs (perhaps with improved accuracy and advanced warhead designs) and other long-range strike systems to substitute for SS-20s (and other missiles to be eliminated by the treaty) in holding targets in Western Europe at risk.

59. Manfred Wörner, "German Minister Discusses NATO's Defense Options," *Aviation Week and Space Technology*, November 17, 1986, p. 79. Wörner's interpretation is not, of course, universally endorsed. A recent British study summarizes the main reasons why ATBM should be regarded as permissible with respect to the ABM Treaty, but concludes as follows: "Notwithstanding these factors, it must be said that Europeans in general, and the UK in particular, set great store by the provisions of the ABM Treaty and there would be great reluctance to undermine it. While it would be difficult to imagine that a full exo-atmospheric ATBM system deployed in Europe would not do so, it might be possible to conceive of some form of endo-atmospheric system that would conform both with the letter and spirit of this Treaty." Wing Commander Graham Cullington, "Anti-tactical Ballistic Missile Defence: The Debate Reborn," *RUSI Journal*, 132 (June 1987), 28.

60. For a discussion of this issue, see Harald Müller, *Strategic Defenses: The End of the Alliance Strategy?* CEPS Paper no. 32 (Brussels: Center for European Policy Studies, 1987), pp. 34–35. Müller argues that "a total ban would not be in the West's interest," and that devising a useful accord would depend in part on clear definitions of systems, plus sufficient intelligence on Soviet capabilities.
61. Office of Technology Assessment, *Ballistic Missile Defense Technologies*, p. 258.
62. *Report of the President's Commission on Strategic Forces*, April 1983, p. 12.
63. Another controversial idea is developing depressed-trajectory SLBMs to be able to attack Soviet LPARs by passing beneath their radar coverage. Michael M. May and John R. Harvey note that a depressed-trajectory capability to threaten LPARs might "help to deter Soviet ABM Treaty breakout." But pursuing such a capability would contradict arms control objectives such as not decreasing SLBM attack warning time and not making attack characterization more difficult. See May and Harvey, "Nuclear Operations and Arms Control," in *Managing Nuclear Operations*, ed. Carter, Steinbruner, and Zraket, pp. 720–722.
64. Howe, "Defense, Deterrence and Arms Control," p. 7. The "balance of prudence" phrase derives from Schelling, *Arms and Influence* (New Haven: Yale University Press, 1966), p. 259; Schelling advances the highway metaphor in "What Went Wrong with Arms Control?" *Foreign Affairs*, 64 (Winter 1985/86), 233.
65. Arnold Kanter, "Thinking about the Strategic Defense Initiative: An Alliance Perspective," *International Affairs*, 61 (Summer 1985), p. 458.
66. Phil Williams, "Meeting Alliance and National Needs," in *The Future of British Defense Policy*, ed. John Roper (Aldershot, England: Gower, 1985), p. 20.
67. For details, see David S. Yost, *France's Deterrent Posture and Security in Europe, Part I: Capabilities and Doctrine*, Adelphi Paper no. 194 (London: International Institute for Strategic Studies, 1984/85), pp. 66, 68.
68. "Declaration on Atlantic Relations Approved by the North Atlantic Council," June 19, 1974, para. 6.
69. Robert W. Komer, "Maritime Strategy vs. Coalition Defense," *Foreign Affairs*, 60 (Summer 1982), p. 1126.
70. General Bernard Rogers has repeatedly pointed out in recent years that, although the conventional capabilities of the Western alliance have steadily improved, "the gap between the conventional force capabilities of NATO and those of the Warsaw Pact gets wider each year." See Rogers, "The Atlantic Alliance: Prescriptions for a Difficult Decade," *Foreign Affairs*, 60 (Summer 1982), 1151. For a detailed analysis, see Phillip A. Karber, "To Lose an Arms Race: The Competition in Conventional Forces Deployed in Central Europe, 1965–1980," in *The Soviet Asset: Military Power in the Competition over Europe*, ed. Uwe Nerlich, vol. 1 of *Soviet Power and Western Negotiating Policies* (Cambridge, Mass.: Ballinger, 1983). For more recent discussions of the problems in assessing conventional force balance trends and the complex implications of these trends for conventional arms control,

see the essays in the annual *Military Balance* of the International Institute for Strategic Studies (particularly the issues published in 1986 and 1987); the interviews with Phillip A. Karber in *Armed Forces Journal International*, May and June 1987; and James A. Thomson and Nanette C. Gantz, *Conventional Arms Control Revisited: Objectives in the New Phase*, R-2697-AF (Santa Monica: Rand Corporation, December 1987).

71. Rogers, "NATO's Strategy: An Undervalued Currency," in *Power and Policy: Doctrine, the Alliance and Arms Control, Part I*, Adelphi Paper no. 205 (London: International Institute for Strategic Studies, 1986), p. 6.

72. See the sources cited in John G. Hines, Phillip A. Petersen, and Notra Trulock III, "Soviet Military Theory from 1945-2000: Implications for NATO," *Washington Quarterly*, 9 (Fall 1986), 134. However, judgments about long-term trends in West European public opinion regarding nuclear employment policies should be qualified, not only because of the usual caveats relating to opinion poll data, but also in view of findings which suggest that the concept of using nuclear weapons to defend West Germany has in fact been controversial since the 1950s. For a detailed analysis, see Stephen F. Szabo, "West Germany: Generations and Changing Security Perspectives," in Stephen F. Szabo, ed., *The Successor Generation: International Perspectives of Postwar Europeans* (London: Butterworths, 1983), pp. 43–75, esp. pp. 50–55.

73. Altenburg interview in *Der Spiegel*, February 10, 1986, p. 75.

74. Wörner, "A Missile Defense for NATO Europe," *Strategic Review*, 14 (Winter 1986), 16.

75. Peter Stratmann, "NATO Doctrine and National Operational Priorities: The Central Front and the Flanks, Part II," in *Power and Policy: Doctrine, the Alliance and Arms Control, Part III*, Adelphi Paper no. 207 (London: International Institute for Strategic Studies, 1986), p. 40.

76. It is widely agreed that, whatever the West's success in improving its conventional-force posture, suitable nuclear retaliatory means will remain indispensable for NATO's strategy of flexible response—for deterrence and war-prevention and for defense, if Soviet aggression cannot be countered by conventional means.

77. Kampelman cited in Charles W. Corddry, "U.S. Negotiations Hint at Easing SDI Obstacle," *Baltimore Sun*, November 5, 1986, p. 1.

78. Howe, "Defense, Deterrence, and Arms Control," p. 7.

79. Commission d'Etudes, *Rapport de synthèse*, p. 5.

80. Kohl, address to the Bundestag, November 6, 1986, pp. 2–3.

81. *Defending America: Building a New Foundation for National Strength* (Washington, D.C.: Democratic Leadership Council, September 1986), p. 15.

82. Nanette C. Brown, *The Strategic Defense Initiative and European Security: A Conference Report*, R-3366-AF (Santa Monica, Calif.: Rand Corporation, January 1986), p. 8. The conference included government officials as well as experts, and was organized by the Rand Corporation, the Stiftung Wissenschaft und Politik, the Institut Français des Relations Internationales, and the Royal Institute of International Affairs.

83. Office of Technology Assessment, *Ballistic Missile Defense Technologies*, p. 241.
84. United Kingdom, House of Commons, *Third Report from the Defence Commit-tee, Defence Commitments and Resources and the Defence Estimates 1985–1986*, vol. 1 (London: Her Majesty's Stationery Office, 1985), p. x.
85. Office of Technology Assessment, *Ballistic Missile Defense Technologies*, p. 34. Francis Pym, a former British Defense Minister, has argued that "It is even possible that their ABM system (together with their air defense programs) could give the Soviet Union a capability to break out of the ABM treaty altogether. Protecting the West against this danger is the most important argument in favor of SDI." Pym, "Containment and the Future: A Euro-pean Perspective," in John Lewis Gaddis and Terry Deibel, eds., *Contain-ment: Policy and Concept* (Washington, D.C.: National Defense University Press, 1986), vol. 2, p. 374.
86. *Report of the President's Commission on Strategic Forces*, April 1983, p. 12.
87. Commission d'Etudes, *Rapport de synthèse*, p. 5.
88. See, among other primary sources, Zbigniew Brzezinski, "A Star Wars Solution," *The New Republic*, July 8, 1985, pp. 16–18; Pete Wilson, "A Missile Defense for NATO: We Must Respond to the Challenge," *Strategic Review*, 14 (Spring 1986), 9–15; Dan Quayle, "Begin to Deploy Incremental SDI Where Possible," *Wall Street Journal*, October 2, 1986; Malcolm Wallop and Jack Kemp, "Perils of Deferring S.D.I.," *New York Times*, August 12, 1986, p. A25; Fred S. Hoffman, *Ballistic Missile Defenses and U.S. National Security: Summary Report* (Washington, D.C.: Future Security Strategy Study, October 1983), pp. 7–12; and Albert Wohlstetter, "Between an Unfree World and None: Increasing our Choices," *Foreign Affairs*, 63 (Summer 1985), 990. Secondary sources include John H. Cushman, Jr., "Conservatives Urge Quick U.S. Action on Missile Defense," *New York Times*, October 3, 1986, p. A13; Eleanor Cleft and Sara Fritz, " 'Star Wars' in Trouble in Congress, Reagan Told," *Los Angeles Times*, August 7, 1986, p. 20; and Rowland Evans and Robert Novak, "SDI: What Will Reagan Decide Now?" *Washington Post*, October 13, 1986, p. A25. The potential advantages of limited-capability BMD deployments are also noted in *Discriminate Deterrence*, the Report of the Commission on Integrated Long-Term Strategy, co-chaired by Fred C. Iklé and Albert Wohlstetter (Washington, D.C.: Government Printing Office, January 1988), pp. 37, 51–52.
89. In May 1972, Gerard Smith spoke on behalf of the U.S. government in underscoring the link between the ABM Treaty and the situation of offensive retaliatory forces: "The U.S. Delegation believes that an objective of the follow-on negotiations should be to constrain and reduce on a long-term basis threats to the survivability of our respective strategic retaliatory forces . . . If an agreement providing for more complete strategic offensive arms limitations were not achieved within five years, U.S. supreme interests could be jeopardized. Should that occur, it would constitute a basis for withdrawal from the ABM Treaty. The U.S. does not wish to see such a situation occur, nor do we believe that the USSR does." Unilateral Statement A by the U.S. delegation, in U.S. Senate, Committee

on Armed Services, *Military Implications of the Treaty on the Limitation of Anti-Ballistic Missile Systems and the Interim Agreement on Limitation of Strategic Offensive Arms*, hearings, 92nd Cong., 2nd sess. (Washington, D.C.: Government Printing Office, 1972), p. 95.

90. President Reagan, *SDI: Progress and Promise*, Current Policy no. 858 (Washington, D.C.: Bureau of Public Affairs, U.S. Department of State, August 6, 1986), p. 2.

91. Reagan interview in *U.S. News and World Report*, September 21, 1987, p. 22. Secretary of Defense Weinberger is also reported to have expressed concern that a U.S. renunciation of the ABM Treaty could accelerate Soviet BMD efforts. See Lou Cannon and Sidney Blumenthal, "Reagan SDI Talk Leaves Conservatives Uneasy," *Washington Post*, August 7, 1986, p. A30.

92. Abrahamson cited in Walter Pincus, " 'Star Wars' Chief Says Deployment, if Feasible, Would Take at Least Decade," *Washington Post*, July 24, 1986, p. A14; and Gordon Smith, deputy director of the SDI organization, cited in David E. Sanger, " 'Star Wars' Facing Cuts and Delays; '92 Goal in Doubt," *New York Times*, November 22, 1987, pp. 1, 14. In February 1988, Secretary of Defense Frank Carlucci described the possible generic components of a Phase I deployment intended to contribute, as part of a lengthy phased deployment, to ultimately "achieving the level of defense contemplated by the President's 1983 directive. "Although the Defense Acquisition Board in September 1987 recommended that some technologies "enter the demonstration and validation phase" of the acquisition process, others remained in the "concept definition" phase, and no decisions for specific BMD deployments during the Reagan administration seemed probable. Carlucci, *Department of Defense Annual Report for Fiscal Year 1989* (Washington, D.C.; Government Printing Office, 1988), pp. 257–261.

93. William F. Buckley, Jr., "A Grand Plan for SDI," *Washington Post*, September 3, 1986, p. A19.

94. For background, see R. L. Maust, G. W. Goodman, Jr., and C. E. McLain, *History of Strategic Defense*, Draft Report SPC 742 (Arlington, Va.: System Planning Corporation, September 1981), pp. 1–14, and Herbert F. York, "Strategic Defense from World War II to the Present," in *Strategic Defense and the Western Alliance*, ed. Sanford Lakoff and Randy Willoughby (Lexington, Mass.: D.C. Heath, 1987), pp. 15–31.

95. Jack Kemp, "How to Proceed with SDI—Deploy Now," *The National Interest*, no. 7 (Spring 1987), pp. 78–79.

96. Senator Sam Nunn, "Interpretation of the ABM Treaty, Part One: The Senate Ratification Proceedings," *Congressional Record*, March 11, 1987, p. 2 of reprint furnished by Senator Nunn's office.

97. William J. Perry, Brent Scowcroft, Joseph S. Nye, Jr., and James A. Schear, "How to Proceed with SDI—Realistic Priorities," *The National Interest*, 7 (Spring 1987), 70, 72.

98. William A. Davis, Jr., *Asymmetries in U.S. and Soviet Strategic Defense Programs: Implications for Near-Term American Deployment Options* (Washington, D.C.: Pergamon-Brassey's, 1986), p. 40.

99. Office of Technology Assessment, *Ballistic Missile Defense Technologies*, p. 257.
100. *White Paper 1985: The Situation and the Development of the Federal Armed Forces* (Bonn, West Germany: Federal Minister of Defence, 1985), p. 31.
101. Wörner has said, for example, that while the vision of a "complete disappearance of nuclear weapons through SDI" is "unachievable" and an "illusion," at least for the foreseeable future, "one can proceed from SDI's relative importance and reduce the threat of a first-strike—which is where danger to our strategic stability and security lies." Wörner interview in *Neue Kronen Zeitung*, Vienna, February 8, 1986, in *FBIS-WE*, daily report, February 11, 1986, p. E1.
102. Sir Geoffrey Howe, "Defence and Security in the Nuclear Age," *RUSI Journal*, 130 (June 1985), 6–7.
103. Ibid., p. 6.
104. Ibid., p. 7. Few West Europeans seem to have mentioned it, but another element of a case against near-term strategic BMD deployments by the United States might be to reject the assumption of some American proponents of such defenses that relatively small BMD deployments could be strategically useful because limited and selective Soviet intercontinental attacks would be more plausible than extensive attacks. While a reasonable and persuasive case for Soviet restraint in the interests of escalation control can be made, another set of arguments points toward large-scale (and potentially preemptive) intercontinental Soviet attacks against U.S. military and C^3I assets as a means of damage limiting, in some circumstances. (Differences of interpretation on this matter may be partly due to the paucity of available evidence.) If such an argument against near-term limited-capability BMD deployments were made, it could be replied that it would be better to defend in an incomplete and uncertain way than not at all and that defenses against small attacks could be steps on the road to capabilities effective against larger attacks. It appears that the principle pointed out by Nathan Leites could nonetheless have multiple applications: a Soviet insistence on the uncontrollability of nuclear operations in their declarations for Western audiences could also make limited BMD capabilities (and other strategic defense measures) appear useless and futile.
105. A few West Europeans suggested in interviews that the SDI could be useful in convincing the Soviets of the risks involved in a BMD competition and in persuading them to resolve reported Treaty infractions and reduce BMD efforts in order to reach an arms control understanding with the United States. A few others noted, however, that one of the unfortunate consequences of what has been perceived as a surprise U.S. initiative in BMD could be the enduring establishment in public perceptions of a misleading impression of U.S. arms race responsibility. This impression could simplify matters for the USSR in the future, they argue, if the Soviets wished to attempt to assign blame for a breakdown of the ABM Treaty regime to the United States.
106. Quilès, cited in *Le Monde*, November 9, 1985, p. 17.

107. Commission d'Etudes, *Rapport de synthèse*, p. 6.

108. Sayre Stevens, "The Soviet Factor in SDI," *Orbis*, 29 (Winter 1986), 699.

109. General Wolfgang Altenburg, "Defense in the Air—NATO's Integrated Air Defense Today and in the Future," *NATO's Sixteen Nations*, 31 (August 1986), 25.

110. Ibid.

111. *Strategic Survey, 1985–1986* (London: International Institute for Strategic Studies, 1986), p. 45.

112. Wörner, "German Minister," p. 79.

113. See the SPD motion against the so-called European Defense Initiative, December 4, 1985, Drucksache 10/4440 of the Bundestag. See also *Der Spiegel*, December 2, 1985, in *FBIS-WE*, daily report, December 3, 1985, p. J2.

114. *Strategic Survey, 1985–1986*, p. 48.

115. Kerry Hines, "Soviet Short-Range Ballistic Missiles: Now a Conventional Deep Strike Mission," *International Defense Review*, 18 (December 1985), 1912.

116. François Heisbourg, "Conventional Defense: Europe's Constraints and Opportunities," in *The Conventional Defense of Europe: New Technologies and New Strategies*, ed. Andrew J. Pierre (New York: Council on Foreign Relations, 1986), p. 91.

117. Wörner, "German Minister," p. 77.

118. Cullington, "Anti-tactical Ballistic Missile Defence," p. 27.

119. Wörner, "Missile Defense for NATO Europe," p. 19.

120. Thomas Enders cited in Michael Feazel, "German Study Encourages Development of Antitactical Ballistic Missiles," *Aviation Week and Space Technology*, July 7, 1986, p. 85.

121. Wörner, "German Minister," p. 77.

122. Altenburg interview in *Der Spiegel*, February 10, 1986, p. 68.

123. Wörner, "'Missile Defense for NATO Europe," p. 19.

124. *Deutsche Weltraumpolitik an der Jahrhundertschwelle, Analyse und Vorschläge für die Zukunft, Bericht einer Expertengruppe* (Bonn: Forschungsinstitut der Deutschen Gesellschaft für Auswärtige Politik, 1986), p. 32.

125. Pierre Hassner. *Europe in the Age of Negotiation*, Washington Paper no. 8 (London and Beverly Hills: Sage Publications, 1973), p. 36.

126. Top-secret memorandum by the secretary of state, Dean Acheson, December 20, 1949, in U.S. Department of State, *Foreign Relations of the United States 1949*, vol. 1, *National Security Affairs, Foreign Economic Policy* (Washington, D.C.: Government Printing Office, 1976), p. 617.

127. See, for example, the speeches by prime minister Laurent Fabius at the Institut des Hautes Etudes de Défense Nationale: "La politique de defense: rassembler et moderniser," *Défense Nationale*, November 1984, p. 14, and "Patriotisme, indépendance, solidarité," *Défense Nationale*, November 1985, pp. 12–14.

128. See, for example, Pierre Lellouche, *L'avenir de la guerre* (Paris: Editions Mazarine, 1985), pp. 282–288. For a detailed discussion of this remarkable

book, see David S. Yost, "Radical Change in French Defense Policy?"
Survival, 28 (January/February 1986), pp. 53–68.

129. Heisbourg, "Europe/Etats-Unis: le couplage stratégique menacé," *Politique Etrangère*, Spring 1987, p. 127. For a review of the noteworthy (but limited) progress in the development of a bilateral relationship that may become one of the foundations of greater West European defense cohesion and effort, see David S. Yost, "Franco-German Defense Cooperation," *Washington Quarterly*, 11 (Spring 1988), pp. 173–195.

130. Except for the highly unlikely prospect of an accident or unauthorized use (and even in such a case, depending on the circumstances, the potential for actual nuclear detonation might be almost nonexistent), the principal nuclear threat to the West is deliberate Soviet use in aggression.

131. Jean-Bernard Raimond, speech at the Council on Foreign Relations, New York, September 22, 1987, text furnished by the French Foreign Ministry, pp. 5, 10.

132. Thomas Enders, *Missile Defense as Part of an Extended NATO Air Defense* (Sankt Augustin bei Bonn, West Germany: Social Science Research Institute of the Konrad-Adenauer-Foundation, May 1986), pp. 6–7.

133. General Franz-Joseph Schulze, in Deutscher Bundestag, *Stenographisches Protokoll der Sitzungen des Auswärtigen Ausschusses und der Verteidigungsausschusses, Offentliche Anhörung zum Thema: "Strategische Verteidigungsinitiative (SDI)*," December 9, 10, 1985, p. 158.

134. Lieutenant General William Odom, "Soviet Force Posture: Dilemmas and Directions," *Problems of Communism*, 34 (July/August 1985), 14.

135. The complete elimination of nuclear weapons does not appear feasible or prudent in the foreseeable future. It would be virtually impossible to verify such an accord, and enormous advantages could redound to a party violating the agreement.

136. James A. Thomson, "The LRTNF Decision: Evolution of US Theatre Nuclear Policy, 1975-9," *International Affairs* (London), 60 (Autumn 1984), 613.

137. Heisbourg, "Conventional Defense," p. 110.

138. Wörner, "Missile Defense for NATO Europe," p. 19.

139. Wörner, "German Minister," p. 79.

140. Some West European experts have acknowledged the hypothetical advantage of devising a U.S.-Soviet military relationship in which less damage might be incurred to the belligerents—and to the global environment—in any future East-West war. In their view, however, the strategic and political disadvantages of a situation of U.S.-Soviet defense dominance outweigh this potential benefit. (Moreover, they judge that the inhibitions discouraging the launching of even small-scale nuclear attacks are likely to remain substantial.) Some U.S. proponents of the SDI have suggested that defense dominance would return the alliance to the situation of the 1950s, prior to *Sputnik* and the development of Soviet ICBMs, in that the United States would regain effective strategic invulnerability and could therefore offer guarantees to allies with unqualified credibility. West European strategists have replied that the pre-*Sputnik* situation did not include the parallel Soviet

invulnerability posited in the defense-dominance vision, and that this would negate the value of U.S. threats to conduct long-range strikes against the USSR in the event of Soviet aggression. For a lucid discussion of the shortcomings (and hypothetical merits) of the defense-dominance concept, see Colin S. Gray, *Nuclear Strategy and National Style* (Lanham, MD.: Hamilton Press, 1986), pp. 286–296.

141. This judgment is shared by Manfred Wörner. See his interview with Elizabeth Pond: "Defense Minister Defends 'Star Wars,'" *Christian Science Monitor*, April 12, 1986.

142. Union pour la Démocratie Française, *Redresser la défense de la France* (Paris: UDF, November 1985), p. 45.

143. The current situation is not, of course, entirely "stable" and satisfactory, in that force balance trends—nuclear and nonnuclear—have been adverse for the West since the 1960s, and the perceived reliability of U.S. nuclear guarantees has been degraded by these trends and by political factors internal to the Western alliance. Critics of the SDI and related U.S. policy initiatives have sometimes failed to acknowledge the deficiencies of the alliance's current military posture.

144. It might also be noted that theories of "arms race stability" based on negotiated constraints on BMD have not held up well, at least as far as the ABM Treaty is concerned, in that the growth of Soviet offensive forces has been far greater than foreseen by ABM Treaty proponents in 1972.

145. David N. Schwartz, "Past and Present: The Historical Legacy," in *Ballistic Missile Defense*, ed. Ashton B. Carter and David N. Schwartz (Washington, D.C.: Brookings Institution, 1984), p. 345.

146. Stephen Peter Rosen, "Foreign Policy and Nuclear Weapons: The Case for Strategic Defenses," in *The Strategic Imperative*, ed. Samuel P. Huntington (Cambridge, Mass.: Ballinger, 1982), pp. 145–146.

147. As François Heisbourg has observed, "it does not appear at all obvious that the new smart weapons and the new concepts will play in favor of the defense rather than the offense: the extension of the size of the battlefield will rather aggravate the geographical asymmetry between a Western Europe without depth . . . and the Soviet empire that continues to dispose of space and therefore of time." Heisbourg, "L'Europe face à la politique militaire américaine," *Politique Etrangère*, Autumn 1984, p. 583.

Index

AAA (antiaircraft artillery), 26, 167
ABM (Antiballistic Missile) Treaty, 3, 5,
7, 8, 115, 172, 185, 303; broad interpretation of, 8, 101, 215, 216, 225,
254; and Western Europe, 9, 19–20;
and Soviet BMD activities, 19–23, 32,
84, 86, 102, 103, 170, 197, 232, 254,
261–262, 285; terms of, 29, 45–46, 97,
101, 193–194, 199, 216, 265; Common Understandings of, 37, 38, 47;
radar restrictions of, 46–54; possible
violations of, 48–50, 70, 105, 194,
200, 201, 213–217, 248, 262, 275;
U.S. vs. Soviet behavior under, 63–69,
78, 80, 120, 211, 233, 257, 261–267,
297; Soviet approval of, 90, 92–102,
107, 128–129, 196, 201, 231, 263,
279; advantages of, for USSR, 197,
198, 199, 201, 210; possible revision
of, 197, 232, 256, 257, 263–264, 266;
compliance with, 213–217, 236, 242,
248, 253, 255, 262, 278, 279, 280,
285; Standing Consultative Commission, 217; nonwithdrawal from, 219,
220, 233, 254, 281; research permitted
in, 219–225, 227, 233, 253, 254,
275; and hypothetical Soviet veto
right over U.S. BMD, 220; and ASAT
weapons, 221, 233, 262; future of,
234, 280–281; definition of ABM
system in, 265; and U.S. BMD, 282,
283. *See also* Breakout; Creepout;
Radar
Abrahamson, Lieutenant General James,
56, 205, 280

ABRES (Advanced Ballistic Reentry System), 66
Acheson, Dean, 293
Adomeit, Hannes, 145, 184
Afghanistan, Soviet invasion of, 136
Aircraft: interceptor, 26, 31, 39, 75, 120;
ground-attack, 119; of Warsaw Pact,
119; fighter, 119, 120, 167, 291; U.S.,
120, 152, 153
Air Defense Committee (NATO), 287
Air defenses: Soviet, 3, 9, 76, 82, 85, 87,
119–120, 155, 198; U.S. vs. Soviet,
26–27, 31–32, 63–64, 69, 75–76, 83,
115, 303, 304; U.S. cutback of, 94; and
arms control, 260. *See also* Defenses,
active; NATO: defenses of; Strategic
defense
Akhromeyev, Marshal Sergei, 113, 160,
217, 222, 226
Aldridge, E. C., 31
Altenburg, General Wolfgang, 164, 247,
273, 290–291
Altunin, Colonel General Alexander,
109
Anureyev, Major General I., 106
Arbatov, Georgi, 187, 214, 228, 229
Arms control, 4, 5, 6, 7, 8, 9; and noncompliance, 36, 37–38, 50; and management of arms race, 78, 84, 98, 101,
128, 149, 288, 296, 297, 300; and U.S.
in Europe, 145; negotiations over, 201,
202, 217–236, 244, 305; Soviet policy
on, 209–241; nuclear, 232–236, 238,
263; Western view of, 251, 254, 256;
principles of, 258–261. *See also* Negoti-

396   **Index**

Arms control (*cont.*)
ations, U.S.-Soviet; SDI: linked with
arms control; *individual treaties*
Arms Control and Disarmament Agency,
U.S., 153, 278
Arms race, 5–7, 71–80, 81, 145, 205;
management of, 95, 130, 149; and defensive systems, 98, 175, 256, 283,
284; in space, 205, 219, 221, 226, 238,
241, 297; trade-offs in, 285–286. *See
also* SDI
Army TACMS (Tactical Missile system),
167, 289. *See also* NATO
ASATs (antisatellite systems), 8, 56–57,
58–59; Soviet, 21, 33, 61, 79, 83, 102,
103, 105, 108, 121; U.S., 105, 222, 233;
French, 175; and SDI, 206, 210, 256;
negotiations over, 218, 221, 222, 231;
and ABM Treaty, 262, 263, 264–265
ASMP (*air-sol moyenne portée*), 120, 177
Aspin, Les, 275
ASW (antisubmarine warfare), 32, 122
ATBMs (antitactical ballistic missiles):
and SAMs, 41, 43, 44, 45, 128, 169–
170, 173; Soviet, 43, 129, 167, 289;
mobile, 61, 198–199; and Western alliance, 205, 234, 242, 266–267, 275,
286, 287, 288, 290, 301; and ABM
Treaty, 262, 265–267, 287; criticisms
of, 287–288 *See also* SAMs
ATMs (antitactical missiles), 286–291
Attacks: long-range nuclear, 3–4, 9, 14,
68, 73, 138–140, 141–142, 153, 161;
preemptive, 4, 25, 78, 94, 122, 126,
127, 138, 190, 197, 288, 289; intercontinental bombing, 17–18, 154, 161; on
Soviet Union, 114, 126, 153, 178–179,
293; Soviet air, on Western Europe,
119, 247, 300; Soviet, on U.S., 138,
147, 156, 247; against nuclear forces,
138–139, 288; limited, 114, 151, 152,
153, 154, 270; nonnuclear, 161, 162,
166, 167–169, 170, 184, 289, 300; tactics of, 174. *See also* FOFA; SRBMs;
Strikes, selective

Ball, Desmond, 123, 124–125
BAOR (British Army of the Rhine), 180
Basov, N. G., 58
Baumel, Jacques, 170
Becker, Abraham, 84, 86

Bellany, Ian, 173, 179
Biryuzov, Marshal S. S., 77
BMD (ballistic missile defense) systems:
Soviet vs. U.S., 1–15, 21–23, 24–69,
79, 80, 83, 93, 100; Galosh, 16–17, 27,
28–29, 34–35, 36, 37, 42, 67, 73, 77,
85, 102, 117, 118, 221; testing of, 25,
281, 282; Safeguard, 29, 30, 34, 93–
94, 100, 101, 280; ABM-X-3, 33, 34–
35, 38–39; Gazelle (SH-08), 34, 35, 36,
37, 38, 67, 85, 177; nuclear-kill, 67;
Nike-Zeus, 77; Sentinel, 100; expansion of Soviet, 150, 162–163, 198, 245,
249, 261. *See also* Moscow defense system; SAMs; Strategic defense
BMEWS (Ballistic Missile Early Warning
System), 29, 42, 44, 48, 51, 54, 214, 215
Bombers: Soviet, 17–18, 73, 75, 87, 116,
119, 167; U.S., 18, 27, 72, 116, 119,
208, 271; long-range intercontinental,
72, 73–74, 115, 116, 119, 132, 154;
and ballistic missiles, 74–75, 154, 268;
West European Tornado, 119; stealth,
152, 208
Bombs, thermonuclear, 79
Breakout (from ABM Treaty constraints),
2, 8, 70–71, 84–85, 90, 193–242, 245,
263, 268; risks of, 69, 198, 200, 209,
247–248; definition of, 69, 84, 193;
incentives for, 133, 149, 183, 194–201,
302; and SDI, 231; response to, 268,
276, 277–278, 279, 281, 282, 284. *See
also* Creepout
Brezhnev, Leonid, 17, 144–146, 187, 189
Brown, Harold, 34, 48, 55, 62, 63, 78–
79, 114–115, 124, 138, 186
Brzezinski, Zbigniew, 278
Buchheim, Robert, 49
Bundy, McGeorge, 158

Carnesale, Albert, 58
Carter, Ashton, 25
Carter, Jimmy, 17, 278
Central Europe, 147–148
Chaff, 35, 43, 177
Chemical forces, 14, 156, 211, 212, 258,
299
Cherednichenko, General, 110
Chervov, Colonel General Nikolai, 105,
223, 250
China, 3, 32, 96, 100, 135, 143, 235